THE OCCUPATION OF IRAQ

THE OCCUPATION
OF IRAQ

WINNING THE WAR, LOSING THE PEACE

ALI A. ALLAWI

YALE UNIVERSITY PRESS
NEW HAVEN AND LONDON

For information about this and other Yale University Press publications, please contact:
U.S. Office: sales.press@yale.edu   www.yalebooks.com
Europe Office: sales @yaleup.co.uk   www.yaleup.co.uk

Set in Minion by J&L Composition, Filey, North Yorkshire
Printed in the United States of America

Library of Congress Cataloging-in-Publication Data

Allawi, Ali A., 1947–
   The occupation of Iraq: winning the war, losing the peace/Ali A. Allawi.
     p. cm.
   Includes bibliographical references and index.
   ISBN 978–0–300–11015–9 (alk. paper)
   1. Iraq War, 2003– 2. Iraq—Politics and government—2003– I. Title.
   DS79.76.A393 2007
   956.7044'3—dc22

                                                              2006039445

A catalogue record for this book is available from the British Library.

10 9 8 7 6 5 4 3 2 1

Contents

Illustrations

Maps   *page*

Preface

I first left Iraq in November 1958, a few months after the Revolution of 14 July, 1958. I had been sent abroad – to boarding school in England, in deepest Sussex – to escape the turmoil of post-revolutionary Baghdad. My extended family had been intimately involved in the affairs of the country, providing ministers, senators, governors and ambassadors to what had been the kingdom of Iraq. But all that suddenly ended. A few mutinous army units had brought our charmed world to an abrupt end. No one resisted the mutineers, apart from the guards at the Royal Palace. The old order simply surrendered to its fate, with hardly a whimper of protest. We were on the wrong side of the revolution, and that was that.

For the next decade, moving from schools in England and then to university in the United States, I always kept a close watch on events in Iraq. In time, my family had made its peace with the new republican order. I ceased to be an exile and became more of an Iraqi student abroad. I was looking forward to resuming my life in Iraq after graduation. But this was not to be. The return of the Ba'ath Party to power on 30 July, 1968 ended whatever hopes I had about returning to Iraq. Instinctively I knew that the new Ba'athist rulers were a different breed from the parade of army officers that had previously run the country. I reckoned that the Ba'athists would rule Iraq with an iron fist. They would impose a totalitarian system that would tolerate no dissent. And this is exactly what they did – but far more virulently and bloodily than I would ever have imagined. A new exile began for me, this time considerably longer, stretching for over thirty years.

Throughout the thirty years of the second exile, I hardly ever stopped thinking about Iraq. Many writers have described the condition of exile, dispossession and wanderings, and exile from totalitarian regimes has additional characteristics: an obsession with travel documents; an exaggerated sensitivity to officialdom; an ambivalent relationship to the culture of one's adopted land; uncertainty about the permanence of the condition of exile itself. All in all, an exile's is a melancholic state of mind, although with elevating moments. The main feature of exile, however, at least for me, was not a sense of loss or a violent dislocation in the pattern of my life. It had more to do with the limitation of possibilities, of reduced choices and opportunities, of few roads that could be taken. There was the feeling that Iraq would have been a far better place if its destiny had not been hijacked by one miserable set of dictators or another; if it had somehow evaded the disastrous experiments in re-engineering societies and economies that characterised the 'revolutionary' states of the Arab world.

It is hope that keeps exiles from either slipping into despondency or finally abandoning the attachment to their native land. In the bleak days of the 1970s, it did not seem that anything could possibly emerge to threaten the stranglehold of the Ba'ath over the country. Year after year in that fateful decade, the regime crushed its internal enemies until no one was left. The flood of oil money made sure that the public would be bought off in a Faustian bargain with its new rulers. But then the unexpected happened. A revolution of enormous significance took place in neighbouring Iran, which frightened the Iraqi ruling elite – not to mention the rest of the world. And the rest, as they say, is history. Saddam Hussein survived the eight-year war with Iran, but he couldn't leave well enough alone.

Throughout this period, I had been working in international development with the World Bank, and later as an investment banker, at the same time maintaining my commitment to opposing Saddam. Trying to keep the two worlds separate was a difficult, even hazardous, task. The Gulf countries of the 1980s, where I spent a great deal of time, were strategically allied to Saddam during that period. (Later, the extent of their enormous financial commitment to the Iraqi war effort would become clear.) Saddam's extraordinary strategic blunders piled up. The world of the Iraqi exiles was turned upside down with the invasion, and then liberation, of Kuwait. Iraqi exiles' hopes rose that the end of Saddam was close at hand, but he, unforgivably, was let off the hook.

The 1990s were heady times. The Iraqi exiles no longer seemed such forlorn, even ridiculous, figures. We started being courted by the media, by chanceries in western and Arab capitals, and some of us even received the ultimate badge of recognition: a White House audience. I moved from one conference and symposium on Iraq to another. The Iraqi opposition had arrived, but we were still incapable of threatening the regime in Baghdad. At least not on our own. We read the tea leaves from Washington and London, but often they were not auspicious.

Then another extraordinary event took place. A few hours after the attacks of 11 September, 2001, I phoned a close friend of mine and told him what I thought would happen next. 'The Americans will overthrow the Taliban; they will have an undeclared war against radical Islam; and they will get rid of

Saddam.' In that order, which is pretty well what happened. I watched the fall of Baghdad on television, unlike my more intrepid or ambitious colleagues. They were out there in Iraq, angling and manoeuvring, almost as soon as the first shots had been fired. I thought that my political career, for whatever it was worth, and which I had spent entirely in opposition, had come to a fitting end. I settled back to watch, from afar, the chaotic events in Iraq unfolding. But this short respite was soon over. Mowaffaq Rubai'e, my great friend and ally, made sure of that. He went on the Governing Council of post-Saddam Iraq and championed me for the Cabinet. 'I am going to put you up for minister of trade,' Mowaffaq said. 'Do you, or do you not, want the job?' He was an eminently practical and no-nonsense man. I hummed and hawed, but then said yes. I don't know precisely why I accepted the offer. I can fairly say it was not ambition, or the thought of glory or power, that encouraged me to do this. I am sure of that. It was more a sense of inevitability. I had spent the best part of four decades ruminating about Iraq. Now was the time to do something about it.

I arrived in Iraq on 11 September, 2003, and spent the next two and a half years in one capacity or another in the government, either as a minister or as a member of parliament. As soon as I had set foot in Baghdad, I began to experience at first hand the chaotic nature of the country and the terrible passions that had been unwittingly, or otherwise, unleashed by the invasion and occupation. The situation was going to unravel, I thought, and with it my entire premise for the ethical justification for the overthrow of the dictatorship by recourse to outsiders. For what other reason can anyone give to warrant the occupation of one's country? I expressed my misgivings to all who were prepared to hear, but no one cared a hoot. Everyone was too busy pursuing his or her own narrow agenda to see clearly what was happening, and the Americans, together with the new Iraqi political class, were all on an altogether different tangent. At the end of the Governing Council's life, I could see the tell-tale signs of disintegration – both in the incoherence of the American 'project' in Iraq, and in the utter mediocrity, incompetence and venality of the new political order. The new Iraq was held together more by the numbing repetition of platitudes and quick-fix nostrums than by any vision. When the Interim Government offered me the ambassadorship to the USA, I could not bring myself to accept it. I knew that I would faithfully have had to represent and reflect the views of a government with which I might be frequently in disagreement.

All this changed when the chance to remedy the errors of the occupation and its aftermath beckoned with the first free elections in January 2005. I found myself on the candidate list of the United Iraqi Alliance, and was duly elected to the Transitional National Assembly. I had wanted to be involved in the drafting of the constitution. I, perhaps naïvely, thought this process was to be the defining feature of the new Iraq. I had also thought that all the component groups of Iraq would come together in a spirited conclave to thrash out their differences, where the great ideas and concerns of the people would be reconciled in a grand, founding document. But I did not even get the chance to participate in the process, which, in retrospect, saved me from another deeply disappointing experience. In spite of a strenuous rearguard action on my part, I was prevailed upon to accept the post of minister of finance. I worked under increasingly difficult and dangerous conditions. My convoy was ambushed twice; the second time was a near-run thing. The sound of the heavy machine guns of my security detail firing back at the assailants still reverberates in my ears. Later, a suicide bomber walked into my bodyguards as they were having their lunch at a popular restaurant. Three were killed, and six others badly wounded. I steadfastly refused to move to the relative safety of the Green Zone, not because of any heroics, but because I felt then – and still do – that the Green Zone is the symbol of all that has gone wrong in Iraq since the occupation. A marooned political class living cheek by jowl with the foreign contingent, both cut off from the terrible, daily anguish of Iraqis.

I knew that my days in politics were drawing to a close. The rot in the 'new' Iraq had set too deep to allow any hope for an increasingly sterile and vacuous political process. I did not seek office for the December 2005 elections, although I did try to help the doomed candidacy of a number of worthy politicians. They were steamrolled into an undeserved fate by the Islamist bandwagon, and the Islamists were immeasurably aided by their skilful exploitation of the 'Sistani' factor. I also made it clear that I would no longer wish to serve in any ministerial post in what I suspected was going to be a flimsy and hastily assembled government. In any case, I probably would have been passed over. All the ministerial posts were doled out by strict adherence to a formula that parcelled out the available positions, which went to stalwarts of the various political parties, on the basis of ethnicity and sect. I had tried to be professional and fair in my running of the Ministry of Finance, but this was not good enough for the hordes of thwarted office-seekers and party hacks that hovered around the new kingpins and power-brokers in Iraq. I believed that Iraq needed an administrative revolution, but I knew that, instead, it would get the lowest common denominator government – which it duly did. I left politics in May 2006, with the end of the Transitional National Government. That government had a bad press. It was unfairly maligned. But it was no worse and, I believe, considerably better, than its predecessors and successor.

At first I did not set out to write a book about my experiences in Iraq. As I became perplexed, however, then astonished, and finally angry at the way that the country was being grotesquely mismanaged and misdirected, I resolved to try to understand and write about how Iraq had ended up in this terrible condition. I knew that I could bring a unique perspective to the exercise: as an Iraqi, as a former oppositionist, and also as a person who knew the ways of the west. For nearly three years I had been near, or in, the centres of power in Iraq, and I could draw not only on personal experiences and relationships but also on the wealth of documents that had come to my attention. I had also kept a diary, and this proved to be an invaluable aid to my memory when the time came to write a book.

Perhaps it is too early to write a definitive account of the occupation of Iraq and its aftermath. But I did want to produce a comprehensive assessment of this momentous episode in Iraqi, and world, history, from the perspective of a contemporary participant in the events.

There have been many books on the recent events in Iraq, and for good reason. None, I dare say, has the broad reach that this book tries to achieve, and none have been written from the perspective of an Iraqi insider. I have tried to provide readers with an objective and dispassionate narrative that can help them understand the forces that led to the calamitous situation in Iraq. The situation in Iraq is complex, dangerous and fraught with poor alternatives. But it is not hopeless. An informed public would not tolerate the half-truths, platitudes and outright deceptions that have characterised the official line on the country. I hope that this book will set the stage for an informed public to demand the necessary changes in policy and direction, to begin to set things right.

Acknowledgements

I cannot adequately thank the numerous individuals who have helped me in the writing of this book. There are a few, however, that I must single out. Dr Mowaffaq Rubai'e, Iraq's National Security Adviser, heads the list. He has been a loyal and steadfast friend. He encouraged me in my project and placed his wealth of experience and keen insights at my disposal. Fred Smith, the senior adviser of the Ministry of Defence during my tenure, also encouraged me with the writing of this book. Fred was the best kind of American to have in Iraq. Quiet, competent, effective, and genuinely caring about the country. There were too few like him in the Occupation administration.

I interviewed many individuals for this book. I have tried to list all of them in the notes, but I would like to mention in particular Sami al-Askari, currently a member of the Iraqi Council of Representatives, and Salem Chalabi, a gifted lawyer and former chief executive of the Iraq Special Tribunal. They were unstinting in their time, and I thank them for their support. My editor at Yale, Heather McCallum, deserves my special thanks for helping me understand the mysterious ways of publishers and gently prodding me in the right direction. Loulou Brown did a wonderful job in her careful editing of the manuscript and made the essential cuts and revisions as painless as possible.

I started thinking about this book in Baghdad, but did most of my writing in London. My gratitude to my wife Munya is limitless. She organised my workspace, made sure that I was not unduly disturbed, and kept the tea flowing. A friend once asked whether Munya was my muse. 'No. She is my judge,' I said. And much more.

People who Appear in this Book

Iraqis

Muhammad Yunus al-Ahmad
Senior Ba'athist rumoured to be living in Syria. One of the key planners of the insurgency.

Ali Allawi
Served as minister of trade and later minister of defence in the Cabinet of the Governing Council. Member of the Transitional National Assembly. Minister of finance in the Transitional National Government.

Ayad Allawi
Former head of the INA. Close to western and Arab governments. Member of the Governing Council. Prime minister of the Interim Government. Head of the *Iraqiyya* parliamentary list.

Massoud Barzani
Son of the legendary Kurdish fighter and leader Mulla Mustafa Barzani. Head of the KDP. A strong advocate of maximum Kurdish autonomy. Leader of the Kurdistan Regional Government.

Ahmad Chalabi
Brilliant but controversial leader of the INC. Served on the Governing Council. Later broke with the Americans, only to re-emerge as deputy prime minister in the Transitional National Government.

Salem Chalabi
Iraqi lawyer and first director of the Iraq Special Tribunal.

Hareth al-Dhari
Leader of the Association of Muslim Scholars. A radical Sunni Arab opponent of the occupation.

Izzat al-Douri
Senior Ba'athist and former vice-president of Iraq. Escaped capture and rumoured to be a linchpin of the insurgency.

Adnan al-Dulaimi
Religious leader and former head of the Sunni Endowment Association. Leader of the Tawaffuq bloc in parliament.

Faisal I, King of Iraq
Ensconced on the Iraqi throne in 1921 by the British. Understood the difficulties of governing Iraq's fractured society, and sought to overcome the divisions of his adopted country by building strong state institutions.

Abdul Aziz al-Hakim
Assumed leadership of SCIRI after the murder of his brother, Ayatollah Baqir al-Hakim. Head of the Shi'a United Iraqi Alliance parliamentary group.

Ayatollah Baqir al-Hakim
Leading Islamist opponent of the Ba'athist regime. Went into exile in Iran. Helped to found SCIRI, which he led for over two decades. Returned to Iraq to popular acclaim in May 2003. Killed by a powerful car bomb in Najaf, August 2003.

Mahdi al-Hakim
Son of the Grand Ayatollah Muhsin al-Hakim. Prominent in organising the Iraqi opposition to Saddam Hussein in the 1980s. Assassinated in 1988 in Khartoum by Ba'ath regime agents.

Tarek al-Hashemi
Leader of the Iraq Islamic Party, an offshoot of the Muslim Brotherhood. Closely connected to the American plan to increase Sunni participation in government. Vice-president of Iraq 2006.

Saddam Hussein
Dictator of Iraq for nearly thirty years. His bloody rule was ended by the Coalition invasion of 2003. Brought in front of the Iraq Special Tribunal on charges of war crimes and crimes against humanity. Sentenced to death in November 2006.

Ibrahim al-Jaafari
Leader of the Da'awa Party and member of the Governing Council. First elected prime minister of Iraq following the January 2005 elections for a Transitional National Assembly. Blocked from a second premiership, to which he had been elected, by a US and British veto.

Grand Ayatollah Abu al-Qasim al-Khoei
The undisputed leader of the world's Shi'a. Followed the 'quiescent' tradition in Shi'a Islam by avoiding political entanglements. Was decisively opposed to the Khomeini proposition of direct rule by learned clerics.

Adel Abd el-Mahdi
Principal SCIRI political strategist. Served as minister of finance in the Interim Government of Ayad Allawi. He was later the vice-president of Iraq.

Kenan Makiya
Writer and public intellectual. Author of *The Republic of Fear*, a powerful indictment of the Ba'ath rule in Iraq.

Nuri (Jawad) al-Maliki
Senior Da'awa Party leader. Spent two decades in Syria in exile before returning to Iraq. Served on the de-Ba'athification Commission and headed the Transitional National Assembly's security committee. Unexpectedly propelled to the premiership in May 2006 after the Anglo-American veto on Jaafari.

Abu Muhammad al-Maqdisi
Palestinian-born Islamist ideologue. A strong influence on *jihadi* thought and a mentor of Zarqawi. Later, he reputedly recanted some of his extremist views.

Adnan al-Pachachi
Veteran liberal politician. Served as foreign minister of Iraq in the 1960s. Member of the Governing Council and elected to the four-year parliament on Ayad Allawi's *Iraqiyya* list.

Latif Rashid
Senior PUK leader. Served as the minister of water resources in all Iraq's governments after the fall of Saddam.

Mowaffaq Rubai'e
Independent Islamist, formerly a senior Da'awa Party leader. Member of the Governing Council. Appointed the national security adviser in 2004. Member of the UIA bloc and close adviser to Nuri al-Maliki.

Ayatollah Muhammad Baqir al-Sadr
A leading figure in Islamic thought of the twentieth century. Associated with the rise of the Iraqi Shi'a Islamist movement. Murdered by the Ba'athist regime in 1980.

Moqtada al-Sadr
Son of Ayatollah Muhammad Sadiq al-Sadr and head of the amorphous anti-occupation Sadrist movement and its Mahdi Army. Leader of a large parliamentary bloc and a force behind the Maliki government.

Ayatollah Muhammad Sadiq al-Sadr
Populist Grand Ayatollah, who built up a massive following in the 1990s. Murdered by assassins from the Saddamist intelligence agencies in 1999. Contrary to expectations, the movement associated with him continued in strength after his death.

Muhammad Shahwani
Former general in the Iraqi army. Implicated in a 1996 coup attempt against the Ba'ath regime. Rumoured to be close to the CIA. Head of the new Iraqi intelligence apparatus.

Grand Ayatollah Sayyid Ali al-Sistani
The acknowledged religious leader of Iraq's Shi'a over the last decade. Played a vital role in pushing for an elected constitutional order after the invasion of Iraq.

Muhammad Redha Sistani
Son of Grand Ayatollah Ali Sistani and head of his private office, from which he wields considerable influence.

Jalal Talabani
Historic Kurdish political leader and head of the PUK. Member of the Governing Council. President of Iraq from 2005 onwards.

Ali al-Wardi
Iraqi sociologist and social historian. Known for his monumental work on Iraq's social history and his dissection of the Iraqi identity.

Abu Musab al-Zarqawi
Jordanian-born terrorist leader and head of the al-Qaeda organisation in Iraq. Killed in a US air-strike in June 2006.

Others
Tony Blair
British prime minister. Abandoned traditional British caution and followed the lead of George W. Bush in advocating war on Iraq.

Lakhdar Brahimi
Algerian diplomat and UN troubleshooter. Involved in the process that led to the formation of the Interim Government and the transfer of sovereignty to Iraq.

Paul Bremer
Diplomat and counter-terrorism expert. Headed the Coalition Provisional Administration, the occupying government in Iraq from May 2003 to June 2004.

George W. Bush
President of the United States. The person most singly responsible for the Iraq war and its aftermath.

Douglas Feith
Neo-conservative lawyer and head of the Pentagon's Office of Special Plans. Was effectively responsible for the planning for Iraq's post-war occupation.

Jay Garner
Retired US Army general and head of ORHA, the first post-war administration for Iraq. Unfairly maligned for his perceived bungling of the job.

Zalmay Khalilzad
Afghan-born American public official and diplomat. Close to neo-conservative circles. Served as liaison with the Iraqi opposition in 2002 and 2003. Appointed the American ambassador to Iraq in 2005.

Bernard Lewis
Leading historian of the Middle East. Wielded great influence on neo-conservative thinking on Iraq and on Vice-President Cheney directly.

Robert Merton
A prominent American sociologist who was instrumental in defining the term 'The Law of Unexpected Consequences'.

Colin Powell
US secretary of state. Maintained a sceptical position on the war, but eventually went along with it.

Condoleezza Rice
US national security adviser and later secretary of state in the second Bush administration.

Donald Rumsfeld
US secretary of defense. Was held responsible for the inadequate size of the American force that occupied Iraq.

Leo Strauss
German-born scholar and philosopher associated with the University of Chicago. His political philosophy was a major influence on a number of senior Bush administration officials

Paul Wolfowitz
US deputy secretary of defense. A strong advocate of the war against Iraq and the implantating of democratic principles into the politics of the Islamic world.

Abbreviations

ACC Arab Cooperation Council
AEI American Enterprise Institute
AFP Association of Free Prisoners
AMS Association of Muslim Scholars
BSA Bureau of Supreme Audit (Iraq)
CBI Central Bank of Iraq
CentCom US Central Command
CIA Central Intelligence Agency (US)
CJTF-7 Combined Joint Task Force Seven
CPA Coalition Provisional Authority
DFI Development Fund for Iraq
DFID Department for International Development
DIA Defense Intelligence Agency (US)
EPCA Emergency Post-Conflict Assistance Plan
EU European Union
EWG Emergency Working Group for Fallujah
FBI Federal Bureau of Investigation
FLN National Liberation Front (Algeria)
FMR Financial Management Regulations (US)
FPS Facilities Protection Service
FREs Former Regime Elements
GAO Government Accountability Office (US)
GCC Gulf Cooperation Council
HRW Human Rights Watch
IAEA International Atomic Energy Agency
ICP Iraqi Communist Party
IEC Independent Electoral Commission of Iraq
IEDs improvised explosive devices
IIA Interim Iraq Authority
IIG Interim Iraqi Government
IIP Iraqi Islamic Party
ILA Iraq Liberation Act
IMF International Monetary Fund
IMN Iraq Media Network
INA Iraq National Accord
INC Iraq National Congress

INDICT (campaign) International campaign to indict Iraqi war criminals
INIS Iraqi National Intelligence Service
IRDC Iraq Reconstruction and Development Council
IRMO Iraq Reconstruction and Management Office
IUM Islamic Unity Movement of Kurdistan
JAC Joint Action Committee
KDP Kurdistan Democratic Party
KRG Kurdistan Regional Government
MEES Middle East Economic Survey
MEIB Middle East Intelligence Bulletin
MEK Mujahedin e Khalq Organisation
MERIP Middle East Research and Information Project
MNF Multinational Force
NATO North Atlantic Treaty Organisation
NDP National Democratic Party (Iraq)
NDRI National Defense Research Institute
NGOs non-governmental organisations
NIE National Intelligence Estimate
NSC National Security Council
OFF 'Oil-for-Food' Programme
OIC Organisation of Islamic Countries
OPEC Organisation of the Petroleum Exporting Countries
OPIC Overseas Private Investment Corporation
ORHA Office for Reconstruction and Humanitarian Affairs
OSP Office for Special Plans
PCO Project and Contracting Office
PDS Public Distribution System
PGI Provisional Government of Iraq
PKK Kurdistan Workers' Party
PNAC Project for the New American Century
PUK Patriotic Union of Kurdistan
RCC Revolutionary Command Council
RPGs rocket-propelled grenades
SAIC Science Applications International Corporation
SAVAK Organisation for Intelligence and National Security (Iran)
SBA Standby Arrangement
SCIRI Supreme Council for the Islamic Revolution in Iraq
SIGIR Special Inspector General for Iraq Reconstruction
SOAS School of Oriental and African Studies (UK)
SOMO State Oil Marketing Organisation
SPITS Special Program on the Implementation of Targeted Sanctions
TAL Transition Administrative Law
TBI Trade Bank of Iraq
TNA Transitional National Assembly
TNG Transitional National Government
UAE United Arab Emirates
UIA United Iraqi Alliance
UK United Kingdom
UN United Nations
UNAMI United Nations Assistance Mission in Iraq
UNDP United Nations Development Programme
UNESCO United Nations Educational Scientific and Cultural Organisation

UNIDO United Nations Industrial Development Organisation
UNMOVIC United Nations Monitoring, Verification and Inspection Commission
UNSCOM United Nations Special Commission
USAID United States Agency for International Development
USIP United States Institute for Peace
WMD weapons of mass destruction
WHO World Health Organisation

Glossary of Arabic Terms

Ahl ul-Bayt 'People of the Household' (the term refers to the immediate family of the Prophet Muhammad and his immediate descendants)
ahzab (plural) Political parties
'alim (singular) A Muslim religious scholar
amir Leader, prince (used by the insurgents in Iraq to denote the leaders of combat cells)
arba'in 'Forty'
'atabat Thresholds (the name given to the shrines of the imams of the Shi'a)
awqaf (plural) Muslim religious endowments
ayatollah A high-ranking Shi'a cleric

bara'a A Quranic term meaning 'disassociation' (as in disassociation from polytheists)
bayan A pronouncement delivered by a *Marji'*
bazaaris A Farsi word meaning wholesale merchants
Buwayhi A ninth-century Persian dynasty in Abbasid Iraq (also a derogatory term for the Shi'a)

chattals Forks or electric junctions

dars al-khariji Outside, or extra-mural, study; refers to the highest degree of scholastic learning in the training of a *mujtahid*
dawla State
din Religion, faith
dustoor Constitution

effendi Official classes

faqih Jurisprudent
fatwa A legal opinion delivered by a Shi'a *mujtahid* or *Marji'*, or by a *mufti* amongst the Sunnis
Fedayeen Saddam Saddam's paramilitary force
fitna Sedition, strife

ghawgha Mob

Hajj The annual pilgrimage to Mecca
hawassim Spoils
hawza Shi'a study circles, akin to university colleges or cloisters
hijab Cover or veil worn by women as customary dress, or to signify modesty and acceptance of Islamic norms
hijri The Muslim lunar calendar year, which marks the time from Muhammad's departure to Medina from Mecca

hizb (singular) Political party
hukm A legally binding opinion on all believers delivered by a *Marji'*
husseiniyya Shi'a meeting hall and venue for prayers and commemorations

ijtihad Independent reasoning
'Ilm al-Rijal Knowledge of men; biographical studies to establish the reliability of narrators of saying of the Prophet or the *imams*
imam Leader (usually refers to prayer leaders)
imam al-Juma'a Friday congregational prayer leader
iqlim Region
irfan Gnosis, a branch of Shi'a metaphysics
ittihad Union

jahiliyya Paganism
jami' Mosque where congregational prayers can be held
jash Donkeys (a slang Kurdish term for government auxiliaries)
jihad Exertion, struggle
jihadis A western term, indicating fighters driven by adherence to extremist Sunni Islam
Jund al-Islam Army of Islam

Kadhimain A northern suburb of Baghdad, site of the shrines of Imams al-Kadhim and al-Jawad
Karbala The city built around the shrines of Imam al-Hussein and al-Abbas
khatib Preacher
Killidar Keeper of the Keys
kufr Infidelity, unbelief, heresy

madrassah An Islamic school
Maghawir Iraqi Interior Ministry Shock Troops
majalis (plural) Conclaves
majlis (singular) Conclave
Maraji' (plural) Shi'a religious authorities
Marji' (singular) Shi'a religious authority
Marji' al-Taqlid The highest Shi'a religious authority, literally, 'worthy of emulation'
Marji'iyya The institution that groups a number of *Maraji'*
masjid Literally, a place of prostration; a centre of prayer, a mosque, but not one where congregational prayers can be held
minbars Pulpits
mujahid (singular) Muslim fighter in a religiously sanctioned cause
mujahiddun (plural) Muslim fighters in a religiously sanctioned cause
mujtahid Qualified interpreter of *Sharia* law
Mukhabarat Ba'athist intelligence services
muqawamma Resistance
muqqalid A follower of a particular *mujtahid*
muta'a Temporary marriage allowed according to Shi'a jurisprudence
al-Mutassimum The infallible ones (usually refers to the Shi'a imams)
muthaqaf Educated person

Najaf The main Shi'a religious city in Iraq, site of the shrine of Imam Ali
nasibi (singular)/*nawasib* (plural) A derogatory term applied by the Shi'a to all extremist Sunnis who are assumed to deny the elevated status of the Household of the Prophet
Nowruz Iranian New Year

rafidhi (singular) Literally, 'rejectionist', that is, a person who rejected the legitimacy of the first three Caliphs of Islam; a derogatory Sunni term applied to the Shi'a

risala al'amaliyya Practical instructions; rulings of a *mujtahid* on matters of religious ritual

sadda (plural) Descendants of the Prophet; in the Shi'a religious hierarchy, *sadda* are entitled to don a black turban and expect to be addressed as such

Safawi The Arabic term for *Safavid*, the rulers of Iran and Iraq in the sixteenth and seventeenth centuries; also, a derogatory name for the Shi'a

salafi Ultra orthodox Sunni Muslim

Samarra A city north of Baghdad, site of the shrines of the two Imams al-Hadi and al-Askari

sayyid (singular) Descendant of the Prophet; in the Shi'a religious hierarchy, a *sayyid* is entitled to don a black turban and expects to be addressed as such

shahid Martyr in a religiously sanctioned cause

Sharia The corpus of Islamic law and ordinances

sheikh (singular) Elder, local leader, also a religious leader; amongst the Shi'a, a *sheikh* is the title applied to a cleric who is not a descendant of the Prophet; he wears a white turban

shoura Consultation

shu'ubi A derogatory term applied to the Shi'a, indicating their partiality to Iran

Shu'ubiya A movement in the Islamic middle centuries that postulated Persian literary superiority over the Arabs

shuyukh (plural) Elders, local leaders, also religious leaders. Amongst the Shi'a, *shuyukh* is the title applied to clerics who are not descendants of the Prophet; they wear white turbans

siddara Hat

souq el-mraydi Local thieves' markets of Baghdad

taba'iyah Dependency; a term that applied to Iraqis who were considered to be Persian dependants according to a 1920s nationalities law

Tafsir Quranic exegesis

ta'ifi Sectarian

ta'ifiya Sectarianism

takfir (singular) Derogatory term applied by the Shi'a to all extremist Sunni who justify the anathemisation or killing of the Shi'a

taqqiyya Dissimulation

tawabin Penitents

tawaffuq Accordance

tekiye Hostel

thawra Revolution

ulema (plural) Muslim religious scholars

umma Nation; also applies to the worldwide community of Muslims

usuli Fundamentalist

Wahhabi (singular) Follower of a fundamentalist Sunni sect of Islam, founded in the eighteenth century by Muhammad ibn Abd el-Wahhab; in Iraq, the term is loosely applied by the Shi'a to all extremist Sunni

wakils Agents

waqf (singular) Muslim religious endowment

Watan Fatherland, country

wilaya Authority; can also apply to an administrative province

Wilayat al-Faqih Literally, the 'Authority of the Jurisprudent'; the term applies to the system in power in Iran

wilayet province

ziyara (singular)/*ziyarat* (plural) Visitations or pilgrimages to the Islamic shrines

Ziyarat al-Arbai'in The term applies to the mass commemoration of the anniversary of forty days of mourning after the death of Imam al-Hussein

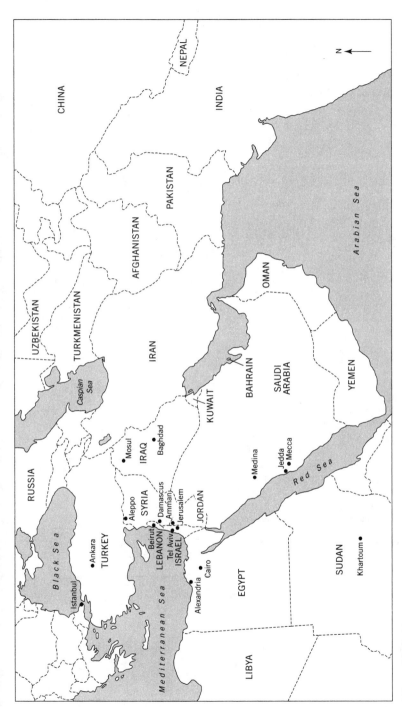

The Middle East

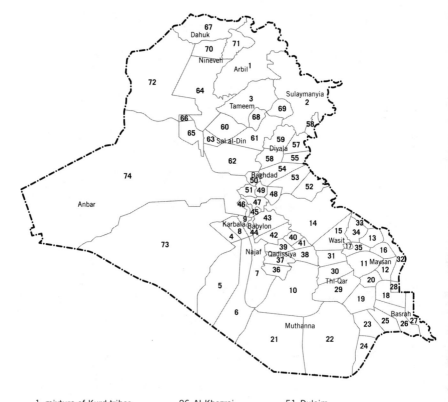

1 mixture of Kurd tribes	26 Al-Khazraj	51 Dulaim
2 mixture of Kurd tribes	27 none shown	52 Al-Jubour
3 Kurd, Turk, and Arab tribes	28 none shown	53 Al-Ssalhi
4 Al-Glall	29 Al Ribad	54 'Ateeghy
5 Al-Glall	30 Bano Hjaim	55 Al-Qarah
6 Al-Hassan	31 Bano Rikab	56 none shown
7 Unizzah	32 none shown	57 Al-Khazraj
8 Al-Hassan	33 none shown	58 Somaida'
9 Unizzah	34 Al-Sawae'id	59 Al-Nifeesah
10 Unizzah	35 Bano Lam	60 Al-Jubour
11 Albu Muhammed	36 Al-Agr'a	61 Al-Takaretah
12 Al-Ozairij	37 Albu Yaser	62 Al-Ddury
13 Bano Bayat	38 Al-Khaz'il	63 Al-Samarraiy
14 Al Zorbaid	39 Al-Fatlah	64 Al-Jubour
15 Al Rabi'h	40 Al-Jubour	65 Al-Samarraiy
16 Albu Timin	41 Al-Laith	66 Al-Samarraiy
17 Al Rabi'h	42 Al-Hawashim	67 Tkrity tribes
18 Al-Montifig	43 Al-Janabi	68 Kurd, Turk, Arab tribes
19 Al-Montifig	44 Unizzah	69 mixture of Kurd tribes
20 Al-Montifig	45 Al-Qaraghoul	70 Sinjar
21 Al-Dufeer	46 Dulaim	71 Sinjar
22 Al-Motairat	47 Al-Qaraghoul	72 Shammar
23 Al-Asdi	48 Al-Ssalhi	73 Dulaim
24 Al-Kindy	49 mixture of tribes	74 Dulaim
25 Bano Malik	50 Al-Ddury	

The Tribes of Iraq
Source: UNAMI

Prologue

'*America does not go abroad in search of monsters to destroy.*' –

John Quincy Adams, Sixth President of the United States of America,
1825–29

In the history of conflicts and wars, there are few instances that match the invasion and occupation of Iraq for complexity of motive and ambiguity of purpose. A seemingly endless chain of causal events have been put forward to explain this most extraordinary episode in contemporary times, but none, it would seem, has provided a satisfying and comprehensive answer. Why did the world's only superpower see fit to marshal its huge military and financial resources, cross the oceans, and overthrow a tyrant and his brutal system of rule, in the teeth of overwhelming international hostility?

The overthrow of the regime that ruled Iraq was achieved in record time, no more than a few weeks of sporadic fighting. The euphoria that accompanied this effortless victory quickly gave way to increasing bewilderment as to what to do with this 'prize', as the occupiers came face to face with the realities of post-Saddam Hussein Iraq and the mysteries of this most complex of countries. Nothing that had preceded the war – certainly nothing coming out of the innumerable conferences and policy papers from think-tanks, Iraqi oppositionists, academic pundits, and the warrens of government – could have prepared the Coalition, that unwieldy term for the United States and its allies, for what they actually found. It would seem that a massive momentum had developed that propelled the USA to war, only to be replaced a few weeks into the occupation by bewilderment and confusion rapidly growing to supplant the purposeful front that had been so carefully crafted.

The hunt for Saddam's elusive weapons of mass destruction (WMD), ostensibly the *casus belli*, was quickly forgotten as it dawned upon the Coalition that there were none to be found. There were no public cheers for democracy, no indications that this was a people hungering for the freedoms and liberties of the west. The most public early demonstrations of what the mass of people appeared to crave were manifestations of popular religiosity that had no counterpart in the west. Equally, the world was not expecting the outbreak of looting on the massive scale that affected not only Baghdad but also far-away oil installations, power lines and Iraqi army bases. The inchoate attacks on government property, the wanton burning of ministries, libraries and even sports stadiums, the images of booty being carted off by frenzied crowds, frequently with TV cameras in tow, somehow didn't quite fit with the behaviour of a grateful people who had just been liberated from tyranny. This grating disjunction between official wisdom on Iraq and Iraqis prior to the war, and the harsher facts of the country and its people, became a recurrent theme in the months and years that followed the fall of the Saddamist regime. And this was not confined to the proponents and apologists of the war. Those who opposed the war, especially in the Arab world, had different, but equally distorted, expectations as to the response of the Iraqi people to the invasion and occupation of their country. The ignominious collapse of the Iraqi army (including the much-vaunted Republican Guard) in a matter of weeks, the evident abandonment by the regime of the Arab 'volunteers' who swarmed into Baghdad to fight the invaders, the reaction of the average Iraqi, who didn't appear to be outraged by the violation of the country's sovereignty and the obvious affront to Arab independence, didn't match the forecasts of the doomsayers. Anyone who had defended Saddam and his regime could only stand shamefacedly in front of the mass graves that were being unearthed almost daily in the aftermath of the war. The barbarism of the Ba'athist state was becoming exposed in all its naked truth. Once again Iraq had confounded its interpreters. The conjunction of forces that came together to propel America to war, and the perplexing reality of the country that became the object of its invading and reforming zeal, has had far-reaching consequences that have reverberated well beyond the borders of Iraq.

The march into this war was to the drumbeat of a triumphalism that curiously manifested itself before, rather than after, the event. There was no doubt who was going to win. The eagerness to embrace war was palpable in large swathes of American public opinion, not least in Washington. Every other option was systematically closed or dismissed, often with no reason given. The targets of this assembling host, the relics of a tottering dictatorship, scurried around the world screaming at whoever would listen – the United Nations (UN), France, the Arab League – exposing themselves for the friendless and abandoned minnows that they were. But although the world was increasingly exasperated by the antics of the Saddamist regime, it was not enough, it would seem, to allow the USA unfettered access into Iraq.

For a long time Iraq had been viewed through a particular prism as regards US foreign policy, not for its own sake, but as part of a larger concern.

Throughout the 1950s, when the country formed part of the anti-communist regional alliance, the Baghdad Pact, Iraq was seen primarily as a staunch and vital ally against Soviet expansionism in the Middle East. Following the overthrow of the monarchy in 1958, American concern was primarily focused on thwarting the drive to power by the Iraqi Communist Party (ICP). When this threat was averted in the early 1960s, the USA settled into a policy bordering on indifference to the goings-on in Baghdad. With the Ba'ath Party having emerged victorious from the scrum of political contenders in 1968, the USA did not materially alter its stance. Throughout the 1970s, US policy towards Iraq was increasingly determined by a new strategic variable: the emergence of the Shah's Iran as a key ally in the area. Whenever the USA was seen to be interfering in Iraq's affairs, it was to enhance the relative power of Iran in the struggle for supremacy in the Gulf. Iraq was relegated to the second drawer of US concerns in the area. All this changed with the collapse of the Shah's rule and the establishment of the virulently anti-American Islamic Republic of Iran. The threat to the Gulf states was too real to ignore, and the hitherto neglected Ba'ath of Iraq, especially after the ascendancy of Saddam Hussein to unchallenged power in 1979, became a crucial instrument in blocking, and possibly reversing, the march of revolutionary Islam.

The war that Iraq fought with Iran (1980–88) was as much to do with protecting and advancing the interests of the west as with local and regional considerations. The USA viewed Saddam's Iraq as the single most valuable, albeit indirect, bulwark against the spread of revolutionary Islam into the Gulf region. After the Iran–Iraq War, the USA once again abandoned an assertive Iraqi policy, leaving the country with a bloated army, huge international debts and an embittered leadership that felt its sacrifices on behalf of others had not been properly acknowledged. In this short twilight period between 1988 and 1990, the USA allowed Iraq to stew in a dangerously delusional and sour condition – until Saddam made the cardinal sin of invading and annexing Kuwait, a major oil producer and an important and long-standing ally of the United States in the Gulf. The direct challenge to vital American and western interests, and the enormous effects this would have if it were not reversed, galvanised America into action. The objective became the expulsion of Iraqi forces from Kuwait and then a strategy to 'contain' Iraq. The latter was designed to disarm, isolate and weaken the regime, remove it as a threat to regional security, and keep it politically off balance. The Ba'ath regime was kept in a state of high anxiety by the USA's support for Kurdish autonomy from the central government, and by the conditional recognition of the disparate Iraqi opposition groups. By and large, in spite of a number of dramatic incidents that somewhat dented this scenario, this policy stayed the course throughout the 1990s, surviving three different administrations in Washington.

The administration of George W. Bush took office in January 2001. It was assumed that because of the bevy of neo-conservative advisers and officials who streamed into government, the strong streak of American ultra-nationalism in a number of key appointments, and the effects of the religious right on Bush personally, fundamental precepts of American policy towards Iraq would change substantially. In spite of the increasing volume of invective against the Saddamist regime, however, initially, there were no major changes in American policy towards Iraq. It took the attacks of 11 September, 2001 on the World Trade Center and the Pentagon to create the breach in the policy ramparts into which marched the proponents of the 'Alternative Discourse'. It was only then that Middle Eastern policy, in particular the policy towards Iraq, began to undergo a fundamental and far-reaching revision.

Several strands of thought, which had previously been consigned to the periphery of official policymaking on Islam and the Middle East in the Washington of the 1980s and 1990s, began to gather serious traction in the White House. Much has been written about the influence of the neo-conservatives, but in reality they were only one of several different, and often clashing, currents. These included 'Wilsonian' internationalists, who prescribed that the USA should be actively engaged with the world to promote the spread of democracy and liberty; the Christian Right with their apoca-lyptic visions; and the proponents of a muscular form of American nation-alism, who believed that the country should not shrink from using its immense global power to promote its narrow interests.

This ascendant and new *zeitgeist*, anchored in a deep loathing and resent-ment for all symbols and verities of the 'soft' liberalism that appeared to infuse American culture and society of the 1960s and 1970s, became, as it were, the forces of the new counter-reformation. Each of these strands saw in the post-9/11 world the possibility of advancing its own parochial points of view, and each catalysed official policymaking into focusing on Iraq as the locus of its plans. Some elements were genuinely concerned with the possibility that Iraq had WMD, ostensibly the only 'legitimate' grounds upon which an aggressive policy of regime change could be based. Such national security interests, not only of the United States, but also of Israel, played a large part in the thinking that underlay the decision to invade Iraq. Other factions had different agendas, including that of implanting the ideals of liberal democracy in the rocky terrain of the Arab world as an antidote to fundamentalist Islamism.

It would take some stretch of the imagination to align the disparate threads that drove the United States into the extraordinary decision to invade Iraq and to turn its own foreign policy on its head. The intellectual underpinnings of the 'Alternative Discourse', however, had been quietly fermenting in the corners of academic departments and obscure postgraduate seminars on political thought and Islamic history for some time. If ever ideas and the advancement of a particular perspective on events were to play a part in the unfolding of decisions of momentous consequence, then a good case could be made for the influence of Leo Strauss and Bernard Lewis. These two scholars probably never met, but their ideas pervaded the American project to refashion Iraq and beyond.

Strauss, a political philospher, believed in the role of the wise elite, schooled in Platonic ideals, exercising power over the mass, who would maintain harmony and quietly propagate the principles of the virtuous state and society. Members of the elite's main tasks were to act as counsellors and guides, preferably discreetly and anonymously, to the rulers who were committed to the shared symbols and ideals of their societies. The mass should be silently directed in subtle ways to protect them from their worst instincts and drives, while preserving their adherence to the basic principles and values of their societies. The fragility of liberal democracy and the ever-present threat of it being fatally undermined by either mass indifference, alarmingly present in modern western consumer societies, or by an aggressive and determined totalitarian adversary, became a recurrent theme in Strauss's writing.

Straussian thought began to take hold in the 1960s and 1970s. His ideas permeated the thinking of the budding counter-attack that emerged within the Reagan administration of the 1980s, and took form as the ideological underpinning of the shift in policy that displaced 'détente' with radical confrontation of the Soviet Union. When the administration of the second Bush was being organised, the Straussians, who had regrouped and strengthened themselves and their policies in various think-tanks and universities during their long exile in the Clinton years, were ready to assume leadership roles in key parts of the government, not least in the Defense and State departments and the National Security Council. The threat to America's national security from radical Islamism fitted exactly into the Straussian construct of what constituted a mortal danger to western democratic values, requiring a forceful and wide-ranging response in the form of the War on Terror. Strauss's followers in important positions in the government provided a philosophic structure and rationale for the way that the War on Terror was going to be fought. This, of course, merged into the other currents of what came to be called 'neo-conservatism', all of which were galvanised by the events of 11 September, 2001 and the predisposition of George W. Bush personally to accept and act upon these arguments.

None of these neo-conservative ideologies was in any way particularly involved with the Middle East, except in the narrow sense that there was a frequent overlap between their concern with American power and national security, and the security and defence of Israel. Nevertheless, the fact that these groups adopted Bernard Lewis's perspective on the Middle East allowed for the formulation of a policy that seemed to have all the ingredients of specificity for the Middle East, and in particular Iraq, when the time came to justify the invasion/liberation of that country.

Bernard Lewis studied at the School of Oriental and African Studies (SOAS) in London, specialising in Islamic history. Lewis developed a particular slant on Islam's encounter with modernity that ran counter to the then prevailing wisdom. The conventional view was that the political oppressiveness, social inequalities and economic backwardness in the Middle East were mainly because of the legacy of western imperialism and the west's incessant interference in the area's affairs. Lewis, however, postulated that the Islamic world's problems were mainly of its own making, driven by a congenital inability of Islamic civilisation to accommodate to its diminished status in the world. 'The Roots of Muslim Rage', the title of Bernard Lewis's now classic essay, was ultimately linked to the failure of Islamic civilisation to accept that it had been relegated to a secondary status by the manifest political and technological superiority of the west. This was even more galling, for this new world was dominated by Islam's historic rival, Christendom. Without this acknowledgement, Muslim societies were unable to rejuvenate themselves and adjust to modernity. Lewis wrote that 'This is no less than a clash of civilisations – the perhaps irrational but surely historic reaction of an ancient rival against our Judeo-Christian heritage, our secular present, and the worldwide expansion of both.'

Lewis's band of admirers grew perceptibly in the 1980s and 1990s and, with the advent of the Bush administration, joined up with the other strands of the 'Alternative Discourse' to dominate Middle East policymaking. Lewis himself put on the mantle of the 'public intellectual', appearing on numerous TV shows, and mentoring and advising all manner of officials in the post 9/11 Bush administration. The 'Lewis doctrine' became official policy, all the more so as Lewis was an enthusiastic advocate of using force to effect change. The invasion of Iraq could now be given a scholarly sheen, carrying the imprimatur of the 'most influential post-war historian of Islam and the Middle East', as Lewis was called by one of his academic followers. The grand scheme of dragging the Middle East, kicking and screaming, into the democratic and secular future designed for it by the 'best and the brightest' of the new Washington, would now begin in earnest. Iraq was in the right place and it was the right time to start the make-over of the region. Lewis and Strauss were profound influences, in deep and subtle ways, on the nexus of advisers, policymakers and war-planners that pushed the USA into invading Iraq.

But in their unseemly drive to war, the invasion's advocates forgot to consider other, more cautionary, narratives. The great sociologist Robert Merton died on 23 February, 2003 at the ripe old age of 92. In 1936 he wrote a seminal paper that should have been read – but probably was not – by the war's planners and boosters entitled 'The Unanticipated Consequences of

Purposive Social Action'. It showed how the actions of peoples and governments always result in unintended consequences, which can distort, negate,
but rarely enhance, the desired outcome. Merton isolated five contributing
factors to unintended consequences, each of which singly, or in combination,
can gravely affect the outcome of collective action or public policy. Merton's
five sources of unanticipated consequences were ignorance of the true conditions pertaining; error in inference; the primacy of immediate interests; the
ideological imperative (or the imperative of 'basic values' as he called it); and
self-fulfilling prophecy, a phrase that he actually coined. The implications
were that if policymakers did not minimise or militate against these factors,
then the outcome of a particular course of policy action would be undesirable,
or at least unexpected. Presumably, if all five variables were ignored, the
outcome might be catastrophic, from the policymaker's perspective. George W.
Bush's war of choice in Iraq was just that: a litany of unintended consequences
– a few astonishing, some surprising, some unwelcome, but most disastrous.
All of Merton's five contributing factors had been, wilfully or otherwise,
neglected in the decision to go to war. Iraq would be the first casualty; then the
region; and finally America itself.

In official Washington, the ignorance of what was going on inside Iraq
before the war was monumental. None of the proponents of the war,
including the neo-conservatives, and also no one in the institutes and think-
tanks that provided the intellectual fodder for the war's justification, had the
faintest idea of the country that they were to occupy. The academics and
researchers who congregated around the Washington think-tanks and the
vice-president's office, who had made Iraq their pet project, were blinkered by
their dogmatic certainties or their bigotries. There was a fundamental misunderstanding about the nature of Iraqi society and the effects on it of decades
of dictatorship. Each strand of American thinking that combined to provide
the basis for the invasion was isolated from any direct, even incidental,
engagement with Iraq. The State Department, supposedly a citadel of realist
thinking, had little first-hand experience of the country, instead relying on
inference and analogous reasoning when trying to unravel the possible
outcomes in the post-war period. The only certainty was provided by the
American military who knew that the Iraqis were no match for their kind of
warfare, and who also knew that they were facing a dispirited and ineffectual
army.

It was not only the absence of any systematic analysis, based on a wealth of
information and experience about the country that was the cause of this
woeful condition. It was more a deliberate revelling in the debunking of
whatever knowledge on Iraq existed. For nearly a decade, Iraq had been the
stomping ground of innumerable UN missions and teams. It had never been
the hermetically sealed country that many had supposed, and embassies and

foreign businesses continued to function throughout the 1990s. But knowledge of the country's internal conditions that might have been gained by these and other sources was never usefully employed to determine the possible outcomes to an invasion of the country. The Iraqi opposition, or at least those people who had access to official Washington, were no better. The exile groups, each with their different agendas, could not and did not provide the USA with a clear and reasonable assessment of the circumstances in Iraq. They were either too parochial in their concerns or simply too eager to assume power after America had removed Saddam. Such groups had no interest in shaking America's resolve by highlighting problems and pitfalls. The British, supposedly the wiser and more jaded of the two partners in the Anglo-American alliance, did not, and would not, play Athens to America's Rome. They were mired in balance-of-power rationalising, and had an obsessive fear of disrupting the status quo in the Middle East. Prime Minister Tony Blair believed that Britain had to be seen as a staunch American ally; he was overly concerned to stay on the right side of a belligerent president, almost irrespective of the merits of the situation. He saw himself as a bridle to Bush's wild horse; in the event, however, he was simply dragged along in whatever direction the horse led. Whatever qualms the British might have had were quietly laid aside. Merton's first rule had been broken. Ignorance of the conditions inside Iraq would very likely set off a cascading chain of unanticipated consequences.

The second of Merton's maxims was that error – in appraisal of a situation, in selecting an appropriate course of action, or in its implementation – would profoundly impact on the outcome of a policy decision. The invasion and occupation of Iraq comprised an index of errors of commission and omission. It would be difficult to catalogue them. There were just too many. They ranged from the numbers of troops deployed, to the type of people who ran the country, to the policy changes, to the off-handedness regarding decisions of monumental consequence. The range, number and pernicious effects of these errors were astounding. Merton might have well been writing of post-war Iraq when he described this type of error as a 'pathological obsession where there is a determined refusal or inability to consider certain elements of the problem'. This was seen time and again in Iraq, where a fixation on one milestone or another, or a determined insistence on pursuing an imagined goal, distorted an objective assessment of the circumstances. Wish-fulfilment was a consequential aspect of the work and pronouncements of the decision-makers in Iraq. This, as Merton said, has to do more with psychiatric literature. The persistence in pursuing erroneous policies – for fear of being off-message; for fear of jeopardising one's career; for fear of the political consequences of 'incorrectness'; or because of an unwillingness to produce, or an incapability of producing, an alternative – was a feature of the entire post-war period.

The third of Merton's tenets was the 'imperious immediacy of interest', where the desire for an outcome is so great that there is a wilful ignoring of its effects. This is, of course, different from ignorance that comes from simply not knowing. Elections were held despite the Sunni boycott; constitutions were delivered in record time, even though there were glaring flaws that had to be rectified. Months after the elections of December 2005, there was still no sign of the promised parliamentary committees to reconsider the offending constitutional articles. The issue of federalism for the South, on which the future of Iraq as a unitary state may well rest, was rammed through with nary a debate. The desire to play out the process according to its original blueprint was so great that it overshadowed, and precluded, any alternative line of reasoning, even when the country's constitution-drafters had to produce a historic document in a few weeks. This was an absurd outcome that reverberated against the entire process. Deals were cut that could not withstand the test of reason or time.

The fourth Merton principle that went unheeded was the effect on decision-making of actions that were driven by a moral or ideological imperative. This was not supposed to happen within the rules of statecraft, where the interests of the state took precedence over other considerations in the formulation of policy. The Bush administration had come into office by castigating the 'immorality' of the previous president, and promised an era of principled government that would be guided by a Higher Authority. 'There is a higher father that I appeal to,' as Bush said. Bush's intense religiosity coloured all his actions, and it certainly played a part in his decision to invade Iraq. In the detailed account of America's march to war, Bob Woodward wrote in his 2004 book, *Plan of Attack*, about Bush's communion with the Almighty that Bush 'was praying for strength to do the Lord's will'. But in a denial that was more of an admission, Bush said, 'I'm surely not going to justify war based upon God. Understand that. Nevertheless, in my case, I pray that I will be as good a messenger of His will as possible.' With a certainty that comes from a burning faith – something that more cynical Europeans could not understand – there was no room to sit and measure out the consequences of faith-driven decisions.

The religiosity of Bush united with an important constituency of the Bush presidency, the Religious Right, who were well represented in both official Washington and the Baghdad occupation authorities. There, it was a belief that the Iraq war was an enactment and harbinger of a number of eschatological prophecies, and that they were the handmaidens for the imminent Second Coming. Other, equally zealous, political ideologues added to the brew of religious verities. None of these groups, which ranged from radical neo-conservatives, champions of frog-marching the Arabs into democracy, geo-politicians intent on 'containing' Iran and militant Islam, would brook any discussion of their ideas, or the assumptions that underlay them. The Iraq war was a godsend – for some literally – as it would allow them to play out their theories and fantasies on the *tabula rasa* of a new Iraq. No one had any time or desire to examine the consequences of the decisions that they were proposing, or pushing for others to adopt. For example, America's toppling of Iran's bitter foe, Saddam, immensely strengthened the influence and power of Iran in Iraq. This was hardly the intended consequence of those who sought to create a democratic bulwark in Iraq as a goad to the Iran of the theocrats. Similarly with democracy itself. The vision of a liberal, secular Iraq governed by elected officials through representative institutions sank with the realisation that democracy might well empower the very groups that were thought to be most hostile to it or those communities that saw the democratic process simply in terms of strengthening their side's control over the state apparatus.

The last of Merton's principles that was ignored was the self-fulfilling prophecy that might come back and haunt the architects of the war. This was especially true in the matter of the War against Terror, Bush's mobilising cry for the American people after the 9/11 attacks. The American public became convinced that there was a link between the Saddam regime and the threat of further terrorist attacks. In fact, the Ba'ath regime, which had a terrible record otherwise, steered clear of being associated with acts of terror against the USA. The WMD argument might possibly have fitted (at its edges) with the War against Terror, if such WMD had indeed existed in Saddam's Iraq. After an exhaustive search for several months by the Iraq Survey Group, however, none was found – and neither was there any incriminating evidence connecting the former regime either with the 9/11 plotters or the al-Qaeda organisation. But then something unexpected happened: Iraq became a centre for global terrorists of the Islamist variety. The fight against terror in Iraq, where previously international terrorists had existed purely as a supposition, now turned into reality. Terrorists were drawn into Iraq not only to fight the USA, but also to fight a host of other enemies that had not been there before the war – mainly the Shi'a ascendancy and the Iranians.

The law of unintended consequences exploded with such force in Iraq because the planners of the war ignored or minimised the hazards of their decisions. Shrewder and/or more perceptive people knew instinctively that the invasion of Iraq would open up the great fissures in Iraqi society, with enormous regional and international consequences. By far the most significant and historically resonant was the tipping of the scales in favour of the Shi'a. The USA may have fallen for the self-serving description of Iraq's Shi'a as a force that was simply waiting to express its democratic proclivities and its gratitude to its liberators. Rather, the invasion achieved what they had thought impossible: the removal of their nemesis by an irresistible external force. Moreover, the new force was eager to seek their community's support and by and large acquiesced in the equitable distribution of power to the Shi'a's clear advantage. But the Shi'a would remain prickly, and their leadership equivocal, about giving the Americans their undivided loyalty – as the other great gainer, the Kurds, appeared willing to do. The truth was that the Shi'a might have been fleetingly grateful to the Americans. Learning from the wrong choices that their leaders had made in 1920, the Shi'a were not going to dump their fortuitous 'leg-up' this time for some *jihadi*-inspired ideology. At the same time, they were not prepared to jettison their collective consciousness or their sense of historic grievance for the sake of the foreigner's goodwill. The weight of the past was too great, and the opportunities to reverse the hand that history had dealt them were too enticing, to fall for the promise of a non-sectarian and liberal Iraq.

The Shi'a identity was connected not only with the legacy of being the victims of the powers that ruled Islamdom but also with the belief that they were the repositories of true Islam. It was this point that was always ignored by analysts when they sought to calibrate the response of the Shi'a to events that were of significance to *all* Muslims. The Shi'a were victims – of despotic rulers, of Wahhabi bigotry, of indifference and often contempt by their Sunni co-religionists – but they were still identifiably and defiantly Muslim. Hostility to Zionism, to imperial designs on Muslim territory and resources, to the infiltration into their societies of western mores and culture, were built into their identity as custodians of true Islam. The Iraqi advocates of the Shi'a's role as the west's natural allies in Iraq and the greater Middle East confused Shi'ism with something else entirely. The heterodoxies of Islam, which were the speciality of scholars such as Bernard Lewis, spawned the argument that the Middle East's outsiders would be the standard bearers of modernism in the Middle East, and therefore the allies of America's project in Iraq. The problem with this way of thinking is that the Shi'a do not see themselves as heterodox; rather, they believe that it is they who uphold the authentic version of Islam and who are therefore responsible for its protection.

Within a few weeks of the invasion and occupation, the reflex action of Iraqis, honed over generations of dealing with tyrants and occupiers, began to kick in. Americans began to experience the ambivalence of the Iraqis in their different guises; the impenetrability of what they truly thought; the bursts of spontaneous violence; the delight in getting the better of the occupier. Also, there was no overlooking the tide of carpetbaggers, con men and camp followers that descended on Baghdad like a plague of locusts. The recasting of the country was supposed to take place within this scene of chaos and confusion, played out against an increasingly violent background. There was no clash of civilisations in Iraq. The actual picture was closer to a chaotic movie, with villains, heroes, and extras wandering on and off the set, and a massive crowd of sullen and dispirited onlookers. This was hardly the vision of the neo-conservatives, or of the starry-eyed dreamers who wanted to 'bring democracy to the Arabs', or of the quick-in-quick-out champions of 'shock and awe'.

Iraq is one of the most invaded and violated territories in the history of the world, and over a long period of time the people who lived in the country had developed survival and accommodation skills that would confound the most determined of occupiers. None of this should have come as a surprise. There were enough pointers in Iraq's recent past to show the likely response of Iraqis to the massive jolt of a physical occupation by foreign powers, and the effects that a violent upending of apparently stable relationships would have on the varied components of its society. The dictatorships and autocracies that had ruled Iraq over the previous half century had tried, through imposing a stultifying uniformity, to smother a true understanding of the country's complex identity. This had been the norm for the rulers of Iraq, in one form or another, for hundreds of years, but it had had little effect on the pattern of the people's affiliations. In an age of nationalisms, the affirmation of the country's basic identity with its dominant Arab ethnicity did not cancel out the existence of other very large populations. Neither did the identification of the state with the prevailing orthodoxies of the broader Islamic world alter the fact that the sectarian affiliation of the majority of the inhabitants, always a crucial factor in the politics of the region, was different from the majority in the Islamic world. The fact remained that the underlying western ethos that governed the thinking about Iraq, prior to and even after the occupation, was essentially derived from schools whose teachings were fundamentally alien to the experiences of the country.

A great deal of anguish, puzzlement and hand-wringing would have been avoided if the pundits and mandarins who were planning for the invasion and the post-war order had paid attention to the lessons and warnings of Ali al-Wardi.

If any single person has come close to unlocking the secrets of the Iraqi character, it is Ali al-Wardi (1913–95). His works on the social psychology of Iraqis and his forays into Iraqi social history made him an eminent – and controversial figure – in his own time. He had frequent brushes with the authorities, especially since his conclusions did not mesh with the official versions of Iraq's history that successive regimes were spinning. His work, however, was overlooked or even dismissed by western academics and experts on the country. In many respects, his writings on the social history of Iraq and his generalisations on the social pathologies of Iraqis did not match western standards of academic scholarship, but this did not detract in any fundamental sense from their profundity and wisdom. No one of consequence in the US administration, or even in that of its ally, Britain, consulted what al-Wardi had spent decades analysing and assessing. His research, his anecdotal style of writing, laced as it was with recollections of farcical and curious episodes in Iraq's social history, was simply ignored. His work did not fit into any category of what was considered acceptable thinking in the west, neither for those who advocated war in the interest of universalising the fruits of democracy nor for those who insisted on the preservation of the balance of power or Arab 'exceptionalism'. He was simply too awkward, too eclectic, in his method to have been taken seriously as an authority on Iraq, Iraqis and 'Iraqiness'.

Ali al-Wardi was born into a well-known family of merchants and *ulema* (religious scholars) in Kadhimain, Iraq. In Kadhimain life revolved around the twin shrines of the seventh and ninth Imams of the Shi'a, which received pilgrims from all over the Muslim world. His early life seems to have been one of considerable hardship and deprivations. Nevertheless, he managed to gain entry to the prestigious American University of Beirut, and went on to receive his Master's and PhD degrees in sociology from the University of Texas in 1950. He returned to Iraq where he joined the faculty of Baghdad University, and rose to become the leading figure in its sociology and social history department.

Ali al-Wardi was a prolific writer. His most notable work was the monumental, multi-volume social history of modern Iraq, misleadingly entitled *Sociological Glimpses from the Modern History of Iraq*, and he summarised the results of his life-long enquiry into the roots of Iraqi society in a volume entitled *Studies in the Nature of Iraqi Society*. Ali al-Wardi rejected the statistically based methodology of modern, mainly Anglo-American, social science, which he found inappropriate for Iraq's conditions. Rather, his methodology followed Max Weber, as he openly admits, but he may have been equally influenced by his readings of the Muslim world's greatest philosopher of history, Ibn Khaldun, whom he called 'the best of references'. It is probably from Ibn Khaldun that he drew his inspirations for his major insight into the nature of Iraqi society, namely the pervasive dichotomy between the city, representing urban civilised values, and the steppes, representing the prevalence of nomadic, tribal values.

Ali al-Wardi insisted that the process of modernisation and urbanisation was skin deep in Iraq, and that tribal values, born of the experience of surviving in the harsh environment of the desert, continued to hold sway for the vast majority of the country's inhabitants. He claimed that the fragility of civilised values in Iraq was partly a response to the frequent invasions that devastated the country. Under such circumstances, Iraq would rapidly shed its civilised veneer and revert to the culture and values of tribal nomadism. The sense of the impermanence of the source of their values drove Iraqis into developing their noted schizoid qualities. The desert could actually or metaphorically encroach on the city, while at the same time, the city could tame the desert by harnessing the country's waters and cultivating its soil. The second key finding of al-Wardi was that Iraqis were ambivalent about the wellsprings of their value systems, which, given the stark contrast between town and desert, obliged them to accommodate conflicting and contradictory perspectives within their persons. The advance of modernity did not decisively supplant one with the other, but merely camouflaged this character bifurcation more adroitly. (The ebb and flow of urban/desert values continued in another manifestation during the last decade of the Ba'athist rule in Iraq, when the values of the tribe were given decisive ascendancy by the regime and became the norm for society.)

This cultural ambivalence has had serious consequences. The state, which is a defining feature of advancing civilisations, stands in contrast to tribal solidarity as an organising principle. The latter celebrates the tribe as the repository of virtues. At the personal level this translates to bigotry, a proneness to disputation and violence, and an exaggerated concern with lineage and status. The tribesman sees the state as a usurper and exploiter, but this has not stopped the tribal migrant to the city from seeking employment in the government as a highly desirable end in itself. The tribesman disdains craftsmanship and most professions, and prefers the prestige of a governmental post to the perceived inferiority of the tradesman's lot. The lackadaisical attitudes to property rights and the rule of law stand in contrast to the perceived glory of seizing property and imposing one's will through force or fear. The latter are eminently tribal traits that persist, even in a modern setting.

The sense of a conflict-strewn society permeates the work of al-Wardi: tribe versus tribe; tribe versus government; intra-urban violence between neighbourhoods; tribe versus town; town versus town; town versus government. The religious divide in society between Shi'a and Sunni also manifests itself in the form of mutual antagonism; however, al-Wardi does not relate this to any innate dogmatic hostility between the sects but sees it as an expression of the tendency of social units and groups in Iraq to divide into antagonistic camps. The rivalries between the Ottomans and the Safavids for control over Iraq exacerbated the Sunni/Shi'a divide, and this fissiparous antipathy continued in different forms into modern times. Ali al-Wardi linked Shi'ism to the south of Iraq, and considered it an urban phenomenon, or at least mostly prevalent in settled populations. Sunnism in Iraq, however, was associated with the prevalence of nomadism and tribalism, and was mainly to be found in the steppes of northwest Iraq. The centre of the country was a stronghold of moderate Sunnism, especially Sufism.

The potential social glue of the Islamic faith, when transposed to the toxic inheritance of the history of the country, became an instrument of control, dispossession and marginalisation. Each episode in Islamic history, instead of forming a shared expression of a common heritage, became infused with a factional perspective and added to the intensity of societal divisions. Iraq was imperfectly modernised, and there remained the ever-present contradictions between cultural values and traits acquired in the alleyways of towns or the hardscrabble life of remote villages, and the imported ideas that accompanied the modernisation process. Transformation of society was a painfully slow process, subject to frequent setbacks and reversals, with old patterns of behaviour often returning to the ascendancy. Here it should be noted that Al-Wardi saw democracy and democratic values always as social rather than political virtues.

Ali al-Wardi invented a new type of sociology, which was that of a fragmented social order interacting within the framework of a tumultuous historic legacy. It emphasised the disjointed nature of Iraqi society, held together by geographic imperatives of coexistence in the same space rather than a common sense of shared history or purpose. This underlying scepticism about the prospects of a quick reform of Iraqi society made him an unacceptable figure to those who proposed to 're-engineer' the country according to the prevailing ideology. That does not necessarily mean that he took a fatalistic position regarding the possibilities of change, rather that he insisted that no social or political project could succeed if it did not take a realistic account of the country's inheritance. In the end, he did come out in favour of a special variety of democracy, one that was based on both recognition of the country's diversity and proportional representation. 'The people of Iraq are divided against themselves and their sectarian, ethnic and tribal struggles exceed those of any other Arab people .... There is no way of resolving this condition better than adopting a democratic system, where each group can participate in power *according to its proportional number* [author's italics].'

The importance of Ali al-Wardi's thesis lies specifically in the possibility that it might have provided a counterbalance to the range of ill-considered and ahistorical assessments of Iraq that governed the planning for the war and its aftermath. Those who drew their lessons from their own engagement with Iraq, notably the British, could have provided the only other alternative reading of Iraq. But their perspective was also flawed, marred as it was by a fear of contradicting the reigning orthodoxies in Washington once the decision to go to war appeared to gather an irreversible momentum. A few voices were raised to remind people of the celebrated 1920 Uprising against British rule as a possible indicator of how Iraqis would respond to occupation. The only lesson drawn from that uprising, which seemed to have appreciative audiences in both the State Department and the Foreign Office, was that an authoritarian minority, preferably drawn from the military, should rule the country. This argument, of course, never got a serious hearing and was summarily brushed aside. It could not withstand the withering contempt from the messianic advocates of full-blown democracy as a precondition for the broader changes to be effected in Iraq and the rest of the Middle East.

People with these views had gained the upper hand, both intellectually and in the corridors of power in Washington, and there was no room for any seriously dissenting views.

When the Coalition arrived in Baghdad on 9 April, 2003, it found a fractured and brutalised society, presided over by a fearful, heavily armed minority. The post 9/11 *jihadi* culture that was subsequently to plague Iraq was just beginning to take root. The institutions of the state were moribund; the state exhausted. The ideology that had held Ba'athist rule had decayed beyond repair. None of this was entirely unexpected, but it masked something more profound. These were the surface manifestations of Iraqi, particularly Iraqi Arab, society. But the real dangers – of divisiveness, vengefulness, deeply held grievances and bottled-up ethnic and sectarian passions – lurked underneath.

1

The Great Divides

'In this regard and with my heart filled with sadness, I have to say that it is my belief that there is no Iraqi people inside Iraq. There are only diverse groups with no national sentiments. They are filled with superstitious and false religious traditions with no common grounds between them. They easily accept rumours and are prone to chaos, prepared always to revolt against any government. It is our responsibility to form out of this mass one people that we would then guide, train and educate. Any person who is aware of the difficult circumstances of this country would appreciate the efforts that have to be exerted to achieve these objectives.' –

Faisal I, King of Iraq, 1932[1]

Conflicts and wars fought on its territory have always been the lot of Iraq. It has had the geographic misfortune of lying across the fault lines of civilisations and empires, and its peoples have suffered the waves of conquerors and battles fought over its lands. The ebb and flow of powers that controlled its destiny always left behind a residue that helped to form the profile of the modern Iraqi. But these were not accretions that melded together to form a common sense of nationhood. The shared history and experiences of Iraqis did not give rise to unifying national myths. The legacy of pre-Islamic civilisations – of Sumer, Babylon and Nineveh – was not one that could be readily adapted to the formation of national identity. The pride that came from knowing that Iraq was the land that gave humanity settled agriculture, its first cities and the alphabet, was not internalised. Iraq's ancient history featured only on the periphery of the identity of Muslim Iraqis.[2] Various modern governments have tried to make the connection and continuity with this heritage – sometimes ludicrously, as when Saddam Hussein appropriated the heritage of the lawmaker Hammurrabi and stuck his name on the (rebuilt) walls of Babylon.[3] But it was never pursued with the intent of forming a national consciousness.

The Terrain and Population of Iraq

Iraq, the land of the two rivers, the Mesopotamia of ancient times, is an amalgam of different landscapes and terrains. The tiny coastline leads to the magnificent waterway of the Shatt al-Arab, the confluence of the two rivers, an area of dense palm groves and lush fields. Above Basra, the main city of Iraq's Deep South, the Shatt al-Arab separates into its two components. There, the marshes of the South begin. It is a landscape of immense expanses of water, of bulrushes, herds of water buffalo and dozens of scattered reed-matted villages. The Tigris River route to Baghdad passes through the cities of 'Amara and Kut, lying in a flat plain. Eastwards, the terrain gently slopes into the hills that lead towards the Iranian plateau. The Euphrates route to Baghdad is more settled, with several towns and cities along the way – Nasiriya, Samawwa, Diwaniya, Hilla, and the shrine cities of Karbala and Najaf. This is a land of rice and barley, and of market gardens and date groves, especially in the Hilla area, on the approach to Baghdad. North of Baghdad, the two rivers separate in ever-widening distances. The Tigris, capricious and flood-prone, has only a few towns of note on its banks – Samarra, Dujail, Tikrit – before the great northern city of Mosul. To the northeast of Baghdad lie the fertile lands of Diyala province – fruit orchards, vegetable farming and cereal cultivation – well watered by a number of tributaries of the Tigris. This is also the start of the undulating hilly, and then mountainous, terrain that marks the territory of Iraqi Kurdistan which stretches like a giant crescent over all of northeastern and northern Iraq. From Fallujah near Baghdad to the Syrian border, the Euphrates harbours a string of small towns on its banks – 'Ana, Rawa, Haditha – but the area is marked by its poor agricultural potential. To the west of the Euphrates lies the great western desert, which effectively separates Iraq from the Arab lands of the Near East. Between the upper reaches of the Euphrates and Tigris rivers lie the steppe-lands of the Jazira, and the grazing and pasture lands of the Arab tribes of the area.

The population of Iraq is equally varied. Arabic is universally spoken outside Iraqi Kurdistan, and Islam is the religion of the vast majority of the people. Over time, the Arab element has assumed primacy, leaving the Kurds, in their hill and mountain country, distinct in their language and culture. The Arab pre-eminence did not completely destroy the ethnic and linguistic identity of the Turkomen and the ancient Christian Assyrian and Chaldean communities, however. The lower reaches of the Tigris and Euphrates valleys are overwhelmingly Shi'a Muslim in faith but Arab in identity. The city of Basra has an important Sunni minority. Migrants from the rural South have overwhelmed Basra, which used to be a polyglot city with large merchant communities from the Indian sub-continent and Iran. Baghdad itself, accounting for a quarter of the population, is a majority Shi'a city. It has a

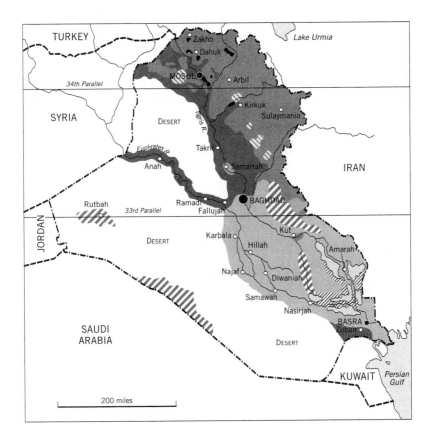

Shi'a Arabs, 55%

Kurds, 21% (Sunni, Shi'a, Yezidi)

Sunni Arabs, 18.5%

Assyrians, Chaldeans, Armenians, 3.5% (Christians)

Turkomen, 2% (Shi'a and Sunni)

Mandians, 0.5% (Sabaens)

Sparsely populated

Notes
Persians, once numerous, were largely expelled in the early 1950s. Armenians are found only
in the major cities.
There are about 400 Jews left in Iraq, post-1950s.

Demographic Map of Iraq

large Sunni Arab population (the majority population in earlier times), with important concentrations of Kurds and Christians. The upper reaches of the Euphrates River are overwhelmingly Sunni Arab, as is the Tigris north of Baghdad – with the exception of the towns of Dujail and Balad, which are two Shi'a enclaves. The north of Iraq is a mosaic of peoples including Arabs, Kurds, Shabak, Chaldeo-Assyrians, and Turkomen. Mosul, lying on the Tigris, is a majority Sunni Arab city, with a large Kurdish east bank and an important Christian community. Turkomen, who are evenly divided between adherents of Shi'a and Sunni Islam, predominate in a few towns, and are historically associated with the city of Kirkuk. In Iraqi Kurdistan, the majority of the people adhere to Sunni Islam. Iraq's total population of about 25 million is divided ethnically between Arabs (perhaps 75 per cent of the population), Kurds about 20 per cent, Turkomen and Chaldeo-Assyrians about 2 per cent each, and smaller groups, such as the Yezidi, Sabaeans and Shabak, accounting for the rest. The population is overwhelmingly Muslim (about 97 per cent of the total). The Arab Shi'a comprise about 60 per cent of the population, the Sunni Arabs about 18 per cent and the Kurds about 20 per cent. The great majority of the Shi'a in Iraq is Arab, but there are also about a million Shi'a Kurds, known as Faylis, as well as the small Shabak community of the Mosul area.

The Genesis of Modern Iraq

The Arab conquest of Iraq and the spread of Islam were distinct breaks from Iraq's ancient past. It is to this period – and to the Ottoman–Persian rivalries that were often played out on its lands – that the modern predicaments of Iraq can be traced. *This* past was not another country. The conflicts that arose from it remained essentially unreconciled and unresolved, even with the passing of centuries. It is true that Iraqis shared in, and often inspired, the glories of Islamic civilisation, but these were insufficient to create a common identity. There was an underside to all of this: of winners and losers; of lost causes clung to, in spite of centuries of repression; of racial and tribal animosities. Too often, what was retained was a violently different version of events, and a culture that celebrated superiority in status and entitlements, as well as past grievances and injuries. For over two millennia, Iraq had either been the centre of a world empire or, more often, part of another country's empire. It was only in modern times that the geopolitical unity of Iraq became established – neither as a contrived state, as many would later claim, nor as a nation in the full sense of the word.

The Kingdom of Iraq emerged out of World War I; it was a state whose boundaries were drawn by Great Britain with little say from its inhabitants.[4] Faisal, son of Sharif Hussein of the Hejaz, was installed as king of Iraq in

August 1921, following a referendum managed by Great Britain, the power mandated to manage the affairs of Iraq at the end of World War I.[5] Iraq had been carved out of the remnants of the Ottoman Empire, and initially included the two Ottoman *wilayets* (provinces) of Baghdad and Basra, to which the northern *wilayet* of Mosul was added in 1926, to form the territorial boundaries of the modern Iraqi state. Faisal had led the Northern Army of his father, the Sharif Hussein of the Hejaz, who, encouraged by the British, and with financial and material support, had revolted against the Ottoman Empire in 1916. Sharif Hussein believed that he had been promised a united Arab kingdom that included modern Syria, Lebanon, Palestine and the Hejaz, as a reward for assisting the Allied war effort against Turkey. His dreams were shattered, however, when he discovered that the British and the French between them had secretly carved out the Ottoman Empire in the Sykes–Picot Agreement.[6] Faisal, who entered Damascus in October 1918 at the head of an Arab army, tried to enforce his father's claims. He was, for a brief period, declared King of Syria, only to be ignominiously expelled by the French in July 1920.[7] Iraq had been a different theatre of war. The British had managed to defeat the Turks only after a long and arduous campaign that stretched over four years. No sooner had the war ended than a major uprising erupted against the British, instigated and led by the Shi'a religious leadership in the shrine towns of Iraq. The revolt, always known afterwards in Iraq as the 1920 Uprising, was a defining moment in modern Iraqi history. It was put down at great human and financial cost. The British subsequently decided to rule the country indirectly. Through a series of intricate negotiations and manoeuvres in Whitehall, Baghdad and Cairo, where Britain's leading Middle East experts had gathered in March 1921 to plan the post-war order in the Middle East, Faisal emerged as the leading candidate for the throne of Iraq.[8]

Faisal had struggled very hard to understand his adopted land, and after over a decade of rule had began to exhibit a subtle appreciation of the intricacies of this heterogeneous country. He had held the ship of state firmly on the course of modernisation and centralisation, in spite of the treacherous politics of his faction-ridden country. He had been squeezed by the often conflicting demands and pressures of the British; the Shi'a religious authorities; the Sunni Arab officers (who formed the backbone of his army and administration); the urban intelligentsia; and the tribal leaders.

In March 1932, Faisal addressed an extraordinary memorandum to the principal political figures in Iraq, asking them to comment on his assessment of the conditions of the country. Although it has appeared from time to time in the texts of a number of historical works on Iraq, only very occasionally has it been accorded its true significance. This is because the memorandum, emanating from such an authoritative source, would have proved deeply embarrassing to an emerging, ideologically driven account of Iraq's social and political history, as it laid bare the real imbalances in the country.

Faisal wrote:

> Iraq is one of those countries that lack a key requirement of a social polity, namely a unity of thought and ideals, and a sense of community. The country is fragmented and divided against itself, and its political leadership needs to be both wise, practical and morally and materially strong. [Its inhabitants] should not be driven by private sensibilities and concerns, or sectarian and extremist considerations. They should be both just and balanced, and strong, with a sense of respect for the people's traditions. They should not be guided by reactionary considerations, or extremist thinking that would draw a violent response.

He continued:

> Iraq is a kingdom that is run by a Sunni Arab government established on the ruins of the Ottoman state. This government rules a Kurdish part, whose majority is ignorant and is led by selfish individuals who incite their compatriots to secede from the state on the grounds that it is not of their kind. The government also rules a Shi'a majority, ignorant in the main, but which is of the same ethnicity. However, the oppression that the Shi'a have suffered at the hands of the Turks did not allow them to share in power and thereby gain the necessary experience in government. This opened a deep chasm between the Arab people of Iraq, divided as they are between these two sects. All this drove this majority – or at least those amongst them who have special interests, clerics, undeserving office-seekers, and those who have not benefited financially from the new order – to claim that they continue to be oppressed simply by being Shi'a. They are being encouraged to abandon the state as an evil entity, and we cannot deny the effect that these people have on the ignorant and simple-minded mass. . . . I do not want to justify the position of the ignorant mass of the Shi'a, and relay what I have heard thousands of times . . . that taxes and death are the Shi'a's lot while the Sunni enjoy the privilege of office. What belongs to the Shi'a then? Even their religious occasions are not sanctioned.[9]

Faisal's melancholic memorandum captured the essence of the country – the great divides between its peoples. It drew a muted response. The politicians were too busy in their power games to step back and look at the country over which they were fighting.

The Shi'a–Sunni Divide

The Shi'a–Sunni split in Islam did not occur, as is often claimed, upon the death of the Prophet Muhammad on 8 June, 632. It evolved over centuries before doctrinal positions hardened and the religious and community distinctiveness of the two groups crystallised. What is indisputable, though, is that the succession to the Prophet formed the basis for this schism. This was when the nascent Muslim community divided between the claims to rulership by Ali, the Prophet's cousin and son-in-law, and those of the three 'Rightly Guided' Caliphs who preceded him as leaders of the Islamic community.[10] From the onset, this division was not simply a case of rival political camps vying for power. It had deep social, tribal, ethnic and religious undertones. To the followers of Ali – the *Shi'a* of Ali – the Household of the Prophet, of whom Ali was the emphatic leader, possessed a certain charisma, bordering on divine sanction, that entitled them not only to spiritual, but temporal, authority over all Muslims. Ali's followers acquiesced, by and large, to the loss of power of their claimant to the first three Caliphs (successors) of the Prophet: Abu Bakr, 'Umar and 'Uthman. Ali himself, while upholding the righteousness of his own position, seemed to accept their rule over Muslims. The murder of the third Caliph, 'Uthman, finally thrust Ali into the Caliphate. But it was a Caliphate that at its outset was bedevilled by hostility and open rebellion by the followers of 'Uthman and the Banu Ummayya, led by the formidable Muawiyya, a relative of 'Uthman, who had been installed as governor in Syria. Ali moved his capital away from Medina to Kufa, in Iraq, on the banks of the Euphrates, to meet the challenge of Muawiyya. Iraq's allegiance to the Household of the Prophet and the veneration of the figure of Ali and his progeny can be directly traced to the momentous decision to move the fulcrum of Muslim power from the Arabian Peninsula to Iraq.

Ali's rule was short-lived. He was beset by mutinies and revolts which soon broke out into full-scale civil war – the so-called *fitna* – between loyalists to his cause and the followers of Muawiyya. Shortly after the inconclusive battle of Siffin with Muawiyya, Ali was assassinated. Ali's son Hassan, son of Fatima, the Prophet's daughter, briefly assumed the mantle of Caliph. He was then prevailed upon to relinquish his claim in favour of Muawiyya. He went into exile where agents of Muawiyya most probably poisoned him. The Ummayyad dynasty, based in Damascus, was born. The events that led to the first schism and its aftermath became one of the defining episodes in the evolution of Shi'a identity. The death of Muawiyya and the accession of his dissolute son Yazid to the Caliphate were contrary to the commitments that Muawiyya made to Hassan to clinch the relinquishing of his claims to the Caliphate. The opposition to the rule of the Ummayyads began to coalesce around Ali's son Hussein, also a son of Fatima, the Prophet's daughter. Hussein left Mecca for

Kufa, to rally his supporters and to lead the struggle against Yazid. He was abandoned, however, by his erstwhile followers in Kufa, who had been cowed into submission by Yazid's governor. Hussein, together with a small band of devoted followers and members of his family, were left stranded in the deserts southwest of the Euphrates River and hounded by Yazid's armies. Hussein brought his party to a final halt near the modern town of Karbala in Iraq, where he prepared to confront the vastly superior numbers of his enemy. The encounter on the desert plains near Karbala, memorialised by most Muslims thereafter by the rites of penitence of the 10th of Muharram – or ʿAshoura – became the most significant date in the history of the Shi'a. Hussein was brutally killed, together with nearly all his male followers, while the women-folk and children were driven away into captivity. The events at Karbala left a permanent scar on the psyche of Muslims. The Prophet's grandson and numerous members of his family had been pitilessly slaughtered and the guilt associated with the act of betrayal and abandonment of Hussein became a recurrent theme in Muslim, especially Shi'a, lore.[11]

Although the Ummayyads had managed to consolidate their power and authority, their legitimacy was constantly challenged by regular insurrections that broke out demanding vengeance for the Household of the Prophet. One of these rebellions, in 750, delivered power not to the direct descendants of the Prophet through Fatima and her sons, Hassan and Hussein, but to the descendants of the Prophet's uncle, al-Abbas. In time, the Abbasids appropriated for themselves the perceived legitimacy that came from being included in the Household of the Prophet, and a majority of Muslims accepted their claim to authority. Nevertheless, a minority rejected the Abbasid compromise, and continued to acknowledge only the spiritual authority of the Shi'a Imams, direct descendants of the martyred Hussein. It was during the five centuries of Abbasid rule that the main outlines of the Shi'a–Sunni schism became established. While the majority tendency coalesced around the four jurisprudential schools of Sunni Islam, which became recognised during the early Abbasid period, it took the Shi'a several centuries before a particular strain – the so-called Imami or Ithna-ʿAshari (Twelver) school – became dominant within Shi'a Islam.[12]

The Abbasids' policies towards the Shi'a varied from a guarded tolerance and accommodation to outright persecution. The Shi'a of the Abbasid period considered themselves an elite, and while they provided numerous functionaries and ministers to the Court, and were prominent in the cultural and commercial life of the Islamic Empire, they kept aloof from the mass, as well as the religious leadership, of the majority Sunni. The detente between the two communities was fragile and punctuated with riots. When the Abbasid Caliphate accommodated the Shi'a, Shi'a symbols and rituals were fully enacted and officially honoured. It was during the Abbasid period that the doctrines of the Shi'a became to a large extent formalised, and set the pattern for the community until the sixteenth century.

The final phase of the crystallisation of modern-day Shi'ism began with the establishment of Safavid power in Iran and the enforced conversion of its people to Imami Shi'ism.[13] The struggles between the Ottomans and Safavids for supremacy in Iraq spilled over into the broader Shi'a–Sunni relationships inside the country, with each community seeking to bolster its position and status with reference to its imperial champion. With the ascendancy of Ottoman power in Iraq in the seventeenth century, the Shi'a were reduced to a subordinate status in the country, and were systematically discriminated against. This became the hallmark for the distribution of power and privilege in the country throughout the Ottoman period.[14]

Two critical tendencies emerged in the eighteenth and nineteenth centuries that had a profound effect on the course of Shi'ism in Iraq. The first was of a doctrinal nature, and was instrumental in cementing the power of the *ulema* over the mainstream Shi'a. Strict traditionalists, known as the *Akhbaris*, insisted on the primacy of the sayings of the Imams of the Shi'a as the basis for jurisprudential rulings and pious actions. They, however, were decisively defeated by those who called for the use of *ijtihad*, or independent reasoning, based on scriptural sources, in promulgating valid religious decisions. The latter group became known as the *usulis*. This, of course, put a premium on scholastic learning and gave an enormous impetus to the rise of an organised class of *ulema*, the *mujtahids*, who could use their knowledge of the source-books of Shi'a Islam as the basis for their authority over the mass of believers. The hierarchy of scholasticism became more pronounced and, at the summit of Shi'a religious life, the position of the *Marji' al-taqlid*, the supreme religious figure, the most learned of the learned, evolved and became institutionalised. In time, it became obligatory for observant Shi'a to emulate the rulings of the learned jurist, through the principle of *taqlid*. The stage was set for the emergence of the institution of the *Marji'iyya*, the grouping of the most learned *mujtahids* of the Shi'a world, in the modern political life of both Iran and Iraq.[15]

The second factor that determined the evolution of the Shi'a community in modern Iraq was the wholesale conversion of the tribes of southern Iraq to the Shi'a Muslim faith. This process started in the eighteenth century and continued throughout the nineteenth century, thus turning the Shi'a into the majority population of Iraq. It also fundamentally altered the characteristics of Shi'ism in the country, and turned what had hitherto been a narrow, urban-based community into one with deep roots in the tribal traditions of southern Iraq. The settlement of tribal nomads as agricultural cultivators on the Euphrates placed them within proximity of the Shi'a shrine towns of Najaf and Karbala, and the influence of the mainly Iranian *ulema* based there. By ensuring their adherence to the Shi'a faith, the *ulema* turned these settled tribes into a vital buffer between the shrine towns and the periodic attacks of the virulently anti-Shi'a Wahhabis of the Arabian Peninsula. By the time the Sunni *ulema* of Iraq, and through them the Ottoman authorities in far-away Istanbul, became aware of this trend, it was too late. The southern Iraq tribes had irrevocably turned to Shi'ism.[16]

The *Marji'iyya* of the Shi'a were previously an ineffectual force outside the Shi'a milieu of Iraq, but they began to take on a leadership role in the affairs of Iraq, following the collapse of Ottoman rule there in 1918 and the subsequent British occupation of the country. The Shi'a *mujtahids* had in fact sided with the Sunni Turks, by calling for a *jihad* against the British. They mobilised a force of nearly 20,000 to fight alongside the Turks, led by a number of *'alims* from the shrine towns, including the later Grand Ayatollah Muhsin al-Hakim. The Islamic identity of the country was under threat, and Sunni and Shi'a were uncommonly united in a joint endeavour against the occupying power.[17] The 1920 Revolt broke out, a seminal event in the history of modern Iraq. The British were able to quell the revolt, but at great cost to themselves. Thereafter, they were determined to reduce, if not eradicate, the power of the Shi'a *mujtahids* to influence the affairs of the modern Iraqi state. The defeated *ulema* of the Shi'a could only retort by denying the legitimacy of the Iraqi state, and enjoining their followers to stay away from the nascent government. It was nearly forty years before the *mujtahids* of the Shi'a would once more begin to consider the need for direct political action.[18]

The Rise of Political Islam

Until the 1950s, the politics of Iraq were devoid of any serious Islamist content.[19] Political Islam actually emerged in Sunni circles, with the spread of the ideologies of the Muslim Brotherhood and the Hizb-ul-Tahrir. Though Sunni in orientation, they each had a number of Shi'a adherents attracted by their Islamist bent.[20] With the rise of a specifically Shi'a Islamist discourse in the 1950s, however, most of their Shi'a followers moved to the newly formed Islamist groups that began to spring up in Shi'a circles at that time. The *Marji'iyya* itself began to be concerned by the spread of alien ideologies amongst the Shi'a youth, especially communism, which established important footholds on university campuses and amongst professional and youth groups. Shi'a political action groups began to be organised in the 1950s, when the idea of a specific Islamist party began to germinate. The Islamic Da'awa Party was born at that time.[21]

The Da'awa Party and Muhammad Baqr al-Sadr

The Islamic Da'awa Party was founded in Karbala in the autumn of 1958. The party became firmly established during the following decade. Although it maintained a semi-clandestine existence, it successfully recruited its stalwarts from students, young professionals and administrators, and became well established on university campuses and in professional associations as a counterpart to the then prevailing currents of Arab nationalism and communism. Nearly all of Iraq's Islamist political parties evolved out of the Da'awa Party, or were somehow connected with it. In its early days, it had the implicit support of the *Marji'iyya*. The great Shi'a *Marji'* of that period, Grand Ayatollah Muhsin al-Hakim, was active in all of its early deliberations and organisational efforts. Its foundation marked three important events. First, the qualified acknowledgement by the highest Shi'a religious authorities of the validity of political action by committed Shi'a in the form of an organised political party. Second, direct participation in the political process of young religious figures, some of whom went on to become major actors in the evolving Iraqi political landscape. The third key development was the emergence of a socio-political discourse at the highest levels of the Shi'a religious hierarchy that set the stage for the emergence of an active, politically engaged, *Marji'iyya*. This was embodied in Sayyid Muhammad Baqir al-Sadr, one of the Da'awa Party's earliest leaders, whose subsequent life and death had a profound effect on the evolution of modern Islamic political thought and action.

Muhammad Baqir al-Sadr[22] was born in 1935 in Kadhimiyya, Baghdad. He came from one of the most prominent Arab Shi'a religious families, with important connections to both Lebanon and Iran. At the age of eleven he left Kadhimiyya for Najaf, where he joined the *hawza* (the Islamic study circles) of several leading *mujtahids*, especially the circle associated with Ayatollah Muhammad Rouhani. He later moved to the *hawza* of the Grand Ayatollah Abu al-Qasim al-Khoei, whose leadership style and priorities, as one of the *Maraji'* of the Shi'a, would be most at odds with him later. Sadr passed through the classic three stages of Najafi religious education in a relatively short period, and was an outstanding student.

Al-Sadr was moved by the apparent stagnation of Islamic thought and its seeming inability to confront the challenges of modernity. He also feared for the future of the traditional institutions of Shi'a Islam and its leadership. He was one of the original organisers of the Da'awa Party, and attended their founding meetings in Najaf in 1957 and Karbala in 1958, both as a principal and as a representative of the Najaf religious hierarchy.

During this period, the *Marji'iyya* of Grand Ayatollah Muhsin al-Hakim was in the ascendancy. Hakim's attitude to the formation of an activist

Islamic political party was cautious. He encouraged the engagement of the Shi'a intelligentsia in political work, but the demarcation between loyalty to a political party and the leadership of the Shi'a community, expressed through the traditional religious authorities, would always be problematic. The early years of the Da'awa Party reflected this tension. Sadr's discourses, writings and pamphleteering provided the bases for the Da'awa Party's organisation and ideological training. By 1960, however, Sadr, and other specifically religious figures inside the organisation, began to come under increasing pressure to distance themselves from the party as the issue of divided loyalties and authority between the party and the *Marji'iyya* escalated. Sadr tried to present the best possible gloss on his departure from the party. This studied ambiguity towards the Da'awa Party – and, in fact, towards other specifically Islamic parties – became the hallmark of the attitude of the *Marji'iyya* to such movements. Grand Ayatollah Muhsin al-Hakim, responding to external pressures from concerned lay Shi'a, as well as to the need to ensure the *Marji'iyya*'s status as the unchallenged authority in the world of the Shi'a, came out with a *fatwa* that neatly bridged this divide. He forbade involvement in political parties that were irreligious, but authorised the joining of an organisation that openly propagated Islam, whose leadership was known and trusted, and was presumably one that was acceptable to, or approved by, the *Marji'iyya*.

The 1960s were a period of growth and expansion for the Islamic movement in Iraq, especially the Da'awa Party. The Da'awa Party's growth was paralleled by the fissiparousness that usually accompanies Shi'a politics. The connections between the *Marji'iyya* and the Da'awa Party were intact, but at a personal rather than an organisational level, which maintained both the ambiguity of the relationship between the two and, at the same time, the ability to deny the relationship, if necessary.

The Ba'ath Party and the Rise of Saddam Hussein

The Ba'ath Party was founded in Damascus in 1947. Initially, it was led by two Syrian intellectuals, Michel Aflaq and Salahedin al-Bitar. In 1952, the party merged with another group in Syria, the Arab Socialist Party of Akram Hawrani, and assumed its final name, the Arab Ba'ath Socialist Party. Aflaq claimed allegiance to democracy and saw Islam as a product of the unique 'genius' of the Arab nation, with the prophet Muhammad as an embodiment of the Arab spirit. The Ba'ath espoused radical Arab nationalism, unity of all Arab lands, secularism, and a socialist economy.

In the 1950s, the Ba'ath grew out of its Syrian base and established branches in several Arab countries, the most important of which was in Iraq.[23] The Ba'ath in Iraq was initially a small part of the opposition to the monarchical regime, but the party grew in size and significance after the 1958 revolution, especially as a counterweight to the rising tide of communism. In 1959, a number of Ba'ath Party militants attempted an unsuccessful assassination of the leader of Iraq, General 'Abd el-Karim Qassim. Amongst the would-be assassins was Saddam Hussein, from the hardscrabble village of 'Auja, near the town of Tikrit. He had joined the party as an enforcer and street thug. Following the botched assassination attempt, the Ba'ath Party in Iraq was reorganised, and fell under the control of another street fighter, Ali Saleh al-Saadi. The Ba'ath also began to infiltrate the armed forces, and in February 1963 was able to launch a successful coup that ended the regime of General Qassim. In November 1963, the Ba'ath's chaotic and bloody rule ended in its overthrow by Arab nationalist officers allied with the president, Abd el-Salam 'Aref, one of the leaders of the 1958 Revolution. The party was suppressed, and, as it went underground, leadership once again switched, this time to a career officer and former prime minister, Ahmad Hassan al-Bakr. Saddam Hussein was put in charge of organising the party's civilian wing, and became the clandestine party's deputy secretary general.

In July 1968, the Ba'ath, in alliance with a few dissident army officers, launched a successful coup against the regime of Abd el-Rahman 'Aref. Using both state and party platforms, and working under the wing of his kinsman, Ahmad Hassan al-Bakr, now the president of Iraq, Saddam was able to consolidate his position in the faction-riven Ba'ath Party. In November 1969, Saddam was appointed as the deputy head of the Revolutionary Command Council, Iraq's supreme governing body. He gathered all the intelligence agencies, the real bulwarks of Ba'athist power, into his hands. The first to go were the non-Ba'athist officers who had executed the coup of 1968. Military and civilian Ba'ath Party rivals were quickly disposed of, through assassinations, mysterious 'accidents', demotions, exile and imprisonment. The Bakr–Saddam partnership faced its first crucial test when the operational head of the intelligence apparatus mounted a failed bid for power in July 1973. Following that episode, the alliance between the two continued mainly unchallenged until 1979. On 16 July, 1979, al-Bakr announced his resignation as president in a move widely interpreted as being instigated by Saddam, who then became president. A fortnight later, a plot against Saddam by senior Ba'athists in league with the Syrian faction of the Ba'ath Party was supposedly uncovered. This resulted in the execution of twenty-two senior Ba'athists, including four members of the Revolutionary Command Council. Some were close friends and associates of Saddam during his rise to power. His ruthlessness, power-drive and cunning won out. Saddam was now the undisputed master of Iraq.

The Ba'ath Party returned to power in 1968 with a determination not to lose control at any cost. It had identified the Islamic movement generally, and the Da'awa Party in particular, as major threats to the regime. In the regional congress, held soon after its coup in July 1968, the Party warned against the spread of religious reactionaries. It was no surprise, therefore, that the intelligence apparatus of the regime, the Ba'ath's main instrument of control, began to develop dossiers on all Islamist activists, including the organisers of religious rituals. It became clear that the regime was determined to either stamp out or co-opt any political opposition. The Ba'ath's first move was against the family and close associates of the Grand Ayatollah Muhsin al-Hakim. His son, Mahdi, was accused of conspiring against the regime and was obliged to flee the country. The Grand Ayatollah himself refrained from any attempt to mobilise public opinion against the regime, correctly gauging that the public was too cowed by the Ba'ath's policy of terror and intimidation. The Grand Ayatollah died in 1970, and the Ba'ath redoubled its campaign of deliberate provocation and harassment against the politically active followers of the *Marji'iyya*. Whatever protective cover had been afforded by the Grand Ayatollah al-Hakim died when he died. The Shi'a Islamic movement in Iraq, and the consciousness that went with it, was now facing its most serious challenge.

Grand Ayatollah Abu al-Qasim al-Khoei

The death of Grand Ayatollah Muhsin al-Hakim was followed by swift recognition of Sayyid Abu al-Qasim al-Khoei as the leader of the *Marji'iyya* in Iraq.[24] The erudition and scholarship of al-Khoei was widely recognised, and it paved the way for the mantle of undisputed religious leadership. Al-Khoei was always opposed to the principle of *Wilayat al-Faqih*, or direct rule by the most learned of jurists, a doctrine formulated in Najaf in the 1970s by the exiled Ayatollah Ruhallah Khomeini.[25] He was aloof from the vicissitudes of Iraqi Islamist politics, and belonged to the quietest school in Shi'a Islam. Al-Khoei played little or no part in the rise of political consciousness amongst the Iraqi Shi'a, denying the necessity for direct engagement in political activity by the learned classes. He believed that political commitments are necessarily dubious and compromising, and that men of religion should steer clear of state affairs.

Grand Ayatollah al-Khoei's advocacy of a limited role of the *Marji' al-Taqlid* for the spiritual and moral guidance of the laity also fitted in with his concern regarding the imbalance of power between the modern state and the traditional religious leadership. When the Ba'ath began to uproot the structures of the Iraqi Islamist movement in earnest, especially the Da'awa Party, through a series of arrests and executions that started in 1971 and culminated in 1974, Grand Ayatollah al-Khoei was left largely undisturbed.

The Ba'ath Regime's Attacks on Shi'a Islamists

Ayatollah Baqir al-Sadr was now pushed into the front lines of defence of the Iraqi Islamist movement, and the Da'awa Party in particular, against the onslaughts of the Ba'ath Party. He responded by redoubling his efforts to establish himself as a *Marji'* in his own right. Al-Sadr's *Marji'iyya* was to be activist and politically engaged and, if necessary, he was to lead the fight against the Ba'athist state. But his *Marji'iyya* never received enough support or traction to threaten the leadership of al-Khoei seriously. Indeed, al-Sadr always acknowledged al-Khoei's superior station and learning. The line that he was pursuing was unusual. At one level, he rejected the quietist, non-political and traditional role of the learned jurist. At another level, he rejected the claims of specifically Islamist political groups, dismissing them as at best secondary and supportive to the role of the *Marji'iyya*. In 1974, he issued a *hukm* (edict) in which he banned religious students of the *hawza* from joining any Islamic political party. Al-Sadr appeared to accept the concept of *Wilayat al-Faqih*, thereby attributing to the most learned *Marji'* an indisputable authority over the polity.

The Iranian Revolution of 1979 precipitated the rise of Saddam to absolute power, and in a pre-emptive strike the Ba'ath regime launched a massive onslaught against the Da'awa Party and its sympathisers, as well as others. This time, the *Marji'iyya* of Ayatollah Baqir al-Sadr itself was targeted. His deputies in Iraq's provinces were rounded up and most of them were later executed. Al-Sadr was placed under house arrest, but then moved to Baghdad, where he and his sister were put to death in April 1980. Thousands of Da'awa Party members, its sympathisers, politically active Islamists and observant Shi'a were rounded up and murdered, while the regime engineered the expulsion of tens of thousands of Iraqi Shi'a to Iran on the grounds of disloyalty to the regime and indeterminate nationality status.[26] The response of al-Khoei to these outrages was exceptionally muted, and this led to severe criticisms being levelled against him for his apparently accommodating silence. There is little doubt, however, that if al-Khoei had responded with a *fatwa* against the Ba'ath, his fate, and probably that of the institution of the *Marji'iyya* itself, would have been sealed.

The Ba'ath Party was intent on not only demonstrating the government's dominance and control over the socio-political life of the country but also on removing the *Marji'iyya* in its entirety as an independent force capable of mobilising the rank and file of the Shi'a. The ease with which the Ba'ath's authority was achieved further increased the regime's sense of invincibility, and it remained unchallenged within Iraq. The Iran–Iraq War, with its immense strategic and regional implications, provided the regime with a huge network of international supporters, including both the United States and the Soviet Union. The fact that the Ba'ath regime was intent on fundamentally altering the allegiances of the Shi'a to its version of history was a matter of little or no consequence to Saddam's supporters. By the end of the decade the Shi'a religious leadership had effectively been subdued – through murders, expulsions and disappearances, as well as through enticements, bribery and inducements.

Within the remnants of the *Marji'iyya* and *hawza*, the political dimensions of Shi'a religious authority became effectively submerged under the quiescent scholasticism of Grand Ayatollah al-Khoei, the acknowledged and unchallenged *Marji' al-Taqlid* of the vast majority of pious Shi'a in Iraq. His vigorous opposition to political action, particularly when it claimed to be based in Shi'a Islamic thought, such as the concept of *Wilayat al-Faqih*, the basic ideological underpinning of Iran's Islamic Republic, ensured that he was, perhaps in spite of his own concerns, at loggerheads with the rulers of Iran. The Iraqi regime, of course, gloated about the intra-Shi'a doctrinal dispute, and frequently used Grand Ayatollah al-Khoei's rulings in its propaganda war against Iran. Saddam was not prepared to openly dismantle a vital Shi'a institution, however. After the destruction of the Shi'a Islamist movement and the muted domestic response to the murder of Ayatollah Baqir al-Sadr, very little could have stopped the Ba'ath regime from destroying the *Marji'iyya* inside Iraq had it so wished. The outbreak of the Iran–Iraq War may have caused it to modify its plans, if for no other reason than that the majority of front-line troops were Shi'a. An open attack on the *Marji'iyya* might have caused serious morale problems amongst soldiers – who were not at all enthusiastic about the war. The presence of the *Marji'iyya* in a clearly subordinate and defensive role was a useful tool.

The Grand Ayatollah worked within the very narrow parameters afforded him. He saw himself as the guardian of its traditional purposes and redoubled the *Marji'iyya*'s efforts in this direction. Student numbers of the *hawza* had dramatically declined since the Ba'ath had come to power in 1968. At one point, the studied indifference of the regime to the much-shrunken Najaf *hawza*, and its frequent harassment of students who were still there, made the question of the *hawza*'s survival in Iraq a big issue. The strains and tensions of managing the *hawza* under such trying circumstances, and the necessary compromises that had to be made with an unsympathetic regime, cast a deep gloom over the *Marji'iyya*.

The Kurds and the Ba'ath

The Kurds, an Indo-European race numbering about 30 million, occupy the mountainous borderlands of a number of Middle Eastern countries, notably Turkey, Iran, Iraq and Syria. Over five million Kurds live in Iraq. Iraqi Kurdistan lies in the north and northeastern parts of the country. The

Kurds frequently say they are the largest nation without a state, and their struggles for national, linguistic and cultural recognition have marked their encounters with the states of the Middle East since the end of the Ottoman period. The origins of the Kurds probably lie in the migration of Indo-European tribes across the Iranian plateau towards the Zagros Mountains, in the middle of the second millennium BC. Over time, a substantial number lost their identity as they merged into the surrounding Turkish, Arab or Persian populations. Similarly, a number of Arab and Turkomen tribes assimilated into the Kurdish cultural milieu and became part of the Kurdish population.

Kurdish national consciousness was late in developing. The Kurdish intelligentsia formed the demand for an ethnically based state after the collapse of the Ottoman Empire. Nearly 75 per cent of Kurds are Sunni Muslims, following the Shafi'i, rather than the Hanafi, rites that prevail amongst the Sunni Arab and Turkish populations. Around 20 per cent of Kurds are followers of Shi'a Islam, in the Imami version that dominates Iran and most of Iraq's Arab population. Several Christian communities coexist within Iraqi Kurdistan, to form part of the Kurdish cultural milieu. Kurds speak two main languages or dialects: Kurmanji, spoken by most northern Kurds, and Surani, spoken by most southern Kurds.

The Kurds had always exhibited a troubled relationship with the central authorities. The Kurdish parts of Iraq were almost entirely contained within the former Ottoman *wilayet* (province) of Mosul, where significant oil deposits had been found. The *wilayet* of Mosul formally acceded to Iraq only in 1926. Under the 1920 Treaty of Sèvres, the Kurds of the Ottoman Empire were to be granted some form of autonomy or even independence, but these promises were quickly forgotten as the western powers began their carve-up of the formerly Ottoman Middle East. The Kurds' lot was to be divided between the successor states of Turkey, Iraq and Syria. Iran also contained a significant number of their fellow Kurds. In Iraq, the Kurds had resisted domination by an Arab government, but the imbalance of power between them and the authorities, now buttressed by the military presence of Great Britain, obliged their leaders to reach a compromise with the central government. The government acknowledged the authority of the Kurds' traditional tribal and feudal leadership (the *aghas*), thereby gaining a modicum of legitimacy for its rule.[27]

Over the following two decades, the Kurds' ruling groups began to integrate within the monarchical system in Iraq and benefit from the involvement. They began to appear in force in some of the key institutions of the Iraqi state, not least the armed forces, and a number achieved ministerial, even prime ministerial, positions. This state of affairs, however, began to be challenged in the 1940s as a result of the growth of an avowedly leftist intelligentsia, often associated with the ICP, that resisted the deepening hold of the traditional classes on the economic and political life of the Kurds. There was also the rise of a specifically nationalist Kurdish movement, centred on the charismatic tribal personality of Mulla Mustafa Barzani. The periodic rebellions, with which he was associated in Iraq, and his legendary defence of the short-lived Mahabad Kurdish Republic, made him a hero for Kurdish nationalists.[28]

The 1958 revolution in Iraq, which overthrew the monarchy and established a republic, appeared to acknowledge Kurdish aspirations. This was a popular event, as most 'progressive' Iraqis had become hostile to the monarchy. The *coup d'état* unleashed tumultuous forces, and rapidly caused the country to polarise. The new constitution defined Iraq, for the first time, as a bi-national Arab/Kurdish state.[29] The rise of the ICP, which counted a large percentage of Kurds in its cadres and leadership, focused attention on Kurdish demands and grievances. The first of many rebellions, led by Mulla Mustafa Barzani, broke out in 1961 in Iraqi Kurdistan, and continued throughout the bewildering coups and countercoups of Iraq during the 1960s. The Ba'ath regime that came to power in 1968, at that time preoccupied by fear of isolation and weakness, decided to negotiate a settlement of convenience with the Kurds. It appeared to concede the issue of the Kurds' insistence on regional autonomy, and through the agreement of March 1970 it secured a peace of sorts with these ever-rebellious people.[30] This relative calm, however, was soon shattered by the outbreak of full-scale hostilities in late 1974. The Kurdish insurrection came to an abrupt end in March 1975, when the Shah of Iran withdrew the logistical and military support that he had previously given to the Kurds. The Kurdish leadership, headed by Mulla Mustafa, left Iraq, and Iraqi Kurdistan was left to the mercy of the central authorities. The Ba'ath regime now began to change the demographic map of Iraqi Kurdistan in earnest, with enforced large-scale population movements and an Arabisation policy. Apart from a few pockets of resistance organised in 1976 by Jalal Talabani and his Patriotic Union of Kurdistan (PUK), part of which included a faction that separated from the main Barzani-contolled Kurdish Democratic Party (KDP), Kurdistan was relatively quiet until the outbreak of the Iran–Iraq War in 1980.[31]

The Iran–Iraq War and the Beginnings of Exile Opposition

The organised opposition to the Ba'ath regime began to take shape in the 1980s. Successive waves of political refugees were created by the Ba'ath's brutality towards its opponents, and by the time of the outbreak of the Iran–Iraq War, a critical mass of the regime's opponents had begun to gather abroad. In time, three centres for the Iraqi opposition became identified:

Tehran, London and Damascus. Gradually a formal Iraqi opposition that identified itself as such emerged, based on the Shi'a Islamist and Kurdish groups, allied to the scattered remnants of Iraq's anti-Saddamist political class, a curious mixture of liberals, Arab nationalists, Ba'athists allied to Syria, socialists and communists. Newspapers began to appear in London and Tehran that reflected the perspectives of the opposition, the most notable being the London-based *Tayar aj-Jadid* (The New Current). A number of conferences were held that highlighted the Ba'ath regime's crimes, and presented the face of the opposition to a less than enthusiastic international public opinion. Nevertheless, the opposition continued to gain ground, buoyed up from time to time by news of imminent breakthroughs of Iranian forces against fortified Iraqi positions, or by the fall of minor towns and villages that seemed to foreshadow the collapse of the regime. Inside Iraq itself, opposition to the regime was concentrated in Iraqi Kurdistan, where the reorganised KDP and PUK started operations against the regime, and in the border marshes with Iran where Iraqi Shi'a Islamist groups launched their guerrilla war against Baghdad. Iran played the largest part in regrouping the ranks of the Islamist parties and, to a lesser extent, the Kurdish groups, while anti-regime Arab nationalists, socialists and communists looked towards Syria and Libya for support.

The Ba'ath regime, however, was far more resilient than had been anticipated by the opposition. In addition, it had the support of the western powers, most of the Arab and Islamic world and the Soviet Union, which were far more concerned about the spread of the Iranian revolution than the dictatorial practices of the Baghdad regime. In many countries, in particular those in the Gulf, the regime's agents were able to operate with impunity and cooperated closely with the intelligence agencies of countries such as Jordan and Kuwait.[32]

During the 1980s a leadership of sorts – loose, uncoordinated, frequently bickering and highly personalised – began to emerge for the Iraqi opposition. There still remained deep divisions and bitterness between opposition groups that profoundly mistrusted each other. The Saddamist Ba'ath was not prepared to compromise at all with its monopoly of power, and was relentless in pursuit of its opponents. The regime also pursued the activist members of the al-Hakim family, particularly the sons of the late Grand Ayatollah Muhsin al-Hakim. Ayatollah Baqir al-Hakim, who fled Iraq in 1980, found his way to Tehran, via Syria. His oppositional activities there, in particular his role in founding the Islamist umbrella group, the Supreme Council for the Islamic Revolution in Iraq (SCIRI), in November 1982, seriously alarmed the Baghdad authorities who tried, through various means, to force him to desist. In 1983, they arrested a large number of the al-Hakim family who were mostly still in Iraq, including rising ayatollahs such as Ayatollah Abd el-Sahib al-Hakim. They executed eighteen members of the family, releasing one of those arrested, Sayyid Hussein al-Hakim, who was forced not only to witness the executions but also to report on them directly to Sayyid Baqir al-Hakim in Tehran.[33] In 1988, Sayyid Mahdi al-Hakim, who had based himself in London after the Iranian revolution, was assassinated in a hotel lobby by Iraqi intelligence operatives while attending an international Islamist conference in Khartoum. He had distanced himself from an exclusively Islamist position and had become a unifying and much-respected figure within exile groups.[34]

The Iraqi opposition, especially the Islamists, established themselves in territory that had been seized by Iranian forces in the Hajj Umran area in Kurdistan. The Ba'ath regime was invariably draconian in its response, and in July 1982 in the town of Dujail, north of Baghdad, an attempt on the life of Saddam by Islamist militants led to mass executions and the razing of large parts of the town in reprisal.[35]

The Ba'ath regime was fearful of further advances in the North by Iranian forces, and rounded up thousands of Barzani tribesmen, banishing them into desert exile where most were subsequently liquidated. Fearful of being caught between an Iran that it distrusted and its bitter KDP rivals, the PUK decided to break ranks with the Iraqi opposition and launched negotiations with the Baghdad regime. By 1983, a ceasefire had been declared between the Ba'ath and the PUK. This was short-lived, however, and hostilities once more broke out in 1985. In May 1987, the KDP and PUK managed to bury their differences and a broad front of Kurdish parties was formed as a prelude to the establishment of a formal Iraqi national opposition. In spite of widespread atrocities, which included the mass murder of hundreds of Kurdish children and youths held as hostages by the regime, as well as the large-scale mobilisation of anti-partisan Kurds (the *jash* who were organised as regime auxiliaries), 1987 saw considerable territorial gains by the Kurdish rebels.

The ICP was the other main non-Kurdish group that was able to mount some resistance to the Ba'athist government in the 1980s. In March 1974, the communists appointed three of their central committee members to the secretariat of the Ba'ath-led National Front. The Ba'ath, however, were determined not to share power, and within a few years the ICP's relationship with the regime became seriously frayed. Persecutions of communists were followed by executions of dozens of its militants. By 1979, the ICP was seriously weakened and driven underground, and it never recovered effectively from the blows dealt by the Ba'ath Party. Its leadership was exiled, hundreds of its cadres were murdered and thousands were incarcerated. In spite of their best efforts at cooperation, therefore, the communists were forced into opposition.

The 1980s crystallised a process in Iraqi politics that had been developing over the past two decades, namely, the emergence of the Islamist movement as the main opposition to the succession of Arab nationalist and Ba'athist governments in Baghdad. This shift in the structure of Iraqi politics, and in the political identity of the majority Shi'a, did not register clearly with observers of the Iraqi scene. It was perhaps fanciful to expect that this process would be accorded any relevance when the Ba'ath appeared to overwhelm the Shi'a Islamist parties decisively in the 1970s, and when the Islamists were unable to achieve much headway during the Iran–Iraq War. The Ba'ath regime recognised the source of the long-term danger to its power and authority, and ferociously tried to extinguish it. However, the paradigms of Arab nationalist and Marxist thought continued to be used to analyse the Iraqi condition. Thus the Arab nationalist/Ba'athist opposition to apparent communist ascendancy in the late 1950s, and the subsequent rivalries and clashes within the Arab nationalist camp, tended to dominate the way Iraqi politics was viewed. The critical role of the military in determining power shifts in Iraq also disguised the emergence of a new mass political awareness and movements that were beginning to make headway amongst the Shi'a. Very few analyses of Iraqi politics gave appropriate weight to the Islamist factor in Iraq. Whenever the influence of religion or sect in relation to Iraqi politics was discussed, it was set against the notion that Iraq as a modernising society had successfully separated state from 'mosque', a meaningless construct in the Iraqi context. For instance, eminent historians of Iraq, such as Hanna Batatu,[36] simply ignored the evolution of the Islamic movement. His book, a major reference work for the social and political history of Iraq, made no mention of the mass executions of Islamists of the 1970s.

Halabja, the *Anfal* and the end of the Iran–Iraq War

In the months preceding the end of the Iran–Iraq War, a number of catastrophes befell the Kurds, the implications of which on the Iraqi opposition in general, and on the Kurds in particular, reverberated for years. In March 1988, PUK and Iranian forces captured the town of Halabja. The Iraqi government forces retaliated by launching a massive chemical weapons attack on the townsfolk of Halabja. Nearly 5,000 civilians were gassed to death.[37] The effect on Kurdish morale was shattering. This was followed by the acceleration of a series of operations against the Kurds that had started in February 1988, code-named *Anfal*. The *Anfal* operations, which did not end until 1989 with the razing of the town of Qala Deza, were conducted with enormous ferocity and barbarity. The entire civilian population of Kurdistan was in one way or another affected. Nearly one-and-a-half million people were displaced, and half the landmass of Kurdistan was depopulated. The savagery of the assaults on innocent civilians was unprecedented. Gas was the weapon of choice. In Bazi Gorge on 29 August, 1988, nearly 3,000 Kurds were gassed to death. All in all, the *Anfal* led to the death of nearly 200,000 civilians in a planned, methodically executed, genocide.[38]

The end of the Iran–Iraq War, the murder of Sayyid Mahdi al-Hakim, and the successful co-opting of some opposition figures by a newly confident regime seemed to mark the death knell for the Iraqi opposition. In particular, the loss of all territory to Iraqi government control, especially after the *Anfal* campaign, and the recovery of all the land that had fallen to the Iranians by the summer of 1988, removed whatever comfort could be gained from operating in liberated Iraqi territory. The total collapse of the Kurdish front, always a source of hope for all oppositionists, was an irreplaceable loss. The opposition sank into a deep despondency, with its ineffectiveness, divisiveness and apparent irrelevance displayed to all.

2

The Rise of the Opposition

'There's another way for the bloodshed to stop, and this is for the Iraqi military and the Iraqi people to take matters into their own hands and force Saddam Hussein, the dictator, to step aside.' –

George Bush, President of the United States, speaking to workers
at the Raytheon Corporation plant, 15 February, 1991

'We didn't expect a general public uprising. . .'

An unnamed Bush aide speaking to CNN after the
March 1991 uprisings in Iraq were crushed

The End of the Iran–Iraq War

The end of the Iran–Iraq War masked the true conditions inside Iraq. Both outside the country and within the regime's own propaganda, it appeared to have emerged triumphant from a titanic struggle that had lasted eight years. During the last few months of the war, a number of events began to turn what seemed an endless stalemate into a decisive Iraqi advantage. The Iraqi forces' recovery in April 1988 of the Fao peninsula at the southern tip of the country; the recapture of most of the strips of territory that had been seized by Iran during the summer of 1988; a more effective deployment of chemical weapons by Iraq; and the 'success' of the *Anfal* campaign in destroying Kurdish resistance, all played a part in the shift of the balance of power in Iraq's favour. What appeared to be most critical for Iran's decision to accept the ceasefire terms of UN Resolution 598, however, was the explicit tilt of the USA against the country.[1] This involved the direct use of American forces against Iranian military and civilian targets in the Gulf area, and culminated in the still unexplained downing of an Iranian passenger airliner flying from Dubai to Iran in July 1988 by a US warship.[2]

The Ba'ath regime began to use its apparent ascendancy in the war to strengthen its claims to leadership in the Middle East. It trumpeted Iraq's ceasefire with Iran as a victory and began to parade as the saviour of the Arab world from the infestation of revolutionary Shi'a Islam and the threat of Iranian expansionism. It claimed a huge political and moral debt from its Arab allies, especially the Gulf States that had played the largest part in bankrolling Iraq's war effort. The reality, though, was somewhat different. The end of the Iran–Iraq War had left Saddam with a bloated army, a lopsided economy and massive external debts. The scale of the resources that were used to fund Iraq's effort, including its own huge oil export revenues, was unprecedented. The war would rank as one of the costliest engagements in modern times. The extent of the participation of the rest of the world in the financing of the Iraqi side of the war would emerge only later, but the destruction wrought on the economies of the two countries involved exceeded a trillion dollars, in direct war damage and lost production.[3]

Saddam had survived a brutal war, and had succeeded in consolidating his power and decimating his opponents. Throughout the war years, the *Marji'iyya* of Grand Ayatollah al-Khoei made virtually no pronouncements on the conflict, and as Saddam became more confident about his domestic front, he began to see the advantage of flaunting his religious credentials, especially with the Shi'a. He refurbished the holy sites of Karbala and Najaf with gold and silver leaf, and played up his own devotional record. The state seemed to be secure in the belief that it might have driven a permanent wedge between the Shi'a Arabs of Iraq and any lingering attachment that they might have had with Iran. The absence of any domestic opposition to the regime encouraged a sense of invincibility and smug superiority. The Ba'ath regime strutted on the regional and world stage, and Baghdad became a port of call for legions of Arab politicians, writers and artists, drawn by the largess of a regime that had become addicted to unaccountable spending. The Gulf states, however, having warded off the dangers from a revolutionary Iran, began to see the threat that might emanate from an over-armed and over-confident Iraq. They started to pull away from the country. Ever sensitive to such developments, Saddam began to seek an alternative pole of influence to the Gulf Cooperation Council (GCC). In February 1989, therefore, Iraq, together with Egypt, Jordan and Yemen, formed the Arab Cooperation Council (ACC), a none-too-subtle regional rival to the GCC. The entire arrangement, though, was ill considered and poorly financed, and could not overcome the inherent difficulties in cobbling together a coherent policy for such a disparate grouping of countries. The ACC would not survive for more than a year.[4]

The Iraqi Opposition and the Rise of Ahmad Chalabi

The external opposition to Saddam languished in limbo. Exhausted by the war effort and anxious to maintain the ceasefire with Iraq, Iran began to scale down its engagement with the Tehran-based Islamist groups. The Kurds were desperately trying to regroup and draw international attention to the geno-cide of the *Anfal* and Halabja gas attacks. These attacks had driven large numbers of Kurds into exile in Iran and, to a lesser extent, into Turkey. In spite of several amnesties announced by the regime, nearly 100,000 Kurdish refugees remained in Iran by 1990.[5] The international response to the regime's human rights abuses was muted. The regime was barely moved by US Secretary of State Shultz's protest against the use of poison gas, a protest that was not carried further in the form of reducing US aid or sanctions against Iraq.[6] In fact the Reagan administration worked vigorously to block the passage of a sanctions bill that would have had the effect of stopping further US assistance to Iraq. The same policy of overlooking Iraq's human rights transgressions and active opposition to any congressional action against Iraq continued from the Reagan to the first Bush administration. The major European powers, especially France, broadly followed the same policy. An international conference held in Paris in January 1989 on the use of chemical weapons, sponsored by France with strong US support, did not even censure Iraq for its violations in the *Anfal* campaign and in Halabja.[7] The USA effectively stymied efforts at the UN Human Rights Commission to hold Iraq to account on similar human rights grounds. It is no wonder that in such an indifferent and hostile environment, the Iraqi opposition to the Ba'ath was unable to make any headway in accessing, let alone influencing, western and Arab policies towards Iraq. Stalwarts of the opposition began to drift away, and a number of their leaders abandoned the struggle and sought asylum as political refugees in the west.

In spite of the enveloping gloom that surrounded the activity of those who opposed the Ba'ath regime, in the two years that followed the ending of the Iran–Iraq War developments were already taking place that would have a profound effect on the struggle for power in Iraq. In Jordan in August 1989, the collapse of a bank under murky circumstances would unleash a force that would help to galvanise the opposition throughout the 1990s and eventually affect the occupation of Iraq. The Chalabi family, Iraqis who had been promi-nent in the political and commercial life of monarchical Iraq, had established Petra Bank in Amman in 1977. Following the 1958 revolution, the Chalabis, under their patriarch Abd el-Hadi al-Chalabi, relocated their prime business interests – to Lebanon, the United Arab Emirates (UAE) and Switzerland. The increasing violence in Lebanon and operational difficulties as the civil war there began to take hold caused the family to seek additional banking oppor-tunities in the Middle East. Jordan, where the family had long-established rela-tions, beckoned as a burgeoning banking market. Petra Bank was entrusted to the management of Ahmad Chalabi, youngest son of Abd el-Hadi. He had already been active in Iraqi opposition politics and had played an important role in a failed coup attempt against the Ba'ath in 1969.[8] He had become a vital link between exiled Iraqi politicians and the Kurdish movement, then led by Mulla Mustafa Barzani. He had also established independent relationships with the stream of Iraqi political and religious figures that regularly visited Lebanon in the 1970s. In Amman, Chalabi settled into building the bank and establishing his relations with Jordan's business classes. During his stay in Jordan (about ten years), Chalabi never lost interest in, or engagement with, Iraqi political affairs, albeit from a difficult position, given Jordan's strategic commitments to Iraq.

Petra Bank prospered throughout the 1980s and rose to challenge the pre-eminence of the Arab Bank in the Jordanian market. By the late 1980s, however, a combination of reduced remittances from expatriate Jordanians and Palestinians, and a sharp fall in Iraqi expenditure in Jordan as the result of the ending of the Iran–Iraq War, pushed Jordan into a serious balance of payments crisis. This was compounded by ill-considered and draconian measures deployed by the Central Bank of Jordan to reduce liquidity in the banking system and to stave off a collapse of the Jordanian dinar. Petra's balance sheet began to unravel and, as the hostility of the Jordanian financial and security authorities to its management grew, Chalabi was forced to leave the country clandestinely for Syria and then London. The Petra affair was to dog Chalabi's footsteps for ever.[9]

Away from Jordan, Chalabi quickly established himself within the Iraqi opposition, having known most of its leading figures for a considerable time. His chosen strategy for attracting attention to the opposition was considerably more subtle and worldly wise than previous opposition methods. He concentrated on building up his connections to the United States and employed his access to its media to full advantage. He wrote a number of opinion pieces that found their way into mainstream American newspapers calling for a democratic, pro-western Iraq, and cautioning readers about Saddam's true intent. In a particularly prescient piece, he envisaged an attack on Kuwait as a likely outlet for the massive war machine that Saddam had built up.

The Invasion of Kuwait and the Iraqi Opposition

The spring of 1990 was the beginning of the countdown to the invasion of Kuwait and with it the rebirth of the opposition's dream of overthrowing the Ba'athist regime. Iraq's massive arms build-up continued apace, in spite of the ending of the war with Iran. This time it appeared to involve the building of a nuclear weapon. A number of arrests were made in London in March 1990 of people connected to Iraq's attempts to procure essential elements for a nuclear weapons programme. Saddam began to flex his muscles. The drive for regional supremacy and the weapons build-up, particularly the possibility of

Iraq working towards the development of a nuclear weapon, seriously alarmed Washington and the Gulf states.

A number of motives drove Saddam to invade Kuwait, ranging from a pathological desire to establish his undisputed leadership of the Arab world, to asserting Iraq's dominance in the oil-producing Gulf region and therefore of the global oil market. Saddam misread the apparent indifference on the part of the USA to minor adjustments to the Iraqi–Kuwait border and seemed to be unaware of what the superpower would think about a full-blown invasion and annexation of the country. He accused Kuwait of 'stealing' Iraqi oil by over-pumping from the jointly owned Rumaila oil field. He then demanded immediate financial redress and write-off of Iraq's debt to Kuwait. An emergency Arab summit conference to resolve the crisis ended in pandemonium. A few days later, Saddam's invasion of Kuwait took place on 1 August, 1990. A week later Kuwait's existence was annulled with its incorporation into Iraq as a province. At that point, the Iraqi opposition, previously mired in petty personality conflicts and nearly moribund, came back to life.

It was not until the build-up of western forces to free Kuwait was nearly complete in November 1990 that the USA and Britain began to seek out Iraqi opposition groups to help in the war and post-war planning.[10] Syria had supported Iran throughout the Iran–Iraq War and had played host to a number of Iraqi opposition political groups, principally the pro-Syrian branch of the Iraqi Ba'ath Party, the communists, assorted leftists and 'democrats', and, critically, the PUK under Jalal Talabani. These groups had been loosely organised by Syria as a National Democratic Front, an entity that proved ineffective. Islamist groups based in Syria, such as the *Harakat-al-Mujahideen* had hitherto been officially ignored. Syria now sought to bring them under some form of coordinating mechanism that it could influence, if not direct. In September 1990, under Syrian prodding, the *Lajnat al'amal al-mushtarrak* (Joint Action Committee) was organised, incorporating Islamists (SCIRI and the Da'awa Party), the main Kurdish parties, the communists, dissident Ba'athists and Arab nationalists. In December 1990, the Joint Action Committee (JAC) in a meeting held in Beirut agreed on a steering committee and secretariat.[11] Within a few weeks, the JAC was expanded to include people and groups sponsored by Saudi Arabia, including the Iraq National Accord (*al-Wifaq*), headed by Dr Ayad Allawi; Salah Omar al-Ali, a former Ba'athist minister who had broken with Saddam; and the London-based Free Iraq Council, led by Saad Salih Jabr.

Ayatollah Baqir al-Hakim and SCIRI

The Supreme Council for the Islamic Revolution in Iraq (SCIRI) was founded in November 1982 in Tehran as an alliance of all the Iraqi Islamist parties that

believed in the establishment of an Islamic state in Iraq.[12] It included the
mainly Shi'a Islamists, such as the Da'awa Party, the Organisation for Islamic
Action, and the Mujahideen Movement, as well as Turkomen and Kurdish
Islamists, such as the Hizbollah grouping led by Mulla Khalid Barzani, brother
of Mulla Mustafa Barzani. The founding of SCIRI came quickly on the heels
of the catastrophic Iraqi reverses on the Khuzestan front in the Iraq–Iran War.
The organisation was set up partly to address the issue of the leadership of a
post-Ba'ath order in Iraq, in the event that the regime in Baghdad would
collapse. Initially, SCIRI had a collective leadership drawn from the leading
Iraqi Islamists based in Tehran, and organised in a sixteen-man consultative
council. Ayatollah Baqir al-Hakim, a prominent Islamist in exile in Iran, and
a son of Grand Ayatollah Muhsin al-Hakim, became spokesman. In time,
Ayatollah Baqir al-Hakim asserted his undivided control over the organisation
and was able to mould the institution to his purposes.

Throughout the period of the Iran–Iraq War, SCIRI acted as an adjunct to
Iranian objectives and plans. It mobilised a number of Iraqi prisoners of war
(the so-called *tawabin*, or penitents) into an organised and well-equipped
military unit – the Badr Corps – that was initially led by officers from the
Iranian Revolutionary Guard. In time, the Badr Corps was placed under
wholly Iraqi leadership, but coordinated through the Iranian upper military
command. The huge numbers of Iraqi refugees in Iran (up to one million
people) also gave SCIRI a population base from which it could draw support,
and for which it could provide services and access to the documents required
for staying, and working, in Iran. The SCIRI's connections to Iran bedevilled
it from the outset. Was it an Iranian front or a genuine Iraqi movement that
had to make necessary compromises, under difficult circumstances, with its
host country? The gradual erosion of SCIRI's role as an umbrella vehicle for
Iraq's Islamists, and its change into an increasingly personalised organisation,
loyal to a single leader, also raised questions as to SCIRI's political
programme, and whether it could be an authentic part of Iraq's Islamist tradition. Ayatollah Baqir al-Hakim never dismissed the similarity of interests
between SCIRI and the Iranian revolution, but insisted that the Iraqi Islamic
movement was separate in its development and that it had preceded the
Iranian Islamic movement by decades. Iran, he maintained, was a natural ally
of Iraqi Islamists, given its long common border with Iraq, the presence of a
large number of Iraqis inside its territory, and shared Islamic and sectarian
affinities. Nevertheless, the realities on the ground had to be acknowledged,
and SCIRI's dependence on Iranian goodwill, as well as financial, logistical
and political support, was clearly necessary for its survival.

The end of the Iran–Iraq War obliged SCIRI to reconsider its role and
strategy, and it began to reach out to other Iraqi opposition organisations,
both Islamists and others, as well as to other countries. The opening came

with the beginning of the Kuwait crisis, and materialised towards the end of the Gulf War. By the end of 1991, Ayatollah al-Hakim had floated a plan to unite the opposition and to call for the overthrow of the regime. The rather vague plan was not well received, but it had the effect of gradually integrating SCIRI, a hitherto aloof force, into the deliberations and plans of other opposition groups, especially those that were reaching out to the USA. By 1992, SCIRI had become a major player in the Iraqi opposition. It also began to evolve a political programme that went beyond the generalities of the Islamist framework. As its relationship with the Kurds changed from that of a tactical wartime alliance into a long-term and strategic relationship, so did its views on federalism, a key Kurdish demand. It began to acknowledge the concept as a valid principle for the restructuring of Iraq's political life, casting it in the framework of the Islamic concept of *wilayet*. SCIRI, however, stood firmly against the threat of the division of Iraq into statelets for the Kurds, Shi'a and Sunni.

SCIRI was a strong proponent of the liberation of Kuwait and offered to mobilise 'a hundred thousand fighters' for the effort to free Kuwait from Saddam Hussein. Ayatollah al-Hakim became a welcome visitor to Kuwait and Saudi Arabia. He was received with near head-of-state protocol, further cementing his status as the pre-eminent opposition leader. In Kuwait, SCIRI was allowed unfettered access to the country's mosques, meeting halls and private salons. Ayatollah al-Hakim's pronouncements were taken seriously, and in spite of a continuing rhetoric that disparaged the sincerity of US efforts to undermine the regime, his position did not veer too far from the international consensus on Saddam. Gradually, SCIRI was weaned from its instinctive hostility to the USA into a position of a grudging acceptance that the superpower might indeed be planning for the overthrow of the regime, but on its own terms and conditions. The USA, in turn, had begun to differentiate between the various Islamist groupings from around the world. The superpower was now clear that the Iraqi Shi'a Islamists – even those that were headquartered in Tehran – had moved away from the position they had adopted in the 1980s and were prepared to cooperate with the United Sates in matters of common interest in Iraq.

The March 1991 Uprisings

The uprising of March 1991, that subsequently became known as the *Sha'aban* Intifada after the Muslim month of Sha'aban, and its brutal crushing by the Ba'athist government, determined the course of Iraqi politics, society and religion for the following decade. The uprising began in Basra on 1 March, as defeated Iraqi army units retreated in chaotic disorder into the city.[13] With troops mulling around the streets and the roads clogged with military traffic, it became clear that the government was losing its authority. Crowds began to assemble, often egged on by armed militants and Islamist sympathisers. The main administrative buildings were soon in rebel hands and fighting broke out where there was resistance by government security personnel or Ba'athist operatives. Within a day, the government had effectively lost control over the city. The news of the fall of Basra quickly spread throughout the south of Iraq and within days insurrectionists had seized the entire region. The pattern throughout the uprising was broadly similar.[14] Crowds, sometimes mobs, stiffened by militants of Islamist parties, defecting soldiers, young clerics or local notables, gathered on the main streets and then marched towards key governmental installations. In some places, the occupants surrendered peacefully, but in others fierce battles broke out. When the rebels seized control over the towns and cities of the South, they first flung open the prison gates. Often, fearsome retribution against the security forces and Ba'ath Party members took place.

The uprisings in southern Iraq were spontaneous and to a large extent unorganised, with no clear leadership. In Najaf,[15] demonstrations against the government began in earnest on 3 March and the city was seized the following day after crowds had grown into thousands and started to lay siege to the main security and party installations. After a day of street fighting the city was secured. Nearly 500 members of the security forces, the dreaded *Mukhabarat* and *Amn al-'Am*, and the Ba'ath Party, were killed in the Najaf insurrection. In Karbala,[16] the uprising took place on 5 March and was led by armed Islamist militants and defecting troops. Crowds assembled in the streets and attacked the main buildings. Key figures of the regime in Karbala were killed, including the deputy governor of the province, the chief of police and high-ranking figures in the Ba'ath Party, and security apparatuses. The shrine of Imam Hussein was used as a rebel headquarters and arms were stored there. It was also used as a court of sorts, where dozens of the regime's enforcers were summarily tried and executed. By 5 March, all the main towns of the South – Basra, Nasiriya, 'Amara, Kut, Hilla, Diwaniya, Samawwa, Najaf and Karbala – were in rebel hands.

In Kurdish areas, the uprising took a different form. Prior to the outbreak of full-scale warfare between the US-led coalition and Iraq, the Kurdish parties had been in continuous contact with the Kurdish auxiliaries who played an important part in maintaining governmental authority in Kurdistan. The uprising in Kurdistan was partly dependent on the neutralisation or defection of these auxiliaries.[17] This, in fact, took place. Suleimaniya was the first Kurdish city to fall to insurgents on 8 March. Lightly armed *pesh merga* (the Kurdish partisan army) attacked the central Security Directorate, which housed the main prison and torture and interrogation centre where thousands of Kurds had lost their lives or freedom. Facing certain death, the security agents and Ba'athists put up serious resistance, and it was only after two days of intensive fighting that the complex fell into rebel hands. Vengeance exacted on government agents was terrifying. Eyewitnesses spoke of 700 people who were executed, hacked or bludgeoned to death just in that one complex alone.[18] Other towns in Kurdistan also quickly fell to the *pesh merga*. Kirkuk, the city that had been the centrepiece of Saddam's Arabisation policies, was the last to fall. The Ba'ath regime had taken precautions against an insurrection there, and had strengthened its defences by widespread pre-emptive arrests and deportations. That, however, did not prevent the city from falling into rebel hands, if only for a few days. On 18 March, 1991 the Kurdish neighbourhoods of the city rose up against the government, and within a day the whole city had fallen under *pesh merga* control. Large-scale killings of security and Ba'ath Party operatives took place.[19]

As the insurrection took hold in the South, the absence of an organisational or leadership framework seriously began to affect its progress and chances of success. The exile political groups did not direct the insurrection. The uprising was supported by the bands of Islamist guerrillas and deserters who had found a refuge in the marshlands of southern Iraq throughout the 1980s. The marshes cover thousands of square kilometres and abut on three southern provinces – and had always been used as places of refuge for political dissenters on the run, and even criminals. In the 1980s the scale of the repression against the Islamists drove hundreds of them into hiding in the marshes where they organised themselves as fighting units. Those fleeing from service, or deserting, during the Iran–Iraq War further augmented their numbers. The tribesmen in the marshlands were a support force, and there may have been several hundred Islamist fighters in the marshes who participated in the uprising. Even so, the exile political groups kept at a safe distance, and none of their leaders set foot in Iraq. SCIRI, in coordination with the Iranian Revolutionary Guards, controlled the entry of large-scale forces from bases in Iran. There was some infiltration into the border towns, especially Basra, where they helped to spread the notion that the uprising was Islamist. Pictures of Khomeini were distributed and banners demanding an Islamic republic were displayed. These created an erroneous impression that pro-Iranian groups controlled the uprising and that its success would considerably extend Iranian influence. This raised alarm bells in Arab capitals, particularly in Saudi Arabia, and played a large part in confirming the decision of the USA and its allies to refuse to give any support to the uprising.[20]

The fall of the important shrine city of Najaf dramatically thrust the *Marji'iyya* of Grand Ayatollah al-Khoei into the limelight. After two decades of assiduously ignoring searing political developments and crises that affected the course of Shi'ism in Iraq and elsewhere, the Ayatollah had to contend with an insurrection on his doorstep. The way that he dealt with it marked the

remaining few years of his spiritual leadership of the Iraqi Shi'a. The Grand
Ayatollah (then in his nineties) issued an innocuous proclamation.[21] He called
on the people of the city to abide by Islamic norms of conduct and bury the
corpses that were littering the streets. He appointed a committee to oversee the
management of Najaf and ensure the continuity of essential services. These
measures were so ambiguous that they could not be construed as giving material or moral support to the uprising or a call to persevere in the struggle. A
parallel military committee had been established, however, probably with the
Grand Ayatollah's knowledge, if not his blessing, to defend the city in the event
of a counter-attack by government forces.

With no real political leadership, however, and little coordination between
the towns and cities that fell to the rebels, and with no prospect of mobilising
the huge moral weight of the *Marji'iyya* in its support, the insurrection had
begun to falter even before Saddam's counter-attack began to take shape.

The Collapse of the March 1991 Uprisings

Saddam's revenge was swift in coming. The scale of the violence in large
swathes throughout the country and the massive destruction and wanton
slaughter that ensued were unprecedented. It was essential for Saddam to
quell the revolt in the South; it directly threatened his hold on power – at one
point the rebels were within fifty miles of Baghdad. It gave the lie to the propaganda fantasy that all Arabs were uniformly in support of the Ba'ath's policies.
It shook the regime's confidence, and at the height of the revolt Saddam began
to be seriously concerned about remaining in power. The ambiguity of the
USA's position towards the regime itself, and whether or not the Allies were
planning to march on to Baghdad immediately after the liberation of Kuwait,
was another reason why the regime lost its nerve in the early days of the
uprising. There was also contradictory evidence about the USA's intentions. On
the one hand, speaking to workers at the Raytheon plant in Massachusetts on
15 February, 1991, Bush had addressed a message to the Iraqi military and
people to rise and overthrow the tyrant.[22] On the other was the unilateral
ceasefire called by the Allies immediately after the expulsion of Iraqi forces
from Kuwait. The issue was settled by the terms of the ceasefire negotiated
between General Schwarzkopf, overall commander of the allied forces, and an
Iraqi military team led by General Sultan Hashim, in the border town of
Safwan on 3 March, 1991. The agreement basically allowed the unhindered
retreat of elite Republican Guard forces into Iraq, with no control over their
redeployment, and the unrestricted use of helicopters, including helicopter
gunships, over Iraqi territory that was not controlled directly by allied forces.[23]

Basra was the first city to come under a sustained counter-attack.
Republican Guard units moved straight from Kuwait into the city, blasting

their way indiscriminately through residential districts and shooting at anything that moved. Women gathering water from the river; children standing on rooftops; knots of bewildered bystanders on the streets; all were mown down. Eyewitnesses reported that the security forces used human shields to protect their tanks. 'I saw that the tank that was leading had three children tied to its front,' as one eyewitness reported to an international human rights organisation. Resistance by the rebels was futile, and although some suburbs held out to the end of March, the city had in fact been secured by mid-March. The carnage, rapine and pillaging in the city by the security forces were dreadful. Arrests of thousands of suspects followed, their fate already sealed. Details of these massacres began to filter out almost immediately, but the scale of the horrors would only emerge much later.[24]

The scene in other towns and cities of the South was not much different. The free use of helicopters made a huge difference to the speed and range of the regime's mobilisation of its forces against the insurgents. Helicopter gunships, authorised under the Safwan ceasefire agreement, were employed extensively and effectively. In Najaf the city was first softened by ground-to-ground missiles and helicopter-fired rockets. Tanks then rolled into the city, firing mainly in the direction of the shrine of Imam Ali, which suffered considerable damage. The main hospitals were attacked and patients as well as doctors routinely executed. Through loudspeakers, the security forces ordered the evacuation of the city, and helicopter gun ships then attacked the assembling throng. By 17 March, the city had fallen. Hundreds of men were executed and several thousand were trucked off to prisons and interrogation centres. More than a hundred *ulema*, including senior ayatollahs, were rounded up, never to be heard of again. The Grand Ayatollah al-Khoei was placed under house arrest and then brought to Baghdad, where he was shown on television, clearly disoriented, alongside Saddam who treated him condescendingly.[25] In Karbala, the fighting was at its most furious and desperate. The rebels, after nearly a week of street fighting, retreated into the area around the shrine of the Imam Hussein. The Republican Guard units then pulverised the area between the two shrines of Imam Hussein and al-Abbas, and the extensive marketplace that connected them. The entire area in the vicinity of the shrines was reduced to rubble, while the shrine of Imam Hussein itself was seriously damaged. By 19 March, the city had fallen under the effective control of the government and the business of retribution and killings began in earnest.[26] The entire South had been reduced to a state of utter subjugation. The Ba'ath regime's battle slogan, attached to the Republican Guard tanks that led the counter-attacks, was *La Shi'a ba'ad il-youm* ('There will be no Shi'a after today').[27]

With the South firmly under control, Saddam then turned his attentions to the Kurdish North. Mindful of the experience of the 1988 *Anfal* campaign and with the large-scale use of poison gas still fresh in their minds, together with the savagery of the regime's reprisals in the South, the Kurdish leadership was taking no chances this time round. As soon as the Ba'ath regime began to bombard Kurdish cities in earnest, the rebel leaders ordered the populations of all Kurdish towns and cities to evacuate towards the Iranian and Turkish frontiers.[28] Within days, a huge human wave of refugees, numbering over a million, descended on the Iranian frontier. Iran let all the refugees in, while Turkey procrastinated until western pressures forced the country to relent. By the end of April, Kurdistan had fallen into government hands, while all along the borderlands of Iran and Turkey, entire tent cities of Kurdish refugees were awaiting their fate. The United States, prodded by extensive media coverage of the refugee crisis, finally took corrective action, but this was limited to the north of Iraq. The Iraqi army was ordered to retreat at least twenty-five miles from the Iraqi frontier with Turkey, and it was announced that the area above the 36th parallel would be a no-fly zone. Meanwhile, the Kurdish leaders began direct negotiations with Baghdad, and a ceasefire was agreed between the two parties. Between April and July the situation in the north of Iraq see-sawed, but buoyed by the no-fly zone, and the presence of an allied monitoring team in Zakho in northern Iraq, the Kurds launched a series of attacks to recapture the key cities of Kurdistan. By the end of July, they had recaptured the cities of Irbil and Suleimaniya, and the Iraqi army effectively ceded control of large parts of Kurdistan to the main Kurdish parties – the KDP in the northern zone and the PUK in the southern zone of Kurdistan.[29]

Opposition Conferences and the Formation of the INC

The collapse of the uprising in the South drove a large number of newly exiled Iraqis into the ranks of the opposition abroad and drastically changed its composition. The preponderance of Islamist factions became an established feature of the opposition and quickly altered the relative balance of power between its various elements. The opposition was now bolstered by three important new considerations. The first was the overt hostility of the USA to the regime in Baghdad. It had sought the overthrow of the regime, but not through a popular uprising. The Saudis and certain Iraqi opposition groups had convinced the superpower that a military coup would be a near certain outcome of the defeat of the regime in Kuwait. Even when this did not materialise, America's commitment to the regime's isolation and possible replacement did not diminish. Second, the establishment of a mainly secure area of Kurdistan under the control of supportive Kurdish parties gave the opposition a possible base of operations against the regime. Third, there was the political isolation of the Ba'ath regime internationally, and the sanctions imposed on it by the United Nations. This made the regime vulnerable to attempts to undermine its authority. The uprising in the South, though it ended in a bloody denouement, significantly raised the profile of the Shi'a Islamist groups and allowed them, for the first time, to reach an international audience that became broadly sympathetic to the plight of the Shi'a of Iraq.

The opposition began to marshal its forces and to seek international recognition. The first port of call was Washington. It was clear that the superpower could bring far more resources to bear, and might prove to be a decisive factor in the success of the opposition's project of overthrowing the regime. Nevertheless, there was great bitterness, especially in Shi'a circles, in what they saw as the indifference, if not downright complicity, of the USA in scuttling the uprising by allowing the Ba'ath regime the wherewithal to crush it. This tension between the need for US support in confronting the regime and the perceived perfidy of the country, particularly manifest in its ambivalence to the uprising in the South and its aftermath, became a recurrent theme amongst Shi'a Islamists during the following decade. America's stated intentions to isolate the regime were held to be suspect, and many senior Islamist leaders would question the USA's real motives behind its rhetoric of confrontation with Saddam.[30]

The expanded JAC organised the first national Iraqi opposition conference in Beirut, immediately after the liberation of Kuwait. All the main leaders attended the conference and made a dramatic show of unity against the Ba'athist regime.

Financed by Saudi money, it was more a show than a substantive effort and achieved very little. Although the State Department had a blanket ban on meeting with any members of the Iraqi opposition in the late 1980s, in time the USA was drawn into opposition politics and the summer and autumn of 1991 saw a steady stream of opposition leaders visiting Washington. The Kurds were far better organised than most in their lobbying, but the emergence of Ahmad Chalabi within the opposition added another dimension. He had developed an extensive range of contacts in Washington and these stood him in good stead in the manoeuvrings that began to take place for influence with the USA. There were two other serious contenders for US attention amongst the non-Kurdish opposition figures. The first was the liberal politician Saad Salih Jabr, an early opponent of Saddam. The second was the Iraqi National Accord (INA) that was set up by Saudi and western intelligence, particularly the British MI6, just before the outbreak of the 1991 Gulf War. The INA, headed by Ayad Allawi, had built-in access to the US government, but through the CIA, which invariably coloured its orientation and prospects.

Ayad Allawi and the Iraqi National Accord

Ayad Allawi was, in many ways, the antithesis of Ahmad Chalabi. Both had assessed the vital role that the USA could play in undermining the regime, and both from their different positions had sought to lead the opposition. But their festering conflicts became one of the principal reasons why the opposition was unable to forge a united front. Ayad Allawi was born in 1945 into one of the prominent Shi'a families of Baghdad. While the Chalabis had mostly left Iraq in the aftermath of the 1958 revolution, Ayad Allawi's family had stayed on. In 1959, the Communist Party appeared to be about to seize power, and sons of the middle and upper middle classes had flocked to the Ba'ath Party, seeing it as the best organised, most effective force to stop the communists. Aged barely 13, Ayad had joined the Ba'ath Party, rising to command a unit in its notorious National Guard. Ayad Allawi was highly active in Ba'ath Party affairs throughout the 1960s. In 1971, he left Iraq for London, ostensibly for postgraduate medical studies, but more likely because he had fallen out with the regime's leadership and especially its rising star, Saddam Hussein. Although he maintained an important party function as a supervisor over the legions of Iraqi students in Europe, his antipathy to Saddam continued without let-up. In 1978, an axe-wielding assassin viciously attacked him at his suburban London home. He had undoubtedly been sent by the regime to liquidate troublesome Ba'ath Party members who would not toe the line. Allawi now became an outright enemy of the regime. He began to establish a network with other like-minded Ba'athists and nationalists who questioned the increasingly violent and dictatorial power of Saddam over the Ba'ath Party and the country.

During the 1980s Ayad Allawi maintained a studied distance from other opposition leaders, and he avoided participation in various Islamist- or Iranian-inspired conferences. Any hint of an Iranian connection would have been anathema to him. He led an active business life during this period, and was always careful to maintain his credentials as an Arab nationalist and reformed Ba'athist, which stood him well in building up his connections in the Gulf countries and Jordan. It was probably during this period that he fashioned his links with western intelligence agencies, particularly MI6. As the Kuwait war loomed, Ayad Allawi formed the Iraq National Accord (INA) in December 1990. The INA, a group comprising former Ba'athists and military and security operatives, had been the brainchild of the western intelligence agencies and their counterparts in the Gulf and Turkey. Ayad Allawi was chosen as its leader.[31]

The Vienna and Salahuddin Conferences

Planning now began in earnest for a substantive opposition conference with US support, with the lead taken by Ahmad Chalabi, closely watched by the INA. The Iraqi opposition's conference in Vienna, held in April 1992, was followed by an enlarged conference to include the Islamists and to be held on

Iraqi territory. This was duly convened on 27 October, 1992 in Salahuddin, with the participation of both SCIRI and the Da'awa Party, and presumably with Iranian blessing. This conference was a milestone in the politics of the opposition. The conference hammered out a structure of leadership and responsibilities that persisted throughout the next decade. It also established the principles of a future Iraq as being democratic, pluralist and federal. The Iraq National Congress (INC), that emerged out of these conferences, developed an explicit formula whereby seats on the various executive bodies were allocated according to sectarian, ethnic and ideological affinities. This formula proved very controversial, as it seemed to enshrine the divisions of society according to communal and ethnic considerations. The INC had a leadership council, comprising a Shi'a, a Kurd and a Sunni. The executive council was also divided proportionately, according to sectarian and ethnic compositions. The chairman of the executive council of the INC was Ahmad Chalabi. Its secretary general was a former communist and human rights advocate, Abd el-Hussein Shaaban, who was later to be accused of being an informer for the Ba'ath regime and dismissed. The INC began its tortuous path of fluctuating between being an umbrella grouping of the Iraqi opposition and a special interest party, beholden to its executive chairman and his allies.

The opposition leadership now began to be received cordially in international capitals. In spite of the clear US source for the INC's funding, the exact relationship between the INC and the US administration remained vague. Washington appeared to consider the INC as only one of many opposition allies and pursued an independent line with other opposition groups, especially the INA and the Kurds. The INC's claims of being the sole coordinator for the Iraqi opposition frequently rang hollow. Intra-Kurdish fighting[32] and the failure of a plan to destabilise Iraqi forces on the Kurdish line triggered widespread dissatisfaction with the progress of the INC. The organisation had always been plagued with disputes, jealousies and divisions, but these had never threatened its survival. Even so, the Da'awa Party and other nationalist and socialist groups quickly pulled out in 1995. The cohesion of the opposition was further challenged by the outbreak of full-scale warfare between the KDP and PUK in 1996, which ultimately resulted in the headquarters of the INC being seized. Several hundred of the organisation's fighters and employees were killed after Irbil was retaken by Iraqi government forces called in to support the KDP. The USA then evacuated others who had earlier been airlifted to Guam from northern Iraq. As a result of these events, Iraqi Kurdistan became divided into two regions, one based in Irbil and controlled by the KDP, while the other, based in Suleimaniya, was controlled by the PUK. But the INC's presence in northern Iraq had ended.[33]

Ayatollah Muhammad Muhammad Sadiq al-Sadr and the Rise of the Internal Opposition

The violent crushing of the 1991 uprising was quickly followed by a concerted campaign, starting in 1991 and continuing for a few months, to undermine the organisational and doctrinal foundations of Shi'ism in Iraq. A large number of *ulema* were arrested and then disappeared; religious schools and mosques were closed; libraries were destroyed; the contents of shrines were looted. The *hawza* barely functioned. The regime, in a series of articles written in 1992 in the government paper *Al-Thawra*, disparaged the 'deviant' doctrines of the Shi'a and cast doubt as to their racial origins.[34] This policy of overt antagonism to the majority of its citizens began to give way to a more carefully crafted plan to build up a Shi'a clerical leadership that was determinedly 'Arab' in its lineage, and one that could be co-opted by the regime. With the death of Grand Ayatollah al-Khoei in August 1992, the regime began to put its plan into action. It released Ayatollah Muhammad Muhammed Sadiq al-Sadr, who had been arrested in the wake of the uprising of 1991. The regime reckoned he would be pliable, given that he was the least known and least popular of the main religious figures. It was a fateful decision.

Ayatollah Muhammad Muhammad Sadiq al-Sadr was born on 23 March, 1943 to a family of noted *ulema* and scholars that could trace its direct descent from the seventh Imam of the Shi'a.[35] He joined the *hawza* at the young age of 11 and studied under a number of scholars, most importantly his relative, Ayatollah Muhammad Baqir al-Sadr, and Ayatollah al-Khoei. He was given the status of *mujtahid* in 1977, when he was only 34 years old, an achievement of note in Shi'a clerical circles. He had also undertaken formal religious studies at the College of Jurisprudence, where he seemed to have been a keen student and reader of history, and where he had picked up a good knowledge of English. He rose further in the religious hierarchy of the Shi'a of Iraq, studying under Khomeini as well as Grand Ayatollah Muhsin al-Hakim. He was acknowledged as a *mujtahid* by a large number of religious figures of the times, which eased his passage into the highest ranks of the Shi'a hierarchy. He was greatly influenced by Ayatollah Baqir al-Sadr, and in his early days was active in politics.[36]

The Ba'athist authorities arrested him twice: first in 1972 and then in 1974, when he was severely tortured. The bouts of imprisonment seemed to have awakened a deep introspection in him, and he turned to *irfan*, the mystical and philosophical dimension of Shi'a Islam. His devotional exercises were so intense and demanding that he drew a reproach from his mentor, Ayatollah Baqir al-Sadr. It was during this period that he wrote a number of mystical works that became an important part of his corpus. As a devotee of a barely understood and not often tolerated form of Islam, he seemed to have consigned himself to a marginal future in the world of hierarchical Shi'ism. According to his own evidence, he was taught this arcane knowledge by a common labourer in Najaf, Hajj Abd el-Zahra al-Gara'wi, an extraordinary admission in a world where the pedigree of one's teacher, and his teachers in turn, is the most valuable accreditation of a man's worth as a *mujtahid*. This partiality to esoteric knowledge must have played an important role in the development of his responses to the challenges that the Shi'a of Iraq were confronting, especially after the 1991 uprising.

Though he maintained a low profile in the 1980s, he established himself as a religious authority with a sufficient number of followers to produce a required compendium of religious rulings, a so-called *risala al-'amaliyya*, that would mark his emergence as an 'object of emulation', a *Marji' al-Taqlid.*[37]

Muhammad Sadiq al-Sadr's release from imprisonment, which coincided with both the death of Grand Ayatollah al-Khoei and the launching of the regime's 'faith campaign', galvanised him into an extraordinary period of activity. He seemed to be operating a carefully considered plan of action. It had several facets, some of which were controversial in terms of both Shi'a jurisprudence and the expected style of discourse between the laity and the religious hierarchy. He changed the concept of *taqqiyya*, or precautionary dissimulation, which had frequently been used to justify hiding one's true beliefs when confronted with danger. Al-Sadr taught that this meaning must be abrogated owing to the trying times that the Shi'a of Iraq were undergoing. He taught that in fact it was obligatory for the religious leader to display publicly his commitment to the symbols of religious faith when conditions were at their most oppressive and dire. He called for the reinstatement of the mass congregational Friday prayers, which he wanted held throughout the country. He himself would lead the Friday prayers at one of the largest mosques in Iraq, the near-abandoned Kufa Mosque, for ever associated with the figure of Imam Ali and his Caliphate based in that city. He called for the revitalisation of the institution of the *Marji'iyya*, after the two decades of quiescence under Grand Ayatollah al-Khoei. In one of his recorded sermons he said: 'We opened our eyes after Sayyid al-Khoei closed his.' He was concerned that the spiritual heirs of Grand Ayatollah al-Khoei, especially Grand Ayatollah Sistani, had chosen to follow the same path of non-involvement in political affairs, thus rendering the Shi'a in Iraq virtually leaderless against the rampant excesses of the state. He established the distinction between the engaged *Marji'iyya* and the quiescent *Marji'iyya*, arguing vehemently in favour of the former. Al-Sadr also firmly believed in the institution of *Wilayat al-Faqih*, or the primacy of the learned jurist in worldly matters, which had been propounded by both Khomeini and Ayatollah Baqir al-Sadr. He rejected the universal primacy of the jurist over all Muslims – a claim that

Iran made for its leader – but acknowledged its validity in a particular setting, thereby succeeding in both affirming his commitment to Islamic government and in avoiding being linked to Iran.[38]

Muhammad Sadiq al-Sadr's programme was based on three main premises: the neutralisation of the state, the mobilisation of the Shi'a masses, and the reform of, or control over, the religious institutions of the Shi'a of Iraq. At first, he established a modus vivendi with the state, which was wrongly understood as an accommodation to the tyranny of the regime and acquiescence in its continued dominance. But Ayatollah al-Sadr, however, was intent on exploiting whatever openings the state offered.

Saddam launched his 'faith campaign' in 1994, when, in a volte-face, the regime adopted the symbols of Islamic piety to buttress its authority and legitimacy. It was an attempt to go beyond the tired slogans of the Ba'ath and tap into a deeper source for the people's loyalties in the hope that it would bolster his regime's credentials. The government began to provide large-scale funding for mandatory Quran classes in schools and government offices. New training centres for preachers and religious studies teachers were established. A new university, Saddam University of Islamic Studies, was launched, and radio and TV stations began to air Quranic recitations, sermons and religious discourses. Alcohol was banned in public places and religiously 'sanctioned' punishments began to be widely employed. Women were encouraged to wear the *hijab*, and within a few years Baghdad had physically changed from an apparently freewheeling city to one where religious symbols and practices dominated. A large number of mosque building and renovation projects were launched, including what was planned to be the largest mosque in the world, on the grounds of the former city airport.

The effects of the 'faith campaign' were profound and far-reaching. The regime now actively sought to infuse religious sentiments into its population and these became an anchor stone of the new, religiously conscious, Ba'ath. The banned Iraqi Islamic Party, an important Sunni political party and an offshoot of the Muslim Brotherhood, was tolerated as it tried to reconstitute its base in a semi-clandestine way. But the Sunni world itself had changed. Moderate Sunnism had been ceding ground to radical Islam everywhere, and this situation had been unwittingly imported into Iraq by a hitherto aggressively secular regime. This had an unintended radicalising effect on society, and encouraged the growth of *salafi* (ultra orthodox) currents in the Sunni community. The regime attempted, somewhat haphazardly and with indifferent results, to control the radical Sunni preachers, but to little avail. They became firmly established in key mosques throughout the country. The government hoped partly to offset this unwanted side-effect of its new-found religiosity by supporting the established Sufi orders, and placing them under the supervision of Izzat al-Douri, Saddam's deputy, a supposed devotee of the orders. The regime spent huge sums of money on the Baghdad shrine of the Sufi saint Abd el-Qadir al-Gailani. The seeds of Sunni Islamic radicalism, laid during the 'faith campaign', were hard to remove.

The Mobilisation of the Shi'a Masses

The Shi'a were seen by the Ba'ath Party to be incorrigible and difficult to peel away from their religious background. The regime wanted to create a pliable Shi'a *Marji'* who would be able to steer the religious life of the Shi'a towards the regime's objectives, rather than try its hand at this directly. The regime's chosen ally was Ayatollah al-Sadr. The Ayatollah himself admitted as much in an interview, when he acknowledged that the state encouraged piety amongst the Shi'a as long as that did not lead to an involvement in political matters. 'They avoid harming us as long as we avoid harming them', he said.[39] It was clear that Ayatollah al-Sadr had been waiting for just such an opportunity to allow him the possibility of openly pursuing his broader agenda. The regime began to treat him deferentially and acknowledged him as a *Marji' al-Taqlid*. They gave him control over the Najaf seminaries and permission to issue residence permits to foreign students of the *hawza*. Having obtained the guarded neutrality of the state, Ayatollah al-Sadr moved on to his next objective – the large-scale mobilising of the Shi'a masses around religious and social works.

The Friday congregational prayers were al-Sadr's chosen vehicle. For a variety of reasons, the institution of the Friday prayers, a vital component of the religious life of Sunni Muslims, had languished in Shi'a Islam.[40] It had been revived in Iran after the revolution, but the conservative *ulemas* of the shrine cities of Iraq had resisted its establishment as an article of faith. Ayatollah al-Sadr brought them back into the heart of Shi'a religious life by using doctrinal, social and barely veiled political arguments to advance his case. He insisted on holding them throughout the country in mosques where his deputies held sway. The Friday prayers became his platform to reach the huge numbers that began to flock into the Shi'a mosques and meeting halls. The Friday sermon, which he delivered personally at the vast, open-air Kufa mosque, was a blend of exhortations, homilies and asides on the pressing matters of the day. The sermons were recorded and widely circulated in Iraq, thus expanding al-Sadr's influence and reach. At first he carefully avoided making comments about the government and its policies, until the tensions between him and the state reached boiling point in early 1999. By that time the congregation at the Kufa Mosque had reached tens of thousands.

The personal delivery of a Friday sermon by a *Marji' al-Taqlid* was an aston-ishing event. Traditionally, the leading divines of the Shi'a world invariably keep their distance from the common man, and in the last two decades they had not even ventured outside the narrow confines of their homes. But here was one of Shi'a Islam's leading authorities addressing the public in their own dialect in a way that was easily understood. The effect was immediate, and the popularity of al-Sadr soared amongst the Shi'a of Iraq, especially the poor, who had felt themselves vulnerable and abandoned in the face of the deprivations of the state. The silence of the traditional *Maraji'* in Najaf about the excesses of the government exacerbated the sense of abandonment, while the distant and irrelevant statements of support and outrage by the exile groups offered little in the way of consolation. Now there was a leader who was prepared to share in the trial and hardships of his people, and who was not afraid to articulate what he perceived to be a more relevant and practical form of Islam.

Al-Sadr also introduced what he called 'jurisprudence for the tribes'. His *fatwas* were direct and pertinent, and tried to reconcile Islamic rulings with tribal customs and practices. Because of the strengthening of tribal traditions in Iraq during the 1990s, and the fact that the majority of poor urban Shi'a – especially in their stronghold of the east Baghdad suburb of Thawra – still maintained strong tribal allegiances, this resonated well with his constituency. He established informal Sharia courts, which adjudicated a wide range of disputes outside the framework of the secular state court system. The pattern he set for the activist *Marji' al-Taqlid* became the leitmotif for the engaged institution that he advocated, and crossed over into the politics of the Shi'a of Iraq during the subsequent decade.

Ayatollah al-Sadr's growing strength and popularity set alarm bells ringing, not only inside the regime's security apparatus but also amongst the traditional *Maraji'* still in Najaf, as well as in the Islamist opposition abroad. The state may have infiltrated his retinue and his deputies with its own agents, to keep watch and report on developments. A number of these people were subsequently exposed, and the charge that the Iraqi *Mukhabarat* (intelligence services) had infiltrated his movement could not be easily dismissed. The exile Islamist groups were at first indifferent to the rise of Ayatollah al-Sadr's *Marji'iyya* inside Iraq. Some, such as the Da'awa Party, tried to establish a point of contact with him, but this was ineffectual. Others, in particular SCIRI, led by Ayatollah Baqir al-Hakim in Tehran, were more sceptical, and by 1999 the scepticism had turned into outright hostility. The antipathy reached a crescendo when SCIRI-connected newspapers in Iran began to accuse Ayatollah al-Sadr and his movement of direct complicity with the regime. In December 1998, a booklet was widely circulated inside and outside Iraq, probably written by SCIRI stalwarts, that detailed a litany of charges and accusations against Ayatollah al-Sadr and his movement, thus deepening the legacy of bitterness between the two camps.[41]

The antagonism between the Sadrist Movement, as it became known, and the traditional *ulema* and *Maraji'* of Najaf became very accentuated by 1999.

Ayatollah al-Sadr's approach to the role and functions of the *Marji'iyya* was revolutionary in many aspects, and affected its entire spectrum of responsibilities and activities. The death of Ayatollah al-Khoei raised the urgent question as to who was likely to replace him as the leading *Marji'* in Iraq. The state began to throw its weight behind Ayatollah al-Sadr, but this did not affect the status of Grand Ayatollah Ali al-Sistani's position as the leading candidate for al-Khoei's mantle. As the most accomplished and learned of Grand Ayatollah al-Khoei's disciples, he was best positioned to be his successor, and this duly became the majority position of observant Iraqi Shi'a. The rapid rise of the Ayatollah al-Sadr, however, threatened Sistani's pre-eminence, and this translated into an escalating war of words between the two camps. On the Sistani side the words were allusive and full of innuendo about the credentials of al-Sadr and his connections to the state. On the al-Sadr side they were more to do with the critique of the disengaged *Marji'iyya* and the need for an Arab, rather than a Persian, *Marji'* for Iraqis. The assassination of two leading ayatollahs, Ayatollah al-Gharawi and Ayatollah Burujurdi in 1998, by regime agents exacerbated the sense of siege inside the Shi'a community.[42] The government blamed the killings on unnamed 'foreign agents', but opponents of Ayatollah al-Sadr indirectly connected him to these murders as an example of his unscrupulous search for power and influence. Ayatollah al-Sadr retaliated against his accusers in a number of his sermons, and recorded private talks, raising other issues such as the disposition of the rumoured fortune derived from religious dues and tithes that Grand Ayatollah al-Khoei had bequeathed to his eponymous foundation. He related bitterly how Grand Ayatollah al-Sistani deliberately snubbed him when he paid the latter a social visit, presumably to mend fences.[43]

The Murder of Ayatollah Muhammad Sadiq al-Sadr and its Aftermath

In the final months of 1998, the looming confrontation between the state and Ayatollah al-Sadr accelerated rapidly. It first began with al-Sadr rejecting the regime's demand that he cancel the annual religious procession to Karbala on security grounds. After being threatened by security agents he relented, but held the government directly responsible for the ban. The government then demanded that he reduce attendance at Friday prayers. His response was to warn government employees against taking any measures that restricted the right of people to attend these prayers. The regime then started to take measures against his prayer leaders and offices throughout the southern provinces and the Shi'a neighbourhoods of Baghdad. Widespread arrests of his deputies, seizure of his movement's mosques and closure of his offices ensued. He met the challenge by calling for the Friday prayer to be held on the streets, if necessary. Demonstrations against the regime's measures broke out in many areas, some of them leading to violent confrontations between al-Sadr's followers and the security forces. In a final attempt to cow the Ayatollah, the regime sent in its heavy guns. Rafii' Diham al-Tikriti, head of the *Mukhabarat*, and Taher Howeish al-Tikriti, Director of General Security, visited him personally in Najaf with the same message: stop the Friday prayers. Al-Sadr refused. A large security force, under the leadership of Muhammed Hamza al-Zubeidi, a notorious senior Ba'athist who had played a leading part in the crushing of the March 1991 uprising, then tried to block the passage of worshippers to the Kufa Mosque. The throng, under instructions from al-Sadr, held their ground. That was the Ayatollah's last sermon. He was put under virtual house arrest. On 18 February, 1999, he was assassinated, together with his two sons, Mustafa and Mu'ammal, as they were driving home from prayers. Approaching a well-known roundabout in Najaf, named after the 1920 Uprising, his car was met with a hail of bullets from a passing vehicle. His sons died immediately. He was taken to hospital where he was left untreated, bleeding to death.[44]

His followers exploded in a paroxysm of rage. In the Thawra stronghold of east Baghdad, thousands took to the streets, congregating around the al-Muhsin Mosque, and calling for the regime's overthrow. The regime's tanks and heavily armed security forces met them. Casualties were in the hundreds. Throughout southern Iraq, city after city was roiled with demonstrations and acts of resistance against the regime. In Nasiriya, the Ba'ath regime relinquished control over the city for a few days as it marshalled its forces to retake it. The regime's ruthlessness and accomplished security apparatus was able to re-establish control. About 120 of al-Sadr's key deputies were arrested. In total, the regime arrested over 3,000 of his supporters. Nearly 450 were subsequently executed. The crisis over the murder of Ayatollah Muhammad al-Sadr had been contained. The regime survived the aftermath, but the Sadrist Movement was to continue in strength as it went underground.

In exile circles, the murder of Ayatollah al-Sadr was met with consternation, puzzlement – and crocodile tears. Those who had been dismissive of his movement as an elaborate scam orchestrated by the *Mukhabarat* could not find any explanation for the escalation of events that culminated in his confrontation with the regime and his subsequent assassination. Members of the Da'awa Party, who considered themselves to be the inheritors of the ideological legacy of Ayatollah Baqir al-Sadr, and who had always thought of his cousin as a theological lightweight, discovered they might have overlooked a powerful social phenomenon that they could have allied themselves with or used to their advantage. SCIRI had taken an overt stance against Ayatollah al-Sadr and had mockingly disparaged his claims to the status of a *Marji' al-Taqlid*. The murder had caught them wrong-footed. The SCIRI media began to refer to him as the martyr and extolled his qualities. They tried to bury any reference to their former vicious dispute with him. But this was insufficient for al-Sadr's followers in Tehran who reacted violently against the murder and held SCIRI and Ayatollah Baqir al-Hakim morally complicit in the crime. The allies of Ayatollah Sistani organised a large-scale media campaign condemning the murder. But there was little doubt that the removal of Ayatollah al-Sadr from the political and religious scene worked to the advantage of a number of people, not least SCIRI and the other exile Islamist groups, and strengthened the massive stature of Ayatollah al-Sistani as the paramount *Marji' al-Taqlid* inside Iraq.

Ayatollah al-Sadr appeared to have instructed his followers that in the event of his death they should accept the leadership of Ayatollah Kadhim al-Haeri, a radical cleric and firm believer in the principle of 'rule of the jurisprudent'. Although a large number of Ayatollah al-Sadr's followers acknowledged Ayatollah al-Haeri's leadership, he was never able to translate this into an effective plan to exert his authority and influence over the entire movement. To the outside world, the leadership of the movement appeared to quickly fragment and the Sadrist Movement ceased to be a factor in the composition of the Iraqi opposition abroad. There were no representatives of the movement in any of the opposition gatherings in the few years preceding the invasion of Iraq, except incidentally, and the exile leadership discounted the political weight of the Sadrists in their deliberations and manoeuvrings. A deep chasm yawned between the Sadrists inside Iraq and the rest of the opposition. The exile opposition considered the Sadrists a spent force and trivialised their political significance inside Iraq. The Sadrists, on the other hand, hounded by the security forces of Saddam and under intense pressure as an organisation, grew increasingly resentful towards the exile groups, whom they accused of abandoning them to stand alone against the regime. Their bitterness would only increase as they contrasted the perceived slights to their fallen leader during his lifetime at the hands of supposed Islamist allies with the loud outpourings of calculated grief that emanated from them in the aftermath of his assassination. There were to be profound, even fatal, consequences as a result of this mutual incomprehension.

3

The Build-up to War

'Given the magnitude of the threat, the current policy [towards Iraq] . . . is dangerously inadequate. . . . In the long term, [the only acceptable strategy] means removing Saddam Hussein and his regime from power. That now needs to become the aim of American foreign policy.' –

Letter sent to President Clinton in January 1998,
signed by eighteen former senior government officials,
including Donald Rumsfeld and Paul Wolfowitz

'It should be the policy of the United States to support efforts to remove the regime headed by Saddam Hussein from power in Iraq and to promote the emergence of a democratic government to replace that regime.' –

Section 3, Iraq Liberation Act, January 1999

The collapse of the INC-led offensive, the debacle of the intra-Kurdish war that brought Saddam back into Kurdistan, albeit temporarily, and the subsequent destruction of the INC's presence in northern Iraq, drove the exile opposition into a cul-de-sac. The momentum that had been established at the Salahudin conference, and the high hopes attached to the formation of the first-ever broad opposition front, dissipated into mutual recrimination and bloody fighting. The INC was never able to institutionalise its efforts, and Chalabi was accused by many of his collaborators of being quirky and uncontrollable. Although he had good working relationships with all the major opposition figures, a residue of distrust and suspicion continued to inform their dealings with him. Nearly all the major opposition groups had established offices in northern Iraq, operating separately from the INC, to which they had been nominally attached as their chosen umbrella group. SCIRI, for example, had already been established in Iraqi Kurdistan, with a field office run by Adel Abd el-Mahdi, a confidant of its chairman, Ayatollah Baqir al-

Hakim. Meanwhile, the INA had been quietly nurturing its links to the intelligence agencies of the USA and UK, and had established its field offices in northern Iraq, as well as an important liaison and control office in Amman, Jordan. An underlying tension existed between Ayad Allawi's INA and Chalabi's INC.[1] This was partly driven by personal rivalries between the two leaders for US support, but mostly because they appealed to different factions in the US government, each of which had fundamentally differing perspectives on the way that the Iraqi regime ought to be handled. The antagonism between the CIA and Chalabi's INC could be traced to the events of 1995 and 1996, when the USA failed to support the INC 'offensive' and allowed the subsequent elimination of the INC's presence in northern Iraq.[2] The rivalry turned into enmity and this was to intensify as the 1990s drew to a close. It entered into the politics of Iraq after the invasion of the country with major consequences.

The INA was dead set against the INC's planned March 1995 offensive, and urged Washington to abandon its support for the project in favour of its own plans for a coup. The INA's theory of regime change coincided with – or reflected – the CIA's own biases for clandestine work with existing power elites inside Saddam's Iraq. It was based on controlling the process by co-opting potential dissidents within the regime's power structures, buttressed by tribal and Ba'ath Party elements, and working through military and intelligence officers who had been 'turned'. This was in accord with pro-western Arab regimes, who were deeply concerned that the process of undermining the regime would unleash uncontrollable forces and open the door for Shi'a and, by inference, Iranian dominance. The INA had been contacted by just such dissidents who were well placed to organise a coup attempt. In 1994, a retired general, Muhammad Shahwani, who had three sons in the Revolutionary Guard, had come up with a coup plan. The CIA adopted this, possibly thereby providing an explanation for its abrupt withdrawal of support at the last minute for the INC's 1995 offensive. The plan was supposed to have been put into effect in June 1996, but the INA coup plan had been penetrated by Saddam's agents, who strung along the coup plotters and then dramatically exposed them. The plotters were arrested, and nearly 120 were subsequently executed, including Shahwani's three sons. Shahwani himself was spirited off to Washington where he continued to work for the CIA. He returned to Baghdad after the fall of the Ba'ath regime. The INA's operating capabilities inside Iraq were severely depleted, but nevertheless it was able to maintain a string of offices in the protected Kurdish zone. In spite of its dependence on material and organisational support from the CIA and MI6, the organisation continued to play a major role in the affairs of the opposition, mainly because of the undoubted political skills and credibility, as well as widespread contacts, of its leader, Ayad Allawi.[3]

Clinton and the Saddam 'Problem'

By the end of 1996, the opposition had reached another low point in its fortunes. The INC's assault on Iraqi army positions had fizzled out; intra-Kurdish fighting essentially led to the partition of Kurdistan between the two big Kurdish parties and the expulsion of the INC from the north of Iraq; the INA's attempted coup had collapsed. Meanwhile, Saddam had agreed to a UN plan to allow resumption of Iraq's oil exports in exchange for authorising the imports of food, medicines and necessary supplies into Iraq. The 'oil-for-food' (OFF) programme, launched in 1996 under UN supervision, appeared to provide the regime with a degree of international legitimacy. It used that to full advantage, manipulating and influencing key individuals, companies and even countries in its campaign to remove sanctions. The USA and the UK continued to be hostile to the regime, but nevertheless the tide seemed to be turning in its favour. Subtle changes were taking place in Washington. In time, this would lead to the formulation of an alternative Iraq policy to the policies that the Clinton administration had been pursuing since it assumed office in 1993. These would have an important effect on the evolution of the principle of regime change, together with the subsequent intensification of the USA's engagement with the Iraqi opposition.

The Clinton administration came to power in 1993, loudly protesting the failure of the preceding Bush administration to address the Saddam 'problem'. The manifest presence of Saddam, after his ignominious defeat in Kuwait, was a taunting reminder that the Kuwait war had not been definitively won. Actually, however, the Clinton administration at its onset had no Iraq policy as such. It was only when members of the administration were confronted with the need to continue Bush's programmes and policies on Iraq and the Iraqi opposition that they proceeded to articulate their own thinking on this issue. The Bush administration had bequeathed a number of commitments on Iraq. These included support for the UN's weapons inspection programme and ensuring that UN sanctions were respected internationally; the continuation of the missions by the US air force over northern Iraq that provided a degree of protection to the Kurds under Operation Provide Comfort II; and support for the Iraqi opposition under the presidential finding of 1991. After some hesitation, the Clinton administration adopted the policy of 'dual containment'. This was announced in May 1993.[4] The policy was designed to isolate Iran and Iraq, politically, economically and militarily. Iraq was recognised as posing the more immediate danger. The preferred tools were diplomatic and political measures, coupled with a rigorous enforcement of UN sanctions against Iraq. Support for the opposition, as a key element in a regime-change strategy, played a secondary and limited role in this unfolding policy. It also signalled the abandonment of balance-of-power considerations, whereby the USA favoured or tilted towards either Iraq or Iran. The balance, if any were needed, was to be provided by a large-scale military US presence in the area.

The effects of sanctions on Iraq were catastrophic. The regime managed to stay in power, but the population suffered greatly from falling incomes, deteriorating services and a collapse of the infrastructure already badly damaged by the war. The sanctions became increasingly controversial as ever more countries questioned their purpose, and whether they achieved their main objective of bringing Iraq into compliance with UN resolutions. The Clinton administration doggedly stuck to them, however, and in the absence of any other policy alternative, dual containment became increasingly questionable as a means to effect regime change. The USA was never prepared to provide the opposition with anything more than token support, and was always afraid of being dragged into an open-ended commitment that might lead it into another war with Iraq.

The Beginnings of an Alternative Iraq Policy

Nevertheless, the germination of a new policy on Iraq had already started in the USA. A group of former government officials, nearly all Republicans and staffers attached to important congressmen, began to question the premises of the policy of dual containment publicly. They were greatly bolstered by the Republican majorities in the Senate and House during Clinton's second administration. In addition, conservative think-tanks in Washington, massively funded by the Right and associated with a vigorous pro-Israel stance, began to seize the debating ground on Middle Eastern policy in general and Iraq policy in particular. In July 1996, a path-breaking report dealing with Israeli strategy entitled 'A Clean Break – A New Strategy for Securing the Realm'[5] was produced. The report had a wide circulation as its signatories were Americans with a record of conservative affiliations and powerful connections inside Washington. It explicitly called for the removal of Saddam Hussein from power as a strategic objective for Israel. The report obliquely referred to the role of the 'Hashemites' (that is, Jordan's monarchy) in redrawing the political map of Iraq. Similarly, the mid-1990s saw the rise of conservative think-tanks such as the American Enterprise Institute (AEI) and the Washington Institute for Near Eastern Policy. They were very well funded by right-wing benefactors, and invariably followed a maximal pro-Israel line. They rapidly eclipsed establishment, often liberal, think-tanks and moulded the parameters of the debate on Iraq policy.

The loss of the INC's field headquarters in Kurdistan drove Ahmad Chalabi to assess the INC's relationships with various Washington sponsors. The CIA appeared to have dropped the INC and instead focused its attentions on the

INA. In the autumn of 1996, Chalabi began to lobby in Washington intensively amongst the groups that had started to challenge Clinton's policy of
dual containment. In light of the realignment of political power in
Washington to the advantage of hawkish Republicans, it was natural that he
would focus on burnishing his credentials with the power brokers on Capitol
Hill and their supporters in the think-tanks, especially the AEI. His key
relationship was with Richard Perle, whom he knew well.

A well-orchestrated campaign to change Iraq policy, aimed at congressmen
and opinion leaders in Washington, was launched, with Chalabi and the INC
as both beneficiaries and principals. A number of sympathetic CIA officers
who had been involved in the preparation of the INC's offensive, notably
Warren Marik, were prevailed upon to give their testimony to congressmen
and the media. They corroborated the INC claim that the CIA abandoned its
obligations to the INC at the last minute. The most pressing issue was the
evacuation of the INC's supporters in Kurdistan after the fall of Irbil to
Saddam's forces. Senator Bob Kerrey, a Clinton confidant, adopted the INC's
cause and played a central part in their final evacuation to Guam. In total, the
USA evacuated nearly 6,000 INC members and supporters, together with
their families.

The think-tanks, led by the AEI, were meanwhile organising conferences
and seminars on Iraq, calling for an overhaul of the policy of dual containment and a more aggressive strategy on the issue of regime change. David
Wurmser, then a fellow of the AEI, had produced a book about Saddam
Hussein called *Tyranny's Ally*, in which he took the CIA to task for their efforts
in Iraq and castigated the INA, their main Iraqi 'asset'. The alliance of
academics, congressional staffers, former Republican office-holders, conservative senators and congressmen, right-wing media personalities, advocates of
a militantly pro-Israel policy, libertarians and even evangelicals became the
government-in-waiting. They were brought together by a combination of
factors: a deep dislike for the supposedly hesitant and weak US response to
international challenges to its supremacy; a fear that Israel's security was being
compromised by the peace process; and concern that Saddam was still bent on
developing nuclear weapons. These groups firmly believed that the traditional
arms of American foreign policy – the State Department and the CIA – were
hopelessly compromised by their discredited alliances in the Middle East and
their reliance on a set of failed policies, notably dual containment. They held
an exaggerated belief in the existence of a cabal of 'Arabists' in the State
Department who manipulated Middle Eastern policies to the disadvantage of
Israel, while at the same time holding the Arabs incapable of developing
democratic institutions.[6] These themes that would come to dominate the
neo-conservative discourse on Iraq were all developed during the late 1990s.

The Iraq Liberation Act

At first, the INC did not make much headway with official Washington. Its access to the State Department was restricted to junior officers. The position as regards the Department of Defense was somewhat better, however, because of the access afforded to it by Richard Perle. Chalabi's media contacts finally led to the airing, in the summer of 1997, of an investigative documentary on ABC news, detailing the circumstances of the 1995 debacle.[7] This had a great impact. Attitudes towards the INC in Washington began to change perceptibly and the organisation was admitted into the burgeoning neo-conservative alliance as its chosen instrument for change in Iraq. The INC and its leader were seen as the most sympathetic of all the opposition groups to their ideas. Chalabi then built on this new relationship and cooperated with leading congressional staffers to produce the Iraq Liberation Act (ILA).[8] Clinton signed it on 31 October, 1998.

The ILA opened a new chapter for the Iraqi opposition and framed its relationship with the USA. It was initially opposed by the administration, especially the State Department, who saw it as an unwarranted interference by the legislative branch in foreign policymaking. The State Department finally came around to adopting the policy, mainly because a number of clauses and amendments had diluted it. These were included at the State Department's insistence as the price for its support for the ILA, which was never intended as a mechanism to finance or engineer the overthrow of Saddam. The Act provided funding for the opposition – defined as parties that supported 'democratic change' in Iraq – and formalised the link between the opposition and the US government. The seven parties identified as comprising the democratic opposition included the INA, the KDP, the PUK, SCIRI, the Islamic Movement of Kurdistan and the Constitutional Monarchy Movement. The INC, which was billing itself as the umbrella organisation for all the opposition, was included, but was treated as just another political party. The total funding available under the ILA was set at $97 million, a pittance compared to the total cost of maintaining the confrontation with Saddam. It carefully excluded 'lethal' training or equipping the opposition. Funds were provided for a Prague-based broadcasting operation, to be run by the USA, called Radio Free Iraq, modelled after Radio Liberty and Radio Free Europe. Other resources were provided for democracy-building, support for the INDICT campaign to bring war crimes charges against Saddam and others in the Ba'ath hierarchy, and for the expansion of the organisational capacity of the Iraqi opposition. A further $8 million was made available for humanitarian relief. The ILA appeared to commit the US government to a policy of regime change, in contradistinction to the policy of dual containment. The reality was somewhat different, however, as its implementation was given to the State

Department which continued to pursue its former cautious policy towards the issue of regime change. The ILA called for the appointment of a 'Special Coordinator for Transition in Iraq', the job of which would be to pull together the various elements within the ILA and to re-establish the efficacy of the Iraqi opposition as a responsible and viable partner in the process of achieving change in Iraq. Frank Ricciardone, a senior career diplomat, who ironically had played a major role in the upgrading and normalisation of US–Iraqi relations in 1984, was appointed as the first such Special Coordinator, otherwise known as the 'Ambassador to the Iraqi opposition'.[9]

The appointment of Ricciardone was well received by most elements of the Iraqi opposition, although there was some lingering scepticism in SCIRI about the USA's 'seriousness' in demanding a regime change. Most of the groups, including the INC, were prepared to work with Ricciardone, given the patent financial and other advantages on offer under the ILA. All conveniently overlooked his earlier engagement with the Saddamist regime. Ricciardone quickly asserted his authority and embarked on wide-ranging consultations with opposition leaders before calling for a new opposition conference. In a number of interviews given at the time, he appeared to be well aware of the difficulty in corralling the opposition in a new umbrella grouping and he maintained a studied vagueness as to the administration's true intentions towards the opposition. It became clear, though, that the military option of arming the opposition was being ruled out in favour of capacity-building measures designed to enhance the opposition's credibility in Washington as a possible alternative government in Iraq. It was unclear as to whether the USA was planning to revitalise the INC as an umbrella group, or create another framework for grouping the opposition. At the same time, Ricciardone gave broad hints that the USA would welcome a coup from within Iraq against the regime – which appeared to work against the avowed principles of the ILA.[10]

The Arab world, with a few exceptions, was hostile to the opposition generally and to the INC in particular. Public opinion in the Middle East had railed against the sanctions policies, which seemed to be aimed at the population rather than at the regime. The intrusive weapons inspection system, no-fly zones and the bombing campaign associated with Operation Desert Fox in December 1998 were viewed as manifestations of a policy designed to weaken, if not destroy, a leading Arab state. The opposition was seen as complicit in a western plan to recolonise the Middle East and ensure permanent Israeli dominance in the area. No Arab country would host the 'Iraqi National Assembly' conference proposed at the INC meeting in April 1999, in spite of strong US representations to its more friendly allies in the area. The hostility of the Arabs to the opposition would prove to be implacable, and would continue, even after the fall of Saddam and the change in status of the opposition.[11]

The New York Conference of the Iraqi Opposition

The 'Iraqi National Assembly' finally convened in New York in October 1999.[12] A number of political groupings that were not represented, or that had not existed when the INC had met seven years previously, were involved in the preparations and deliberations of the enlarged assembly. A group of senators and congressmen who had led the fight for the ILA had addressed a strongly critical letter to Clinton, accusing the administration of 'drift' in its Iraq policy. They deplored the administration's unwillingness to provide security assurances to the opposition's plans to hold a conference inside Iraq. They demanded that the administration implement the provisions of the ILA and start providing military assistance to the INC and other opposition parties. The letter called for the USA to recognise and support the INC's efforts to hold the National Assembly meeting in northern Iraq. As a result, the State Department rushed to organise the conference, to which nearly 350 delegates were invited. It sent the Under Secretary of State Thomas Pickering and Ricciardone to hover over the proceedings.

The conference produced a new sixty-five-member executive council for the reconstituted Iraq National Assembly and a seven-person leadership council, including Ayad Allawi, Ahmad Chalabi, Latif Rashid (of the PUK), Hoshyar Zibari (of the KDP), Sharif Ali ibn al-Hussein (of the Constitutional Monarchists), Riyadh al-Yawar (an independent Sunni) and Sheikh Muhammad Muhammad Ali, who represented the independent Shi'a Islamists. Neither SCIRI nor the Da'awa Party sent any delegates to the conference and they refused to be represented on the executive council. But the Islamists kept one eye cocked at the new opposition leadership, knowing full well that it was backed politically, and financed directly, by the USA.

Ricciardone had to tread a fine line with SCIRI[13] as it was the most important Shi'a Islamist grouping in the opposition and the one most sceptical of US intentions. The experience of the March 1991 uprising had severely affected the organisation and left it suspicious and frequently hostile to the USA's policy in Iraq. Publicly, it rejected the policy of sanctions and dual containment. Its presence in Tehran and the clear support it had from the Islamic Republic made it open to Iranian influence. The stature of Ayatollah Baqir al-Hakim, however, ensured that SCIRI would be seen not merely as an appendage of Iran but rather as an autonomous political group with clear priorities when it came to Iraq.

By the end of the 1990s, SCIRI had undoubtedly become the most important opposition group with which nearly all the other parties sought an accommodation. No effective opposition grouping or policy initiative would work without its involvement. In fact, no US plan involving the opposition would have been considered credible without SCIRI's active participation.

One of Ricciardone's main priorities, therefore, was to maintain a line of communication with SCIRI and to draw the organisation into the plans that the USA was preparing for the opposition.

The Undermining of Sanctions and Weapons Inspections

Two of the main pillars that guided the USA in its dealings with Iraq throughout the 1990s were beginning to fray, notwithstanding the passage of the ILA and the escalation of air strikes. Saddam was brazenly manipulating the OFF programme to which the USA had reluctantly acceded. He was holding out the enticing possibilities of preferential treatment to compliant companies and countries, and was busy busting sanctions and bribing politicians and other public figures.[14] The clamour of demands for removing sanctions was becoming incessant, and convincing arguments were being deployed to the effect that they were destroying not only the economy but also the fabric of Iraqi society. Humanitarian groups were reporting on the dire conditions in the slums of east Baghdad and in the South, with the regime claiming that 5,000 children per month were dying as a result of the sanctions. Within the space of a few months starting in July 1999, a number of Arab countries, led by Jordan, and followed in quick succession by Yemen, Morocco, Tunisia, Algeria, the UAE and Egypt, began to break the ban on flying into Baghdad airport with a number of humanitarian flights. Public opinion in the west also began to be affected by the graphic images of human suffering in Iraq, and there was considerable pressure on western governments to relax the sanctions regime.[15] In December 1999, the UN Security Council gave Iraq permission to sell unlimited amounts of oil under the OFF programme. Even inside the US Congress, the situation was beginning to shift in favour of Iraq, and in February 2000, seventy congressmen signed a petition addressed to Clinton calling for the end to UN sanctions.

The Iraqi opposition was divided about the sanctions policy. A number, especially the SCIRI Islamists and the Da'awa Party, called for their immediate removal. The Kurds, who were establishing the backbone of their autonomous regional government, were also vocal against the continuation of the sanctions. Other elements in the opposition, however, especially the INC and the INA, were more equivocal, linking continuation of the sanctions to the regime's non-compliance with UN resolutions. But the sanctions were hated inside Iraq, and there were few voices that were raised in their defence as a price for weakening the regime.

The weapons inspection programme, on the other hand, had come to an abrupt end, and Iraq was not prepared to accept the UN terms for the return of the inspection teams. The Clinton administration stood strongly behind the UN's extensive and intrusive weapons inspection programmes, designed to uncover and eliminate Iraq's WMD. The UN programme had destroyed a great deal of biological, chemical and other material for WMD, and had uncovered a number of sites that were implicated in Saddam's weapons programme. The UN weapons monitoring effort in Iraq entailed a running battle of wits between the inspectors of the United Nations Special Commission (UNSCOM) team and the Iraqi authorities who had fiercely resisted the UN's programme. There were several tense stand-offs that invariably culminated in Iraqi capitulation, but by 1998 the regime had become sufficiently emboldened to challenge the UN's insistence directly on the continuation of the inspection and monitoring programme. On 5 August, 1998 the regime suspended cooperation with UNSCOM and the International Atomic Energy Agency (IAEA), linking any future resumption of their activities with a removal of sanctions, and the insulation of the inspection team from the possibility of compromise by US intelligence. By the end of October, 1999, Iraq had asked for the departure of the weapons inspection team from its territory, but then in an about-turn announced its intention to cooperate unconditionally with UNSCOM. This was not sufficient, however, to stop the UNSCOM chairman, Richard Butler, from declaring that Iraq was withholding its full cooperation.

On 16 December, 1998 Clinton ordered large-scale air strikes against Iraq, aimed not only at weapons sites but at the heart of the regime's security and military apparatus. Operation Desert Fox was designed not only to punish the regime for non-cooperation with UNSCOM but also to create the conditions for the regime's overthrow. For the first time since the end of the Gulf War, the USA took specific military measures to undermine the regime of Saddam Hussein, and to encourage elements from inside Iraq to rise up and topple the Ba'ath Party from power. The weapons inspection programme had been effectively terminated. UNSCOM itself became mired in controversy as one of its inspectors, Scott Ritter, openly accused the USA of subverting the process by planting intelligence operatives on the inspectors' team. Barred from Iraq, UNSCOM's mandate ended when a UN panel concluded, in March 1999, that the bulk of Iraq's weapons programmes had been dismantled, but that Iraq continued to require an ongoing monitoring and verification system for whatever WMD might have eluded UNSCOM's inspectors. In December 1999, the UN Security Council authorised the setting up of United Nations Monitoring, Verification and Inspection Commission (UNMOVIC) to monitor Iraq's weapons programmes and to identify any remaining disarmament tasks. Hans Blix, a veteran Swedish diplomat and former director general of the IAEA, was put in charge of UNMOVIC. As a result of the lack of hard evidence concerning WMD emerging from Iraq, the veracity of which could be tested through the aegis of UNSCOM, the world had to rely on indirect evidence, most of which would later prove to be inaccurate, false or exaggerated.

Richard Butler and Rolf Ekeus, his predecessor as the head of UNSCOM, had warned that Iraq might have reconstituted its nuclear weapons programme in the absence of UN inspectors, but Blix had dismissed the possibility of Iraq re-launching its programme in such a short period of time. Nevertheless, the fear of what Saddam might be hiding haunted the USA.[16]

Debates About the Future of Iraq

The 1990s saw within the Iraqi diaspora and beyond an explosion in ideas, proposals and plans for the future of Iraq and its various communities – many had previously seemed outlandish. Gradually a number of clear tendencies crystallised to inform the debate, and these formulations were carried over into Iraq after the invasion in 2003. Broadly, the evolution of the political ideas of exiled Iraqis fell into three categories: communitarian thinking; a reformed Islamism; and a liberal, secularised democracy. All ideologically based thinking, be it communism, socialism or Arab nationalism, was in rapid retreat. Iraqis began to explore the interplay of democracy and Islam, and there was a substantial revision in the thinking of former radical Islamists about their doctrines and political programmes.

Concepts such as federalism, constitutional government, human rights and democratic institutions were widely discussed, and formed the basis for a number of conferences and seminars.[17] The issue of Iraq's reform and political overhaul became a widespread topic in the international media. The only group that seemed left out of this debate was, significantly, the Sunni Arabs of Iraq, probably reflecting their paucity of numbers in the Diaspora, as well as their association, rightly or wrongly, with the policies of the Ba'ath in power.

The proponents of a secular, liberal democracy for Iraq grew rapidly in number in the 1990s. They were a motley collection as there was no serious liberal and democratic tradition in Iraq to draw on. Political groups such as the Iraqi Independent Democrats were mostly drawn from the ranks of former Marxists. They remained rooted in an aggressive secularism and dogmatic 'modernism', though, and refused to acknowledge the significance of the increasing religiosity of the mass of Iraqis. Others, such as the writer and public intellectual Kenan Makiya, trod a solitary path in a campaign to mobilise Iraqis in exile behind a post-modern, somewhat ethereal, vision of a tolerant and pluralist Iraq. His book *The Republic of Fear*, written in the late 1980s under a pseudonym, was an incisive examination of the terror state of the Ba'ath, and became an overnight best-seller after the invasion of Kuwait.

It was the emergence of Adnan al-Pachachi, however, a former foreign minister, and long-term foreign policy adviser to Sheikh Zayed of Abu Dhabi, on the Iraqi opposition stage that galvanised the liberal democrats. He brought not only enormous name recognition (his father, Muzzahim, had been a prime minister in the days of the monarchy), but also experience in diplomacy and high-level politics. He was well regarded throughout western and Gulf capitals, had a deep reservoir of funding, and brought prodigious energy, professionalism and political skills to the table.

Communitarian thinking became most developed with the Kurds. Their years of struggle against the central government, and the unprecedented ferocity of the regime's attacks on their civilian population, raised serious doubts in the minds of most Kurds about the desirability of any connection with the Iraqi state. The break from the central government ever since the 1991 uprising fostered in the Kurds a sense of exceptionalism, and advanced the growth of a separate national consciousness. This was accelerated as the structures of an autonomous regional authority for Kurdistan began to be put in place, a process which had begun in earnest after the end of the Kurdish civil war of 1996. In opposition circles and conferences, the Kurdish leaders insisted on a form of federalism that to all intents and purposes was an association of two separate states, while at the same time maintaining an insipid commitment to the unitary Iraqi state. They acknowledged the need for a continuing formal link to the Baghdad government, but insisted on their right to opt out of any its policies, laws and institutions that might harm their regional interests. By the time of the October 1999 'Iraqi National Assembly' meeting in New York, the Kurds had won critical concessions from the opposition on the issue of federalism that went beyond the 1992 Salahuddin Conference. It was now a cardinal principle of the Iraqi opposition that the Kurds of Iraq would be entitled to a high degree of autonomy in any post-Saddam order. The Kurds had also won the argument in Washington and other western capitals. Irrespective of the US and UK governments' often-voiced commitment to a unitary Iraqi state, it was accepted that the Kurds would have a federal relationship with the central government in the event of the regime's downfall.

Islamism and the Emergence of an Explicit Shi'a Consciousness

The Iraqi Islamists abroad underwent a metamorphosis in the 1990s. The groups that had championed the cause of the Islamic revolution in Iran found themselves in a doctrinal and political cul-de-sac. During the Rafsanjani era, the Iranian revolution was maturing and gradually abandoning its revolutionary rhetoric in favour of more pragmatic domestic policies. At the same time, radical Islamism, especially the Sunni variety, was being seen increasingly as a dangerously destabilising force, and had assumed an unacceptable harshness in countries in which it had prevailed, such as Sudan and Afghanistan. Sunni Islamism around the world was also developing a strong anti-Shi'a bias, which made it even more problematic for Iraq's Shi'a Islamists to acknowledge the same ideological roots. Western governments that had hitherto been hostile to Iraqi Islamists began to change their attitude in response to the Kuwait crisis. They signalled that they were prepared to deal with Islamist parties, provided they renounced terrorism and modified their political platforms. The main Islamic parties that were either connected to Iran or that had spearheaded the Islamic movement in Iraq began to change their discourse perceptibly. Thus the Da'awa Party, which had been classified as a terrorist party by the State Department in 1985, and had had to be removed from the Department's list before the USA could undertake any serious contacts with it, now reviewed its ideological programme and produced a new manifesto that turned it into an acceptable social democratic party, with Islamic religious roots.[18] Talk of an Islamic republic was toned down, and revolutionary posturing was replaced with sober business suits and trim beards. It was a far cry from the party that had once claimed to be the ideological heir of the legacy of Ayatollah Baqir al-Sadr.

SCIRI also began to accept the pragmatist imperative in its dealings with the west. In the UK, it had established relations with the Foreign Office. In Washington Ayatollah Baqir al-Hakim stressed that although he personally believed in the premise of an Islamic republic for Iraq, he would never impose it by force. Without formally accepting the principles of political democracy, he would inch very close to its substance, to the point where SCIRI could satisfy the US criterion of being a part of the 'democratic opposition'. SCIRI's political programme remained vague, beyond an insistence that the 'Muslim Iraqi people would choose an Islamic form of government' in a free election. It became, for all practical purposes, a party with a potential mass following led by a charismatic religious leader. Islamist intellectuals also began to question the impossibility of reconciling Islamism with democracy. A number of publications, some edited by Iraqis (such as *Islam 21*), began openly to make a connection between democratic values and Islam. They paved the way for a large-scale adoption of the formal principles of democracy by exile Iraqi Shi'a Islamists.

It was in the 1990s, though, that another current would emerge in the exile Iraqi Shi'a community that became a vital force in the politics of post-Saddam Iraq. The idea that there existed a special Shi'a identity, or consciousness, was a subject that had never seriously been mooted in the modern history of Iraq. In fact the opposite had been the case. The Shi'a had always sought to express their political aspirations through any number of ideologies that variously included Arab nationalism, Islamism, liberalism, communism and even Iraqi 'nativism' – but never specifically in Shi'a form. There had been an avoidance of expressing or discussing sectarianism. The turning point came with the March 1991 uprising, its ruthless crushing and the subsequent massacres specifically targeting the southern (Shi'a) population.

The first tentative signs arrived with the formation of the Public Affairs Committee for Shi'a Muslims, an offshoot of the London-based al-Khoei Foundation. The Foundation was established in 1988 by Grand Ayatollah al-Khoei as an international charity for educational and religious works under the supervision of the *Marji'iyya*. The al-Khoei Foundation, well funded and with large institutional premises, established an excellent network of relationships at all levels of government in the UK and elsewhere. It became increasingly involved in Iraqi affairs.

In the summer of 1992, the foundation hosted a seminar on 'The Shi'a of Iraq at the Cross-roads'. It was well attended, and a number of pioneering studies were presented. They explored the identity of the Shi'a of Iraq, their shared history of oppression at the hands of successive governments and, for the first time, a federal structure for the Shi'a of Iraq was proposed as a solution to the issue of their disempowerment. The seminar had a very powerful impact in the Iraqi Shi'a diaspora as it was the first time that the spotlight was focused, controversially, on the specific problem of the Shi'a of Iraq. It elicited broad support for its claim that they were now united in adversity against the idea of a central state. Other political groups, especially Arab nationalists and liberals, however, did not easily accept this position. The dam, however, had broken. It was no longer considered forbidden or bad form to discuss this problem in a candid way.

The focus on issues that disproportionately affected the Shi'a of Iraq, which included the environmental catastrophe of the draining of the marshlands and many specific human rights abuses, also accelerated the formation of an evolving Shi'a political identity. Dr Sahib al-Hakim uncovered many violations and published a detailed exposé of how Saddam's regime had committed atrocities against 4,000 Shi'a women, through a systematic campaign of rape, torture and murder. By the end of the 1990s, the ranks of those who were calling for a special status for the Shi'a of Iraq had swelled enormously.

These evolving currents of a separate Shi'a consciousness found their most complete expression in a manifesto entitled 'The Declaration of the Shi'a of Iraq', issued in July 2002.[19] It was written by Mowaffaq al-Rubai'e, Ali Allawi and Sahib al-Hakim. The Declaration drew in a wide range of participants from academic, professional, religious, tribal and military backgrounds. Over 400 Iraqi Shi'a opinion leaders in exile signed it. The Declaration called for a new Iraq based on the three principles of democracy, federalism and community rights. While not explicitly demanding a Shi'a region, the 'Declaration' did not rule this out. It stressed that the Iraqi state was inherently sectarian in nature and that the structures of institutional discrimination against the Shi'a had to be completely dismantled.

The 1990s ended with an Iraqi opposition that was fundamentally different from the one that was present at the beginning of the decade. The main actors were still there, but their relative power had shifted. Above all, the involvement of the USA in the affairs of Iraq after the Gulf War had changed all the rules. The USA believed that a formal opposition, broadly supportive of US objectives in Iraq, would be an important adjunct to its own drive to isolate and contain the country. It also gave the opposition the means to propel their activities to an altogether different plane. At the same time, the US involvement with the Iraqi opposition generated its own problems and anxieties. The opposition continued to fret about the real intentions of the USA towards Saddam, and whether aggressive containment policies would persist in the indefinite future. More important, the regime change implied in the ILA somehow had to be substantiated. It was not, by a long shot, a foregone conclusion that the regime would crumble under this pressure.

4

The Invasion

'*I don't think it's unreasonable to think that Iraq, properly managed – and it's going to take a lot of attention, and the stakes are enormous . . . it really could turn out to be, I hesitate to say it, the first Arab democracy . . . I think the more we are committed to influencing the outcome, the more chance there could be that it would be something quite significant for Iraq. And I think if it's significant for Iraq, it's going to cast a very large shadow, starting with Syria and Iran, but across the whole Arab world, I think.*' –

Paul Wolfowitz, Deputy Secretary of Defense, September 2002, speaking to Bill Keller, a *New York Times* reporter

A Discordant Opposition

The attempt to create a united opposition was short-lived. The largest Islamist groups had boycotted the New York Conference, and the INA's covert whispering campaign against Chalabi, orchestrated through the CIA, was matched by the INC's open undermining of the INA. Tensions had reached boiling point. The INC's allies amongst the Washington rightward-leaning power brokers were publicly denouncing the INA, and repeating the charge that Saddam's agents had infiltrated the latter organisation. This mutual antipathy between the two 'secular' liberal stalwarts of the opposition was mirrored in Washington by the increasing polarisation of opinion on Iraq in two antagonistic camps. The first camp, led by the State Department and the CIA, was supposedly 'realist' in its approach to Iraq. It emphasised the difficulties in planting democratic values in Arab/Islamic cultures; it was wary of radical change that would disrupt the delicate sectarian and ethnic balances inside Iraq; and it was concerned about the adverse effects of such change on the stability and interests of US Arab allies in the area, and Turkey. The other camp, led by conservative congressmen and senators, and with some support from a few individuals in the Clinton administration, called for a radical over-haul of the Middle East's political culture and the vigorous espousal of democracy and human rights as the levers to modernise the societies therein. Iraq was to be a test case for this new direction in US foreign policy.

The former policy necessarily led to support for the INA. Its emphasis was on co-opting military and security elements inside the regime and buttressing them by dissident tribesmen and cooperative Kurdish parties. The aim was for a coup, or some form of organised military mutiny. This fitted well with the belief that changes in Iraq should be carefully managed and controlled, in case the demons of Iraq's history were let loose. And with the emergence of Adnan al-Pachachi on the Iraqi opposition scene, the State Department had a cham-pion who enjoyed great credibility and support from the USA's traditional Arab allies, especially in the Gulf. The INC, however, played to the latter camp. Its cultivation of the proponents of the alternative Iraq policy paid off during the second Clinton administration, which was coming under a concerted attack by the Republican Right and its allies. Amongst Iraqi opposition circles, the INC was seen as the party that pushed for the ILA, and therefore breathed new life into the opposition's work, and it was not bashful about ascribing to itself the entire credit for this change in fortunes for the opposition.

Ricciardone worked hard to draw together the groups that had come together briefly in New York. It was an uphill struggle. The INA began to boycott the INC's meetings. It considered the upcoming executive council meeting in London, scheduled for 7 July, 2000, to be illegal, and suspended its membership of the INC.[1] The executive council meeting went ahead in any event, but it was a truncated affair, with the Islamists as well as the INA staying away. The opposition sank back into a confused jumble of parties, each trying to cultivate its privileged status, especially with the US government or one of its agencies. The Islamists, on the other hand, having stayed away from the New York conference, began to develop second thoughts about the 'serious-ness' of the United States in its challenge to the Saddam regime. The two main Islamist parties, the Da'awa Party and SCIRI, quietly encouraged the develop-ment of Islamist front organisations that might, at some later date, carve a place for them in the new US-supported opposition firmament.

The Early Bush Administration

The Bush administration that came to office on January 2001 was packed with proponents of a more aggressive policy on Iraq. All departments of govern-ment that dealt with Middle Eastern policy or Iraq were thoroughly over-hauled, and a large number of individuals associated with the radical wing of the Republican Party or conservative and pro-Israel think-tanks moved into the inner sanctums of power. The 'Alternative Iraq Discourse' became *the* discourse. Straussians, evangelicals, American nationalists, neo-conservatives, libertarians, even Wilsonian internationalists, began to populate the upper reaches of the Pentagon, National Security Council and the vice-president's staff. For a while the State Department was not so affected, while the CIA continued to be led by George Tenet, a leftover from the Clinton administration. A number of the fifteen signatories of the January 1998 letter to Clinton demanding an aggressive anti-Saddam policy found top-level jobs in the Bush administration.[2] Other prominent individuals associated with the former alternative Iraq policy were nominated to senior positions throughout the new administration.

The elaboration of an actual new policy for Iraq, however, was slow in coming. Within a short space of time, the divisions between the realists at the State Department, now headed by Colin Powell, and the radicals at the Pentagon and the vice-president's office became all too evident. The State Department relented on a number of issues, such as releasing funds to the INC, but remained sceptical about the ability of the opposition to foment a rebellion or to organise a confrontation with Saddam. The administration did, however, increase the range and force of its air campaign against Iraqi anti-aircraft positions. In February 2001, large-scale raids, larger than the limited responses of the Clinton years, appeared to signal a more confrontational posture with Iraq, but these were not followed up with more wide-ranging steps to challenge the Ba'ath regime. The State Department fell to adopting a policy of 'smart sanctions' against Iraq, designed to remove most goods and services from the trade embargo, while simultaneously strengthening the monitoring of Iraq's porous borders.[3] At the same time, Iraq had managed to neutralise its neighbours with a policy of preferential trade treatment, reaching billions of dollars, with countries such as Syria, Turkey, Jordan, Egypt and even Saudi Arabia. Smuggling and sanctions-busting began to draw Iraq's neighbours away from possibly supporting a more aggressive policy towards Iraq, thus undermining the administration's efforts to build up regional support for its smart sanctions proposals. In July 2001 in the UN Security Council, the administration was obliged to withdraw its smart sanctions resolution fronted by the UK, because of Russian opposition. So a key element in the revamped State Department's approach to Iraq was left in shambles.

By September 2001, sanctions imposed against Iraq appeared to be no longer acceptable to a wide range of international opinion. They were being ignored, circumvented and subverted on a daily basis by major powers, companies and individuals. And the opposition itself was coming under increasingly sceptical scrutiny. It was, for all intents and purposes, ostracised in the countries of the Middle East with the exception of Kuwait and Iran. Probes by the State Department into the INC's US-provided finances seemed to uncover sloppy, if not dishonest, internal controls. Colin Powell publicly disavowed the possibility that the Iraqi opposition would be militarily enabled to challenge the regime, and claimed its role would be limited to 'public diplomacy' and humanitarian work. Assistant Secretary of State Edward Walker was careful to meet not only INC-connected exiles but also other non-INC groups. Meanwhile, Dick Cheney's office was issuing statements that gave the INC '100%' support and calling for Saddam's overthrow. The administration seemed to be inconsistent with regard to its Iraq policy, with no particular power centre being able to dominate the policy agenda. Chalabi himself began to appear to be a divisive figure, with both strong advocates and detractors in Washington.

Iraq Policy in the Aftermath of the 11 September Attacks

The terrorist attacks on the Twin Towers and the Pentagon on 11 September, 2001 changed the entire political landscape of the world, and with it the administration's policy on Iraq. The previous uncertainty of the direction that this policy was to take was quickly dispelled. Within a few weeks of the attacks, it became clear the Bush administration was gunning for Saddam.[4] Iraq was emphatically implicated in the war against terrorism, and was added to the Taliban regime of Afghanistan and al-Qaeda as the USA's main targets. In a series of war planning sessions, Bush and his closest advisers appeared to have settled on military action to deal with the Saddam 'problem'.[5] The public tone on Iraq began to change perceptibly, with an escalation of the rhetoric against the regime, forcefully linking it to various terrorist plots, including the 9/11 attacks. The advocates of the hardest line decisively won the debate on Iraq inside the administration. In November 2001 Bush instructed Defense Secretary Donald Rumsfeld to begin planning for war with Iraq. Before the year was out, General Tommy Franks, the head of the US Central Command, had presented Bush with a detailed war plan. Colin Powell and the State Department had to manage as best they could with a pre-scripted agenda set by the neo-conservatives and their supporters both inside and outside government. A fundamental decision on Iraq had been made. The Saddam regime had to go within a relatively short period of time. This target was linked to the US war plan against international terrorism. The decision was made, irrespective of the existence of any conclusive evidence to link Saddam to international terrorism or to his possession of WMD. The choice was either military action or an escalation of diplomatic pressure, mainly through a new and more intrusive UNMOVIC presence in Iraq.

The momentum towards a decisive confrontation with the Baghdad regime began to develop inexorably throughout 2002. The initial salvoes of the Bush administration in this campaign were to reopen the WMD file and to demand the return of the UN's inspectors. Intelligence began to be gathered and leaked, or made public, to strengthen the case for the inspectors' return and to keep the regime on the defensive. The CIA was charged with coordinating the intelligence material that might implicate Saddam and make the case for either internationally sanctioned disarmament of Iraq or, failing that, regime change through other – including military – means. The intelligence on WMD was ambiguous at best and perceptive analysts had leaned towards the belief that the UN's inspection teams in the 1990s had uncovered and destroyed most of what had been left of Iraq's WMD programme.[6] Irrespective of where the intelligence would lead, however, the policy decision to remove Saddam from power one way or another had already been taken. The Bush administration did not use its intelligence resources to inform policy; rather, it selectively applied potentially damaging, but inconclusive, intelligence information to strengthen its case against the Ba'ath regime. In this regard, information on Iraq's WMD that originated from, or passed through, the opposition (notably the INC) was uncritically accepted and used to bolster the case for war.[7]

The Pentagon played an important part in thwarting any flow of intelligence that might weaken the hawks. Shortly after 9/11, Paul Wolfowitz, the deputy secretary of defense and a key figure in the neo-conservative alliance in government, authorised the establishment of a special unit that would generate damning intelligence on Iraq. This unit turned into the Office for Special Plans (OSP), under Abram Shulsky, and reported to William Luti, the deputy under secretary of defense. Shulsky was a devotee of Leo Strauss, and a contributor to the Project for the New American Century (PNAC). Shulsky had worked in intelligence for a number of years and had co-authored an essay on the application of Straussian thinking to intelligence analysis. It called for seeking out an adversary's intentions, rather than simply accumulating facts. It was necessary to burrow under the mounds of information to uncover an opponent's hidden purposes. With regard to Iraq, Saddam's intentions were clearly aggressive and in view of this he had to be treated aggressively. The OSP developed a counter-dossier to that of the CIA, and even that of the Pentagon's own Defense Intelligence Agency. It relied partly on information about Saddam's WMD provided by Iraqi defectors to make the case that Saddam did possess WMD and that the regime had links to al-Qaeda.[8]

Iraqi Exiles and the Gathering War Clouds

The signals emanating from Washington agitated the Iraqi exiles. With the overthrow of the regime now a distinct possibility, the opposition groups began to jockey for greater influence with the power centres inside the administration. Chalabi's INC once again allied itself to the groups that were responsible for the passage of the ILA, and made new and even more powerful friends. Meanwhile, the INA grew in stature, in tandem with the raised CIA profile within the administration. The CIA had proved itself in the Afghan war by mobilising and directing the Northern Alliance in their successful campaign against the Taliban, with minimal US casualties and cost.[9] The Northern Alliance model became a serious working template for the over-throw of the regime in the event that hostilities commenced. The CIA regained its credibility inside the inner councils of the Bush administration and became a key player in planning for the subversion and overthrow of the Baghdad regime. Other groups, especially the Kurds, redoubled their efforts with their Washington friends and allies. The Kurds played on the Northern Alliance model, casting themselves as the Iraqi equivalent of the Tajik community in Afghanistan, and claiming a disproportionate share of the war planners' attention, especially the CIA.

The British also had a hand in mobilising the opposition, and their efforts mirrored those in the USA with one major difference: the British had no equivalent to the neo-conservatives inside their government. There were a few individuals with access to the prime minister's office who might have shared some of the neo-conservatives' opinions, but they were in clearly subordinate roles. The Foreign Office was hugely sceptical about the possibility of demo-cratic change in Iraq, and while not explicitly saying so, was cynical, if not contemptuous, about the more rosy prognoses of the neo-conservatives regarding a post-Saddam Iraq.[10] MI6, on the other hand, stuck close to the CIA, and had early settled on the INA as its most suitable opposition partner.

In August 2002, the main leaders of the opposition were invited to Washington to meet with Under Secretaries Marc Grossman of the State Department and Douglas Feith of the Pentagon. The failure of Bush's top leadership to meet with the opposition was interpreted as signalling a cautious US commitment to it as an alternative to the Baghdad regime. It was during closed-door sessions, however, that the Bush administration encouraged the opposition to organise a broad conference of exiles in preparation for the possibility of military action to overthrow the regime. In these meetings, both Rumsfeld and General Richard Myers, the Chairman of the Joint Chiefs of Staff, made an appearance to underline the seriousness of the USA's commit-ment to challenge Saddam. An opposition conference was set for December 2002 in London.

Visions for a Post-war Iraq

As the build-up to the war progressed, the role of Deputy Defense Secretary Paul Wolfowitz loomed large in war planning. Wolfowitz had been one of the most vociferous supporters of the view that the United States had a special role to play on the world stage. It was in the USA's strategic interest to advance the cause of democracy and to implant the values of liberalism, pluralism and human rights.[11] On Iraq, he publicly affirmed his belief that American policy should be guided by the Ba'ath regime's *intentions* rather than by the standards required to prove or disprove its possession of WMD. The group that Wolfowitz assembled around him in the Pentagon was firmly wedded to this perspective, notably the Under Secretary for Defense Policy, Douglas Feith. Feith had been given overall control over post-war Iraq planning. He had peculiar qualifications for a person charged with determining the fate of an Arab state as he was a committed Zionist and supporter of the Likud Party of Israel, and his career had been enmeshed with the issues of Israeli security. He carried into his job an extreme version of the usual neo-conservative associations with right-wing policy institutes. Feith had a belief that the post 9/11 order gave the USA a unique opportunity to alter the political landscape in the 'greater' Middle East, that is, all countries between Morocco and Pakistan.

The State Department adopted a more sober approach to the impending likelihood of a post-Saddam era in Iraq. In April 2002, it set in motion a series of meetings and working groups made up of Iraqi exiles, which examined various aspects of Iraq's society and economy, and prepared a number of policy prescriptions for a possible new government in Iraq. Technical groups were organised around a number of thematic issues, including public health and humanitarian needs; transitional justice; public finances; and oil. The project, grandly titled the 'Future of Iraq Project', was placed under the control of Tom Warrick, a senior State Department officer at its Bureau of Near Eastern Affairs.

The State Department was plagued from the start by bureaucratic wrangling and turf wars with the Defense Department. The INC was firmly against any such State Department-led initiative, fearing that it would lead to strengthening the hand of the State Department's protégés in the struggle for supremacy inside the Iraqi opposition. The INC's position coincided with the Defense Department's own suspicions about the groups that were being sponsored by the State Department. The project faced funding problems, and moved in fits and starts.

The tug of war between the State and Defense departments over control of the administration and governance of Iraq masked a far more serious issue. The entire process of planning for a post-war Iraq was mired in ineptitude, poor organisation and indifference. The 'Future of Iraq Project' was a half-hearted and unreal attempt to tackle the issues that would confront the overseers of a country with a devastated economy and a dictatorial political culture. Most of the groups dealt with issues on which the participants had no up-to-date information, or any immediate experience. The real importance attached to the project was reflected in the State Department's allocation of a single basement office to act as the 'control' centre. The lack of clarity about the administration's true intentions in post-Saddam Iraq may have contributed to the confusion about the plans for the governance of the country. By the time the military option appeared to have been definitively selected, it was too late to start seriously thinking about the administration of a post-war Iraq.

'The Transition to Democracy' report compiled by the Democratic Principles Group and edited by Salem Chalabi and Kenan Makiya was the most complete statement of what the liberal and westernised groups within the opposition sought for Iraq's political future.[12] It was a reflection of the political and constitutional thoughts of a radical democratic bloc, at that time associated with the INC. To a large extent, it also seemed to reflect the direction of thinking on Iraq in the Pentagon. A number of issues that would later prove contentious were first mooted in the report, including the extent of de-Ba'athification, the scope of federalism, the desirability of a bill of rights, and, critically, the nature of a transitional government following the overthrow of the regime. De-Ba'athification, or the process of eliminating the ideology of the Ba'ath Party and its adherents from Iraq's body politic, was raised in a paper that compared Iraq's experience with the Ba'ath to that of Germany's with the Nazis, and sought similar mechanisms for dismantling the legacy of totalitarian rule.[13] The entire drift of the report was for a complete break with Iraq's political traditions of strongman rule, centralisation, and scant respect for human, minority and community rights. A number of voices from within the Democratic Principles Group, however, were critical of Makiya's attempt to present the report as a collective effort, and refused to acknowledge it as more than the work of a few fringe elements. The fracas over the report carried over into the nature of the conference that the opposition was organising with US assistance at the end of the year. If the report were to have any significance, it should be recognised by the conference as a draft for a working blueprint on the political future of Iraq. The political parties strongly objected to using the report as a foundation stone for a new political compact between the opposition parties. Ghassan al-Attiyya, an important political thinker and writer, argued that the form that any transitional authority would take would be directly dependent on the way that the regime was overthrown. If it were under some form of UN approval, the UN would have the final say on the nature of Iraq's transitional authority. Similarly, if it were as a result of unilateral action by an Anglo-American coalition, the coalition would be the arbiters of the transitional authority.

The December 2002 London Conference of the Iraqi Opposition

Preparatory work for the grand conference of the opposition was bedevilled by ongoing battles about what it was expected to achieve. There were three key directions that the conference could take. The first, represented by idealists who congregated around Chalabi and the INC, wanted a conference that would ensure the opposition mapped out a new course for Iraq. Their chosen handle was the 'Transition to Democracy' report, and their tactic was to have the conference adopt some, or all, of the report's recommendations, thus binding the likely new leaders of Iraq to a set of agreed principles and policies.

The second course that the conference might take was a public relations exercise, designed to show wide Iraqi support for the US policy of escalation with Saddam and to bless any military action that might be taken against the Ba'ath regime. This was the plan of the 'realists' in the administration, who needed an Iraqi cover for the evolving plan to attack Saddam. No commitments would be made at the conference beyond general statements of encouragement for democratic rule and respect for civil and human rights. It was clear that at this point the United States had ruled out handing over the country to the opposition. Irrespective of the Pentagon's support for the INC, the dominant administration view was that the opposition was essentially disunited. As a group, it did not merit the support of the United States as an alternative to Saddam.

The third course for the conference was what the leaders of the opposition parties expected to achieve as far as their own narrow interests were concerned. Washington held limited expectations for the conference, but this did not stop the main opposition groups from using it as a forum for cementing their control over the political process and forming a mechanism that would coordinate with the USA in the run-up to the war. The conference would also be used to reintegrate within its formal structures important groups that had stayed away from the New York Conference, especially the Islamists of SCIRI and the Da'awa Party. The leaders' main concern was to ensure the continued primacy of the main opposition parties, while acknowledging the need to broaden the representation base inside the conference. SCIRI in particular had feared that an American military government would effectively consign the organisation to a position of powerlessness.

The London Conference opened on 14 December, 2002.[14] There was a sense that an event of historic importance was taking place. Several countries sent observers to the conference, including Iran, Turkey, the UK and the EU.[15] The USA sent a large observer delegation, led by Zalmay Khalilzad, the new special envoy to 'Free Iraqis'. He had been chosen to fill the vacuum left by the reassignment of Ricciardone to an ambassadorial position, and had been brought in fresh from his successful shepherding of Afghanistan's myriad groups into a new political compact.[16] There was an a priori rejection by the USA of any suggestion of a provisional government being set up, or even planned, at the conference, and this veto was relayed in no uncertain terms to the participants. The US delegation had wanted to establish a small opposition leadership group with which it could discuss and coordinate the pending action against Saddam, but it was left purposefully vague as to whether such a coordinating group would have any serious influence on the direction of events. This uncertainty, with some attendees at the conference seemingly privy to the USA's true intentions, and others anxious and fearful about being accorded an out-of-the-race position, exacerbated a situation that was already confused. Several participants openly expressed their fear that a military occupation was in the offing, and called for international acceptance of the opposition as a government, or parliament, in exile.

The desirability of a provisional government based on the opposition was not broadly accepted. Some groups, such as Chalabi's INC, wanted a provisional government to be established before any military action took place.[17] Others, such as the Kurds, wanted to form a government after the regime was overthrown. The INA and its supporters were silent on this issue, but worked against the idea of a provisional government formed without taking into account the 'internal' opposition to Saddam. The CIA and its supporters insisted that a military insurrection or a palace coup were the most likely routes for overthrowing the regime. The formation of any provisional government based on exile groups, before the overthrow of the regime, might very well alienate the 'internal' opposition and dissuade it from any attempt to change the regime. America was also deeply suspicious about Iran and its role in succouring the opposition.[18]

As it was, the conference recognised that, irrespective of US intentions, it was necessary to come up with a committee of sorts that would place a mantle of legitimacy on the opposition and meet one of the conditions for possible participation in a post-Saddam administration. Finally, a sixty-five-person committee was selected by the leaders of the main political groups, broadly reflecting the changes in the composition of the opposition over the previous decade. Although independent Shi'a Islamists staged a walkout, claiming that SCIRI had appropriated the role of sole arbiter of the Shi'a Islamists for itself, the conference nevertheless ended on a high note and appeared to have succeeded in preparing for an eventual role for the exiles in the post-Saddam order. But a serious discussion of a number of vital issues had been avoided. The possible overhaul of a Sunni-dominated system; federalism as a halfway house to Kurdish separatism; the role of religion in Iraq's public life; the extent of Iranian influence in a post-Ba'ath order; the scope of de-Ba'athification – these were all issues that were kept firmly off the conference's agenda. The sixty-five-person follow-up committee was invited to meet again soon after the New Year in Iraqi Kurdistan.[19]

The Aftermath of the London Conference

Meanwhile, the Pentagon had sent its Deputy Assistant Secretary of Defense, William Luti, and General David Barno to London to meet with eleven opposition officials to discuss the training of about a thousand Iraqis as military auxiliaries in the event of war.[20] All the opposition groups mentioned in the ILA were invited to send names of trainees, but in the event, only the INC submitted a large enough number of candidates to escape the stringent vetting designed to weed out Islamists and infiltrators. The purpose of this force was not clear. It was meant to be a unit to which Iraqi army would-be deserters could defect, and its members to act as liaisons, translators and interpreters to the US army in an invasion of Iraq. Opposition groups such as SCIRI were sceptical, and refused to send any candidates. Others thought this an attempt on the part of the pro-INC Pentagon cabal to give the INC a military advantage.

Following on from the London conference, the USA invited a number of opposition leaders for discussions in Washington in early January 2003. The administration had redoubled its efforts to include the Da'awa Party in its war planning, hoping at least to have a positive response from the party regarding any American military action.[21] The sixty-five-man committee was scheduled to meet in Salahuddin in Iraqi Kurdistan, on 22 January, 2003.[22] The Kurdish groups had demanded that the USA provide adequate security for the meeting, but the Bush administration was initially hesitant to extend its security commitments beyond the flights patrolling the no-fly zone. In addition, the superpower might not have been prepared to acknowledge publicly the deliberations of an opposition committee that saw itself as a nucleus for a new transitional government.[23] The Salahuddin meeting took place on 25 February, 2003. The INA did not formally boycott the meeting, but Ayad Allawi was in Ankara at the time, holding talks with the Turkish government. He made it clear that the INA stood four-square against the idea of a government-in-exile.[24] A government-in-exile was, in fact, one of the two main issues that dominated the meeting. The other was the looming threat that Turkey might be induced to join the war coalition and invade northern Iraq. This rang loud alarm bells amongst the Kurds. They not only feared the tipping of the balance against them in disputed territories such as Kirkuk, in favour of Iraqi Turkomen who were supported by Turkey, but also the possibility of being disarmed. The USA was actively wooing Turkey. In December 2002, Deputy Defense Secretary Wolfowitz and Under Secretary of State Marc Grossman visited Ankara, trying to elicit Turkish military support for the invasion of

Iraq and encouraging the Turks to open channels with the Iraqi opposition. Within Turkey, however, the possibility that the country might join a US-led coalition in the invasion of Iraq was a very controversial and highly unpopular issue. The Turkish government insisted that any Turkish involvement had to be amply offset by taking into account the political, economic and diplomatic costs that Turkey would incur as a result.

Khalilzad, who had arrived from Turkey, presided over the meeting in Salahuddin. He was at pains to downplay the possibility of a formal military occupation of Iraq, stating that the USA had no desire to govern Iraq directly.[25] He talked about a 'rolling transition', whereby the US military would hand over occupied territory to Iraqi 'representatives' as soon as the security and military situation would allow, but he couldn't dispel the notion that the USA was not wholly committed to a sovereign government of Iraqis. Ahmad Chalabi demanded sovereignty – Iraqi sovereignty over Iraqi soil. SCIRI's Abd el-Aziz al-Hakim raised the spectre of foreign occupation and insisted that the Iraqi people would resist it. The USA, however, was adamant that there would be no provisional government declared from Salahuddin – and had prepared for the arrest of the proponents of such a government, in the event that the committee declared it.[26] The Kurds began to withdraw their support for such a move, and the idea of a provisional government collapsed. Even so, the committee endorsed the Kurdish demand that no intervention by regional powers would be tolerated. Eventually, the follow-up committee settled on the formation of a six-man leadership council, composed of Talabani, Barzani, Chalabi, Abd el-Aziz al-Hakim, Ayad Allawi and Pachachi.

By the time the Salahuddin Conference had ended, war had become imminent. Saddam had presented a massive document to the UN, claiming that he had no WMD. Hans Blix had corroborated this, by stating to the Security Council on 14 February, 2003, that the UN team had found no WMD in Iraq. Bush rejected these findings, however, insisting that Saddam must go or be removed from power by military action. The USA had mobilised a large force – just how large a force became a subject of much debate later – and was poised to invade Iraq from the south, through Kuwait, and via Turkey. The Turkish parliament, though, voted against the government's proposal to allow US troops through Turkish territory, and the much-expected Iraqi northern front did not materialise. In spite of the build-up of troops, America was still expecting a regime change through the action of agents inside Iraq, and through 'decapitation' of the regime by surgical strikes against the leadership. (Great hope was pinned on the 'smart' bombs that allowed for pinpoint bombing, which was supposed to take out the top leadership.) In late February 2003, the USA fired cruise missiles at a bunker in Baghdad, expecting to kill Saddam and other regime figures. This was to be the first of many attempts to decapitate the regime, none of which were successful. It was clear from the missile strike that the CIA plan for assassinating Saddam and other top leaders in the Iraqi government was still supported by most of official Washington.

The Invasion and the Iraqi Opposition Forces

The invasion of Iraq was launched on March 19, 2003 by American forces led by the Third Infantry Division, with British support, from Kuwait into Iraqi territory. The war was fought fitfully over a three-week period. There was no doubt about the final outcome, even if at certain points there appeared to be some resistance. But this was quickly overcome. In Basra, the British had effectively surrounded the city in the first week, but did not actually establish control until the end of March. Meanwhile, the Americans had met unexpected resistance in the city of Nasiriya, mainly from the *Fedayeen Saddam*, a militia loyal to Saddam and his family. The march to Baghdad was halted by sandstorms in the central Euphrates area, and also by running skirmishes and ambushes. But the Iraqi army and the vaunted Republican Guard simply melted away. The troops did not surrender en masse as had been expected – they simply went home. The Coalition intelligence had expected that entire units would switch sides and form the core of a future loyal military force with which they could cooperate. Apart from very few exceptions, however, this did not happen. Reports of wholesale surrender of Iraqi army units were simply unfounded. By the time the vanguard of the US invading force had reached the outskirts of Baghdad, the armed forces of Iraq had almost disintegrated. The regime tried to use the Arab 'volunteers' who had flocked to join the battle against the invaders. Some 4,000 were reportedly in Baghdad, awaiting orders from the Iraqi High Command. They were thrown into a hopeless battle in the airport area against the Americans, and were decimated. Large-scale operations ended when the US army entered Baghdad in force on 9 April, 2003, and in a symbolic gesture pulled down the statue of Saddam in Firdaus square in the heart of the city.[27]

The involvement of exile Iraqis in the planning and execution of the war had been negligible. The Kurds had been effectively sidelined by the decision not to open a northern front, but their *pesh merga* forces did play an important supporting role to US Special Forces that were earlier deployed in Iraqi Kurdistan.[28] There were, in addition, three other possible groups that could have contributed an 'Iraqi' element to the coalition forces: the Badr Brigade, the INC, and the INA people who were armed. The group that was finally trained in Hungary had far fewer recruits than had been expected, and its members were allocated to the various US and British frontline units as interpreters and liaison officers. The Badr Brigade was prepared to enter Iraq, but the USA had sent a forceful message to SCIRI warning that if any organised force from Badr were to enter the battle it would be considered an enemy combatant and treated accordingly. This, however, did not stop Badr from infiltrating its units into a number of towns and cities near the eastern borders with Iran that were outside the main invasion routes of the US army. In mid-April, Badr forces seized Baqubah, the capital of Diyala province, while a SCIRI cleric, protected by Badr gunmen, occupied the government buildings in Kut, the capital of Wasit province.[29] In the west, Ayad Allawi's INA moved into the tribal areas of the Anbar province. The INA had no armed wing as such and relied on winning over tribal elements that it had cultivated over the years from its Jordan base. This was part of INA's plan of co-opting Sunni Arab tribes that had been alienated from the regime, or whose loyalty could be bought. It was part of the grand strategy that evolved with the CIA, which included the use of dissident military and security officers, Ba'ath Party leaders and tribal chiefs to undermine key props of the regime's power structure. There was, in fact, very little to show for INA's effort, except for minimal resistance to the presence of the occupying armies in the very early days after the war in the western and northern parts of the country.[30]

The INC also tried, from its temporary headquarters in the Dokan area of Kurdistan, to recruit a force that could help it in the looming struggle for power and influence in Baghdad. The organisation had maintained regular contact during the early days of the war with both the Pentagon and United States Central Command (CentCom) in Qatar. The resistance in Nasiriya by *Fedayeen Saddam* to the advancing American army appeared to show up the absence of Iraqi participation in the war against Saddam. At that point, the Pentagon decided to fly the INC contingent down from Kurdistan to Nasiriya, as part of the effort to put an Iraqi Arab face to the Coalition forces, for both symbolic and tactical reasons. After a few days of training, the Free Iraqi Forces, as it was now named, was attached to US Special Forces. It was used in a few engagements in the marshlands, notably in the Shatra area, where it appeared to have uncovered a large cache of arms. The publicity effect of this move was enormous. A number of groups saw this as a Pentagon attempt to load the dice in favour of the INC. But the reality was somewhat different. The group stayed isolated in an abandoned camp, and had to scrounge for transport. On 16 April, Chalabi and his small force arrived in Baghdad and ensconced themselves in the Hunting Club.[31]

The Rise of the Islamists and the Murder of Sayyid Abd el-Majid al-Khoei

Iraq's inhabitants did not meet the invasion with joyous scenes of welcome for a liberating army. The collapse of the decades-old dictatorship left a power vacuum, especially in the South and in the poor Shi'a suburbs of Baghdad.

Islamist forces and their allies, who laid claim to the loyalty of the population, quickly filled the power vacuum. Parallel power structures evolved in nearly all towns and cities of southern Iraq, but they remained undetected by officials installed by the occupying authorities. In places such as Sadr City, the giant Shi'a slum of east Baghdad, the dormant Sadrist Movement, about whose existence virtually nothing was known by the west before the war, sprang to life, and within days after the fall of Baghdad it had secured the area. The movement had not been quashed by the former regime, as many had thought, but had simply gone underground. The speed and extent of the Islamist wave that swept over Shi'a Iraq was as if a tsunami had silently and very rapidly spread to cover the South. No one had predicted the strength of this wave and the depth of support that it engendered amongst the poor and deprived population of the area. In Baghdad, with the occupation forces settling in to run the country, the goings-on in the South, or even in Sadr City, were matters of very little concern. The USA had quickly defeated the Iraqi armed forces and could now nudge and cajole its allies in the opposition and inside the country to work together to produce an acceptable governing formula for the country.

Clashes between the shadow local governments and the administrative structures that were being put in place by the Coalition were not slow in coming. Frequently, the struggle for local control of the southern towns was between proxies of the Coalition, some of whom had come with the invading armies, and others that had been hand-picked by local commanders or who had been suggested by the field operatives of the CIA or British intelligence. The individuals selected to run these towns had little sensitivity or knowledge about local conditions. In nearly every southern province, as well as in Sadr City, the original administration that had been put in place in the wake of the invasion fell apart, and power seeped to the newly emergent Islamists and their local allies. The failure to establish local control, especially in the larger cities that had been bypassed by the invasion force, was an issue that was to come back to haunt the Coalition, time and again. To a large extent, this was because of the insufficient number of troops that had been committed to the invasion. General Eric Shineski, the retiring US army commander, had suggested in congressional hearings before the war that Iraq would need a force of nearly 500,000 troops to pacify and control the country properly after the fighting. Wolfowitz and Rumsfeld, however, had dismissed his views. A larger force would have given the Coalition's local proxies the wherewithal to at least face up to the challenge of the Islamists more forcefully.

The assertion of local power by underground Islamist forces was first manifested, with tragic consequences, in the holy city of Najaf. Sayyid Abd el-Majid al-Khoei, the secretary general of the Khoei Foundation, had developed strong relationships with western governments and agencies throughout the decade that he spent in London after the collapse of the March 1991 uprising. The Foundation was seen as a moderating force in the world of Shi'a Islam, and a useful counterweight to the Iranian regime. As the war with Iraq became ever more likely, al-Khoei, who had studiously avoided any direct involvement in the politics of Iraq, began to show a marked interest in Iraqi affairs. In late 2002, he had even floated the idea of institutionalising the position of the Shi'a in Iraq by forming a Shi'a council that would oversee the civilian affairs of the community after the fall of the regime. His approach was basically communitarian.

As war became imminent, he had been approached by the CIA to help in the effort of controlling the city of Najaf and establishing a conduit between the *Maraji'* of Najaf and the Coalition.[32] He eagerly accepted the challenge. On 3 April, 2003 he was flown by a US Marine helicopter with his group into Najaf. He established himself in an abandoned house and began a series of visits to the city's leading Ayatollahs, including Grand Ayatollah Ali al-Sistani who had recently issued a statement advising Iraqis not to hinder the progress of the Coalition's troops. Al-Khoei appeared to be well supported and funded in this effort. He quickly organised a civilian council and set himself the task of returning basic services to the city's population.

With the support of the US military, plenty of resources at hand, and an illustrious name, al-Khoei believed that he would be able to master the politics of the city. But he made two cardinal errors. First, in his keenness to bind the disparate groups in Najaf, he reached out to the Saddam-appointed custodian of the Holy Shrine of Imam Ali, the so-called *Killidar* (Keeper of the Keys), Haider al-Rufaii, who had been cowering inside the compound of his house since the fall of the regime. He was deeply unpopular, not only because it was believed he had taken some of the shrine's treasures and donations, but also because he had been a member of the Ba'ath Party, as well as a member of the defunct, rubber stamp National Assembly. The other mistake made by al-Khoei related to his treatment of Moqtada al-Sadr and his followers in Najaf. He belittled their significance, as he was essentially ignorant of the changed power relations in Najaf because of the rise of the movement associated with the murdered Ayatollah Muhammed Sadiq al-Sadr.

On 10 April, al-Khoei, together with an armed escort, accompanied Haider al-Rufaii to the shrine of Imam Ali. There, while the two were in the custodian's offices, they were accosted by a mob of angry supporters of Moqtada al-Sadr. After an exchange of gunfire and throwing of grenades, the mob seized al-Khoei and al-Rufaii. Al-Rufaii was hacked to death in front of the gates of the shrine. Al-Khoei was killed later, apparently after failing to receive protection in Moqtada al-Sadr's house nearby. Although one of al-Khoei's entourage managed to contact the US military and the CIA, al-Khoei's erstwhile protectors did not interfere to stop the mêlée at the shrine. (It was later admitted that the US commanders in the area had had instructions not to approach the heart of the city lest it be interpreted as an infringement of the sanctity of the shrine.)[33]

The murder of Abd el-Majid al-Khoei left a deep impression, not only in Najaf but also throughout Iraq. He had been a well-known and respected figure throughout the Iraqi exile community, even though his recent engagement in politics had not been universally welcomed. Islamists found in him a potential rival, and his strong links with western agencies were held against him. In the complex interrelationships of the religious families of Najaf, his name carried significant weight. At the same time, his early advocacy of the *Marji'iyya* of Grand Ayatollah Ali al-Sistani made him a powerful contender as one of the gateways to the Grand Ayatollah. After his murder, the Grand Ayatollah barricaded himself in his house, surrounded by a posse of armed supporters. Later, a mob tried to force Grand Ayatollah al-Sistani and Muhammad Said al-Hakim to leave Najaf, on the grounds that they were of Iranian origin. It was only after a tribal force of 1,500 armed men was assembled who swore to protect the Grand Ayatollahs that the immediate threat to the *Marji'iyya* diminished. Moqtada al-Sadr, whose relationships with the assailants were unclear, had definitely established himself as a leader in the tortuous politics of the city and therefore of Shi'a Iraq as a whole. The murder of al-Khoei and the circumstances surrounding it would feature constantly in the battles between the Coalition and Moqtada al-Sadr, as al-Khoei's murder was pinned to the Sadrists.

The Collapse of Central Authority

The circumstances of the emergence of local power groups in other towns and cities of the Shi'a south were not so dramatic as the tragic events of Najaf. In Nasiriya, the city fell under the tutelage of local tribesmen allied with the Da'awa Party and a returning ayatollah, Muhammad Baqir al-Nasiri.[34] In the string of towns and villages adjoining the border with Iran, a motley collection of disparate Islamists and tribesmen seized control of places such as Badra. 'Amara, the capital of Maysan province, was initially controlled by Abd el-Karim Mahoud al-Muhammaddawi,[35] a guerrilla fighter whose exploits in the marshlands earned him the title 'Lord of the Marshes'. In Basra, a variety of groups associated with the Sadrist movement, including a breakaway faction called the Fadhila Party, and SCIRI, established their authority. In Sadr City, the Sadr movement was irresistible and enjoyed huge local support. In Karbala, the authority of the followers of Ayatollah Taqi Mudarressi and his Islamic Action Organisation became evident, but the group had to share control of the city with Islamists of the Da'awa Party and SCIRI. This uneasy admixture of a formal occupation authority and local power groups with profoundly different agendas marked the emergence of provincial politics in the newly enfranchised Shi'a south.

The pattern in other parts of the country was completely different. In the Sunni Arab provinces, as well as in parts of Baghdad, antipathy to the invasion and a serious fear of disempowerment marked the emergence of an entirely separate consciousness – that of resistance to the occupation. In Iraqi Kurdistan, there were no serious attempts to displace the governing structures of the Kurdistan Regional Government by the Coalition. The main problems that were confronted at local and provincial levels involved attempts by the Kurds to extend the scope of their control into Kirkuk, parts of the city of Mosul and Nineveh province, and southwards into the mixed areas of Diyala province and eastern Wasit. The imposition of Kurdish control over disputed territory became a central feature of Kurdish attempts to define the territorial limits of Iraqi Kurdistan.

The collapse of central authority in Baghdad and the rest of Iraq in the weeks preceding and following the fall of Baghdad on 9 April, 2003 led to outbreaks of looting and property destruction on a huge scale. The looters were not confined to any particular stratum of society, and they responded in the classic fashion described by Ali al-Wardi when law and order breaks down in Iraq's civil society. CentCom ignored the call for the Coalition to have a strong military police presence in all areas falling under the Coalition's control. When looters saw that the new authority was unwilling or incapable of projecting its power, all inhibitions previously constraining the looters disappeared. Nearly every ministerial building was systematically stripped of its contents, and fires were ignited in the buildings, both to hide the crimes and to burn down hated symbols of the state's power. Hotels, palaces, villas of the elite, embassies, hospitals, barracks, power stations, water works, were all targeted and mostly looted, vandalised and burned down. The National Library with its priceless manuscript collection was looted and the building set on fire. Thousands of vehicles and construction equipment were stolen and spirited off, mainly through the Kurdish north, and sold on to smugglers and dealers in Iran, Turkey, Syria and Jordan. Baghdad's police force, normally 40,000 strong, had disappeared, and there were no firefighters to dampen the flames. Fires raged out of control for days on end, and Baghdad was strewn with a large number of gutted and burnt-out buildings. The scene of devastation was striking, and had never been anticipated by the war's planners. The nonchalance of the Coalition's soldiers and officers in the face of brazen theft and plunder, reportedly because of the lack of orders to intervene and stop the looting, gave rise to the charge of the Coalition's indifference to the widespread destruction of Iraq's cultural legacy and infrastructure. The looting and destruction of Iraq's cultural heritage became something of an international cause célèbre and played into the hands of the war's many opponents around the world. The first, highly exaggerated and alarmist, reports suggested a calculated plunder of the National Museum's contents, which set off wild alarm bells ringing in international antiquities markets. The reports were given some credence by western archaeologists who had cautioned that the war might devastate Iraq's antiquities. A number had been in the vanguard of opposition to the war, and their ranks were stiffened by Iraqi archaeologists who also appeared to give credence to these reports. There was in fact considerable theft from the National Museum's treasures, but never to the extent originally claimed. The museum's director quietly scaled down his estimate of loss, but not before the FBI had been called in to examine the case.

The first weeks after the fall of Baghdad had set the stage for the drama that had only just started. The mostly Shi'a population of the South had stubbornly refused to make the connection between the overthrow of a hated regime and the invasion and occupation of the country. The Sunni Arabs were alienated, sullen and resentful, and bided their time for an appropriate response. The Kurds were determined to maximise their gains and to set themselves up as the Coalition's indispensable allies.

5

Occupation Authorities

'We will demonstrate to the Iraqi people and the world that the United States wants to liberate Iraq, not to occupy Iraq or control Iraqis or their economic resources.' –

Under Secretary of State for Political Affairs Marc Grossman, speaking to the Senate Foreign Relations Committee, 11 February, 2003

The United States had invaded Iraq with no plan as to how to actually administer the country, even though the issue of the post-war governance of Iraq had been discussed well before the invasion. The Iraqi opposition were divided on the problem, with some groups advocating the formation of a provisional government that would assume power immediately after the overthrow of the regime. But the reality was that Iraqi exiles had been mainly concerned with the political arrangements and structures through which they would assume or inherit power, not with the actual task of running the country on a day-to-day basis. The detailed requirements for the transfer of control from a centralised, dictatorial and perverse Ba'athist-led Iraq to a form of effective governing body had been left to the USA to consider. This, however, the superpower totally failed to address.

The Testimony of Marc Grossman and Douglas Feith, February 2003

The first public exposition of what the USA was planning for a post-Saddam Iraq came in a series of hearings held by the Foreign Relations Committee of the US Senate in February 2003. Under Secretary of State Marc Grossman and Under Secretary of Defense Douglas Feith testified as to arrangements being considered for a post-war Iraq.[1] The premise that underlay their testimony was that the conflict would be short-lived, and that the main issues that would arise would relate to humanitarian and reconstruction needs. Little understanding was shown about the nature of the Iraqi state, and whether its administrative mechanisms would be able or reliable enough to manage the demands of a post-conflict situation. Grossman talked about the task of coordinating the humanitarian effort, supervised by a team drawn from the US Office of Management and Budget and the National Security Council. A sum of $40 million was allocated for this endeavour. He lauded the progress of the 'Future of Iraq' project, and endorsed its findings as the basis of a reconstruction and restructuring programme. He outlined a three-stage transfer of authority from an immediate post-war military administration that would seek to secure and stabilise the country; a gradual transfer of power to an Iraqi transitional authority; and the development of a constitution upon which a democratic government would be based. Feith detailed the workings of the new Office for Reconstruction and Humanitarian Affairs (ORHA), over which he had primary responsibility.

The ORHA had been established in response to Bush's decision to give the Pentagon control over post-war planning for Iraq. It was organised in four line departments, focusing on humanitarian relief, reconstruction, civil administration and logistics, and finance. Feith hinted at a number of steps that might be taken following the overthrow of the Ba'ath regime. They included the establishment of a commission to write a new constitution and the vetting of senior ministerial personnel, together with the removal of those who might have been implicated in the crimes committed by the regime, or with whom the new authorities could not cooperate.[2] From their testimony, it was evident that Grossman and Feith had no idea about the functioning of the state that the USA and its allies were going to inherit inside Iraq. The working model had been that of a quick war, followed by a seamless assumption of power by Iraqis from inside and outside the country, all working under the benign tutelage of a short-term occupation authority. Services would be quickly established; oil production would be increased; local elections would be soon held; and the occupying powers would then depart quickly. The entire process of managing the affairs of a country of over twenty-five million people that had been enmeshed in wars, sanctions and dictatorship was reduced to an office that had been established less than eight weeks before the invasion of the country.

Senator Joseph Biden, the ranking Democrat on the Committee, had been scathing of this cavalier approach to a post-war Iraq, and took the administration to task for belittling the scale of the problems that it anticipated in a post-war situation. The issue of whether Iraq should be administered by a UN transitional authority was raised by Biden, but Grossman basically dismissed the notion. Feith's answers to pointed questions about securing Iraq's borders after the fall of the regime, and whether the US would deploy sufficient troops for this task, were evasive. Both Feith and Grossman were hesitant and vague about the detailed arrangements for the post-war security, political and administrative situation. It became clear that the USA had done very little preparatory work for the administration and securing of the country after the overthrow of the regime. All the planning had gone into details of the military campaign. The military itself was insufficiently concerned with post-hostilities planning – the 'Phase IV' – and CentCom dealing with post-combat stabilisation had produced no operational plan.[3]

Jay Garner and the ORHA

The head of the ORHA, the focal point of the US post-war planning in the weeks preceding the invasion of Iraq, was Jay Garner, a retired general. His experience of Iraq had been limited to 'Operation Provide Comfort' along the Turkish–Iraqi border in 1991, to support the Kurds who had fled Iraq to the Iranian and Turkish frontiers in a mass wave after the collapse of their uprising. After a few weeks in Washington, Garner and his small team decamped for Kuwait in mid-March 2003, just before the war was officially launched.

Although Garner reported to the CentCom commander, General Tommy Franks, it was mainly Rumsfeld, Wolfowitz and Feith in the Pentagon who set key policy and personnel decisions. The US military in Iraq had very little to do with Garner. General David McKiernan, the commander of the Coalition's land forces, and in effect the military governor of Iraq, had imposed martial law after the fall of Baghdad. He had declared himself to be the effective ruler of the country, but the military interpreted this in strictly security terms.[4] McKiernan had no political programme as such, and the military's forays into public administration were haphazard and ineffectual.

The ORHA was operating with an ambiguous mandate, reflecting the confused and often contradictory statements from Washington regarding the nature and degree of autonomy of a new Iraqi administration. At first, considerable credence was given to the reports that the USA had decided to appoint 'advisers', drawn from experienced State and Defense Department officials, in all of the Iraqi ministries to act as a shadow government to a nominally Iraqi administration.[5] The division of authority between the advisers and the formal government, however, was a point of contention inside Washington. The Pentagon's civilian administrators had wanted the advisers to be the spearheads for changing the political culture of the country and a tool in the process of democratising Iraq. These various ideas and plans coalesced under the rubric of the Interim Iraqi Administration (IIA), a shorthand for the indistinct decision-making structures that the USA wanted to introduce into post-war Iraq. It was still unclear, however, whether the interim administration would be the new Iraqi government, overseen by shadowy 'advisers', or whether the interim administration would act as an advisory body to a Coalition-run Iraqi administration. But signals were already apparent that the USA planned an extensive interim period, lasting over two years, before power was to be transferred to an Iraqi-led government.

Garner began to recruit a hybrid organisation. The ORHA staff comprised mainly Americans, Iraqi-Americans and exiles, and British and Australian personnel. They planned for a flood of refugees and displaced persons that never materialised. Garner divided Iraq into three regions. The southern and northern regions were given to retired generals while the important central region of Baghdad was assigned to Barbara Bodine, a former ambassador to Yemen. Feith had managed to insinuate his special legal adviser Michael Mobbs as the ORHA's coordinator for civil administration.[6] Mobbs had earlier been involved in providing the legal opinion for the doctrine that allowed the incarceration of 'enemy combatants' in Guantanamo, a vague concept in international law. He was assumed to be responsible for selecting the individuals, Iraqis or otherwise, to staff the senior ministerial posts in Baghdad, and acted as Feith's 'inside' person in the ORHA hierarchy.

The well-meaning Garner could not protect the ORHA from the ongoing feuding between the State and Defense departments on control over post-war Iraq policy. Lower-grade State Department officers had a deep-seated fear that the Pentagon was determined to hand over the direction of Iraq to the INC and its supporters, while the Defense Department was concerned that Garner might succumb to pressure from the State Department's 'Arabists' and place their experts in important administrative posts in Iraq. In the event, there was continuing friction and antagonism within the ORHA's management, and Garner was not altogether free in his personnel selection. He had to reverse a number of appointments that he had made.[7] Tom Warrick, who had supervised the State Department's 'Future of Iraq' project, was assigned to join the ORHA, but his appointment was vetoed by Rumsfeld, probably prompted by the vice-president's office.[8] James Woolsey, a controversial figure associated with the neo-conservatives and the INC, and a former head of the CIA, was also vetoed, presumably by the State Department, from joining the ORHA.

Iraq Reconstruction and Development Council

The ORHA's effort was bolstered by a number of Iraqi-Americans and Iraqi exiles, who found themselves attached to the Garner team in Kuwait. Some had been involved in the 'Future of Iraq' project, or were associated with the INC, while others were recruited by a group called the Iraq Reconstruction and Development Council (IRDC), headed by an Iraqi-American named Emad Dhia. In 1998, he, together with others, had founded the Iraqi Forum for Democracy, which aimed to propagate the ideas of liberal democracy within the context of the Iraqi opposition. The IRDC was supervised by Abram Shulsky's Office of Special Plans unit in the Pentagon. Dhia had spent the best part of two months before the invasion recruiting professional Iraqis abroad as part of the plan to staff Iraqi ministries with relevant expertise. His job was now to integrate Iraqi recruits into senior levels of government inside Iraq. It was at first unclear whether the IRDC staff would operate as the nucleus of a new administrative machinery for Iraq and how their work would be coordinated with a future interim administration or the Coalition-provided advisers. Dhia himself was a highly effective and dedicated manager, but he was obliged to recruit staff at short notice and with insufficient background checks on individuals' competence and professionalism. A number of Iraqis were nominated – or planted – by the exile political groups into the IRDC, while others falsified their credentials or expertise to land high-paying jobs in a new Iraqi administration. Having spent the weeks before the war in IRDC's Virginia offices working on post-war planning, about a hundred such Iraqi exiles were flown into Kuwait and then into Iraq. They were part of the professional 'rapid deployment' team that was to directly manage, or assist in the management of, Iraq's ministries. The IRDC team was sidelined. Few in the ORHA's structure knew how to relate to a group that was not wholly western, or governmental, or indigenous. The plans for its deployment as a policy-making force fizzled out in the face of the enormity of the problems of governing Iraq. Eventually, the IRDC settled down into a support service for Iraq's new ministers, thus losing its original purpose of forming a nucleus for revamping the administration of the country.[9]

The Interim Iraqi Authority and the Nasiriya Conference

Washington was concerned about the issue of the formation of an IIA, as the administration had to deflect growing criticism that it had no plans to manage Iraq's affairs. While still in Kuwait, Feith had been in intense discussions with like-minded Iraqis attached to the ORHA, about the various permutations that an IIA might assume.[10] The Pentagon maintained that its core should consist of the six-man leadership council that had been selected by the opposition in Kurdistan the previous February. One of the proposals that was being seriously considered was that the six-man council would select a further seven individuals from inside Iraq, who would then form a thirteen-man steering committee. This, in turn, would select a further sixteen individuals to form a twenty-nine-member Interim Iraqi Authority, roughly approximating the number of Iraqi ministries. The assumption was that the IIA would form the government of Iraq. This method of selection would, of course, provide the exile groups, and especially the INC, with a head start in the final make-up of the government of the country.[11]

In response to these pressures, the State Department hurriedly organised a conference on the future government of Iraq to be held in Nasiriya.[12] Zalmay Khalilzad led the US side. The State Department sent a high-level contingent to the conference, headed by Ryan Crocker, the Deputy Assistant Secretary for Near Eastern Affairs, who also acted as the conference's moderator. The conference opened on 15 April, 2003. Jay Garner made his first public appearance to the assembled Iraqis. The organisers had invited the entire leadership council of the Salahuddin Conference. (SCIRI and the Da'awa Party – the latter was not in the leadership council – declined to attend.) The conference was accompanied by Islamist demonstrations in Nasiriya.

The conference adopted a thirteen-point programme, calling for democracy, a federal system for Iraq, and respect for the rule of law.[13] It also demanded the dissolution of the Ba'ath Party. More contentious issues, such as the role of religion in the state, were deferred to a subsequent meeting. Colin Powell suggested in an interview that participants were chosen by the US military.[14] Several speakers insisted on depicting the future Iraq as a benign, secular and liberal society, emphasising issues that were dear to the hearts of the war's planners: pluralism; constitutionalism; a market economy; human and gender rights. It took some time before this rosy picture was hacked away by brutal actualities of life in Iraq. While the Nasiriya Conference was taking place, demonstrators in the city of Mosul were being fired on by US troops. Ten were killed and sixteen wounded.[15] This was a harbinger of much worse to come. The Nasiriya Conference achieved very little practical progress towards the formation of the IIA. Another conference was planned to take place in Baghdad a fortnight later. It would include the leaders of the major political groups.

Jay Garner in Baghdad

The ORHA's ambiguous mandate made it unclear as to whether it was an aid and reconstruction body, an interim governing authority, or the civilian adjunct to a military government, ultimately reporting to General Franks and the Pentagon. The British had always envisioned a greater role for the UN in post-war Iraq, and were wary of the ORHA and its Pentagon civilian backers. They pushed for a greater degree of coordination between the ORHA and the UN, which already had a humanitarian coordinator in Baghdad. Garner had overseen the rapid development of the ORHA's staff, but their numbers were clearly insufficient to run the country's affairs. By the time the ORHA had assembled in the Republican Palace in Baghdad in mid-April, it had about 450 staff members, not counting the 100 or so members of the IRDC. The speed with which the staff had to be assembled necessarily led to an uneven quality of personnel. Although it had some dedicated, competent and effective officers, it also had its share of incompetent and corrupt adventurers, who relished the idea of playing a commanding role in an occupied country. Excepting the IRDC staff, there were very few Arabic speakers. Those who claimed to speak Arabic – who had been deemed 'fluent' by Washington – were poor speakers or unintelligible to Iraqis, with their distinct Arabic dialect. Initially, the ORHA team was left marooned in the palace with unclear lines of demarcation between it and the military, which gave it scant attention. Garner was insufficiently versed in the world of shady deals and insider dealing, a standard feature of the Iraqi business scene. While still in Kuwait, he had been besieged by contractors seeking lucrative deals with the US military and the ORHA. He had imprudently allowed himself to be hosted by a variety of local businessmen, some of whom had had previous associations with the Ba'ath regime, which raised serious questions about his judgement and choice of associates. In the conspiratorial minds of many, these meetings raised the possibility that the USA had secret designs that might include manoeuvring former Ba'athists back into power.

Garner did not reach Baghdad until 21 April. By then the ORHA had established its northern office in Irbil and its southern office in Basra. Garner had made a number of statements that appeared to downplay the ORHA's central role in the governance of Iraq. He talked about transferring authority to an interim Iraqi authority as soon as possible. The retired general appeared to be out of his depth in both Iraqi politics and the battle for supremacy over Iraq policy between various US government entities. He made a number of inept statements and gaffes. His sporty, casual dress did not engender the necessary respect with the Iraqi public, accustomed as they were to their leaders appearing in stiff, formal attire. Garner's public statements were mainly focused on the need to provide basic services, and to bring power generation up to an acceptable level. At his first press conference in Baghdad, he avoided discussion of political issues, concentrating on the problems of reconstruction, restarting oil exports and the provision of services.[16] One of his first decisions in Baghdad was to have the self-proclaimed Mayor of Baghdad, Muhammad al-Zubaidi, a former INC official, arrested, thus ending an endemic power struggle that had paralysed the work of the municipality.[17] Garner exercised the Coalition's authority over all ministries by circulating directives instructing senior ministerial officials not to accept any instructions except directly from the Coalition. But the lawlessness and chaos that were engulfing Baghdad and most of the country soon overwhelmed the early efforts by the ORHA to re-establish essential services.

Garner could not dispel the impression that the scale of the problems was overwhelming him. He began talking about the limited mission of the ORHA, saying that it would hand over effective power to an interim Iraqi authority within three months. The idea of a provisional government was seriously raised again, partly in response to the absence of any viable models for running the country. While he was meeting privately with the Kurdish leadership during a trip to the north of Iraq, Garner stated clearly that he had been authorised by Rumsfeld to fill the political and security vacuum in the country. He explicitly said that Rumsfeld had agreed to the formation of a Provisional Government of Iraq (PGI), based on the leadership council that had been selected in Salahuddin in February. The Kurds then asked Larry DiRita, a naval officer with strong Republican affiliations who was also Rumsfeld's senior aide in Iraq, to call Rumsfeld directly to receive confirmation for Garner's statement. Rumsfeld confirmed that the Department of Defense would support the formation of a provisional government based on the expanded leadership council of the Salahuddin meeting.[18] Zalmay Khalilzad, whose status as a presidential special envoy on Iraq continued after the fall of Baghdad, and whose organisational relationship with Garner was vague, picked up on the indication of a provisional government. Both Garner and Khalilzad began to hint openly at the possibility of a provisional government.[19] The British, always concerned that the exile opposition leaders would move to control a provisional government, were alarmed at this prospect and moved to thwart it. But another, more potent, storm was about to hit the ORHA and end its short life. Garner's mandate, and the ORHA itself, would be terminated within less than three weeks after his arrival in Baghdad.

The Baghdad Conference

Initially, the Baghdad Conference was to have been an enlarged forum for bringing together a broad spectrum of Iraqis, both from inside the country and former exiles, to thrash out the form of an interim administration. But its timing coincided with rising speculation about the formation of a provisional government, and though the links between the two could not be formally made, the conference was buzzing with rumours about the formation of an Iraqi-led provisional government.[20] The entire drift of the conference was towards the formation of an Iraqi government within a short while. The conference opened on 28 April with about 300 representatives drawn from Iraq's various ethnic, religious and political groups.[21] Both Garner and Khalilzad attended the meeting. Michael O'Brien, the British Minister of State for Foreign Affairs, was also in attendance. All the main former opposition leaders stayed away, partly to allow space for other delegates to appear in the media. The conference voted overwhelmingly to form an Iraqi-led government, and called for another, larger conference in a month's time to select the post-war transitional government. The meeting constantly referred to the need for a government and not an administration, underlining the drive towards securing sovereignty for a new Iraqi government. Khalilzad endorsed the conference's resolutions. He declared that the following conference would decide if the country were to have a prime ministerial or presidential style of government.[22] It was clear to the participants that the USA had shifted its strategy and was keen to accelerate the process that would lead to an Iraqi-led government. The Pentagon, with the support of the vice-president's office, appeared to have won the argument for a rapid transfer of power to an Iraqi government.[23]

A series of further meetings of the leading political figures were held to discuss the composition of the provisional government. At this point, Ibrahim al-Eshaiker, spokesman for the Da'awa Party who went by the underground *nom de guerre* of Ibrahim al-Jaafari, was invited to join in the deliberations for the provisional government. His inclusion in the original six-person leadership council was not universally popular, but people who disagreed with his inclusion, notably those from SCIRI, acceded to the majority view on condition that the Da'awa Party would be totally committed to the new course of action. Discussions also began with representatives of the leading Sunni Islamic group, the Iraqi Islamic Party, and one of its leading lights, Professor Muhsin Abd el-Hamid. His deputy, Hachim al-Hassani, a US-educated economist, joined him in these discussions. Another candidate for a leadership role in the future provisional government was Naseer al-Chadirchi, a septuagenarian liberal lawyer, who had remained in Baghdad throughout the Ba'ath period.

Both Khalilzad and Garner were privy to these discussions, and both were supportive of the idea of a provisional government. Garner wanted to hurry the process and regularly enquired whether the group had finalised its deliberations. Garner had suggested that the core leadership group that emerged out of the February Salahuddin Conference should be maintained as the axis for any enlargement to the leadership council. On 5 May, he announced that a collective nine-person Iraqi leadership, which would be the nucleus of an Iraqi-led government, would be in place by mid-May. Later in the day, however, the American interlocutors, Garner, Khalilzad and Ryan Crocker, began to express some unease about vague signals emanating from Washington that might influence the direction in which the negotiations for a provisional government were taking. Garner began to drop broad hints that he might soon be leaving.[24]

Garner and the ORHA were blamed for not curtailing the wild looting; for their inability to provide adequate public services; for not stemming lawlessness; and for tolerating the presence of senior Ba'athists in positions of power. The statistics that tumbled out of his office listing the ORHA's achievements rang very hollow compared to the physical hardship that the population had to continue to endure. Claims about electricity production being better than ever and the improvement in water supplies did not match the experience of the population, especially in the Baghdad area. Garner later complained about the inadequacy of his organisation's financial appropriations and held bureaucratic wrangling in Washington as partly responsible for its poor performance. The Garner weeks were uniformly dismissed as a disaster, and it was acknowledged by political commentators that Garner had been the wrong person for the job, driving the normally careful John Sawers, Blair's special envoy to Iraq, to describe it as an 'unbelievable mess'. In a May 2003 memo to Blair's advisers, he described ORHA as having 'no leadership, no strategy, no coordination, no structure, and inaccessible to ordinary Iraqis'.[25]

The Coalition Provisional Authority

News began to filter from Washington that a high-level diplomat would soon be appointed to oversee the political process in Iraq.[26] On 6 May, Bush announced that Paul Bremer would become the top civilian administrator in Iraq. On 8 May, Powell announced that the USA and UK were sponsoring a UN resolution that would, in effect, give them the status of occupying powers in Iraq. The Iraqis were completely flabbergasted by this reversal. Within the space of a few days, the entire process that was to lead to a provisional Iraqi government had been abruptly stopped, and then upended.

The dramatic shift in American policy was the result of several factors. Foremost of these was Colin Powell's reassertion of the influence of the State Department with Bush. The decision-making process in the Bush administration was complex, with different power centres vying for the President's ear. Bush tended to make a final decision by himself, and once a decision had been taken he would not tolerate any dissent. A few people were able to influence his thinking directly, notably the British Prime Minister Tony Blair. It subsequently became clear that British requests for the need for a clear UN resolution that would regulate the Coalition's powers and presence in Iraq had won Bush over. Working with Powell's State Department, Blair had convinced Bush that for the future course of events in Iraq to unfold in an acceptable fashion, some form of UN and international support for the Coalition's efforts would be required. This change of direction was signalled to some of the Coalition participants in the Baghdad talks on the formation of a provisional government. Ryan Crocker later intimated as much to one of the key negotiators in Baghdad, Hoshyar Zibari, then the KDP's principal foreign affairs spokesman, and later Iraq's foreign minister. Crocker said that, when they had reported to the National Security Council on the progress of talks on the formation of an Iraqi-led government, National Security Advisor Rice had informed him that the National Security Council was working on 'other ideas'. It soon became clear what these 'other ideas' were. There was also considerable unease in the State Department and the CIA about the reliability of the proposed Iraqi leadership, notably Ahmad Chalabi. A further explanation for the abrupt shift in policy and the resort to a UN resolution was the issue of the legality of the Coalition's use of Iraqi funds and assets under international law. The legal aspects of the occupation loomed very large in the thinking of both the State Department and the Foreign Office. With a prolonged Coalition military and civilian presence in the offing, it would not be possible to draw on Iraqi resources without some form of an enabling UN resolution.

The Coalition Provisional Authority (CPA) was authorised under UN Resolution 1483, on 22 May, 2003. News of its existence had been dribbling out of Washington. Early reports first dealt with the appointment of Ambassador Bremer as the President's envoy, who was to oversee the 'reconstruction process' and the building of new 'institutions and governing structures'. On 13 May, it was announced that Rumsfeld had appointed Bremer as CPA administrator. There was no official announcement that the ORHA had been superseded, or that Garner was to be replaced. It was implied that the ORHA's work would now fall under the new CPA, and that Garner would come under Bremer's overall authority as CPA administrator. Whether the CPA was a federal agency of the USA or whether it was an entity responsible to the UN Security Council was never definitively established. The USA and UK had addressed a letter to the president of the UN's Security Council on 8 May, informing him that the Coalition had created an authority that would subsume the work of the ORHA. In practice, the CPA was always treated as part of the US federal government. Bremer himself reported to the secretary of defense through the secretary of the army. The preamble to UN Resolution 1483 acknowledged the existence of the CPA, prior to the enactment of the resolution. The ambiguous nature of the CPA in international law proved useful for the Coalition in deflecting criticisms (and lawsuits), while maintaining direct American control over its executive levers. The resolution also allowed for the creation of a 'Development Fund for Iraq' into which Iraq's oil revenues would be paid. It established a special body of international monitors to report on the activities of the Development Fund; instructed the secretary general of the UN to appoint a special representative for Iraq who would spearhead the UN's return to the country; and lifted sanctions on Iraq. On the issue of a provisional government, the resolution was clear. The CPA was the occupying authority, leaving the issue of an interim administration to be sorted out under the guidance of the CPA and the UN's special representative. The UN's explicit involvement in the formation of a future Iraqi government was a victory for the British and for those who shared the same perspectives within the new Iraqi political class.

Khalilzad had left Baghdad shortly before the public announcement of Bremer's appointment. It was understood that his absence would be brief, as he was to consult with his principals in Washington and return with a detailed US response to the impending formation of an Iraqi-led government.

Khalilzad, of course, did not return to Baghdad. Bremer's appointment came as a thunderbolt out of the blue to the assembled leaders in Baghdad, and was greeted with indignation by most of the main political figures. Uncertainty reigned, while there was dark talk about the imposition of a colonial regime. Many Iraqi leaders felt that the USA had been duplicitous in its negotiations and that there had always been a parallel track that aimed at the installation of a 'pro-consul' figure. No one in Baghdad had heard of Bremer. His career path did not include the Middle East; even seasoned Washington insiders from the Kurds and the Chalabi camp had not been aware of him.[27] They rushed to find out what they could about Bremer and, more importantly, what his appointment signified in terms of changes in the US policy on the governing of Iraq. The US policy planners had apparently earlier considered the appointment of a senior civilian governor, to fill in the period between the ending of Garner's assignment and the installation of an Iraqi-led government. Retrospectively, it is difficult to tell if this had been the USA's plan all along or if it was only under the pressure of events that such an abrupt reversal of policy did in fact take place. The fact remains, however, that Bremer was interviewed for the job before the end of April, while negotiations for a provisional government were taking place in Baghdad. This was a clear indication that the USA might not have been eager to accept the creation of a provisional government within a timetable that was not of its choosing. Bush, Rumsfeld and Powell had all interviewed Bremer and had approved his appointment.

Paul Bremer, the US Overseer of Iraq

Paul Bremer was plucked from relative obscurity to become the US overseer of Iraq. Born in 1941 in Connecticut, he joined the Foreign Service in 1966 and was first posted to Afghanistan. Between 1972 and 1976, he served as an assistant to Secretary of State Henry Kissinger. He also served in a number of overseas postings, including deputy chief of mission in Norway (1976–79). In 1983 he was named as the US ambassador to the Netherlands. Along the way, Bremer seems to have developed an expertise in the issues of terrorism and counter-terrorism. In 1999, Dennis Hastert, the Speaker of the House of Representatives, appointed Bremer to be the Chairman of the bi-partisan National Commission on Terrorism. Bremer joined the Marsh and McClellan Group, an insurance giant, in 2000, rising to head its crisis-consulting unit. The 9/11 attacks on the World Trade Center directly affected the Marsh Group, with nearly 300 of its employees lost in the attacks. Irrespective of his personal qualities, Bremer was not in the first division of American career diplomats or Republican foreign policy experts. He appeared to have been selected precisely because of his lack of prior involvement in the Iraq crisis. He apparently straddled two antagonistic camps – the realists and the neo-conservatives – who vied with each other in the making of Iraq policy. Bremer's character was in marked contrast to that of the genial and informal Garner. He was more 'telegenic' and comported himself with the *gravitas* expected of a representative of a superpower.

The process that led to his appointment was short and hasty. It amply confirmed the chaotic and off-handed way in which decisions of momentous significance for Iraq were taken. The recruitment process for the leadership of a country of over twenty-five million people would not have passed muster with even the most indifferent of corporate headhunters.

The First Days of Bremer and the CPA

Bremer arrived in Baghdad on 12 May, 2003.[28] He was accompanied by Garner and by General Richard Meyers, the chairman of the Joint Chiefs of Staff. He quickly seized the initiative and upstaged the hapless Garner.[29] Bremer had immersed himself in briefing papers while still in Washington and wanted to make a dramatic impact soon after his arrival. He also wanted to establish his authority quickly, and to sharpen the contrast in style and substance with the ORHA. Garner's status became indeterminate, although he was still technically Bremer's deputy until his assigned departure date of 1 July. But he left by the end of May, embittered by his experiences and saddled with the responsibility for the calamitous turn of events in Iraq. Most of the ORHA staff were absorbed into the structures, and became the core, of the new CPA.[30] Garner and his staff became increasingly isolated inside the palace as the security situation deteriorated.[31]

Bremer had brought with him his own team, including Ambassador Clay McManaway as his deputy, and a number of staff assistants. Nearly all of Garner's senior staff were to be replaced. A new, more image-conscious, more purposeful organisation appeared to be taking shape. To underline his determination to tackle pressing law and order issues, Bremer brought along Bernard Kerik, lately the police commissioner for New York, now designated the person responsible for tackling the lawlessness in Baghdad. On the day of Bremer's arrival, Massoud Barzani, expressing the views of most of the Iraqi leadership council, spoke of his concern and disappointment at the turn of events.[32] The departure of Garner, whom the Kurds considered a special friend from the days of 'Operation Provide Comfort', gave them further cause for anxiety. The leadership council bided its time until Bremer was ready to meet with them and, it was hoped, dispel the fog that had descended on the Coalition's intentions.

The meeting between Bremer and the Iraqi leadership council was set for 16 May. The leadership council, now known as the G-7, included Talabani, Barzani, Chalabi and Ayad Allawi. Naseer al-Chadirchi and the Da'awa Party spokesman, Ibrahim al-Jaafari, had been recently added to the leadership council. Adel Abd el-Mahdi was representing SCIRI in the absence of Abd el-Aziz al-Hakim. The Coalition was represented by Bremer, Garner, General McKiernan, the military commander of Iraq, and General Abizaid, deputy to CentCom's chief General Franks. John Sawers, the British special envoy, was in attendance. The State Department was represented by Ryan Crocker and Hume Horan, a retired ambassador, who had, controversially, been replaced as ambassador to Saudi Arabia in 1988 at the personal request of King Fahd.[33]

Horan had spent his Foreign Service career in the Middle East and spoke excellent Arabic. He was the CPA's senior religious affairs adviser and showed considerable knowledge of the intricacies of the Shi'a and Sunni Islamist worlds in Iraq, and the nature of Islamic religiosity. His perspective on the Middle East emerged straight from the Bernard Lewis thesis of multiple identities at play. To Horan, Iraq's identity was that of a mosaic that had been rudely shattered and had to be painstakingly reassembled. This vision informed Bremer's thinking – and, through him, that of the CPA. Horan's influence could be detected whenever Bremer spoke of Iraq's past and future in idyllic terms, superimposing an imagined country on the harsh reality of its current ethnic and sectarian divisions. In a telling article after his departure from the CPA, Horan mused about the possibility – and desirability – of an Iraq, Israel, a democratised Iran and Turkey axis at play in the Middle East, a vision fully endorsed by the neo-conservatives in Washington. Such an axis, he believed, would act as an exemplar to the rest of the Arab states of the area, soften the edges of their religion – and even encourage their 'reformation' – and ease their acceptance of, and transition into, the modern world.[34] This type of jaundiced reasoning, based on ideologically driven motives and a selective reading of history, was very prevalent in Baghdad in the early days of the CPA. It conveniently underplayed the significance of tendencies and actual events that fell outside the framework of analysis.

Bremer's meeting with the G-7 was one in which he was to invoke his powers in no uncertain terms, and set the relationship between the CPA, the dominant party, with himself in charge, and the Iraqi leadership group, the subordinate party. Bremer stated emphatically that his orders had the force of law under the powers that the USA and UN had given him. The CPA was to set overall policy and assume responsibility for managing the country's affairs. Throughout, Bremer had talked about broadening the base of the Iraqi leadership council, claiming that the exiles were not sufficiently representative of the people. Talabani asked what the function of the G-7 would be, now that the possibility of a provisional government had been postponed to an indefinite date, and whether the status of the G-7 would be compromised by the dilution of the leadership group with unknown new members. Barzani, who had been nominated by the G-7 to act as their spokesman, pointedly asked if the Coalition was still committed to the enlarged conference that was being planned for later in May. Bremer and Garner both avoided giving a direct answer, thus implicitly confirming that the conference would not be likely to be held at all. Bremer aggressively added that while the G-7 were free to hold whatever conference they wanted, the CPA would still be the final arbiters.

Soon after his first meeting with the G-7, Bremer invited the group to Baghdad's Conference Centre where he reconfirmed that the Coalition had no intention of agreeing to the formation of a provisional government. He talked about the need for the G-7 to be more inclusive and to reach out to new people to join the leadership council. All the G-7 members were vehemently opposed to the dropping of the idea of a provisional government, and warned Bremer that the CPA would most certainly fail if there were no parallel Iraqi-led governmental authority with which it could liaise. At a later meeting, Bremer introduced the G-7 to three others whom the Coalition had selected for possible inclusion in an enlarged leadership council. They included Aqila al-Hashemi, an ambassador-level staff member in the Foreign Ministry. She was a well-respected diplomat, trained in France, and had been a confidante of Saddam's foreign minister, Tariq Aziz. The other two were Thamer Ghadhban, a senior director general at the Oil Ministry, and Sayyid Farqat al-Qazwini, an imposing cleric from the Hilla district, rumoured to be close to the CIA. This enlarged group was to be Bremer's interlocutor with Iraq's political classes, but at the same time he was careful to disabuse the group's members from any impression that they were to be the core of the next government.

A bewildering sequence of events led to the imposition of an occupation authority in Iraq. The Bush administration's position on Iraq, in the immediate aftermath of the war, was riddled with expedient decision-making, departmental in-fighting, conflicting strategies and policy incoherence. All of these ineptitudes featured prominently in the erratic path to the formation of the CPA, which was played out against the background of a prostrate country that was awaiting a signal as to what the conquering armies were planning for its future. The volte-face on the determination to form a provisional government was the most difficult to understand. It effectively undermined the credibility of the parties with which the USA had been engaged, with varying degrees of enthusiasm, for the better part of a decade. In the event, the CPA had to deal with the same cast of characters. The CPA was only explicable in terms of a cover for sorting out a post-war 'Iraq policy', when none had existed prior to the invasion. The half-hearted occupation, which tried to maintain the rhetoric of liberation while acting unilaterally and without accountability to Iraqis, evolved into the slapdash administration of the CPA. Iraq became a victim of a chaotic scramble to impose conflicting agendas on the government of the country, ranging from the neo-conservative warriors on the one hand, to the hard-headed 'realists' of the national security state on the other.

The Return of Ayatollah Muhammad Baqir al-Hakim

A few days before Bremer's arrival in Baghdad on 12 May, an event of greater significance to most Iraqis was taking place. Ayatollah Muhammad Baqir al-Hakim made his fateful decision to return to Iraq from his decades-long exile in Iran. The Ayatollah had been biding his time in Tehran, awaiting clear signals as to the direction of events. At first, he had been uncertain whether the Coalition would allow any free political activity. His brother, Abd el-Aziz, doubled up as the leader of the Badr Brigade and his spokesman and was already engaged in discreet talks with the Coalition about Iraq's political future. SCIRI's main political adviser, Adel Abd el-Mahdi, had been deeply involved in the politics of the G-7. Ayatollah Baqir al-Hakim, however, was preparing the blueprint for a radical form of Islamist political work.[35] The Ayatollah crossed into Iraq near Basra in a hundred-car convoy on 10 May. SCIRI was already well established in Basra, and a crowd of nearly 10,000 turned up to hear Ayatollah Baqir al-Hakim give his first public speech inside Iraq. His convoy then wound its way through several Shi'a towns and cities in the South before reaching its final destination in Najaf.[36] In Najaf, the Ayatollah was greeted by tens of thousands of supporters and well-wishers. All his speeches called for the rapid transfer of power to Iraqis; an end to the occupation; and the establishment of a constitutional government where Islamic values and precepts would be honoured.[37] He spoke of a tolerant and just society, but clearly in Islamic rather than democratic or secular terms. The Ayatollah was preparing a unique role for himself of political authority over the rank and file of the Shi'a. Recognising that the concept of *Wilayat al-Faqih*, or direct rule of the jurisprudent, in its Iranian variant, would not be acceptable to most Iraqis and to the Coalition, and perhaps chastened by the experience of clerics in power in Iran, he put forward a different form of political organisation for Islamists. His plan, which he seemed to have discussed with the leading Ayatollahs of Najaf, including Ayatollah Sistani, was based on refining the concept of the *Marji'iyya* to give it two clearly distinct identities: one religious and spiritual, and the other political.[38]

The problem of political authority in Shi'a Islamist politics in Iraq had arisen from the inherent conflict between acknowledgement of the *Marji*'s ultimate power over political decisions, and the reluctance of the traditional *Maraji*' to become directly involved in worldly matters. This could be reconciled only if the Islamist political parties recognised the authority of a *Marji*' who was determinedly political, such as Ayatollah Baqir al-Sadr. Such an authority might allow the formation of an organised political party, if it recognised his ultimate control over political decisions, or if the *Marji'* himself refused to become involved in political matters (except *in extremis*) but did not refute the legitimacy of a political party with an Islamist programme. The Da'awa Party had finessed the issue by formally acknowledging the theoretical authority of a *Marji'*, but nevertheless appropriating the right to make key political decisions for its leadership on the grounds that they were best equipped to evaluate the bases for such decisions. Thus, they acknowledged the *Marji'iyya* of al-Khoei on religious and spiritual matters, but did not accept his political quietism. This line of reasoning became ever harder to follow when the party reconstituted itself inside Iraq. Grand Ayatollah Sistani, the acknowledged senior *Marji' al-Taqlid,* was neither wholly quietist nor actively or publicly engaged in political matters. Ayatollah Baqir al-Hakim and SCIRI had to follow a different course, not least because its leader was himself a religious authority.

Ayatollah Hakim had tried to elevate his status to a *Marji'*, especially in the mid-1990s, when he began to attend the final stages of advanced religious learning in the Shi'a Islamic tradition, namely the so-called *dars al-khariji.* But for a variety of reasons, including his unwillingness to abandon full-time politics for the dedicated life of a would-be scholar, he did not achieve an unchallenged religious status, and was not recognised, upon his return to Iraq, as belonging to the highest ranks of learned ayatollahs. He did, however, establish for himself a unique status that combined the unification of a political orientation with advanced religious training. The way in which he comported himself when the Iraqi opposition was in exile was to distinguish himself from others in the leadership class. His claims were not seen as a pretentious affectation, but were to a large extent honoured by most leaders in the opposition. The challenge now was to carve out for himself a religiously sanctioned status as a political *Marji'*. This would be a departure from traditional doctrine. A political *Marji'* would be one who could declare opinions and decide on political matters, and who could make rulings that would be binding, but who nevertheless would be subordinate, in matters of religious dogma, to the classic *Marji' al-Taqlid.* The assumption was that the *Maraji' al-Taqlid* would approve the emergence of such an institution and would accept its judgement on political matters. In this way, the traditional institutions of the Shi'a *Maraji'* would not be compromised by their direct involvement in politics. At the same time, the leading Shi'a political authority would be trained in the *hawza*, as well as having direct experience and proficiency in the art of politics. The underlying premise was that by separating the two functions, there would be a realisation of the need to subordinate political decisions to the ultimate safeguards of the religious authorities of the Shi'a.[39]

The tension between the religious authority of the *Maraji'* and the demands placed on them to become involved in worldly matters had been unsatisfactorily resolved by the institution of the *hashiya*, or entourage, of the *Marji'*. The entourage frequently comprised his immediate family, mostly sons, who played the intermediary role between the religious world and the profane world of government and power. Ayatollah al-Hakim essentially wanted to do away with the influence of the *hashiya* on the worldly decisions of a grand ayatollah – even though his own power had originated partly as a son of the Grand Ayatollah Muhsin al-Hakim. Judging the moment opportune to advance the idea of a political *Marji'*, he began a series of intensive consultations in Najaf with Grand Ayatollah Sistani and other grand ayatollahs in Najaf, such as Said al-Hakim, Ishaq Fayyadh and Bashir al-Najafi. The indications were that he was making headway in convincing them that he could play the role of the political *Marji'*, faithfully interpreting the religious boundaries of the Najaf ayatollahs, while at the same time bringing his undoubted political skills to bear on the major issues affecting Iraq.

6

A Collapsed State – a Ruined Economy – a Damaged Society

'The oil revenues of that country could bring between $50 and $100 billion over the course of the next two or three years. Now, there are a lot of claims on that money, but . . . . We are dealing with a country that can really finance its own reconstruction and relatively soon.' –

Paul Wolfowitz, Testimony to the US House Appropriations
Committee, 27 March, 2003

The country that the Coalition occupied was in an advanced state of decay. A fifth of its territory and population had been outside central government control for over a decade. Huge swathes of the South had been deliberately starved of funds for development and basic services, and the standard of living had precipitously crashed. The 1990s had seen a dramatic fall in incomes and quality of life throughout Iraq. Although Baghdad and the western and northern provinces had been kept supplied with resources to maintain a modicum of services, they were only marginally better off. Since the end of the Gulf War in 1991, the state's administrative machinery had been radically refashioned to meet the security needs of the government and the paucity of resources, and to simultaneously abide by, and subvert, the terms of the UN sanctions. The state, society and economy were all under siege. The measures taken to manage this decade-long crisis marked both the state and society in fundamental ways, and produced distortions that few outsiders could comprehend. The Coalition and exile oppositionists' ignorance of the actual conditions inside Iraq on the eve of invasion was one of the gravest errors of omission committed.

The Iraqi State in the Immediate Post-war Period

The reports and studies on Iraq that underpinned the planning for the war were woefully inadequate and ill informed about the parlous condition of the machinery of government.[1] The state had, in effect, withdrawn from the detailed management of the country, except in a few vital areas necessary for the immediate survival and continuation of the regime. On the eve of war, the Iraqi state was divided into four functional areas: security; provision of basic services; managing the sanctions regime and international isolation; and management of day-to-day affairs of government. Security took precedence over all other considerations, and the range and reach of Saddam's security networks had grown to grotesque proportions. Representatives of the *Mukhabarat*, the main intelligence agency, were planted, openly as well as covertly, in every layer of the departments of government.[2] Some combined their intelligence responsibilities with actual line management, so that there were often ministers who were high-ranking officials in the *Mukhabarat*. By the time the war had ended, the more brazen intelligence operatives had escaped – either going underground or leaving the country – but the second and lower layers of the security apparatus continued to function within the ministries. Bremer's order that banned senior intelligence officers from continuing in their government jobs affected a few thousand people, but a much larger number stayed in their positions awaiting developments. Covert intelligence officers expected their colleagues in government to be too afraid or indifferent to their positions to expose them.

Theft, Looting and Arson

The database of the Iraqi government was one of the first items to be targeted by the former regime's security elements, operating under the cover of looters and arsonists after the collapse of law and order in Baghdad that had accompanied the invasion. The destruction of files, records, documents and databases was achieved methodically, and affected nearly all the ministries and government departments. The intention was both to destroy any paper trail that could be used against individuals and entities, and to make the task of governing Iraq that much more difficult. Ministries were not only methodically picked over, but were then ransacked and burnt down. In a few government departments, enterprising individuals were able to spirit away key records or kept a back-up system operating. Frequently, they took valuable documents to their private homes for safekeeping, at great personal risk. The loss of important documents and records hampered the re-establishment of normal operating procedures after the end of hostilities. The Coalition laboriously had to reassemble organisational charts and decision-making structures in an environment of great fear and uncertainty for the bureaucracy.[3]

The reconstitution of the administrative structures of the government was further complicated by the disappearance of top bureaucratic cadres, who had either fled the country or had sat at home awaiting developments. The destruction of the communications infrastructure and the delay in establishing a newly functioning communications system made this task even more difficult. Apart from the Ministry of Oil complex, which was guarded by the Coalition to preserve the records of Iraq's all-important oil sector, nearly all other departments of the government suffered considerable damage. The Ministry of Trade, which managed the entire supply chain for the universal food subsidy programme, upon which the entire population depended, was left unguarded and open to looters. This was in spite of the fact that the Coalition had decided very early on to keep the food rations programme continuing. The main building of the Ministry of Trade was set on fire several times, and most of its original records were wiped out in the fires that engulfed the edifice. Purely by chance, however, arsonists and wreckers never reached another building where the computer banks for the food rations programme were kept. The full roster of names of ration-card holders was saved intact. The ration cards were a critical statistical tool, since they were the only near-complete system of recording the population in the absence of official census figures.[4] In spite of gaps in a full reckoning of the number of beneficiaries, they were nevertheless remarkably accurate, and proved extremely useful as the statistical basis for any number of socio-economic programmes in the post-war period. It would have been catastrophic for both the population and the occupation authorities if the records had been destroyed.

The rest of the Ministry of Trade's enterprises fared much worse. Nearly all were systematically looted and burnt down, including shopping centres scattered throughout Baghdad, food and construction materials warehouses, and the huge vehicle maintenance complex. Facilities belonging to other ministries suffered a similar, if not worse, fate. Hospitals, barracks, construction equipment, power plants, transmission cables, water works, oil field equipment – the list was endless. Stolen goods and equipment flooded into nearby countries. Copper and aluminium prices in regional markets such as Kuwait or Iran fell precipitously owing to the flow of metals from melted down cables coming out of Iraq.[5] The stolen goods were passed to 'fences' and dealers, frequently in the Kurdistan region, who then arranged for their disposal and transport out of the country. Markets for household goods, building materials and foodstuffs sprang up in Baghdad and elsewhere to handle the flood of stolen goods. They fell under the generic name of *hawassim* (spoils), Saddam's name for the 'epic' battle with the Coalition.

The scale, method and focus of the looting and destruction betrayed the existence of considerable organisation and premeditation. The systematic theft and targeted destruction could not have been only the work of mobs of wild looters who seized or burnt whatever was at hand. (It is not possible to dismantle complex machinery and complete factories – such as the huge repair works of the government's car imports monopoly – without an organisation that is able to define its target, and arrange for its storage, transport and disposal.) It subsequently became established that the more targeted and purposeful looting was organised by insiders, either from former ministries or in former security agencies. The objectives were manifold, and included sowing the seeds of administrative chaos and disorganisation, and monetary gain. In many ministries, individual managers were responsible for organising and directing the theft and burning of their departments. Some, three or four months after the invasion, left Iraq and retired to other countries. The CPA overlooked these transgressions, and never acknowledged that its mismanagement, naïveté, and poor recruiting practices were responsible for the empowerment of both bureaucrats and returning exiles who had been involved in stealing public assets, or who were bent on abusing their position. Some of these corrupt people were agents of the Coalition's intelligence services and were therefore placed in positions of authority, irrespective of the damage that they might cause to the integrity of the post-war order.[6]

The Old Bureaucracy Inside the 'New Iraq'

The ORHA team that first landed in Baghdad had tried to entice senior bureaucrats back into ministerial service. A few proved loyal to the new order, and genuinely welcomed the overthrow of the regime. Most, however, were passive or actively hostile to the changes. The senior- and middle-ranking layers of the bureaucracy were drawn from the Sunni Arab elite, who had collaborated, often willingly, with the defunct dictatorship.[7] The very limited turnover of ministers during the Ba'athist era had turned some ministries into virtual fiefdoms for particular ministers, their friends and cronies, and their kinsmen. (The Ministry of Trade, for example, had eleven of its fourteen directors general drawn from the Sunni Arab community, especially from Rawa, the former Ba'athist minister's hometown.) These senior bureaucrats had not taken kindly to the violent overthrow of the regime by foreign forces, and bided their time for more propitious circumstances. Others tried to ingratiate themselves with the new ruling power, and became adjuncts of the CPA.[8] They cut themselves off from their ministries, while becoming indispensable as interlocutors and fixers for the ORHA or the CPA. The Coalition had no way of vetting these people properly, given their inadequate knowledge of the actual situation existing in the country, and intense pressures to restart the government machinery. Some of these senior bureaucrats were given huge powers and allowed to make key decisions affecting their ministries, or latitude to recommend multimillion-dollar purchases. They were doubly important to the new occupiers if they spoke fluent English. In time, a nexus evolved that dragged many people, including CPA officers and the military, into a web of corruption. The ignorance, inexperience and simple anxiety about the unknown that was the mark of many newly arrived administrators from the Coalition played into the hands of crafty and skilled manipulators from the totalitarian bureaucracy.

The reliance on old-line administrators to overcome the Coalition's uncertainty about Iraq's governmental machinery may have been a need born out of necessity. The effortless transfer of loyalty on the part of these senior bureaucrats was based on their confidence that they possessed the knowledge and experience that would be vital to run the Byzantine machinery of the inherited state. The CPA, partly because of its indeterminate mandate, made no move to initiate serious administrative reforms, or to introduce new structures and processes that might signal its commitment to a fresh start. The chaos and confusion of the early post-war weeks simply added to the absence of any workable or realistic plan to run the country. The end result was the perpetuation of a system with ingrained working habits and practices, overseen by a bureaucracy that was fundamentally little different from its predecessor. The underlying reality was that the profoundly undemocratic, labyrinthine and dysfunctional machinery of government was allowed to continue with only a few ineffectual changes at its top. An unintended side-effect was the exponential increase in corruption. Ironically, the bureaucracy's corrupt practices had partly been kept in check by the fear of draconian sanctions in the Saddam era, in the event that individuals were caught out. With the dissolution of the security services and the removal of the watchful eye of the Ba'ath Party, bureaucrats had no need to worry about the consequences of being discovered.

The exiles who returned with the expectations of overhauling, modernising and democratising the state were confronted with entrenched bureaucratic systems, and a CPA driven mainly by expediency and political considerations.

Provincial and Local Government

At local government level, the collapse of the administrative framework was more obvious, especially in the South. Local administrators who filled senior posts in provincial towns and cities were frequently from outside the area, or Ba'athists, or both. Most of the higher-ranking staff fled after the beginning of hostilities. During the Ba'ath regime, a system operated that was highly centralised, where no local decisions could be made without reference to the relevant ministries in Baghdad. When the military occupied territory it tried to re-establish basic governance structures, using a variety of methods. Most involved a crude consultation scheme. Meetings to select a local governing council would be announced, and candidates would be selected from whoever showed up. In the larger cities, local leaders might have been selected as a result of the intervention of the military or the intelligence services to promote specific candidates. In several instances, glaring errors of judgement were made, where criminals, high-ranking Ba'athists and outsiders were elevated to positions of power and authority. In Basra, the first governor appointed by the British was drummed out of office by widespread protests. In Najaf, the governor turned out to be a person with a criminal record, who had to be arrested by the very Marines who had originally installed him. The attempt to re-establish local services at first fell on the civil affairs units of the military.[9] They gave way to a series of local government experts, mainly private contractors working for the main US aid agency, United States Agency for International Development (USAID).

The CPA began to introduce governing structures throughout the country that reflected its role as the occupying authority and helped it to spread its writ across Iraq. From the outset, there was a lack of clarity about the ultimate objective. The local government structures were considered 'interim', while the people were being prepared for full-fledged elections. The need to introduce some local accountability and preference was frequently at odds with the appointment of provincial CPA administrators, who acted as de facto governors. The CPA had a stranglehold over financing, in terms of its absolute discretionary control over both Iraqi funds and US appropriations for administering the country. This made it difficult to claim that local autonomy and empowerment were taking place when the attendant financial resources needed to make this possible were not forthcoming. At first, selecting a local government usually followed a 'town hall meeting'. Cities were divided into districts and neighbourhoods. Each neighbourhood selected its representative council. The council, in turn, would select a district council which, again in turn, would select the provincial council. The only 'direct' election was at the neighbourhood level.[10] The provincial councils were coordinated with the CPA through the local governance teams, which would have included, apart from consultants and contractors, representatives of the military and other agencies. Interpreters were needed, given the poor language capabilities of the CPA local teams. The results were broadly acceptable at the neighbourhood level, but as the pyramid rose to the district and provincial levels serious issues emerged.

The provincial councils were seen as tools of the occupation and were not considered as either representative or democratically elected. The objectives of local government reform – autonomy, local accountability, improvement of services – soon clashed with the CPA's pressing need to re-establish central government. When that was reconstituted along its traditional, centralised patterns of decision-making, the experiment in autonomous local government collapsed. No local administrator was prepared to take any decisions that ran against the writ of the central ministry in Baghdad. The issue of ferreting out criminals, people with a suspicious background and senior Ba'athists was never handled either appropriately or satisfactorily. A large number of councillors slipped underneath the incomplete vetting procedures, and there were continual protests at the type of people who claimed high positions in the CPA's local government administrations. The CPA tried to rectify the early mistakes, not by direct elections, but by what was called the 'refreshment' process. The idea was to weed out obvious miscreants and ensure that the councils would be broadly supportive of the CPA.[11] This would later prove highly contentious when the CPA tried to promote the use of provincial councils in lieu of elections for a process that would lead to a new sovereign authority.

CPA Advisers and Staffers, and the Administration of Iraq

The patterns of interaction between the occupation authority and the central bureaucracy was set in the early days of the ORHA, and continued, mainly undisturbed, with the CPA. A team of advisers was attached to specific ministries. The advisers came from agencies of the US, UK and Australian governments, and the private sector. The US Army Corps of Engineers provided the first advisers to the Health, Electricity and Housing ministries. USAID provided advisers to the Labour and Education ministries. The State Department provided ex-ambassadors throughout the ministerial spectrum. The agricultural adviser was Trevor Flugge, an Australian and former chief executive of AWB, an Australian wheat exporter and the largest supplier to Iraq in the sanctions period. Conflicts of interest abounded, and some came to light after the advisers had left Iraq. For example, the AWB was accused of having a number of key Ministry of Trade executives on its payroll in the sanctions period, and connived in kickback schemes to the former regime.[12]

The advisers acted not so much as liaisons but as actual administrators, even though some insisted on maintaining the fiction of Iraqi involvement in key decisions. The senior Iraqi bureaucrats dealt with them as representatives of the powers-that-be. The advisers, in turn, were supported by a group of staff housed in the Republican Palace, which doubled up as both the administrative and the political heart of the Coalition. The staff, who were organised as virtual shadow ministries, were certainly hard-working and dedicated, but they were of hugely variable quality. Some were quite competent and effective. Others were inexperienced, or ideologically driven, or employed because of whom they knew in Washington. The more glaring of the inappropriate appointments would ultimately leave, or be asked to leave, but in the early days of the CPA they were to be found at all levels. It was notable that those who felt driven by the ideological perspectives of the neo-conservatives, or those who wanted to prove themselves in the imagined country of their fantasies, were incapable of making the adjustment to the real conditions in the country. They tended to gravitate towards areas that ideologically were disputatious or controversial, driven by dreams of a cultural makeover of the country. A few lasted beyond their minimal contractual obligations.[13] Their continued presence would prove controversial as the CPA settled into the humdrum business of running the country. In contrast to the ideological variety, however, those who were idealists were persistent and courageous, seeking provincial assignments and difficult projects.[14] A few, such as Fern Holland, a CPA worker on women's issues, gave their lives for their work in trying to improve the lot of Iraqis or raise their political or social awareness.[15]

The Iraqi Economy in the Aftermath of War

The economy that the CPA now presided over had been devastated by war, sanctions and grotesque distortions. The decline of the Iraqi economy had started well before the Gulf War of 1991. The costs of the Iran–Iraq War had been hidden from the public by huge overseas borrowings and cash dollops from the Gulf countries. The infrastructure had already begun to seriously fray during the 1980s as the state diverted ever more resources to fund the war effort against Iran and the expansion of military industries inside Iraq. In the Gulf War the Allies had deliberately targeted the country's infrastructure in a programme of sustained and ruinous bombing. At the end of that conflict Iraq was left with a degraded or destroyed infrastructure, and with stringent international sanctions that replaced the embargo that followed the invasion of Kuwait. Many Iraqis were impoverished.

The UN demanded that Iraq comply with a list of requirements mainly relating to the issues resulting from the liberation of Kuwait and Iraq's WMD programme before sanctions could be lifted. In the event, Iraq was allowed to import foodstuffs, but the embargo on Iraq's oil exports continued, except on a case-by-case basis, primarily to finance the UN's own operations inside Iraq. The concession on foodstuff imports was of limited value as Iraq was unable to generate any serious export earnings to finance any significant imports. Iraq had to rely on assistance from the international aid community for its basic needs. The humanitarian crisis inside Iraq became deeper. To address this, the UN passed another resolution in 1995, authorising an increase in Iraq's oil export levels. Iraq, however, rejected the resolution as part of its campaign to have the sanctions removed entirely. The economy continued to deteriorate, with little foreign exchange earnings, an effective trade embargo and a ruinous monetary policy that resulted in hyperinflation and a collapse of the currency. Further negotiations with the UN finally led to

Iraq's adoption of the terms of the 1995 UN Resolution 986. Oil exports were resumed at a higher level, with the UN managing a programme for the import and distribution of essential commodities. This was the genesis of the OFF programme.[16] The quantitative restrictions on Iraq's oil exports were removed in stages and by 1999 none remained. Iraq could freely export its oil.

The OFF programme defined the development of the Iraqi economy in the period between 1996 and the start of the war in 2003. The total amount of oil exported under the programme reached $64 billion, of which 30 per cent was withheld by the UN Compensation Commission for war reparations arising from Iraq's invasion of Kuwait and its aftermath. Roughly 15 per cent of the total proceeds was spent under UN supervision in the autonomous Kurdistan region, while about 55 per cent was in the form of authorised imports by the Iraqi government. The UN and its contractors mired the OFF programme in corruption and mismanagement. Inside Iraq, the state fashioned an economy that was built around the exigencies of the OFF programme. First, and most crucially, was a system of universal subsidies that covered the entire population. Each Iraqi family was entitled to a fixed quantity of basic foodstuffs and other essential commodities on a regular monthly basis. The fixed ration covered a high percentage of the daily calorific requirements of Iraqis and could be stretched to cover a family's entire monthly needs.[17] In addition, petroleum products and all utilities were provided at virtually no cost. Health services were mainly free as were the cost of basic medicines. Although the average Iraqi monetary income was low, it did not account for the value of free (or nearly free) goods and services that were received from the state. Official salaries became ludicrous, for instance a university professor would earn the equivalent of $20 per month. There was no financial incentive to stay in paid state employment, particularly as the government provided a completely subsidised system for basic necessities. With most of the state's revenues providing for subsidies, there was little left over for maintenance and repair of infrastructure, let alone new capital investments.

The system was kept going by marked favouritism shown to Ba'ath Party members, security and military personnel, and intelligence operatives, who not only received massively higher salaries but also enjoyed special allowances and privileges. There was also a skewing of expenditure towards the more favoured regions, which provided the regime's foot soldiers and its base of support. The numbers of those who were overtly favoured created a class of several million who owed their status and standard of living to the largess of the regime. By providing for the basic needs of the population, the regime abdicated responsibility for managing the economy, which was allowed to deteriorate uncontrollably. Crime rapidly increased, with regime-connected mafias proliferating in every corner. The OFF programme allowed for the development of corrupt procurement networks that favoured regime cronies, operating from foreign bases such as Amman and Beirut, and employing regime front companies and favoured individuals. These networks spread right into the heart of the bureaucracy which was responsible for evaluating and approving multi-million contracts funded through the OFF programme. The rampant oil smuggling coordinated through the intelligence apparatuses was another source of large-scale revenues for the government. In the process, it created a group of wealthy sanctions-busters and oil smugglers.

The abysmal salaries in the public sector drove many people to leave the country during this period. Perhaps two million people emigrated from Iraq during the 1990s. Low salaries encouraged the growth of corruption inside the ministries. Governmental services that were nominally free were frequently rationed according to people's ability to pay. Commodities and medicines in public warehouses were skimmed before they reached their final destinations. By the time Iraq was occupied in 2003, the country had one of the most dysfunctional and distorted economies of the world.

Early Economic and Financial Policies of the CPA

The CPA's economic team was charged with restarting economic activity and beginning the process of reforming and restructuring the economy. At first the main issues were relatively mundane, relating to organising the payments system and ensuring that salaries of civil servants were paid on time. The ORHA and the CPA had utilised the frozen Iraqi assets in the USA, which had been released for this specific purpose.[18] They amounted to nearly $1 billion and with additional funds from seized assets inside Iraq – mainly cash – held in the Central Bank, the commercial banks, and from stashes of money found in Saddam's palaces, the working capital initially available to the Coalition was over $3 billion. One of the first tasks of the Coalition was to revamp the salary structures and eliminate glaring pay level discrepancies between ministries, to keep the dinar/dollar rate at a stable level and not to 'dollarise' the economy. Salaries were increased by a huge margin, partly to reflect the need to pay a living wage, and partly to gain popularity with the very large class of civil servants. Funding of the CPA's operations and projects was never an issue during the early stages of the occupation. The CPA preferred to use Iraqi funds – from the so-called Development Fund for Iraq – as these did not have to go through the same degree of scrutiny and control before being disbursed as would have been the case with US funds.[19]

Cash began to slosh around the economy, ostensibly to kick-start development. In practice, however, this led to massive waste and corruption.[20] It became the subject of detailed investigation by various US agencies, including Congress. The economic policy of the CPA was a blend of wild-eyed and hopelessly unrealistic radical reforms, supposedly to introduce a liberal market economy, and a sober, methodical attempt to get the main engines of Iraq's economy gradually functioning again. Priority had to be given to restarting the work of Iraq's ministries, in spite of their glaring shortcomings, and relaunching the oil industry, as well as increasing production and exports. The latter task was assigned to the main defence contractors, who were given mandates to undertake the necessary repairs to the oil infrastructure to start large-scale production. Both the CPA and the ORHA had carelessly promised the Iraqi public far more than they could realistically deliver. The gap between the results achieved and what the public had been led to expect grew ever larger over time. More jobs had been promised; higher living standards; a growing level and increased quality of public services. These were reiterated time and again as the natural and expected consequence of Iraq's liberation from the tyranny of Saddam. As the CPA consistently failed to reach the performance standards it had set itself, Iraqis became cynical about its promises. Quick results and quick fixes came to dominate the CPA's economic policy discussions, which in time led to another fear: that genuine economic reform would prove unpopular and ought not to be attempted. Much ideologically driven reform was mooted – then abruptly abandoned when the political consequences were thought to prove too great or too risky.

Work on the economy and finances of Iraq had not featured significantly in the pre-war planning at the Pentagon or State Department. There was little hard information on the overall physical conditions of the infrastructure, the actual state of the governmental machinery, and the extent of deterioration in the public services sector. A great deal of the information generated on Iraq was by non-governmental organisations (NGOs), some of which followed a parochial, or even ideological, agenda, and UN agencies that were active in Iraq in the days of sanctions.[21] The regime had manipulated the undoubted humanitarian crisis in Iraq to its advantage, and banner headline figures about the death of half a million Iraqi children as a direct result of sanctions became an accepted fact. This fed into an already prevalent tendency within the US administration generally, and the neo-conservative camp in particular, to doubt the neutrality of the UN agencies and NGOs when it came to Iraq. The Pentagon displayed a sneering, dismissive attitude to these institutions, and their staff were generally distrusted and made to feel unwelcome in the corridors of the ORHA and the early CPA although, with the passing of UN Resolution 1483, the CPA did begin to seek the UN's advice and the involvement of specialist international bodies such as the World Bank and the International Monetary Fund (IMF) became sought after.

By June 2003, the UN agencies, the World Bank and IMF had established a significant presence in Iraq. Faced with the fait accompli of the invasion and occupation, the UN's agencies dropped whatever reservations they might previously have had and began to collaborate with the occupation authorities in drawing up a balance sheet of Iraq's economy and pinpointing the areas where immediate attention was required. The UN had developed intimate line relationships with key technical staff in the Iraqi ministries, and these were carried on into the post-war era, and placed at the disposal of the new CPA administrators.[22]

The reconstruction of Iraq loomed as a major challenge and extremely daunting task. Policies had to be developed that catered not only for immediate emergency needs but also for the reform and restructuring of sclerotic institutions, macroeconomic and financial stabilisation, and the introduction of new principles of market reform and liberalisation. This hugely ambitious and radical scheme was supposed to be achieved by a recently constructed occupation authority, with a limited and legally uncertain mandate, and a staff that had been thrown haphazardly together that was not up to the challenges it encountered.

The CPA embarked on a series of impractical market-inspired reforms, mostly culled from the East European model of 'shock therapy',[23] which took no account of the repercussions engendered. Government entities' deposits and liabilities were offset with the state-owned commercial banks. This denied liquidity to certain enterprises while removing financial obligations from others. Although the purpose was to cut the Gordian knot of who owed what and to whom, the end result was a paralysis in the financing of enterprises and the transfer of their financing to the budget directly. Thus, the Ministry of Finance became directly responsible for meeting all the financial needs of state-owned enterprises, as they lost access to their funds or conversely found themselves with written-off debt. It also had the unintended consequence of massively increasing the net worth of the bankrupt state-owned banks. The financing of the state-owned sector remained an unresolved issue that carried from budget to budget.

The CPA rushed into passing a mass of worthy investor-friendly laws, but none had the desired effect of stimulating investments or encouraging the inflow of foreign capital. Foreign investors were hesitant about visiting the country, let alone investing in it. There was a naïve belief that changes in the regulatory and institutional structures of the country would automatically elevate Iraq to the top of investors' lists. The equally misplaced assumption that the private sector would be the engine for growth and change in Iraq allowed the commercial gangs that monopolised business in Saddam's Iraq to continue. They could now claim to be the vanguard of the new private sector, and contracts flowed to businessmen linked to the former regime. At the same time, Iraq became a magnet for foreign charlatans and adventurers who came into the country on the back of the CPA, and were given unrestricted access to Iraqi ministries and institutions. Some surfaced as instigators and beneficiaries of major scams financed by the uncontrolled flood of cash that moved around the economy in the early days of occupation. In a report on the CPA's early economic successes, most of the achievements listed were either chimerical or ran counter to the CPA's stated policies. For example, the CPA decided not to tamper with the subsidy programme, and re-established the food distribution system mainly along the lines of the Saddam-era procedures, together with all their shortcomings and flaws. Its free trade policy, partly as a result of the collapse of all border controls, resulted in a chaotic expansion of imports, primarily second-hand cars that added to the misery and pollution of Baghdad. (Iraq became a dumping ground for the surplus used-car stocks of all nearby countries.) At the same time, Iraq's looted capital equipment was spirited away and saleable goods, such as scrap metal, found their way beyond the country's frontiers.

The CPA also began to import and distribute petroleum products, which it subsequently allowed to be sold at official give-away prices. This not only opened the way for unrestricted state imports of oil derivatives, it indefinitely postponed the need to reform their price structure. The latter was one of the key props of price reform that was vigorously advocated by the CPA reformers. The CPA also trumpeted its overhaul of the financial system but in fact reforms were marginal. The CPA authorised the entry of foreign banks, but did not undertake any measures at all to restructure the state-owned banks, which accounted for over 90 per cent of the deposits in the system. Tax reform was also meaningless in an environment where few, if any, paid any personal income tax. There seemed to be an ideological preference for a flat tax rate, rather than any formula designed to encourage production and investment.

The one undoubted success was the management of the currency reform, and the introduction of new Iraqi dinar banknotes.[24] This was achieved with the support of the newly independent Central Bank. The installation of a nationwide system of mobile phones played an important part in introducing Iraqis to modern telecommunications systems, although the awards of the contracts were mired in controversy. These 'successes' seemed to point to the recasting of Iraq as a determined economic 'tiger', purposefully and successfully following the best international practice and cutting-edge economic thinking. But there was little or no domestic resonance. Iraqi audiences could not relate the flow of optimistic pronouncements from the CPA to the erratic and falling supply of electricity and other public services. The irony is that group-think began to infect the entire CPA organisation, nowhere more so than in the economic arena. The CPA developed attitudes and methods of working that frequently ignored bad news. The obsession with putting a positive note on all but the more dire events obstructed the development of coherent long-term plans with realistic and realisable targets.

The Collapse of the Middle Classes

The fabric of Iraq's society seriously began to unravel during the 1990s. The effects of sanctions, war, dictatorship and unremitting state violence were felt at all levels of society. Exiles who returned to Iraq after the fall of the Ba'ath regime were shocked by the degree to which the country had changed. For those who had spent decades abroad, the changes were incomprehensible. The country that they remembered, and about which they had spent years reminiscing, simply no longer existed. Even for those who had left in the early or mid-1990s, the conditions in Iraq had deteriorated or changed considerably. The changes affected the middle classes more than any other group. Because of the 1970s oil boom, the Iraqi middle classes and personal incomes had grown substantially during this decade. Indices of car, appliance and home ownership all expanded considerably. For the first time for a large number of people, foreign travel to nearby countries became possible. Many middle-class Iraqis considered the 1970s to be a 'golden period', in spite of the regime's increasing brutality.

The regime mitigated the effects of the Iran–Iraq War on living standards by massive foreign borrowing, so that by the end of the 1980s living and social conditions for the middle classes had not seriously deteriorated. Observers frequently pointed out that the Iraqi middle classes showed clear evidence of Iraq's success in moving beyond sectarian, ethnic, tribal and religious identity politics. They were held out as examples of successful modernising and 'nation-building'. Their status also perpetuated the notion that an exclusively Iraqi identity, forged partly by the Ba'ath, and transcending other affiliations, was now the dominant characteristic of at least the Arab majority of Iraq. A false impression was given about the strength of the middle classes who purportedly shared a common, secular outlook that defined the 'real' Iraq. As evidence, proponents of this view talked about the wide scope of inter-sectarian marriages. (It later transpired, however, that the number of inter-sectarian marriage households was insignificant, certainly never more than a few percentage points of all households.)

The supposed existence of a potentially large middle class in Iraq formed the basis for the political outlook of the liberal democratic and secular groups that emerged after the collapse of the Ba'ath regime. In fact, the middle classes were fragile, and their precarious hold on prosperity was seriously challenged in the 1990s. Sanctions and hyperinflation effectively destroyed them. By the end of the decade, they had effectively disposed of their movable assets to compensate for the collapse of their personal incomes. Auction markets sprang up in Baghdad to sell furniture, bric-à-brac, heirlooms and appliances. The Iraqi dinar collapsed from a rate of nearly one dinar to three dollars in the 1980s, to one dollar to two thousand dinars. Salaries did not keep pace with inflation. At the time of the outbreak of war, a schoolteacher, a quintessential member of the Iraqi middle classes, was earning the equivalent of about five dollars per month. As a result, the 1990s saw a mass exodus of professionals – engineers, doctors, administrators – either to the west or to the few Arab countries, such as Jordan, Libya and Yemen, which would take them. The country suffered an enormous brain drain in the 1990s, the effects of which would feature prominently in the post-war era.

Poverty, Subsidies and the Decline of Social Services

The eroding economy drove an increasing number of families to abandon or postpone education for their children. By 2000, nearly a quarter of the school-age population had dropped out of school, mainly for financial reasons, as children were called upon to find some work to help supplement the resources of their families.[25] Child beggars and street pedlars (for example, children trying to sell cigarettes or boxes of tissues) swarmed on to the main streets of the cities, especially Baghdad. Literacy rates plummeted. By 2003, nearly half the adult population was illiterate.[26] The sanctions pushed for a self-sufficient economy. In practice, this proved difficult to manage. In agriculture, for example, the regime tried to increase domestic grain production by signifi-cantly raising prices paid to farmers. Although total yields began to reach 1980s levels, the yields per hectare were still substantially less, partly because sanctions limited supplies of agricultural implements and dual-use agricul-tural inputs such as fertilisers and pesticides. In 2003, the agricultural sector was still a long way from providing the needed foodstuffs for the average Iraqi. The dependence on food imports continued at a very high level. Domestic production of wheat was 300,000 tons, while imports ran to nearly 3.3 million tons. A similar pattern ranged across the entire commodity spectrum. For example, 99 per cent of sugar was imported; 96 per cent of rice; and 93 per cent of cooking oil.

The system of food rationing was thus a lifeline for Iraqi households, and became a sacrosanct element in society, creating complex and negative psychological responses when the CPA first publicly discussed the possible alteration of the inherited system. The system had grown quietly in the 1990s, and had then taken its all-encompassing shape with the launch of the OFF programme in 1996. By 2003, the system was probably the only tool available that was able to manage the serious impoverishment of the people, and it made a crucial difference to the lives of Iraqis. However, the entire nexus of suppliers, transporters, middlemen, commission agents, warehousemen and grocers who administered the operation was both corrupt and inefficient.

The culture of dependency that it engendered became a recurrent issue in post-war Iraq.

Some sectors suffered grievously in the 1990s, and the effects of their suffering were clearly evident. For instance, the WHO described Iraq prior to 1990 as having 'one of the region's best health care systems'.[27] At that time, doctors occupied the highest strata of society, and Iraqi medical education was considered the best in the Arab world. But all this changed during the 1990s. The degradation of the infrastructure, especially the water treatment and sewerage facilities, impacted on the panoply of water-borne diseases that infected the population, in particular children. In Baghdad, for example, nearly 500,000 tons of raw sewage was dumped into the River Tigris every day. Child mortality doubled in the South of Iraq. The health system under sanctions evolved to accommodate the chronic underfunding. The OFF programme offered the opportunity of re-equipping some of the hospitals and clinics, and providing them with much-needed medicines. At the same time, the later Saddam state tried to generate revenues from an impoverished population by modifying or abandoning the free welfare system, thus forcing the hospitals into a fee-paying system that eliminated the universal free health care to which the public had become accustomed. Corruption became rampant as doctors and other health workers sought to augment their ridiculously low state salaries with extra income from patient charges. There were other extortions, such as allowing patients in need of emergency services to wait until a bribe had been paid, or denying them hospital beds or food unless a payment had been extracted.

Women, Unemployment and Social Dislocation

The Ba'ath regime systematically undermined its own policies that claimed to encourage women's rights. Iraq was never the land of feminism, as portrayed by the media. The oppressive and domineering state-sponsored women's movements counterbalanced women's rights. In the 1990s the regime's increased emphasis on social and religious conservatism particularly affected women. Women's dress began to change, with the emphasis on religious observance and codes of conduct, and women began to wear the *hijab* in ever-greater numbers. What had previously been seen by the Ba'ath as an aberration of extremely conservative (and backward) social groups became the norm in the 1990s. Women, who previously might have had an apparently independent career, became far more rooted in traditional roles prescribed for them. With very high unemployment, whatever jobs there were were given to their menfolk as a matter of priority. At the same time, women ended up as heads of households in ever-growing numbers, either because they had been abandoned, or because their menfolk had been killed in Saddam's various wars, or murdered, or forced into exile. Some women were driven into prostitution, a frightening prospect in Iraq's tribal and religious culture. (The prevalence of open and covert prostitution on a very large scale was one of the features of the Baghdad landscape after the ending of formal hostilities.) Nevertheless, the Iraqi family unit continued to be resilient, in spite of the prevailing harsh circumstances. Psychological problems, however, were increasing, and the use of anti-depressants, anxiety-alleviation drugs and tranquillisers soared. In the immediate post-war period, a leading Iraqi consultant psychiatrist estimated that a quarter of the total population of Iraqis suffered from psychological illnesses or disturbances.[28]

Throughout the 1990s, the unemployment situation was dire. Mass unemployment was a fact of life. Between 30 to 50 per cent of the labour force was unemployed, with significant regional variations. In the Baghdad slums nearly 60 per cent of the labour force was unemployed. The sense of job insecurity in an environment where the state seemed to have abdicated its responsibility for managing the economy added to people's woes. The CPA was confronted by legions of unemployed demanding a solution to their plight. The early attempts to soak up the problem had an insignificant effect on the overall unemployment level, in spite of grandiose claims that the unemployment issue was at the top of the economic agenda.[29]

The Ba'ath campaign against the Marsh Arabs resulted in the destruction of their habitat and 300,000 displaced persons.[30] This number was added to the nearly 500,000 displaced people in the Kurdish areas from the regime's campaigns against the Kurds. The regime also targeted the Turkomen and Assyrian communities who, for reasons of security and Arabisation, were driven out of their ancestral villages and towns. The Marsh Arabs were driven into the slum fringes of the towns and cities of the South, and into Baghdad, where they festered in intolerable conditions, with little prospect of employment or government support. With the fall of the regime, the Kurds began to repopulate the areas from which they had been evicted, while the Marsh dwellers demanded the restitution of their habitats.

The terrible social legacy of the previous two decades was hardly recognised by American troops who entered Baghdad on 9 April, 2003. Neither did returning Iraqis fully fathom the changes that had taken place in their country, and the fundamental change that the Iraqi psyche had undergone over the decades of dictatorship, war and sanctions. The naïve, ideological or self-serving analysis of Iraq, conducted from the vantage points of Washington or London, bore little relationship to the facts on the ground. The CPA was handed this legacy to manage. It was not only hampered by its own weaknesses and shortcomings but was also bewildered by the total strangeness of the Iraqi social, political, institutional and economic landscape. The CPA was driving itself ever more into a physical and psychological ghetto, even before the external violence became insupportable. The task of administering, let alone reforming, Iraq in the face of such hurdles, was well nigh impossible.

7

Deepening Rifts in a Brittle Society

'They started to bring groups of innocent people to this graveyard and began executing them here. . . . They brought people here in buses – each group was between 120 and 150 people. They would bring three groups of this size each day. Before they brought these people, they would bring a bulldozer to dig holes. . . . When they brought the people, they pushed them into the holes with their hands tied and their eyes covered. When they pushed them into the holes, they would start shooting massively. Afterwards, they would bring the bulldozers to bury the people. . . . This operation lasted from March 7 until April 6, 1991.' –

Eyewitness to the 1991 Mahawil massacres of Shi'a, as reported to
Human Rights Watch, May 2003

For the first time in modern history, the fall of the regime confronted Iraqis with the question of where their true loyalties and identities lay. The public airing of community differences and grievances had previously been taboo. Any mention of them, or any suggestion that the state was institutionally biased against certain communities, was drowned in a sea of vituperative condemnation, and was equated with treasonous talk that aimed at under-mining national unity.[1] Even a casual acknowledgement of sectarian and ethnic grievances would open the country to the dreaded threat of *fitna* (sedi-tion). This would inevitably lead to partition. The airing of sectarian issues was tantamount to condoning the division of the country into mini-states, thereby ensuring the continued dominance of foreign powers, especially Israel. The charge of *ta'ifi* (sectarian) was difficult to live down, and was frequently used to smother the possibility of any debate about the sectarian issue in Iraq. The political discourse in Iraq was therefore channelled in any number of directions – into Arab nationalism, socialism, modernism – but never into an examination of the sectarian basis of power.[2] The denial of sectarianism was so potent and deep-rooted that it pushed discussion of this problem to the outer limits of acceptable dialogue. In time, this denial created its own reality, and became an article of faith.[3]

The Kurds had managed to slip out of this straitjacket because of a grudging acknowledgement of their 'peculiar' status. Also, their decade of semi-independence confirmed their demands for special treatment within a federal Iraqi state. The Shi'a, however, were another matter altogether. Their attitudes and beliefs in terms of their loyalty to religion, sect, race or nation would be critical in determining the course of Iraq's political future. The Iraqi state, dominated by the Sunni Arabs, of which Faisal I had spoken, and which had continued unchanged in its basic form for decades, had come crashing down. What kind of state would replace it would be partly dependent on how individual Iraqis felt they had been treated, whether they had gained or lost by the state's existence over the years; also, whether they could be convinced that the state could be reformed, so that it would become more fair and just to all its citizens. In short, did a national compact still exist between Iraqis and their state, in spite of the abuses and injustices that had been visited on most of the state's citizens at one time or another?

The issue was not so much to do with the occupation of the country by outside forces. Careless predictions were made that the Coalition would be met with a wall of resistance by Iraqis, who would transcend their differences in a common front against the invader. The media – even 'embedded' journalists on the front line – reported any form of resistance during the war as a sign of the impending clash between an aroused people and the country's occupier. The initially disorganised and random attacks against the Coalition were portrayed, especially in the Arabic language press, as the beginning of the much-awaited 'national liberation war'.[4] There was resistance, and this would grow, but it had as much to do with the violent disruptions of the power structures in Iraq caused by the invasion as with any rejection of the foreigner in Iraq's midst.

The occupation of Iraq overturned a laboriously constructed system of rule and authority that had become grotesquely distorted during the last decade of the Ba'ath. The system appeared to be monolithic and impervious to change; in the final analysis, it was held together by the threat and use of extreme force and brutality. Saddam had succeeded, to an extent that would only later become apparent, in instilling fear and anxiety as the governing, all-dominant, parameters in Iraqi society and politics. The raw and naked fissures inside Iraqi society became wider and deeper in the decades of Ba'athist rule, and with the removal of the heavy hand of the dictatorship they emerged into the light of day. At first, the signals were confused. The scattered crowds of onlookers that greeted the Coalition's armies seemed perplexed and anxious, unsure of how the overthrow of the government would affect them. The crowds' response to the pulling down of Saddam's statue in Baghdad's central

Firdaus Square on 9 April, 2003 (with the help of US Marines) appeared stilted and stage-managed.[5] But the spontaneous public outbursts of joy in the Shi'ite slums surrounding Baghdad and the southern towns were genuine enough.

The Kurds and the Invasion of Iraq

The Kurds were undoubtedly the most enthusiastic about the invasion of the country. With the exception of extreme Islamists, they enthusiastically welcomed the new order. The *pesh merga* had participated effectively with US Special Forces before and during the war in securing installations and key neighbourhoods in northern cities such as Kirkuk and Mosul.[6] When Garner, and later Bremer, first visited Kurdistan, they were received as heroes and liberators, not invaders or occupiers.[7] There were almost no acts of resistance or violence against the Coalition in any of the Kurdish areas. Whatever insurgency did take place was instigated by outsiders, or associated with the elements in Kurdistan that had been allied to the al-Qaeda network.

Kurdish Islamists were a peculiar mixture of Saudi-sponsored groups, such as the Islamic Unity Movement of Kurdistan (IUM), traditional Sufi brotherhoods (*tariqas*), and shadowy *jihadi* organisations that traced their origins back to the war in Afghanistan.[8] The IUM had managed to secure an electoral base in a number of towns and villages close to the Iranian frontier, especially the town of Halabja, site of the notorious 1988 gas attack. The organisation was broadly neutral about the presence of the Coalition, later cooperating with the CPA in the formation of a post-war governing authority. The Sufi brotherhoods were represented by the Qadiris and Naqshabandis and were always active and popular in Kurdistan. The Kasnazani Qadiri brotherhood became the most widespread and had a mass following, not only in Kurdistan but in other parts of Iraq, and elements of the branch maintained strong links with the occupation authorities.

The *jihadis* were drawn to Kurdistan for a number of reasons. The terrain of the borderlands with Iran and Turkey was mountainous and inaccessible. Immediately after 9/11, a group calling itself *Jund al-Islam* (The Army of Islam) established itself in a mountainous area near the town of Halabja. It was clear that the group was linked to al-Qaeda. The group subsequently merged with another extremist Islamist party to form *Ansar al-Islam* (The Partisans of Islam). In March 2003, as part of the campaign in Iraq, the Coalition bombed the *Ansar*'s bases in Biyara, killing over 250 of its members.[9] The rest regrouped and formed one of the first insurgent/terrorist groups, attacking a variety of targets in Kurdistan and later in the rest of Iraq.

Sunni Arabs and the Invasion

The Sunni Arab community of Iraq had deliberately avoided using a sectarian label, and never acknowledged that Iraqi politics was based on sectarian advantage. The slaughter that accompanied the suppression of the 1991 uprising was never condemned by Sunni Arab oppositionists for what it was: an indiscriminate terror campaign against the Shi'a *qua* Shi'a. Many liberal individuals could not bring themselves to accept that the state might commit such horrors in the interests of maintaining itself in power and, by inference, maintaining the dominance of the Sunni Arab community. The slaughter was explained away as the errant behaviour of a regime whose crimes did not spare any sect or group.[10] The invasion of Iraq swept away this comforting fantasy. For the first time in the modern history of Iraq, the Sunni Arabs were forced to confront the loss of their ascendant power *as a community*.

Most Sunni exiles had stayed away from direct involvement with the opposition's formal structures, but as the USA became increasingly committed to regime change, key Sunni exiles became engaged in the process. They broadly continued to avoid creating a 'Sunni bloc' akin to the Shi'a and Kurdish blocs, and this reluctance to assume the garb of sectarian or identity politics continued into the post-war era.

Sunni Arab opinion divided into three broad trends as a result of the occupation of Iraq. The first was the position adopted by those who, belatedly, had joined the ranks of the opposition, and who accepted the principle of regime change at the hands of foreign powers. They clung to a liberal, secular and democratic political line. Publicly they sought to move the basis of Iraqi politics away from ethnicity and sectarianism to a fulcrum that revolved around issues such as human and gender rights, democratic institution-building, the continuation of Iraq's Arab links and a strongly pro-western orientation. This was by far the weakest current in post-war Sunni thinking, because very few Iraqis had been steeped in the liberal democratic tradition. The second current of opinion was held by Sunni Arabs who had stayed in Iraq and had stood against the Ba'ath regime, either in public or in private. The regime had tolerated the presence of these individuals: the expression of mild criticism and concern might prove the regime's tolerance of opposition and its willingness to enter into dialogue with 'honourable' dissidents. This current of opinion was adopted by liberal lawyers and professionals, academics, and also significant political parties such as the Iraqi Islamic Party (IIP).

The third, held by far the largest group of Sunni Arabs, rejected the occupation and the premises upon which it was built. This group spanned the leadership class of the old Ba'athist order, including senior bureaucrats and diplomats, various categories of administrators, academics, cashiered officers, intelligence officials, businessmen, traders and tribal chiefs. These people formed the base from which violent resistance was to be organised.

The rejection of the terms of the new politics – especially the apparent ascendancy of sectarian consciousness amongst the Shi'a – was a common denominator in the thinking of all Sunni Arabs, irrespective of their attitude to the war and occupation per se. Many had undoubtedly shunned the Ba'athists, feeling that they had betrayed the hopes of true Arab nationalism and the non-sectarian promise of Iraq. In spite of their position on the decades of Ba'athist rule, all were united in their refusal to accept that the ground rules of Iraqi politics were about to be recast along sectarian identity. The fear of marginalisation and impotence in the face of both a rising Shi'a militancy and a powerful occupying force kept most Sunni Arabs in a state of active or passive hostility to the new order. There was a general sense that an unnatural, alien, force had overthrown an entire system of power and authority. It had no connection to Iraq's history or experience and could not therefore be considered a legitimate arbiter of the country's destiny. There was also the underlying unease that was felt about the loss of privileges and advantages with which the previous regime had disproportionately favoured the Sunni Arabs. They had no wherewithal with which to address these issues; their reading of Iraq's history and identity flew in the face of the unfolding drama. They had never before been called upon to consider themselves as Sunni Arabs. To them, Iraq had always been an Arab country; sectarian differences were a throwback to the dark ages; Iraq was a unitary and centralised state; and a powerful army was necessary to fend off foreign invaders, especially if they were Persians.

This was the story of Iraq of which they felt themselves to be the custodians. Its outlines were set out in the 1920s, with the educational policies of the Arab nationalist pedagogue, and transplanted Syrian, Sati' al-Husri.[11] His successors had reiterated essentially the same message over the following eighty years. The Ba'ath Party had embellished this story, putting itself at its centre. There was no other version. Any alternatives would only have led to mayhem, bloodshed, chaos and, finally, the dissolution of the country. This was the legacy carried by those Sunni Arabs who would not adjust to the new conditions in Iraq. They were determined to defend their idea of Iraq, violently if necessary. The prospect of Kurdish autonomy, however, and even full-fledged independence, did not seem to exercise the Sunni Arabs to the same extent as the rise of the Shi'a: they seemed to have resigned themselves to accept the inevitability of some form of regional autonomy for the Kurds.

There was a short-lived moment when a pan-Islamic appeal was thought to bridge the gap between the sects.[12] Calls for Islamic unity poured out of the mosques during the early days of the occupation. A number of religious leaders, both Shi'a and Sunni, made a show of presenting a united façade, and organised demonstrations took place that featured prominent leaders from both sects. Preachers frequently made formulaic references to Sunni–Shi'a unity, but they could not disguise the deep chasm that had opened up between the sects. Sunni leaders, perhaps anticipating an acceleration of the sectarian trend in Iraqi politics, began to question whether the Shi'a did in fact constitute a majority of the population, and overtly wondered whether Iraqis would accept 'Iranian' (by implication, Shi'a) rule over them. Amongst the Shi'a, the Sadrists were the most insistent on maintaining a common front with the Sunni Islamists, partly to distinguish themselves from the seemingly more sectarian SCIRI, and partly for genuine patriotic reasons and rejection of the occupation. The Sadrists always claimed that they were Iraqi nationalists, and therefore publicly eschewed sectarian differences between the Shi'a and the Sunni. They also, like the Sunni Arabs, wholeheartedly rejected the occupation and refused to countenance cooperating with the Coalition. They were also mostly at odds with the Shi'a religious hierarchy. SCIRI, on the other hand, was more connected with the Shi'a religious hierarchy and Iran, and was therefore more determinedly 'Shi'a' in its public posture.

The Shi'a and the Invasion

The post-war era opened up the prospect for changing the political circumstances of the Shi'a of Iraq. They suddenly found that their nemesis had been removed. Throughout the 1990s, the Shi'a had undergone a major change. The 1991 uprising and its brutal suppression, together with the extreme hardships suffered by the Iraqi people in the 1990s, which disproportionately affected Shi'a areas, had led to a serious questioning as to what it meant to be a Shi'a inside Iraq. The legacy of the Iran–Iraq War was to keep the Shi'a of Iraq outside effective power. The Arab and Islamic worlds seemed supremely indifferent to the plight of the Shi'a. These factors conspired to mould a new Shi'a political consciousness and identity. The movement associated with Ayatollah Mohammad Sadiq al-Sadr was much more than an example of rivalry between the prominent religious families of Iraq. A 'tipping point' had been reached, which would manifest only after the removal of the Ba'athist regime. The grudging acquiescence in a Sunni-dominated state, the hallmark of previous generations of Shi'a political leaders, would now be rejected outright. The key shift in Shi'a thinking, however, was a move from the politics of 'victimisation' to an insistence on their rights as a majority. This went beyond the simple assertion of majority rights and extended to the heart of the Iraqi state itself, and the redefinition of the identity of the country.

All these currents, most still in the formative stage, emerged into the light of day after the fall of the Ba'ath regime.[13] A simple acknowledgement of democracy and democratic rules of practice would no longer be sufficient to assuage the majority of the Shi'a. The Iraqi state under the Ba'ath regime had all but declared war against the majority of its citizens and had come very close to destroying their religious leadership and institutions. To prevent this happening again, the Shi'a would now insist on moulding the state to their own perceptions and requirements.[14] Not all the Shi'a subscribed to this new definition, but a very large majority did so, moving the fulcrum of political identity and loyalty away from secular groups and towards Islamists and sectarian figures. The pattern of Iraqi political life had decisively altered.

In the first weeks after the fall of Baghdad, glimpses could be seen of the way that the mass of the Shi'a would behave in the future. The signs were not to the liking of the Coalition, the secular politicians, or the Sunni Arab community. Rather than celebrate their release from the Ba'athist dictatorship and acknowledge the vital role of the USA in this process, most of the Shi'a gravitated towards their religious leadership, and to explicitly Islamist groups.[15] In many towns in the South, demonstrations were held demanding 'Islamic Rule'. In Baghdad, the Sadrists seized control over the poor Shi'a neighbourhoods, especially Sadr City which housed over two million inhabitants. The first Friday prayers after the collapse of the regime saw many thousands congregating in the mosques and meeting halls of the Shi'a to hear preachers and prayer leaders call for the establishment of an Islamic order in Iraq.[16] The immediate post-war period also coincided with one of Shi'a Islam's most evocative dates: the commemoration of the fortieth day after the date of Imam Hussein's death at Karbala, the *Ziyarat al-Arbai'in*. Traditionally, this would take the form of a march on foot by believers to the shrine of Imam Hussein in Karbala. This would be the first time for decades that the commemoration would have been held as previously it had been banned by the Ba'athist authorities. It would be the first indication of the strength of religious allegiances and feelings of Iraq's Shi'a. In the event, hundreds of thousands, possibly up to a million, made the march on foot to Karbala.[17] They were watched by American helicopters.

The Street Power of the Shi'a

The emergence of the Sadrists coincided with, or caused, the involvement of large numbers of people in the movement's support base, and manifested in the mobilisation of people for demonstrations, protests and commemorations: the Shi'a had taken to street power. The movement was still raw and prone to violence. But the Sadrists' relative immaturity was more than compensated for by their overwhelming support in the poor neighbourhoods of Baghdad and in many towns across the South, including Najaf. Moqtada al-Sadr, the putative leader of the Sadrists, was ensconced in that city. He had only recently emerged from the shadows, and few knew what to make of him.[18] He had none of the authority in religious matters that senior ayatollahs commanded, but nevertheless led the Friday prayers at his father's bastion, the Kufa Grand Mosque, to which tens of thousands of the poor, labourers and farmers, would flock. These prayers were an important political tool. Al-Sadr was contemptuously and arrogantly dismissed as an upstart, not least by the circles close to the grand ayatollahs of Najaf. But they, and many others, seriously underestimated the Sadrist movement's appeal.

The emphasis on the provision of social services also became a feature of the areas that fell under the sway of Shi'a Islamists. Schools, hospitals, water-works, electricity sub-stations were all under the control of local political Islamists. When the CPA eventually managed to wrest control over these facil-ities and transfer them to local authority or ministerial administration, the political parties nevertheless continued to exert a strong influence over these entities. In the major urban centres, the Shi'a Islamists had insinuated them-selves at all levels of the local administration, well before their presence and significance became generally realised.[19] By then, it would be too late to change the structure and personnel of these organisations, except in the most reprehensible cases.

The Rise of the Shi'a Militias

The Shi'a militias seriously began to infiltrate the main towns and cities soon after the fall of the Ba'ath regime. Not all the Islamist groups had organised militias. Some were no more than local vigilante groups that sprang up to take over towns before the Coalition arrived, or organised to support local politi-cians and authority figures. They would prove temporary and disappear as the powers of their sponsors melted away or were absorbed into larger groups. Some were co-opted by the Coalition. The Badr forces associated with SCIRI proved a most valuable asset in the tussle for local control. SCIRI wisely chose not to confront the Coalition with a heavily armed force. Badr entered Iraq unhindered by the Coalition, having left heavy weaponry, such as tanks and artillery pieces, in Iran.[20] The weaponry would not only have proved provoca-tive to the Coalition but would have been virtually useless against the Coalition's immensely greater firepower. There were plenty of light, and even heavy, arms available to SCIRI from the looting of the depots of the Iraqi army and the Ba'ath Party militias. About 10,000 trained and disciplined Badr fighters entered Iraq, either unarmed or armed only with light weapons, and reassembled in various towns and cities as the fighting arm of SCIRI.[21] Their ranks were swollen by local recruiting drives that turned Badr, now renamed the Badr Organisation, into the largest Shi'a Islamist militia.

The Sadrist militia was slower in forming. It grew in those areas where the Sadrists preponderated, or where they were determined to make a show of strength, such as the vital, religiously symbolic city of Najaf. In time, these militias would become coordinated, and with a proper, albeit primitive, command structure, to be renamed the Mahdi Army. The Da'awa Party never had a formal militia as such, although its organised armed groups contained hundreds of militants. They were never deployed tactically or strategically to gain advantage, but were used mainly as a defensive force. The real strength of the Da'awa Party inside Iraq was considerably less than what had been predicted. Not quite a mass party, it had spawned a number of splinter groups, some of which had grown into major foci of power that had often eclipsed the mother party. In Basra, for example, it was the Basra offshoot of the Da'awa that was prominent. The Da'awa was a party of the intellectual elites, and found it difficult to move into the realm of mass politics. It nevertheless managed to turn its immense legacy as one of the earliest and most determined of the Ba'ath's opponents to significant political advantage, particularly amongst the better-educated Islamists. Ill-informed reports, such as that the Da'awa 'controlled' the city of Nasiriya, were untrue; in fact, the Da'awa had to struggle to make its presence felt in the face of the better-organised and funded SCIRI, and the mass appeal of the Sadrists.

The arming of the militias proved a remarkably easy task.[22] At the end of the war, Iraq was awash with weapons, a by-product of one of the most militarised societies in the world. Estimates of Iraq's pre-war weapons stockpiles were in excess of 650,000 tons. The Coalition had secured or destroyed about 400,000 tons, leaving 250,000 tons of weaponry unaccounted for. The weapons caches, numbering tens of thousands, were an easy target for militias, armed groups and the nucleus of what would later be called 'the insurgency'. Some of the unsecured caches contained the very type of weapons that the Coalition had stated would constitute WMD. Hundreds of surface-to-surface warheads, stored at a military college near Baqubah, each of which contained fifty-seven pounds of high explosives, simply vanished. (In a cause célèbre that featured in the 2004 presidential elections, 377 tons of high-grade explosives stored at the al-Qaqa'a site, south of Baghdad, which had been flagged by international weapons inspectors, simply disappeared.) Heavy armour and artillery were easy to locate and secure. The Kurdish *pesh merga*, taking advantage of their ambiguous status between a militia and a formal military force, kept the tanks and artillery pieces that they seized and moved them to storage depots in Kurdistan. Altogether, perhaps one-third of Iraq's total weaponry was seized by private groups and militias, contributing immensely to the relative power of various political parties.

Mass Graves and the Hardening of Shi'a Consciousness

The discovery and excavation of mass graves, and the seizure of huge caches of documents from Saddam's security agencies in the early post-war period, crystallised the reality of the crimes committed against the Shi'a and the Kurds. It hardened the determination of the Shi'a to carve for themselves a commanding role in the new Iraq.

Prior to the invasion, the existence of mass graves had been generally acknowledged by international bodies and human rights organisations, but there was no clear documentary or physical evidence that could irrefutably prove their presence. The fall of the regime, however, allowed for a flood of disclosures that put paid to any doubts about the Ba'ath regime's human rights record. The Americans had flown millions of pages of documents to Qatar, and then to the USA. But the chaotic conditions after the fall of Baghdad had allowed a huge pile of other governmental, Ba'ath Party and security archives to fall into the hands of political parties, NGOs, private citizens' groups and individuals. In some cases the whereabouts of these archives had been known beforehand and they fell, mainly intact, into the hands of political groups. The Kurds, for example, located documents that gave precise details about the thousands of 'disappeared' Kurds, mainly from the Barzan tribe who had been rounded up in the early 1980s. Two mass graves were located in the south of the country that held the remains of nearly 2,500 of these 'disappeared'.

A particularly large cache of documents, some eighteen million pieces, fell into the hands of the *Jamiat al-Sujjana' al-Ahrar* (Association of Free Prisoners – AFP), a grouping of mainly Shi'a former political detainees. These were mainly the documents of the *Amn al-'Am* (The General Securities Directorate). By July 2003, the AFP had confirmed the murder of 300,000 people, just from the files of the General Securities Directorate. It had also seized a sizeable cache of documents from the Military Intelligence Department, which no doubt would reveal further executions. The offices of the AFP were jammed with distraught people seeking information about disappearances, or confirmation about the death, of their loved ones. The AFP's walls were covered with lists of individuals who had been executed. The CPA tried to keep track of the activities of these NGOs, most of which were set up after the end of the war, but plans to centralise the documentation record about executions and human rights abuses came to nothing.

The Iraq Memory Foundation, a group founded by the writer-activist Kenan Makiya, gained control over the records of the Regional Command of the Ba'ath Party. Other NGOs were underfunded and, to varying degrees, amateurish. The documents were poorly stored and suffered from deterioration, damage and loss. Some of the less scrupulous organisations began to sell documents of value to families and individuals. The Iraq Memory Foundation called for a more coordinated and systematic approach to document collection and storage, but the CPA declined to cooperate, and established its own department for this purpose.

A more graphic indictment of the Ba'ath regime would emerge as a result of the discovery of a large number of mass graves scattered around the country.[23] For over a decade, the fate of the thousands of the 'disappeared' in the aftermath of the quashing of the 1991 uprising had been a taboo subject. People were simply too afraid to probe and the Ba'ath regime would deny that there were any 'disappeared', and would hint that these people were still incarcerated. The first mass grave was uncovered near the city of Hilla, south of Baghdad, in early May 2003. By the standards of later mass graves, this one, in the village of Imam Bakr, was small, containing nearly fifty bodies. However, the US military, which controlled the area, soon concluded that tens of thousands of people were buried in mass graves in the Hilla area.

On 13 May, 2003, two large mass graves containing thousands of people were located in the area of Mahawil near Hilla.[24] Many of those arrested in the uprising of 1991 had been detained there. The US military at first tried to secure the site, but the pressure of the crowds seeking information about their loved ones caused them to relent and civilians swarmed over the mass grave sites, which were then exhumed by mechanical diggers. Execution squads from the Special Republican Guard had done most of the killings. Other organs of the regime had participated, including local branches of the Ba'ath Party, the police, intelligence services and pro-government tribes. It would later prove difficult to develop forensic evidence, as a result of the damage caused to the burial sites, but numerous people, including local farmers, had witnessed the killings. Many of the culprits would also flee, and the chaos in the early days after the war also contributed to the problems in apprehending suspects. For example, the head of the Albu Alwan tribe, Sheikh Mohammad Jawad al-Naifus, was arrested near Hilla on 26 April, 2003 by US Marines. Members of his tribe had been implicated in the execution of prisoners at Mahawil. Local people had identified him as one of the main officials who had supervised the executions. He was taken to the large internment camp at Camp Bucca, near the port of Umm Qasr and screened by interrogators from the US Judge Advocate's Office. By an extraordinary turn of events, he was released on 18 May, 2003. That a person who by all accounts was one of the prime suspects in the mass murders at Mahawil could be released, after he had been identified as such and arrested, is a revealing example of the confused state of the transitional justice system in Iraq.

The Mahawil discovery caused uproar inside Iraq. It confirmed without a shadow of a doubt the existence of mass graves, and the Ba'ath regime's complicity in crimes against humanity. Terrible stories from the few survivors of the Mahawil executions began to emerge, confirming people's worst fears. Mahawil was only the first of a series of mass graves that were quickly unearthed. In May 2003 alone, mass graves were found near Basra, Radhwaniyya near Baghdad, and in Kirkuk and Mosul. The entire country seemed to contain mass graves, and more continued to be found well into 2006. The vast desert areas of Anbar province held the bodies of thousands of Kurds and Shi'a. Eyewitnesses spoke of a line of prisoners three kilometres long. The prisoners were shot and dumped into ditches. The mass graves outside Kirkuk held nearly 2,000 Kurds.

The numbers of dead in the mass graves of Iraq were never satisfactorily determined, and this became an issue that festered. The exhumations uncovered perhaps 10,000 bodies, but the gravesites themselves certainly held far more. In the remote desert areas of Anbar and Samawwa provinces, to which it was known that thousands of prisoners had been taken, mass graves are suspected, but have not as yet been found. Human rights organisations have floated figures in the 300,000 range, while the USA has claimed 400,000. The final tally will never be known, but it most likely exceeds 100,000 people. About 270 reported mass graves sites were recorded, most of them being in the southern and central parts of the country. A number of former guards and burial workers came forward with information about the location of mass graves. Even a few executioners, overcome with remorse or seeking immunity, voluntarily confessed their grisly work and helped investigators to identify sites and people killed. International volunteers and forensic examiners from a number of countries began the arduous task of protecting the sites, training Iraqis in forensic archaeology, and gathering incriminating evidence to help in prosecuting the planners and perpetrators of these atrocities. Their work would provide the basic evidence for the Iraqi Special Tribunal, a court that would be later set up to try cases of war crimes, genocide and crimes against humanity.

The psychological impact of the mass graves was immense. To some extent, the Kurds had become inured to the horrors of the Ba'ath regime. Their isolation from Baghdad for over a decade may have helped to foster a more measured response to the discovery of even more evidence that confirmed the regime's crimes. Prior to 1991, the violence of the regime had been specifically targeted and the population at large had been insulated from its effects. By painting the Kurds as seditionists and the opposition as treasonable, the Ba'ath were able to 'justify' to the general public that its measures were part of its duties to maintain public order and defend the national interest. Iraqis may have been aware of the regime's atrocities, but only through rumour and innuendo rather than direct first-hand experience. Most people avoided thinking about this issue, while others accepted the regime's propaganda about its enemies. The deportations to Iran in the 1970s and 1980s were accompanied by public distribution of the properties of these unfortunates as booty, or its sale at give-away prices. A similar fate befell the property of dispossessed or murdered Kurdish families. This created a counter-narrative that justified the expulsions, killings and sequestrations as necessary, or even desirable, outcomes for people who were treated as fifth-columnists or separatists. The larger the circle of beneficiaries from the regime's crimes, the greater the public willingness to accept the official version of events.

The Iran–Iraq War provided further justification of state interest to explain away the regime's violations. Thus, the displacement of people in the Iranian borderlands, or the use of execution squads to stop front-line soldiers from retreating in battle, were seen as perfectly justifiable measures in a national emergency. It was not until the 1991 uprising, however, that the regime began to employ mass and indiscriminate terror tactics against the population outside the confines of Kurdistan. This time, the official version was not easily digestible, if for no other reason than that the physical evidence of destruction was there for all to see. The Ba'ath kept people's anger and scepticism at bay by the simple expedient of fear. Its story line that the uprising was caused by the *ghawgha* (mob) was never convincing, especially as a huge number of people fell under the regime's definition of 'mob'. The anger and resentment were suppressed, and could not be vented until the occupation by the Coalition. The discovery of the mass graves was the release mechanism. The catharsis was short-lived, however, as Iraq would soon spin into another cycle of violence.

Revenge Killings

The dismantling of the Ba'ath apparatus of terror and control and the cancellation of unjust and punitive laws had an immediate and positive impact on human rights in Iraq. But the inability of the Coalition to impose law and order created another set of issues and problems that gave rise to wide-scale human rights abuses. Lawlessness was accompanied by a rise in kidnappings, abductions and rape. The numbers of street children increased markedly as the Coalition mistakenly 'liberated' orphanages and released inmates of juvenile prisons.

At first, assassinations and murders driven by revenge or settling of old scores were not as common as most people feared, given Iraq's long history of vengeance-seeking. A few weeks into the occupation, however, saw the emergence of reports about politically motivated killings.[25] The most vulnerable were known members of the former security apparatus, and Ba'ath Party operatives who had not fled their areas or who had felt that they had some form of protection or immunity. The rate of such killings began to increase, after news of the mass graves had spread and after the orders banning the

Ba'ath Party and calls for de-Ba'athification were promulgated. In May 2003, unofficial tallies of politically motivated murders in Baghdad alone had reached several hundred. The demand for vengeance was more pronounced in areas in the South and Sadr City that had suffered most from Ba'athist repression. The killings were to some extent the response of people who were seeking justice and had lost confidence in the Coalition's ability or willingness to bring the culprits to justice. The ill-thought-out decision to bring known Ba'athists back into government service added to the ambiguity of the Coalition's purpose regarding the former regime's administrators and enforcers. The USA seemed more concerned about arresting leading members of the regime – the so-called 'pack of cards' – rather than pursuing those who were directly responsible for implementing the former regime's murderous orders. Religious leaders appeared to sanction the killings, in spite of brave efforts on the part of a few to put a stop to them.

The killing spree against former regime operatives soon went beyond those who could be clearly identified by their victims or by their reputation. The membership lists of the Ba'ath Party and intelligence operatives began to be widely circulated, following the seizure of document caches after the fall of Baghdad. Death squads started to work on these lists and, by June 2003, the killings began to include academics, teachers, bureaucrats, artists, journalists and professionals who were seen to be part of the regime's control and repression apparatus.

The cracks inside Iraqi society began to appear shortly after the fall of Baghdad. Iraq had never had a grand national compact, such as an overarching constitution to which all subscribed, or even an 'understanding' between its component groups. The 'idea' of Iraq took root unevenly throughout the country. The narrative of Iraq fashioned by its leaders and pedagogues was compromised for many of its citizens who did not share in, or resonate to, its founding symbols. Nevertheless, some form of accommodation between the state and most of its citizens had been reached by the 1950s. Essentially, it was based on the recognition by the Shi'a elite that they might have some share of central power, within limits that would satisfy the more ambitious of their leaders. But they should not aspire to control or run the state, even though their numbers might warrant this. At the same time, the state, dominated by the Sunni Arabs, would recognise and acknowledge the props of Shi'a identity, and would not move to alter or shrink them in any significant way. Essentially, the Sunni Arabs controlled the state, while the Shi'a were allowed to keep their civil, mercantile and religious traditions. It was a precarious balance, but it held the potential for improvement and progress towards a common sense of citizenship, duties and entitlements. Successive governments in the 1960s and 1970s, however, foolishly destroyed this. The state removed the elements that kept a vigorous Shi'a identity alive in parallel to a Sunni-dominated state. Nationalisations, emigration and expulsions destroyed the Shi'a mercantilist class; the state monopoly on education, publishing and the media removed the cultural underpinnings of Shi'a life; and the attack on Najaf and the religious hierarchy came close to completely eliminating the *hawzas* of Iraq. When the state embarked on its mass killings after the 1991 uprisings, Iraq became hopelessly compromised in the minds of most of the Shi'a. If the former Iraqi state defined Iraq, then few people in the Shi'a community – and fewer still amongst the Kurds – would have anything to do with it. The last overlords of the old Iraqi state, Saddam and his Ba'ath Party, had given Iraq little apart from misgovernment, defeats and disasters, culminating in the occupation of the country by foreigners. The opportunity to build a fair and just state now presented itself. But it was a race against time as to whether something new could be fashioned out of the wreckage of the old state.

8

Dismantling the Ba'athist State

'There is a duality in Baathists. You can find a Baathist who is a killer, but at home, with his family, he's completely normal. It's like they split their day into two twelve-hour blocks. When people say about someone I know to be a Baathist criminal, 'No, he's a good neighbor!' I believe them. The Baath Party is like the Nazi Party, or like the Mafia. If you meet them, they are simpatico. And this is why it's very difficult for us to do our work, which is to change – really change – Iraqi society.' –

Mithal Alusi, Director, De-Ba'athification Commission, November 2004[1]

It was broadly accepted that the new Iraq had to be built on a democratic platform, where individual and civil rights would be protected and where the relationships between state and society would be decisively shifted away from an overweening, authoritarian government. The treatment of former Ba'athists caused much bitter recrimination within the new Iraqi political class. The arguments in favour of a drastic 'cleansing' of Ba'athists from Iraq were countered by the assertion that most of its members had been coerced into joining, and collectively could not be held responsible for the crimes of the former regime. By and large, the camp that sought a thoroughgoing de-Ba'athification included the INC and Shi'a Islamist parties, backed by civilians in the Pentagon. Those who called for a narrow and selective definition of culpable Ba'athists included the INA and the liberals grouped around Adnan al-Pachachi. The Kurds insisted on de-Ba'athification, but held out so many exceptions that it was difficult to gauge what they really wanted. Garner had chosen to ignore the issue, and in practice, therefore, allowed the continuing presence of former Ba'athists in the government machinery.

Bremer, on the other hand, was determined to implement broad de-Ba'athification, dismantle the entire edifice of the Ba'athist state, and enshrine all freedoms associated with a modern, liberal state. The arrival of Bremer seemed to promise a new beginning. Soon after arriving in Baghdad, he started to give TV addresses to the Iraqi public, explaining his policies and hopes for the future. Very few Iraqis could relate to what he was trying to convey. The US slogans and catch phrases of his media advisers did not resonate with his public. Words such as 'liberty' and 'freedom' translated poorly into the customary political usage of most Iraqis, and did not carry the same meaning or significance in Arabic. The belaboured turns of phrase of liberal ideology had no roots in the Iraqi political culture and, though worthy in their intent, left most people indifferent to what he was saying. Unfortunately, the CPA insisted on forcing its own image of what Iraq was or should be, and buttressing its representations by copious reference to polls and focus groups. The press releases in Arabic, the TV spots, the staged announcements were all imbued with the same alien rhetoric.

The End of the Ba'ath Party

The end of the rule of the Ba'ath Party triggered a great deal of emotion inside Iraq. There was little doubt that a dispassionate analysis of the years of Ba'athist rule would have shown the Party to be an unmitigated disaster. The Ba'ath, after all, had provided the scaffolding for Saddam's rule. It administered one of the worst terror states in modern times; mismanaged its economy; and supported the rulers who drove the country into three disastrous wars. But the indictments of the Ba'ath Party that might have been expected were not dispassionate and were not universally shared. It was insufficient to simply equate its years in power with the calamities that had befallen Iraq. The Ba'ath Party had metamorphosed into something else. It became symbolic shorthand that covered more complex loyalties. The fact remained that the Coalition did not conquer Iraq and annihilate its opponents. The Iraqi army was not destroyed in battle; it refused to fight and simply faded away. The structures of government were allowed to continue as they were. The Coalition tried to live up to the rhetoric of a liberator. The often hesitant, indecisive and inconclusive nature of the occupation created ambiguities that were exploited by Ba'athists and their fellow-travellers. The comparison with the Nazi Party's treatment after World War II would not apply to the Ba'ath. The Nazi Party as an institution was smashed, and no one would tolerate a counter-narrative of its history. Individuals with a Nazi past were accommodated, but not if they in any way continued their allegiance to the Nazi Party or its dogmas. This, however, was not the case with the Ba'ath. People believed that Saddam had usurped the Ba'ath and had distorted its otherwise 'credible' record to suit his own purposes. After all, were not Ba'athists also victims of his terror? The argument began to be made that there were both 'good' and 'bad' Ba'athists; that most members joined the Party to secure, keep or procure advancement in a job; that the Ba'ath Party had played a useful role in 'modernising' society, and so on. At the same time, there was the opinion, especially in the Sunni Arab community, that de-Ba'athification was shorthand for removing Sunni Arabs from positions of power and influence.

The Ba'ath Party had over two million members by the time the regime was overthrown. It was by no means exclusively, or even predominantly, Sunni Arab. Shi'a, and even Turkomen and a few Kurds were well represented throughout the Party structure, but the Party's upper echelons, and its key organisational and security units, were disproportionately Sunni Arab. The Party had only a few hundred followers in 1968 when it seized power, but it had had more than three decades to organise Iraq according to its own image. It reached into every nook and cranny of the lives of Iraqis. It controlled the state machinery, the professional and academic institutions, and the media, and had its own militia. Positions of influence in the government would rarely be open to non-Ba'athists, and in the more sensitive ministries adherence to the Party was a condition of employment. In the diplomatic service, one of the most desirable and competitive of careers in the government, the high prevalence of former Ba'athists in the senior posts caused a quandary for the CPA. It had to make a number of exceptions to its stated policy of de-Ba'athification, simply to keep the Foreign Affairs Ministry functioning. This would be the case for a number of sensitive ministries, where exceptions were made that appeared to create a precedent. This, in turn, opened the way for a flood of complaints and demands for special treatment by ex-Ba'athists, some of which were accommodated through influence and privileged access to the CPA. Nevertheless, up to ten thousand individuals were summarily removed from ministries by the Bremer Order in the first three months of the CPA, on the grounds that they were members of the four highest ranks of the Party. Most could not disguise their Party membership, but some camouflaged their status by a variety of ruses. It was not always clear where an individual stood in the Party hierarchy, as often his or her status would not be publicly acknowledged or even known, except to a handful of people. Hearsay and gossip were frequently used by malcontents to point out high-ranking Ba'athists, but it is likely that a number of people dismissed may have been entirely innocent of the charge that they were militant Ba'athists.

The Ba'ath never fully lost its penchant for secrecy at the highest level, even having ruled the country for thirty-five years. The task of ferreting out senior Ba'athists was difficult because of the destruction of records. Payroll records in particular were important in determining what person was a high-ranking Ba'athist. Ba'athists would normally be paid multiples of the pitiful wage rates prevalent in the public sector, up to fifty times in certain instances. For example, a primary school teacher would ordinarily be paid the equivalent of £2 per month, whereas a Ba'athist in the same post would be paid £100 per month. Inclusion in foreign trips and all expenses paid trips, a mark of privilege in the Iraqi bureaucracy, would also be a fair indicator of a person's ranking in the Party. Payroll records and the recording of privileges were used to make a case against individuals who had denied that they were high-ranking members of the Party.

De-Ba'athification in the early days of the CPA proceeded in a generally straightforward way. The vast majority of individuals caught in the first round of dismissals were those who could be clearly identified in the higher levels of the Party ranks, and the case against them was clear cut. It was only after the process had been transferred to Iraqi control, with the formation of the Supreme Council on de-Ba'athification, that the issue became contentious.[2]

The De-Ba'athification Order

The policies on de-Ba'athification, promulgated in Bremer's first act as Administrator, his CPA Order 1, issued on 16 May, 2003 and entitled 'De-Ba'athification of Iraqi Society',[3] angered large numbers of people. The Order called for the implementation of the previous CPA decision to disestablish the Ba'ath Party. It removed the four top echelons of the membership of the Party from all government posts and banned their future employment in the public sector. The lowest grade encompassed by the Order was the *firqah* (group) member, and it included the next three grades of *shu'bah* (section) member, *far'* (branch) member and the highest rank of membership, that of the Regional Command of the Party. All in all, about 30,000 people would be directly included in the de-Ba'athification Order. (In a subsequent Order, all the property and assets of the Ba'ath Party were seized and transferred to the CPA for their administration.)

The policy had been mooted long before the invasion of Iraq. It featured as a prominent part of the exile literature that was evolving on the Ba'ath Party and its totalitarian and iniquitous characteristics.[4] The outrages of the Ba'ath Party and its brutal enforcers as the handmaiden of power in Saddam's Iraq became more openly acknowledged in the 1990s as the regime came under intense international scrutiny for its human rights violations. As the momentum towards war developed and the imminence of the regime's overthrow grew nearer, loud voices began to be raised about the imperative of dissolving the Ba'ath Party and ridding Iraq of Ba'athist ideology and Ba'athists. A section on de-Ba'athification was included in the Future of Iraq report by the Democratic Principles Working Group. A thorough de-Ba'athification was demanded by the main Shi'a Islamist parties and the Kurds. Ahmad Chalabi and the INC had also been vociferous proponents of de-Ba'athification, and carried the cause into the leadership council. In the early days of the post-war political environment there were few voices raised against the principle of de-Ba'athification. Thus, when Bremer informed the G-7 of the details of his first Order, it was received with unanimous approval. But sober voices that had been consulted on the process of de-Nazification in Germany after World War II, including leading historians and experts on the subject, had been cautious in their advocacy of such a policy. In fact some had warned about the possibility of serious divisions in the country if such a policy were to be enforced.[5]

Arab nationalists and former Ba'athists, however, were more sceptical about de-Ba'athification. Within the US administration, de-Ba'athification was adopted by the Pentagon's Office of Special Plans and by its head, Douglas Feith. Bremer stated in his memoirs that Feith told him of the policy before he took up his office as the CPA Administrator.[6] It was presented to him as a draft order that he was to announce upon his arrival in Baghdad. On the day before Bremer signed the de-Ba'athification Order, Feith gave testimony in front of the House International Relations Committee on the conditions inside Iraq. He explicitly rejected the possibility of keeping senior Ba'athists in office as a price for maintaining the proper functioning of government. 'Our policy', he said, 'is "De-Baathification" – that is the disestablishment of the Ba'ath Party, the elimination of its structures, and the removal of its high-ranking members from positions of authority in Iraq.'[7]

De-Ba'athification was central for the plan to remake Iraq into a new democracy, and to produce a new political culture that would replace the authoritarian and nationalist models of the past. But its proponents had not adequately considered the deep roots that the Ba'ath had developed in Iraq after nearly thirty-five years of power, or how the upper echelons of the Party had become dominated by Sunni Arabs from the towns and villages of the upper reaches of the Tigris and Euphrates rivers. The function of the Party as administrative glue and the fact that considerable numbers of people had joined it for nothing more than personal advancement, or even survival, were only tangentially acknowledged by the CPA, and more generally by the proponents of full-scale de-Ba'athification amongst Iraqi political figures. Ayad Allawi had always argued against sweeping de-Ba'athification, claiming that most who joined the Party did so as a '"vehicle to live," a means of obtaining and keeping their jobs and other state perks'.[8] Vengeance, or ideological distaste, were the guiding sentiments for most of the advocates of de-Ba'athification in the Iraqi opposition. The planners of the war, especially those in the Pentagon and the vice-president's office, saw the Ba'ath Party as an ideological block that had to be removed and its influence excised, a Nazi Party in all but name.[9] The State Department, to some extent influenced by the British, its Arab interlocutors and the INA, may have accepted the principle of removing close supporters of Saddam from power, but not wholesale de-Ba'athification as such. Ba'athists rather than the Party per se could be useful to the running of Iraq and might provide a counterweight to any takeover of the government by Islamists.

De-Ba'athification was also equated with 'de-Sunnification', as some observers called it, and its unrestricted application would exacerbate sectarian tensions in post-war Iraq. No serious discussions were held in the pre-war period to examine the role of the Ba'ath Party in post-war Iraq: planning was left to a few decision-makers inside the Pentagon's Office for Special Plans. Opinion divided into three camps. The first called for a targeted culling of the upper reaches of the government. Only hardline 'guilty' 'Saddamists', irrespective of whether they held any Party rank, would be purged, rather than Ba'athists as such. The purge of these 'Saddamist' elements would probably not have exceeded a few hundred individuals. A second group called for the removal of the upper layers of the Party from the government (the policy that was in fact subsequently adopted) with a campaign to educate the remaining membership about the excesses of the Party. The success of such a policy would be dependent on the fairness with which it was implemented. The last group wanted the complete erasure of the Party and its legacy from public and private life. It was thought that the Party was an unmitigated evil, and that any acknowledgement of its existence, even in an indirect way, would seriously compromise the reform of Iraqi society and politics.

Garner had no specific de-Ba'athification policy. In fact he seemed to have decided that he would avail himself of the skills and assistance of any person who would be useful and who would willingly cooperate with the new administration. He allowed senior Ba'athists to continue in their posts, and actually appointed notorious Ba'athists to positions of influence and authority. There were a number of demonstrations against some of his more ill-considered appointments. Dr Ali al-Janabi, a senior Ba'athist, was appointed to be the acting chief of the Ministry of Health. He was driven out of his job by widespread protests by the ministry's staff because of his alleged corruption and mistreatment of employees.[10] Bremer's first Order was a dramatic move that signalled a decisive commitment to the reordering of Iraq's society along democratic lines. But like most of the CPA's pronouncements, there was a great deal of wishful thinking, poor implementation and insufficient consideration regarding the consequences or the Order. In the event, it would prove one of the most controversial of the CPA's decisions. The Iraqi Leadership Council did not express any serious disagreement with the Order when Bremer first presented it to them. But since the Order was pitched between two extremes, the way in which it was implemented would play a large part in determining the outcome of de-Ba'athification. The escape clause that gave hope to the proponents of a more lax attitude to de-Ba'athification was the power given to the administrator (Bremer) to make exceptions to the Order.

The swift elimination of the higher rungs of Ba'ath Party members in the ministries did not necessarily eliminate either the presence of Ba'athist sympathisers, or include the most egregious cases, however. The blunder-buss approach did not destroy the network of sympathisers, and even fifth-columnists, in the most important ministries. Frequently, these groups would mount an open challenge to the Coalition's authority on one pretext or another.

A Media Explosion

The removal of controls on a free press was an essential component of the political strategy of the CPA. Variety, topicality, critical and investigative reporting were all absent in the media of the Ba'ath regime. The virtues of an open society could be easily demonstrated by authorising free and uncensored journalism, which, it was thought, would more endear Iraqis to the ways of the new order. One of the immediate and most noticeable changes after the fall of the Ba'athist regime was the explosive growth of a newly free press and media. The stultifying media that had existed for decades, a key element in Ba'athist control, were swept away. Within weeks of the occupation, tens of newspapers were started, and there were at least eighty-five new titles by the end of June 2003.[11] Most of the newspapers were launched on a shoestring, and though claiming to be dailies were produced erratically. Nearly all the major political parties had their own newspapers, and competed for the reader's attention. The Kurds extended their Arabic language dailies to Baghdad, but all the other former opposition parties launched new newspapers. The journal *Baghdad* was produced by the INA; *al-Muttamar* by the INC; the Sadrists produced the *Hawza* newspaper; SCIRI had *al-Adala*. The main independent newspaper in the early days of the occupation was *Azzamman*, edited by Sa'ad al-Bazzaz, a former crony of Saddam's son Uday, and reputedly backed by Gulf funding. Al-Bazzaz toed a mild Arab nationalist line, and sought to build a media empire in the country.[12] The pan-Arab press based in London and the Gulf became available in Baghdad, although the Saudi paper *Asharq al-Awsat* did start a Baghdad edition of its own by the autumn of 2003.

The newly enfranchised press had a serious credibility problem. With one or two exceptions, such as *al-Mada* newspaper, founded by the former communist Fakhri Karim, the press did not inspire much confidence. It reflected the prevailing party line, manufactured news, or distorted the news to fit a preconceived political plan. Newspapers such as *Bayanna al-Jadida* (loosely connected to SCIRI, but funded mainly through blackmail and payoffs from ministers) specialised in rumours and scurrilous stories. With weak libel laws and no way of enforcing them, it could print almost whatever it wanted. Most people preferred news from the satellite channels, especially the pan-Arab channels, al-Jazeera and al-Arabiyya. With the fall of the regime, entire streets and markets became devoted to the sale, repair and installation of satellite dishes.[13] The cost of an imported dish or a crude domestic variant remained reasonable.[14] These channels had taken a uniformly anti-war stance, especially al-Jazeera, which was run from Qatar and funded by the Qatari government. They began to play up incidents of resistance to the occupation and the conditions of chaos and insecurity inside Iraq. The effects of the pan-Arab satellite channels on Iraqi opinion would later become a controversial subject. The CPA would later close down a number of these stations' Baghdad bureaux for malicious or inflammatory reporting. All the main international media had their Baghdad contingents. Iran also jumped into the fray, establishing an Arabic-language station, al-Alam, which targeted the Iraqi, especially Shi'a, audience. There were correspondents from the main global newspapers and news agencies, but after a few months the foreign media presence, though still large, would be reduced. For the first time, Internet access became possible. By the summer of 2003, Baghdad had over thirty cybercafés, providing access through service providers based in Kurdistan. In time, Internet access and usage would explode. Iraqis would quickly adjust to the world of the World Wide Web. Some intrepid Internet stalwarts, such as the blogger SalamPax, became worldwide celebrities.[15] Blogging became a fast-growing industry in Iraq.[16]

The Coalition put its media policy into practice as soon as its armies had entered Iraq. They first launched a radio station from the newly occupied port of Umm Qasr, which beamed nationwide, with a mixture of entertainment and promotional ads. This was the handiwork of the ORHA's Office for the Iraqi Media, and was called the 'Indigenous Media Project'. This officially turned into the Iraq Media Network (IMN).[17] The idea was that the IMN would be the cornerstone of Iraq's new media efforts. In the second of Bremer's orders, issued on 23 May, the Ministry of Information was dissolved. The IMN was given the buildings and equipment of the former regime's media, and it took on about 400 of the former employees of the Ministry of Information. The rest, numbering over 4,000, and mostly active or nominal Ba'athists, were sacked. They were reckoned to be too close to the former regime, justifying and promoting its policies and actions, and acting as sycophantic trumpet-blowers for Saddam and the Ba'ath.

The IMN claimed to be modelled on public broadcasting stations in the USA and the UK, but in truth it was a mouthpiece for the CPA. Its TV station initially broadcast for about six hours per day, but in spite of having a monopoly over terrestrial TV in Iraq, the station was hardly ever watched. Iraqis preferred to get their news from the pan-Arab satellite channels, or from al-Alam. The IMN's newspaper was widely circulated. Both the IMN and the CPA would soon run into controversy with accusations of waste and ineffectiveness dogging their every step. Control over the CPA's media policy by the US Department of Defense became a serious issue on Capitol Hill. But the conundrum confronting the IMN was whether it was an arm of the CPA or a genuine, independent public broadcaster. The CPA seemed to settle the issue with its Order 14, issued in June 2003, which proscribed a number of media activities, including reporting on incidents or events that could be construed as undermining the CPA. Several journalists left the IMN, frustrated with the CPA's control over the media's activities, and by its apparently contradictory goals.[18]

The Dissolution of the Armed Forces

In his second Order, CPA Order 2,[19] Bremer dissolved all the formal armed and security units of the state, including the regular armed forces, the Republican Guard units, the intelligence and security services, and the ministries associated with administering and supervising them. The Order also specified that a 'New Iraqi Corps' would be formed at a future date as a first step in forming a 'self-defence capability' for Iraq. This was another of Bremer's most controversial decisions, the repercussions of which would be felt later.

Bremer would later defend his position by stating that the army had in any case dissolved itself as most of its formations had simply melted away during, and immediately after, the war.[20] He claimed that the Kurds were extremely suspicious of the armed forces, given their decades of struggle against the central authority in Baghdad and the army's massive butchery of the Kurds during the *Anfal* campaign. He also said that the Shi'a were hostile to the old armed forces, which had a traditional built-in bias against the Shi'a.[21] Another unstated premise behind the decision to dissolve the old Iraqi army was the belief held in many neo-conservative circles in the USA that the army in Iraq was both an instrument of control and the propagator of an ideology that was aggressive and disruptive to both stability and peace in the Middle East.

The Iraqi army had played an almost mystical role in the narrative of modern Iraqi history.[22] The Iraqi public was never told of the army's excesses in its various campaigns against tribes, Kurds, Assyrians, and other rebellious groups. It was seen as a preserver of the nation's core values, and heroic myths were built around its supposed victories and triumphs. In the 1930s the army had developed a notable pro-German tendency, culminating in a disastrous decision by Iraq to declare war against Britain in 1941, following a coup by nationalist officers.[23] Its battles in the 1948 war in Palestine and in the 1973 October war[24] were given an epic dimension, and schoolboys were drilled in the virtues of the armed forces as upholders of martial values and pan-Arabism. This, of course, continued into the eight-year Iran–Iraq War, where the army, in the Ba'athist regime's propaganda, was given the additional role of 'guardians' over the eastern gateway of the entire Arab world.

The militarisation of Iraqi public life went hand in hand with the cult of the armed forces, and the tempo increased as the Ba'ath seized power. Almost the entire male population of the country was in one way or another involved in the armed forces, the paramilitary forces, or the militias, as conscripts, recruits and volunteers. Donning of military uniform became standard practice for senior officials in the government. As society became militarised, so the army became politicised. Every coup and counter-coup in Iraqi history was accompanied by widespread purges of the officer corps, but it was only with the advent of the Ba'ath that political activity in the officer corps became banned, under the penalty of death – except for the Ba'ath Party. The Party began to infiltrate poorly trained, but loyal, Party members into the officer corps, to keep the army in check. These people would play an important part in controlling the officer corps during the Iran–Iraq War, when the armed forces were massively expanded. They reached a combined total of perhaps a million people, in a country whose population in 1988, when the war ended, did not exceed twenty million. The armed forces were only partly demobilised in the 1988–90 period – only to be plunged once again into war during the Kuwait crisis.

All the army's campaigns and wars were given evocative titles. The Iran–Iraq War became the *Qadissiya*, in memory of the victory of the Arabs over a Persian adversary in the early period of the expansion of Islam. The Kuwait war became *Umm al-Maarik* (the 'Mother of All Battles'), a ridiculous epithet for a military and political disaster. By the time the 2003 invasion had taken place, the armed forces were a shadow of their former self. At the top of the hierarchy of military formations were the Special Republican Guard, numbering about 25,000 well-paid, well-armed and well-equipped formations that guarded the Ba'ath regime and Baghdad. Most of its Sunni Arab members were drawn from the tribes and clans of the upper reaches of the Tigris, Saddam's own tribal territory. Below them were the once elite units of the Republican Guard, a multi-division-size formation whose armaments and *esprit de corps* had degraded during the 1990s. Its officer corps was drawn mainly from the broader network of Sunni Arab tribes and regions. At the bottom were the largest formations of the Iraqi army proper. These had deteriorated considerably, and in many respects had ceased to be effective fighting formations. Most of the troops, however, were drawn from the Shi'a regions.

The officer corps in all these units, except the Special Republican Guard, had lost nearly all their previous privileges and elevated status, and had been reduced to impoverishment as the sanctions of the 1990s dragged on. The cars, access to special shops, subsidised housing, pension and salary privileges that they had enjoyed during the Iran–Iraq War were things of the past. Also, the bloated nature of the armed forces gave rise to remarkable statistics. There were about 20,000 general officers for an army of about 400,000.[25] The composition of the officer cadres in the regular army, skewed as they were towards the city of Mosul, was also a notable feature. This city provided something like half the general officers, and a third of the other officer ranks of the army. The dissolution of the armed forces would have a profound impact on the city. These were the armed forces that Bremer had ordered dissolved.

The dissolution of the armed forces and the intelligence services involved the dismissal of at least 400,000 people.[26] The effects of this order were far greater than the removal of the top-ranking Ba'athists from office. The response of Iraqis to this action was also far more complex. On the one hand, the Ba'ath was uniformly detested in Kurdistan and amongst most of the population of the South of Iraq. The arguments employed to question de-Ba'athification were more to do with keeping the machinery of government going and the fairness with which it was applied than with the desirability of keeping the Party and its institutions alive. The security services were detested, and very few could muster any arguments for keeping them. The armed forces, on the other hand, generated considerable sympathy and respect throughout Iraq. Only in Kurdistan was the decision to dissolve the armed forces uniformly popular. The Shi'a had a more ambivalent attitude. A minority supported the dissolution of the army, but not along the lines that the Order implied. The Order basically postulated a *tabula rasa* upon which a new army, structured along modern, professional lines, would be built. It was implicit that the CPA, and by inference the Coalition, would model it along the lines that they saw fit. The new Iraqi army, which the Order said would be a self-defence force, was one that would be shorn of most of the offensive capabilities of a modern army. This was not the army that most of the Shi'a, especially the Islamists, wanted. The Shi'a aimed to remove the biases against themselves in the military institutions of the state, but not to diminish or eliminate the army's fighting capabilities.[27] While the CPA (and presumably Washington) wanted a military force that would not pose a serious threat to its neighbours, and that would be kept small and dependent, Shi'a Islamists wanted a strong army, but only in the context of a state in which they would predominate. The Bremer Order therefore came as a shock to most Iraqis in terms of its sweep and implications. The decades of indoctrination about the Iraqi armed forces had left a deep impression on the public at large, who reckoned that the army was an integral part of the identity of the state of Iraq. For the officers, the army had been essentially a noble institution. It would prove difficult, even for the Shi'a, to accept a wholesale dissolution of the armed forces and to leave the country bereft of an army.

The Sunni Arab community was clearly most affected by the dissolution of the armed forces. Even in its reduced and bedraggled state, the army still gave its troops their only means of livelihood. For the tens of thousands of cashiered officers, the army was their home and only career, and to be suddenly and unceremoniously dumped greatly affected their sense of self-worth. Loss of dignity was added to their impoverishment, and an anxious and resentful multitude retired to their homes nursing their grievances about the new order. Officers were considerably embittered at the way in which the Iraqi army was portrayed. Saddam had used it for his own ends, and it was thought that it should not have to be saddled with his crimes. A number of the army's units, such as the 51st Division, which had surrendered to British forces near Basra early in the fighting, had even indirectly cooperated with the invasion force by responding to the Coalition's call not to fight.[28] For the rank and file of soldiers, the dissolution of the army was less traumatic, but they still depended on it for their pay, despite it being a pittance. Hundreds of thousands of mainly conscript soldiers were now thrown into unemployment. At first, there were small-scale demonstrations by soldiers and low-grade officers at the decisions taken. They would gather in front of the gates of the heavily guarded Republican Palace to air their grievances. But by June, the intensity of these demonstrations gathered strength. In one such case, riots erupted, and two former Iraqi army officers were shot dead.[29] The Order had called for the payment of a one-month stipend to the cashiered force. Following the riots, however, and under pressure from a number of Iraqi politicians, Bremer changed his decision. Nearly 250,000 former servicemen were to be paid a monthly stipend of $50 to $150 per person for the indefinite future.

Bremer's adviser on the Iraqi military, Walter Slocombe, a former under secretary of defense under Clinton, talked about creating a 40,000 man 'New Iraqi Army' within a three-year period.[30] He promised to field a division-size force of light infantry by the end of 2003, some 12,000 strong. General Paul Eaton was placed in charge of the recruitment and training of the New Iraqi Army, although the actual work was to be done by military contractors. But this new army would be a pale reflection of the old one. Deep suspicions began to be harboured as to the true intentions of the Coalition in fielding such a patently inadequate force for a country with a population of over twenty-five million in a difficult region. Further suspicions were aroused when General McKiernan, the top American military commander in Iraq, issued a disarmament order in May, which seemed to cover all groups and parties. But he pointedly exempted the Kurdish *pesh merga* forces from this order. The *pesh merga* had, in addition to their light weaponry, a sizeable arsenal of tanks and artillery. To the angry officers of the old Iraqi army, this seemed a deliberate attempt to create an imbalance in military capabilities between the centre in Baghdad and the Kurdish regions. Some talked darkly about the disarmament order being the harbinger of the dismemberment of the country.

The twin Orders of de-Ba'athification and the dissolution of the army were later seen as the vital ingredients that launched the insurgency. Bremer was held directly responsible for this apparent strategic blunder. But though the Orders carried his signature, the policy decisions were not his. It would have been difficult for him, with less than a few weeks on the job, to have developed these policies or to have been able to countermand these decisions, if they had been taken by others, with any authority. Ultimately, the blame, or credit, for these decisions has to lie elsewhere. The policy on de-Ba'athification was clearly developed prior to Bremer's assumption of office. The dissolution of the army also fitted into a preconceived notion of how the future Iraq would emerge. In such a vision, there was no place for a nationalist, pan-Arab institution that could be used to threaten Iraq's neighbours and block the plan to 'democratise' the Middle East. The disintegration of the army justified the decision to dissolve it on the grounds that it had simply ceased to exist. When the decision to dissolve the armed forces was taken, there was little consideration given to the rise of an insurgency or resistance, which might have been contained and crushed by a well-equipped and friendly Iraqi army.

Reforms of the Justice System

One of the main issues that the Coalition had to contend with was the status of the Iraqi justice system. The Ba'athist regime, as in most single party dictatorships, had sought a legitimising legal process for its repressiveness and violence. The Iraqi legal system was based on a strange blend of criminal codes derived from European, mainly French, models, via the legal codes of Egypt and Syria.[31] With the exception of personal status laws, which were largely drawn according to the Sharia,[32] the codes were wholly secular in nature, with some accommodation made to traditional tribal laws. The main criminal codes and codes for criminal procedures were redrawn after the Ba'ath came to power. Before the Party assumed power in 1968, the judiciary in Iraq had long been established and was proud of its heritage of independence. After 1968, judges had to be approved by the Ba'ath Party, and the entire institution became compromised. The judiciary was remoulded to fit the policies and requirements of the Party. In an innovation that had far-reaching consequences for the administration of justice, the supreme authority in Ba'athist Iraq, the Revolutionary Command Council (RCC), attributed to itself the power to issue decrees with the force of law. These decrees accumulated over time, and frequently contradicted or contravened established rules and procedures in the criminal and civil codes. The RCC established a number of special courts, entirely outside the framework of the established law, and gave these courts extraordinary powers to try and sentence defendants.[33] These exceptional courts were part and parcel of the plan to crush all political opposition or any individual or group that stood in the way of the Ba'athist programme. They went beyond the infamous *Mahkamat al-Thawra*, the revolutionary court that was periodically used by Iraq's republican regimes to try the opponents of the government. Under the Ba'ath, the intelligence, security and military services all had their own special courts, which tried and sentenced tens of thousands of people with no regard to due process, or even the formal codes, of law. Rule by decree and sentences passed by special tribunals were the hallmarks of the latter Ba'ath period. When the regime fell, the Iraqi judiciary was hopelessly complicit in the crimes of the regime and in fact acted as one its main props. Reform of the justice system was therefore a key element in the process of dismantling the Ba'athist state. This added to the clamour for justice from the thousands of victims of the Ba'ath regime, and the demands for war crimes tribunals to try the top hierarchy of Ba'athists and regime stalwarts.[34]

In a series of Orders issued between April and June 2003, the CPA tackled the problem of the judicial inheritance from the Ba'athist years. It established a committee, half of whose members were drawn from the CPA, to vet judges, to suspend the application of most of the 1969 Ba'athist penal code, to ban torture and suspend capital punishment. It also separated the judiciary from control by the Ministry of Justice, and established it as an independent third arm of the state. In a June 2003 public notice, the CPA exempted itself, the military and foreign contractors from coming under the jurisdiction of Iraqi laws. Most Iraqis could not miss the irony that the CPA had replaced Saddam's rule by decree with yet another form of arbitrary authority, albeit apparently sanctioned by international law and mostly benign in its intent. The 'legality' of Bremer's Orders was always a contentious issue. The Iraqi judiciary was loath to implement the more controversial aspects of Bremer's decrees, and a number of them were left to gather dust. A frequent ploy was to insist that Orders were reproduced in the official gazette before they could have the force of law. When the CPA announced a definite end date to its occupation mandate, Iraqi lawyers and judges began to procrastinate in implementing or interpreting the law, preferring the established Iraqi version, even if it contravened the Bremer Orders. Enforcement of the Orders, except where they impinged on security or other vital matters, was an ongoing problem.

Difficulties in Reforming the Iraqi State

The dismantling of the Ba'athist state proved far more difficult than had been anticipated. The structures of control, the routines and procedures of government, and the reward and punishment system kept the country firmly in the grip of the Ba'athist regime for nearly thirty-five years. These could not be uprooted overnight through a series of administrative orders. The entire country was ensnared in the webs of these structures, which defined the inter-relationships within ministries and between the ministries and various other units of government. It was a hierarchical, highly centralised, formal structure of organisation that was shadowed, at various levels, by other, often fearsome, power relationships. The 'other' government was that of the intelligence and security apparatus and the network of clan and tribal connections to the regime's leading figures, and to Saddam's inner circle of close family and sons. The system as a whole would tolerate no opposition to its routines and procedures unless they were in some way connected to this other, shadowy government.

The CPA thought that by removing culpable individuals and dismantling the central institutions of the Ba'athist state, the edifice of government would accommodate itself to the new post-war order and the economy and services would kick-start. The working model, in fact, was the removal of the top layer of dedicated Ba'athists and their temporary replacement by the expatriate Iraqis recruited under the IRDC programme, stiffened and monitored by the CPA's corps of professional advisers. This was a blunder of the first order of magnitude, which contributed mightily to the mass of problems that arose later in the management of the machinery of government. The amount of manpower, energy and resources that had been needed to make the state conform to the Ba'athist design was enormous. The CPA did not demolish the state that it had inherited and then start to rebuild it along the lines that it prescribed. This was the usual way of working in countries that had been totally defeated in war and then occupied. But the CPA insisted on keeping the form and most of the content of Iraq's government intact. This was partly owing to a conscious policy decision to keep disruptive change to a minimum, in keeping with the premise that the formal occupation would be short-lived, and that only minimal interference in the legal and administrative framework of the country would be accepted by international opinion. The CPA's legal advisers, and the British, were exceptionally sensitive to the CPA's changing of laws and methods of government.

Another contributing factor that stymied any attempt to reorder Iraq's laws and government fundamentally was the fact that the CPA was simply not given the go-ahead to undertake such wholesale reforms. Stabilising and directly administering post-war Iraq did not feature in the CPA's mandate. It would have clashed with the doctrine of the Pentagon's civilian leadership and that of the neo-conservatives strewn across various departments of the US administration. A full-blown occupation would have undermined the notion of liberation, and would have exposed the American public to the potentially open-ended nature of the occupation. The unwillingness to treat the Ba'ath legacy for what it was – a totalitarian state with a privileged elite – and therefore in need of a radical overhaul, made the CPA reforms essentially tentative and nominal. It was as if a huge, decrepit building had been struck unevenly by a demolition ball that succeeded in inflicting only minor damage to the edifice. The foundations, and a considerable part of the superstructure of the dysfunctional state, remained.

The removal of senior Ba'athists from office did not always result in their replacement by competent, or even honest, people. The CPA had sought out senior civil servants who for one reason or another had been marginalised or dismissed by the previous regime. One of the facts that later became established, often through bitter experience, was that not all those bureaucrats who had been sidelined were worthy of high office. Some had been dismissed for malpractice, corruption or incompetence. Others had been opposed to the regime in one way or another, or had said the wrong words at the wrong time. They found their way back into office by appealing to the CPA on the grounds of 'political persecution'. At the same time many bureaucrats, who acted as the linchpins of corrupt practices, remained in their jobs, maintaining their connections and networks.[35] This time, however, there were no prying eyes of the dreaded *Mukhabarat* to keep them in check. Corruption in the post-war era, at first surreptitiously, but later brazenly, continued to infect the entire apparatus of the government. The web of corruption that was the mainstay of the later Ba'athist state continued, though often with new players. Very few individuals were prosecuted, or even censured, during the CPA's tenure in power, even when corruption or gross mismanagement was all too evident. This can be directly attributable to the timid and inadequate restructuring of the Iraqi government. A massive opportunity was lost, and with the escalating pressure to bring things to 'normal', the old ways reasserted themselves. In far too many cases, whatever the changes that were made to the governance of the country, it was simply a matter of reshuffling of names and faces within the same tired, inefficient and deeply corrupt structures of the state.

9

The Formation of the Governing Council and the Rise of the Insurgency

'We reject this occupation . . . . No country would accept an occupation. We have lost our dignity. Until now we have not seen anything . . . except killing, searches and curfews. There is a reaction for every action. If you are choking me, I will also choke you. We have a resistance just like the Palestinians, Chechens and Afghans.' –

Sheikh Mudhafar al-Ani, Imam of a mosque in al-Qaim, Anbar province, speaking to Nir Rosen of the *Asia Times*, October 2003

The passage of UN Resolution 1483 opened the way for the re-entry of the UN to the political process in post-war Iraq. The acrimonious disagreements in the Security Council, between the American-led Coalition and the anti-war front led by France, Russia and Germany, seemed on the way to being papered over. The Resolution was preceded by swift and generally cooperative negotiations between all the major powers, with concessions being made by all the concerned groups. The USA agreed to an enhanced UN role in the political process, by accepting the creation of the post of a Special Representative of the Secretary General to assist in the formation of an interim Iraqi authority.[1]

The Appointment of Sergio Vieira de Mello

Sergio Vieira de Mello, a Brazilian, who was then the UN High Commissioner for Refugees was selected as the UN Special Representative. He arrived in Baghdad on 2 June, 2003. Before he left New York, he stated at a press conference with Kofi Annan on 27 May, 2003 that he gave himself two strategic targets. 'As I hit the ground priority number one will be to establish contacts with . . . representative Iraqis, Iraqi leaders, representatives of the media, of civil society, and there are many,' de Mello said.[2] His second priority was to 'establish good working relations' with the USA and British occupying powers, and their coalition partners. De Mello set to work on nudging Bremer and the CPA towards a more empowered group that could be granted some serious oversight role over the government. He stressed the need 'to empower the free people of Iraq as soon as possible. The sooner the Iraqi people govern themselves, the better,' he told reporters.[3] De Mello was working on an agenda that called for the rapid normalisation of the political situation in Iraq and the removal of the face of occupation. The manifestations of the occupation of Iraq, which the UN as an institution had grudgingly acknowledged but whose legality it never fully accepted, had to be quickly erased. The CPA was obviously working on a different plan, with far wider implications. A common ground had to be struck between the two versions in the short term if the conditions of UN Resolution 1483 were to be honoured.

With the arrival of de Mello, the perception inside Iraq was positive, if for no other reason than the public's general familiarity with the UN and its operations, and its utter bewilderment at the CPA and the strangeness of the fact of occupation. A glimmer of hope arose that, with the involvement of the UN, the situation would be quickly normalised and that the occupation would soon end.

The Formation of the Iraqi Governing Council

It is not clear who could claim responsibility for the final form of what eventually became the Governing Council, but the presence of de Mello clearly pushed the debate away from a purely advisory body – Bremer's inclination – to the hybrid form that it eventually took.

The decision to expand the G-7 to include a more 'representative' grouping of Iraqis in the leadership council had been anticipated. The argument had been endlessly made that the G-7 was unrepresentative, self-appointed and dominated by exiles. The selection of the twenty-five members of what was to become the Iraqi Governing Council was done according to certain established formulas. These continued to govern the distribution of power subsequently. The first 'cut' was to accept the principle of ethnic and sectarian balance in the governing authority. The Shi'a as a group would hold a slim majority in the Council, reflecting their numerical majority in the country. The Kurds and Sunni Arabs would each have a roughly equal share of 20 per cent plus of the seats, again reflecting their relative weighting in the country. Minorities such as the Turkomen and Christian communities would need to be represented. The second 'cut' was the political affiliations of the Council members, as between Islamists, Kurdish parties, secularists and liberal democrats. Representing the affiliations of the Sunni Arabs was somewhat problematic but this was finessed. Most of their representatives fell into the 'liberal democratic' category, with the exception of the predominantly Sunni Iraqi Islamic Party. The third 'cut' involved finding tribal representatives and, importantly, representatives of Iraqi women. Considerations of gender were prominent in the public relations toolkit of the CPA and empowering Iraqi women was frequently cited as one of its important objectives.

Apart from the seven members of the leadership council, the selection of the other members of the new Governing Council followed a circuitous route. Some, such as the moderate Islamist Dr Mowaffaq al-Rubai'e, had already staked a position for himself by ceaseless networking activity after the fall of the regime, and played an important part in bridging the gap between the Islamists and the CPA. The senior religious figure, Sayyid Muhammad Bahr ul-Uloom, was a leading Shi'a moderate with a long-established presence in the counsels of the Iraqi opposition.

The selection of the Sunni Arabs for the Governing Council included, predictably, Dr al-Pachachi and Naseer al-Chadirchi, but also a few surprises. Sheikh Ghazi al-Yawar, an engineer, had not been notable for his public opposition to the Ba'athist regime. Samir al-Sumaidaei, although a long-standing member of the Iraqi opposition, had been publicly inactive for some time. He would prove a very articulate and effective member of the Governing Council. Dr Aqila al-Hashemi was a senior diplomat in the Iraqi Foreign Service, and a confidante of Ba'athist Iraq's Deputy Prime Minister, Tariq Aziz. She was a very active and committed member of the Governing Council. Her vociferous championing of the new order clashed with her previous association with the defunct regime, and opened her to accusations of opportunism. On 20 September, 2003, Aqila al-Hashemi was shot in the abdomen as she was leaving to attend a meeting of the Governing Council. Hashemi was to join a delegation that was heading for the annual meeting of the UN General Assembly. Part of her brief was to press the case for granting greater international recognition for the Governing Council. As one of the few women on the Governing Council and a senior diplomat, she had the right profile to present the face of the 'New Iraq'. She would be defending a council that had been widely condemned as being unrepresentative, if not quite a stooge of the occupying powers. But this was not to be. Nine assailants attacked her outside her house. She died three days later. Her security detail, mainly relatives, were insufficiently trained and inadequately armed to provide any serious protection.[4]

The lackadaisical way in which security was provided for key Iraqi officials who were cooperating with the Coalition became a contentious issue. Apart from the main political leaders, who had their own militias and small armies of bodyguards to protect them, the Coalition provided little or no protection for leading Iraqis in the early days of the post-war period.[5] The cost of providing personal security was prohibitive for the less well-endowed Governing Council members, who had to rely on immediate members of their family or clan for protection. Some Governing Council members, incredibly, had to take a taxi or public transport to their job, thus exposing them to huge personal safety risks. Others had to take the embarrassing recourse of borrowing money and weapons from their better-funded and better-supplied colleagues.[6] The CPA did not believe that there was an organised and determined resistance embarking on a systematic campaign of murders, assassinations and bombings. The provision of visible security for the Governing Council and for other key government officials would have possibly undermined this preconception. The fact that the CPA denied that the Governing Council members and other senior officials were a potential target for insurgents led the Coalition to take measures that reduced their personal safety. The Coalition's troops often forcibly disarmed, or even arrested, bodyguards and the security detail of Governing Council members. It took the assassination of Aqila al-Hashemi to accelerate the implementation of security measures for the Governing Council and other senior officials.

The Governing Council negotiated a number of powers for itself. These included the right to nominate twenty-five Cabinet ministers and to supervise their work.[7] But on key matters, such as control over financial resources and security and military matters, their powers were either undefined or circumscribed. Bremer was not going to sign away the main rights and prerogatives of the CPA as the UN-sanctioned occupying authority. The tension between the demands of the Governing Council to act as a fully empowered body and Bremer's CPA as the occupying authority became a recurring feature of the interrelationships between the two entities. It compounded the distaste, bordering on contempt, that Bremer personally felt for a number of the Iraqi political leadership, especially the returned exiles. This aversion grew with time, and eventually came near to poisoning the relationship between the Governing Council and Bremer.

The Governing Council assembled in Baghdad's main conference centre for its first public exposure on 13 July, 2003. The group, rather than the CPA, announced its own formation, partly to preserve the fiction that the measure was an all-Iraqi affair.[8]

Public opinion in the Arab world was overwhelmingly hostile to the invasion of Iraq and this translated into a deeply held conviction by the so-called Arab 'street' that the Governing Council was simply another instrument of control of the occupation. This viewpoint necessarily impacted on the governments of the concerned states and they had to balance this public hostility to the Governing Council with the pragmatic requirement of maintaining a co-operative relationship with the USA when it came to Iraq. De Mello had to contend with this context when he made his tour of Iraq's neighbours. He stressed that the Governing Council was the beginning of a process that would include the appointment of a Cabinet, the drafting of a constitution and the holding of nationwide elections. He did not deny that the Governing Council was ultimately responsible to the CPA, but sought to portray the formation of the Governing Council as an integral part in the process that would end the occupation.

The Governing Council quickly sought to stamp its authority, at least outside the security and military areas. Its pronouncements took on an independent slant and its leaders struggled to portray themselves as a legitimate and representative authority that was working diligently to end the occupation and to take responsibility for alleviating the concerns of the Iraqi public. In one of its earliest sessions the Governing Council denounced the occupation forces for 'cruelty and violence used against citizens whose homes were being searched by the Coalition forces'.[9]

The Governing Council was invited to take up Iraq's seat at the UN without specifically being recognised as the government of the country.[10] On 14 August, in a 14-0 vote, with Syria abstaining, the UN Security Council passed Resolution 1500 that 'welcomed' the formation of the Governing Council, but left the question of a sovereign Iraqi government till later.

The 'Moqtada Problem'

During the negotiations that preceded the formation of the Governing Council, Bremer and the Coalition had to contend with the increasingly alarming issue of the so-called 'Moqtada Problem'. With the virtual absence of any public services in the poorer quarters of Baghdad, the Sadrists were organising the collection of garbage, the clearing out of water mains, and the provision of security for hospitals and schools.[11] They were making their presence felt throughout the country with their launch of a number of newspapers and magazines. The Coalition was visibly concerned about their growing influence. Bremer in particular, seemed to have developed a visceral dislike for the person of Moqtada al-Sadr. 'Muqtada al-Sadr has the potential of ripping this country apart . . . We can't let that happen,' wrote Bremer in his memoirs.[12]

The military was also aggressively confrontational whenever they came across the Sadrists. Within a short span of time, Moqtada al-Sadr and his movement became the face of the enemy, well before the Coalition identified the existence of an Sunni Arab-led insurgency that had little connection with the Sadrists. An enterprising investigative judge, Ra'ed Juhi, who would later work with the CPA, began a secret investigation into the circumstances of al-Khoei's murder, and unearthed evidence that seemed directly to implicate Moqtada al-Sadr. A warrant was then quietly issued for his arrest alongside a number of alleged accomplices. Iraqi liberals and secularists, who still wielded considerable influence on the CPA in its early days, encouraged the isolation of the Sadrists from the political process and their exclusion from the Governing Council.

The Najaf hierarchy's conditional acknowledgement of the CPA-led political process, starting with the formation of the Governing Council, gave Moqtada al-Sadr an important opening that he would fully exploit. His became the only Shi'a movement that voiced not only an uncompromising position on the occupation, but one that called for an alliance across sectarian boundaries to confront it. His supporters organised numerous public marches and demonstrations denouncing the occupation, and demanding the establishment of an Islamic government with clerical oversight.[13]

The CPA and Grand Ayatollah al-Sistani

The relationships of the occupying authorities and Grand Ayatollah al-Sistani were on an altogether different plane. The CPA considered the continuing acquiescence of the Grand Ayatollah in the broader outlines of the CPA's policies on the governing of Iraq, especially in the process that would lead to the transfer of full sovereignty to an Iraqi-led government, to be a matter of the highest importance. The Coalition simply could not afford to alienate the Najaf hierarchy, knowing full well that a simple decision or *fatwa* on the part of Sistani could derail the entire Coalition project. Sistani, however, scrupulously maintained a formal distance from the occupying authorities. He refused to meet any person associated directly with the Coalition, preferring to meet with intermediaries and Iraqi politicians.

Sistani's son, Muhammad Reza al-Sistani, a scholar in his own right, was the critical conduit to the Grand Ayatollah. He was perhaps the single most important influence on his thinking, even though Sistani would ultimately make the final decisions. Sistani frequently consulted with the other three grand ayatollahs of Najaf, all of whom discreetly gave precedence to his views and succeeded in maintaining a united front for the *Marji'iyya* of Najaf. Sistani had adopted a few key positions. First he had distanced himself from any overt support for the occupation. In subsequent rulings, he ordered an end to looting, the return of stolen property to local authorities, and forbade the revenge killings of Ba'athists.[14] Crucially, he called for the *ulema* of Iraq not to accept any positions of administrative or executive responsibility in any layer of government.[15] He expressed great unease about the ultimate motive for the invasion of Iraq and stressed the vital need to transfer power back to Iraqis as soon as possible.[16]

The CPA never fully appreciated Sistani's fidelity to preserving Islam's role in society and government, and confused his bare acknowledgement of the occupation with tolerance of the CPA's more controversial proposals. The CPA, in some instances resentfully,[17] admitted his power and mostly sought to accommodate him, but they never fully accepted the fact that a septuagenarian recluse, sitting on threadbare carpets on the floor of a modest house in Najaf, could block their plans. The first signs of a looming crisis between the CPA and Najaf related to the issue of drafting a new constitution for Iraq. Bremer had proposed that the new constitution be drawn up by expert Iraqis, and then presented to the public and endorsed by a referendum. This would be part of the process that would include the formation of an interim Iraqi administration – and that would conclude with the election of a sovereign government under the new constitution. Ayatollah Sistani, in a widely circulated *fatwa* of 1 July, categorically rejected the proposal to have the constitution written by unelected experts.

He then called for elections for a constituent assembly that would draft the constitution and then offer it to a referendum. Bremer tried to take the Ayatollah's edict in his stride, but insisted that no elections were possible in the near term given the absence of a census, a voter registration roll and any electoral boundaries.

The battle lines were drawn. Was Iraq's new constitution to be drawn up by experts, some under the influence of the CPA or who, anyway, shared their vision of Iraq; or was it to be drafted by an elected assembly that was likely to be dominated by Islamists?

First Rumblings of the Insurgency

The lawlessness in Baghdad and in most of the country did not equate to a political resistance as such, and was mainly due to criminality. It was clear that most of the Shi'a went along with the occupation for the time being. The Sunni Arabs were another matter, though. The first indications of Sunni Arab attitudes to the occupation occurred in Fallujah. Fallujah, in the middle of the tribal heartland of the Anbar province, was known for its conservative religious culture. The city had taken exception to the arrival of the troops who had taken up positions in the main municipal buildings and in a number of schools. Rumours began to circulate that the US army had been equipped with special binoculars that could see through people's clothes. This compounded the apparently heavy-handed patrolling and searches of homes, and led to a heightening of tensions.[18]

A series of demonstrations against the US presence culminated in a major incident in front of one of the schools occupied by the US army. Shooting broke out and nearly seventeen people were killed and over seventy-five wounded. In a follow-up demonstration, a further three people were killed by US fire. Grenades were thrown at the building, injuring seven US servicemen. The pattern of incidents continued in the town in the month of May and June 2003. By the end of summer, the people of Fallujah were openly boasting that they were in outright rebellion against the occupation.

In May, many reports mentioned hostility to the occupation in the towns and villages of the Upper Euphrates.[19] In Hit, US soldiers were confronted with angry crowds demanding a cessation of the ubiquitous search operations. They attacked both the town's municipal building and its police station, and burnt them down. In Ramadi, the capital of Anbar, drive-by shootings at American soldiers became a regular occurrence. In Baghdad's predominantly Sunni neighbourhood of al-Adhamiyya shoot-outs between US troops and armed groups erupted at the Abu Hanifa Mosque. The Imam of the mosque, in a sermon delivered on 6 June, 2003, openly called for resistance to the occupation.[20] His message was endorsed by scores of Sunni prayer leaders throughout the country. A series of small-scale attacks against American military convoys and checkpoints took place mainly in the Sunni triangle, and in the small towns and villages in the southern approaches to Baghdad. Iraqis cooperating with the CPA became assassination targets. By the end of June 2003, central Iraq appeared to be in the midst of a low-level, decentralised insurgency. This was vehemently denied by the CPA, the military and the politicians in Washington and London. Even star reporters talked about resistance and guerrilla attacks, but not an organised insurgency. It would take a brave and prescient academic, Professor Ahmed Hashim, to declare that Iraq was indeed in the throes of an insurgency.[21]

August 2003 was the month during which the actual dimensions of the insurgency, and its potential for derailing the plans for the occupation, began to emerge. On 7 August, a powerful car bomb tore into the Jordanian Embassy in Baghdad, killing eighteen people.[22] It was the worst attack on a non-military target since the end of formal hostilities. The motives for the bombing were not clear at first. Several theories were put forward, for instance that it was the work of the former regime's security agents or al-Qaeda operatives. The work was also attributed to groups that shared in the widespread anti-Jordanian sentiments in the country due to Jordan's apparent partiality to the former regime, and its recent decision to grant asylum to two of Saddam's daughters. By mid-August alarming reports began to be received by the CPA that al-Qaeda-related groups, especially the *Ansar al-Islam*, were planning an escalation of terrorist attacks.

Attack on the UN Headquarters in Baghdad and the Death of Sergio Vieira de Mello

On the afternoon of 19 August, a flatbed truck carrying about a ton of high explosives was detonated at the UN's Baghdad headquarters at the Canal Hotel. Twenty-two people were killed and 150 injured, some very seriously. Sergio de Mello was among those killed.[23] The bomb had exploded immediately below his office, which was demolished. The attack was the work of a suicide bomber. Eyewitnesses talked about a truck careering towards the building at high speed before exploding at the foot of de Mello's office. A group affiliated with al-Qaeda took credit for the operation. The UN in Baghdad was left leaderless, with its staff shocked and seriously demoralised. The UN had mistakenly believed that its neutrality and evident support for a quick restoration of sovereignty to Iraq would make it somehow 'different' from the occupiers and therefore immune to attack.

The logic of the incipient insurgency worked, however, in an altogether separate dimension. The UN, like all other international agencies operating in Iraq, was a soft target, and attacking it would drive home the insecurity and violence in the country. The UN did not respond immediately to the massive provocations of the attack on its headquarters. Its staff were still being augmented by new arrivals and there was no noticeable increase in security consciousness on the part of the staff. The CPA strengthened its perimeter defences around the UN compound, but Kofi Annan discounted evacuation. It took another suicide bomber to convince him otherwise. On 22 September, a bomb exploded in the parking lot, killing several Iraqi policemen. The UN senior directors in Baghdad then unanimously recommended to Kofi Annan the evacuation of all UN staff from Iraq. Kofi Annan accepted this but nevertheless kept a residual UN presence of about thirty international staffers in the country. The UN had effectively withdrawn from Iraq. As an institution it was traumatised by the bombing, the worst in its history.[24] Many blamed the UN Secretary General for agreeing to the Coalition's wish to allow the UN to re-enter Iraq with inadequate security arrangements, simply to send a 'business-as-usual' message.

The Murder of Ayatollah Baqir al-Hakim

On 24 August, in an ominous portent of things to come, Grand Ayatollah Muhammad Said al-Hakim was hurt by flying glass from a bomb that exploded as he was ending his evening prayers at his quarters in Najaf.[25] Three of his guards were killed by a further explosion. Some tried to portray it as part of an ongoing challenge to the authority of the senior Najaf Grand Ayatollahs by the followers of Moqtada al-Sadr. Thinly veiled accusations levelled against the Sadrists from both the established Shi'a political groups and the followers of the *Marji'iyya* became more vocal. Muhammad Baqir al-Mihri said, 'The majority of the Shi'a follow Sistani except the supporters of Moqtada al-Sadr. They have abandoned [the majority] because of the presence of former Ba'athists in their midst.' He went on to demand the arrest of the murderers of al-Khoei, and in a clear reference to Moqtada added 'even if the murderer wears religious garb and has an important social status'.[26] The more established Shi'a groups were concerned that the Coalition might be alienated from the Shi'a generally by the confrontational methods of the volatile Sadrists. There was a consensus amongst both the Najaf hierarchy and the leaders of the main Shi'a political groups that events were working to the advantage of the Shi'a and consolidation of their power. Al-Sadr's direct challenge to the Coalition was therefore an unwelcome diversion. This became even more pronounced when Moqtada al-Sadr called for the formation of a new Islamic army, the 'Jaysh al-Mahdi' or the Mahdi Army.[27] This would present a double challenge – to the Coalition and to the established parties – but none of the Shi'a establishment would directly challenge Moqtada al-Sadr and his as yet untested strength with the Shi'a masses.

On Friday, 29 August, as Ayatollah Baqir al-Hakim was emerging from the south entrance to the shrine of Imam Ali in Najaf, having just delivered the weekly sermon, he and nearly a hundred other people were killed by a powerful car bomb.[28] Chaos and pandemonium broke out as worshippers, fearing another bomb, struggled to leave the shrine area. His death was at first received with shock and disbelief, and then with anger and sorrow. In the few weeks before his death the Ayatollah had established himself as the key Shi'a political leader and, by his carefully crafted statements, as the voice of moderation. While formally rejecting the occupation, Ayatollah Baqir al-Hakim had sought a limited degree of cooperation with the CPA, and had placed considerable hopes on the Governing Council as a preparatory step on the way to the transfer of full sovereignty. No one took responsibility for the blast. Wild theories proliferated, with some holding the Sadrists as the prime suspects. But it was clear that, given the sophistication of the device and the split second timing of the blast, it could only have been perpetrated by experts in explosives. The police investigation into the bombing concluded that it had the same markings as the UN bombing earlier that month. Fingers were pointed at the intelligence operatives of the former regime or elements from al-Qaeda. The Governing Council was at first unsure how to handle the disaster.[29] Eventually it declared three days of public mourning. Nearly half a million people attended Ayatollah Baqir al-Hakim's funeral procession in Najaf.

The murder of Ayatollah Baqir al-Hakim was a devastating blow to the Shi'a Islamists and of course to SCIRI itself. The Ayatollah had moulded SCIRI around his person, and his leadership was unquestioned. His position on the occupation and his guarded cooperation with the Coalition established the precedent that allowed for an acceptable degree of engagement between Shi'a Islamists and the CPA. While his speeches were peppered with often unfavourable remarks about the Coalition and the need to transfer authority to Iraqis as soon as possible, his true position was far more nuanced. The complex of motives that governed his decision-making ranged across potentially contradictory objectives. Thus an early departure of the Coalition had to be balanced against the possibility that the Ba'ath and its new-found allies amongst radical Sunni Islamists could mount a comeback. Ignoring the US-sponsored Governing Council could result in Shi'a Islamists being excluded from power as well as possibly alienating the Coalition as a useful ally in the post-war power struggle with other groups. His legacy to the Iraqi opposition was immense and it was under his tutelage that a number of strategic relationships were forged.

The murder of Ayatollah Baqir al-Hakim capped a month of escalating violence. The bombings in particular crystallised the nature of the resistance that the Coalition was about to face, but few were prepared to acknowledge a persistent pattern. This could provide a basis for arguing that an insurgency existed or was about to be born, which would undermine their sunny composure. The attacks were seen as the work of 'dead-enders', or by what became euphemistically known as FREs – former regime elements. It would have been a dangerous volte-face if any other explanation to the persistent insecurity in Iraq was admitted. There was always the perception that the invading force would be widely welcomed by a grateful Iraqi public. To link the continuing violence in post-war Iraq to a possible miscalculation about the response of Iraqis, Arabs and Muslims to this exceptional act was to risk opening once again the whole debate about the war. But this had to be confronted. After the initial shock of occupation wore off, the politics of the country began to be overwhelmed by power struggles pitting all kinds of groups against each other, of which the CPA was wilfully ignorant. The problem was that the Coalition's project for Iraq was ill thought out and poorly executed. Its opponents knew what they wanted – or more accurately, they knew exactly what they didn't want.

The Insurgency Crystallises

At first it was unclear whether Saddam planned the growing resistance to the presence of Coalition forces and to the radical plans in prospect for the new Iraq as part of a post-war strategy.[30] The former regime was not capable of mounting a serious military challenge to an invasion force. The absence of any WMD in Iraq's arsenal was known for certain by the top leadership of the Ba'athist regime, and without unconventional weapons the Iraqi forces were no match for the Coalition. In the summer of 2003, however, reports were still heard of the existence of a detailed post-war resistance plan, minutely crafted by the Ba'ath Party and involving the widespread looting and destruction of state property and vital records after the fall of Baghdad. The reality, which only emerged much later, was different. The Ba'ath regime was in fact preoccupied with two very different issues. The first was how to deal with the ever-growing threat from the United States. The last weeks of the Saddamist regime were based on a denial of the imminence of war and the dismissal by Saddam (until it was too late) of any plans for the defence of strategic sites, let alone the country as a whole. Saddam's fear, which permeated the entire military and intelligence apparatus, was that a replay of the 1991 uprising would take place – and that this time it would be successful.[31] He countered the possibility of another Shi'a insurrection by creating and arming the *Fedayeen Saddam*, paramilitary units under the command of his son, Uday. These were issued with light weapons, inadequate to meet a serious military threat, but sufficient to guard Ba'ath Party offices effectively and keep any uprising at bay. Saddam was greatly concerned that the American strategy was not so much about invading the country; rather, through intensive bombings and undercover sabotage, to create the conditions for a Shi'a uprising.

The fear of a serious domestic challenge to its power was what governed the military strategy of the former regime. This led to the dispersal of the main *Fedayeen Saddam* force to the towns and villages of the South, not to counter an invasion, which it was patently incapable of doing, but to keep the population in check. Similarly, Saddam's deployment of the regular army soldiers was not so much to block the progress of an invading force but more to do with keeping Iran out of Iraq in case of a breakdown in general law and order, which is what happened in 1991. The fearful and confused response to the Coalition's invading force was a clear indication that the Ba'ath regime did not expect the US threats to actually materialise in the form of an invasion. It is therefore improbable to attribute to Saddam and the Ba'ath Party planners any role in the post-war insurgency that actually materialised. To talk of Saddam's post-war strategy is to deny the clear evidence that he was planning to counter an uprising, and not a military occupation of the country. When the invasion did take place, his fear of an uprising continued to dominate his thinking, and he refused to counter any deployment of his main military units that might have had the potential of weakening his response to a popular uprising. The fact that Saddam was unsure how to respond to an invasion once it had taken place, however, does not invalidate the preparations that the regime had made to resist its own possible overthrow. The Ba'ath had always been paranoid about its removal from power – by coup, assassination, civil war or insurrection. Former Ba'athists amply confirmed the existence of elaborate contingency plans for the Ba'ath Party's return to power in the event of its overthrow, including activation of sleeper cells, establishing second- and third-tier command structures, and the stashing of funds in foreign accounts. The Ba'ath regime prepared for an insurgency in the event of its overthrow and established the patterns of resistance, communications and organisation that would make that possible. The actual insurgency evolved partly as a result of the existence of such contingency arrangements, but mostly as a result of an amalgam of other forces that came together, jointly and separately, to oppose the Coalition.

There was huge weapons stockpiling in secret locations, and a core of regime loyalists were trained in sabotage and covert operations in the eventuality that they had to fight their way back to power.[32] It was this disparate group of select Ba'ath Party operatives, security agents, officers in the elite military formations, *Fedayeen Saddam* members and a few tribal leaders, shored up by criminal elements, that formed the nucleus of the insurgency. Evidence that such plans existed emerged in the investigative work done in the immediate post-war period by the myriad agencies that collected military, security and political information on the former regime. The Iraq Survey Group, the Defense Intelligence Agency, the CIA and British intelligence had all gathered together a huge trove of documents on the former regime's inner workings, and had interviewed hundreds, if not thousands, of people associated with it. In the autumn of 2002, the Ba'ath regime had trained over 1,000 selected officers from the intelligence services in guerrilla warfare and terrorist tactics. They were specifically instructed to prepare themselves to reconnect with each other in the event of the regime's collapse, and to operate within the framework of a decentralised, networked structure. A secret communications system, code-worded Project 111, was developed for this purpose. Another plan, Plan 459, evolved to attack water plants throughout the country.

The insurgency began to gel in the summer of 2003. Scattered attacks against the Coalition's forces in the early days did not augur the beginning of a long-term resistance. But the steady beat of assaults on the infrastructure of the country, especially the oil facilities, was another matter. It did not make sense to attack the country's infrastructure, except in the context of reducing the capacity of the state to manage the country's affairs. The destruction of the electricity pylons and transmission lines, and looting of key infrastructure facilities could be explained by the simple criminality of gangs that sought to profit from the melting down of metals for resale and the theft of expensive capital equipment. But destroying pipelines and pumping stations had no direct material benefit to the perpetrators; it could only be explained as part of a plan to reduce the resource base of the governing authorities and to increase the cost of occupation. On 12 June, 2003, the main pipeline carrying Iraqi crude from the northern oil fields to Ceyhan in Turkey was attacked, launching the 'pipeline war'. This war was a constant struggle between saboteurs trying to shut down Iraq's oil exports and repair crews, and a variety of installation protection forces trying to stop them from doing so.[33] A few days later, there was an explosion at the main refinery in Baiji. This became the harbinger of numerous attacks and explosions on Iraq's refinery capacity and the pipelines that fed them with fuel stock. The infrastructure war began in earnest in the summer of 2003, aimed at creating a fuel shortage inside Iraq, reducing the revenue base of the country and impeding the supply of power to the public. The political advantages of such terrorist attacks would multiply as they began to reveal the inability of the occupying power to provide a basic level of services to the public.

In the first four months after the fall of Baghdad, there were about 200 serious incidents of armed resistance across the country.[34] Their effects on the Coalition were minimal, but their lethal effects grew over time. Most attacks were in the form of shooting incidents, but the number of ambushes was also significant, increasing markedly over the period. The use of rocket-propelled grenades (RPGs) also increased, raising the threshold of attacks as RPGs were especially effective against lightly armoured vehicles. So-called 'quality' attacks, those implying a high degree of organisation and control, began to emerge during this period. The majority of such attacks were in the Baghdad area and in the Sunni Triangle. It was difficult for the Coalition to discern the existence of any command organisation behind these attacks. There was clearly no national resistance structure that one could point to. At the same time, although some attacks were by individuals using widely available weaponry, the inference could not be drawn that they were the work of isolated people as individual responses to the occupation. Most attacks were effected by small groups, frequently not exceeding ten people, who would mount squad-size attacks in a fairly sophisticated and coordinated way, and would then disperse into the local community.[35] Certain towns had a number of these groups, which suggested that there existed if not regional, at least town or city-wide, organisation. By the end of August 2003, the military's public estimate of active resisters to the occupation ranged from a low of 5,000 to a high of about 10,000 people. But private estimates about the tenacity of the insurgency were more alarming. It was not so much because of the large numbers of fighters who were involved in the insurgency but because of the assessment as to the depth and nature of support for the insurgents.

Support for the Insurgency

Support for the insurgency crossed a number of hitherto separate boundaries and stirred deeply held passions.[36] At the most pedestrian level, it was a simple yearning for a return to power by those who had exercised it for far too long. But at another level, the appropriation by the insurgents of the symbols and rhetoric of national resistance to the foreign occupier masked a far more complex array of motives, not all of them noble. The easiest to understand was Iraqi patriotism, a revulsion at the invasion of the country by foreign armies, and a feeling that Iraq's integrity as a country had been violated. But this was a minority view. The Kurds welcomed the invasion of the country and could not, by any stretch of the imagination, be considered as proponents of the Iraqi patriotic line. Their connection to the Iraqi state was non-existent and their loyalty to Iraq as a country was sorely tested by their oppression by the state over the previous thirty years.

The loyalty of the majority Shi'a was to the country, not to the state. The state, which they may have briefly equated with the country during the Iran–Iraq War, ceased to command their support and respect. The overthrow of a tyrannical regime to some extent balanced their reluctance to admit to a long-term presence of foreign armies in Iraq. They conditionally tolerated the Coalition's presence and their toleration was determined by the extent to which their relative power as a community would be enhanced by a guarded cooperation with the Coalition. Any resistance on their part in the early days was more connected to the ongoing factional struggles for power within the Shi'a community, in particular the rise of the Sadrist Movement as a potent force and a major player in Iraqi politics. The anti-Coalition stance of Moqtada al-Sadr never extended to a systematic campaign against the presence of foreign forces in Iraq. It was more to do with the use of force to accompany the claims of the movement to a dominant place in Shi'a, if not Iraqi, politics. Even so, although they would never acknowledge any debt that they may have had to the Coalition for overthrowing Saddam, the Sadrists' public posture was based on a patriotic rejection of the occupation. No other Shi'a group shared the Sadrists' rejection of dealing with the Coalition and their frequently violent resistance to it.

The Iraqi 'nationalist' resistance was thus a misnomer. The appellation conveniently overlooked the fact that the majority – specifically the Kurdish and most of the Shi'a population – did not support violent resistance to the Coalition. It was the Sunni Arabs who rejected the occupation in its entirety and refused to countenance any long-term changes to the political structure of the country that were based on it. The early policies of the Coalition regarding de-Ba'athification and the dissolution of the Iraqi armed forces may have provided a valid justification for the growing acts of resistance to the occupation, but the fact remained that it was the Sunni Arab community that felt most threatened by the new arrangements. Whatever the policies were that the Coalition chose to pursue would have been met with the same degree of suspicion and hostility by the Sunni Arabs – short of a return to the status quo ante. There was a widespread feeling in the Sunni Arab community that it was by a freak of history that a decades-old, if not centuries-old, order had been unnaturally overturned. Whatever individuals might have felt about the directions in which Saddam and the Ba'ath Party were taking Iraq, it could not warrant acceptance of such a dramatic upending of the political order. It was this sense of loss and disempowerment that fed the main wellsprings of the 'nationalist' resistance.

The main protagonists in the early days of the insurgency were former Ba'athists – colonels and majors from the elite formations and their equivalent ranks in the intelligence, security and Ba'ath Party apparatus.[37] Small groups began to coalesce around leaders drawn from the middle ranks of the former regime. They were loosely coordinated with Ba'ath Party leaders who were still on the run, and who were able to provide them with direction and funds. It is unclear how far Saddam himself played a part in mobilising these teams, but it is known that a number of clandestine meetings were held between him and leaders of these groups during the insurgency's early period. The role of Saddam's deputy, Izzat al-Douri, who remained at liberty, may also have been important in these crucial first weeks.[38] Money was not a problem,[39] and an elaborate chain for funnelling the required resources was developed to cater to the financial requirements of these small insurgent groups. The early insurgency was very much an Iraqi-led affair, designed to create conditions of chaos and insecurity in the country and to act as the nucleus for expanding the scale and scope of the insurrection. If it had a political programme, it was more to do with the distant hope of returning the Ba'ath Party to power. Epithets, such as *Hizb al-ʿAwda* (the Party of Return), which were used by the insurgents to take credit for certain operations indicated the early insurgents' Ba'athist roots. But in the long term, the Ba'athists had little hope of galvanising the resistance. The former regime was too unpopular and its ideology too full of holes to be taken seriously as a rallying unit for a prolonged war of resistance. What the Ba'ath Party could do, however, was to provide the entry point into the various units of government, relying on the tens of thousands of its members who still retained a residual loyalty to the former regime. They would prove the invaluable insiders for the insurgency as it grew in size and sophistication.

The Scope of the Insurgency

The denial of the existence of an insurgency permeated the entire CPA-governing apparatus throughout the early period. Underlying this smug indifference was a misplaced confidence in the ability of the Coalition to contain and defeat what were still thought of as the desperate acts of the remnants of a defunct regime. Very little thought was given to the root causes behind the violence and the palpable hostility of the Sunni Arabs to the new order. The absence of any overarching structure to the insurgency diminished its significance. The insurgent groups that went under a bewildering array of names were seen as little more than ad hoc bodies, and destined to disappear as the post-war order consolidated itself. In fact, it was the very dispersion of the insurgents into a myriad of organisations and groups that proved its true strength and capacity for long-term resistance.

The failure of the intelligence apparatus of the Coalition, both military and civilian, to penetrate the insurgency and to forestall its increasingly lethal attacks was also marked. This was partly owing to the absence of any serious planning for post-war stabilisation operations, which would have certainly included measures to prevent the rise of an insurgency. At the same time, the obsession with finding WMD diverted a great deal of resources and manpower from the vital task of intelligence-gathering, allowing precious time for the consolidation of the insurgency. The feeble resources at the disposal of the Iraqi government could in no way fill the glaring vacuum in intelligence on the insurgency. The police were barely functioning, while the intelligence-gathering capabilities of the political parties were either poor or were concentrated on other tasks. The Kurdish parties, with perhaps the most sophisticated intelligence-gathering operations, were naturally focused on security in Kurdistan. The Islamist parties, whose own intelligence-gathering activities were bolstered by Iranian operatives, were also far more concerned with securing their own control over Shi'a territories and uncovering Ba'athists in their midst. This left the smaller parties such as the INC and INA to provide what little information they could gather, but the onus of intelligence-gathering fell to the intelligence officers of the military and the CIA.

The CIA had started its mission in Iraq with less than a hundred operatives.[40] Its operations in Iraq were hampered by a shortage of trained personnel who were Arabic speakers, and by the high turnover in its staff. The increasing insecurity also hampered the operations of the Agency. Officers of the CIA could not freely travel without conspicuous armed bodyguards. This severely impacted on the Agency's ability to recruit Iraqi spies and to monitor and supervise their operations. As one officer said, 'How do you do your job that way? You can't . . . They don't know what's going on out there.'[41] Three separate CIA station chiefs served in the brief nine-month period after the fall of the regime. The second may have been replaced because of the leak of a pessimistic CIA report that appeared in November 2003. The report stated that a growing number of Iraqis were supporting the resistance, and believed that the insurgency would be able to defeat the USA.[42] The failure of the CIA to come to grips with the insurgency was in sharp contrast to its success in helping to locate most of the Saddam regime's leadership. Belatedly, the CIA expanded its scope of operations in Iraq until, by the spring of 2004, it had more than 300 full-time case officers, and over 500 personnel in total. The CIA office in Iraq became the biggest in the world.[43] But the CIA still faced the same difficulties in penetrating the insurgency and gaining 'actionable' intelligence on it.

The insurgency that the CIA and other intelligence agencies were supposed to penetrate was a complex of organisations and groups that kept a decentralised and amorphous structure to their operations.[44] Broadly, they were

divided into two major constellations. The first was grouped around the operations of the al-Qaeda affiliate in Iraq, now under the command of Zarqawi,
comprising al-Qaeda and groups bearing names such as *Jaysh Ahl-ul-Sunna*,
(The Army of the People of the Sunna) and *Jaysh al-Taifa al-Mansoura* (The
Army of the Victorious Party). They would later be formally organised under
the rubric of *Majlis Shoura al-Mujahideen* (The *Mujahideen* Advisory
Council). This element of the insurgency specialised in spectacular terrorist
acts, including car bombings, suicide bombings, and mass killings of innocent
civilians. They also launched the brutal beheadings that were taped and widely
circulated to the media. It mainly comprised foreign and Iraqi terrorists,
committed to the utilisation of terror as a form of warfare of choice. It was
organised according to the principle of *Imara*, the appointment of *Amirs*, a
theological term for an undisputed local leader, to command local cells of
fighters. The second constellation of insurgents was more diversified and
overwhelmingly Iraqi in composition. It included over ten identified groups,
with numerous sub-divisions, operating in various parts of central and
northern Iraq. The most prominent were the *Jaysh al-Islami al-Iraqi* (The
Islamic Army of Iraq), *Jaysh 'Umar* (The Army of Omar), *Jaysh Muhammad*
(The Army of Muhammad) and *Kataib Thawrat al-'Ishrin* (The Battalions of
the 1920 Uprising). Some of these groups were primarily tribal affiliations;
others were organised by the former regime's intelligence officers or by regular
military officers. *Jaysh 'Umar*, for example, was founded by a former colonel
in Saddam's *Mukhabarat*, Khudhair Abbas al-Obaidi. Its modus operandi
involved the extensive use of improvised explosive devises (IEDs) against
Coalition forces, and targeted killings of police officers. It numbered about
3,000 people, including nearly a hundred from a single extended family. The
leadership of this group was primarily drawn from former senior officers
in the dissolved army. The Islamic Army of Iraq included mainly Salafist
insurgents under the leadership of former intelligence officers. According to
a French journalist, Georges Malbrunot, who had been abducted by the group
and held captive for nearly four months, the Islamic Army had upwards of
15,000 members. The group appeared to him to be well organised, well
equipped and well funded.[45]

Insurgents were held together by three factors: family loyalties, tribal affiliations or a commitment to an extreme form of Islamism – and frequently all
three – which made these groups difficult to penetrate. They also benefited
from the implicit support that was given them by broad swathes of opinion in
the Sunni Arab community, which made the recruitment of spies and infiltrators into their ranks an even more difficult task. The cell-like organisation
that formed and disbanded for particular tasks also contributed to the problems in penetrating these organisations. After the Fallujah battles, the insurgents avoided set-piece encounters with the US military, preferring to follow

a strategy of oozing into territory that was insufficiently guarded and melting away when the Coalition attacked in force. The many arrests of insurgent suspects, reaching at some point to over 20,000 able-bodied males in custody, did not significantly drain away the recruitment pool. Neither did the large fatalities incurred by the insurgents whenever they encountered an American force seem to dent their abilities to replenish their losses.

The insurgency's bombing campaign began in the summer of 2003. The summer's car bombs were nearly all rigged by Abu Umar al-Kurdi, a Zarqawi associate. After his arrest in early 2005, al-Kurdi confessed to the car bombs that targeted the Jordanian Embassy in July 2003, the UN headquarters in August 2003 and the devastating car bomb that killed Ayatollah Baqir al-Hakim.[46] Al-Kurdi's services were available to the burgeoning insurgent groups, and they often employed him in the early days on targets against police stations and recruitment centres. The former *Mukhabarat* was also put to use by the insurgent groups. They quickly discovered who was supportive of or collaborating with the new order. Intimidation could then be quickly employed against these people and those who might follow in their steps, through warnings, abductions, death threats and assassinations. Whenever large numbers of such people had assembled, as in recruitment centres for the police or the military, suicide bombings might be used. The killing sprees targeted all manners of people, from local and provincial officials, teachers, truck drivers carrying supplies to the military or the CPA, canteen workers to day-labourers, cleaners and laundresses. The aim was to force the government to lose control over the streets, and to create a sense of foreboding and perpetual anxiety. The momentum in this direction grew to irresistible levels by the end of 2003, even though the CPA, the Governing Council and the Cabinet were still ignorant about the scope of the insurgency. Whole neighbourhoods slipped into the insurgents' control as they began to flaunt their power publicly. In some neighbourhoods, 'renunciation' centres were formed, where those who had been warned could publicly dissociate themselves from the CPA and the government.[47] The insurgency began to shape the public mind to its inevitable victory.

Militant Sunni Islam and the Insurgency

In the summer of 2003, the home-grown Islamist/Salafist trend amongst Iraq's Sunni Arabs arose to stake a claim to the leadership of the insurgency. They combined the rhetoric of the nationalists with a commitment to militant Sunni Islam, motivating their fighters with a hatred for the occupation and a religious requirement to struggle against it. Their best-known organisation was the Army of Muhammad, a group that had a connection with former regime elements, but which had developed an overlay of Islamist ideology to distinguish itself. Its reputed leader was a former Republican Guard Chief of

Staff. These Islamist/nationalist groups took advantage of the increased religiosity of Sunni society in Iraq of the later Saddam period, and were able to recruit from a pool of young people who had imbibed the message of Saddam's Faith Campaign. They referred to themselves as *mujahideen* (faith warriors), thus clearly imbuing their fight with the Coalition with religious imagery. Their relations with Saddam loyalists were often frayed, as they evolved from two separate traditions.

Sunni Islamists had frequently been treated harshly by the Saddam regime. But faced with a common enemy and a fear that Iraq was to be handed over to the Shi'a made the Sunni Islamists and former Ba'athists allies – at least until the early Ba'athist-led insurgency became overshadowed by the Islamists.[48] They had sunk deep roots into the heartland of al-Anbar province, the city of Mosul, in the towns and villages that covered Baghdad's southern approaches, and in the Sunni neighbourhoods of Baghdad. These roots were further strengthened by the network of family, clan and tribal relations that are critical to the functioning and ordering of Iraqi society. Mosques were the most effective recruiting centres for these groups. Major mosques, such as Baghdad's Umm-ul-Qura Mosque and the historic Abu Hanifa complex were important elements in mobilising Sunni Arab opinion.[49] They became open centres for insurgents' proselytising and fund-raising. Friday prayer leaders used their *minbars* to extol the virtues of the 'resistance', and to encourage the congregation to support it by word and deed. The Sunni Arab *ulema* had been noticeably less politically active than their Shi'a counterparts, but the rise of a purist or Salafi strain within Sunni Islam, encouraged mainly by Saudi Arabia, led to the emergence of a class of politically active and intolerant clerics. This phenomenon, with important modifications, had migrated to Iraq in the last years of Saddam. It led to the rise of Sunni clerics who were prepared to challenge the assumptions of their own community aggressively. Not only did they disparage their own community for its 'laxness' and poor religious observance, but they began to ridicule the Shi'a and their rituals publicly. This undoubtedly contributed to the escalation in sectarian thinking and the erosion of the degree of intercommunal tolerance that was essential for maintaining social stability in Iraq. Some Sunni Arabs openly rejected the Coalition and the occupation, including the most important hard-line Sunni Arab political organisation, *Haya'at 'Ulama al-Muslimin* (Association of Muslim Scholars, AMS).

Association of Muslim Scholars

The Association of Muslim Scholars (AMS) was founded immediately after the fall of Baghdad. The group took over the massive *Umm-al-Maarik* (Mother of All Battles) Mosque in Baghdad, which they renamed the *Umm-*

ul-Qura (The Mother of all Cities, the Quranic name for Mecca) Mosque. (The mosque's minarets were designed by Saddam in the shape of Scud missiles.) The AMS grouped a number of leading clerics, including the imams of the mosques of Abu Hanifa and the Gailani shrine, under the leadership of Hareth al-Dhari. He had attended the Sunni world's most prestigious religious institution, Cairo's Al-Azhar University. Dhari seemed to have come up against Saddam in the late 1990s, and was forced to flee the country, only to return after the fall of the regime. Hareth's son, Muthanna al-Dhari, also played a prominent role in the AMS, mainly as its indefatigable advocate in the regional media. Abd el-Salam al-Kubaisi acted as the AMS's official spokesman.[50]

The AMS soon laid claim to the mantle of implacable resistance to the occupation. In a series of articles, it developed the theme of *fiqh al-muqawamma* (the jurisprudence of resistance).[51] The AMS's chief ideologue, Muhammad 'Ayash al-Kubaisi, developed the Islamic basis of the insurgency, rooting it in the inalienable right of people to resist invaders, irrespective of the invaders' motives. He proclaimed resistance to be a form of *jihad* and considered it a *fardh'ayn*, an obligatory duty on each and every believer. This stands in stark contrast to another principle in Islamic jurisprudence of *fardh kifaya*, a duty whose obligatory nature is discharged if anyone else is under-taking it. Thus joining the resistance becomes an insistent duty that is in the same category as the normal obligatory acts of a believer, such as prayer or fasting. The AMS was careful, however, to reject random acts of violence against innocents within its exposition on the legal doctrine of resistance. It insisted that legitimate resistance could only target the occupier and his allies. For a while the AMS seemed to be the only Sunni institution not connected with the former regime that was not co-opted in one way or another by the CPA.

The AMS was the only Sunni Arab organisation prepared to support the insurgency openly, while at the same time eschewing its own recourse to violence. It tried to set itself up as the guardian of both Sunni Arab and Iraqi interests, using its anti-occupation stance to reach out to the Shi'a, especially to the apparently like-minded Sadrists. The AMS developed the principle of refusing to participate in any political process under the tutelage of the occupation authorities, and refused to countenance or legitimate any formal dealings with the CPA and the Governing Council.

Foreign *Jihadis*

Another strand to the evolving insurgency was the flow of foreign Islamist, mainly Arab, fighters into Iraq, the so-called *jihadis*. These groups were not of the same ilk as those that had assembled in Baghdad to fend off the American army in the last days of the Ba'ath regime before the fall of Baghdad. Those who had escaped capture or death made their way back from whence they had come, deeply disillusioned by their experience and their apparent betrayal by the Saddamist forces. The new *jihadis* flowing into Iraq were far more dangerous, disciplined and ruthless than the ragtag groups that thought they were defending Arab honour at the gates of Baghdad. A steady stream of these people began to seep into Iraq during the summer of 2003. They were mainly young Arabs fired by preachers in their home country who had portrayed Iraq as a land of *jihad* where the forces of evil have to be confronted. The *jihadis* would often arrive in Damascus and then be transported via circuitous routes into western Iraq, where they would be housed and assigned to one of the insurgent cells. This network had to rely on an extensive financial and logistical support system, both inside Iraq and in neighbouring countries, notably Syria. The Coalition's inexcusable abandonment of Iraq's frontiers, without any border controls, facilitated the task of moving these *jihadis* into Iraq. For several months after the fall of Baghdad no entry requirements of any kind were required for people coming into the country. They only had to present (frequently forged) travel documents to a Coalition patrol or checkpoint, undergo a cursory inspection, and they were then allowed in. The CPA had no strict population control measures. Documents such as passports, identity cards and weapons permits were not standardised, and the CPA continued to allow the use of Saddam-era documents, which were easily forged.

The CPA claimed that it had 2,500 personnel guarding Iraq's frontiers in August 2003 – a clearly insufficient number. On the Iraq–Iran frontier, Iranian pilgrims heading for Iraq's holy sites swamped border crossings. Arab fighters, frequently coming from Afghanistan and using clandestine routes, might easily mingle with the crowds and gain access into Iraq. The CPA created the Department of Border Enforcement, which was given a large variety of functions, some of which, such as customs, later had to be transferred back into the more appropriate ministries. In spite of the house-cleaning that supposedly took place as a result of the formation of the Border Enforcement Department, a large number of its staff were connected to the insurgency, criminal rackets or local tribal strongmen – and frequently all three. The borders stayed porous, enforcement was weak, and the flow of foreign insurgents continued unabated. The build-up of the foreign fighters was gradual over the summer and autumn of 2003. In the summer of 2003, the foreign fighters had not yet honed their tactics of suicide bombings and beheadings that characterised their later operations. They were still an auxiliary force to be used, usually as cannon fodder, at the behest of the mainly Ba'athist-dominated insurgency.

The *Ansar al-Islam* group that was active in Iraqi Kurdistan regrouped after the US bombing of their bases. In the spring and summer of 2003, small groups of the Ansar returned via Iran. They roamed the country seeking suitable targets for their attacks, and linked up with a number of insurgent cells, especially those connected with former regime loyalists. They appeared to have coordinated their terrorist attacks with the al-Qaeda network, and had accepted the military leadership of Abu Musab al-Zarqawi. By the end of 2003, the terrorist network associated with Zarqawi began to take shape, and it was to call the shots thereafter for all foreign terrorist organisations operating in Iraq.

The Coalition, the CPA and the Evolving Insurgency

The CPA ignored the threats from the evolving insurgency. A link of sorts was made between the provision of jobs for the masses of unemployed and the persistence of violent resistance – if there were no jobs, the unemployed would be likely to persist in violent resistance. This became a mantra for a while. But the CPA persisted in maintaining its blindly optimistic interpretation of events because of a deep unwillingness to veer from the scripted lines. Straying from the received version of events was unacceptable, and this rigid thinking compounded the entrapment of most senior officials into a 'group-think'. The CPA, reflecting its Washington overseers, was not prepared to indulge in 'nuanced' thinking, a term of opprobrium in the Bush inner circles. This would have opened the door to rendering the analysis of Iraq's conditions as extremely complex, and in the process would undermine the official US thinking about Iraq. This was that the invasion of Iraq was liberation; the vast majority of people welcomed the Coalition; Iraqis who resisted were standing against the forces of freedom and democracy; and reconstruction and prosperity were just around the corner. The reality of the situation was paid scant attention, at least publicly. This was that thirty years of dictatorship, one-party rule and militarisation of society had its own, sizeable, community of adherents; that up-ending established power relations built over decades, if not centuries, was bound to have a dramatic effect; that freeing bottled-up passions ranging from thwarted national aspirations to a deeply felt sense of victimisation might boil over into radical political demands. There was also the negative response of Arab and Islamic countries to the brazen intrusion of a superpower into the heart of the Middle East. The CPA was using a simple, if not simplistic, navigational chart to guide its progress in dangerous waters, and the comfort and cushion provided by the Coalition's forces were insufficient.

The CPA veered from its 'dead-enders' description of the insurgency to one where the culprits were foreign *jihadis* and terrorists in alliance with former Ba'athist loyalists. It also insisted on trivialising its opponents. For example, progress was measured against arrests or the killing of the names and faces on a deck of cards that was produced to embody the 'enemy'. The dwindling number of faces on the cards still at large did not seem to have a noticeable effect on the level of violence. For example, the killing of Saddam's two sons, Uday and Qusay, in an intense fire fight inside a safe-house in Mosul in late July 2003 did not materially affect the insurgency. It was claimed, however, that they were linchpins of the insurgency and their death presented as extremely important. '[The death of Uday and Qusay] was a landmark day for the people and for the future of Iraq. Every single day we get closer to a secure and stable environment that will allow this country to flourish,' exulted General Ricardo Sanchez in a news conference.[52]

This categorisation of the insurgents translated into ineffective military actions against the insurgency. With the dismantling of the armed forces and the security apparatus, the Coalition had no Iraqi component to its security strategy. The measures that were used to confront the insurgents were mainly ineffective. They were also deeply offensive to the cultural and religious mores of what was still a tribal society. It is not so much that the US forces deliberately trampled over these sensibilities, rather that they were generally ignorant of them. The searching of homes without the presence of a male head of household, body searches of women, the use of sniffer dogs, degrading treatment of prisoners, public humiliation of the elderly and notables, all contributed to the view that the Americans had only disdain and contempt for Iraq's traditions. These stories of American insensitivity to local customs grew in the telling and became in the hands of the insurgents and their sympathisers a deliberate programme on the part of the USA to undermine the religious and cultural roots of the country. Such stories would grow in scale and effect after details emerged of the humiliation and degradation of prisoners in the notorious Abu Ghraib prison. It would take some time before the Coalition would wake up to the consequences of its poor appreciation of local values. But in the summer and early autumn of 2003, the insurgency was seen as narrowly based on the former regime elements and Rumsfeld's notions of 'dead-enders'. By November 2003, however, the persistent frequency of attacks against the Coalition, now numbering twenty to thirty per day, resulted in a reassessment of the source of violence in the country, at least by the military and the intelligence community.

In October 2003, a major study on the insurgency, embodied in a US National Intelligence Estimate (NIE), concluded that the insurgency was driven by local factors, and that it drew its strength from deep grievances and a widespread hostility to the presence of foreign troops. This came on the heel of a steady flow of intelligence reports that the insurgency was becoming rooted and spreading. But the Bush administration policymakers, who continued to repeat their conviction that the violent resistance was the work of former regime elements and foreign *jihadis*, essentially ignored the NIE. Robert Hutchings, then chairman of the National Intelligence Council, said, 'Frankly, senior officials simply weren't ready to pay attention to analysis that didn't conform to their own optimistic scenarios.'[53] In August 2003, Bush commented on the insurgency by making fatuous remarks such as 'There are some who feel like the conditions are such that they can attack us there. My answer is bring 'em on. . . . We've got the force necessary to deal with the security situation.'[54] Almost the entire US intelligence community, including the CIA, Defense Intelligence Agency (DIA) and the State Department's own intelligence bureau, had concluded that the insurgency was dangerous and might derail the Coalition's plans for building democracy and improving the economic situation. The National Intelligence Estimate which had been requested by the US military's Central Command could not break through the complacency barrier that prevailed in official policymaking circles.[55] It would have been too much of a volte-face in orthodox thinking, too soon after the overthrow of the Ba'ath regime.

The Absence of Shi'a–Sunni Coordination

One of the few encouraging signs for the policymakers in Washington and the CPA was the absence of any widespread cooperation between the Sunni and Shi'a communities in formulating a joint anti-Coalition strategy. The fact remained that while the vast majority of Sunni remained hostile to the Coalition's occupation, the majority of Shi'a felt that they could gain more by a guarded engagement with it, distasteful as that might be. Foreign forces were mainly concentrated in the Sunni Arab areas, and their absence from predominantly Shi'a areas removed a potential focus for Shi'a discontent. With the exception of a few incidents in Sadr City, the military kept well out of the major Shi'a concentrations in Baghdad and the cities of the South. In the three southernmost provinces, the British were primarily responsible for security. Their style of patrolling, as well as their paucity of numbers, resulted in very few confrontations with the overwhelmingly Shi'a population of the southern provinces. The intrusive and frequently oppressive presence of US troops in the Sunni Triangle had no equivalent in the Shi'a areas. The Shi'a were not subject to the heavy-handed security measures that played a large part in crystallising anti-Coalition feelings in the Sunni areas. Shi'a leaders were cautious in their public response to the insurgency. While mouthing platitudes about the rights of resistance to an invader, they were careful not to provide any legitimacy to an insurgency that carried the signatures of two of their most implacable enemies: the former Ba'athist ruling class, and the intolerant, Salafi-minded, Islamists.

Nevertheless, the potential for the growth in Shi'a resistance to the occupation was always there. It depended on progress – or lack of progress – on three vital areas of concern to the Shi'a. First, there was the issue of restoring power and sovereignty to Iraqis and, by inference, the redistribution of power in favour of the Shi'a majority. Second, there were bread-and-butter issues related to the restoration of basic services, reducing unemployment and improving living standards. Third, there were the issues related to the re-imposition of law and order, the containment of terrorism and making sure the return of the old order, in whatever guise, did not occur. In the summer and autumn of 2003, from the Shi'a perspective there did not seem to be sufficient grounds to withhold support for the political process. The formation of the Governing Council and the Cabinet, and the open acknowledgement by the CPA of its desire to introduce a constitutional and democratic order in Iraq appeared to address the issue of returning political control over the country back into indigenous hands. As a result, as far as the Shi'a were concerned, the Sadrists were the only people who were openly discontented during this period. The inability of the CPA to restore basic services and to staunch the deterioration in the law and order sectors worked to the advantage of the most radical elements in the Shi'a community. The Sadrists cemented their hold over Sadr City as they began to replace the absent state in providing basic services.

The New Iraqi Security Forces

The growing insurgency, continuing lawlessness and the evident stretching of the Coalition's forces led to an acceleration of the plans to construct and deploy new Iraqi security forces. The CPA had anticipated this and planned to develop a 'New Iraqi Army', but this could not be trained, equipped and deployed until well into the future. The more immediate security needs required the reconstitution of the old police forces and the creation of a military auxiliary force that would free the Coalition forces to fight insurgents. The Ba'athist police force had been notorious for its corruption and incompetence. The Coalition tried to rely on the old police force to preserve the peace, but within a short while it became clear that the police were completely incapable of providing security.

In early encounters with insurgents, the police were hopelessly outclassed and outgunned. The Coalition had called on former policemen to report for duty who had supposedly been vetted by CPA civilian advisers. The actual responsibility for oversight of the Iraqi police, however, was allocated to the Coalition's military police, who disregarded the competence and skills of these recruits.[56] The CPA quickly found that it had employed a large number of people who had criminal records, no police experience, or who were illiterate.

A basic three-week course was deemed sufficient to 'graduate' new police officers. The results were at best perfunctory. Seeking a long-term transformation
of the Iraqi police, the CPA embarked on an expensive training programme
for thousands of police recruits in specially constructed facilities in Jordan.
Allegations of theft and corruption dogged the programme. The state of the
Iraqi police by the end of 2003 was deplorable. Weak, poorly led and
equipped, corrupt and infiltrated, they were no match for the insurgents.

It was not only the break-up of the army and the former security services
that opened the way for the insurgents to organise themselves. A security
vacuum was allowed to develop. The catalogue of errors – in planning, judgement, understanding and execution – was so wide-ranging as to border on the
inexplicably negligent. They stretched from inadequate on-the-ground forces,
failure to break up the security and intelligence services of the old regime, lax
border controls, toleration of looting and property destruction, insufficient
understanding of the consequences of disbanding the armed forces, to incompetent and corrupt military contractors. The insurgency was not inevitable by
any stretch of the imagination, even though some form of ongoing resistance
would have been probable. But there was no reason why it could not have been
contained, and possibly defeated, at its inception.

The early counter-insurgency campaign was notably ineffective. Indeed some
have concluded that the faulty US counter-insurgency strategy and tactics
played a part in cementing the insurgency.[57] A combination of a blinkered and
dogmatic framework for analysing Iraq, and an inflexible military doctrine
conspired to produce a uniquely ineffective counter-insurgency operation.
There was little understanding of who the enemy was, and poor intelligence
on its numbers, organisation, deployment, leadership and modus operandi.
American counter-insurgency tactics fluctuated from excessive force and
coercion to gross cultural insensitivity. All the while, the US military had
insufficient numbers to control and pacify insurgent areas, allowing the insurgents to reassert control whenever the military would move on elsewhere. In
time, the military would improve its strategy and techniques, but in 2003 and
early 2004, American counter-insurgency operations unwittingly fed the insurgency. Iraqis watched helplessly as the insurgency took root. Most, though not
all, were alarmed at the rise of violent resistance to the occupation. In the
Sunni Arab areas, however, the number of those who supported what was
deemed to be a resistance increased to a large majority. Iraq was heading for a
dangerous polarisation of opinion.

10

The Shadow of Real Power

'We reached a point where we started asking ourselves: are we informers or advisers? Being an adviser means that you sit around the committee table devising the orders, but we were implementing orders without being consulted in their devising. So we were not seen as advisers, let alone as decision-makers. All the big decisions – dissolving the Iraqi army and the security apparatus, privatisation, oil policy, the banking system, the restructuring of the media – were made [by the CPA] behind closed doors.'–

Isam al-Khafaji, former IRDC member, who resigned from his post in protest, speaking in an interview, August 2003

Landscapes of an Occupied Country

The power of the CPA was now acknowledged in international law, but the slapped-together administration that Bremer had set up was unsure of what its tasks and objectives were. It veered uncomfortably between considering itself a caretaker administration to being a benign tutor for Iraq's induction into the democratic camp. It sought a radical overhaul of the country's laws, institutions and political culture. It combined the elements of imperial 'indirect rule', by officially ceding some power to the Governing Council, but ensuring that the Governing Council was shorn of resources and legal authority, rendering it dependent on the CPA, which never trusted its Iraqi partners in government sufficiently to provide them with the leeway to make decisions and policy without reference to the 'Palace'. An uncomfortable relationship was fostered between the CPA, the Governing Council and the Cabinet. The real power of the CPA, its unchallenged authority and its control over money and military force, overshadowed the 'virtual' authority of the Governing Council and the Cabinet. But this power was not calibrated or strengthened by a coherent governing policy. A chaotic, contradictory and often secretive CPA would spring its decisions on unsuspecting Governing

Council members or ministers. Months of laborious work would be suddenly cancelled by Bremer's expedient of refusing to sign decisions made into law, or of refusing resources to allow the decisions to be effective. The effects of this on the administration and progress of Iraq were pronounced.

Bremer, the Governing Council and International Recognition

The relations between Bremer and the Governing Council were fragile and frequently acrimonious. The powers that Bremer appropriated for the CPA were in keeping with UN Resolution 1483, but the leaders of the Governing Council had primed themselves to take over power as the linchpins of a provisional government. Bremer's distaste for certain key figures in the Governing Council is clear from his own memoirs, and it was privately reciprocated by a number of them.[1] Bremer had to deal with an entity that he had created, but which had a life and mind of its own. A number of factors played a vital part in the making of this relationship. On the Governing Council side, there was extreme sensitivity to the charges that were levelled against it by opponents of the war and the occupation, who considered the Governing Council as a rubber-stamp, toothless entity with members who were no better than quislings.[2] Proving the Governing Council's independence and its ability to set policy and influence the direction of events became very important to it. This opened the way to confrontations between the Governing Council and Bremer.

It proved impossible to select a single leader for the Governing Council, and it was finally settled that a representative group of nine would form an executive council. The leaders chosen were Abd el-Aziz al-Hakim (SCIRI); Ibrahim al-Jaafari (Da'awa Party); Muhammad Bahr ul-Uloom (Independent Islamist); Ahmad Chalabi (INC); Ayad Allawi (INA); Adnan al-Pachachi (independent liberal); Muhsin Abd el-Hamid (Iraqi Islamic Party); Jalal Talabani (PUK); and Massoud Barzani (KDP). Of the nine, five were Shi'a, two Sunni Arabs, and two Kurds. Three were Shi'a Islamists and one was a Sunni Islamist. It was decided that members of the leadership council would take turns, alphabetically and on a monthly basis, as head of the Governing Council. The first head during the month of August 2003 was to be Dr Ibrahim al-Jaafari.

The issue of sovereignty of the state exercised a number of the Governing Council members, especially Adnan al-Pachachi and Ahmad Chalabi. Pachachi was a commanding figure in the ranks of the liberals and secularists inside the opposition. Diplomatically skilful and very well connected, he was a favourite of the diplomats of the State Department and the chanceries of the USA's moderate Arab allies, especially the UAE. From the onset,

Pachachi had been conscious of the need to have formal powers assigned to the Governing Council so that the stigma of occupation was removed from Iraq. He was highly sensitive to the potential loss of Iraq's sovereignty. It had been galling for him to see Iraq reduced to the ranks of occupied countries. He was acutely aware that the resolution of a great number of issues hinged on this matter.

Soon after the Governing Council's formation, Pachachi headed a Governing Council delegation, in September, to the UN Security Council, which was presided over by Spain's foreign minister, Ana Palacios, a strong defender of the war. In his speech to the UN's General Assembly on 24 September, 2003, Pachachi stated that 'Iraq had not lost its sovereignty. Its sovereignty was held in abeyance until full powers were restored to an Iraqi authority . . . . My appearance here means that Iraq has regained its government and its right to be represented at international forums.'[3] The push to grant sovereignty back to an Iraqi government was identified with the Governing Council, which was seen as the locus of Iraq's government. But this was not necessarily the way that the CPA saw matters. The confrontation bubbled to the surface during a meeting of the Security Council's permanent members, called by Kofi Annan in Geneva in September 2003 to discuss the upcoming US-sponsored resolution on Iraq. The Iraqis had pushed to be observers at this meeting, and Adnan al-Pachachi had presented a revised draft of the resolution that gave the Governing Council the right of embodying Iraq's sovereignty. This caused considerable tension between the US Secretary of State, Colin Powell, and the French and Germans and their allies in the Iraqi Governing Council. Ahmad Chalabi had to deflect the impression that the CPA and the Governing Council were on a collision course by saying: 'We have no disagreement with the United States Government. We are not at odds with the United States.'[4]

UN Security Council Resolution 1511

The US version of the status of the Governing Council partly won out and became the basis of UN Resolution 1511. The Resolution finessed the issue of power and sovereignty. While granting the Governing Council and the Cabinet the right to embody Iraq's sovereignty, it maintained the powers of the CPA as the effective arbiter of Iraq's affairs until a representative government was formed. The Resolution stated clearly that 'obligations under applicable international law recognized and set forth in Resolution 1483 (2003) . . . will cease when an internationally recognized, representative government established by the people of Iraq is sworn in and assumes the responsibilities of the Authority'.[5] The CPA would continue in business until a representative government, but certainly not the Governing Council at that point, was formed. But Resolution 1511 also gave recognition to the Governing Council's attempts to carry Iraq's sovereignty and stated that 'the Governing Council and its ministers are the principal bodies of the Iraqi interim administration'. The Resolution called for the preparation of a timeline that would lead to the formation of a representative government, and linked that process to the preparation of a constitution. This was a key American demand, that no representative government to which the CPA's power would be transferred was possible without a constitution. The Resolution wanted the Governing Council to provide to the Security Council, no later than 15 December, 2003, for its review, 'a timetable and a program for the drafting of a new constitution for Iraq and for the holding of democratic elections under that constitution'. This was a major plank in American occupation policy in Iraq, to which the Governing Council frequently objected. The CPA, in particular Bremer, was of the opinion that the Governing Council was not representative, and could never be representative, and he was not prepared to transfer power to an unelected, unconstitutional body.[6]

Deliberations and Decisions of the Governing Council

In its early sessions, the Governing Council authorised the formation of a committee to work on the draft of a new constitution. The deteriorating security conditions in the country, however, were a cause of never-ending concern. Throughout the month of August 2003, the security conditions began to threaten the safety of the individual Governing Council members. The Islamist Governing Council member Izzedine Salim provided a graphic account of the collapse in law and order in Basra, and the rise of organised criminal gangs involved in racketeering, kidnapping, extortion and smuggling. Both he and another Governing Council member, the lawyer Naseer al-Chadirchi, had been subject to armed attacks aimed at their convoys and homes. The issues of adequate security and funding for the Governing Council members became top priority. On 3 August, 2003, the Governing Council, in one of its more important decisions, formed a Security Committee and charged Ayad Allawi with its leadership.[7]

It was clear, even in those early days, that the Governing Council was not a government-in-waiting. Rather, it was a hybrid, which fitted awkwardly into the governing structures of an occupied country. All the data and information base of the Iraqi state were under the control of the CPA, and what was released to the Governing Council was only what was thought necessary or convenient. For example, in the early August sessions of the Governing Council, the CPA's officer responsible for the budget, David Oliver, gave a most perfunctory description of the state of Iraq's finances.[8] The budget for the rest of the year, which was in the process of being finalised, had been created without any serious involvement by the Governing Council.

The 2003 Iraq Budget and Supplemental Appropriations

The CPA budget was produced in early July and called for expenditures of about $6.1 billion for the balance of the year, mainly funded by oil exports of about $3.5 billion.[9] The budget was an amateur and unrealistic affair, hastily put together by ministries that had no idea of modern budget preparation requirements, and a CPA staff that was barely aware of the true needs and resources of the Iraqi state. The Iraqi ministries of Finance and Planning were drawn into a process that in the previous regime had been discharged in the utmost secrecy. They persuaded the CPA staff to prepare the budget in the old command economy format, rather than embark on an overhaul of the budgeting process. The Ministry of Finance was nothing more than an accounting and recording bureau. The Planning Ministry, on the other hand, was where the regime's technocratic elite had converged, and it was they who had held the upper hand in the management of the centralised economy. The imprint of the Planning Ministry was all over the budget, clearly establishing the ministry as a powerful rival to the CPA's technical and advisory staff. The CPA chose the line of least resistance, and where it mattered most, the old ways were kept going for the sake of expediency. The Governing Council was supposed to have responsibility for budget-setting but was denied appropriate information by the CPA. In any case, the Iraqi-funded budget was a bit of a red herring. Iraqi budgetary rules or constraints did not govern the real expenditures. They were the direct expenditures inside Iraq from funds seized by the Coalition, and thus outside the remit of the budget-makers, together with funds that were appropriated by the US Congress for reconstruction and related expenditures in Iraq. Bremer was soon to demand a huge increase in the appropriations for the reconstruction of the Iraqi economy.

The supplemental appropriations sought by Bremer in August amounted to nearly $20 billion. That went far beyond his original estimate to Bush of only a month previously of $5 billion.[10] What Bremer was seeking in supplementary funds far exceeded any congressional estimate of what would be needed for Iraq's reconstruction. It also directly challenged the assumption that Iraq's oil revenues could pay for the country's reconstruction. The costs of reconstruction had been completely unknown before the invasion. The estimates were wild, and wildly variant. Bush had appropriated an additional $2.4 billion for Iraq's reconstruction in a supplemental appropriation in March 2003. This was added to the $1.1 billion earlier approved by Congress for Iraq's reconstruction. In September 2002, the total cost of a conflict with Iraq and its subsequent reconstruction had been estimated at $100–200 billion by the White House economic adviser, Lawrence Lindsey.[11] The US Office of Management and Budget questioned this as being 'very, very high'.

The CPA could not rely on the Iraqi ministries themselves for a guide to the reconstruction needs of the country. The ministries had been gutted and could not produce effective spending plans and proposals. The years of sanctions had degraded their ability to plan coherently in an environment of extreme scarcity of resources. The CPA staff was too inexperienced, did not have the right talent and had too little prior exposure to the working environment in Iraq to be able to provide the CPA with a reliable assessment. Ultimately, the CPA had to depend on the work that was being done by the UN agencies and the World Bank in determining an acceptable basis for estimating the total costs of Iraq's reconstruction. They had laid most of the groundwork for establishing the needs of the Iraqi economy before the invasion. It was also politically expedient to have the World Bank and the UN on board if the Coalition were to expand the basis of donors for Iraq's reconstruction. What was shocking, however, was the total absence of both any Iraqi public debate on the country's reconstruction needs and the integration of the Governing Council into these discussions. A 'we know best' attitude, with a profoundly anti-democratic ethos, prevailed. Iraqis were spoon-fed the programme, with the underlying assumption that they should not look a gift horse in the mouth, and this manner continued into the formation of the Cabinet.

The Formation of the Cabinet

The formation of the Cabinet was one of the urgent tasks of the Governing Council. A Cabinet would take the operational responsibility for the running of the government. It was eventually decided that each Governing Council member could nominate one representative, who would be chosen if there were no insurmountable objections by others to his nomination. In this way, the carefully crafted balance between various ethnic, sectarian and ideological groups would be kept in roughly the same proportion as that which existed in the Governing Council.

The Cabinet reflected the complex way in which the interests of twenty-five people could be accommodated. The result, which led to curious, not necessarily happy, choices, was nevertheless workable. Certain individuals were patently unsuitable for the jobs they had been allocated, while others were determined to implement specific party agendas. Also, the ministers did not know to whom collectively they were to report. Was it the Governing Council and, if so, who inside the Governing Council? Was it the rotating chairman, the heads of the Governing Council's committees, or the nine-person leadership council? Or was it Bremer and the CPA who had by far and away the greatest direct interaction with the ministries, both from the financial point of view – the CPA did, after all, control the money – and through the legion of foreign advisers both inside and outside the ministries?

Iraq ran the risk of having three governments – the CPA, the Governing Council and the Cabinet – through the uncontrolled actions and decisions of individual Cabinet ministers. This confused state of affairs became public when a number of Iraqi ministers attended the annual conference of the World Bank and the IMF held in Dubai in late September 2003.

The international community was keen to see the Iraqi delegation and to hear its views on the economic and social conditions of Iraq. The Iraqi delegation was headed by Adel Abd el-Mahdi, in his capacity as the deputy to the SCIRI representative on the Governing Council, Abd el-Aziz al-Hakim. The Iraqi delegation comprised the main economic ministries, including the ministers of finance, agriculture, planning, health, education and trade, and the governor of the Central Bank of Iraq. The CPA, however, brought along a parallel delegation, much larger than the Iraqi delegation, which shadowed the latter and tried to pull the strings from behind the scenes. The Iraqi team, hastily assembled and with little or no previous exposure to international conferences, had no choice but to accept the CPA tutelage. The Iraqi delegation had arrived in Dubai on board an American military aeroplane, and had been received by members of the US and British diplomatic missions in the UAE. Its status was subject to some dispute. Were the delegates representatives of a sovereign government? Who could speak on behalf of Iraq – the ministers or the CPA? In the end, the conference organisers assigned the Iraqi ministerial team the strange category of 'special invitees'. In fact, this was a CPA delegation in all but name. This bizarre state of affairs where one country's official delegation travels on board a military plane belonging to another country, and looks to the accompanying foreign team for guidance and direction, was not lost on the more alert reporters in Dubai.[12] The CPA wanted to use this forum to outline Iraq's economic policies and to put the best possible gloss on events since the fall of Baghdad, at least in terms of the economy. This was to be a test of the effectiveness of the new Iraq's economic team and its commitment to bold economic reforms. There would be no place for surprises and the Iraqi team was held on to a tight media leash.

Bremer had recently enacted a number of Orders that might have profound economic significance. One, Order 39, dealt with the dismantling of nearly all controls over non-oil foreign investments, with the exception of the banking sector, and allowed unimpeded access to the Iraqi market by foreign investors. On the surface, this example of neo-liberal thinking appeared innocuous enough, given the manifest need of the Iraqi economy for investment, technological transfers and upgrading of management skills. Proponents of a more open and market-based economy might have supported it. But the Order was made with little discussion with the Governing Council, and emerged fully formed from the warren of CPA offices dealing with the economy. Bremer signed it into law on 19 September, 2003, just as the Dubai IMF/World Bank annual conference was about to start. This Order was an essential part of the gamut of measures that the CPA hoped would turn Iraq's economy from a state-centred to an open market economy. The underlying philosophy behind the thinking was clear, but it raised serious alarms in a number of quarters. First, the legal issue was raised of whether the CPA, as the occupation authority, had the right to change any of the fundamental laws of the country. Second, the Arab and international press began to play up the 'Iraq-for-Sale' angle, making lurid remarks about how Iraq's most cherished assets would be bought for a song by foreign interests.[13] This played into the hands of the opponents of the war.[14] Third, and most important, the Order was overwhelmingly rejected by the very group which should have supported it, namely the Iraqi private sector. Iraqi businessmen were not interested in increasing competition from better-heeled and better-managed companies in a market which, for all its faults and weaknesses, had until then been theirs and theirs alone.[15] There was not one voice raised in support of the CPA's radical economic plans.[16]

The Politics of Reconstruction

The CPA had another agenda item for which it sought international support. The reconstruction needs of the Iraqi economy were running far ahead of their original estimates. The Bush administration had just gone public with its supplemental budget request from Congress, which earmarked nearly $20 billion of grant aid for Iraq's reconstruction. Bremer had pitched in with a statement on 22 September, 2003, to the House Appropriations Committee, where he made a strong, even grandiloquent, case for the supplemental budget, linking it to the fight against global terrorism and the USA's historic support for freedom and democracy.

> If we fail to recreate Iraq with a sovereign democracy sustained by a solid economy we will have provided the terrorists with an incredible advantage in their war against us . . . . The $20.3 billion in grants to Iraq the President seeks as part of this $87 billion supplemental bespeak grandeur of vision equal to the one which created the free world at the end of World War II. Iraqis living in freedom with dignity will set an example in this troubled region which so often spawns terrorists. A stable peaceful economically productive Iraq will serve American interests by making America safer.[17]

The Americans wanted the international community to share in the burden of Iraq's regeneration, and the Dubai venue was the first and most important forum to achieve this objective. The sidelining of the UN and its agencies in the run-up to the war came back to haunt the CPA. The key document to having the UN and its agencies committed to Iraq's reconstruction was the UN/World Bank 'Joint Needs Assessment Report on Iraq'. Iraqi ministers were barely consulted on this. The draft of the document was available by the time of the conference and it was vital for the USA to agree with the UN and World Bank on the final version before an upcoming donors' conference in Madrid in October.

Although privately sidelining them, the CPA had to present the Iraqi ministers in the best possible light to the international community, and especially to the media. All the ministers at the Dubai convention were sent to carefully prepared press conferences and TV appearances, where the CPA's recently promulgated orders were dramatically presented to the assembled audiences by the Iraqis, as if the initiatives were entirely of their own making. The policies seemed to emerge straight out of the right-wing think-tanks and the neo-liberal 'Washington Consensus'. A statement read by the Finance Minister, al-Gailani, but prepared by the CPA advisers, gave the impression that it had been a carefully constructed and Iraq-led process. The statement read in part: 'Following recent extensive discussions between the Iraqi Governing Council and the Coalition Provisional Authority, I am pleased to announce a series of significant economic and financial reforms.' But there had been no extensive discussions between the CPA and the Governing Council. McPherson, Bremer's economic adviser, rammed his package through the finance subcommittee of the Governing Council, headed by Ahmad Chalabi, and it was approved with scant debate at the Governing Council itself. In fact, a few days after al-Gailani made his statement, the Governing Council issued an astonishing disclaimer about Bremer's Orders, saying that al-Gailani was expressing his personal views and not those of the Governing Council. The net result of this tussle between the CPA and the Governing Council was to confuse the public even more as to the direction and intent of economic policy.

The Economic Policy Prescriptions of the CPA

The muted power struggle masked another issue. The policy prescriptions of the CPA were frequently a minority perspective, even in the USA, barely understood by the American public, and foisted on Iraq with no regard to local conditions. In very broad outline, they could be defended. But the kind of raw and unfettered Darwinian capitalism that the more radical of the CPA advisers were trying to promote was totally unsuitable for Iraq in its current bankrupt state.[18] The backlash from the Iraqi business community was fearsome. The Iraqi ministerial team met with representatives of the important Iraqi business community in the UAE. It was unanimously agreed that the new investment regulations, which basically put foreigners and Iraqis on a par with each other, would work to the detriment of the Iraqi private sector. Some ministers tried to alleviate the sector's concerns but it was a futile effort. The Iraqi private sector believed it was entitled to grow fat behind high tariff walls, import quotas and rigged markets – just like the private sector in the Gulf countries.

The Iraqi private sector was sharply divided. On the one hand, there was a mass of small businessmen and 'industrialists' – where a toothbrush factory would count as a major enterprise – on the other, a small coterie of Ba'ath cronies who feasted on sanctions-busting deals, smuggling, and outright theft of state assets. The resurgence of these near-criminal elements as part of the drive to open up the economy was a constant worry for the more aware ministers. The CPA's proposed panoply of radical economic measures made their emergence as linchpins of the new, liberalised economy nearly certain. The CPA already seemed indifferent to the large number of lucrative post-war contracts awarded to former Ba'ath regime business associates. Incredibly, some senior CPA advisers looked favourably on the East European and Russian models of economic transformation after the collapse of the Soviet empire. In one instance, a senior staffer for the Senate Finance Committee who was visiting Baghdad encouraged black market operators during the Saddam era to emerge as legitimate businessmen.[19] The seizure of large segments of the economy by criminal gangs, allied with corrupt politicians, was apparently seen as an evil but necessary condition for the successful transition of a state-dominated economy to a more open economy. Even in the autumn of 2003, a number of investment groups dominated by Ba'ath cronies had sprung up, some based in Dubai and apparently well capitalised. The process of co-opting the new Iraqi political class by the business groups associated with the defunct regime would soon begin in earnest. The stage was being set for more looting of Iraq's assets.

The International Development Community and the Madrid Conference

The international development community was thrown into crisis as a result of the invasion of Iraq, and the aftershocks were still being felt during the Dubai Conference. Jim Wolfensohn, the then World Bank president, met a number of the Iraqi senior team, and focused on the need to get Iraq's debt renegotiated at the earliest possible time, linking that effort to a successful outcome for the donors' conference in Madrid. He was clearly upset that the CPA had not consulted the World Bank in any way when it developed its sweeping economic reforms package, and suggested that the Iraqis seek the help of the World Bank and the EU in creating a counterbalance to America's dominance of Iraq's economic agenda. Wolfensohn was especially concerned that if the EU/US stand-off on Iraq were not resolved soon, the Madrid donors' conference would end in disaster. The Iraqi team also met with a number of Arab and Gulf delegations at the Dubai Conference, to seek their views and support for the economic reconstruction plans for the country. Behind a façade of ceremonial *politesse*, however, the Arabs were uniformly unsympathetic to Iraq's plight and could barely disguise their hostility to the invasion and their resentment at its consequences. The Arabs did not attach any significance or legitimacy to the Governing Council and its Cabinet, and would have barely deigned to notice the Iraqis in Dubai were it not for the overweening presence of the Americans. Their lack of sympathy and suspicions of the Iraqis was almost palpable, and it was clear that their support for Iraq's reconstruction in the Madrid Conference would only be token.

The Madrid Conference of donors for Iraq's reconstruction was held on 23 and 24 October, 2003. The Iraqi delegation was led by Ayad Allawi, the president of the Governing Council during October. Colin Powell headed the large US delegation, including that of the CPA. Most of the USA's other Coalition partners fielded sizeable delegations, and were represented by senior political figures. Kofi Annan gave the opening speech. 'We all look forward to the earliest possible establishment of a sovereign Iraqi government, but a start to reconstruction cannot be deferred until that day.' The Japanese, by far the most important donor after the USA, had pledged $5 billion to Iraq's reconstruction. The USA finally relented on the management of donor funds, and agreed to channel them through two trust funds managed by the World Bank and the UN respectively. Countries that had opposed the war were not prepared to hand over their contributions to a US-led organisation, and their participation was essential to broaden the base of international support to Iraq's reconstruction efforts. 'I need the money so bad we have to move off our principled opposition to the international community being in charge,' said Bremer.[20]

Although the conference was declared a success, it could not mask the fragility of the international consensus on Iraq. Pledges reached $33 billion, but $18 billion of that were the USA's supplemental budget commitments. A further $10 billion was supposed to come from the World Bank and the IMF, but this was open-ended and was governed by the stringent project and programme loan criteria of these institutions. Japan's contribution of $5 billion was certainly impressive, but nothing was pledged by France and Russia, while Germany's commitment was a paltry $100 million. The UK pledged nearly $450 million in additional funding for Iraq's reconstruction. However, a huge gap usually emerges between pledges and actual disbursements at conferences such as that of Madrid. The Iraqi Madrid delegation, the Governing Council and the Cabinet would all trumpet the headline figures pledged in Madrid without telling Iraqis the flimsy basis for such optimism. The fact was that it was the USA, with Japan in tow, that was contributing most of the money pledged in Madrid, and it was the USA, in particular, that had already appropriated the funds and was poised to spend them. Nevertheless, by any reckoning, America's contribution to the reconstruction of Iraq was financially impressive. It dwarfed any other commitment made to a non-European country. It was not the generosity of the US taxpayer that was to be questioned, but the way in which the money was actually spent.

CPA Unilateralism in the Making of Economic and Financial Policy

Within a few weeks of the formation of the Cabinet, it became clear that the CPA was not prepared to relinquish control over key aspects of the Iraqi economy. This was not only the case in the area of international economic cooperation but also in terms of a proprietary interest in certain sectors which the USA had considered priority areas. For example, in the matter of the reso- lution of Iraq's debt, the CPA entered into a series of binding agreements with investment banks and lawyers, and acknowledged the legitimacy of Saddam- era debts. Neither the Central Bank nor the Ministry of Finance was judged competent enough to question the conclusions of the US Treasury. The CPA adopted a particular path for debt restructuring that might not have been freely chosen by a sovereign Iraqi government. The governor of the Central Bank, for example, had been a leading member of the Jubilee Fund initiative which called for repudiation of 'odious debt', that is, debt incurred by dicta- torships and tyrannies for wars and internal repression. His views were not sought when the debt-restructuring plan was being developed. The Ministry of Finance was not consulted whatsoever on this momentous decision, partly because there were no competent bodies inside the ministry that could make a considered judgement on the matter. Similarly, the Trade Ministry, nomi- nally responsible for the management of the food supply chain for Iraq's universal rationing system, was completely by-passed in the procurement, shipping and distribution of the imported foodstuffs. The programme was run by the CPA and the UN's World Food Programme, essentially continuing to use similar methods as the previous OFF programme, with its massive corruption and inefficiencies. The situation was not rectified until well into 2004, when the Ministry of Trade was given responsibility for managing the imports for the country's food ration system.

   In the matter of Iraq's international economic policies and the relations with multilateral agencies and donor countries, it was the CPA that developed the strategies and plans, with Iraqis following in its wake. The package of economic policies that Iraq was expected to follow, ranging from accession to the World Trade Organisation to Central Bank independence, were eminently reasonable, but it was the secretive and unilateral manner in which they were introduced that marred their acceptability. In a meeting with the Governing Council on September 4, 2003 Bremer made clear his displeasure at Iraqi ministers traipsing all over the world, meeting with donors, and trying to raise money for their department's reconstruction needs. 'The ensuing confusion could severely disrupt the functioning of the CPA's own carefully modulated approach to donors,' he said in meetings with the Governing Council.[21] It was thought that Iraqis could not understand the complexity of donor relations or the rehabilitation of the power sector and that their interference in the process would only cause problems.

CPA Control over Security Policies

It was not only in the economic sectors that the CPA's work overshadowed, by-passed or ignored that of the Iraqi ministries. With the dissolution of the army and the intelligence services of the former regime, the Ministry of Interior became the only official Iraqi ministry involved in the area of security work. The deterioration in security, especially after the UN bombings and the murder of Ayatollah Baqir al-Hakim, opened the floodgates of popular discontent at the Coalition's inability to control the abysmal situation. The office of Grand Ayatollah al-Sistani issued a scathing bulletin, holding the occupying authority responsible for the collapse of law and order in Iraq.[22] A number of Governing Council members had given statements to the press about the Coalition's dereliction of its responsibilities, and held the Coalition's force directly accountable for the spate of suicide and car bombings plaguing the country. Bremer was incensed at these remarks, and pointedly demanded that the Governing Council should desist in making such inflammatory comments.[23] This was the beginning of a prolonged quarrel between the CPA and the Governing Council about control over security and general security policy. It peaked whenever some outrage had occurred. The Ministry of Interior, nominally in charge of the Iraqi police, soon entered into a confrontation with Bremer over the recruitment and training of paramilitary forces. These so-called rapid intervention forces of the Ministry of Interior were seen as threatening by the Coalition commanders. The CPA money spigot was turned off and that was that. Another issue that the Ministry of Interior tried to tackle early on was control over Iraq's borders, but the CPA vetoed the rather draconian measures that the minister was proposing.[24] The training of Iraqi police was a crucial policy decision over which Iraqis had no control. The entire programme became thoroughly discredited, after the police force collapsed in a number of cities when seriously challenged by insurgents.

The confused lines of authority and responsibility often led to serious situations developing between ministers, the CPA and the Governing Council. In particular, the military seemed to be operating under its own steam and could basically do whatever it saw fit. Most ministries had a special liaison officer assigned from the Coalition to oversee the security arrangements for ministerial installations and key personnel. This person would normally oversee the Facilities Protection Service (FPS), the security guards service that was initiated by the Coalition and under the nominal control of the Ministry of Interior. The FPS force grew to about 40,000 by the end of 2003, but their effectiveness was questioned in spite of the undoubted loyalty and bravery of some FPS men.[25] They underwent three days of intensive training, and were contracted out to various government departments. They would normally provide the first point of contact between the Coalition forces and the ministries in times of crisis.[26]

It was the shadow government that caused the greatest problems in the day-to-day management of the ministries. The CPA did not see it as a systemic problem, because of its patchy understanding of the internal dynamics of the government machinery. Neither for that matter did most of the new ministers. Some had come in with specific party agendas, and did their best to turn the ministries into fiefdoms. Others, unsure of how long either the CPA or the Governing Council would last, had divided loyalties – to both the Governing Council and the CPA. By the end of 2003, Iraq was governed by a hodgepodge of authorities: the formal and increasingly remote occupation powers at the 'Palace'; the Governing Council that felt suffocated by the CPA's restrictions and conditions; and a Cabinet that was controlled by the CPA's purse. There were also the parallel, often dangerous, networks inside the government that continued to function, that owed their loyalties to the former Ba'ath regime, to political parties, to criminal gangs or to themselves alone.

11

The Enigma of Ayatollah Sistani

Question addressed to Grand Ayatollah Ali al-Sistani by a group of his followers on 20 June, 2003:

'The Occupation Authorities in Iraq have stated that they have decided to form a council that would write the new Iraqi constitution; and that they will appoint members to this council in consultation with political and social groups in the country, after which the constitution that will be drafted by this council will be presented for approval by a referendum. Could you inform us of the religious ruling on this project and what believers ought to do regarding the manner in which the new Iraqi constitution is to be drawn?'

Official answer provided by Grand Ayatollah Ali al-Sistani on 26 June, 2003:

'Those forces have no jurisdiction whatsoever to appoint members of the Constitution preparation assembly. Also there is no guarantee either that this assembly will prepare a constitution that serves the best interests of the Iraqi people or that it expresses their national identity whose backbone is sound Islamic religion and noble social values. The said plan is unacceptable from the outset. First of all there must be a general election so that every Iraqi citizen who is eligible to vote can choose someone to represent him in a foundational Constitution preparation assembly. Then the drafted Constitution can be put to a referendum. All believers must insist on the accomplishment of this crucial matter and contribute to achieving it in the best way possible.'

The passage of UN Security Council Resolution 1511 placed a framework on the process of transferring power and sovereignty back into Iraqi hands. The Resolution specified the date by which the details of the matter were to be presented to the Security Council – and it was assumed the CPA would manage it. The Resolution also seemed to put paid to the argument proposed by many in the Arab world and in Europe that the USA was planning a long-term occupation, although suspicions of CPA micromanagement remained. The struggle for controlling the pathways to the constitution under which an Iraqi government was to be re-empowered became a defining feature of Iraq's political scene. It was not only the Governing Council but sub-groups within the Governing Council, which represented ethnic and sectarian communities, that began to demand a role in the process. The religious leadership of the Shi'a in Najaf were also extremely concerned about the outcome, and demanded their say in defining the key milestones of this process. Those who were excluded from the process, in particular the Sadrists, also sought to influence events, while the Sunni Arab community that was not engaged in support for the insurgency maintained a close interest in the unfolding events.

The Shi'a House

The Shi'a in the Governing Council, prompted by the Shi'a Islamists in the Governing Council, started a caucus called *Al-Bayt Al-Shi'i* (The Shi'a House), thinking that the Kurds and Sunni had organised themselves similarly.[1] The Shi'a House became an important, and surprisingly cohesive, coordinating body. All the Shi'a in the Governing Council, including Hamid Moussa, the Communist Party leader, and the secular Ayad Allawi, were invited to join this informal grouping.

The Islamists took the lead in the Shi'a House deliberations. SCIRI's ever-present representative, Adel Abd el-Mahdi, was committed to the principle of a common Shi'a position on all issues, and worked diligently to ensure that the Shi'a House became the sole political reference point for coordinating the policy positions of the Shi'a in government. Shi'a House meetings were open to other opinion leaders in the Shi'a community, and were regularly attended by Shi'a in the cabinet. It was powerful discussion forum and the opinions expressed became instrumental in forging a common Shi'a position on a variety of issues.

The Shi'a House also provided a vital mechanism for relaying the messages of the Najaf hierarchy to the gatherings, and vice versa. Regular updates were provided to the religious authorities, especially to the office of Grand Ayatollah Sistani, the acknowledged senior *Marji' al-Taqlid* who kept abreast of developments almost on a daily, if not hourly, basis.[2] The Shi'a House members were determined not to repeat what they thought to be the disastrous decisions of their forebears during the 1920s. It was a commonplace amongst the Shi'a that by failing to cooperate with the British mandate authorities in the 1920s, and resisting occupation on the grounds of patriotism, they effectively handed over the governing of Iraq to the Sunni Arabs. A leading Shi'a polemicist, Hassan al-'Alawi, coined a memorable phrase regarding the 1920 Uprising, that the 'Shi'a's ultra nationalism cost them [control over] the nation'.[3] The Shi'a interlocutors would not alienate the Coalition at this stage. This was also the line taken by the Najaf *Marji'iyya*, who were equally determined that the Shi'a must not confront the Coalition, even at the expense of being accused of 'collaboration'. This was a fine line to tread, for the CPA was not keen to hand over power to a Shi'a-led government under the control of Islamists. What the CPA considered to be the ideal outcome for Iraq's governance had no resonance with the Shi'a Islamists, but this was neither the time nor the place to confront the Coalition on this matter. This temporary partnership was expedient for both groups. Sistani's muted acquiescence to the presence of foreign troops was not support for the occupation per se, but a pragmatic choice, based on his assessment that this was the Shi'a's historic moment to redress the balance of power inside the country. This was balanced by his deeper commitment to Islam and to the doctrines that he expounded and defended on behalf of millions of his followers. The Coalition, on the other hand, knew that Sistani held the loyalty of millions in his hand, and that he could make the occupation far more costly and turbulent if he so chose. At the same time, the Coalition had an alternative political vision for Iraq.

Grand Ayatollah Ali al-Sistani

Sistani's political philosophy was an enigma. To westerners, his entire persona was an enigma, but that was partly because they had no first-hand access to him.[4] He refused to meet anyone from the CPA, and, in fact, anyone else remotely connected with the occupation powers. But every year he did see dozens of delegations from all walks of life, not only from Iraq but also from the huge Shi'a community in Iran, the Gulf countries and the Indian sub-continent who drew their guidance from him. The Grand Ayatollah spoke only through his acknowledged representatives or through his son, Muhammad Redha Sistani. Several senior members of the Governing Council outside the clerical class, such as Mowaffaq Rubai'e, did have direct access to the Grand Ayatollah and from time to time were used as go-betweens. The fact remained that the CPA could only indirectly gauge the views and reactions of Sistani to their policy measures and proposals.

Sistani was born in Mashhad, Iran, in August 1930, equivalent to the month of *Rabi' al-Awal* 1349 in the Islamic (*hijri*) calendar.[5] He came from a long line of religious notables in Iran. His grandfather, also named Sayyid Ali, was a renowned scholar and teacher of jurisprudence in the Mashhad *hawza*. At the age of 5, the future Grand Ayatollah was taught the Quran by a woman; by the time he was 11, he had enrolled in a traditional school to start the decades-long process of the scholastic education of a *mujtahid*. In 1948, Sistani left for Iran's centre of classical Shi'a learning in Qum, where he continued his advanced studies in jurisprudence and the doctrines of Shi'a Islam. In 1951, he left Iran for the holy cities of Iraq and settled in Najaf to complete his religious studies at the hands of scholars such as Ayatollah al-Khoei and Sheikh Hussein al-Hilli. Nearly a decade later, Sistani returned to his birthplace with the coveted status of a *mujtahid*. He was granted his degree and also received a separate certification of his status as an accomplished scholar of traditions from the Prophet and the Imams of the Shi'a. He was also acknowledged as having expertise in the specialist religious science of *'Ilm al-Rijal* – knowledge of the biographies of narrators of religious traditions and sayings. Armed with these accreditations, Sistani was well on his way to becoming a leading authority in the world of Shi'a Islam. His sojourn in Mashhad was brief, however. In the following year, probably urged by Ayatollah al-Khoei, he returned to Najaf, where he began to give lessons to seminary students. Early on, he was marked by Ayatollah al-Khoei as a worthy successor to his legacy. In 1987, al-Khoei assigned Sistani the leadership of the famous Khadra Mosque in Najaf, where he himself had led the prayers. Ayatollah Sistani continued to lead the prayers at the Khadra Mosque until its closure by the Ba'athist authorities in 1993. It was Sistani's association with Ayatollah al-Khoei, his scrupulous avoidance of any political gesture during the days of the Ba'ath, and his prolonged house arrest in the late 1990s that caused many people to misunderstand his political philosophy. This perception was further reinforced by the few pronouncements that he issued on the arrival of the Coalition, and his ambiguous position during the early months of the occupation.

The position of Grand Ayatollah Sistani as the undisputed head of the Najaf hierarchy was unassailable. The Najaf grand ayatollahs were united and other ayatollahs outside the Najaf hierarchy did not seriously dispute Najaf's preponderance or Sistani's pre-eminence. The murder of Grand Ayatollah Muhammad al-Sadr had removed the guiding spirit for the Shi'a masses of the cities. The followers of non-Iraq-based ayatollahs were few and could not be counted on to mount a serious challenge to Sistani's supremacy. Neither the Iranian politico-religious leadership, represented by Ayatollah Khamane'i, nor the Lebanon-based Grand Ayatollah Muhammad Hussein Fadhlalla had any substantial following in Iraq. Iran, where Sistani had a large following, carefully monitored the situation in Iraq and had judged it politic to leave Sistani in overall control over the responses of the Shi'a to the most vital issues.

Sistani and the Relationship Between Religion and the State

The virtual seclusion of Sistani during the last decade of Ba'athist rule in Iraq added to the mystery of his views on the role of religion in the modern state. His communications with outsiders during these years were strictly limited to his rulings on matters of religion, and he did not give one public statement (a *bayan*) that could be construed as political in content. He did, however, make a strongly worded pronouncement in April 2002, denouncing the Israeli action against the Palestinians in the occupied territories, condemning what he said was American support for it, and demanding a united Muslim response. It was the absence of any substantial information on Sistani's political position that gave rise to speculation as to his real intentions.

Many linked Sistani to the 'quietist' tradition in Shi'a Islam, even attributing to him a belief in the separation of 'mosque and state', a ludicrous interpolation of a western secular concept into an entirely different tradition.[6] This became part of the ideological arsenal of the neo-conservatives and their allies, who tried to invent a non-interventionist, even secular, bent to the Najaf establishment. This quiescent Najaf became contrasted with the Iranian model of clerical rule, and all kinds of wishful thinking was aired about Najaf replacing Iran as the global pivot of Shi'a Islam.[7] This line of thinking may also have been helped by the Sadrists' talk of the 'active' *Marji'iyya* and the 'passive' *Marji'iyya*, with the latter clearly associated with Sistani. Another thread that led people to equate Sistani with the 'quietist' school in Shi'a Islam was his long association with Grand Ayatollah al-Khoei. The best pre-2003 record of Sistani's political views emerges from an obscure exchange between Grand Ayatollah Sistani and Professor Abdul Aziz Sachedina, a scholar of Islam at the University of Virginia.

Professor Abdul Aziz Sachedina, a practising Shi'a originating from the East African Khoja Shi'a Muslim community, was a noted expert on Shi'a jurisprudence. He had published a number of seminal works on Shi'a Islam, including *The Just Ruler in Shi'ite Islam* and a detailed analysis of al-Khoei's Quranic exegesis, *The Prolegomena to the Quran*. Sachedina had proposed a number of non-traditional approaches to understanding Islam, which appeared to irritate his community which then sought to stop him from public lecturing and discoursing on Islam. Sachedina, rather innocently, decided to seek recourse with Ayatollah Sistani, and to subject his teachings to the Ayatollah's scrutiny, and, he hoped, obtain his understanding and approval for continuing in his way. In August 1998, Sachedina travelled to Iraq and had intensive discussions with the Grand Ayatollah. The exchanges between Sachedina and Sistani took place over a period of two days, in which Sistani's views on a number of crucial issues became clear. The meetings were later outlined in an account by Sachedina, entitled 'What Happened in Najaf?'[8] They are an excellent primer to the inherent potential of conflict between religious reformers and intellectuals on the one hand, and the authority of the religious establishment on the other. Far from being the detached and ethereal figure of the imagined 'quietest' tradition, in these discussions Sistani is shown to have some vigorous opinions on the primacy of the *Marji'* in matters of doctrine. He made scathing remarks about the experiment in 'reformist Islam' under President Khatami, and was sceptical about religious pluralism and coexistence. Revealingly, Sistani also pointed out that he had had disagreements with al-Khoei on matters of juridical principles, but 'had abstained from mentioning these disagreements in public'.[9]

Sistani emerges as someone who is vitally concerned with the role of Islam in state and society, and one who does not advocate a benign negligence or avoidance of all things to do with the state or government. The argument that is usually trotted out by those who make a claim for the lack of interest of the Shi'a in worldly power is that the Shi'a have no resonance with the modern state. To them no state is legitimate. Legitimate power is the sole prerogative of the Hidden Imam who, upon his return from occultation, will establish the perfect state. This line of reasoning, however, had no attraction for Sistani. The Grand Ayatollah was certainly not a proponent of the detached *Marji'iyya*, indifferent to the state and worldly power, and concerned only with the way Shi'a Muslims should obey their religious injunctions in a profane world. Neither was he a narrowly sectarian religious leader. He made it clear to Sachedina that he considered the institution of the *Marji'iyya* and its rulings to be valid for all Muslims, not only the Shi'a. To Sistani, the state was necessary to protect Islam, but that was a far cry from demanding the direct rule of the *ulema* as a precondition to ensuring the Islamic identity of the country. Sistani's views were far more subtle than the crude division between 'quietist' and 'activist' *ulema*.

The linking of Sistani to the non-interventionist school in Shi'a Islam went hand in hand with an attempt to see a commitment to democratic principles inside the Najaf *Marji'iyya*. The idea was that, at bottom, the *Marji'iyya* had to be democratic. Democracy implies the rule of the majority and that the Shi'a, by adhering to democratic norms, would inevitably attain power. This led to another bout of wishful thinking on the part of the CPA and Iraqi secularists who, curiously, refused to relate Sistani's views on the state and government to a far more meaningful set of markers, namely, the evolution of his political theory within the traditions of Shi'a scholasticism.[10] In this regard, the most important innovation in recent times, and the theoretical and jurisprudential underpinning of the Islamic Republic in Iran, was the rise of the doctrine of *Wilayat al-Faqih* ('Guardianship of the Jurisprudent'). Sistani stood between the two polar extremes in modern Shi'a religious politics: the apolitical, inward-looking, strain best exemplified by Ayatollah al-Khoei, and the interventionist and activist strain associated with Ayatollah Khomeini. Al-Khoei barely acknowledged the concept of 'Guardianship of the Jurisprudent', and limited it to authority over a minor. Sistani, on the other hand, expanded the notion drastically, and admitted the idea of the 'Guardianship of the Jurisprudent' to cover all matters that affect the Islamic social system. The ruling of the *faqih* (jurisprudent) would be paramount in all matters social and political, and all believers, including other *mujtahids*, have to abide by them. In his *fatwas* on this matter, Sistani was careful to limit the scope of authority of the *faqih* over social matters; but actually his definition of social effectively covered all facets of Islamic society, including its politics.[11] Where he differed from Khomeini was in his willingness to accept the involvement of clerics in the management of political affairs, and he did not agree with Khomeini's insistence that the *faqih*'s political skills have to be added to his religious authority to complete the requirements of the position. Without explicitly saying so, Sistani was concerned with the corrupting effects of politics on the reputation and authority of the *ulema*, rather than any theological arguments against politics per se. His *Wilayat al-Faqih* was in many ways designed to ensure the primacy of the rulings of the *faqih* in essential matters of state, without risking direct engagement in the political process. In this framework, democracy is not an end in itself but a process by which the scaffolding of an Islamic state can be established. Eventually, this state will have to acknowledge the involvement of the *Marji'iyya* in all critical matters, even though it would not formally enshrine this role in its constitutional make-up.[12]

Sistani, the Constitution, and the Transition Process

In the weeks after the fall of the Ba'ath regime, Sistani issued a number of *fatwas* that dealt with subsidiary issues. One of them, aimed at clerics, specifically cautioned them to avoid becoming entangled in politics and to confine their role to providing 'general guidance' to their followers. This was seized upon as positive evidence of Sistani's commitment to a depoliticised clergy. His calls to his followers to return looted state property, and to desist in hunting down former regime operatives until a proper court was established were also interpreted in this vein. The CPA thought that it had won Sistani's neutrality for its plans to fashion a constitution for Iraq. Sistani's 26 June *fatwa* therefore arrived as a bombshell. It demolished the idea of a distant and aloof *Marji'* and brought Sistani into the heart of the unfolding political drama. However, the CPA effectively ignored the implication of Sistani's *fatwa* and continued to pursue the goal of an appointed constitution-writing body. It was clear that the CPA was following a patently undemocratic route, no matter how much gloss Bremer tried to put on it.

The CPA wanted control and to structure the framework of the state along western constitutional precepts. The Sistani *fatwa*, by insisting on direct elections to a constituent assembly, put the CPA in a quandary. Either it accepted an elected body that might not prove amenable to its pressures, or it had to face the possibility of rejection of the constitution if it were produced by an appointed group, no matter how 'representative' they appeared to be. The CPA would not abandon its scheme yet. By charging the Governing Council, some of whose members were close to Sistani, with the task of forming a preparatory committee to explore the possibilities for an appointed constitutional convention, the CPA thought that it would neutralise Sistani, but the Governing Council would not defy Sistani, or the legal and democratic logic of the *fatwa*. In addition, voices inside the *Marji'iyya* itself began to dissent publicly on the issue of Coalition troops and Sistani's apparent policy of constructive engagement. In early October, Grand Ayatollah Bashir al-Najafi said, 'Iraqis should be taught never to believe the promises and slogans of the US-led coalition forces. Most injustices inflicted on Muslims everywhere can be traced to the politics of arrogance pursued by the United States and surrogate regimes.'[13] Beset on all sides and by these issues, the CPA abruptly switched course. It did so when Moqtada al-Sadr's movement burst on the stage, presenting the CPA with another serious challenge.

Moqatda al-Sadr and the Transition Process

The Coalition had never anticipated a populist movement challenging its authority in post-war Iraq. In fact, the CPA had consistently downplayed the importance of the Sadrists, and had tried to dismiss them as an ephemeral phenomenon that would soon pass away. Underlying the CPA's dismissiveness and hostility towards the Sadrists was an underlying contempt, bordering on hatred, on the part of the CPA leadership for Moqtada al-Sadr personally and for the movement generally. In a conversation with Bremer about the significance of the Sadrists as an expression of the disempowerment of the Shi'a poor, Bremer angrily retorted that he 'didn't care a damn about the underclass and what they [the Sadrists] represented!'[14]

The grudging acknowledgement of the Sadrists did not translate into concrete measures to entice them into the political process. Rather, the reverse happened. A policy of isolation and confrontation was chosen by the CPA to shrink, if not destroy, the Sadrists' power. This policy was tacitly supported or tolerated by the Governing Council. The Sadrists themselves did not shirk from the looming confrontation and in some ways chose to precipitate a crisis, both to demonstrate their strength and to test the resolve of their adversaries and the limits to which they would be prepared to go. In early October 2003, the first units of the new Mahdi Army paraded in a graduation ceremony in Basra in the presence of Moqtada al-Sadr. A number of clashes between Coalition troops and supporters of the Sadrists quickly took place in and around Sadr City, with fatalities on both sides. The Sadrists organised large street demonstration in protest and on 11 October, Moqtada al-Sadr announced that he had formed an 'alternative government', complete with ministers, in a direct challenge to the Governing Council and the CPA.[15] These events coincided with a vast crowd of hundreds of thousand of pilgrims converging on Karbala to commemorate the birth of the twelfth Imam of the Shi'a, the Mahdi, who had gone into occultation.

The timing of Moqtada's announcement of his alternative cabinet and the throngs in Karbala were clearly aimed at creating a symbolic connection with the millenarian expectations associated with the return of the Imam al-Mahdi. On 14 October, two days after the commemoration of the Imam al-Mahdi's birth, clashes broke out between the Mahdi Army and guards loyal to Grand Ayatollah Sistani, who were protecting the shrine of Imam Hussein in Karbala. About a hundred fighters from the Mahdi Army tried to seize control of the shrine complex, from which Moqtada's supporters had been evicted a month earlier. This attack, which was aimed directly at Sistani and his Karbala representatives who controlled the shrines of the city, was repulsed partly with the help of Bulgarian troops from the Coalition, who sealed the entrances to Karbala, blocking Sadrist reinforcements from reaching the city. Two of Sistani's Karbala representatives lambasted Moqtada and even accused Moqtada's movement of harbouring Ba'athists and former intelligence officers. In Sadr City, his followers retook over the municipality building. Coalition forces moved tanks into Sadr City and retook control over the municipal building, but in Basra the reverse happened. Sadrists who had been evicted from their headquarters by British troops succeeded in taking back control of the building. Moqtada had announced his re-entry into the political fray in Iraq and the CPA was having nothing to do with it. Moqtada's threat to the military moved from vocal rejection of the occupation to small-scale encounters and ambushes of US troops.

There was also the need to bolster the authority of Sistani in the face of armed challenges by the Sadrists. Sistani had made a number of statements condemning the uncontrolled flow of arms into private hands. The shrine guards loyal to Sistani simply did not have the firepower to withstand sustained attacks from the Sadrists. The possibility that the Sadrists would evolve into a version of the Lebanese Hizbollah was emerging. This exercised the planners in Washington and the CPA no end and nipping the Sadrists in the bud became an essential objective.[16] The CPA began to believe that the entire prospect for a future pro-western and moderate Iraq would be seriously compromised if the Sadrists transformed themselves into a disciplined, armed mass movement, outside the Coalition-sanctioned political process. The fact that it was connected to Iran made it doubly dangerous. It was above all this fear that drove the Coalition's long-term policies on the 'Moqtada Problem'. Reports began to circulate in late October 2003 that a crackdown on the Sadrists was imminent. Moqtada al-Sadr himself appears to have recognised the gathering forces ranged against him, and made a series of tactical retreats. In a Friday sermon in early November he proclaimed that 'it was Saddam Hussein and not the Americans who were the enemies of Iraq' and stated that the American military were 'guests of Iraq'.[17] The CPA seemed to have been mollified for the moment, and held off from any serious measures against the movement.

Early Plans for Restoration of Sovereignty

The drive to restore sovereignty to an Iraqi govenment was shared by the Coalition, the Governing Council, Iraqi politicians who were prepared to go along with the political process, and the Najaf hierarchy. The Americans were divided as to the best way forward, but Bremer's plan was broadly accepted in Washington. The main points of Bremer's proposals, which he unveiled in the *Washington Post* on 8 September, followed a path to sovereignty that called for the writing of a constitution *prior* to the transfer of sovereignty. The plan called for the formation of the Governing Council, appointing a Cabinet, nominating a committee to examine the pathways to a new constitution, drafting a constitution, holding a referendum on the constitution, and then elections for a new government to which sovereignty would be transferred. There were technical arguments used to justify the delay in holding elections and a genuine concern that an elected constitutional assembly would result in a majority of Islamists, both Shi'a and Sunni, who would derail the entire project of enshrining western constitutional and political principles in Iraq's new constitution. It became increasingly problematic for the CPA to maintain a commitment to democratic principles while at the same time denying the impeccable democratic arguments for a popularly elected constitutional assembly.

Both Pachachi and Chalabi emphasised sovereignty transfer as a precondition for any meaningful movement in the restoration of full independence. The argument used was that writing a constitution under a formal occupation would be unacceptable to the Iraqi public and would taint the process. This line was also used, paradoxically, by those who rejected the occupation in its entirety, such as the AMS. The Governing Council had discussed a number of other mechanisms for the transfer of power from the CPA to a sovereign Iraqi government, but these proposals were not taken seriously by the CPA, which insisted on a detailed management of the proposals that were being considered by Washington and London.

Towards the November 15 Agreement

The challenge that confronted Bremer and the leaders in Washington and London was how to reconcile these conflicting currents while controlling the process and at the same time maintaining a forward momentum towards the normalisation of Iraq's political life. Eventually, a complex formula was developed that seemed to resolve these problems.

Key figures in the Governing Council had accepted an unstated, but basic, premise of the CPA, namely, that the risk of Islamist domination of the constitution-writing process be mitigated. 'I think it is very reasonable and necessary to have a provisional government before having a constitution,' commented Jalal Talabani.[18] To assuage other critics who might balk at the prospect of a provisional government without any constitutional safeguards, the idea of a fundamental law was broached. This 'basic' law would serve a dual purpose: to set the parameters of power for an interim government, but more importantly, from the CPA and the Kurds' perspective, to lay out broad principles of power, administration and governance that no constitution-writing, freely elected assembly, could breach in the future. The Kurds' insistence on a formal recognition of their demands for a federal Iraq had to be included in any transitional governance arrangements. In essence, the fundamental platform of what subsequently became the November 15 Agreement was the drafting of a basic law by an unelected authority as a roadmap for the transitional process.

The essence of the plan involved the drafting of a basic law for the transition period by 1 March, 2004. This was to be written mainly by the CPA, although the process was to be under the nominal tutelage of the Governing Council. Elections for a transitional assembly and government would then be held in July 2004, and a constitutional convention would be elected in January 2005. The plan was soon dropped in favour of holding 'caucuses' that would select the transitional government. The direct elections route was deemed impractical in the time frame that the Coalition wanted to impose on the return of sovereignty to Iraq: 30 June, 2004.[19]

The agreement had five basic provisions. The first element was the drafting of a 'Fundamental Law', which was intended to provide the legal framework for the government of Iraq. It included a bill of rights, a commitment to a federalist Iraq, an independent judiciary, civil control over the military, and a statement that the fundamental law could not be amended. The second element was a provision to reach an accord between the CPA and the Governing Council on the status of Coalition forces in Iraq. The third and most controversial provision was the selection process for a Transitional National Assembly (TNA). It specifically stated that the TNA would not be an extension of the Governing Council. The members of the TNA were to be selected through a caucus system in the eighteen governorates of Iraq. The fourth provision involved the restoration of Iraqi sovereignty by 30 June, 2004, through the nomination of a government by the TNA. The final provision was to set out a detailed timetable for an elected convention that would write Iraq's new constitution which would be subject to referendum. A new set of elections for an Iraqi government would be held no later than 31 December, 2005.

The CPA held considerable sway over the provincial and local councils, having nominated, selected or approved most of their members. The caucus process was therefore naturally seen to be a surrogate for CPA control over the selection of the TNA, which was to nominate the sovereign Iraqi government. The Governing Council came under considerable pressure from Washington to go along with the proposal. Jalal Talabani, who held the rotating presidency of the Governing Council for November, signed the agreement with Bremer on 15 November. 'We agree with the CPA on establishing a unified, federal, democratic system and on forming an interim government,' said Talabani. Commenting on the difference between the Governing Council and the proposed interim government, Talabani said, 'There is a big difference, since the interim government will be elected by a transitional assembly that will comprise representatives from the provinces. It will enjoy full authority and not [be] controlled by any party.'[20] The CPA trumpeted the agreement as a milestone in the transfer of power back to Iraqis, and as heralding a democratic future. It launched a wide-ranging media campaign to sell the idea to the public. Nevertheless, in spite of early statements of support from most of the Governing Council members, the agreement soon came under sustained attack. In particular, the Shi'a Islamists feared that a controlled caucus system, by skirting around elections, would rob them of the possibility of power that was beckoning from their numerical majority.[21] The office of Grand Ayatollah Sistani had issued a statement in late October, reinforcing the earlier *fatwa* that dismissed the legitimacy of any unelected constitutional body.[22]

Opposition to the November 15 Agreement

In reply to written questions from the *Washington Post*, Sistani rejected the idea of a caucus system to select the TNA: 'The mechanism in place to choose members of the transitional legislative assembly does not guarantee the establishment of an assembly that truly represents the Iraqi people.'[23] The absence of any reference to Islam in the November 15 Agreement was also a point of contention. The SCIRI leader Abd el-Aziz al-Hakim said in reference to the Shi'a concerns about the November 15 Agreement, 'There will be real problems if our reservations are not taken into account.'[24] Some Governing

Council members were also concerned, in case the new proposals for an elected assembly would leave them jobless. Views of the Governing Council had not yet hardened, and initially there was considerable support for the agreement as it had been signed by both Bremer and Talabani. Although al-Hakim clearly expressed his reservations, others, who would later reverse their position, appeared to accept its broad outlines. Chalabi, for example, tried to build on its positive aspects, such as the transfer of sovereignty. He empha-sised the imperative of reforming the provincial councils prior to holding the caucuses as another safety valve for ensuring the relative independence of the delegate-selection process.[25] Underlying the discussions was a deep anxiety about the fate of the Governing Council if the process did not specifically mandate its continuation in the post-sovereignty transfer period.

The CPA applied considerable pressure to ensure that the Agreement was ratified by the full Governing Council, and began to work behind the scenes to raise the spectre of a Shi'a dominance of the political system if there were no prior safeguards before elections were to be held. In this they were assisted by the increasing anxieties of the Sunni members of the Governing Council regarding the Sistani position on elections. The fear of holding elections in an uncertain environment affected all the Sunni Muslim representatives on the Governing Council. Abd el-Hamid said, 'It is impossible, before the coming July, to establish a Basic Law by the will of the entire Iraqi people, because organizing elections requires a census of the population, as well as a guarantee of security and stability, and these factors are neither available nor possible right now.'[26] Ghazi al-Yawar stated that 'It is impossible to hold elections under present conditions.'[27] Women on the Governing Council, too, were mobilised against the Sistani demand for elections, wanting special provisions for women in the basic law.

The UN Re-enters the Political Process

The possibility of a confrontation with the Shi'a on the Governing Council in general, and with Sistani in particular, made the CPA hesitant about pressing ahead with the plan regardless. Bremer had strongly resisted changes to the November 15 Agreement and was unprepared initially to concede the all-important caucus procedure for selecting the traditional assembly. Nevertheless, he had to factor in the risks of alienating the Shi'a and Sistani. A number of demonstrations against the November 15 Agreement took place. In Washington, the National Security Council began to explore the possibility of re-engaging the UN. Sistani's position also began to modify, as the CPA were insistent that elections could not be held in the time-frame that had been outlined in the agreement. Sistani signalled that he would entertain an inde-pendent adjudicator on this matter, and was willing to accept a UN mission that would review and report on the feasibility of holding elections within a few months, and this was confirmed by a Governing Council delegation visit in December.[28] The ground was being laid for the re-entry of the UN into the Iraqi political process.

Kofi Annan, who had corresponded with Sistani on the elections issue, questioned the practicality of holding elections in the short time available. He appeared reluctant to challenge the CPA's contention on this matter, and was vague about the UN's involvement in the Iraqi political process. Meanwhile, the number of street demonstrations in favour of Sistani's position on elections increased markedly over the following weeks with major demonstrations in Basra and Baghdad.[29] But the stand-off continued. The threat of a Shi'a boycott of the political process became real. The Coalition had to weigh the risks of continuing with the November 15 Agreement without Sistani's support, or acknowledging his demands without appearing to give him a veto on the entire effort.

The argument began to be advanced by those close to the Najaf hierarchy that a flawed election was better than none. Sheikh Ali Ruba'i, a leading cleric from Najaf, clearly expressed this view. 'We believe that even if it is an 80 per cent election, it is still more legitimate than a zero per cent election,' he said.[30] Bremer and the UK's special representative on Iraq, Sir Jeremy Greenstock, met with Annan in New York on 19 January, 2004 to discuss the issue of the UN's involvement in Iraq. Hovering in the background was the figure of Lakhdar Brahimi, lately the UN's special envoy in Afghanistan. Both the USA and the UK had wanted him to become personally involved in the resolution of the looming crisis on the elections issue, and help to diffuse it. Annan had to weigh the security problems and the traumatic after-effects of the bombing of the UN headquarters in Baghdad against the rapidly unravelling political situation in the country. Leading Shi'a politicians increased the tempo of their demands for the UN's involvement. Abdul Aziz al-Hakim announced that, 'There should be a real participation of the people through elections in choosing this council.'[31] The conclusions of the UN team 'would be respected' by Ayatollah Sistani. Ahmad Chalabi said, 'The view that we hold in Iraq now is this, that democracy is associated with elections. What some people are trying to do now is to try to explain how we can have democracy without elections.'[32] Pachachi, on the other hand, reiterated his early position of sovereignty before elections. 'We'd much rather have the end of occupation and getting back our sovereignty than waiting until elections are held. If you can get sovereignty without elections, fine,' he said. The sectarian divide on this matter was becoming deeper by the day, and involving the UN seemed to be the only way out. Greenstock piled on the pressure for the re-entry of the UN into the political process.[33] Annan began to relent.

On 23 January, 2004 a small advance team from the UN arrived in Baghdad to liaise with the CPA on the security problems that might face a possible enlarged UN presence in Iraq. Brahimi was also invited to Washington to discuss the UN's involvement in the elections issue, while in Iraq, Ayatollah Sistani called on his followers to cease their demonstrations. The pressure for the UN's re-engagement with Iraq had its effect on Annan. Swallowing his reluctance to have the UN return to Iraq under conditions which did not ensure the security of the UN's team, he finally said he intended to send a team to assess the different ways to select a new Iraqi sovereign government. 'I have concluded that the United Nations can play a constructive role in helping to break the current impasse,' he said. 'I will send a mission to Iraq.'[34] Ayatollah's Sistani's demands were going to be met, but no one was sure how the UN team would report.

12

A Constitution in Waiting

'Grand Ayatollah Sistani has already clarified his observations on the agreement of November 15th [and maintains] that any law prepared for the transitional period will not gain legitimacy except after it is endorsed by an elected national assembly. Additionally, this law places obstacles in the path of reaching a permanent constitution for the country that maintains its unity and the rights of its sons of all ethnicities and sects.' –

Statement by the office of Grand Ayatollah Ali al-Sistani
on the Transitional Administrative Law, 8 March, 2004

'The Transitional Administrative Law, written and approved by the Iraqi Governing Council . . . lays out the path Iraqis will follow to sovereignty, elections and democracy.' –

Paul Bremer, 24 March, 2004

The November 15 Agreement had been drafted in a hurry and addressed the CPA's two main concerns.[1] First, that the transition process would be governed by a law that would in effect be a crypto-constitution. The CPA had wanted this basic law to deal with substantive constitutional issues, although it was a law that would govern for only a transitional period, because it had calculated that the basic transitional law would set markers for any new permanent constitution, and that any future attempts to challenge the principles established in this law could be thwarted. The Kurds shared this view. Second, the CPA was adamantly opposed to holding elections for a legislative body that would oversee an interim transitional government. There was a lurking fear that elections held in such an uncertain environment ran the risk of electing individuals who might compromise the principles of the transitional constitution.

Differing Visions for a Transitional Process

The battle over the transition to sovereignty masked a fundamental conflict between differing visions of a future Iraq. The Coalition's constitutional project for Iraq, with the principles of liberal democracy as a loose framework, was visibly fraying, a victim of both its poor articulation and the mounting difficulties of governing the country. A number of premises had governed the Coalition's policies. There was the belief that there was a broad centre ground in Iraqi politics that was both modern-minded and non-sectarian. This centre, it was thought, would serve to buttress the Coalition's own policy prescriptions, and would stand firm against divisive sectarianism and Islamism. A second current reasoned that the Coalition's status in Iraq would be undermined if it were to clash with either the Kurds or the political and religious leadership of the Shi'a.

The alienation of the Sunni community was for the moment taken for granted. There were many Sunni Arab groups outside the Governing Council, such as the AMS, various Friday prayer leaders, tribal chiefs, former military officers, academics and professionals. But they simply did not have the clout or the desire to demand a place at the negotiating table. The Governing Council was seen by the Sunni Arabs to be a hopelessly sectarian entity, and the entire transition process appeared to be rigged against them. Sunni Arab political leaders had actually chosen a different route for manifesting their interests, as they began to regroup after the debacle they had suffered with the overthrow of the former regime. They had to tread a very narrow path between unrelenting hostility to the occupation and a very guarded and tentative engagement with the CPA. The presence of the Iraqi Islamic Party as the most organised Sunni group inside the Governing Council, afforded them a seat from which they could calibrate their responses to events. An idea of an Iraq with which they would be deeply uncomfortable was beginning to emerge, however. The twin threats of Kurdish separatism and the political implications of an acknowledgement of the Shi'a's demographic majority were increasingly dominating the discourse on the transition process.

The Drafting of the Transition Administrative Law

The tangled thicket of conflicting visions and ideas about Iraq was supposed to be reconciled in a single document: the fundamental law, or what later became known as the Transition Administrative Law (TAL). Moreover, the TAL dealt with procedural issues, such as timetables for handing over powers to a new Iraqi government and election deadlines, as well as substantive issues such as agreements on the status of Coalition forces.[2] It was a tall order even under the most favourable conditions – and these were certainly not evident in Iraq.

Shortly after the signing of the November 15 Agreement, the Governing Council established three committees that covered the drafting of the fundamental transitional law, the practicability of holding elections in the near term, and relations with the United Nations. The Kurds presented their own version of the constitution, which, understandably, pushed for their very partisan vision of the country. Within a short space of time, the 'liberal' bloc associated with Adnan al-Pachachi presented their own ideas for a transitional law, which was followed by a separate document presented by Ayad Allawi's INA group.[3] The Shi'a bloc had no version to present. They were prevailed upon by SCIRI's Abd el-Mahdi not to present one, preferring to rely on the drafts produced by others. The meetings of the constitutional committee were frequently heated, and little progress was made on an agreed working draft for the transitional constitution. The CPA became concerned about the lack of progress. With a looming deadline of 28 February, 2004 for the production of what would be in effect the transitional framework, and a clear risk that the conflicting drafts would not be reconciled in time, it took over the drafting process. Bremer held a decisive meeting with Adnan al-Pachachi, where agreement was reached that it would in fact be the CPA that would produce the working draft for the transitional constitution. Essentially, the TAL was drafted by a committee that had little connection with Islamists and the *Marji'iyya*, was greatly influenced by western notions of constitutional process, and was constructed with English as the operative language. The Iraqis on the drafting committee were all exiles, and had no feel for the prevailing sentiments of the majority Iraqis. The vital issue of Kurdish rights, which by implication could be used to recast the entire framework of the country, was left to bilateral deals between the CPA and the Kurds. In a crucial move, the CPA appropriated for itself exclusively the negotiations with the Kurds.[4]

There was deep concern in the CPA that the Kurdish/Arab divide might have grown too wide, and that the role of the CPA as an interlocutor was essential for the success of the project. Bremer visited Kurdistan on three separate occasions, where he conferred with both Barzani and Talabani on this matter. The Kurds had retained Peter Galbraith, a former US Ambassador in Croatia, as their main adviser on the transitional constitution. Galbraith was known for his position as an advocate of a loose Iraqi confederation, and was strongly in favour of Kurdish autonomy.[5] The drafting committee, led by Salem Chalabi and Faisal Isterabadi, worked on the document while they were effectively kept in the dark about the scope of Kurdish demands. Strangely, the draft of what became the TAL progressed without any serious Shi'a participation. Sistani, who was lulled into complacency by the assurances of the Shi'a House that the process was under control, did not interfere in the drafting. Bremer presented the Kurdish demands to the TAL drafting committee very late in the process, and only after strenuous demands that he should do so from Salem Chalabi and Isterabadi.

By early February 2004, the committee had prepared the main outlines of the draft that incorporated the agreed positions of the Kurds as negotiated between them and Bremer. It was only at this stage that the Shi'a woke up to the TAL implications, and hastily agreed to form a committee of their own to examine the draft.[6] Bremer, presumably under Washington pressure, refused to countenance any delay to the 28 February deadline for the conclusion of the TAL. A series of marathon meetings then ensued.

The text of the draft TAL enshrined principles that were supposed to guide the transitional process, and even the constitutional framework, of Iraq. Even its preamble was worded in stirring terms, reminiscent of permanent constitutions – and utterly alien in construction and phraseology from the Arabic language and the Iraqi experience. 'The people of Iraq, striving to reclaim their freedom . . .' the TAL began. It talked about pluralism, gender rights, separation of powers and civilian control over the armed forces – none of which were even remotely familiar terms in Iraq. The TAL embodied western, specifically American notions, and was carefully supervised by the CPA. Each significant point had been pre-cleared with the NSC in Washington.[7] Neither the CPA nor its drafters envisaged it as anything less than the basic model for Iraq's permanent constitution. The Kurds certainly viewed it as such, and were vigorous in defending the positions that they had developed in their bilateral negotiations with Bremer. The Sunni Arabs on the Governing Council also worked on the assumption that the TAL would provide the basis for any constitutional order in Iraq. The involvement of Pachachi as the main Governing Council leader who was charged with the drafting of the TAL ensured that the Sunni Arab perspective, together with Pachachi's commitment to secularism and liberalism, would not be lost in the final text. In spite of their heterogeneity, the Sunni Arabs on the Governing Council began to organise themselves as a consciously Sunni caucus and developed joint positions on the draft.[8]

A Contentious Article in the TAL

The pressures to accept the document with minor modifications became irresistible. A key Kurdish demand was slipped in as article 61(c) of the TAL, at the tail end of the drafting committee's work. It allowed the Kurds the possibility of rejecting any permanent constitution in a referendum, if two-thirds of the voters of three provinces so decided. The Kurds dominated the three provinces within the Kurdistan Regional Government. By legislating for the inviolability of this principle in any future constitutional negotiations, the Kurds had a veto power on any constitution that veered too far from the accepted norms of the TAL. The Sunni Arabs also accepted this controversial article, seeing it as a way of limiting Shi'a power, and possibly also providing the Sunnis with the ability to block any future constitution not to their liking.[9] The final draft was presented to the Governing Council which, surprisingly, approved it unanimously. A committee was formed to go over the document for typographic and drafting errors, working on the assumption that there would be no substantive alterations to the document. The Shi'a caucus had not done their homework.[10] Article 61(c) suddenly loomed as an issue, and there were hurried consultations between SCIRI's Hakim and the Najaf hierarchy. When word of the draft TAL reached Najaf, the response of the *Marji'iyya* was scathing. Sistani had major reservations about the implicit claims of the TAL to being a crypto-constitution, and considered any such designation as usurping the democratic right of Iraqis to choose their own constitution.[11] In Najaf's reckoning, 61(c) gave the right of a minority to block the will of the majority of Iraqis, and to force on them a series of concessions of principle as a price for having a working agreement for the country. The *Marji'iyya* was, of course, concerned about two main issues: the primacy of Islam and Iraq's Islamic identity, and cementing the empowerment of the Shi'a majority within a decidedly Islamic character for Iraq's state and society.

The Shi'a caucus had to scramble to explain its approval of the draft TAL to the *Marji'iyya*, while at the same time announcing to its partners in the Governing Council that they now had reservations about a document that they had agreed to only a few days previously.[12] The Kurds refused to accept any modifications to the TAL, especially to the offending article 61(c), with Barzani stating that the Kurdish parliament had already approved the draft TAL and would not tolerate any changes to it.[13] Meanwhile, the CPA had prepared for a grand signing ceremony for the TAL which had to be suddenly and embarrassingly postponed when word came that the Shi'a caucus was not prepared to sign the document.[14] Immense pressures were then exerted on the Shi'a caucus to yield to the demands of the CPA, the Kurds and the Sunni Arabs, and to circumvent the *Marji'iyya*'s deeply felt qualms about the document. Washington would not brook any further delay. The TAL was too important a milestone in the November 15 Agreement. Finally, a compromise of sorts was cobbled together between the Shi'a caucus and the Najaf hierarchy that allowed for the signing of the TAL. In a clumsy move, the Shi'a leaders on the Governing Council signed the document – only to hold a press conference later in the day to express their reservations about the TAL, especially article 61(c). The *Marji'iyya* was deeply perturbed about this episode, rightly suspecting that the TAL would determine the course of Iraq's constitutional passage and resentful at the bungling of the Shi'a caucus in managing the TAL drafting process.

The TAL was deeply resented by a large majority of Iraqis, not least by Shi'a lawyers, academics and professionals who had remained in Iraq during the Saddamist years. Its obviously western provenance and its Kurdo-centrism seemed to open the country to dismantling its Arab identity and to partition. To a broad cross-section of Iraqis, the TAL's laudable statements of rights and freedoms could not dispel the overall impression of a flawed document, written by a foreign occupier with Iraqi fellow-travellers in tow.

The Transition Administrative Law

With the signing of the TAL on 8 March, 2004, the CPA seemed to have resolved a particularly difficult issue. In public, the CPA maintained that they might have been upstaged by Sistani, but the reality was very different. The CPA got its Iraqi interlocutors, the Governing Council, to put their names to a document that had built-in safeguards against the possibility of a permanent constitution differing greatly in content from the TAL. The TAL had the usual checks and balances expected of a democratic constitution, but it went one step further by having supermajorities required at a number of critical junctures. It could only be amended by a three-quarters majority of the TNA and the unanimous approval of the three-man Presidential Council (article 3). This would be a practical impossibility. Since the Presidential Council itself required a two-thirds affirmative vote in the TNA, the Kurds had effective veto power on the people who might be candidates for this post. A grudging acknowledgement of the role of Islam in the country was made, but the Islamist demand that Islam be considered the main, or only, source of legislation was rejected. Instead, Islam became only one of many sources of legislation (article 7(a)). In an obvious dig at Arab nationalists, Iraq was not identified as an Arab state. Instead, the Arabs of Iraq were deemed to be part of the Arab nation (article 7(b)), an absurd construct. The Kurdish language was elevated to the status of an official language (article 9) as part of a panoply of measures that gave recognition to the Kurds' de facto government, the Kurdistan Regional Government (KRG), and to its juridical and financial independence from the centre in Baghdad.

In spite of its many shortcomings, however, the TAL granted unheard-of freedoms, in one of the most far-reaching expressions of democratic, human and civil rights present in any single document. Even so, the spectre of occupation remained due to the presence of Iraqi forces under the command of the Coalition.

The TAL called for the election of the TNA by no later than 31 January, 2005. Having decided that the transfer of sovereignty to an Iraqi government was to take place by 30 June, 2004, a hiatus developed for the period between 30 June, 2004 and the elections for the TNA as to the nature of the governing authority during this period. Bremer had little confidence in the organising and leadership qualities of the Governing Council, and believed that it was incapable of improvement and reform.[15] Talking about the Governing Council to Deputy Defense Secretary Paul Wolfowitz, Bremer said, 'These people couldn't organize a parade, let alone run a country'.[16] He would frequently by-pass the Governing Council in his dealings with specific ministers. Ministers who were connected to the CPA ignored the Governing Council by their direct links to Bremer, and built on this privileged relationship to cement and enhance their control over their ministries.[17] There were two interconnected issues that deeply concerned the CPA. First, whether elections for the TNA could be held by the time sovereignty was to be transferred on 30 June, 2004, and second, in the event that elections could not be organised in time, what authority was to be created and empowered to exercise sovereignty for the interim period. The arguments were not only technical in nature but also went to the heart of control over the transition process, to ensure an outcome that would not run counter to the interests of a myriad of parties, the most important and powerful of which was the USA.

Fears of the Role of Islam in the New Iraqi State

Behind the sanctimonious statements about democracy and freedom, the USA and its Allies were extremely wary of a government that might be dominated by Islamists, and that would be open to Iranian influence. The composition of the Governing Council was dictated by the dynamics of the former Iraqi opposition and the exigencies of the situation in Iraq in the summer of 2003. With the experience of nearly six months behind it, however, the CPA was uneasy about the extent of Islamist influence on the Governing Council. In particular, the CPA was taken aback by a Governing Council decision to reintroduce religious law as the basis for Iraq's personal and familial codes. The measure was passed on 14 January, 2004 during the tenure of Abd el-Aziz al-Hakim's presidency of the Governing Council and in the absence of the liberal member Adnan al-Pachachi. Secular women's groups, abetted by the only female minister Nasreen Barwari, took to the streets, denouncing the measure as retrograde. In the event, and after considerable CPA pressure, the Governing Council dropped the clause. In another public display of the CPA's anxiety about the extent of Islamist influence on the Governing Council, Bremer made it clear that he would veto the fundamental law – the TAL to be – if it designated Islam as the main source of legislation. When asked if the TAL would push Iraq into becoming an Islamic republic, Bremer answered, 'Don't worry, this won't be an Islamic constitution'.[18] In another manifestation of the concern about the Islamic drift of the country, the TAL adopted the interpretation of the concept of 'freedom of religion' as implying the right of an individual to change his or her religion. This was a fraught issue under Sharia law, as it was generally considered that a Muslim could not change his religious affiliations. Under Muslim law, the crime of apostasy is punishable by death. The right to proselytise in Iraq had been one of the demands of the Christian Right in America, and a number of evangelical and fundamentalist Christian organisations were active in Iraq in the wake of the invasion. Senator Brownback of Kansas, a leader of the Christian Right in Congress, wrote to the CPA insisting that the right of religious freedom be included in the TAL.[19] Bush himself took an interest in this matter, for both personal and political reasons.[20] The Christian Right had marked Iraq as a frontline state in its proselytising mission. Kyle Fisk, the executive administrator of the National Association of Evangelicals, announced, 'Iraq will become the centre for spreading the gospel of Jesus Christ to Iran, Libya, throughout the Middle East . . . President Bush said democracy will spread from Iraq to nearby countries. A free Iraq also allows us to spread Jesus Christ's teachings even in nations where the laws keep us out.'[21] With a looming deadline for the transfer of sovereignty, evangelicals redoubled their efforts in Iraq, frequently combining proselytising with humanitarian aid. The CPA had a number of middle-level staff members who were fundamentalist Christians and who played a part in formulating the legal structures that were designed to thwart the creeping Islamisation of the state. The sense of urgency on the part of those who were not Islamist, that measures had to be taken quickly to block this unwelcome development, became all-pervasive.[22]

The unstated fear was that the UN mission would concur with Sistani's demand that elections could and should be held before the transfer of sovereignty on 30 June, 2004. With the TAL in place as a crypto-constitution, the Coalition adopted a two-pronged strategy to counter the risks of holding premature elections. The first part involved careful monitoring of the UN mission to ascertain the practicability of holding elections and influencing the outcome in favour of delaying any elections. The second part was a persistent questioning of the credibility of the Governing Council as the basis for an interim sovereign authority. The key to the strategy that was being pursued by Washington and London was to be Lakhdar Brahimi, the UN's envoy to Iraq.

The Brahimi Mission

Lakhdar Brahimi had joined Algeria's national liberation movement (FLN) soon after the war against the French began in 1954. Following the Algerian coup of 1991, Brahimi was appointed the junta's foreign minister and served on its six-man High Security Council. In 1993, he was forced out of office after an internal dispute with the Algerian prime minister. He then started a long career with the UN as a special envoy and troubleshooter in many countries. From 1997 he was key to the successful UN mission to Afghanistan. He won important allies in the USA and the UK, a result of the respect he had earned for his achievements, especially in post-Taliban Afghanistan.

Although Adnan al-Pachachi had welcomed the UN's involvement in the Iraqi political process and had seen Brahimi's appointment as a very positive development,[23] elements of the neo-conservative lobby in Washington saw him in a different light. His involvement with the Arab League marked him out as an Arab nationalist and therefore implicitly anti-Israel, while his role as an apologist for the Algerian military junta labelled him as a supporter of the Arab penchant for authoritarian military governments and centralised state control. However, the *Marji'iyya* was prepared to give both him and the UN team the benefit of the doubt, and eagerly awaited the results of their mission to establish the practicability of holding elections before the end of the June 2004 deadline.

The UN mission, led by Brahimi, arrived in Iraq on 6 February, 2004 and stayed for a week. Brahimi held a number of meetings with the main protagonists in Baghdad before going to Najaf to see Grand Ayatollah Sistani. His team fanned out and met many Iraqi public figures, including tribal leaders, academics, Sunni and Shi'a religious figures, women's groups, journalists and human rights organisers. Brahimi could sense the mounting divisions in the country, and its fragmented and polarised political scene. This drove him to mention the possibility of civil war, if the political class did not wake up to its responsibilities. At a press conference Brahimi warned members of the Governing Council to be 'conscious that civil wars do not happen because a person makes a decision [to start a civil war] .... Civil wars erupt because people are reckless, people are selfish, because people think more of themselves than they do of their country.'[24]

The Governing Council itself was split along sectarian and ethnic lines. All the Shi'a members, with the exception of Ayad Allawi and Hamid Moussa of the Communist Party, stuck to the Sistani line, and insisted that elections could be held before the 30 June deadline. But Sunni Arabs, including Pachachi, Yawar and Chadirchi, were adamant that elections were not feasible at such short notice. Even the Kurds, fearing that elections would bring to power an uncontrolled Shi'a majority, came out against the idea of elections by the end of June. All, of course, paid lip service to the idea of elections as the underpinning of a constituent assembly, but none was prepared to take the plunge before safety measures were in place against what they feared would be a 'tyranny of the majority'. 'No one in his right mind would reject the elections in principle ... but at the same time we don't want to have nominal or hasty elections and pay a hefty price for that,' the AMS said in a statement after it had met with Brahimi.[25] The mood in the UN camp was decidedly sceptical about the possibility of holding elections by the end of June. It also appeared to reject the CPA's caucus system for electing the delegates to the TNA. The mission returned to New York and on 23 February, 2004 Kofi Annan released Brahimi's report to the Security Council.[26]

The Brahimi Report to the UN Security Council

The Brahimi report confirmed that the caucus system was not workable, and that it should be dropped as a mechanism for selecting the national legislative body. At the same time, while acknowledging that elections were the only valid manner for selecting members for the legislative and constituent assembly, the UN team deemed it impossible to hold elections by the date of the handover of sovereignty. The report also raised a number of concerns on the political situation inside Iraq, talking about a 'growing fragmentation of the political class'; entrenched sectarianism; and a polarisation of the political environment. Surprisingly, the report also touched on the most sensitive issue of the major divides in Iraqi society and politics, thus breaking one of the main taboos in Arab politics in a most public way. For the first time, the UN dealt openly with the sectarian and ethnic problems in Iraq as the determinants of its political life. 'In the Sunni community and among the secular elite, there are perceptions that they are witnessing a decisive shift in the balance of power as a result of which they will lose in the new political arrangements that are being put in place,' the report intoned. The Shi'a were described as determined not to repeat the mistakes of their predecessors following the abortive 1920 Uprising. 'They [the Shi'a] are committed to correcting this and ensuring the political emancipation of the Shi'a community.' The Kurds, on the other hand, were described as having 'made numerous gains since the early 1980s and after the first Gulf War but fear that new arrangements will be at the expense of what they have now'. Minority groups felt that a 'majoritarian system' would 'put them at a huge disadvantage', while women's groups were described as being 'concerned that the gains made under the secular regimes of the past are under threat from a new system dominated by religious-based parties'.

The Brahimi report also noted the high level of violence and instability throughout a number of provinces, including Baghdad, which would have a marked impact on the ability to hold elections. There would be a concerted attempt by insurgents to disrupt such elections, and the level of participation would be clearly affected by an organised boycott campaign, if necessary enforced by violent measures. There was no assurance that a delay in the elections could be warranted simply because of the hope that the insurgency might wind down in the future and therefore improve the security environment for holding elections. In fact, an opposite case could be made.

The report was an extraordinary admission on the part of the UN of the divisions and conflicts inside Iraqi society, and of the difficulties of the way ahead. In some respects, the UN confirmed its hostility to the American-led war, but it also implicitly recognised that the management of the transition period was critical for ensuring an 'acceptable' outcome. What that outcome was going to be was determined by the position that the UN were to take on the practicability of elections in the short term and the nature of the interim government that would be handed sovereignty after 30 June, 2004. The report concluded that 'a provisional government will need to be formed by 30 June 2004 through some mechanism other than direct elections.' The caucus system for electing a transitional assembly to nominate a provisional government was dropped. At the same time, the UN did not insist on a consultative assembly for nominating the new government. The appointment of the provisional government was left to an undefined mechanism. The report did discuss the range of alternatives inconclusively. The report stated that the provisional government would have to be of short duration, but by leaving its formation to an unspecified process, allowed the Coalition the opportunity to manage the transition process. Implicit in the report was the need to ensure an eventual outcome that would not materially differ from the objectives of the USA and its Allies, as well as groups inside Iraq. The desired outcome was to be achieved through the appointment of an unelected provisional government and the postponement of the elections to at least six months into the life of the provisional government.

The Brahimi report was approved by nearly all groups except the Shi'a. A number of the Governing Council's Shi'a members, in particular Ahmad Chalabi, mistrusted the purpose of the entire mission. Brahimi was seen to be too close to the ruling groups in the Arab world which had supported the Ba'ath regime until the last possible moment and were scathing about the prospects of democracy in Iraq. They were now fearful that Iraq might slip entirely out of the orbit of Arab countries. The hostility of most Arab rulers to the post-Saddam order in Iraq was assumed to be shared by Brahimi, and this inference, partly supported by Brahimi's own vehement stand against the war, would greatly influence the attitudes of the majority of the Shi'a about him. The Shi'a Islamists saw him in a somewhat different light. Brahimi was believed to favour, if not the continuation of Sunni dominance, at least ensuring that they would enjoy a disproportionate share of power. What mattered most now was whether the Najaf hierarchy in the person of Grand Ayatollah Sistani would accept the conclusions of the Brahimi report, and the continuing role of the UN as an impartial arbiter in Iraq.

Sistani, Brahimi and the Transition Process

Sistani was certainly dismayed when the UN confirmed the impracticability of holding elections by 30 June. However, he had made sure the caucus system was jettisoned, and had obtained the UN's sanction on the principle of elections as the basis for establishing the transitional assembly. Sistani finally agreed to Kofi Annan's suggestion that elections could be held by the end of the year, or by 31 January, 2005 at the latest. Now the main concern of the *Marji'iyya* was to ensure that the TAL, which was signed within a fortnight of the Brahimi report, would not completely dominate the political and constitutional agenda of Iraq. A continuing role of the UN in the political transition process was seen as one of the essential safeguards for stopping this from happening. There had been widespread demonstrations against the TAL in a number of Shi'a towns and cities, and scathing statements against it were made by people close to the *Marji'iyya*. No one, however, with the exception of the Sadrists, pushed for the outright repudiation of the TAL. Once it had been signed, however, the *Marji'iyya*'s main concern was to deny it international legitimacy as the only valid political roadmap for the transition period. On 19 March, 2004, Sistani addressed a letter to Lakhdar Brahimi in which the Ayatollah clearly set out his views on the TAL and his concerns lest it receive a formal UN endorsement.[27] Sistani stated that it was through the efforts of the *Marji'iyya* that the UN was brought back into the Iraqi political process. It had hoped that an elected assembly would act as the ultimate authority during the transition period, but as a result of the TAL, 'the National Assembly will be shackled by a host of restrictions .... An unelected body, the Governing Council, in coordination with the occupying authority has imposed a strange law for the administration of the country during the transition period. And what is more dangerous has imposed . . . a set of principles and processes on the manner in which the permanent constitution is to be written.' The Ayatollah went on to state that the TAL did not enjoy the support of the majority of Iraqis, and that it forfeited the rights of the elected representatives of the people in an unparalleled manner. He was clearly referring to article 61(c) that provided a veto right on the permanent constitution to three provinces if they reject it in a referendum. The letter then clearly spelt out the *Marji'iyya*'s objection to any attempt to give international credence to the TAL by including it in a future UN resolution. 'We warn that such a step will not be accepted by most of the Iraqi people, and will have dangerous repercussions. We ask you to so notify the members of the Security Council.'[28]

The Brahimi mission was dogged with the charge that it had carved a space for the USA and its Allies to manage the transition process, while appearing to be impartial as to the mission's methods and purposes. The *Marji'iyya*, however, continued to believe in the good intentions of the UN and Brahimi,

the Zarqawi strategy was in fact related to the escalating tensions between the sects in Iraq, and a determination to exacerbate them. The increasing bitterness of relations between Iraq's sects was smothered underneath a rhetoric of denial. Nevertheless, Zarqawi's organisation, which was to become the most notorious of the foreign terrorist groups operating in Iraq, began to displace al-Qaeda at the top of the Coalition's anti-terrorist propaganda. It formed part of the tripartite mantra that the insurgents were a combination of 'former regime elements', radical Islamists, and foreign terrorists and *jihadis*. None of the legs of this tripod was deemed to have any domestic base and it seemed to be a matter of time before these 'anti-Iraqi' forces were to be crushed. In private, however, more sober and realistic analysts were beginning to discern the seeds of a more lasting conflict.

The effects of decades of concentrated Wahhabi, and less extreme Salafi, teachings hurled at the Sunni world of Iraq were beginning to have a lasting effect on Sunni Arab opinion.[7] With the Shi'a in a clearly subordinate position during the decades of Saddam's rule, there was no need to couch the sectarian divide in openly antagonistic terms. The sudden collapse of Ba'athist rule and with it the disempowerment of the Sunni Arab community, however, crystallised the threats in no uncertain terms. Wahhabi teachings began to make some sense after all, and seeped into the mindset of a large number of Sunni Arabs, who had hitherto been indifferent or hostile to Wahhabi, or even religious, thinking. Throughout the 1990s there had been a dangerous escalation of the animosity between the Shi'a and the Sunni throughout the eastern Islamic lands. In Afghanistan, for instance, the sectarian conflict was exacerbated by the fact that most Shi'a were of the ethnic Hazara group. The Taliban indulged in wanton acts of murder specifically against the Hazara community, culminating in a particularly horrifying massacre in 1998. The concept of *takfir*, or levelling the charge of infidelity to Islam to the Shi'a as a group, was introduced. The charge of *takfir* was not an easy one to make or even suggest. Under Muslim canonical law, this charge could only be applied under highly restrictive and narrow conditions.[8] Those accused of *kufr* (heresy) can theoretically be banished from the community of Islam – and even put to death. A number of Wahhabi preachers and even academics issued a *fatwa* authorising a *jihad* against the Shi'a.[9]

The deterioration in Shi'a–Sunni relations in the 1990s, and into the decade of the 2000s, stood in marked contrast to the earlier efforts by leading religious authorities in the Sunni and Shi'a worlds to bring the two sects closer. Throughout the pre-World War II era and well into the 1960s the relationships between the two communities were, if not ideal, at least amicable. Iraqi religious leaders were at the forefront of this movement of ecumenism.[10] Al-Azhar University, the acknowledged leader of official worldwide Sunni orthodoxy, under the leadership of Sheikh Mahmoud Shaltut, issued a famous *fatwa* in 1959 confirming that the sect of Twelver Shi'a Islam, to which the overwhelming majority of Shi'a subscribe, is religiously correct.[11] Shi'a throughout the Middle East were euphoric about this declaration and felt that the age of sectarian rivalries was finally over. This sense of benign indifference between the sects was the norm in Iraq until the 1970s, and coloured the perceptions of many people as to the true relationship between the communities. It was therefore not surprising that many returning exiles, especially secularists who had spent their formative years in Iraq of the 1950s to the 1970s, were shocked by the deterioration of intercommunal relations, and were extremely reluctant to acknowledge that the dreaded disease of sectarianism might have overwhelmed their country of memory.

Radicalisation of Iraqi Sunni and Shi'a Islam

The barrage of anti-Shi'a literature emanating from Saudi-sponsored schools, universities and seminaries became required reading for the recently energised Sunni Muslims of Iraq. The bookstalls outside Baghdad's main Sunni mosques, such as the ones around the Imam Abu Hanifa Mosque in 'Adhamiyya, displayed mainly Salafist or Wahhabi-inspired literature, mostly imported from Saudi Arabia.[12] These tracts generally ignored the Shi'a perspective, and contributed to the polarising of opinion in a country that was already dividing along sectarian lines. A noticeable change in the topics and delivery of sermons affected all the main Sunni mosques of Baghdad and elsewhere, and laid the groundwork for the overthrow of the mild form of religious orthodoxy prevalent in Iraq by a more arid and doctrinally inflexible form of Sunni Islam.[13] Some of the preachers were careful to maintain a public posture of sectarian accommodation, but others began to use code words behind which they could hide their true inclinations and fears. In the year after the invasion, words that implicated the Shi'a of Iraq in one 'crime' or another began to filter into common usage. The words *Safawi* and *Buwayhi* were used interchangeably to imply the Shi'a. Both of these terms referred to alien dynasties, in particular to Iran. The implication was that the Shi'a of Iraq were close to Iran, and that their loyalty to the homeland was suspect or even that they were transplanted Iranians.

The campaign by the *jihadi* Salafists and Wahhabis to dominate the world of Sunni Islam with their intolerant and frequently perverse version of religion was not limited to vilification of the Shi'a. They also denounced moderates in their midst, especially the Sufi orders. In Zarqawi's letter, he devotes a particularly bilious section to Sufis, drawing on both the Wahhabi horror of shrine visitation and the Islamic modernists' caricature of Sufis as drugged debauchees and gluttons. In the demonology of the Wahhabis, the Sufis are apostates, only one step removed from the Shi'a. The letter stated, in reference to the quiescent *ulema* of the Sunni, 'These are mostly Sufis doomed to perdition. Their part of religion is an anniversary in which they sing and dance to the chanting of a camel driver, with a fatty banquet at the end. In truth, these are narcotic opiate[s] and deceitful guides for an [Islamic] nation that is feeling its way on a pitch-black night. As for the spirit of *jihad* and the jurisprudence of martyrdom and disavowal of the infidel, they are innocent of all of that.' The insurgents began a bombing and intimidation campaign against the Sufi orders. In April 2004, they blew up a Sufi *tekiye* (hostel) in the city of Ramadi, and this continued with further destruction of Sufi shrines in western Iraq and the murder of a number of Sufi leaders. The campaign against Sufis really took off in earnest in 2005, however, when they received the insurgents' ultimate accolade – a suicide bombing.[14]

The Muslim Brotherhood, the pan-Islamist movement originating in Egypt, also had followers in Iraq. The Iraqi Islamic Party, though not formally connected to the Brotherhood, was also in Zarqawi's firing line. They were castigated for prevarication and duplicity, and their involvement in the Governing Council was seen as a power ploy that would undermine the insurgents' cause. The letter stated, 'Their [The Muslim Brotherhood's] whole effort is to extend political control and seize the posts of Sunni representation in the government . . . while taking care in secret to get control of the mujahideen groups through financial support . . . . It is their habit to grab the stick in the middle and change as the political climate changes. Their religion is mercurial. They have no firm principles, and they do not start from enduring legal bases.'

The CPA continued to ignore the ever-mounting signals that the insurgency was turning dangerously close to becoming a general Sunni insurrection with the most grotesque acts of violence being carried out in the name of so-called 'national' resistance. The assertion that the insurgency could be somehow contained without tackling the underlying fears of the Sunni was becoming increasingly awkward.

The Shi'a of Iraq went through their own metamorphosis. Shi'a mosques, especially those that fell outside the direct control of the *Marji'iyya*, began to exercise their new-found freedoms. The sermons of the Friday preachers became more politically charged. The carnage caused by the unrelenting pace of car and suicide bombing gave the sermon leaders a pretext to levy accusations not only at the insurgents but also at what were seen as their apologists and fellow-travellers. In particular, the AMS maintained a studied ambiguity about its positions on violence, and its condemnation of the insurgents' outrages was at best lukewarm. It drew the most anger from the Shi'a *minbars* (pulpits). The radicalisation of the Shi'a was more political than doctrinal, however, in the sense that the Shi'a did not push to the forefront their juridical and doctrinal arguments with the Sunni. The Shi'a retort to the Wahhabi threat was more defensive. Shi'a doctrine did express deep reservations about the Sunni version of historical events, but there was also an acute awareness that the Shi'a were a minority in Islam as a whole. Their ideological attacks on the Sunni were more hesitant, and conditioned partly by the fear of an irreversible drift of the Shi'a from the main body of Islam if their doctrines were seen to be too different. The Shi'a concentrated their campaign against Wahhabism per se and not against the world of mainstream Sunnism. The gradual erosion of traditional Sunnism in Iraq and elsewhere, and the rise of militant anti-Shi'ism as an element of modern Sunni thought, made the task of differentiation increasingly difficult. What used to be a slanging match between Wahhabism and Shi'ism – and in some ways containable – developed into one between an increasingly radicalised Sunni Islam and the Shi'a. The Shi'a resurrected the term *nawasib* (those with a particular hatred for the Prophet's household) to attach to the extreme insurgents.

Abu Musab al-Zarqawi and the Ideology of Abu Muhammad al-Maqdisi

The Coalition had never anticipated the rise of Zarqawi as an insurgent. He had been a little-noticed figure before the war. In his speech to the UN's Security Council in early February 2003, Colin Powell explicitly connected Zarqawi with the Ba'athist authorities, to fortify the claims of the regime's complicity with al-Qaeda and international terrorism. 'During Zarqawi's stay in Baghdad, nearly two dozen of his associates set up a base of operations in the capital to move people, money and supplies throughout the country . . . . They've now been operating freely in the capital for more than eight months,'[15] Powell said. After the war, however, the charge of his connections with the former regime was quietly allowed to die.

Zarqawi was a Jordanian, whose real name was Ahmad Fadheel Nazal al-Khalayla of the Bani Hassan tribe.[16] He was born in October 1966 in the grimy town of Zarqa – hence the alias of 'Zarqawi' by which he was later known. His childhood and youth were spent in the squalor and poverty of a Jordanian backwater. He dropped out of school and drifted into a life of criminality. He was jailed in the 1980s, but when released in 1989 made his way to Afghanistan, just as the war against the Soviets was coming to an end. He based himself in the western city of Herat and seems to have befriended Osama bin Laden. He also met the man who would be his ideological mentor, Abu Muhammad al-Maqdisi. Returning to Jordan, he was involved in petty trade, but kept his *jihadi* credentials. He was implicated in a conspiracy with his mentor, Maqdisi, and the two were arrested in early 1994 and sentenced to life imprisonment. In 1999, Zarqawi was released in a general amnesty following the coronation of the new Jordanian king, Abdullah. The time spent in Jordan's jails seems to have had a profound impact on Zarqawi. He became exposed to a strain of Salafi thought that was being developed by Maqdisi and that became the foundation for the ideology of the *jihadi* Salafists. The alliance between Zarqawi and Maqdisi in jail was more than that between a teacher and a star pupil. Zarqawi was also the enforcer for the group around Maqdisi, and was used to good effect in the turf wars between the various Islamist and criminal gangs in prison. The extreme ideology that Zarqawi adopted, especially his rabid hatred for the Shi'a and anyone who collaborated with the 'crusaders', the *jihadi* Salafist term for the Coalition, could be traced directly to his period in prison in the company of Maqdisi.

Maqdisi was one of those figures in modern Islamism whose importance is only discovered late in the day.[17] Agencies concentrated their attentions almost exclusively on the terrorist acts of al-Qaeda and the primitive obscurantism of the Taliban, ignoring the rise of the *takfiri* trend in Salafi thought. It was above all the polemics and writings of Maqdisi that demarcated the boundaries of the new thinking, and opened the way for the extraordinary violence that has been employed in Iraq.

Maqdisi's parents emigrated to Kuwait soon after he was born, and it was in Kuwait that he was raised and schooled. Kuwait in that period was a hothouse of Palestinian activism. Most politically conscious Palestinian youth, in that heyday of radical Palestinian nationalism, tended to gravitate towards leftist and nationalist parties. There was, however, a small core of Islamist Palestinians who became influenced by the thought of extremist clerics based in the Wahhabi stronghold of Buraida in Saudi Arabia. What put Maqdisi on the map of the evolving *jihadi* Salafi movement was a tract that he wrote entitled *Millat Ibrahim* (The People of Abraham). Out of this Quranic verse, the ideologue of the new *jihadi* Salafism spun a complete doctrine of renunciation of governments that do not follow a narrow path of obeisance to the 'true religion', as seen through the eyes of the medieval literalist Ibn Taymiyya and his modern followers in the Wahhabi and Salafi movements. The practice of *bara'a* (distancing oneself from governments, systems and groups that do not subscribe to this perspective) became a religious obligation.

It was only a small step after that to link renunciation with actual physical resistance and obligatory struggle against such systems. *Takfir* became not only an act of withdrawal from contaminating cultures and ideas – but an active struggle, violent if necessary, against offending institutions and groups. It was left to Maqdisi and his followers to define the countries, dynasties and sects that fell foul of the narrow path of obeisance to the 'true religion'. In November 1995 Maqdisi went in and out of jail in Jordan. In a satellite television interview with the al-Jazeera channel in July 2005, he seemed to have recanted some of his more extreme pronouncements. In 2004, he issued a letter from jail where he took pains to distance himself from the extreme actions of his erstwhile pupil Zarqawi. He insisted that, for a Muslim, the charge of *takfir* was a very serious one, and should not be lightly brought. In particular, he took issue with the wholesale murder of the Shi'a in Iraq and the indiscriminate use of suicide bombing as a tactic, which was increasingly becoming Zarqawi's stock-in-trade. In essence, he called for a cautious and nuanced response to the challenges that the *jihadi* Salafists saw around them, and for them not to be drawn into confrontations and battles.

Zarqawi brought this '*takfiri*' ideology into his war in Iraq, taking it to a higher pitch of violence and destructiveness. He also appeared to have swapped ideological mentors as Maqdisi rejected the consequences of his own teachings. The letter that Maqdisi addressed from jail appeared to have taken Zarqawi by surprise.[18] Zarqawi took it upon himself to reply to his former teacher and responded in ways that claimed for himself a scholarly status. He distanced himself from the newly cautious Maqdisi, insisting that *jihad* in Iraq was an obligatory act.[19] As for the Shi'a, the attacks on them were entirely warranted by what Zarqawi claimed were *fatwas* from *jihadi* Salafi scholars that confirmed that the Shi'a must be fought.[20] The apparent split in the *jihadi* Salafi movement was not of sufficient consequence to disrupt the operations of Zarqawi. If anything, Zarqawi, as the field commander of the *jihadi* Salafists, appeared to be gaining further support in the months to follow for his unbendingly violent ways. One wing of the insurgency, the most vicious and deadly, was coalescing around Zarqawi and his *Tawhid and Jihad* organisation. It would soon become the operating arm of the al-Qaeda network as Zarqawi moved decisively from Maqdisi and gave his allegiance to Bin Laden later in 2004.

The Insurgency Gathers Steam[21]

The other aspects of the insurgency also began to crystallise in the final months of 2003 and early 2004. The depiction of the insurgency as 'dead-enders' and former regime elements began to appear ridiculously inappropriate. Nevertheless, the CPA and the Pentagon continued to deny publicly that what they had on their hands in Iraq was the germination of a full-scale insurrection of the Sunni Arabs of Iraq. As one of the former Ba'athist regime's enforcers said to a *Washington Post* reporter, referring to the Sunni Arabs generally, 'We were on top of the system. We had dreams. Now we are the losers. We lost our positions, our status, the security of our families, stability. Curse the Americans. Curse them . . . . Was being a Baathist some sort of disease? Was serving the country some sort of crime?'[22] The former intelligence officer went on to say, 'These people with turbans are going to run the country', in a clear reference to the Shi'a clerics. This statement encapsulated the views of the great majority of Sunni Arabs, and captured their sense of loss and anxiety at the future. Their very identity was under serious threat as the country which they had fashioned in their own image appeared to be slipping totally outside their control and understanding. Identity was inextricably linked to power, status and privilege, just as the social historian Ali al-Wardi had said. But in early 2004, the CPA would hear none of this. The British were beginning to reassess the true conditions inside Iraq, but the situation had not yet deteriorated to the point where they could challenge entrenched American thinking on this policy.

The drift of most Sunni Arabs towards the adoption of a variant of Salafi Islam to buttress their identity and as a mobilising factor against the occupation and its consequences was accelerating in the final months of 2003 and in early 2004. Ba'athism, Arab nationalism, liberalism were useless as effective mobilising ideas for a community trying to recover its balance. Apart from a few die-hard loyalists, there was little love lost for Saddam Hussein and his family, but the Ba'ath Party continued to serve as a useful mechanism for organising the resistance to the occupation. It was always able to operate and indeed thrive in a clandestine atmosphere, and the loss of power did not completely paralyse its operations. It had lost nearly all of its top leadership; only Saddam Hussein and the elusive Izzat al-Douri were still at large by December 2003. Although some of its second- and third-tier membership was targeted for assassination by hit squads attached to the Kurds and to the Shi'a religious parties, Ba'athist cells were able to re-establish themselves and conduct small-scale operations against the Coalition. There was no doubt that the funds, and even some of the arms, in the early days of the insurgency were provided by clandestine Ba'ath Party cells, individuals from Saddam's extended family, even Saddam himself.

The ideology of the Party also changed in opposition, partly to accommodate the increased religiosity of its mainly Sunni base and partly because its own membership had turned more pious. The Party positioned itself as the bearer of the standard of heroic Arabs in defence of their country, and its use of religious imagery played to its increasingly receptive Sunni Arab base. The more Salafist insurgents and those with Ba'athist roots diverged considerably in their beliefs, however. The religious credentials of the Ba'ath were suspect, and some Islamist insurgents took pains to distance themselves from the former regime and its institutions. The capture of Saddam Hussein on 13 December, 2003 in humiliating circumstances caused a setback to Ba'athist insurgents, but had little impact on the insurgency as a whole. The triumphalist tone with which his capture was reported – Bremer, on announcing the news in a press conference, exclaimed 'Ladies and gentlemen, we got him!' – was a sign of wilfully ignoring the facts of the insurgency and, worse, a trivialisation and personalisation of its causes.

Saddam Hussein had been captured on 13 December, 2003 by elements of the USA's 4th Infantry Division, while hiding in a six-foot-deep hole in a farm in the village of Daur, close to his hometown of al-'Auja. The hole was covered by a trap door. His dishevelled, heavily bearded, and haggard face was beamed to the world, with a Coalition doctor alternately poking a tongue depressor into his mouth or searching for vermin in his hair. It was an ignominious end to the career of one of the world's most feared and hated figures. After a thorough medical examination, he was cleaned up, and then four members of the Governing Council, Chalabi, Pachachi, Rubai'e and Abd el-Mahdi, saw him. The meeting between Saddam and the Governing Council members was tense. It was allowed by the CPA partly to confirm his identity. Saddam, when he deigned to respond, treated Governing Council members as interlopers and agents of foreign powers. He showed absolutely no remorse when confronted with a series of accusatory remarks about his murder of the Hakim and Sadr families, or about his invasion of Kuwait.[23] He continued to insist on his position as the legitimate president of Iraq. The capture of Saddam was met with jubilation in most of Iraq, but in the predominantly Sunni parts of the country it passed without much notice. The CPA thought it had achieved a major breakthrough in its attempts to damp the insurgency, but this was not so. Saddam had inspired only a part of the insurgency, and that part adjusted itself to his capture, continuing in its lethal ways with a new political agenda.

The capture of Sadddam brought a closure to only one aspect of the war: the war to depose Saddam. Otherwise, it was only a blip on the insurgency's radar screen. On the other hand, it took the CPA several months to acknowledge that the capture of Saddam was not the overwhelming victory it had previously thought it to be, even though his capture had been the result of remarkable detective work by a special US military intelligence team that had been assigned to track him.

The small part of the insurgency that had called for the restoration of Saddam to power now ended. But other, far broader, streams, also rooted in the loss of power and privilege of the Sunni Arab community, fed into the insurgency. The disbanding of the army and intelligence services pushed a large number of professional soldiers and officers into the ranks of the unemployed. The sense of wounded pride and loss of income and status drove a number of them into the insurgency, not necessarily as its foot soldiers but more as its planners and logistical experts. Evidence began to mount in late 2003 of the prevalence of former military and intelligence officers in some of the insurgent groups, especially *Jaysh Muhammad* (the Army of Muhammad). *Jaysh Muhammad* was the insurgent group that combined all these elements of nationalism, defence of honour, and an orthodox Islamism into one of the largest insurgent forces. In a profile of the insurgents of *Jaysh*

Muhammad in their early days, the correspondent for *Newsweek* wrote in August 2003 that the insurgents were inspired by Sunni Islamism, nationalism and anti-Semitism. Reading from a prepared statement, one of the insurgents said, 'The Americans have occupied our land under a false pretext, and without any international authorization. They kill our women and children and old men. They want to bring the Jews to our holy land in order to control Iraq, to achieve the Jewish dream.'[24]

The oft-made claim that the disbanding of the army had released a flood of recruits for the insurgency was not the only, or even the main, underpinning of the insurgency. The reality was more complex, as were the motives that drove apparently gainfully employed former senior officers into insurgency work. In a detailed article on the evolving insurgency written in early 2004, Christian Parenti described a meeting with insurgent leaders and fighters in the Sunni area of 'Adhamiyya in Baghdad. One of them, a former general in the Iraqi army, was openly contemptuous of the Shi'a and demanded the restoration of Sunni power. 'The Shi'a know nothing! The Sunni must govern Iraq,' he said.[25] Another, apparently an officer who was now in charge of a team of fighters, admitted that his group was in contact with remnants of the *Fedayeen Saddam* paramilitary force. His reasons for joining the resistance were more straightforward. He said he was fighting because the war had shamed and destroyed the army, and because the occupation was abusing and humiliating Iraqis and Islam. No one admitted they were fighting because they had nothing better to do, or because they were in need of money. A sense of aggrieved pride and loss of face and honour was a contributing factor that drove people into the insurgency. This blended into notions of patriotism and the religious injunction to fight aggressors and occupiers. Zaki Chehab, writing in the *Guardian,* profiled a number of insurgents in the Ramadi area in October 2003.[26] Most of them seemed to be simply aggrieved at the occupation of the country, and had little connection with the Ba'ath Party or its leadership. 'We do not want to see our country occupied by forces clearly pursuing their own interests, rather than being poised to return Iraq to the Iraqis,' one said. They were indifferent to the possible capture of Saddam Hussein and its effects on the insurgency, claiming that his capture would finally sever the links between Saddam and the resistance movement.

Tribes and the Insurgency

The tribal confederations of western Iraq that played a large part in the former regime's power structure were also significant contributors to the insurgency.[27] There are very few tribes in Iraq that have hierarchical command structures, and tribal authority is a far more diffuse matter than simple allegiance to a paramount sheikh. The idea of paramount sheikhs was in itself an outdated concept, for the retribalisation of Iraq under the latter years of the Saddamist regime did not imply the wholesale readoption of the authority of traditional tribal leaders. Some tribal 'leaders' doubled up as businessmen, growing fat in the smuggling and sanctions-busting decade of the 1990s. The loss of enormous smuggling revenues and lucrative rackets could not be easily compensated for in the post-war era. Some tribal leaders were openly driven to cooperate with the CPA for strictly financial reasons. Others used the threat of the insurgency to draw support from the Coalition to strengthen their own hold on their tribe. In the Fallujah area, the Albu-Issa tribe were prominent in the insurgency. They were the least urbanised of the major Sunni tribes, as they predominated in the rural areas. The Dulaim tribal confederation, numbering hundreds of thousands of people, was to be found in the string of towns along the upper reaches of the Euphrates. They had been viewed suspiciously by Saddam as a number of Dulaimi officers had been involved in a major plot against the regime. They were drawn into the insurgency in spite of concerted efforts by the CPA and former political exiles to include them in the new order. The Dulaimi tribes may also have been deeply affected by the Coalition's bombing of a farmhouse during the war, in which nearly twenty members of the prominent Dulaimi clan of al-Kharbit were killed. Another large tribe, the Janabi, had been encouraged to settle by the previous regime in the string of villages and small towns just south of Baghdad, partly to impede access between Baghdad and the Shi'a cities of the South. The tribal chiefs of the main Janabi clans were given rich agricultural lands in and around the towns of Latifiyya, Yousoufiyya, and Mahmoudiyya. The area was connected to the main western highway passing through the Sunni Anbar province, by-passing Baghdad. An area that previously had been predominantly Shi'a changed over a twenty-year period into a Janabi stronghold. It became known as the 'Triangle of Death' for its incessant insurgent activities against Coalition forces and for the frequent attacks on travellers between Baghdad and the cities of the South. It effectively controlled access to the holy cities of Karbala and Najaf.[28]

The support that the tribes gave to the insurgency cannot be explained away by simply taking into consideration the Coalition's cultural insensitivity to tribal customs or codes of honour, important though this might have been. It was also because of real losses in income, status and influence. A large number of Saddam's elite forces of officers and men had been drawn from these tribes, and this was an added factor in their sense of grievance. The tribes also fancied themselves as upholders of tradition and real Islamic values, and frequently they conflated the two. Thus, a particularly gauche Coalition house search might offend tribal honour, as well as convey a sense of trespass on Islamic boundaries. This is what apparently happened in Hit, where roughly conducted US house searches led to a near insurrection in the town.[29] The pull of Salafi Islam, especially on their youth, was not to be belittled, and a number would be drawn into the insurgency for religious motives. The tribes, however, as a whole kept a fair distance from the *jihadi* Salafists and tensions would be rife between the two groups on many occasions.

Sunni Thinkers, *Ulema* and the Insurgency

The rise of the traditionally docile Sunni *ulema* class was a major contributory factor to the insurgency. The Sunni clerical class had always been intimately associated with power and the Ministry of Religious Endowments (*Awqaf*) traditionally took direct responsibility for the staffing, paying and directing of the nearly 7,000 Sunni mosques under its jurisdiction. Shortly after the Governing Council was created, it was decided to abolish, under strong Sunni protest, the Ministry of *Awqaf*. The ministry had traditionally been dominated by Sunnis. The division of the *Awqaf* into semi-independent Shi'a and Sunni commissions, albeit funded by the state, removed a great deal of power over the institutional religious affairs of the country from the official Sunni *ulema*. This pushed the Sunni clerical class into a more open engagement with politics. This became evident soon after the occupation, as a disoriented Sunni community, reeling from the sudden collapse of Ba'athist authority, streamed into mosques seeking solace, guidance and encouragement.

Apart from a few outbursts by radical clerics, there was very little in the way of outright exhortation to their congregations to oppose the occupation directly, let alone take up arms against it. A common theme emanating from the Sunni mosques was that the occupation was a form of divine retribution for Muslims for having ignored their religious duties. The Ba'ath regime had no defenders from the pulpits, but neither did the occupation. Sunni clerics were groping to find the new power balance; there was a general sense that with the clear rise of the Shi'a on the Iraqi political scene, it would be advisable to adhere to a call for inter-sectarian Islamic harmony, which is what happened in the immediate months after the fall of the regime. By the summer of 2003, however, the situation had radically altered. The CPA's anointment of sectarian and ethnic quotas as the basis for the Governing Council's composition may have given the Sunni Arabs a proportional representation, but it was a psychological shock for them to consider how their relative power had so drastically dwindled. The response from the Sunni mosques was uniformly negative. Other factors also played a part in radicalising the official Sunni *ulema* class. They were distraught at the Coalition's inability to stop the appropriation of large state (Sunni) mosques in majority Shi'a areas, such as Hilla and Karbala, by a variety of Shi'a groups.[30] The return of the Iran-based Shi'a parties was viewed with open hostility and fear as they seemed to be a harbinger of extensive Iranian influence in the country. The intentions of the USA in Iraq were increasingly unclear, as the official explanation for the motives for the occupation seemed to change frequently: thus, for example, search for WMD gave way to promotion of democracy, which gave way to fighting terrorism. There were increased suspicions that the USA was planning a permanent presence, by which Iraq would be refashioned as a secular, ultra-capitalist, democracy with a strategic alliance with the west and Israel. The summer and autumn of 2003 saw large-scale raids by Coalition forces on Sunni mosques, and the arrest of a number of radical Friday prayer leaders. The limited political activism of the Sunni mosques in the early days of the occupation gave way to an assertive involvement in political affairs. It was only a small step from this to advocating struggle openly against the new conditions and support for what was termed the *muqawamma* (resistance).

The drift towards piety in the world of Iraqi Sunni Islam, which had been encouraged by an embattled state in the 1990s, was reflected in the dominance of the Wahhabi/Salafi strain. A number of Sunni Islamist writers and thinkers whose works had been banned during the high noon of Ba'athist secularism had been once again allowed to circulate as part of the former regime's attempts to bolster its religious credentials. The works of Muhammad Ahmad al-Rashid of the Muslim Brotherhood became particularly important.[31] Rashid called for the postponement, but not abandonment, of *jihad* in conditions where the governments were too strong, or where society was not yet sufficiently prepared for an Islamic government. In his construct, Iraq under Saddam had been just such a state. It was inadvisable and dangerous for the Islamists to confront the state directly there, but Iraq was fertile ground for the special brand of proselytising that he advocated, a watered-down version of Salafism, in line with the Brotherhood's own brand of politics – to work within systems that they disapprove of, while simultaneously maintaining their distance from regimes mired in *jahiliyya* (paganism), the Salafi term for secular Arab states. Rashid's writings also skirted around the issue of sectarianism, and essentially ignored the Shi'a's doctrines, refusing to attach any significance to their presence in Iraq – this allowed Sunni Arab Islamists simultaneously to take advantage of the opening offered by Saddam's 'Faith Campaign' while laying the foundations for a more direct challenge to the state. So Islamist Sunni political activism remained imperceptible during the 1990s but would break out into the open after the fall of the regime.

The Coalition was unprepared for the emergence of Islamism as an important force in Iraq's Sunni Arab community. The indifference to politics that marked the posture of Islamists during the 1990s changed perceptibly after the fall of the Ba'ath regime. *Jihad*, in the sense of armed struggle against a 'pagan' order, was now obligatory, and the fact that this order was linked to foreign occupiers made it doubly so. When Islamist political and social activity broke out in earnest in Mosul, just after the fall of the regime,

Coalition officials put it down to the sudden freedoms that the population now enjoyed. It was claimed to be a passing fancy that would disappear when jobs, democracy and security were provided. One Coalition official stated that 'there is a certain amount of novelty to this.... This will decrease over time.'[32]

In the extraordinarily changed circumstances of post-war Iraq, it was the Salafi clerics who began to seize the initiative in expressing the fears and concerns of their congregations. Mosques began to be used as centres for the dissemination of *jihad* literature and anti-Shi'a tracts. Arms caches ranging from machine guns, to grenades, and even small rockets were found in mosques. Sermons became more overtly anti-Coalition, and though no preacher would openly call for *jihad* against the Americans, the sermons left little room for doubt.[33] Imams also began to act as go-betweens with insurgent groups, and connected like-minded worshippers in networks that supported the insurgency or launched a group themselves. Under interrogation, many insurgents admitted that they were encouraged or guided in their work by radical Sunni imams. The status of the Sunni *ulema* class rose perceptibly in the months following the occupation, and they enjoyed an unprecedented level of trust and support from their community: they became the cheerleaders of the insurgency.

The Sunni *ulemas* were far more cautious, however, when it came to approving attacks against civilians, or when the insurgency strayed into dangerous sectarian territory. Attacks against the Shi'a were condemned, but never without these outrages being linked to the legitimacy of resistance to the occupation. It was clear that no progress on any front was possible before the removal of the stain of occupation.[34] The radicalisation of the Sunni *ulema* class and its fusion of Islamist and nationalist rhetoric was a rebirth of an old identity. Arab nationalism had been conflated with Islam in the minds of many people in the pre-World War II period.[35] This identity of interests, however, was abandoned by the second wave of Arab nationalist ideology that dominated the Middle East in the 1950s through to the 1980s, where Islam was kept firmly at bay. In Iraq, apart from the brief interlude of the 'Aref brothers in the 1960s, when Sunni Islam had achieved a favoured status inside the military-dominated regime, religion was not an element of the official Arab nationalist doctrine of the Ba'ath. In some ways, therefore, the fusion of the two ideological currents harked back to the struggle against direct foreign control. It was a potent mixture, and one that proved very attractive to dispirited former Ba'athists, cashiered army officers, and restless youth seeking to make their mark against foreign occupiers.

A more aware and better-led government, with appropriate policies consistently applied, might have defused part of the anger of the would-be insurgents. In fact, the often chaotic, incoherent and even bizarre administration of the CPA, and its ineffective reconstruction efforts, encouraged the insurgents. The promise of 'good times' around the corner was made once too often. Iraqis became increasingly exasperated and frustrated at the CPA's inability to deliver even the most basic services. The new order was seen to fail even in this arena and the economy did not spring to life. The fact that insurgents had begun to attack basic infrastructure and rendered reconstruction even more difficult did not detract from this argument in the mind of the Iraqis.

The delicate weave that had kept Iraq's social fabric intact over the years began to unravel. Hitherto, fringe or extreme elements sought to redefine the identity of the communities in ways that shrank the common middle ground which had always existed between the sects and ethnicities. The goal was nothing less than the elimination of Iraq's historic *convivencia*, which had become dangerously brittle as a result of the overt sectarian practices of the latter Saddamist years. The Wahhabi and Salafi ascendancy amongst the Sunni Muslims was matched by an aggressive assertion of Shi'a consciousness, both of which played to the fears and anxieties of the mass of the people. Strains began to appear at the most basic level: in families that had both Shi'a and Sunni members; in neighbourhoods that were mixed; in towns and villages that crossed sectarian or ethnic dividing lines. The seeds of an incipient civil war were laid at this, the most elemental, level. The relentless attacks on civilian targets were not only a key insurgent strategy, designed to show the inability of the USA and the central government to protect the people; they was also important in stoking the fires of sectarian hatreds. In many ways, the desired effect of polarising the population into hostile sectarian camps would succeed. It was only a matter of time before the Shi'a militias would spring into action as defenders of Shi'a lives and property, while the insurgents would don the mantle of protectors of Sunni Arabs. Sectarian violence would now be added to the war of resistance against the occupiers that the insurgents claimed they were waging.

14

A Marshall Plan for Iraq?

'It would be neither fitting nor efficacious for this Government to undertake to draw up unilaterally a program designed to place Europe on its feet economically. This is the business of the Europeans. The initiative, I think, must come from Europe. The role of this country should consist of friendly aid in the drafting of a European program so far as it may be practical for us to do so. The program should be a joint one, agreed to by a number, if not all European nations.' –

George C. Marshall, addressing the commencement class of Harvard University, 5 June, 1947

'Our strategy in Iraq will require new resources . . . I will soon submit to Congress a request for $87 billion. This budget request will also support our commitment to helping the Iraqi and Afghan people rebuild their own nations, after decades of oppression and mismanagement. We will provide funds to help them improve security. And we will help them to restore basic services, such as electricity and water, and to build new schools, roads, and medical clinics. This effort is essential to the stability of those nations, and therefore, to our own security.' –

George W. Bush, addressing the American people, 3 September, 2003

'[The CPA] didn't have [monitoring] systems set up. They were very dismissive of these processes . . . .The CPA didn't hire the best people . . . . We were just watching it unfold. They [the CPA] were constantly hitting at our people, screaming at them. They were abusive.' –

Andrew Natsios, former administrator of USAID, in an interview with *Newsweek*, 22 March, 2006

The Marshall Plan, officially the 'European Recovery Program', was one the most important foreign policy successes of the United States after World War II.[1] It was the yardstick by which all major economic assistance programmes for reconstruction and development had to be measured, as it combined enlightened self-interest with a massive transfer of resources to the war-ravaged economies of post-war Europe. It was, alongside NATO, the centre-piece of the USA's strategy to strengthen the western anti-communist alliance and to fight the Cold War.[2]

The realisation that Iraq would need massive funds for reconstruction only dawned on the Coalition nearly four months into the occupation. The opti-mistic prognosis of the neo-conservatives that Iraq's oil exports would be mainly sufficient to fund Iraq's reconstruction needs had been given a further fillip by Andrew Natsios, the administrator of USAID. In a TV interview on 23 April, 2003, Natsios went so far as to disparage any comparisons between the aid that the USA was planning to provide Iraq and the Marshall Plan. 'No, no. This doesn't even compare remotely with the size of the Marshall Plan,' he remonstrated. He clearly stated that the USA was budgeting for only $1.7 billion in economic assistance to Iraq. He continued, 'Well, in terms of the American taxpayers' contribution, I do [think so] . . . this is it for the US. The rest of the rebuilding of Iraq will be done by other countries . . . and Iraqi oil revenues . . . They're going to get in $20 billion a year in oil revenues. But the American part of this will be 1.7 billion. We have no plans for any further-on funding for this.'[3] By the time Bremer had spent a few weeks in Baghdad, however, the figure would rise to $5 billion, and by the end of August 2003 the CPA had put in a supplemental budgetary request for $20 billion for Iraq's reconstruction.[4] Bush clearly linked the supplemental budget request with the fight against terror, bringing democracy to Iraq, and the broader goals of progress and peace in the Middle East. Bush sought to put the assistance to Iraq in the same grand, overarching vision of the Marshall Plan. The war against terror was substituted for the Cold War; Iraq became a frontline state in this war; and the supplemental budget, slapped together by the CPA in a few weeks, became Iraq's 'Marshall Plan'.

Reconstruction of Iraq and Comparisons with the Marshall Plan

There was no doubt that the Iraqi economy was devastated and that immense sums would be required for its reconstruction. The scale of the planned US aid for Iraq's economic rehabilitation was huge by any standards. On a per capita basis, in 2003 dollars, the aid would be larger than what had been received by any single country under the Marshall Plan. The average assistance per capita for the European recipients of Marshall Plan aid over its four-year life was about $350 in adjusted 2003 figures.[5] The equivalent level for Iraq was about $900 per capita for a one-year level of assistance. The proposed amounts of aid were unprecedented, and dwarfed any other ongoing US assistance to a developing country. In Iraq, the inept way in which the US aid programme was presented to the public by the CPA was symptomatic of the problems and troubles that would overwhelm this act of extraordinary generosity. The effects of these massive transfers, as well as the CPA's own access to Iraqi funds, would be whittled away by an unbelievable combination of amateur programming, poor execution, incompetence, corruption and waste. The problems were compounded by a rapidly deteriorating security situation and the targeted attacks on Iraq's infrastructure and on reconstruction projects and teams. But the primary failure was policy planning and management.

The breathless comparisons with the Marshall Plan were hugely overblown. The Madrid Conference of donors simply increased the resource pool for Iraq, but the implementation mechanism for managing these large inflows remained woefully inadequate.[6] On the US side, it would seem that none of the admirable lessons of the Marshall Plan had been taken into account. The Marshall Plan had been a culmination of a nearly two-year-long debate on the conditions of the European economies and the prospects for their recovery. CPA officers who had absolutely no prior knowledge of the Iraqi economy or any meaningful experience in Iraq announced the Iraqi plan after a few weeks of back-office work.[7]

The Marshall Plan was developed after long and protracted negotiations with the beneficiaries. The Iraqi plan was entirely unilateral. The USA or, more accurately, a group of CPA officials with some help from the Pentagon's Office of Special Plans determined the needs, defined the areas of concern, and drove the process in record time. Iraqis looked on, some in wonder, others in indifference or incomprehension, at what the USA was proposing to do in Iraq. Some Iraqis kept silent, because of fears of appearing ungrateful at this unexpected munificence. Others, such as a number of Islamists, questioned the dark motives behind the huge appropriation requests of the Supplemental Budget. The Governing Council in its minutes made only a perfunctory mention of the CPA's budgetary request. This showed an extraordinary indifference to a matter of vital concern to Iraqis, but equally, it revealed the fact that only one or two people on the Governing Council were able to understand the significance of the American proposal. Some ministers were later encouraged to mouth platitudes about Iraqi engagement with the CPA in this matter, but this was manifestly untrue. They did not participate in defining the programme. Because Iraqis had not been involved in the process, they felt complacent, and even entitled to the aid. Many in the CPA often spoke about the unappreciative Iraqis, without acknowledging that the process itself, because of their own actions, was flawed from the outset. The lack of involvement of Iraqis in any aspects of the American reconstruction plan was a glaring mistake. The chaotic staffing policies of the CPA and the flow of politically connected, but inexperienced, personnel overwhelmed the excellence exhibited by a number of individuals. Inter-agency disputes in Washington further reduced the effectiveness of the reconstruction programme.

The reality was that the United States had committed itself to an unparalleled reconstruction effort in an unstable and dangerous environment. In sector after sector – oil, electricity, water and sanitation – targets were consistently missed, ignored or changed. Iraqis continued to suffer from increasing blackouts and untreated sewage. The 'disconnect' between what the CPA publicly trumpeted and the experience of the average Iraqi was almost total. The resulting performance gap was managed by a tiresome campaign of media manipulation, insipid retelling of 'success' stories, and rigid denial of shortcomings and flaws. It was only a matter of time before the hounds of investigative journalism and congressional oversight committees, as well as the CPA's own inspector general, would uncover the huge black hole that lay underneath.

Strategy, Funding and Implementation of Iraq's Reconstruction

From the outset, it was not clear what source of funds was to be used to finance what expenditures. Contracts were awarded by a number of US government entities, as well as the CPA. The Pentagon, mainly through the US Army Corps of Engineers, and USAID were the major agencies that awarded reconstruction or reconstruction-related contracts prior to the establishment of the CPA. On 24 March, 2003 the Pentagon announced that it had awarded a contract to Kellogg Brown and Root (KBR), the engineering subsidiary of the multinational energy services company, Halliburton, for a sum that might total $7 billion. The contracts were to rebuild Iraq's oil infrastructure and, controversially, to import fuel for the domestic Iraqi market. Dick Cheney, the US vice-president, had served as Halliburton's chairman in the 1990s, and the company could never quite shake off the allegations of shady dealing and cronyism that accompanied the award of these contracts. KBR employees were subsequently indicted for hugely overcharging for fuel supplies to the Iraqi market.[8] There were also a number of massive awards to Pentagon-related companies, the 'military' contractors. These favoured companies, that formed a charmed circle and seemed to follow the US military around the world, were awarded contracts affecting a large number of vital sectors, including the repair of Iraq's electricity distribution infrastructure. A number of companies that benefited from the Pentagon's military contracts were also connected to firms that were well positioned to receive civilian contracts.

The Pentagon's military contractors were a world on their own in the Iraqi reconstruction scene. Access to them by Iraqi subcontractors was always highly restricted, and a culture of secrecy permeated the entire sector.[9] The US military had favoured individuals and companies. A number of these suppliers, based in the Gulf countries or Turkey, Lebanon and Jordan, would reap huge fortunes from the expenditures of the Coalition in Iraq. But Iraqi companies, except for a very few, were kept well at bay. The exceptions were primarily companies associated with the old regime such as the Bunnia Group.[10] Less well-connected Iraqi companies and their employees were untried and untested, and therefore not to be trusted with the supply of provisions and services that the military expected. The Ministry of Trade's attempts to open up the procurement of the US military to Iraqi companies were first ignored and then rebuffed.[11] In the early days of the occupation, it was Kuwaiti, Egyptian and Korean subcontractors, Saudi and Turkish transport companies, Jordanian food brokers, Pakistani and Indian labour contractors, and Lebanese middle-men who ruled the subcontract world of the US military. The Pentagon preferred to deal with these, rather than Iraqi, subcontractors.[12]

The USAID, which was well managed, was charged with managing the initial pre-war appropriations of $3.3 billion for disaster relief and infrastructure rehabilitation. Its programme was spread across a number of sectors and included significant 'capacity'-building work, improving local governance and supporting democracy-building in Iraq. USAID awarded a large $600 million multipurpose contract to Bechtel Corporation in April 2003 for infrastructure repair, including power, roads and bridges and transport facilities, and in total Bechtel would receive about $2.3 billion in contracts from USAID.[13]

It was the CPA, however, using Iraqi funds from the Development Fund for Iraq (DFI) as well as funds from the $18.4 billion supplemental budget approved for fiscal year 2004, which handled the bulk of the reconstruction programme. The CPA was responsible, as the effective UN-sanctioned administration of Iraq, for Iraq's investment budget until the handover of sovereignty in June 2004. After that period, the US reconstruction effort in Iraq was passed on to the US Embassy, which divided the work into two separate departments: the Iraq Reconstruction and Management Office (IRMO) and the Project and Contracting Office (PCO). The former reported to the State Department and was responsible for the continuing strategic direction and management of US-funded projects; the latter, on the other hand, reported to the Department of Defense, and was responsible for contracting and project management.

The US reconstruction effort in Iraq did not significantly draw on the $18.4 billion supplemental budget appropriations until well into 2004. The initial funding for reconstruction was derived primarily from Iraqi vested assets, which had been transferred to the US Treasury at the outbreak of the war; assets, primarily cash, seized in Iraq from treasure troves kept by Saddam; and the revenues from Iraq's oil exports. The CPA controlled about $23 billion in Iraqi revenues and assets from the May 2003 to June 2004 period.[14] It allocated about $7 billion from these funds for reconstruction efforts. The confusion as to the actual source of disbursed funds for Iraq's reconstruction under the CPA originated from the jumble between the various pools that the CPA could draw upon.

Two underlying premises lay behind the USA's reconstruction plans for Iraq: to concentrate on rebuilding the country's infrastructure and to step up the level of oil production and exports. This was to dovetail with a mass of economic and policy reforms that would establish the institutional and legal framework for transforming Iraq into a modern, capitalist economy. The strategic vision was reasonable and allowed the superpower to concentrate its efforts on sectors essential to the functioning of the economy, the development of which would reflect well on the occupation authorities. The early plans, however, had little or no component that dealt directly with Iraq's endemic and massive unemployment. It was only later, when the insurgency had taken hold, that measures were enacted to alleviate unemployment, measures considered essential to the reconstruction effort. By that time, it would prove difficult to tackle the problem in any but the most blunt and rudimentary fashion, with large ad hoc allocations to unemployment hotspots that were connected, one way or another, to insurgent activity.

Unfortunately, in each of the key sectors that were the linchpins of the reconstruction plan, namely oil, power, water and health, serious shortcomings in project definition, design and execution adversely affected the overall effectiveness of the investment expenditures. In other, 'soft' sectors of reconstruction work, such as in governance, ministerial and administrative reform, and integration into the global economy, all of them vital for increasing the efficiency of government and improving economic growth, the outcome of the huge expenditures on consultants and advisers was equally uncertain. Consultant contracts ate up nearly a billion dollars of USAID's assistance budget.

The Oil Sector

The US efforts in the oil sector focused on three interrelated areas: first, to restore Iraq's oil production and exports; second, to supply the domestic market with petroleum products and derivatives; and third to ensure that pipeline maintenance and security kept pace with changing circumstances. The USA utilised nearly $5.5 billion from various funding pools on the oil sector. Nearly half of that came from Iraqi funds drawn from the DFI.[15]

Projects to enhance oil sector production and exports were identified prior to the war. They included the restoration of a water injection and treatment plant at Qarmat Ali in the South. This was vital to the creation and maintenance of pressure in the major southern oil field of Rumaila. The plant had been damaged and looted during the war. Another major oil production and export-related project included the repair of a critical pipeline-crossing terminal at al-Fathah, near the northern oil fields in Kirkuk. There were other important projects for oil and gas separation plants in both the southern and northern oil fields, as well as the restoration of wells, pumping stations and export terminals. Some needed modernisation and equipment upgrade or replacement, while others had to be re-equipped entirely because of widespread looting.

War damage to Iraq's refineries had been minimal, but the refineries themselves were in dire need of modernisation. Some had been built in the 1950s and their successive upgrading could not bring them to the operational efficiency of modern refineries. Iraq's all-important oil sector had suffered from serious underinvestment during the 1990s and a critical shortage of spare parts and materials. By the time of the outbreak of the 2003 war, however, Iraq's oil production had reached about 2.5 million barrels per day (bbd).[16] The level of Iraq's oil production became an issue in the run-up to the war, as US congressional sceptics questioned whether the administration had a notion of the true condition of Iraq's finances. Paul Wolfowitz had stated that Iraq would be able to generate oil export revenues of between $50 to $100 billion between 2004 and 2006. He was putting forward a strong case for the costs of the occupation and reconstruction to be borne through Iraqi-generated revenues, and not by the US taxpayer. 'We are dealing with a country that can really finance its own reconstruction and relatively soon', said Wolfowitz.[17] This, however, ran counter to an internal US government report produced by a Pentagon task force that showed the true, decrepit condition of the oil sector. The overconfidence about Iraq's oil production capacity led to a serious misrepresentation by the US administration of the true costs of Iraq's reconstruction and financing. There was considerable fear amongst the war planners that Saddam would set Iraq's oil fields on fire, in the same way as he had treated Kuwait's oil fields on leaving the country in 1991. As it was, there were only a few well fires, which were quickly put out. But the extensive looting of oil field equipment, specialised transport equipment, and separation and water treatment plants, had a profound effect on the capacity of the sector. Declining power supply also impacted on oil operations, to the point where power was needed to continue oil operations and fuel was needed to supply power stations. Oil production plummeted, and by the summer of 2003 sabotages of oil equipment, especially pipelines, began to hamper production and exports. Although the CPA had hired private contractors to guard Iraq's oil facilities, the nearly 14,000 security guards employed were hastily recruited, poorly trained, poorly led and often infiltrated by insurgents. The revenues generated from oil exports in 2003 did not exceed $8 billion, a far cry from what the war planners had anticipated.

Demand for refined products, especially gasoline and diesel fuels, pushed the CPA into undertaking a major fuel import programme. This had not been factored into the reconstruction budget prior to the war. There had been little anticipation of the explosion in demand, as a result of the post-war doubling of Iraq's car population in a few months. There was also the increased demand for diesel fuel as a result of the ubiquitous installation of generators in homes to provide electricity to households when the power supplies were cut off. By the middle of 2004, Iraq was consuming nearly 20 million litres per day of gasoline while producing only 12 million litres per day. The balance had to be imported.[18] The marked fall in domestic refinery output was mainly due to poor procurement practices and contractors' shortcomings. The funds allocated for fuel imports were essentially wasted, as there was virtually no recovery from their resale. Iraq under Saddam had maintained the lowest petrol product prices in the world and the CPA, in spite of the fine rhetoric on the need for market pricing, maintained the massive subsidy to this sector. Most of the funds utilised from the DFI for the oil sector, nearly $2.3 billion out of $ 2.7 billion, were used to finance petroleum products imports.[19] This figure would grow alarmingly by the end of 2005 to an annualised rate of $6 billion.

The expenditures on the oil sector had little effect on the level of oil production and exports. By the time the CPA was dissolved, oil production and exports had fallen to levels that were far lower than pre-war figures. The target figures, which were based on pre-war production and exports, were 2.6 million bbd and 2.1 million bbd, respectively. The CPA ignored investments in the oil production and export sectors, relying on the ongoing programme of the US Army Corps of Engineers and its prime contractor KBR to revitalise oil production and exports. The CPA essentially withheld investment allocations to the Ministry of Oil in 2003 and 2004. The ministry had no autonomous ability to fund its investment projects and in the main awaited the realisation of the KBR and other CPA-approved contracts. These contracts themselves were afflicted with a host of problems. The effect on oil production and export levels was immediate. It was not until November 2004 that the Ministry of Oil was consulted on a reconstituted project list that would partly supplant the early list of projects.

The CPA had adopted a policy of supporting the involvement of international oil companies in Iraq's oil sector – without actually doing anything about it. Part of the CPA's oil sector thinking, in fact, was to defer expenditures on refineries and the development of new oil fields, so that foreign companies could undertake the necessary investment. At the same time, the Ministry of Oil was dissuaded from undertaking any investments in refinery improvements or new oil field developments so as to keep open the possibility of reordering Iraq's oil sector and opening it up to foreign investment. The cost of replacing Iraq's antiquated refineries was estimated at $6 billion to $7 billion.

Electricity Supply and Demand

The CPA began to take credit, prematurely as it transpired, for restoring power and oil production to their pre-war levels. Electricity supply became a major issue in the early post-war period, with a huge expansion in power demand, caused mainly by the substantial improvement in the purchasing power of civil servants. Their huge increase in salaries translated into a far greater demand for electrical appliances such as air conditioners.

During the Ba'ath regime the electricity supply system had used a few large power-generating units that allowed for central control over power supply and distribution.[20] In the early days of the sanctions on Iraq the power sector had been hit badly, but the situation became somewhat better after the launch of the OFF programme in 1996. By the time the 2003 conflict had ended, Iraq had negotiated nearly $2 billion in power contracts under the OFF, which were awaiting final contract approvals and funding. The CPA continued with a centralised power-generating system rather than opting for a more dispersed system, which would have made far more sense in the light of Iraq's changed political scene. Under the Ba'ath regime, electricity had been used as a political tool and rationed to favour particular regions and cities. Thus, for example, in the summer of 2002, Baghdad had uninterrupted power supplies, while other parts of the country had none. When the war ended, regions that felt they were deprived of power supplies, especially those which had large power-generating plants or transmission lines within their boundaries, began to cut off supplies to Baghdad as a result of their resentment at their past deprivations. The outages were exacerbated by the destruction of transmission lines by looting and incipient insurgency activities, leaving a power sector barely able to meet a few hours of supply on a nationwide basis. The CPA did manage to increase production to nearly 4,000 MW by the autumn of 2003, but this proved insufficient to meet both burgeoning demand and the resupply of power on an equitable basis throughout the country. Baghdad became subject to ever-more lengthy power blackouts. At the same time, saboteurs found the transmission and distribution of Iraq's centralised system an easy target.

A central plank in the USA's reconstruction strategy was the restoration and upgrading of Iraq's electricity system. In fact the power supply was seen as a litmus test of the efficacy of the entire reconstruction effort. The power sector in Iraq was provided with nearly $5.7 billion in resources, the bulk of which came from US appropriated funds. The CPA used about $800 million in DFI funds for the electricity sector. The bulk of the resources were utilised for restoring or constructing power generation, transmission and distribution systems. Nevertheless, power generation over the course of the two years following the occupation never reached the pre-war level of 4,500 MW. The USA was committed to increase electricity production by a further 3,100 MW by June 2005. The figure actually achieved was only 1,900 MW.[21] The promises of the CPA and subsequent Iraqi governments to restore electricity production rang increasingly hollow as Baghdadis sweltered without power during the long hot summers of Iraq. The travails of the power sector ran into many hurdles: the poor choice of technologies for the new generating equipment; an inappropriate electricity generating and distribution design system and architecture; poor operations and maintenance on the part of the Ministry of Electricity; decay and degradation of the inherited power supply and distribution systems; insurgency damage to power infrastructure; corruption in procurement and operations management; incompetent management and administration of the system; power theft from illegal connections; and shortages of money.

It was the CPA and its successors that were primarily responsible for the chaotic conditions in the power sector. Isam al-Khalisi, one of Iraq's most noted electricity experts, wrote a long critique of the electricity sector in the post-war era, saying that: 'Inept preparation and lack of knowledge of the intimate working of the system became apparent within days of the start of the occupation .... Diffused authority, confused management and, at times, a foreign army residing inside a power station have all contributed to the destabilization.'[22] He criticised the CPA's decision to transfer responsibility over the sector from a semi-independent commission to a ministry headed by a CPA favourite. 'Politicisation of top management of an industrially based organisation of national strategic importance increases the potential for short term thinking, mediocrity and even corruption.' The rapid turnover of senior CPA personnel responsible for the power sector was also held responsible for the poor performance in the sector. In less than a year seven different people were responsible for the electricity sector.[23]

The US Government's Accountability Office (GAO) detailed the shortcomings of the electricity sector in a report of July 2005 to a number of congressional committees. It questioned the choice of gas combustion turbines technology to operate several Iraqi power plants, given the limited access to natural gas supplies. The training that was given to Iraqi personnel on the new equipment was inadequate and led to numerous breakdowns and power outages.[24] Security problems afflicted the electricity grid on a regular basis, especially attacks on transmission towers. (By September 2003, nearly 600 towers had been knocked down, and no sooner would repair crews reinstall them than they would be attacked again.) A CPA attempt to improve security of the national grid failed when a contract to train 6,000 guards for the electricity sector was abandoned after fewer than 340 guards were trained.[25]

These electricity supply problems were compounded further by the massive increase in demand after the removal of UN sanctions in 2003. Electricity demand had passed 8,500 MW, while the supply kept to less than the pre-war level of 4,500 MW. This, together with the redistribution of power more evenly across the various regions of Iraq, led to the massive outages that Baghdad and hitherto favoured areas had avoided before the war. They now had to endure what other regions, especially the South, had experienced during the last years of the Saddamist era. For example, the average pre-war level for power supply for the whole of Iraq was between four to eight hours per day. In Baghdad, the equivalent pre-war level had been between sixteen and twenty-four hours per day. By the end of 2005, Baghdad's power supply averaged eight hours per day, while the average for Iraq as a whole was sixteen hours per day. This, of course, increased the anger and frustration in the metropolis. The insurgents would target the power supply to Baghdad as a matter of strategic priority throughout 2005 and 2006.

Other Sectors

A similar range of problems affected other sectors on which the US reconstruction effort focused. The water and sanitation sectors saw their aid allocations reduced significantly as funds were diverted to finance increased security costs. The disbursements were agonisingly slow.[26] By March 2005, only 12 per cent of the funds allocated to the water and sanitation sector had actually been disbursed. There was also significant cost creep. The GAO 2005 report stated alarmingly, 'Agency metrics for tracking progress in the water and sanitation sector do not show how the US program is affecting the Iraqi people.'[27] A key sewerage project was the rehabilitation of the Rustamiya sewerage treatment plant that covered all of east Baghdad. The UN had been working, gratis, to repair the complex, given the critical importance of clean water in preventing water-borne diseases. For inexplicable reasons, the CPA ordered the UN to abandon the job. USAID then awarded the contract for the complex's repair to Bechtel in the summer of 2003. A team from the USA's NBC news visited the site in the spring of 2004, fully eight months after the contract was awarded, but saw 'no heavy equipment, no laborers or replacement parts for the pumps and machinery at the Rustamiya site'.[28] Iraqi state-owned companies with considerable experience in the water treatment sector were not allowed to bid on important water works contracts. Bechtel was the main contractor for the majority of the water and sewage treatment plants.

Mismanagement, Theft and Looting of Infrastructure Projects

The problems, however, were not only due to serious miscalculation and poor planning on the part of the CPA and its successors. Iraqis were often unable to manage the facilities that were being handed over to them by the USA. The GAO reported that, 'as of June 2005, approximately $52 million of the $200 million in completed large-scale water and sanitation projects either were not operating or were operating at lower capacity due to looting of key equipment and shortages of reliable power, trained Iraqi staff, and required chemicals and supplies.'[29] A report in the Los Angeles Times on 10 April, 2005 on the reconstruction efforts described how 'Iraqi officials have crippled scores of water, sewage and electrical plants refurbished with U.S. funds by failing to maintain and operate them properly, wasting millions of American taxpayer dollars in the process.'[30] Bechtel was quoted as saying that out of forty projects in the water sector, not one was operating properly. The Los Angeles Times report continued, drawing on internal documents from contractors and USAID. It quoted from one report, 'This is the antithesis of our base strategy and a waste not only of taxpayer funds, but it deprives the most needy of safe drinking water and of streets free from raw sewerage.' The 'sustainability' problems of complex projects that required sophisticated operations and maintenance talent were issues that affected all the large-scale reconstruction projects undertaken by the USA. Iraqis accused the Americans of excluding them from the early stages of project planning and of insufficiently providing for the projects' upkeep and maintenance. The State Department acknowledged these issues and, in a report to Congress in 2005, proposed to increase the operations and maintenance budgets for US-backed projects by over $600 million. USAID's director for the water sector, Mark Oviatt, said, 'This has been my biggest problem and concern in Iraq. Americans are investing hundreds of millions in Iraq. The capacity is not there to maintain it.'[31]

The issues that afflicted the USA's reconstruction programme in Iraq went to the heart of the 'capacity' problem. This was a euphemism that camouflaged the true dimensions of the problem. The Iraqi state inherited by the CPA and by subsequent Iraqi governments was a dysfunctional organism. There was no doubt of the individual qualities of Iraqi engineers and managers, who could be found in key positions in businesses and enterprises throughout the Middle East and the west. Even in Iraq, they had quickly been able to rebuild a great deal of the infrastructure damage after the first Gulf War. But the ensuing decade of sanctions and institutional decay had had a terrible effect on the quality of Iraq's governing structures. Complete isolation from the world had had a major impact on the ability of Iraq's engineers and managers to keep abreast of best international practices in their field of expertise. This made most of them defensive when dealing with assertive foreign consultants and advisers, and pushed them to adopt a 'we-know-best' attitude. In some instances they did know better, as in the practical problems of how to assess costs and manage the Iraqi bureaucratic system. In other areas, however, they were woefully unprepared, and felt intimidated by the hordes of experts who descended on them.

Language was also a serious problem. The decades of war and sanctions had brought about a drastic diminution of linguistic standards at Iraq's universities and technical colleges. By the time of the invasion, the only fluent English-speaking Iraqi engineers and technocrats were those in their fifties and sixties, who had been trained abroad and had maintained their language skills. The subsequent generation had poor or non-existent language skills. As a result, their technical skills had atrophied; they had been cut off from developments in their disciplines, and the scale of rebuilding now was vastly more complicated than the situation that Iraq faced after the Gulf War. The bluster of Iraqi politicians when it came to claims that they could have managed reconstruction more efficiently was glaringly at odds with the abysmal machinery of state and its gross inefficiencies, inequalities and outdated practices. The degradation of the administrative system in Iraq in the past two decades was now compounded by the unfamiliar management practices of Iraq's new masters, corrupt public officials, and the harsh politicisation of hiring, staffing and routine technical and management decisions in Iraq's ministries.

The Development Fund for Iraq (DFI)

The CPA's stewardship of funds in Iraq's account at the Federal Reserve Bank of New York, the Development Fund for Iraq (DFI) account, also came under intense scrutiny. Funds from this account were what fuelled most of the expenditures on reconstruction during the CPA days. A report from the advisory board charged with oversight of the DFI account was scathing in its comments. The internationally renowned firm of accountants and auditors KPMG was retained by the International Advisory Board to audit the accounts of the DFI, as part of the UN Resolution 1483. The CPA was initially hostile to this, seeing it as an attempt to curtail its discretionary spending powers as the internationally sanctioned occupation authority. The main point of contention was whether the International Advisory Board should passively audit the expenditures from the DFI, or have additional authority to examine the use and allocation of funds. The deadlock between the CPA and the International Advisory Board continued to the end of 2003. The CPA tried to nominate an auditor for the International Advisory Board, a tiny firm,

North Star Consultants that operated out of a private home near San Diego.[32] This company was awarded a $1.4 million contract to review the CPA's internal controls, but according to a July 2004 report of the US Government's Special Inspector General for Iraq Reconstruction (SIGIR), they did not perform this task at all. This rather silly ruse was patently insufficient to quell the demand for proper auditing of the CPA's use of DFI funds. Accordingly, the International Advisory Board was finally authorised to recruit from an international pool of qualified bidders. Its report covered the period from the establishment of the DFI until the dissolution of the CPA. The CPA staff was also notably uncooperative with the auditors, frequently citing other priorities for not providing KPMG with the required information.

The CPA would, as a matter of choice, draw on funds from the DFI for disbursement rather than US-sourced funds. The reasons were clear: the standards of accounting and reporting of US funds had to comply with rigorous rules under the Department of Defense's Financial Management Regulations (FMR). Iraqi rules for disbursement of funds were also strict, but could be conveniently ignored or overlooked. In any case it was improbable that Iraqi rules would apply to the DFI. This was particularly true when it came to handling large dollops of cash, which was the preferred CPA method of paying local contractors and suppliers. The CPA had shipped nearly $12 billion in cash from Iraq's DFI account to Baghdad. The audit report of KPMG found serious shortcomings in the CPA's reporting and control mechanisms over Iraqi funds drawn from the DFI. A March 2004 audit by SIGIR, for example, found that the contracting procedures of the CPA, and its predecessor, the ORHA, did not follow the US government's procurement rules in 22 out of 24 contracts. By April 2004, the CPA had awarded nearly 2,000 contracts valued at over $1 billion, paid for overwhelmingly by funds drawn from the DFI. The KPMG report identified weaknesses in controls over oil production and exports, which were not metered in spite of many calls to introduce proper metering. This obliged KPMG to qualify the DFI's statement of cash inflows and outflows, a serious indictment by auditing standards. The report also pointed out the poor control systems in Iraqi ministries which were the main spending units. These compounded the problems of the proper control, reporting and evaluation of the DFI funds used for Iraq's reconstruction.

The CPA's Economic Mismanagement and Policy Failures

The CPA's economic mismanagement was not admitted until nearly a year later when its own inspector general's office, SIGIR, and the Government Accountability Office began to produce detailed reports on waste, mismanagement and possible corruption.[33] The political costs of acknowledging the

1 Ali al-Wardi (1913–95), an eminent social historian whose work opposed the versions of history promoted by successive regimes and analysed the social psyche of the Iraqi people. His scholarship – penetrating, eclectic and idiosyncratic – was largely ignored by the West.

2 Sayyid Muhammad Baqir al-Sadr was a prolific scholar and one of the originators and earliest leaders of the Islamic Da'awa Party. Acknowledging the validity of political action by committed Shi'a and reinforcing the importance of a politically-engaged religious hierarchy, Sadr was one of the thousands of Shi'a executed by the Ba'ath regime.

3 A Kurd father cradles his infant son on their doorstep in Halabja. Both were killed by the Iraqi chemical attack on the city, 150 miles north-east of Baghdad, on 16 March, 1988, which claimed the lives of 5,000 civilians, three-quarters of them women and children. This image has now become iconic of the cold brutality of Saddam Hussein's *Anfal* campaign.

4 On 16 January, 1991, an allied military operation to liberate Kuwait from the leadership of Iraq was launched. Codenamed Operation Desert Storm, a US-led coalition force drove Saddam Hussein's army out of the country it had occupied since August 1990, leaving 50,000 Iraqis dead and the oil fields of Kuwait aflame.

5 Ayad Allawi and Ahmad Chalabi voting to expand the Iraqi National Congress in 1999. Then opposition leaders, both men would find places on the Iraq Interim Governing Council and become transitional Prime Minister and Deputy Prime Minister respectively.

6 Cereals being unloaded in Umm Qasr as part of the United Nations Oil-for-Food programme. Established in 1995, the programme was designed to provide humanitarian needs (food and medicine) for Iraqi civilians whilst upholding the economic sanctions that would enforce the demilitarisation of Iraq. It continues to provoke controversy even after its termination in 2003.

7 In a symbolic gesture, Iraqi men demolish the statue of Saddam Hussein that stood in Firdaus Square after US troops enter the city on 9 April, 2003.

8 Usurping the role of Jay Garner in the Office for Reconstruction, Paul Bremer was announced Administrator of the Coalition Provisional Authority in May 2003, backed by a UN resolution. The abrupt reversal in policy, as well as Bremer's brusque authority, was shocking to those confident in their ability to establish a native provisional government on their own terms.

9 The social policy in Iraq had always been divided along sectarian lines, but the war exacerbated Shi'a–Sunni antipathy. Violence, protest and counter-aggression, targeting specific symbols of the religious factions, have marred daily life.

10 CentCom's unwillingness or inability to provide a strong military presence in Coalition-controlled areas after the fall of Baghdad led to a massive outbreak of looting and property destruction. It was utterly unexpected. As well as symbols of the state's power (ministerial buildings, embassies and palaces), manifestations of Iraq's cultural heritage were destroyed – the National Museum was plundered and, above, Basra University Library's reading room was gutted.

11 The Central Bank of Iraq, ransacked during the war, is guarded by US troops. Although state-owned banks accounted for well over 90 per cent of deposits, they were virtually bankrupt and unable to function effectively.

12 Grand Ayatollah Ali al-Sistani, the top Iraqi Shi'a cleric, a man of wisdom and few words who exuded the charisma and authority to influence and direct events. He distanced himself from any overt support for the occupation but accepted the foreign force as a necessary cost of overthrowing tyranny. Stressing the vital need for transferring power back to Iraqis as soon as possible, he issued a fatwa rejecting Bremer's proposal to have the constitution written by un-elected experts.

13 The Iraqi Governing Council signed the country's interim constitution (known as the Transitional Administrative Law) on 8 March, 2004, to take effect until sovereignty was restored to a caretaker government. The creation of a constitution was a key American demand, and Bremer insisted on an appointed constitution-writing body. Elections were not only difficult to arrange – their outcomes were beyond the CPA's control.

14 The city of Fallujah, in a photograph taken one year after the crisis in April 2004, shows the decimation of this bastion of insurgency. The offensive began in retribution for numerous attacks on the coalition, including the ambush and murder of four guards, two of whose charred bodies were strung up on a bridge.

15 Radical Shi'a cleric Moqtada al-Sadr was the putative leader of the Sadrists, a raw and violent mass political movement that galvanised huge support. The son of Ayatollah Muhammad Sadiq al-Sadr, who was assassinated in 1999, he led the Friday prayers at his father's bastion, the Kufa Grand Mosque, dressed in a burial shroud to proclaim his faith publicly – a Sadrist stance of renouncing quiescence and quietism.

16 Members of the Mahdi army in Imam Ali shrine, Najaf. Entrenched Sadrists and militiamen stockpiled weapons in preparation for the eruption of fighting, and occupied the shrine with Moqtada al-Sadr in August 2004 to protest against the government. The question of who was to have control of the shrines in Iraq was contentious.

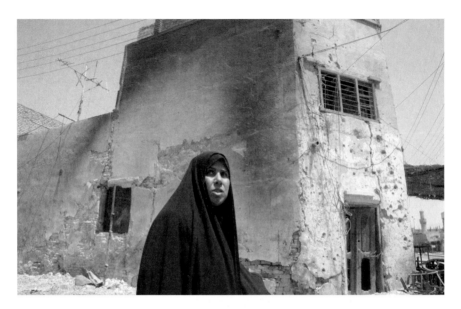

17 The crisis in Najaf was the biggest challenge to Ayad Allawi since his interim government took full power. Moqtada al-Sadr's army battled against multinational forces for more than two weeks, devastating the surrounding streets. With Sadrist control of the shrine and Shi'a in-fighting, it took Sistani to intervene and open negotiations, but the stand-off remained unresolved.

18 The Green Zone, a heavily fortified ten-kilometre-square oasis of calm in the middle of Baghdad. It accommodated the successive Iraqi administrations, housed almost all the senior politicians and served as the headquarters for the US Embassy which operated from the Republican Palace (pictured). The 'bubble' became increasingly barricaded against the hardships and dangers of Baghdad – a symbol of a besieged administration blind to the realities of the rest of Iraq.

19 The aftermath of a suicide bombing in Baghdad, 2005.

20 An Iraqi couple, proudly displaying their ink-stained fingers despite the threats from insurgents, vote on 30 January, 2005 in the first free national election in Iraq for fifty years.

21 US Army and Iraqi National Guard soldiers patrol the Haifa streets in 2005. A concurrent deployment of the country's army and multinational forces remained necessary as the timelines for withdrawal were instigated and perpetually deferred.

22 Iraqi Prime Minister Ibrahim Jaafari (centre) stands with other parliamentarians to take oath at the start of the first session of Iraqi parliament on 16 March, 2006 in Baghdad. The formation of the new government was under discussion.

23 The first elected government of Iraq since the fall of Saddam Hussein's regime convened on 20 May, 2006. Prime Minister Nuri al-Maliki (centre), a staunch supporter of Jaafari, nevertheless recognised that for the past five months the management of Iraq had been inefficient and harmful.

24 On 19 October, 2006, Saddam Hussein's long-delayed trial opened. Charges of genocide and human rights abuses during the *Anfal* campaign against the Kurds in the 1980s were brought against him. Although the case was infamous for its histrionics and tortuous progress, it represented an attempted introduction of a new Iraq to the world's media, as a country where its people's rights would be respected. It was not only the trial of one man's past, but a country's future.

inadequacies of the CPA's economic stewardship over Iraq were too high. Even institutions such as the United States Institute of Peace (USIP), part of the trio of congressionally established advocacy institutes that were active in Iraq, exaggerated the CPA's reconstruction successes.[34]

The US reconstruction effort was placed on a sounder footing after the dissolution of the CPA and the transfer of its responsibilities to the US Embassy. The relative power balance between the Pentagon and the more specialised US agencies shifted decisively in favour of the latter and with that, more professionalism and accountability was introduced into the reconstruction programme. The best-qualified staff were those who had been seconded or recruited by the US Treasury. By its very nature the Treasury team was highly specialised and worked on compartmentalised issues of public finance and central banking. They could not, and were not, easily second-guessed by the political appointees on the CPA's roster. Treasury and USAID staff successfully worked on currency and financial sector reform, banking regulations and supervision, and Iraq's international economic relations. They understood the need to focus on human and technical parameters that made projects successful, as well as good policies. The rank amateurism and swaggering arrogance of too many of the CPA's recruits contrasted with the professionalism of the established development and reconstruction agencies, both of the USA and other supporting countries, particularly those from the UK, Australia and Poland.[35]

The policy environment under which reconstruction was taking place went through two distinct phases before the transfer of authority to the Interim Iraqi Government. The first phase culminated in the mass of policy measures to open up the economy, such as the foreign investment law, allowing foreign banks access to the Iraqi market, trade liberalisation and tariff reform. It was naïvely hoped that foreign investment would be quickly attracted to Iraq in sizeable amounts and that the economy would be restructured under the pressure of competition and open markets. However, major foreign investors, ranging from the multinational oil and resource companies to regional groups based in the Gulf countries, showed little interest in these reforms per se. The second phase of the policy reforms debate tried to concentrate on areas where change was essential but would not be costly in political or social terms. Here the CPA's promise of root-and-branch reform fell flat, a casualty of pusillanimity and increasing policy paralysis.

The CPA failed in three distinct areas where policy reform was essential to create the enabling environment for reconstruction. The first area was the reform of the price support and subsidies system that dominated the state's expenditures. At no time did the CPA seriously question the wisdom of continuing Saddam's policy of providing basically free fuel to the Iraqi public. On the contrary, the CPA embarked on an import programme for petroleum products to meet the demands of the growing domestic markets, and continued to 'sell' the fuel at give-away prices. The unwillingness of the CPA to confront this most brazen form of price distortion meant this poisoned chalice was handed on to future Iraqi governments. It was not until December 2005 that the Transitional Iraqi Government began to tackle the problem.

Another crucial area of reform was the Public Distribution System (PDS) – or the food ration programme. The system was distorted and inefficient. Ultimately, after considerable time and effort had been expended to develop a cash substitute for the PDS, the US Treasury and CPA did nothing on the grounds that 'it was no longer the US's policy to introduce any major reforms into the Iraqi economy'.[36] Therefore, an opportunity to break the nexus associated with the food ration programme, which included massive corruption at all levels of the supply chain, was lost.

The CPA also shirked from undertaking any reforms of the state-owned enterprises. These entities were financial black holes, costing the Iraqi budget upwards of a billion dollars in subsidies. Loud noises were made in the early days of the CPA about the need to restructure and sell state-owned companies as part of the market liberalisation reforms that were going to be implemented. In the event, the CPA did nothing but compound the operating problems of these companies by denying them access to their own funds. The hysteria from the domestic and international media when the possible privatisation of state-owned enterprises was first mooted had the desired effect of scaring the CPA from undertaking any changes. Once again advanced plans by a number of ministries for limited rationalisation and privatisation of state-owned companies were left with no champion in the CPA, when the policy parameters changed. These and numerous other cases of policy reforms that were shelved marked the huge gap between the CPA's liberalising rhetoric and the actual policies that were pursued. It was a marked failure of will and betrayed the hopes of those Iraqis who had championed the cause of market reforms. The original radical reformist agenda of the CPA was abandoned as soon as the political costs began to appear in the calculations.

In spite of the CPA's lack of resolve to implement reforms that would have had a substantial impact on the reconstruction programme, there were a number of very important institutional decisions that were made that did improve the management and efficiency of the economy and government. Bremer's order regarding the establishment of a Public Integrity Commission was a notable achievement, and created the framework for seriously tackling the exploding levels of high- and low-level corruption in the country. The most important economic and financial reform that the CPA introduced, however, was the promulgation of the Financial Management Law. This was a profound and far-sighted piece of legislation that set the framework for writing balanced budgets, with public accountability for all government expenditures. The Law played a vital part in establishing the parameters of budget preparation and made unauthorised expenditures – the bane of Iraqi budget managers – a culpable act. The fact that its provisions were subsequently grossly breached did not detract from its importance as a powerful tool for ordering Iraq's public finances. The CPA or, more accurately, the US Treasury, also began the process of tackling Iraq's massive $130 billion in foreign indebtedness. The effects of this effort would not emerge until later, but it was one of the great success stories of the USA's involvement with Iraq.

15

April 2004 – the Turning Point

*'America has unsheathed its fangs and its despicable intentions and the
conscientious Iraqi people cannot remain silent at all. They must defend
their rights as they see fit.'* –

Statement by Moqtada al-Sadr, 6 April, 2004

Two separate incidents on Wednesday, 31 March, 2004 marked the beginning
of the most serious crisis that the Coalition had faced since its arrival in Iraq
a year before. As the drama unfolded, it seemed that Iraq was witnessing a
nationwide insurrection against the occupation. One part of the crisis was
connected to the perennial 'Moqtada problem', the other to the evolving insurgency that was growing deadlier and more widespread by the hour, leading to
yet another confrontation in the city of Fallujah. For the first time, important
constituencies in both the Shi'a and Sunni communities simultaneously rose
up in arms in two widely separate locations. At the time, these two incidents
appeared unconnected, but they would play a large part in determining the
course of events in Iraq over the following months. They coincided with the
launch, with much fanfare, of a new, rebranded Iraqi army and security services structure that would face their first test only days after they came into
being. In the background, the UN's special envoy, Lakhdar Brahimi, working
closely with Robert Blackwill, the NSC's point man on Iraq, were putting the
final touches to what would become Iraq's Interim Government. It was this
government to which sovereignty was to be transferred. These crucial developments would be packed together in April 2004, in the final few weeks of the
CPA's life.

By the end of 2003, Moqtada al-Sadr appeared to be retreating from an
openly hostile position on the CPA and the occupation. He had made a
number of conciliatory statements that had appeased the CPA, and by the
start of the New Year had moved away from centre stage.[1] The 'bad boy' of
Iraqi politics appeared to be tamer and more conscious of the disparity of

power between his movement and the Coalition. Sistani's dominant role in the events leading up to the November 15 Agreement, and his campaign against its terms, also gave Sistani an undisputed mastery over the Shi'a political response and, by extension, over the entire Iraqi political scene. Both the UN and the CPA anxiously waited for his words and pronouncements on the political transition. Moqtada was nowhere to be seen in these crucial negotiations. He had been accorded his true, limited, stature on the Iraqi political scene. Or at least that was what was thought. The CPA and the Iraqis on the Governing Council had made yet another blunder in their assessment and judgement of the Sadrists. The CPA had wilfully ignored the scale of Moqtada's support among the Shi'a underclass, and had refused to countenance its significance. It had treated him as a ruffian and his supporters as no better than thugs and extortionists. The Governing Council politicians, especially the Islamists, were more circumspect in their attitude to Moqtada, simultaneously wary of his street power and condescending towards his ambitions. In public they would damn him with faint praise; in private they were fearful and often panic-stricken whenever his movement appeared to erupt out of its main enclave in Sadr City. For it was in Sadr City that Moqtada ruled supreme.

Sadr City

The CPA and the military's reconstruction teams had made occasional forays into Sadr City, but these had been hesitant, small scale or unsustained. There had been some achievements especially with the renovation of schools: the CPA had repaired about 100 of the 270 schools in the area.[2] In most other areas relating to the city's infrastructure and services provisions, however, the efforts were of no consequence, given the massive range of Sadr City's problems. It is probably the biggest city in Iraq, though its true size has never been statistically measured and has been masked for political reasons. It would have been dangerous to acknowledge publicly that a supposedly Shi'a suburb of Baghdad was now nearly as big as the metropolis itself.[3] By 2004, two to two-and-a-half million people were estimated to live there, although the actual number is unknown.[4]

Sadr City originated as a slum in the 1950s. It occupies an area of about thirty square kilometres, and while accounting for less than 10 per cent of the area of Baghdad, it contains more than one-third of the greater Baghdad population. By the spring of 2004, the mood in Sadr City had turned distinctly sour against the occupation. The initial high expectations that the population had had regarding the Coalition and improvements in their living standards and habitat had been unfulfilled, leaving an increasingly embittered people. Local sheikhs had estimated unemployment at over 70 per cent of the labour force.[5] Education and literacy rates were well below the national averages. Infrastructure had crumbled. Sadr City's water and sewerage systems were abominable, with raw, liquid sewage oozing onto the streets from broken pipes. Solid waste collected in the streets for months on end. Only 40 per cent of the water available was estimated to be drinkable. The electrical grid relied on cables that were strung across the ground in a haphazard fashion. Only half the households were connected to the grid, and the city's residents received only two-thirds of the power that Baghdad received. Roads collapsed and could not be repaired, partly owing to the constant flooding of the streets and the concentrations of sewage. There were only two general hospitals, together with a paediatrics hospital and an obstetrics hospital.

The local politics of Sadr City evolved in atypical ways. The incomplete urbanisation of migrants and the poor provision of state services kept the inhabitants loyal to their tribal roots and traditions. Nearly 98 per cent of the population of Sadr City was Shi'a, nearly all from the tribal rural areas of southern Iraq. All the main tribes of the south, that is, up to 164 different tribes and clans, were represented.[6] The power of the local tribal leaders, numbering over 300, was generally acknowledged, but with the rise of the Grand Ayatollah Muhammad al-Sadr, who had specifically reached out to the inhabitants of Sadr City, most of the tribal elders had deferred to his over-arching authority. Following his murder, the network of religious, tribal, and also, surprisingly, professional leaders associated with the late Grand Ayatollah, reconstituted their power in the city.[7] The Coalition tried to skirt around the Sadrists when it set up district and neighbourhood councils as part of its local government initiatives. The Sadr City District Council cooperated with the military, but came under widespread suspicion for corruption and theft of funds marked for infrastructure and social improvement.[8] The chairman of the District Council was murdered, presumably for working with the Coalition. Throughout the latter part of 2003 and early 2004, the Sadrists quietly built up their power base in their militia arm, the *Jaysh al-Mahdi* (the Mahdi Army), and effectively controlled the political life of the city. In July 2003, Moqtada paid his first visit to Sadr City since the fall of the Ba'athist regime. Ecstatic crowds numbering tens of thousands, and carrying tribal and Iraqi banners, met him.[9] Meanwhile, his stalwarts had seized all the main mosques and meeting halls in Sadr City, and in most of the other major concentrations of poor Shi'as in Baghdad, such as the Shuula district. The main Friday congregational mosque in Sadr City, the Muhsin mosque, was led by Sayyid Hassan Naji al-Moussawi, who doubled up as the head of the Mahdi Army's units in Baghdad.[10]

The CPA and the Sadrists

In spite of the grudging acquiescence of Moqtada to the inevitable passage of the TAL, the Sadrists were far from withdrawing from the public arena. Moqtada developed a deliberate and far-reaching strategy to gain political supremacy. The Sadrists had begun to deepen their involvement in community-related work and in providing a modicum of social services in those areas where they prevailed. They even went so far as to set up eight religious courts that meted out rough and ready justice in Sadr City, Najaf and other localities throughout the country. At the same time, work was continuing apace on building up the Mahdi Army's capabilities. The CPA knew all this, and was extremely apprehensive about Moqtada's plans. It had not given up hope of pinning the murder of Abd el-Majid al-Khoei directly on to Moqtada. The investigative judge, Ra'ed Juhi, had issued the warrant for his arrest in November 2003. Juhi now began to give the Governing Council and certain ministers a private viewing of the gruesome photographs of al-Khoei's murder, together with a detailed exposé of the circumstances of the crime.[11] At the same time, the CPA began to sound out more moderate senior clerics, such as the Kadhimain-based Ayatollah Hussein al-Sadr, a close relative of Moqtada, about the repercussions if the arrest warrant were actually implemented.[12] The response from the moderate senior clergy, including those who were close to the Marji'iyya, was uniformly encouraging to the CPA. The CPA had reckoned it had received the 'green light' from the senior Shi'a clergy to move directly against Moqtada.

In the first few weeks of 2004, the Sadrists picked on popular issues around which to organise marches and demonstrations that would not directly challenge the Coalition. The activities were meant more in the way of displaying the street power of the Sadrist movement, and were focused both at the Coalition and rival Shi'a power centres. However, the tempo of the Sadrists' demonstrations soon picked up. An associate of Moqtada al-Sadr in Kadhimain, Sayyid Hazem al-'Araji, accused the USA of collusion with terrorists by not preventing a grenade attack against the shrines of Kadhimain. 'We think the Americans know the people who did this but they want to hide it. They hide it to make a sectarian war,' he said.[13] Following the murderous suicide bombings in Kadhimain and Karbala in March, that marked the occasion of Ashoura, the Mahdi Army began to provide 'security' in the teeming Shi'a areas of Baghdad and elsewhere in the country, notably in Karbala and Najaf. The CPA decided to tackle the 'Moqtada problem' up front.

The actual justification was provided by a series of inflammatory articles written in the Sadrists' mouthpiece, the weekly al-Hawza newspaper. Al-Hawza's circulation was limited to 15,000 copies, mainly aimed at Sadrist militants.[14] (Its influence was negligible outside these rather narrow circles.)

On 28 March, 2004, Bremer signed an order to shut down the paper for sixty days, and the newspaper's offices were padlocked. The editor was served a letter explaining that the newspaper had violated a ban on fomenting violence. *Al-Hawza* articles were indeed pejorative, and made a number of outrageous claims about Masonic plots and outlandish Zionist conspiracies.[15] But they were no more vitriolic than any number of similar accusations made by Baghdad's gutter press that had blossomed after the fall of the former regime. The closure of *Al-Hawza* was believed to be a deliberate and measured move on the part of the CPA to contain Moqtada, and to draw him out where he could be arrested. It was widely condemned by both supporters and opponents of the CPA. Most thought it would strengthen Moqtada's hand and provide him with an excuse to denounce the CPA's victimisation of his movement and its double standards. With reference to the Karbala bombings Moqtada said, 'America benefited from the events in Karbala to make war against me.'[16]

Anti-American feeling amongst the Shi'a rank and file increased markedly during the first few months of 2004. The imbroglio over the November 15 Agreement and the calls for marches and demonstrations by the *Marji'iyya* and the Sadrists inflamed already impassioned opinion. Many CDs of the aftermath of the Karbala and Kadhimain bombings were widely distributed, showing bereaved and shocked people blaming the Coalition. Mosque loudspeakers in the Shi'a neighbourhoods were heard to call for *jihad*. One said, 'We blame the Americans, let's expel the Americans, let's unite to expel them from Iraq'.[17] Eschatological fever gripped a large number of people in the Sadrist neighbourhoods, with many believing that the Imam al-Mahdi, the Twelfth Imam of the Shi'a who, it was believed, had gone into occultation, was about to reappear. In response to the growing unrest, the CPA committed another blunder. They arrested Sheikh Mustafa al-Yaqoubi, an influential acolyte of Moqtada, on 3 April, on charges of complicity in Khoei's murder. On the following day, demonstrators from Najaf converged on the nearby Spanish security base and in the confused situation that followed a major fire fight broke out. Nearly 22 Iraqis were killed and over 200 wounded.[18] In response to the fighting, Bremer said, 'This morning, a group of people in Najaf have crossed the line and they have moved to violence . . . This will not be tolerated by the Iraqi people and this will not be tolerated by the Iraqi security forces.'[19]

Moqtada, sensing impending danger, at first took sanctuary in the Kufa Mosque, and then moved to his office in Najaf, where he issued a defiant statement. He cannily aligned himself with Sistani, hoping to bolster his credibility, saying, 'I proclaim my solidarity with Ali Sistani, and he should know that I am his military wing in Iraq.'[20] On 5 April, Dan Senor, the CPA's spokesman, announced that an Iraqi judge had issued an arrest warrant for the 'Shi'ite cleric Muqtada al-Sadr' in connection with the 2003 murder of 'another cleric' at a mosque in Najaf. Senor, and later Brigadier Kimmitt, tried to portray the arrest warrant as a purely Iraqi judicial affair. Kimmitt was the deputy director of coalition operations for Combined Joint Task Force-Seven (CJTF-7). Kimmitt said, 'The cleric can surrender at any Iraqi police station or wait to have the warrant served . . . . Whatever al-Sadr decides, he will be treated with dignity and respect . . . the same way every other alleged criminal in the Iraqi justice system is treated.' [21]

The Uprising of the Sadrists

In the previous forty-eight hours the Mahdi Army had risen in a number of southern cities, and in a coordinated series of actions had taken over municipal buildings, bridges and police stations. In Nasiriya, Italian troops clashed with the Mahdi Army as the Sadrists tried to seize bridges across the Euphrates. In Amara, the Mahdi Army was involved in a series of clashes with British troops. In Karbala, Bulgarian and Polish troops of the Coalition came under intense fire from Sadr's supporters. In Sadr City itself, Coalition forces came under regular attack, even while crowds milled around the Sadrists' headquarters waving flags and chanting Moqtada's name.[22] But the uprising of the Mahdi Army was met with an indifference bordering on stony-faced hostility by the militias of the other main Shi'a groups, such as SCIRI's Badr Brigade. They simply watched and waited, while the Mahdi Army took on the Coalition.

The CPA was caught completely wrong-footed. They had calculated that a combination of bellicosity, the public airing of the arrest warrant against Moqtada, the fear of the Sadrists' rising popularity by the more mainstream Shi'a Islamists and the tacit support of the Marji'iyya to the crackdown, would isolate Moqtada and make his arrest possible. What was clear, however, was the CPA's, in particular Bremer's, disdain for the Sadrists. Intelligence reports had been streaming in about the broad base of support for the Sadrists, the increasing anti-American sentiments in the Shi'a areas, and, most threateningly, signs of cooperation between the Sunni insurgents and the Mahdi Army. The Sunni insurgency heartland of Anbar province had exploded once again, and Fallujah was in the grips of a major anti-Coalition rebellion. The CPA had just finished putting the final touches to the national security structure for Iraq. A new defence minister, Ali Allawi, had recently been appointed to the post, in addition to his Trade Ministry portfolio. There was a new head of the Iraq National Intelligence Service (INIS), and a new National Security Advisor. A Coordinating Committee for National Security, which consisted of key CPA personnel and Iraqi national security ministers as well as other concerned ministers, had started to meet regularly. A few days after its inception it was faced with the most dangerous security situation since the fall of the Ba'ath regime.

By 7 April, the Mahdi Army rebellion had assumed dangerous proportions. Unsubstantiated reports began to filter in of Iranian involvement in the uprising, but these were vague and inconclusive. Iranian intelligence had established deep roots in southern Iraq, but it was unclear whether they had a hand in the actual decision to foment an uprising.[23] The scale of the disturbances was exaggerated. The Mahdi Army had seized control over sensitive points and installations, but poorly trained and motivated Iraqi police had mainly surrendered these. In Kut and Nasiriya, the takeover of sensitive facilities by the Mahdi Army took place after Coalition troops had left these positions. The Sadrists were not itching for a fight. Their control over these cities was tenuous at best and they would not be able to withstand any serious Coalition attempts to retake them. In spite of the widespread nature of the rebellion, the Mahdi Army was mainly concentrated in Najaf, where it had effective control over the shrine complex of Imam Ali. They also had a degree of control in Kut. In Sadr City, their presence was felt everywhere, but they did not mount a direct challenge to the Coalition's control over Baghdad. The Sadrists' plan was to combine just enough of a military challenge, with control over the city of Najaf, the symbolic capital of the Iraqi Shi'a. They were quite sure that a seize-and-hold strategy, with continuous harassment, street demonstrations and the sowing of civil disorder, would eventually wear out the CPA, fearful as it would be of the adverse consequences of a frontal assault on their positions. This would be especially true if the Coalition tried to force them out of the shrine in Najaf. Religious leaders on the Governing Council and the *Marji'iyya* were horrified at the possible effects of a full-blown attack on the shrine to dislodge the Mahdi Army.

At first, negotiations with Moqtada were firmly rejected by the CPA. Although the Security Committee held detailed discussions, it was clear that decisions were taken elsewhere, notably by Bremer and his small coterie of American national security advisers, and on the military side by the top brass of the awkwardly named Combined Joint Task Force-Seven.[24] Bremer's national security advisers were of uneven quality. A few, such as Christopher Ross, were skilled negotiators with strong political insights. Others approached the problem holding the stilted formulations of security theory derived from think-tanks and political science departments, having little feeling for, or understanding of, the underlying issues in Iraq. Unfortunately, it was the latter category of advisers who predominated. Their dedication did not counteract their inappropriate advice. Bremer was on poor terms with General Sanchez, of CJTF-7, and was frequently surprised and upset about decisions apparently reached unilaterally by the military.

The Iraqis on the Security Committee were generally more sensitive to the complexities of the issues, but were insufficiently experienced and had no power or actual resources. The CPA and the military called the shots, pursuing their own plans and schemes. In many respects therefore, the Security Committee was an entirely fictitious arrangement, designed to assume tasks for which it had no takers. Its role in the Moqtada and later Fallujah crises was marginal but it still served some propaganda value for the CPA. It put an Iraqi face on the CPA's and the military's decisions.

Ministers on the Security Committee had to defend publicly policies which they had no hand in formulating. Often they would be confronted with CPA or military decisions that ran diametrically opposed to what they had proposed. The obsession to micro-manage all aspects of the media spread to the instructions given to the Security Committee. Ministers were told not to use the term 'Mahdi Army' but rather 'Moqtada's Militia', in an attempt to downplay the significance of the rebellion and to eschew the word 'uprising'. All were told to toe the earlier Bremer line that the 'armed sedition of the Moqtada Militia will not be tolerated'. There was a wide gulf between the realities on the ground and the 'themes' of the CPA's media managers. The Iraqi police force disintegrated, or did not resist when confronted by the Mahdi Army; Iraqi military units were nowhere evident in the fight to recover towns, cities and installations that fell to the Mahdi Army; and the Security Committee, supposedly the main national security decision-making body, was continually sidelined by the CPA, the military, and even the Governing Council.

The Stand-off in Najaf [25]

By mid-April, however, the Coalition had regained control over nearly all the towns that had fallen to the Mahdi Army, leaving Moqtada inside Najaf and Kufa, and in parts of Karbala. The hopeless mismatch in firepower between the Mahdi Army and the Coalition, and its poor leadership and training, led to its inevitable defeat. Wherever the two sides met, brave but chaotic and ill-disciplined militiamen could not seriously withstand the determined and deliberate power of the US military. Moqtada was now bottled up in the city of Najaf, and proposals to mediate the crisis began to arrive. The CPA presented a plan for Moqtada, to include the disarming of the Mahdi Army, respect for the institutions of the state, and the removal of his armed supporters from the streets.[26] Following Bremer's bombastic claims that Moqtada would either 'be killed or captured', the CPA's proposals were seen as a climbdown. Moqtada predictably countered with a set of his own proposals, which included the withdrawal of the military from the holy cities. With the stand-off continuing throughout the latter part of April, the CPA worked on a detailed blueprint for defeating Moqtada and the Mahdi Army, using mainly political measures. The aim of the plan was to drive a wedge between the population of Najaf and the Sadrists. It was premised on the belief that the shopkeepers and hostel-owners of the shrine city, severely affected by the falloff in pilgrimage traffic, would welcome the reimposition of law and order. Information was accumulating that the population in Najaf was unhappy about the presence of the Mahdi Army, and that the *Marji'iyya* would not be averse to action against the Sadrists. Rather optimistically, one of the plan's objectives was to isolate Moqtada from the Mahdi Army. How this was to be done was left vague, but presumably it would have involved making financial inducements to the Mahdi Army and Moqtada's key clerical supporters to abandon his cause.

Other plans included allowing him to escape to Iran and pledges of reconstruction funds in Najaf. The only aspect of the plan that had any effect was the military one. Regular raids and precision attacks on Mahdi Army positions in Najaf became very damaging to the Sadrists. Hundreds of fighters of the Mahdi Army were killed, wounded or arrested in these fire fights. By the middle of May 2004, Moqtada's supporters were concentrated only in the centre of the city, in and around the shrine of Imam Ali. Negotiations then began in earnest to dislodge the Sadrists from their last bastions. A game of chicken began, with Moqtada knowing that the Coalition might not be prepared to mount a frontal assault on the shrine, while the CPA banked on the isolation and difficult conditions of Moqtada in the centre of Najaf. At this point, the Shi'a caucus at the Governing Council, the 'Shi'a House', entered the fray.

Throughout April and May of 2004, the Shi'a House, which was now Islamist dominated, acted as an intermediary between the Coalition and Sadr, holed up as he was in the Najaf shrine. Ambassador Ross was the main CPA interlocutor, working closely with the recently appointed National Security Advisor, Dr Mowaffaq Rubai'e. The latter played a pivotal role in the negotiations with the Sadrists. Ayatollah Sistani's son, Muhammad Redha Sistani, who wielded considerable influence both with the CPA and the Shi'a House, entered the negotiations. The *Marji'iyya* had initially taken a hostile position to the Sadrists and the occupation of the shrine. The possibility was floated that tribal forces, loyal to the *Marji'iyya*, could take over the city, with tacit help from the CIA. Although the CPA signalled its approval of this initiative, it led nowhere.

The stand-off in Najaf was dangerously accentuated when a stray shell landed on the dome of the shrine. The *Marji'iyya* came under pressure from opinion leaders in the worldwide Shi'a community to take a firm position, one way or another, on the occupation of the shrine. These communities were naturally concerned in case the fighting escalated to the point where the shrine itself might become seriously damaged. The *Marji'iyya* signalled that it was unwilling to accept that the disarming and dissolution of the Mahdi Army, a key Coalition demand, should be linked to the evacuation of the shrine itself. Fortified by the *Marji'iyya*'s position, the Shi'a House, acting through Rubai'e, saw an opening, and offered an outline of a settlement to Moqtada. This involved a four-point plan, which Moqtada accepted, and included both the withdrawal of the Mahdi Army from Najaf and the return of the Coalition's forces in Najaf to their bases. Crucially, Sadr was firm in refusing to entertain the disarming and dispersion of the Mahdi Army. After some hesitation, the CPA accepted the broad outlines of the Shi'a House's proposals, and decoupled the disarming and disbanding of the Mahdi Army from its withdrawal from the shrine itself and the city of Najaf. The Coalition ceased its offensive operations against the Mahdi Army. The issue of the arrest warrant against Moqtada al-Sadr was allowed to quietly die away. Indeed, the CPA, in a letter to the Najaf governor outlining the terms of the agreement, was almost effusive about the turn of events. The renegade cleric of yesterday suddenly had the honorific of 'Sayyid' attached to his name, and his response to the Shi'a House proposals were viewed as a 'positive and constructive step towards the peaceful solution which [the CPA] have been advocating'.[27]

The apparent climb down by the CPA regarding the arrest of Moqtada al-Sadr and the dissolution of the Mahdi Army was not only prompted by the hesitancy of the *Marji'iyya* to countenance a full-blown assault on the Sadrist forces. It was also related to the fear of a 'two-front' insurgency. The spectre of Shi'a–Sunni cooperation in countering the occupation was raised in early April, when the Moqtada uprising coincided with the increased hostilities in Fallujah. Sanchez, the commander of the occupation forces, admitted as much. 'The danger is we believe there is a linkage that may be occurring at the very lowest levels between the Sunni and the Shi'a. We have to work very hard to ensure that it remains at the tactical level.'[28]

The Fallujah Crisis[29]

The Fallujah crisis of April 2004 had its genesis with the ambush and murder of four American private security guards as they were driving through the city after taking a wrong turn.[30] Their vehicle was burned, their bodies mutilated and dragged through the streets. Two of the charred corpses were strung up on a nearby bridge. The killings of the guards had followed in the wake of a whole string of attacks against Coalition forces or civilians over the previous few months. In one such attack on 12 February, 2004, CentCom's chief, General Abizaid, escaped an assassination attempt when his convoy came under fire from insurgents with rocket-propelled grenades.[31] Fallujah had, in the intervening period, effectively slipped out of Coalition control. US troops decamped to bases outside the city. A few days before the attack on the US security guards, the US Marines' First Expeditionary Force had taken control of the Fallujah area from the US Army's 82nd Airborne Division, with promises of a less aggressive, more targeted, counter-insurgency strategy.[32]

The CPA's initial response to these murders, whose gruesome images were being constantly rebroadcast by the satellite channels, was measured. But soon thereafter, both Bremer and the White House began to express altogether different sentiments. They considered these outrages as an affront to the Coalition, and a direct challenge to the power and resolve of the USA. Bremer promised that the murders would 'not go unpunished'. The struggle for control over Fallujah was nothing less than the 'struggle between human dignity and barbarism'.[33] The Marines' commander in western Iraq, General James Conway, was more circumspect about pursuing retribution against the perpetrators of this atrocity, but Rumsfeld overruled him. It was decided to attack Fallujah, and root out the insurgents who had turned the city into their stronghold.

Fallujah was divided into two sectors, northern and southern, and two Marine battalions would take each sector. By 5 April, the Marines' operation was well underway, but the insurgents put up stiff resistance. As the fighting dragged on with no quick victory in sight, the battle for Fallujah began to dominate the airwaves. The al-Jazeera satellite channel had a correspondent inside the city. He relentlessly focused his cameras on the civilian casualties and the destruction that was being visited on the town.

The combination of hard fighting, increasing civilian casualties, sensationalist reporting by the Arab satellite channels and serious grumblings from the few Sunni on the Governing Council, as well as the intercession of Hashim al-Hassani of the IIP, exerted a powerful influence on the course of events. The bravado of Bremer and the CPA fizzled out as they began to seek ways out of a morass of their own making.

A further embarrassing event that dampened the fighting mood in the CPA was the effective desertion of the only Iraqi army unit deployed in the battle. The second battalion of the nascent 'New Iraq Army' simply refused to fight. In another instance, a unit of the civil defence corps, mobilised to join the fighting, simply jumped off from trucks transporting them to the battle scene and drifted back to their base in Baghdad. The battle for Fallujah became a cause célèbre for the insurgents, as well as the serried ranks of Arab satellite channels who built it up into a heroic defence of a beleaguered city in the face of overwhelming US power. Within a remarkably short period of time, the enterprise of retribution and cleansing the city of insurgents ran the risk of generating precisely the opposite of what had been expected. For the insurgents, Fallujah became a rallying cry, and a powerful recruiting tool. The Sunni Arabs who were cooperating with the CPA were neither grateful for this attempt to root out insurgents, nor cowed by the Coalition's show of force. A particularly poignant and principled response came from the competent

Minister of Human Rights, Abd el-Basit Turki, who challenged the entire project and resigned in protest.

The Fallujah crisis coincided with the arrival of the UN envoy Lakhdar Brahimi for consultations on the formation of the Interim Government. He was immediately caught up in the swirl of events as various politicians tried to impress on him the gravity of the situation and its deleterious effects on his mission. Brahimi was incensed, and called the offensive a form of 'collective punishment' and 'not acceptable'.[34] Shi'a politicians on the other hand, with the notable exception of the Sadrists, who were fitfully trying to make common cause with the Fallujah insurgents, were more circumspect. There was plenty of public hand wringing, but in private they were more forthcoming about their desire to see the end of the insurgents' stronghold in Fallujah and the car-bomb factories that were rumoured to abound there. The three Sunni members on the Governing Council (Pachachi, Yawar and Hassani, acting as deputy for Muhsin Abd el-Hamid), however, met and agreed to resign from the Governing Council collectively if the Coalition was not prepared for a ceasefire and to embark on serious negotiations to end the fighting with the insurgents or their representatives. Bremer became seriously alarmed at this turn of events, while in Washington pressure was mounting on the President, especially from Blair, to stop the offensive. On 9 April, the Coalition declared a unilateral ceasefire. The US Marines, having initially opposed the operation, were incensed. They had captured nearly a third of the city with few casualties, and felt that the politicians had let them down. Later, General Conway would declare, 'Once you commit, you've got to stay committed'.[35] The siege of the city was relaxed and its inhabitants were allowed to leave, in case they were afraid that the fighting might resume and they would find themselves in the middle of running battles. The insurgents, a motley collection but including significant numbers of locals who fought in defence of their honour and city, continued to operate there.

With a ceasefire of sorts in place, various parties began to look for a way out of the impasse. The relations between Bremer and Sanchez had deteriorated to the point where their barely concealed antipathy broke out for all to see at the various high-level meetings which they both had to attend.[36] Bremer continued to work through the official structures of the new national security system, and his position at these meetings was consistent in his insistence that the insurgents had to be confronted and destroyed. But the Security Committee was essentially toothless. It produced a mass of initiatives to 'resolve' the crisis, none of which materialised.

General Muhammad Shahwani, the newly appointed head of Iraq's nascent security and intelligence services (INIS), which were directly connected to the CIA and funded by the USA, had begun secret negotiations on behalf of the US Marines to bring the siege to a close. A former senior general in the

Saddam-era armed forces, Shahwani had long been a major asset of the CIA. His appointment to the Iraqi Intelligence Service was shrouded in mystery.

Shahwani was a firm believer in the virtues of integrating the officer elite of the former regime into the structures of power in the new order. The US Marines were also apparently impressed by the fact that a large number of fighters in Fallujah did not fit the catch-all description of dead-enders and foreign terrorists, but rather were military types who presumably responded to military discipline. Conway began to look for senior officers from the former regime's army with whom he could cooperate in reimposing order on the city and tackling the insurgents. Shahwani was in direct contact with Conway, and within a few days produced two senior officers from the former regime's army, Generals Muhammad Latif and Jassim Saleh. Latif was a Baghdad native while Saleh was from Fallujah. Saleh also, it emerged later, had ties to the insurgency. Nevertheless, Conway proceeded to work out the details of forming a special 'auxiliary' force of former soldiers and officers under the command of Latif and Saleh who would take over security in Fallujah. On 29 April, Conway authorised the formation of the 'Fallujah Brigade', a force of local men under the command of Latif and Saleh. Only a day before, Conway had addressed a meeting of senior Iraqi officials to plan for a large humanitarian operation in Fallujah, clearly indicating that the US Marines were going to resume large-scale operations in Fallujah in the near future. The fighting was expected to result in a large-scale displacement of people from Fallujah.

The 'Fallujah Brigade'

None of these ongoing discussions between the US Marines and Shahwani were known to the interim ministers, the Governing Council, the CPA or even Bremer. In fact, even the Pentagon was only perfunctorily briefed on the US Marines' plans with Shahwani and when the terms of the deal to form a 'Fallujah Brigade' were announced, it came as a bolt from the blue. Rumsfeld accepted the deal as a fait accompli, and marked it down to a commander's field prerogatives. Bremer, on the other hand, was livid, particularly, as he later explained, as he had learned about it from newspaper reports. Ali Allawi, the Iraqi Minister of Defence, and the National Security Advisor were outraged that the deal had been struck behind their backs, and at the serious implications of handing over security of a key city to a force of questionable composition and loyalties. The Defence Minister went on television, denouncing the Fallujah Brigade and refusing any Ministry of Defence association with, or financial commitment to, it. Several Governing Council members backed this position, issuing a statement condemning the formation of the Fallujah Brigade. The fear was that the 'Fallujah Brigade' experiment would be expediently replicated in other insurgent strongholds – thus effectively handing over control to the insurgents, operating under the guise of formal military units, over large swathes of Iraqi territory. 'It was the equivalent of the poachers becoming the gamekeepers,' said Allawi, the defence minister.[37] A series of emergency meetings were held between the security ministers, Bremer, Sanchez and Shahwani, to try to address the concerns of both the Iraqis and the CPA, but to no avail. The Fallujah Brigade was constituted, ostensibly under the ultimate control of the US Marines, as an auxiliary force.

All the fears of the nay-sayers were realised. The 'Fallujah Brigade', after a few weeks of apparent cooperation with the Marines, began to act as the core of a national liberation army. Any pretence that they were rooting out insurgents was dropped. In fact, the opposite happened. By the end of June, Fallujah had once again become an insurgent stronghold, with leaders of the 'Fallujah Brigade' openly aligning with the insurgency and calling for Islamic government in the city. A fusion between the insurgents, the Fallujah Brigade, the police and the imams of the mosques developed into a form of Islamic rule in the city. The Coalition resumed its bombing raids on insurgent hideouts in the city, with the inevitable civilian collateral deaths further inflaming passions. By the time the Interim Iraqi Government had been ensconced, the ramifications of the Fallujah problem had grown. There was little hope that a much more violent confrontation, between the Iraqi government and the MNF on one side and the insurgents of Fallujah on the other, could be avoided. The hasty and poorly considered decision to form the ill-fated Fallujah Brigade would lead to a far more violent and destructive battle a few months later. Bremer, to his credit, was acutely aware of the dangers of the US Marines' decision to hand over control of Fallujah to this 'auxiliary force'. The possibility that the last days of the CPA would witness destructive attacks on both Sunni and Shi'a insurgents, in Fallujah and Najaf, was an unpalatable outcome. A new Iraqi government was being formed and its success would be seriously jeopardised if it were to start its life in the aftermath of devastating battles.

The twin crises in April 2004 revealed the inherent weakness of the Coalition's position vis à vis both the Sadrists and the insurgents. Not only did hesitancy and uncertainty mark the Coalition's decisions about the appropriate course to follow but the CPA was also operating under a time fuse that would lead to its own demise within a few weeks. Not only did the CPA lose face by its turnabout from its original bellicosity but it also left the two antagonists that it faced in a much stronger position. The chaotic planning, personality clashes, the confused lines of authority, and the huge number of uncoordinated actors were all symptomatic of the larger failure of the CPA to establish its credibility as a consistent and purposeful administration. The final few weeks of the CPA's life effectively summarised its essential incoherence.

16

The Interim Iraqi Government

*'I will not say who was my first choice, and who was not my first choice . . .
I will remind you that the Americans are governing this country.'*

Lakhdar Brahimi, June 2004

The April crises added to the sense that the CPA had effectively run its course
and that the formation of a new Iraqi government was not only a formal
requirement for the restitution of sovereignty but an essential component for
stabilising the country. The CPA itself began to have a *fin de siècle* feel to it,
with a noticeable thinning out of its ranks. A number of senior personnel
slipped away to their former jobs, or to new positions on the back of their
valuable Iraq experience, while the more junior staff were busily preparing
their resumés for graduate and business schools and fast-track careers. In May
2004, the end of the CPA could be sensed in the eerily quiet corridors and hall-
ways of the former Republican Palace. The legal form of the US presence in
Iraq had not yet changed, but the advance guard of State Department officers
were already in Iraq to prepare for the establishment of the US Embassy. The
Governing Council was also facing its inevitable demise, and members began
either to jockey for positions in the interim government or at least to assure
themselves of some association with the post-sovereignty order. The Shi'a of
the Governing Council, and a number of cabinet officers, were hoping to be
on the radar screen of the two kingmakers, Robert Blackwill and Lakhdar
Brahimi, as potential prime ministerial candidates. The Kurds had apparently
got wind of the strong predilection on the part of the USA and the UK to
appoint a Sunni Arab as president, in a conciliatory gesture to the Arab world
and as an accommodating signal to the insurgents. It was felt that a Sunni
Arab as head of state would send a reassuring message to the population of
Iraq that the occupation was not designed to change its essential character.[1]
Both Jalal Talabani and Massoud Barzani ruled themselves out of any central
governmental role and assigned their deputies to the senior posts reserved for

the Kurds. Barzani wanted to stay in Kurdistan as head of the regional government, while Talabani sought the presidency of Iraq. It was in this atmosphere of anticipation, scheming and foreboding that the new interim government was being hammered out. The only clear loser in this phase was Ahmad Chalabi.

The Marginalisation of Ahmad Chalabi

By the time the CPA era drew to a close, Chalabi found himself increasingly alienated from the CPA and the power centres in Washington. He moved from the supposed favourite of the Pentagon to being an isolated and harassed figure. This was owing to a combination of some poorly timed, even maladroit, moves on his part, together with a deteriorating security situation that was partly blamed on the excesses of de-Ba'athification. The credibility of the war's earlier proponents amongst the neo-conservative cabal in Washington was rapidly dwindling as the insurgency increased in virulence. The tangled politics of post-invasion Iraq and the persistent violence and instability gave a fresh impetus to the role of the State Department and the intelligence services in the making of Iraq policy. The latter had always looked askance at Chalabi, and undermining his credibility in Washington and Baghdad had been a recurrent theme in their dealings with him.

A number of factors played a part in the declining position of Chalabi as one of Iraq's movers and shakers. First, Chalabi had uncovered a treasure trove of incriminating documents that connected senior western, Arab and UN figures with massive corruption in the UN's OFF programme.[2] Apart from seeking restitution for Iraq from these scams, his constant probing and unearthing of incriminating documents began to grate on the CPA. The CPA had maintained most of the UN's supply chain to Iraq under the OFF programme, and had continued to work with companies and individuals who were the main culprits in the corruption and subversion of the programme. The amounts that were stolen, misused and corruptly obtained in the OFF programme ran into billions.[3] The entire programme had been financed by Iraqi oil revenues, and the funds that had been misappropriated properly belonged to the Iraqi people. But Bremer blocked any further funding for the Governing Council investigation, and asserted that any enquiry into the propriety of the UN programme would be under the CPA's aegis. The possibility of the UN being drawn into an investigation of its practices that might implicate key individuals was extremely unwelcome, especially as the UN was being recalled, under US prodding, back into the Iraqi political scene. It would have been too damning to the UN's role as a credible arbiter if it was demonstrated that it had wilfully allowed the oil-for-food programme to be abused.

Chalabi had always been leery of the UN, rightly or wrongly seeing it as institutionally biased towards the status quo in the Middle East and opposed to the root-and-branch reform of the Middle East order that he had been advocating for over a decade. The UN position on the Middle East and Iraq was, in fact, highly complex. However, the UN's perfectly understandable concern with the appropriateness and degree of its re-engagement with Iraq raised alarm bells inside the Shi'a caucus. Some leaders, in particular Ahmad Chalabi, considered the UN's 'soul-searching' a mask behind which the UN would pursue a policy of restoring the status quo ante, or at least a tilt towards the more moderate Sunnis.

Chalabi expressed his views forcefully to the *Marji'iyya* and others who cared to listen. He went public with his misgivings about the UN and Brahimi. In an interview with Fox News on 25 April, 2004 he referred to Brahimi as 'a controversial figure. He's not a unifying figure . . . I believe that he should be more sensitive to the realities of Iraq.'[4] The USA had backed the Brahimi mission, and was relying on his cooperation and direct involvement in selecting the interim government, while Chalabi's rearguard actions against the UN and Brahimi mission no longer resonated with Washington. In fact, they were seen to be positively damaging as they ran counter to the USA's revised policy on the UN's involvement in Iraq. Chalabi moved from being a valuable, though prickly, ally, to being a nuisance and a potential threat to the UN's involvement in developing the transition to sovereignty. Bremer had always harboured deep misgivings about him.[5] In late April, a meeting in the White House was convened to discuss a memo drawn up by the NSC's Robert Blackwill entitled 'Marginalizing Chalabi'.[6] The memo listed all the usual charges against Chalabi, including that of providing false information on WMD. The gist of it was, however, as its title implied, to deny Chalabi any serious role in the transfer of power to an interim government.

A third factor in the decline of Chalabi so far as the CPA and Washington were concerned related to his increasing involvement with Iran. Chalabi had never hidden his relationships with the key figures of the Islamic Republic, and his contacts there were long-standing and deep. In fact, he had put them to good use when he controversially received an exceptional authorisation from the US government to use funds from the ILA to finance the INC's office in Tehran. In early 2004, the tempo of his contacts with Iran increased, although they were held in public view. Iranian diplomats and visitors called on his headquarters or at his private residence in full view of the CPA and other Iraqi leaders. There was nothing secret about them, but even so they would provide valuable ammunition for his critics. News began to leak out of Washington from intelligence agencies to the effect that Chalabi had provided Iran with 'sensitive' information about US political plans in Iraq and detailed information on US security operations. Apparently Chalabi had told the

Iranian intelligence station chief in Baghdad that the USA had broken their secret codes and was privy to all their communications. The FBI was charged with investigating these allegations, but they fizzled out once Chalabi had been effectively shut out of the transition process. The suspicion remained that the investigations were part of an orchestrated campaign to discredit him.

The marginalisation of Chalabi appeared complete when his headquarters were raided on 20 May by US-led forces and his home searched for incriminating evidence about alleged misdeeds in the Ministry of Finance.[7] Bremer was certainly aware of the raid, as were key officials in Washington.[8] Chalabi-bashers in the world's media, and especially the Arab press and satellite channels, were having a field day. Their prime hate figure was now on the ropes, and his days as one of Iraq's new crop of leaders were believed to be numbered.

Brahimi was clearly nettled by the charges that he was antipathetic to the Shi'a. In a US television interview in late April 2004, Brahimi was asked what he thought about the criticism levelled against him that being a Sunni Muslim might affect his impartiality in selecting the new Iraqi prime minister. 'I am a UN man. I am definitely a Muslim. And I come from a country where, you know, there are no problems of Sunni and Shias . . . . Frankly, I think it's silly, you know, to suggest that I may have a problem because I am Sunni, that I favour the Sunnis against – on the Shi'as. Why should I do that?' But even with the abrupt departure of Chalabi as a serious contender for the prime ministerial post, Brahimi had to contend with a number of other knotty issues. Under the TAL the prime minister was the chief executive of the Interim Government, and by common consent, had to be drawn from the Shi'a community. The Interim Government itself had to be credible domestically, regionally and internationally, and provide substance to the notion of sovereignty transfer. The *Marji'iyya* had to be consulted, the Kurds mollified and the Sunni Arabs, who were embittered by their exclusion from power after the invasion, needed to be accorded a more significant role in the government. Bremer had recently sounded off about the 'excesses' of de-Ba'athification, in an implicit admission that the Sunni Arabs should have been given a more prominent role in the governance of Iraq.[9] With the eclipse of Chalabi, a great deal of the blame for the de-Ba'athification policies could be laid at his doorstep as he had been the head of the de-Ba'athification Commission.

Ayad Allawi as Prime Minister

Throughout April and May 2004, Brahimi and Blackwill met with a huge number of Iraqi politicians, professionals and religious leaders before getting down to the business of selecting the prime minister and Cabinet. Bremer and the British contingent in Baghdad played a strong supporting role, while behind the scenes the intelligence agencies were preparing master lists of their own candidates for senior positions in the Interim Government. One of the earliest issues that emerged was whether the Interim Government should be drawn up as a stopgap administration with limited functions and duties. This was broached by Brahimi when he talked about a government of non-political 'technocrats'. In discussions with Blackwill, the then Minister of Defence Ali Allawi urged the UN team and Blackwill to consider a small interim government, not exceeding twelve to fifteen technocratic ministers, with the highly defined task of preparing for the January 2005 constitutional assembly elections. The Interim Government would then effectively be depoliticised, and its head would be committed not to seek any elected political office, at least until a new constitution was set in place. The security functions of the Cabinet would devolve on to an interim national security council, which would include the leaders of the main political parties as well as the security ministers and the prime minister. Blackwill appeared to reject this suggestion, and strongly indicated that the USA would not allow the transfer of power to a government that would not try to control the political process during the interim period: the USA, at least, would favour a government of politicians that would be susceptible to its influences. Nevertheless, Brahimi continued to talk of a neutral, technocratic government.

The final selection of Ayad Allawi assumed certain inevitability, even though, according to Pachachi's discussions with Brahimi, 'Ayad Allawi was not even being considered seriously' in the early days.[10] The increased tensions in Fallujah and Najaf worked in favour of Ayad Allawi's candidature. A security-minded person was seen as an essential requirement for vigorously prosecuting the war against the insurgents and Moqtada. The unresolved stand-off in Najaf and the evident disintegration of the Fallujah Brigade as a Marines auxiliary force and its transformation into an insurgency tool promised an unavoidable confrontation. A prime minister who, above all else, could understand the imperative of establishing security and who might be called upon to authorise the use of large-scale force, would be a critical element in the difficult transition period. Ayad Allawi fitted the profile in nearly every respect. The natural choice of the security-minded establishment in both London and Washington, he was also the 'last man standing'. It now only needed Sistani's approval, and Najaf indicated that the *Marji'iyya* would not object if Ayad Allawi was the UN team's final choice. (Sistani accepted him – just, because all the Islamists had been vetoed, and Chalabi was out of the running. Also, Sistani was banking on a quick transition to the constitutional elections.)

Before the choice could be finalised by Brahimi, the Governing Council decided to pre-empt the announcement of Ayad Allawi as the new prime minister. The Governing Council used a sleight of hand that made it appear as if he was their choice, and that it was they who were actually in control over the selection process. The Governing Council seized the initiative. In a specially convened meeting, it approved the selection of Ayad Allawi as its candidate for prime minister, presenting Brahimi with what appeared to be a fait accompli.[11] On 28 May the Governing Council announced that Ayad Allawi was going to be Iraq's interim prime minister. Soon after the announcement was made, Bremer, closely followed by Brahimi, entered the Governing Council chambers to congratulate Allawi. The UN statement issued on the occasion stated that Brahimi 'is perfectly comfortable with how the process is proceeding thus far'.[12]

The Presidency and the Ministerial Team of the Interim Iraqi Government

The presidency was to be offered to a Sunni Arab, in spite of objections by the Kurds. The Kurdish leaders were incensed and fired off an angry letter to Bush on 1 June. This rebuff added fuel to their anxieties that their achievements in post-Ba'ath Iraq were being compromised. The TAL was the anchor stone of Kurdish aspirations in Iraq. They viewed it as a sacrosanct 'roadmap' for the transition period, and well beyond. It was not included in the UN resolution that authorised the end of occupation and the formation of the interim government. This was done partly to assuage the bad feelings that the Najaf hierarchy had about the TAL, especially its clause 61(c).

The Kurds threatened non-cooperation, and even non-participation, in the interim government, but pressure from Washington and comforting sounds from Ayad Allawi mollified them. Allawi was unequivocal in agreeing to implement the terms of the TAL during the transition period. Eventually the Kurds accepted a number of senior posts, including the vice-presidency and the offices of deputy prime minister and minister of foreign affairs.

Both Brahimi and Blackwill had wanted Adnan Pachachi for the job of president, and his appointment seemed certain. He appeared to be an ideal figure. A moderate liberal democrat with huge international credibility, he seemed the perfect face for the interim presidency. Brahimi had made up his mind about Pachachi and had relayed the news to him that he was to be the interim president of Iraq. Brahimi's preference was also made clear to leading members of the Governing Council. A series of backroom manoeuvres inside the Governing Council, however, together with mismanagement of the candidacy by Pachachi himself, led to an unexpected outcome. Parachi's standing with Brahimi, Blackwill and Bremer was used against him by members of the Governing Council, and the Council selected Ghazi al-Yawer as the interim president. Pachachi himself credits Ahmad Chalabi with leading the 'conspiracy' to deny him the presidency.[13]

The final stages in selecting the Interim Iraqi Government involved the choice of ministers. Brahimi's preferred 'government of technocrats' meta-morphosed over time into a hybrid of something else. In spite of weeks of intensive consultations and cv-gathering, the final form of the Interim Government Cabinet was very little different to the one it was to replace. There were, however, important differences as to the personalities selected for ministerial appointments. First, the proportion of Islamists was reduced from that of the Governing Council Cabinet, in a deliberate attempt to limit their influence. Second, the intelligence agencies had directly selected a number of ministers who were connected to them in one way or another. Third, the CPA, which had developed some awareness of the range of professional capabilities available inside Iraq, also pitched in with their candidates. Ayad Allawi was given a list of two or three choices of ministers for each ministry, and was allowed to veto only those whom he felt he could not accept. He was not allowed to propose candidates himself. Given that he had only a limited first-hand knowledge of most of the names that were being proposed, he could only intervene in the few instances where he found a particular ministerial candidate objectionable. It was not a Cabinet that was designed for either cohesiveness or consistency of approach and policy.

In late May, all ministers of the Governing Council were curtly informed by Bremer that they should tender their resignations. The Interim Government was to assume power nearly a month before the formal transfer of sovereignty at the end of June. This was inexplicable. For a month, not only would Iraq have a government that would operate in a legal limbo, but incoming minis-ters would not be briefed about the functions of their ministries. Bremer's dislike of the Governing Council and his wish to see the back of it may have played a part in the decision to establish the Interim Government fully four weeks before the start of its legally mandated period.

The Interim Government was inaugurated on 2 June, 2004, in front of a huge throng of assembled officials and dignitaries and the world press. The insurgency was raging and Baghdad was even more insecure, but Iraqis broadly welcomed the Interim Government. A glimmer of hope had arisen with the impending return of sovereignty, and in spite of the evident absence of Iraqi control over the process of the Interim Government's formation, its inauguration nevertheless augured a better future. The office of Grand Ayatollah Sistani expressed lukewarm and heavily qualified support for the Interim Government. In a statement issued on 2 June, 2004, Sistani said that he 'repeatedly affirmed the necessity for the Iraqi government to possess a sovereignty that derives from free and honest elections in which the Iraqi people participate in a general way'.[14] He went on to complain that, 'the option of holding [early] elections was rejected, for many well known reasons . . . Thus, the process has become one of appointment, in order to form a new

government, without achieving the legitimacy of having been elected . . . .
Even so, it is to be hoped that this government will establish its worthiness
and probity and its unwavering determination to shoulder the immense
burdens now facing it.'[15]

The fact remained, however, that an interim government was an unnecessary interlude between the handover of sovereignty in June and the constitutional elections by the end of the year. Nobody could satisfactorily explain why
the appointed Governing Council and its government should have any less
legitimacy in the public eye than a similarly appointed Interim Government.
They were both collaborative compromises. The Governing Council was
demonised in the Arab media. By the end of the CPA, no one could be found
to have a good word to say about the Governing Council.

In contrast, the Interim Government, through the media managers of
Washington, London and the CPA, was repeatedly presented as a fresh hope
for Iraq's emergence into a democracy and abandonment of the divisive
policies of the Governing Council. It didn't matter one jot that the Interim
Government's senior appointments were all drawn from either the Governing
Council or its Cabinet. The politics of reducing the definition of progress to a
set of rigidly observed milestones had already set in. The milestones that
were cast in the TAL became hallowed and had to be met, otherwise the
'message' would become confused. The formation of the Interim Government
was such a milestone, and was therefore indicative of the seriousness of
progress towards a satisfactory resolution of the Iraq issue. Whether the artificial attainment of milestone objectives had any real significance was an altogether different matter. Image frequently overwhelmed substance as the USA
set one symbolic goal after another in the political process. The political
process lurched forward within the tight constraints of artificial dates and
deadlines.

Powers and Functions of the Interim Government and Security

The Interim Government inherited a whole range of unresolved issues and
problems from the CPA. It was not that the transfer of sovereignty meant that
the burden of the state's administration was going to be transferred lock, stock
and barrel to the new government. The CPA was about to be dissolved, but its
more important tasks were seamlessly transferred to the new US Embassy,
headed by John Negroponte, a career diplomat and former UN ambassador.
The Interim Government did, however, inherit a number of powers, tasks and
responsibilities that had been exercised by the CPA as the occupying authority.
The most important was probably control over Iraq's oil exports and
financing. The budget for 2004 had already been established, but signatory
powers and sole control over Iraq's main accounts at the Federal Reserve Bank

of New York were transferred from the CPA to the Interim Government, as was control of the ministries. The CPA had simulated the transfer of sovereignty to Iraqi ministries in the few weeks prior to the formation of the Interim Government, but the most important spending and revenue-generating ministries, namely Trade and Oil, continued under direct CPA control until just before the date of sovereignty transfer. The situation with the Defence and Interior ministries was somewhat more complex.

The terms of the UN Resolution that endorsed the formation of the Interim Iraqi Government were explicit in their treatment of the status of the Coalition forces in Iraq. UN Security Council Resolution 1546 stated 'that the multinational force shall have the authority to take all necessary measures to contribute to the maintenance of security and stability in Iraq'.[16] The Resolution had two letters appended to it, the first from Ayad Allawi in his capacity as Iraq's new prime minister, and the second from Colin Powell, the US Secretary of State. Allawi's letter requested an extension of the mandate of the MNF and said, 'Until we are able to provide security for ourselves, including the defence of Iraq's land, sea and air space, we ask for the support of the Security Council and the international community in this endeavour. We seek a new resolution on the Multinational Force mandate to contribute to maintaining security in Iraq .... The Government requests that the Security Council review the mandate of the Multinational Force at the request of the Transitional Government of Iraq, or twelve months from the date on which such a resolution is adopted.'[17]

Colin Powell in his letter to the UN Security Council made explicit what the MNF's role would entail. He said, 'On the implementation of this policy, recognizing that Iraqi security forces are responsible to the appropriate Iraqi ministers, the Multinational Force will coordinate with Iraqi security forces at all levels – national, regional, and local – in order to achieve unity of command of military operations in which Iraqi forces are engaged with the Multinational Force.'[18] Iraq's fledgling forces would come under the administrative control of the Ministry of Defence, but operationally would be part of the command structure of the MNF. In effect, the Iraqi armed forces could not be deployed without formal MNF approval. In addition, the UN Resolution made it clear that the Interim Government was indeed just that: a sovereign but temporary government whose main political purpose was to organise national elections before the end of January 2005. Effective military power remained with the MNF – in effect, the United States – and the occupation would continue under another guise.

Ayad Allawi's letter also affirmed the enhanced role that Iraq was to have in the fight against terrorists and insurgents, and the Interim Government's determination to build adequate and appropriate security forces and structures. The national security structures established under Bremer would continue and would be the mainstay of the security system under the Interim Government. There was no mention whatsoever, either in the Resolution or its appendices, of the TAL.

Policies of the Interim Government

The formation of the Interim Government coincided with a dramatic shift in American policy in Iraq. The persistence of the insurgency and the unalloyed hostility of the Sunni Arabs to the occupation forced a strategic rethink. It began with the return of the UN to centre stage in Iraq and ended with an acknowledgement that stability in Iraq might require the involvement of the Sunni Arabs, and even the main props of the Ba'ath regime, in the transition process. At the same time, the neo-conservatives in Washington were losing ground to the traditional power centres, who were reasserting their authority and control over Iraq policy. The composition of the Interim Government finally reflected this shift in emphasis. Out of thirty-five ministers, only one, the Minister of Youth, was an Islamist in the full sense of the word. The other 'Islamist' was Abd el-Mahdi of SCIRI as Minister of Finance, but he was hardly an Islamist, given his chequered background as a former Marxist and then Ba'athist. The marginalisation of the Shi'a Islamist parties was deliberate, and reflected a desire to overturn the power distribution formula of the early CPA days. On the other hand, the two key security ministries of Defence and Interior were awarded to people who were intimately connected with the efforts by the CPA and the intelligence agencies to exercise control over Iraq's provinces. Hazem Sha'alan at the Ministry of Defence and Falah al-Naqib of the Interior would prove controversial figures in the Interim Government, Sha'alan because of his entanglement in a massive, even world-class, corruption case at the Ministry of Defence; Naqib because he was alleged to have packed the Interior Ministry with cronies and former Ba'athists.

The Interim Government had ministers who were active, or who had held senior positions, in the former regime, and their commitment to the new order was suspect. This would particularly be the case for the new ministers of trade and higher education and a minister for the state – all serious ex-Ba'athists. The new Cabinet also reversed the dismissals of a large number of senior Ba'athists who had been removed under de-Ba'athification orders or corruption charges. The Interim Government was being used to reconfigure Iraqi politics towards a new adjustment with the forces who had been alienated by the radical demilitarisation and de-Ba'athification measures of the CPA and the Governing Council. It was a forlorn and doomed attempt to undercut the appeal and spread of the insurgency by appeasing and empowering part of its 'moderate' political base. At the same time, a new, more accommodating, stance was developed towards Arab countries, especially those that had security connections with the USA. This fitted in well with Ayad Allawi's own inclinations. He had developed excellent relationships with the network of strategic allies that the USA had forged in the Middle East. These notably included Jordan, the UAE and Egypt, as well Rafiq Hariri's Lebanon. The official response from these countries was enthusiastic towards the Interim Government, seeing it as the type of regime that they wanted to see established in Iraq. The Interim Government was poised to change the terms of Iraq's politics and give the non-Islamist, and even anti-Islamist groups – the so-called secular liberals and nationalists – a strong chance to dominate the state and to manage the upcoming elections to their advantage.

But there was no let-up in the insurgency, which flared ever more virulently even as the Interim Government was settling in to power.

The Legacy of the CPA

Ayad Allawi inherited a country that had visibly deteriorated under the CPA's stewardship. It was not only the security conditions that were becoming ever more violent; the average lot of the citizenry was pitiful. The shocking mismanagement of the country was plain for all to see, but the true extent would only appear later as the documentary evidence began to mount. The main thoroughfares of Baghdad were potholed and litter-strewn. The formerly plush suburbs of Mansour and Jaddiriya had taken on a frayed and subdued look. Baghdad's parks had been abandoned and were covered with weeds. The river-front cafés and restaurants that had done a roaring trade in the early days of the occupation were now frequented only by the intrepid. At night they became the haunts of faintly menacing-looking men, huddled over bottles of beer or whisky. The situation in the poorer areas of Baghdad and the rest of the country was abysmal. The CPA had inaugurated a number of show-case social and urban improvement schemes throughout the country, but their effects had been minimal. A riverside park in Baghdad that had been rehabilitated by the CPA at a cost of $1 million was soon abandoned to thieves who stripped it bare of its fixtures and children's amusement rides.

Allawi and the Insurgency

The Interim Government did not pursue de-Ba'athification and reintegrated former Ba'athists. Ayad Allawi had started his premiership by publicly stating the Interim Government's intention of providing amnesty for insurgents, including Moqtada al-Sadr. In fact in an interview with the *Washington Post* shortly after his accession to power, Allawi said that he had frequent meetings with insurgent leaders in his house to persuade them to join the political process.[19] The groups apparently included senior officers from the Special

Republican Guard, staunch Saddamist supporters and radical Islamists. In the interview, Allawi claimed that these meetings had a beneficial effect in that they separated the 'nationalist' insurgents from the foreign terrorists, such as al-Qaeda's affiliates in Iraq. There was no doubt that these meetings were held with the full knowledge of the western intelligence agencies in Iraq, as they explored ways of reducing the virulence and spread of the insurgency. The spurious division of the insurgents into two baskets, the first domestic and patriotic, and the second foreign and terrorist, informed the position of many Iraqis and foreign observers who saw the possibility of co-opting the home-grown variety of the insurgency into the political process.

The insurgents, however, had a different plan. Throughout the late spring and early summer of 2004 they were developing a strategy that involved the encircling of Baghdad.[20] The strategy was multi-layered, and included the establishment of safe zones where the inhabitants would either be supportive to the insurgents or at least neutral. To effect the creation of a friendly environment, these areas had to be cleared of their Shi'a population. Reports were mounting of a quiet form of ethnic cleansing in the 'Sunni Triangle', especially in the towns and villages to the southwest of Baghdad. Shi'a were being killed and their meeting halls and mosques attacked with the intention of driving them out of the areas adjacent to the Triangle. In Samarra, a shrine city of the Shi'a to the north of Baghdad but populated mainly by Sunni, sectarian relationships in the past had been reasonably cordial, if not quite harmonious. But a calculated escalation of sectarian feelings took place in the weeks preceding the formation of the Interim Government that culminated in a pro-Saddam demonstration on 2 July, 2004. A premature withdrawal of the MNF from key control points in Samarra left the poorly trained police and elements of the National Guard, the renamed ICDC, in charge. Insurgents came out in force and by mid-July imposed their control over the city. They began to distribute leaflets demanding the expulsion of the Shi'a. According to eyewitnesses, the police began to take their orders from the insurgents, while the National Guard simply disappeared from the streets.[21] The city was slipping under the control of radical Islamists, and was about to join Fallujah and the towns and villages of Anbar province as a bastion of the insurgency. The security situation threatened to become even more serious.

Allawi was now faced with the legacy of the unresolved stand-off in Najaf, the surreptitious spread of insurgency power in Fallujah as a result of the systematic subversion of the Fallujah Brigade, and the strong possibility that Samarra might fall into the category of an insurgent-controlled city. It was imperative that the developing cordon around Baghdad be broken, a task that was understood by the MNF's new commander, General George Casey, who had replaced Sanchez. Throughout the summer of 2004 a debate was raging inside both the Interim Government and the MNF about whether or not the

292 THE OCCUPATION OF IRAQ

Iraqi forces were prepared to take direct action against insurgents in the scope and scale envisaged. The MNF was acutely conscious of the propaganda benefit of Iraqi-led forces taking the initiative and bearing the brunt of the fighting. But it was also aware that the fight against the insurgents could not withstand another calamitous collapse in the fighting capabilities of Iraqi government forces such as had occurred with the Fallujah crisis earlier in the year. The entire summer and early autumn of 2004 were taken up by a series of violent confrontations with insurgents, designed to bring Fallujah and Samarra back under MNF and Iraqi government control.

In July 2004, Ayad Allawi embarked on a tour of the neighbouring Arab countries to introduce the new government, elicit their support and encourage their involvement in stabilising the conditions in Iraq. A main concern was to stop the flow of terrorists and insurgents across the Syrian and, to a lesser extent, Jordanian frontiers.[22] The tour was supposed to include Iran and Turkey but these were deferred until later. The involvement of Syria – or at least its covert intelligence units – in the Iraqi insurgency was becoming an ever more troubling issue. Hoshyar Zebari, the Foreign Minister, did not officially accuse Syria – or Iran – of direct support for the insurgents, but that was clearly his meaning. In a statement issued in Dubai in early July, Zebari stated that there was foreign support for the insurgents, but that the Interim Government was planning to tackle the issue through dialogue and discussions with the countries concerned. The most explicit statements of support for the Interim Government came from Jordan's king. Jordan's role as a crucial support base for the invasion of Iraq and its subsequent willingness to continue in its support of the Coalition clashed with public sentiments in the country, which were overwhelmingly hostile to the invasion and occupation of Iraq, and saw the Governing Council as 'collaborators' and rank traitors to the Arab and Islamic cause.

The foreign policy of the Interim Government would crystallise a number of the conflicts that were inherent in the Iraqi condition. Many had lain dormant while the Coalition had directly occupied the country. Now that a sovereign government was supposedly in charge, the attitude of foreign countries especially the neighbouring Arab countries and Iran, to developments inside Iraq, became crucial in determining the chances of stability. The struggles between Arabs and Persians for the 'soul' of Iraq were a replay, in a different guise, of the age-old problems that had plagued Iraq and undermined its stability and security. Once again the ghost of Ali al-Wardi hovered over the landscape of an Iraq in conflict.

The Interim Government was the culmination of a long process that started soon after the cessation of hostilities. The terms under which authority was to be ceded to an Iraqi-led government had to be carefully crafted almost immediately. This issue exercised a great deal of the energies of policymakers in Washington, London and the UN, as well as Baghdad politicians and the Najaf hierarchy. The process took all manner of twists and turns, but eventually the Interim Government took the form it did for two underlying reasons. The first was that the USA was only prepared to cede power to a friendly government that would dominate the transition period and control the pace of change. The second was that the final composition of the Interim Government reflected a fundamental change of direction in Washington. The incompetence of the CPA, and the fundamental misreading of the conditions in Iraq by the war alliance led by the neo-conservatives, shifted the relative power over Iraq policymaking towards the State Department and the CIA. Not only was the idea of a caretaker government jettisoned, but the Interim Government was skewed in favour of the re-establishment of a version of the authoritarian state in Iraq. By selecting Ayad Allawi as the prime minister, however, the creators of the Interim Government structure brought in someone who had his own ideas on how to run Iraq. He had lain low throughout the period of the Governing Council, but all the time he had been observing events and calibrating his response. He would now have the opportunity to reverse or alter some of the key decisions that were taken by the CPA, and stamp on the Interim Government his authority and vision of the new Iraq.

17

Arabs and Persians

'The gates of hell are open in Iraq.'–

Amr Moussa, Arab League's Secretary General, September 2004

'To us it seems out of this world that you do this. We fought a war together to keep Iran from occupying Iraq after Iraq was driven out of Kuwait. Now we are handing the whole country over to Iran without reason.' –

Prince Saud al-Faisal, Saudi Foreign Minister, speaking at the Council of Foreign Relations in New York, 23 September, 2005

The CPA and Washington determined the foreign policy of Iraq during the direct occupation period in all matters of significance. Travel documents of Iraqi officials were clearly stamped with the CPA's insignia, and on official missions it was the CPA or Washington's representative who was accorded the status of real decision-makers. Iraqi ministers were treated by and large correctly, but it was clear that their status was subordinate to their CPA 'minders'. In fact, in many countries the US Embassy doubled up as Iraq's alternative diplomatic mission and when issues or problems arose that affected Iraq, it was the US Embassy that was called upon to resolve them. The Governing Council's ministers were frequently denied entry to countries to which they had been officially invited to attend conferences or some other function. In one egregious blunder, the Minister of Refugees was detained in Beirut airport for hours on end and then transferred to a hotel where he was kept under virtual house arrest. Visas to western countries, even for members of the Coalition, were hard to obtain for those with only Iraqi documents. There were many instances where ministers were left to cool their heels in a transit country, while awaiting the issue of their entry permits to meetings or conferences in the USA or western Europe. Ministers with dual nationality, of which there were a significant number, preferred to travel using their western documents rather than their Iraqi passports with their dubious legality. This bemused foreign officials who received these ministers, who were purportedly representing Iraq while using the documents of another country to travel with. These ministers would, of course, be seen as lacking in authority and *gravitas*. All these issues added to the difficulties in establishing the bona fide credentials of the post-invasion Iraqi government and made the task of establishing its legitimacy that much more difficult.

This state of affairs was not helped by the formation of the supposedly sovereign Interim Government. In spite of ringing endorsements from the UN, and from a number of hitherto hostile countries in the Middle East, the Interim Government was not universally accorded the treatment of an independent government. The indefatigable Foreign Minister Hoshyar Zebari travelled everywhere to raise the profile of the new order and to elicit support from the international community. His task during the CPA era was dictated by the facts of occupation. His diplomatic task as foreign minister was mainly concerned with explaining the terms of the various political milestones that governed the transition process, and seeking support for them. His main targets were the Arabs, for it had been the Arabs who had been the most alienated by the invasion of Iraq and who were contributing, in various guises and forms, to the instability in the country. Kuwait had been the only country that was unequivocal in its support for the invasion and that wished good riddance to the Ba'ath regime. But it kept its distance from the new political establishment as a group, while continuing to receive and support individual ministers and party leaders. Other regional Arab powers ranged from outright hostility and support for the insurgency, such as Syria, to an apparent accommodation with the new reality of Iraq's occupation, one that seemed to presage a more dangerous and assertive American involvement with the area.

The Arab States and Post-War Iraq

This outward adjustment to the belligerent intrusion of the USA into the affairs of the Middle East masked an even more frightening prospect – the possibility of the marginalisation of the Sunni Arabs in a state dominated by the Shi'a and Kurds. It might even herald the break-up of Iraq. In reality, the Arabs divided into three camps when dealing with the post-invasion options in Iraq. In the first camp was Syria, which had its own unique perspective on the Iraq crisis, driven by fears about US intentions as regards Syria, following the demise of a kindred, though rival, regime in Baghdad.[1] The second camp included the USA's main 'security' partners in the area. These states, such as Egypt, Jordan, the UAE and Qatar, had invested a great deal in cementing a privileged relationship with the USA, and had developed close links with the superpower in security and military matters. The invasion of Iraq created a conundrum for them. On the one hand, their dependence in varying degrees on the USA's security umbrella obliged them to water down any public misgivings that they might have had about the invasion. On the other, they had real anxieties about the direction of the USA's post-9/11 policy approach in the Middle East. The rhetoric of democracy promotion, which the USA was increasingly using in the Middle East, might harm their rulers' hold on power.[2] The occupation of Iraq was in fact profoundly unpopular throughout the Middle East. Public opinion sympathised with the 'resistance', the universally applied epithet given by the Arab media to the insurgency. The third camp was Saudi Arabia, a state that felt profoundly threatened by the invasion of Iraq, but for different reasons to Syria. The neo-conservatives in Washington, who played a prominent role in providing the ideological basis for the invasion of Iraq, were generally hostile to Saudi Arabia and its version of state-sponsored Islam. The Saudis were fearful of the changing balance of power in Iraq in favour of the Shi'a, an anathemised sect in Wahhabi doctrine, and its effects on both the regional balance of power and on Saudi Arabia's own Shi'a minority.[3] They were also concerned lest Saudi and other *jihadis* radicalised by the war in Iraq might turn their attention to Saudi Arabia and cross back from Iraq along the huge desert frontiers between the two countries.[4] Overlaying all these fears, the Arabs, apart from Syria, shared a deep concern that the rise of the Shi'a inside Iraq, supposedly natural allies, and to some seen as stooges, of Iran, would lead to Iranian domination of the area.

The Interim Government offered the anxious Arabs the best way out of their dilemma. The manner in which the Interim Government was formed appeared to indicate a more sober American assessment about the way out of the Iraq crisis, and a major modification of the USA's original, neo-conservative-tinged vision for Iraq. The last days of the CPA seemed to augur a recognition that the earlier sweep of de-Ba'athification (or 'de-Sunnification' as some in the Arab media tried to portray it) and de-militarisation policies might have been misguided, and even foolhardy. The composition of the Interim Government could also be construed as a form of peace-offering to nervous Arab countries. Ayad Allawi was well known for his pan-Arab credentials, for his orientation towards security and intelligence work, economic and social liberalism, and caution towards Iraq-wide federalism. His Shi'ism was of a strictly non-political variety, while his relationship with the Najaf hierarchy was correct, though distant.[5] He was also a foe, and perceived to be a foe, of Iran, and frequently decried what he saw as dangerous Iranian meddling in Iraqi affairs. His Cabinet was tailor-made to repair Iraq's relationships with the Arab world, and in particular with those countries that shared in America's strategic alliances in the Middle East. He was received most sympathetically in Jordan, Egypt and the UAE. Lebanon, which under Rafiq Hariri was stirring against its Syrian overlords, also sought an opening with him.

In spite of Allawi's determined efforts to bring the Arabs on board as supporters of his version of post-war Iraq, they were still cautious about the longevity of the Interim Government and his staying power as head of government. Elections had been promised for the year's end; no one was sure what the outcome would be. The fears and anxieties of the Arabs were not to be assuaged simply by whirlwind diplomacy and fine-sounding statements. These fears were of an existential nature, and no country was more aware of the potentially revolutionary effects of the cataclysmic changes in Iraq than Saudi Arabia. The official silence of Saudi Arabia on developments in Iraq throughout the CPA period was deafening. Prince Saud al-Faisal made a hesitant promise of reconstruction aid during the Madrid Donors Conference, but there was precious little to indicate the country's true policy. The large numbers of Saudi nationals who were caught up in Iraq's insurgency – as fighters and suicide bombers – were much commented upon. In a two-year period between June 2003 and June 2005, nearly 55 per cent of the foreign fighters killed in Iraq were Saudi.[6] It gave credence to the charge that official Saudi Arabia allowed, if not actively encouraged, the insurgency. Rumours abounded regarding the flow of monies from Saudi 'charities', merchants and businessmen to the Iraqi insurgency. The increasingly conservative Salafist and Wahhabist strain in the Sunni Arab community of Iraq deepened the bonds between them and the Wahhabi establishment in Saudi Arabia. Several leading Sunni clerics made regular trips to Saudi Arabia, where they discussed the plight of the Sunni of Iraq and the options that lay ahead.

Saudi Arabian Attitudes to Post-War Iraq

The Saudis were driven by four considerations when facing the occupation, violence and instability in Iraq. The most immediate was the fear that instability might spread into Saudi Arabia itself as a result of the turmoil in its neighbouring country. While Iraqis and Americans were concerned about the flow of Saudi *jihadis* into Iraq, the Saudi authorities were more worried about the reverse flow from Iraq into Saudi Arabia. The borders between Saudi Arabia and Iraq were long, porous and sparsely inhabited, and the roaming tribes had uncertain national allegiances. Fighters steeled by the Iraqi insurgency could easily cross them and carry the war into Saudi Arabia. Prince Nayef, the Saudi Interior Minister, admitted as much when he said, 'We expect the worse from those who went to Iraq.'[7] The issue of returning Saudi *jihadis* and the control of the borders between Iraq and Saudi Arabia was frequently brought up in discussions between Saudi authorities and the USA. Evidently the Saudis did not have much faith in the ability of the Iraqi authorities and security forces to protect the frontiers. This was corroborated by senior

American diplomats, who had approached the Saudis to increase their finan-cial and security commitment to Iraq as well as their support for the Interim Government. The Saudis' concern with the risk of terrorists flowing into their country from Iraq was paramount. A second issue related to the possibility that Iraq might become a proxy battleground of regional interests trying to compete for influence. In practice, this meant Iran, for the Saudis were not too exercised by the possibility of Turkish intrusions into Iraq because of Turkey's fears of Kurdish separatism. The Saudis had direct influence on the Kurds, mainly through the Kurdish Islamist movement, and their relationship with the traditional Kurdish leadership was cordial.

Iran was another matter. The deep distrust that existed between revolu-tionary Iran and Saudi Arabia was never easily dispelled, in spite of both countries' antipathy to the regime of Saddam Hussein. The fear that Iran would subvert the institutions of the new Iraqi state through its Shi'a allies and proxies was always there. Prince Saud al-Faisal, the Saudi Foreign Minister, expressed his anxieties clearly in a speech to the Council of Foreign Relations in New York. 'The Iranians now go in this pacified area that the American forces have pacified, and they go into every government of Iraq, pay money, install their own people, put their own – even establish police forces for them, arms and militias that are there and reinforce their presence in these areas.'[8] A third factor that influenced Saudi policy towards Iraq related to the oil sector. Saudi Arabia was perched on top of the world's oil industry as the pivot producer and the inevitable partner with the developed countries in meeting their energy demands. The much-vaunted estimate of Iraq's potential oil reserves and its expected rivalry to Saudi Arabia led to Saudi uneasiness about the future management of international oil supplies, intra-OPEC strug-gles for influence, and stability of oil prices. But Iraq was in no condition to challenge any oil producer seriously as it struggled to maintain even its present low output of about two million bbd. The oil dimension for Saudi concerns was more of a long-term issue.[9]

The most worrying of the Saudis' immediate concerns was the rise of Shi'a power in Iraq, because it might challenge the basic identity of the Saudi state, built as it was on the bedrock of a puritanical Wahhabist religious affiliation. The Saudis found it awkward to discuss the Shi'a issue in Iraq, preferring to hide behind the platitude that the Shi'a of Iraq were Arabs and patriots, and thus implicitly hostile to Iranian ambitions in Iraq. But partly in response to the threat of the Islamic revolution in Iran, a great deal of Saudi propaganda effort had gone into linking a supposedly schismatic Shi'ism as an exclusive preserve of non-Arab Iran, thereby devaluing and de-legitimising Shi'ism as an authentic strain within Islam. The marginalisation of Shi'a Islam, and, in fact, its demonisation, was a recurrent theme in the radical Wahhabi discourse. It infected the Saudi educational curriculum and was a deeply held prejudice of the traditional *ulema* classes of Saudi Arabia.[10] It led to an adoption of anti-Shi'a policies in the religious sphere that would be difficult to dispel without the risk of rupture with the Wahhabi clerical class, a main prop of the Saudi regime. The challenge of Shi'ism in power in a majority Arab country was one that the Saudis would find deeply problematic. Moreover, the Arab country was Iraq, a historic heartland of Islam and inextricably linked with the glories of Muslim and Arab civilisation. It would be the first time in modern history that the Shi'a of the Arab world would have had control over the territory they inhabited. The spillover effects of Shi'a predominance in Iraq on to the Shi'a populations of the Gulf and Saudi Arabia might therefore be immensely destabilising.

The Saudi dilemma was not one-sided. Iraqi Shi'a, too, were contending with the novel idea of being in power and dealing with the mighty religious authority of Saudi Arabia on an equal footing. The existing tensions were kept under control in the days of the CPA and the Interim Government, but they would erupt during the Transitional Government. In fact, the Saudi government pursued an accommodating policy in areas where there was a requirement for a direct engagement with Iraq, such as in the management of the annual *Hajj* quotas.

The policy of the Saudis towards the Interim Government, in particular to the person of Ayad Allawi, was inexplicably stand-offish. The Interim Government was probably the least objectionable outcome for a new Iraqi governing structure and the most likely to keep the Saudis' demons of instability and direct Shi'a rule at bay. In fact, the underlying premise of the Interim Government was strictly to limit the links between Iran and Iraq, and to maintain a pan-Arab profile for the country. This policy was partly designed to keep Iraq in step with the US policy of isolating Iran, but it was also one that was willingly subscribed to by the main players in the new government. The strengthening of the Interim Government, in spite of the Shi'a identity of its leader, and the sprinkling of Islamists in the structure of government, was manifestly in the interest of those Arabs, notably those in Saudi Arabia, who were wary of Iran's intentions. But the idea that the Interim Government was merely a way station in a democratic process the outcome of which was still unknown kept the Saudis sitting on the fence. This was not the case, however, with the smaller Gulf countries, in particular the UAE. They correctly saw the potential of the Interim Government under Ayad Allawi of playing the role of foil to Iran. The Interim Government also held the promise of 'managing' the transition process, limiting religious Shi'a influences on the government and rebuilding the centralised Iraqi state, or at least the majority Arab component. The UAE and Qatari support for the Interim Government was explicit, and continued into support for the electoral campaign of Ayad Allawi in the January 2005 elections.

Jordan, Egypt and the Interim Government

Jordan and Egypt also recognised the value of buttressing the Interim Government and the political line elaborated by Ayad Allawi. Jordan became a prominent and vocal supporter. Coordination between the Jordanian military, police and intelligence apparatus and the new Iraqi security institutions was increased. The Interim Government also reintroduced, and in some cases strengthened, the Ba'ath-era commercial and economic ties with Jordan. A memorandum of economic and financial cooperation was signed between the two countries. Promises of building a pipeline from Iraq's northern oil fields to terminate in Aqaba were made, promoted by a scion of the Gaoud clan from Iraq's Anbar region. This was justified partly by the need to placate the Sunni tribes of Anbar province, who were prone to support the insurgency. It made little economic sense as a west-directed Iraqi oil pipeline should have ended in the Mediterranean, not in a Red Sea port. Iraq had already built pipelines to Saudi Arabia's Red Sea port of Yanbu during the Iran–Iraq War. They were now disused, and might be recommissioned if Saudi–Iraqi relationships were stabilised. The use of Jordanian intermediaries and banks, such as the Housing Bank and the Jordan National Bank, in various Iraqi government deals became ever more pronounced. Jordanian businessmen began to dream of the halcyon days when Jordan was Iraq's main access to the outside world; they had profited handsomely from this privileged relationship. By the end of the Interim Government, the nexus of relationships between Iraq and Jordan, with many of the same actors as in the sanctions-busting period, looked dangerously close to being replicated. Jordan, it would later emerge, was a key conduit in a whole range of suspicious and corrupt business deals involving Iraqi high officials. The country had invested a great deal in the success of the Interim Government and in Ayad Allawi's electoral strategy.

Egypt was geographically distant from the Iraqi scene, but nevertheless believed that its influence as a leading Arab power needed to be felt. On the surface, Egypt had few leverage points on Iraq and there were few Egyptian companies or individuals who had serious interests in the country. Nevertheless, the Egyptian security chief Omar Suleiman maintained a close watch on Iraqi affairs and had a good working relationship with the new Iraqi prime minister. In October 2004, Egypt announced that it would host a conference on Iraq that would include representatives from two dozen nations and international organisations. It would be held in late November 2004 at the resort of Sharm el-Sheikh.

All Iraq's neighbours were invited, as well as the G-8 countries, China and a variety of international and regional organisations such as the UN, the EU, the Arab League and the Organization of Islamic Countries (OIC). But the conference's objectives clashed with the Interim Government's main concern at that time of gaining international support for its muted proposals to postpone the elections scheduled for January 2005. There were strong signals that the electoral list headed by Ayad Allawi might face certain defeat in the upcoming elections, thus jeopardising the entire political programme of the Interim Government and rendering the conference's decisions and recommendations meaningless. In fact, earlier that month, King Abdullah of Jordan had expressed doubts about the difficulty – though what he had really meant was desirability – of holding elections on time. 'It seems impossible to me to organise indisputable elections in the chaos we see today [in Iraq]', he said.[11] An Iraqi diplomat went one step further. The Interim Government, he intimated, was against the conference if it reiterated the terms of the TAL and sought international support for the election datelines. '[The Interim Government] is against this conference and . . . would consider a postponement of the elections, rather than plans to secure holding them on time, more appropriate to their interests.'[12] An attempt at developing a momentum to postpone the elections faltered, however. The USA would have none of it. The conference produced a set of insipid proposals. Egyptian diplomacy saw the limits of its ability to seriously influence events in Iraq when it was faced with a determined opposing stance by its larger and much more involved ally, the USA. What appeared to join the USA and the Arabs was a common suspicion of Iran's motives and the expansion of Iranian influence into Iraq.

The Arab League and Iraq

The Arab League had previously expressed deep misgivings about the impending invasion of Iraq, and Amr Moussa, its secretary general and former Egyptian foreign minister, was vociferous in denouncing the occupation. In fact, only a few days into the conflict, the Arab League issued a ringing condemnation of the 'aggression' against Iraq. All Arab League countries with the exception of Kuwait adopted the resolution. Observers were left greatly puzzled as to how Bahrain, Qatar, Jordan and the UAE could all express outrage at the 'aggression', while simultaneously providing assistance to the invading forces.[13] A deep cynicism, bordering on contempt, was the most common Arab 'street' sentiment regarding the League.

The first crisis between the Arab League proper and the occupation authorities came when the League refused to recognise the Governing Council as the effective representative of Iraq. The League disingenuously stated that the Governing Council was not an elected entity, despite the fact that the majority of the League's member states were dictatorships or unelected monarchies. In reality, the Arab League did not want to grant any legitimacy to the occupation and to Iraqi governing institutions emanating from it. It took a month of wrangling and special pleading by Hoshyar Zebari (and American pressure behind the scenes) to modify the League's stance. In September 2003, the Arab League relented and the Governing Council was allowed to occupy Iraq's seat at the Arab League, albeit for a year only.

The tensions between the League and the Governing Council continued unabated. Both the Kurds and the Shi'a on the Governing Council harboured deep suspicions about the League, and especially about Amr Moussa. He was seen as duplicitous and unwilling to adjust to the loss of power by the Sunni Arabs of Iraq. Moussa reciprocated in his dislike of the Governing Council and its 'collusion' with the occupation authorities. In March 2004, Moussa rejected a proposal raised by Zebari for the Arab League to join in sending peace-keeping forces to Iraq. Moussa declared that it was 'impossible', given that such a request could only be lodged by a 'legitimate government', clearly implying that the Governing Council and its government were illegitimate. He said, 'What is certain is that Arab troops cannot join with troops occupying another Arab country.'[14] At a number of points the statements from the Arab League's secretary general seemed to endorse the 'resistance' and the legitimacy of opposition to the government in Baghdad. In June 2004, Moussa declared that the 'resistance should be transformed into an opposition', and called for a national reconciliation conference.

The sourness of the Arab League towards the post-invasion order continued well into the formation of the Interim Government, ostensibly the government to which sovereignty was returned under a UN Resolution. Nevertheless, Moussa would comment in a meeting of Arab foreign ministers in September 2004, three months after the transfer of sovereignty, that, 'The situation is getting more complicated and tense. We have to help Iraq to overcome this crisis and move events in a positive direction that could help Iraq regain its full sovereignty, fortify its unity, end the occupation and rebuild its institutions according to its free will and sovereign rights as a member state of the League.'[15]

Moussa also gave the League's stamp of approval to the so-called national resistance in Iraq, clearly differentiating its professed acts of resistance to the presence of foreign forces from the brutal terror of al-Qaeda and its ilk. In the same meeting, he said, 'Listen, resistance against occupation is natural, but this does not include cutting off people's heads without any justification . . . We should distinguish between obvious terrorist operations and resistance against occupation troops.' Even the Interim Government with its pan-Arab orientations began to feel that the Arab League was moving from being a potentially impartial interlocutor to an advocate for the insurgency. In December 2004, as the Interim Government was preparing for the upcoming elections, the Arab League unwisely received a delegation of Iraqi figures who claimed they formed part of the 'national resistance'. The delegation repeated the slogan of there being no possibility of security before the withdrawal of foreign forces, a position that paralleled Moussa's. The League had hurried to embrace opposition to the Interim Government and the new order, while it had not opposed Saddam for many years while he was in power.

The evident support of the Arab League for the opposition and the national resistance, however, considerably emboldened those Sunni Arabs who were prepared to engage critically with the Iraqi government and the US Embassy. The persistent refusal of the Arab League to accord full recognition to the Iraqi governments that emerged out of the political process continued. No Arab League mission visited Iraq until October 2005. Predictably, the Arab League was praised by the leaders of the Sunni Arab community for its concern with Iraq's sovereignty and for averting civil war. At the same time, it was condemned by the Shi'a religious and secular groups for ignoring the indiscriminate terror of insurgents. The Kurds, who throughout had been sceptical of the Arab League, were considerably mollified by the changed tune of the League regarding Kurdish demands for federalism. The Arab League reflected the increased willingness on the part of the Arab regimes to countenance, and even support, Kurdish demands for autonomy. This was a signal to show that the Arab world could accommodate an effectively confederal Iraq, but that it would not countenance a Shi'a-dominated Iraq or a three-way federal state with a weak centre. The bogeyman of Iran and the Shi'a's assumed subservience to that country would simply not go away.

Iran and Post-War Iraq

Although Iran had officially opposed the invasion of Iraq, unofficially it had welcomed the overthrow of the Ba'ath regime, an attitude tempered with extreme wariness about US designs on Iraq and their implications for the Tehran regime. In contrast to its limited involvement in the war to overthrow the Taliban of Afghanistan, mainly by supplying intelligence to the USA on the activities of al-Qaeda members, Iran did not take any direct role in supporting US actions in Iraq. The Iranians advised their supporters and allies in Iraq to stand aside in the war and not act in any provocative or threatening way towards the Coalition. After the formation of the Governing Council and its government, the relationships between Iran and Iraq, at the official level, followed two parallel tracks. At the CPA level, the relationship was stiff and strictly constrained, but this did not spill over into overblown statements about Iranian infiltration of Iraq or denunciations of the Iranian regime. If anything, the CPA wanted to ensure that Iran's influence over a number of key actors, including the Shi'a Islamists and the Najaf hierarchy, was used constructively in support of the transition process. There were a few incidents that sent mixed signals to Iran, notably the disarming, but not expulsion, of the Mujahedin e Khalq Organisation (MEK), based in Diyala province. The MEK was a long-standing opponent of the Tehran government and had participated in an ill-fated invasion of Iran during the last weeks of the Iran–Iraq War. The organisation had committed itself to armed struggle against the Iranian regime, and had allowed itself to be used by Saddam in repressing the 1991 uprising and as a tool to pressurise Iran. In exchange, Saddam allowed the MEK the use of a military base in Diyala province, where it had maintained a brigade-sized armoured force, under strict Iraqi control. The MEK was deemed to be a terrorist organisation by the State Department, and the fact that it was allowed to remain in Iraq after the invasion indicated that its usefulness as a pressurising tool had not been exhausted.[16]

The Governing Council's relationships with Iran, however, were more cordial, even effusive. Both the Shi'a Islamists and the PUK publicly acknowledged and honoured Iran's role in harbouring the opposition to Saddam, and supporting them in times of distress. There was a strong desire on the part of the Governing Counci to recast the relationships between the two countries on a constructive, even strategic, basis. Sayyid Abd el-Aziz al-Hakim of SCIRI went so far as to state that Iraq should accept the principle of paying reparations to Iran for the damage caused by Saddam's invasion of the country.[17] A number of delegations visited Iran, and Iraqi ministers were frequently in Tehran signing protocols of cooperation and exchanges and bilateral agreements in the industrial, trade, transport and financial arenas. But it was the CPA that called the shots, and these agreements were never implemented in the way that its signatories had wanted. The USA was not prepared to put its seal of approval on agreements that would bind Iraq closer to Iran in anything other than that which was absolutely necessary.

The limited, but correct, relationships between Iran and occupied Iraq began to change as the date of handover of sovereignty approached. The electoral bases for the political transition, in spite of determined efforts on the part of the TAL to qualify the meaning of majority rule, clearly favoured the parties that could claim a mass following. The fear that Iran would exploit this opening and try to advance its interests by helping the Shi'a parties into power became one of the factors that determined the composition of the Interim Government. Within weeks of its formation, the Interim Government, through its Minister of Defence, Hazem Sha'alan, fired a volley at Iran that went well beyond any reasonable concern about Iran's intentions. Sha'alan was propelled into his ministry by backroom machinations of the intelligence agencies, and his statement bore the hallmarks of the beginning of a concerted campaign to demonise Iran's role in Iraq. Sha'alan's denunciations of Iran were sweeping. 'Iran is Iraq's number one enemy . . . [Iran] is interfering in Iraq's affairs to kill democracy . . . Iran has seized border posts, sent spies and saboteurs [into Iraq] and has infiltrated the new Iraqi government.'[18] Presumably, he meant that the Minister of Youth and Sports, a high-ranking SCIRI official and the only Islamist in the government, was actually an Iranian agent.

This extraordinary outburst was quickly followed by other accusations levelled against Iran by the Interim Government, which reached a crescendo as the election date of 30 January, 2005 loomed nearer. Feeling that the CPA had taken a too benign approach to Iran, the anti-Iranian cohort in the Interim Government, fortified by an increasingly aggressive US policy towards Iran's nuclear programme, increased the tempo of their attacks. In October 2004 Muhammad Shahwani, the head of Iraq's intelligence services, an agency directly funded by the CIA and outside the purview of the Iraqi government, stated that Iran was responsible for the assassination of a number of his agents. His agents had raided a number of safe houses in Baghdad and had found a 'treasure trove' of documents incriminating Iran in acts of subversion in Iraq.[19] These documents, however, were never released, and nothing came of this accusation. The credibility of Iraq's intelligence agencies was somewhat suspect. Previously, Shahwani had accused the National Security Adviser, Mowaffaq al-Rubai'e, of being in league with the Iranians. He claimed that his agents had tracked Rubai'e to a house in Kadhimain, where he had met secretly with the Iranian ambassador. This supposedly happened at the very same time as Rubai'e was having dinner with, of all people, Bremer.[20] In December 2004, King Abdullah of Jordan chimed in with a sweeping attack on Iran and its expansionist aims in Iraq.[21] The entire panoply of anti-Iranian charges that anchored the Arab nationalist discourse and that had formed the ideological underpinning of the Iran–Iraq War was being rehashed. A comingling of the political ascendancy of the Shi'a with a purported Iranian subversion of Iraq was a time-honoured canard that was being deliberately resurrected.

Iran's interests in Iraq, in spite of the repetitive claims of Arab nationalists to the contrary, did not include territorial expansion. The battles, both rhetorical and military, of defining the Iran–Iraq frontier and the Shatt-al-Arab waterway stretched from the 1930s. They did not, in fact, amount to more than a few square miles of disputed territory and did not add up to an 'irredentist' claim on Iraq. But Iran did have vital interests in Iraq which it was determined to pursue, and the country did have pressure points and huge leverage inside Iraq to achieve this end. Iranian interests in Iraq after the fall of the Ba'ath could be reduced to four basic objectives. First, to ensure that Iraq maintained its territorial integrity and did not break up as a state; second, to avoid instability that would spill over into its own territory; third, to encourage the rise of a friendly, Shi'a-dominated state, and to consolidate such a state; and, lastly, to ensure that the US presence in Iraq did not lead to

undermining the Islamic republic.[22] In pursuit of these goals, Iran had to
fashion a carefully calibrated strategy to deal with post-invasion Iraq that was
built on a number of policies. The first was to ensure that the Shi'a, as a political bloc, stayed united throughout the various stages of the political process.
The evolution of democracy in Iraq, especially as regards electoral politics,
worked to the advantage of Iranian interests, in that the possibility of a united
Shi'a electoral alliance might ensure the Shi'a's political ascendancy in Iraq.
Iran therefore became a great proponent of free elections. A second fixture of
Iranian policy in Iraq was the spread of its support to a myriad of political
groups and individuals. These ranged across the entire political spectrum, and
included secular liberals such as Ahmad Chalabi and his INC, Kurdish politicians, including Jalal Talabani and his PUK, as well as the anchor stone of the
Iranian network of Iraqi alliances, the Shi'a Islamist parties. These included
not only SCIRI, which had pride of place in Iran's cavalcade of allies, but also
the various wings of the Da'awa Party, and other Islamist groups with a
regional basis in southern Iraq. Iran also cultivated close relationships with
Moqtada al-Sadr's movement, which began to feature prominently in Iran's
plans for Iraq. The third aspect of Iran's policies was to keep the threat from
the USA at bay. This would concentrate the US mind about the threat that
Iran might pose to Iraq's security and keep the USA from taking drastic steps.
How this could be achieved with the increasingly belligerent calls in
Washington to do something about Iran's nuclear programme was not altogether clear. The best way was to continue to hint at Iran's capability for
mischief-making and to encourage just enough resistance to the American
presence in Iraq to keep the threat alive. The fact remained that Iran had far
more at stake in the successful unfolding of a democratic order under Shi'a
dominance than in a clandestine war to drive the USA out of Iraq.

   No objective analysis of Iran's interests in Iraq, however, could overcome
the visceral, almost atavistic, fears that the Arab nationalist, Sunni Arab political leadership and the insurgents had regarding Iran's motives and its
supposed ubiquitous fifth-columnists buried inside Iraqi society. These
deeply ingrained prejudices were trotted out regularly to inflame the political
landscape in Iraq. The key charge, as in all similar conspiracy theories,
involved disparaging the loyalty of often-persecuted and harassed groups and
questioning their allegiances to the homeland. Returning exiles who had been
expelled to Iran during the Ba'athist period on the spurious charge of having
'Persian antecedents' – a terrible legacy of Iraq's discriminatory early nationality laws – were accused of being Iranians masquerading as Iraqis, and of
inflating the electoral rolls. Refugees fleeing Saddam's terror, mainly from the
marshlands and the southern provinces, returned to Iraq only to find that
they were included in the catch-all category of Iranian infiltrators. Clerics and
political groups who were exiled in Iran were accused of introducing 'Iranian

style' social mores and dress codes, including the widespread adoption of the custom of temporary marriage: *muta'a*. Senior Shi'a politicians with Iranian-sounding surnames, such as Hussein Shahristani, whose family had resided in Iraq for hundreds of years, were labelled Iranian agents. The ever-voluble Sha'alan, the Interim Government's Minister of Defence, accused Shahristani of working on the Iranian nuclear programme. 'He now has the pretension of becoming the head of the Iraqi government but we will not allow that?!' Sha'alan was quoted as saying.[23] Another favourite charge was to portray the Badr Brigade of SCIRI as an Iranian cat's paw, and to attribute unexplained assassinations of Ba'athists and former regime operatives to this Iranian-trained force.[24] These claims of Iranian perfidy multiplied incessantly, until they crystallised in the oft-repeated charge that Iran had surreptitiously planted a million of its people in Iraq to distort the electoral rolls. It was a ludicrous claim as it conflated the number of Iranian pilgrims in Iraq with returning exiles and refugees, to produce an alarming headline number. But these reports fell on willing ears and played their part in deepening the fears about Iran's intentions in Iraq.

Even so, not all the concerns about Iran and its intentions were unfounded. Iran was determined to be intimately involved in Iraq's affairs, and to shape the landscape to suit its interests. It adopted a policy of 'keeping the pot simmering' the better to be its keeper and manager. This strategy had been called a 'managed chaos', and implied that Iran would use its influence, power and money to continue to keep conditions from permanently stabilising until such time as the US threat was diminished and the Shi'a's political primacy was assured.[25] The policy had its dangers and limits. Chaotic conditions, almost by definition, are not prone to control, and at some point they might serve the insurgents' interests. Similarly, a carefully calibrated destabilisation might easily run foul of the USA, which might respond in an aggravated manner. Striking the right balance would challenge Iranian strategists. This was not lost on a number of shrewd observers of the political scene in Iraq. In a detailed review of Iran's strategy in Iraq, the International Crisis Group interviewed the former Governing Council member Naseer Chadirchi, who said, 'I don't think the Iranians want to create uncontrollable chaos in Iraq.... They want a manageable chaos, and they share this approach with other neighbouring states.'[26] In the same report, a Tehran-based EU diplomat was quoted as saying, '[The Iranians] are trying to balance between chaos and civil war. But they do not have a clear idea where the balance lies.'

The troubled relationship with Iran during the Interim Government went to the heart of the Iraqi dilemma. It reflected Iraq's immense historic difficulties in establishing a confident, cooperative and unthreatening exchange with Iran. Apart from a brief interlude in the 1950s when monarchical Iraq joined Pahlavi Iran in the anti-communist Baghdad Pact, the relationships ranged from formally correct to bellicose. The truth was that while the Shi'a of Iraq had been disempowered, it helped the ruling elites, whether military, nationalist or sectarian, to hang the charge of *taba'iyya*h – the dreaded charge that implied Iranian origin or dependence – on any Shi'a group or movement that sought political redress.[27] The various regimes, especially that of Saddam, became skilled at manipulating the subtle links between Shi'ism in Iraq and Iran, and blurring the patriotism of Iraqis who had connections in any form with Iran. The Iran–Iraq War was felt to have 'forged' an Iraqi identity as Shi'a conscript soldiers bore the brunt of the fighting and casualties without mutinying or fleeing the battlefield. This episode in Iraqi–Iranian relationships continued to be used as a retort by well-meaning apologists to claims that the Shi'a of Iraq were intrinsically more loyal to Iran than to Iraq.

The 'problem' of Shi'a loyalties and identity in Iraq was raised once again in the Interim Government period, but this time in reverse. Now it was being postulated that Iran was grossly interfering in Iraq's affairs, and that those who supported it were, *ipso facto,* suspect in their loyalties. Not all Shi'a clerics, even those who had been exiled in Iran, were partial to the Islamic Republic. One such person, Sayyid Ayad Jamaluddin, was not only a staunch believer in the separation of state from religious authority, but was also a vehement critic of the Islamic Republic, which he described as a religious dictatorship. He said, 'The leadership of the jurist as in Iran is unique in the history of the Shi'a sect . . . Ayatollah Khomeini did not rely on specific religious texts to implement the doctrine of the rule of the jurist . . . . It is estimated the vast majority of the Shi'a, from the days of the great occultation until today reject the principle of the rule of the jurist. Khomeini was the first leader to put this theory into practice.'[28] He would later join Ayad Allawi's electoral list for the December 2005 elections. Other Shi'a clerics extolled their Arab pedigree and attacked Iran's interference in Iraqi affairs. They added some credence to the argument that the accusations currently levelled against Iran were not part of a plan to keep Iraq's Shi'a in a subordinate situation, but rather were being made because the national security of Iraq and the chances for peace and tranquillity were being jeopardised by Iran's actions.

The Interim Government was a serious threat to Iran's strategy in Iraq. From Iran's perspective, it heralded the return of the mindset that had governed successive Iraqi regimes from the military dictatorship of the Aref brothers to the Ba'ath and the Saddamist years. This time, however, the lead was not coming from a minority-controlled government, but one in which Shi'a predominated. The anti-Iranian posturing on the part of the government was more to do with the internal power struggle within the Shi'a for electoral dominance, rather than a genuine concern with alleged Iranian subversion or infiltration or aversion to Iran. It was a careful balancing act, where the role of the 'heavy' was given to the three security leaders, the Defence Ministry's

Sha'alan, the Interior Ministry's Naqib and the spy chief Shahwani. It could be reasonably inferred, therefore, that, given the close connections of these three parties to the western intelligence services, the shrill anti-Iranian line was developed in cooperation with these agencies. By painting Iran as a threat to Iraq's stability and recovery, Shi'a public opinion might then be mobilised in revulsion against the country. As the election date neared, disparagement of the Islamist parties as Iranian proxies and tools became more marked, but Iraqi Shi'a opinion was having none of this. In spite of real misgivings about Iran's role in Iraq – many public opinion polls showed Iraqis still suspicious of Iran and its intentions – there were other, far more important, considerations in the upcoming constitutional assembly elections. No matter how much the Interim Government tried to pin the blame on Iran, it could not dent the immense authority of Ayatollah Sistani and the growing street power of the Islamist parties. It was Ayatollah Sistani who was listened to by the Shi'a masses, and anti-Iranian policies were not on his agenda.

Iran also wielded an immense amount of 'soft' power, that is, the nexus of cultural, social and trade relationships that allowed it to extend its influence into Iraq. These had been severely disrupted during the three decades of Ba'athist rule. Expulsions, expropriations, border closures and war had greatly affected the flow of people, goods and ideas. These factors had played a part in recasting the former cosmopolitan shrine cities, and parts of Baghdad itself, into a new environment dominated by tribal Arabs, albeit from the Shi'a South. The Ba'athist years also led to the burial of cultural and linguistic links to Iran. Those who knew it, fearful that it might indicate partiality to Iran and its culture, had suppressed knowledge of Persian, a common second language in parts of Iraq. Relatives in Iran were quietly forgotten. Financial and other incentives were given to Iraqis to divorce their Iranian spouses. That even included Iraqi spouses who had wrongly been considered to have Persian antecedents. Iranian cultural manifestations that overlaid certain Iraqi Shi'a customs were also suppressed. (For example urban Arab Shi'a used to play out the rituals of the Iranian New Year, *Nowruz*. This ceased, and *Nowruz* became a purely Kurdish holiday.) It seemed that the Ba'ath, through brutality and a concerted *Kulturkampf*, was going to sever the cultural and social links between Iraq's Shi'a and Iran.

The overthrow of the Ba'ath regime stopped the suppression of Iraq's cultural links with Iran, but it was nevertheless difficult to replicate the old and, in many ways, easy interaction between the two peoples. The collapse of border controls allowed a flood of Iranian pilgrims to visit the shrine cities. Within months the shrine cities began to take on, deceptively, part of their former cosmopolitan vitality. But the underlying base of facilities, tradesmen, permanently resident Iranians and knowledge of Farsi had badly atrophied. The flow of Iraqi exiles in Iran back to their towns and cities helped, in time, to re-establish an aspect of the old multicultural ways of the shrine cities. Trade also sprang to life after the stifling controls of the former regime on the regulation of pilgrim traffic. Iran could now openly sell the religious artefacts and literature associated with the ritual of *ziyara* (the visitation of the tombs and shrines of the Shi'a imams).

At the same time, Ashoura commemorations, together with the previously banned public displays of grief, were reconstituted with fervour born of decades of suppression. Some of the more dramatic rituals were not so much 'imported' from Iran but owed a great deal of their current character to their unfettered display in that country. In particular, this included the serried ranks of flagellants, divided into neighbourhoods, professions, and youth – with youth groups having their own processions. They marched in their tens of thousands, all dressed in black with green headbands, under huge banners, carrying tributes to the martyrs of Karbala and excoriating their tormentors. The crowds, often bleeding from the marks of ritual swords on their heads and showing the bloody scars from the repetitive beating of their backs with chains, also served to demonstrate publicly the power and religious passion of the Shi'a of Iraq. Political parties and neighbourhood groups competed to produce the most striking and fervent marchers. There were mutterings that these were Iranian customs that had nothing to do with 'true' Shi'ism, but they fell on deaf ears. What were genuinely imported features of the 'new' Ashoura commemorations were the artefacts used by the marchers that had been refined in Iran. These included three types of chains for self-flagellation: a lightweight version used by children and the elderly; a heavy-duty version used by the mass of marchers; and a 'special' version with serrated chain-links for the more zealous marchers. Ritual swords with a flattened edge were used to draw blood from the edge of the scalp, and through repeated light blows these kept the blood flowing, causing the disturbing, though not seriously dangerous, images of bloodied men and children. Arabic language books, published in Iran, flooded the market, undercutting the usual suppliers from Beirut and Cairo. They catered for the hunger for Shi'a religious works that had been proscribed during the former regime. Works of, or about, the murdered ayatollahs of Iraq, especially Ayatollah Baqir al-Sadr and Muhammad al-Sadr, were ubiquitous, as were books dealing with the more peculiarly Iranian slant on Islamic government. These books now became the staple of the numerous booksellers on Mutannabi Street, Baghdad's main book market. The cultural onslaught included book fairs promoted by the Iranian government, which took place at Baghdad's universities and other such locales, and which were avidly attended. Anti-Iranian politicians used these innocuous affairs as proof of Iran's evil intentions.

The Shi'a religious revival, which had been going on for over a decade, received a new fillip from Iran in other, unexpected, areas. Iran's relative technical sophistication in media management, web design and the Internet allowed the grand ayatollahs of Iraq, especially Grand Ayatollah Sistani, the possibility of using their Qom offices for propagating their views, pronouncements and *fatwas*. Sistani's Iran office, managed by his son-in-law Sayyid Jawad Shahristani, produced a comprehensive, updated website which catered not only for Iraqis but also for the large and increasing number of Iranians who followed his religious lead. Anecdotal evidence even suggested that Grand Ayatollah Sistani was the *Marji'* with the greatest following in Iran, and received a higher amount of religious tithes than all the grand ayatollahs resident in Iran. This did not create the tension that had been forecast between the institution of *Wilayat al-Faqih* of Iran, under the leadership of Ayatollah Ali Khamane'i, and the Najaf hierarchy. Previously, wishful assessments had been made by neo-conservatives and think-tanks that the empowerment of Iraq's Shi'a would strengthen the Najaf hierarchy and thereby create a competing pole to Qom for the loyalties of the world's Shi'a. This was used to deflect the opposite argument that the empowerment of Iraq's Shi'a would deliver Iraq to an aggressive and nuclear-armed Iran. Najaf was portrayed as the 'Vatican' of the Shi'a world and Qom's ascendancy was seen as temporary and owing to aberrant conditions. This was a highly simplistic and misleading reading of Shi'a religious institutions and the interaction within the religious hierarchies of the Shi'a world.

The relationship between Grand Ayatollah Sistani and Iran was complex, and not easily pigeon-holed. It included a number of strands, none of them sufficient in and of themselves to explain fully its multifaceted nature. Personal, family, scholarly and linguistic bonds pulled in one direction, but, pulling in another direction, the status of a grand ayatollah demanded, as a religious duty, absolute fealty to advancing the precepts of Islam according to the particular *mujtahid*'s own reasoning. This might have conflicted with the concept of the *Wilayat al-Faqih* as propounded by Ayatollah Khamane'i and become elaborated during the years of the Iranian Islamic regime's formation. But difference of opinion, even on vital matters, was easily accommodated, even expected, in the Shi'a hierarchy. Grand Ayatollah Sistani approached the Iraqi crisis from the perspective of his religious duty to the Iraqi people, a position that most Iraqis acknowledged. The mutterings from disgruntled politicians about an 'Iranian' ayatollah dictating the terms for Iraq's political settlement found absolutely no resonance with the mass of Iraqi Shi'a.

A far more serious charge was made, however, regarding the involvement of the *Marji'iyya* itself in politics of any kind. Sayyid Ayad Jamaluddin used the argument that the religious hierarchy would become tarnished if it became involved in the rough and tumble of politics. 'It is dangerous to exploit religious legitimacy in politics,' he said. 'The Shi'a are courting catastrophe when the name of the religious leadership is exploited in politics.'[29] Distancing the *Marji'iyya* from the crucial political issues at hand was a self-serving assertion by politicians concerned about the effects of Sistani's pronouncement on their electoral chances. None of these people mentioned Sistani's involvement in pushing the process forward during the Bremer days, when Sistani was the only person with stature to demand the acceleration of the political process and the holding of elections. One thing was absolutely clear though: Iran never tried to subvert the authority of Grand Ayatollah Sistani. It quietly welcomed his involvement in steering the broad direction of the Iraqi political process towards elections, and never questioned his ultimate decisions. Although Sistani might have been critical of the finer details of Iran's Islamic government, he was, by calling for elections and democratic rule, helping to put a majority Shi'a government in power in Iraq.

Trade between Iran and Iraq increased very rapidly after the fall of the regime. The border posts of Mehran and Mundhirriya/Qasr Shirin saw the incessant flow of Iranian goods into Iraq, mainly consumer goods, foodstuffs, chemicals and building materials. In November 2003, the Iranian Trade Minister stated to the visiting Iraqi delegation that Iran–Iraq trade was reaching a level of a billion dollars on an annualised basis.[30] The CPA was clearly unwilling to offer Iran any access to Iraq's public sector purchases, especially the food basket, and Iran was shut out from these markets at least for the duration of the CPA period. Some electricity purchase contracts had been negotiated during the CPA era, as Iraq's power crisis became aggravated, but they were implemented only later. Iranian exports went mainly to the private sector and were accompanied by a number of Iranian trade delegations from the public, cooperative and private sectors. The relationships between Iraqi and Iranian merchants were rapidly being re-established, in spite of the CPA's suspicions of Iraq's deepening economic relationships with Iran and the lethargy and chaotic policy planning on the part of the Governing Council government. The November 2003 Talabani-led mission also signed a number of protocols in the transport, construction, investments and oil sectors, and the groundwork was being laid for the use of Iranian ports and transhipment facilities for goods coming into Iraq.

There was a powerful movement afoot to reorient Iraq's economic and trade axis away from the Saddam era linkages with near eastern Arab countries, into a north western/south eastern orientation, focusing on Iraq's historic trade and investment relations with Turkey, Iran and the Gulf countries. These formed Iraq's natural trading partners, rather than the markets of the Near East which lay hundreds of miles across deserts from Iraq's centres of population. Many ministers believed that Iraq's trade patterns were deliberately distorted in the past to serve politically motivated economic policies, to the detriment of Iraq's economy and welfare. Arab countries, especially Jordan, looked on with alarm at Iraq's burgeoning trade with Iran, seeing in it a diminution of Jordan's role in the Iraqi economy. Arabs were afraid that Iraq might act out its desire to diversify its trading links and rebuild its relationships with its neighbours to the east and south. This was resented as another example of Iraq 'drifting' away from its Arab roots, despite the fact that numerous Arab countries such as Morocco, Egypt and even Jordan, with their bilateral agreements with the USA and EU, developed similar policies of diversification. This, of course, added to the notion that the Arab countries were not so much concerned with Iraq's trade diversification as they were exercised by any signs of Iraq's tilt towards Iran. While the CPA had been in charge, however, it had not been prepared to implement these agreements, at least for the imports for which it was responsible, deferring the matter to later governments. The Interim Government tried to halt the deepening of Iraq's trade relationships with Iran, and tried to breathe new life into the Saddam-era trade and economic links with countries such as Jordan, Lebanon and Egypt.

Iran's knowledge of Iraq was all-encompassing and unsurpassed. To the legion of its people with first-hand experience in Iraq, Iran had a number in its upper-leadership echelons who were actually Iraqi by birth, or who had spent their formative years in the country. A number of senior commanders of the Iranian Revolutionary Guards, the *Pasderan*, including a deputy commander, were born and raised in Iraq. The judiciary in particular was packed with Iraqi-born Iranians. Some important Iraqi businessmen who had been expelled to Iran in the 1980s on spurious charges had been able to re-establish themselves in Iran's economy. They would prove adept at quickly staking their claim in the new Iraqi economic order. They would also provide the vital buffer between Iran's merchants – the famous *bazaaris* – and the evolving Iraqi private sector, especially the newly enfranchised Shi'a merchants and traders. There was also a surreptitious side to Iran's deep involvement in Iraq. Thousands of Iraqis were recruited into the intelligence-gathering network of Iran, thus affording Iran the detailed, on-the-ground, information base that would allow it to further refine its policies and tactics. The range and scope of Iran's access to Iraq easily exceeded that of the USA and the Arab countries. How this access and influence was to be used worried the Americans and the Interim Government.

Turkey, Iraq and the Kurds

Turkey's relationships with Saddam Hussein's Iraq were a thicket of inter-locking interests that were barely concealed by Turkey's formal commitment to the UN sanctions regime. Turkey had deepened its economic and trade interests with Iraq ever since the launch of the Iran–Iraq War, with Iraq opening a vital oil export line to Ceyhan, on Turkey's Mediterranean coast. Throughout the 1990s, Turkey did not seriously interrupt the work of myriad smugglers and sanctions-busters operating from Turkish territory, even as it was providing the base for the operations of the flights that were patrolling the no-fly zone. These parallel tracks – formal support for the policy of containing Iraq and exploiting the trade and other opportunities afforded it by the Iraqi regime's isolation – were a recognised and accepted feature of Turkey's Iraq policy in the 1990s. With the launch of the UN OFF programme, Turkey's trade with Iraq exploded, with Turkey providing the largest component of Iraq's imports. Turkey was also Iraq's main land conduit and vital truck route to western Europe.

As the Bush administration moved from containment of Iraq to outright belligerence towards the country, however, Turkey became seriously alarmed at the huge risks to its own security that war with Iraq would entail. Turkey had always supported a strong centralised government in Iraq as the best bulwark against the possibility that a weakened Iraqi state might unleash forces that would jeopardise Turkey's own security and vital national interests. By far the greatest of Turkey's fears was the possibility that a weakened or divided Iraq would give rise to a Kurdish state in northern Iraq that would act as a magnet for similar claims by its own substantial Kurdish population, nearly twelve million strong. The consolidation of the Kurdish parties' hold on Iraqi Kurdistan, and the vital role that the Kurds played as the USA's main strategic ally inside Iraq, seriously concerned the authorities in Ankara. The Turks watched with increasing alarm as the demands for a federal Iraq became legitimated in the TAL. Thwarting the plans for an emergent Kurdish state or an Iraqi confederation became a main feature of Turkey's policy in Iraq, even while it appeared to accept that some degree of autonomy for Iraq's Kurds would be inevitable. The re-formation of Turkey's main Kurdish insurgent group, the PKK, against which the Turkish army had fought a decades-long dirty war, in northeastern Iraq, was also looming as a critical Turkish national security problem.

The Kurdish issue directly affected Turkey's other main concerns in Iraq. They included the status of Iraq's Turkomen, who were concentrated in the North of Iraq, and who were contenders with the Kurds (and Arabs) for control over the vital oil city of Kirkuk. Turkey had recently taken an interest in promoting the rights of Iraq's Turkomen population, both as fellow Turkic speakers and as a useful tool to counter the Kurds. Turkey was instrumental in creating the Iraq Turkomen Front, as an umbrella organisation for Iraq's Turkomen. Iraq's Turkomen themselves were divided, however, as nearly half were Shi'a who did not necessarily see eye to eye with Turkey. Nevertheless, the cause of Iraq's Turkomen, a popular one inside Turkey itself, gave Turkey a platform to advance its claims that it had legitimate interests in northern Iraq. This also dovetailed with Turkey's concern that Kirkuk's oil fields might fall under the control of a Kurdish government, providing it with the wherewithal to finance an independent Kurdish state. At another level, both the 'deep state' in Turkey – the nexus of senior officers and civil servants who were the backbone of the secular order that had been founded by Mustafa Kemal – and the mildly Islamic but staunchly Sunni ruling party of Prime Minister Erdogan were concerned about the loss of power of Iraq's Sunni Arabs and the rise of militant Shi'ism. The possibility that Iraqi Shi'a religious parties aligned to Iran would come to power alarmed both Turkey's secularists and Sunni Islamists, creating yet another knotty issue to unravel. Turkey had to balance all these factors into a coherent policy, all the while maintaining a deep suspicion of US designs for Iraq and the fear that the USA, its erstwhile NATO ally, might be acquiescing, inadvertently or otherwise, in the rise of a Kurdish state. As a result Turkey was both driven to interfere in Iraq to protect its vital interests – it frequently made noises about occupying northern Iraq – and was anxious that deepening its involvement in Iraq might drag it into a quagmire.

The crucial test of where Iraqis' loyalties lay was to be in the elections promised by the end of January 2005. The Shi'a on the whole were conscious that the holding of elections on time would work to their advantage. Islamists and liberals such as Ahmad Chalabi were acutely aware that early elections were their best chance to reverse the flow of the Interim Government's policies. In turn, the Interim Government was conscious that it was working against time. The only justification for delaying the elections – and thereby enhancing its chances of returning to power – was whether the violence and instability in Iraq would warrant the postponement of the elections. The Interim Government was confronted with an escalating series of problems in Najaf, Samarra and then Fallujah, all of which added to the uncertainty of whether elections could, or should, be held on time.

18

Showdown at the Shrine

'The Iraqi Government will not stand idly by in the face of this mutiny.' –

Ayad Allawi, Prime Minister of Iraq, August 2004, referring to the
occupation of the Imam Ali shrine in Najaf by the Mahdi Army[1]

The CPA left the Interim Government with two unresolved crises that were
more akin to poisoned chalices. The stand-off in Najaf continued throughout
the summer of 2004, with a cat-and-mouse game being played between the
Mahdi Army and the MNF, with Iraqi detachments in tow.[2] Also, once again,
Fallujah had become an insurgent stronghold after the complete subversion of
the Fallujah Brigade and its ineffectual commander, General Muhammad
Latif. The first to break was the Najaf confrontation. It was also the one that
was most fraught with risk as its resolution required a firm position by Ayad
Allawi on a number of sensitive and controversial issues. These included the
role of the militias in the new Iraqi state; the status of the Sadrist movement;
the manipulation of religious symbols for political ends; the ultimate control
over religious shrines; and the role of the *Marji'iyya* in the Shi'a political landscape, and its power over the problematic Sadrists. A wrong step or miscalculation on any of these issues could threaten Allawi's premiership and seriously
jeopardise his electoral prospects. The resolution of these issues would
indelibly mark his premiership.

Disarming the Militias

The disarming, demobilisation and reintegration of the militias – the 'DDR'
of the security professionals – was an issue that had been only belatedly
broached by the CPA. The militias of the two Kurdish parties had evolved
into something like a regular force, with proper training and discipline, and
with their own ministry at the Kurdistan Regional Government. The Kurds
had insisted that their *pesh merga* were not strictly militias but rather an

armed force responsible for security in Kurdistan and a self-defence forma-tion. They resented any attempt to label the militia an irregular force, and refused to have their *pesh merga* subject to the same rules that governed other, 'lesser', militias. Immediately after the fall of the Ba'athist regime, the Coalition assigned the task of DDR of the militias to a veteran USAID offi-cial, Larry Crandall.[3] But he never took up his post because the Pentagon cancelled his assignment. The militia problem devolved on to the incoming CPA adviser on national security, Walter Slocombe. Neither Slocombe nor the military viewed the militias a serious security threat and never went further than making platitudinous remarks about their unacceptability in the new Iraq. The Coalition's military commander, General Ricardo Sanchez, said in September 2003, 'We are not going to allow private militias to operate in the country'.[4] The military, however, did nothing about them, and Slocombe said that he didn't think the militias at that time 'were a very big problem'.[5]

The lack of firm resolve on the militias issue gave a decided boost to the Shi'a Islamist parties, who redoubled their efforts to establish their own secu-rity forces on the ground. The most formidable of these groups was the Badr Brigade, affiliated to SCIRI. By the summer of 2004, it had grown to a trained force of nearly 15,000 people, and was active in the southern provinces. The Badr Brigade had established itself as a force to be reckoned with in numerous southern towns and cities. The November 15 Agreement and the impending TAL finally concentrated the CPA's mind on the militia problem, as it woke up to the potential threat that might emanate from uncontrolled militia forces. In February 2004, Terrence Kelly, who had worked in both the Clinton and Bush White House in the Office of Science and Technology, was recruited by the CPA. He joined the CPA's national security with explicit instructions to work out a policy on the militias within a few weeks.

Kelly identified nine militia groups that appeared willing to work with the CPA in the political transition process.[6] By the far the most important were the Kurdish *pesh merga* and the Badr Brigade, but there were other militias associ-ated with the INC, INA, the ICP, the Da'awa Party and its large splinter group, the Da'awa Party–Iraq Organisation, and a force linked with the Iraqi Hizbollah party that was active in the southernmost provinces. Kelly proposed a three-pronged strategy that became the basis for CPA Order 91. The Order effectively banned militia activity. The strategy involved recruiting qualified militiamen into the nascent security forces; retiring and paying pension or disability benefits to older militiamen; and integrating former militiamen into civilian life through job-training schemes. The INC militia was pretty much a bodyguard force, and its formal dissolution was easily achieved. This was also the case with the INA and Da'awa Party militias, both of whose leaders were aspiring to high office in the post-sovereignty government. The maintenance of a militia under these circumstances would have been problematic for their candidature.

The Kurds, however, were unprepared to accede to a national militia policy, and continued to run their *pesh merga* as a regional security force, answerable only to the Kurdistan Regional Government. Kelly found that most of his work focused on the resolution of the Shi'a militia problem, especially the Badr Brigade. SCIRI always maintained that the fact that the Badr Brigade had been based in Iran had not been a matter of choice. Iran was the only neighbouring country of Iraq that had been prepared to lend its territory to an armed resistance to Saddam. The Badr Brigade was therefore a bona fide resistance army, and should be accorded the same treatment as the Kurds' *pesh merga*.

The USA was left in something of a quandary. The Kurds were prepared to go along in theory with the DDR policies developed by Kelly, while at the same time insistently pressing their case for exceptional treatment. The Badr Brigade was not prepared to disarm and disband without receiving assurances that the security of the Shi'a population would not be compromised. This evolved into an elaborate game being played between the CPA and SCIRI, with the former trying to entice the latter to enter the militia DDR process, and the Badr Brigade holding out for more substantive assurances and further incentives. The Coalition was fully aware that Badr could be, and was in fact being, used as a political tool to extend the reach of the Shi'a Islamists, but could not, without serious risk, embark on a plan of its forcible disarmament. SCIRI was also concerned about the loss of its armed wing into security structures the composition of which was still uncertain, especially when the Mahdi Army, which it viewed as a direct threat to its pre-eminence, was expanding without any hindrance not least because of the previous laissez-faire policy adopted by the CPA. The Mahdi Army was decidedly not on Kelly's approved militia list for DDR treatment.

The proposals for the militias' disarmament evolved into a detailed strategy and implementation note, which was used as the basis for ongoing negotiations with the political parties at the time of the CPA's dissolution.[7] A major plank of the policy involved the individual recruitment of suitable militiamen directly into the new security forces. It was always a central tenet of Kelly's proposals that militiamen be recruited as individuals rather than as a corporate block. This would prevent the infiltration of militiamen as organised units into the security forces. This policy, of course, did not apply to the Kurds, who effortlessly transformed themselves, en masse, from irregular forces into a regional security force. The process of integrating militiamen into the new Iraqi security forces began in earnest in April 2004 under the first civilian Minister of Defence but then ran into serious obstacles when the Interim Government's new Minister of Defence, Hazem Sha'alan, refused to recruit militiamen associated with Islamist parties into the army.[8] Sha'alan was busy recruiting former Ba'athist officers and NCOs into the armed forces, and was not too keen to see his plans compromised. There was a firm belief on the part of the Interim Government and the Anglo-American intelligence agencies that Iraq's reconstituted security forces should be built, as far as possible, on elements of the former army and intelligence services, irrespective of their degree of involvement with the former Ba'ath regime. The presence of militiamen from the Islamist parties, some of whom might have participated in the Iran–Iraq War on the Iranian side, was seen as an affront to the professional officers of the Ba'athist armed forces, whom they were trying to entice into the new security structures.

The Interim Government's security strategy implied the adoption of a policy that would take months, if not years, to implement, especially as it was based on two highly controversial premises. The first was the large-scale induction of professional officers from the former security and armed forces into the new Iraqi security forces. The second was to rely on the tribal and clan affiliations of the main Interim Government protagonists and flood the new Iraqi security forces with these recruits.

The process was carried to its furthest extent in the Ministry of Interior, where a new Special Police Commando unit was organised by the Interim Government's Minister of Interior's uncle. General Adnan Thabit was brought in by the minister, Falah al-Naqib, whose roots were in the city of Samarra. Adnan Thabit was a Saddam-era general who had fallen foul of the former regime and had been imprisoned and sentenced to death.[9] His anti-Saddamist credentials were impeccable, but nevertheless he had been a former Ba'athist. His profile almost exactly fitted the type of person that the Interim Government and its advisers wanted to bring into the new security structures: tough-talking, with a military or security background, and part of the leadership structure of the former regime without being associated with Saddam and his inner circle. The Special Police Commandos, drawn from former Saddam-era special forces and the Republican Guard, would feature importantly in various counter-insurgency operations in late 2004 and early 2005, notably in the Samarra area. They were the first elite-type units of the new security forces upon which so much hope was being pinned by the Interim Government and its supporters. They would be the harbingers of a new post-CPA order in Iraq – security-conscious, disciplined and focused on rebuilding the state. Or at least that was what the official line would have the world believe. The reality was somewhat different. The Ministry of Interior's elite units might easily have heralded something else entirely: the growth of a death squad culture under official sanction.[10] Later, of course, this very accusation would be laid at the doorstep of the Ministry of Interior in Dr Jaafari's Transitional National Government, but its genesis was in the Interim

Government's toleration of the special forces attached to the security ministries.

The Struggle Over Control of Najaf

The Interim Government began to be buffeted by serious security problems, even before the final transfer of sovereignty on 28 June, 2004. This date had been advanced by two days to avoid any public handing-over ceremonies. Bremer left surreptitiously, soon after he formally transferred power to the Interim Government. In his memoirs, Bremer stated that security considerations prompted the change in the transfer of sovereignty date and his own departure plans. But Iraqis did not see his departure in this way. He appeared to be slipping out of the country that he had ruled for over a year. The CPA's legacy in Iraq was, at best, spotty. The regime had not been accepted by the Iraqi public; few had good words to say about this strange episode in Iraq's history. The locus of activity now shifted decisively to the Interim Government as the US Embassy deliberately maintained a low profile under Ambassador Negroponte.

The first signs of an impending breakdown and an escalation of the confrontation between the Mahdi Army and the MNF were not in Najaf but in Sadr City, where in early June five US servicemen were killed after encountering a roadside bomb.[11] The rhetoric from the Sadrists began to take on more confrontational and menacing tones. In a sermon delivered on his behalf by an associate in the Kufa Mosque, Moqtada rejected Allawi's government as illegitimate because it had been 'appointed by the occupier'.[12] The statement went on to demand an immediate withdrawal of the MNF as 'there is no freedom or democracy without independence'. It was in Najaf that the Interim Government would face its first major problem, however, regarding the forces of Moqtada al-Sadr. The ceasefire between the Mahdi Army and the MNF that had been negotiated earlier by the Shi'a House had been fitfully observed. The situation in Najaf was becoming more serious by the day. The governor of Najaf, Adnan al-Zurufi, a Coalition appointee, sensed that a confrontation was imminent when he said, 'They need to finish this story pretty quickly. We need to finish this story pretty quickly'.[13]

A complex struggle for control of Najaf began. It pitted a myriad of forces against each other. The Sadrists, who were at the centre of the crisis, sought to use their hold on Najaf to demonstrate their ineluctable rise as a force amongst the Shi'a; to force their way on to the political landscape as a potent movement; and to steal a march on the other Shi'a Islamists. It was also a subtle signal to the USA that the costs of ignoring or harassing the Sadrists were too high, and that they should be accorded a position of respect in the evolving political line-up in Iraq. At the same time, they sought to test the limits of power of Grand Ayatollah Sistani and his ability to control the Shi'a masses. It was not so much a frontal assault on the *Marji'iyya* as such, in spite of the Sadrists' rhetoric on the 'silent' versus the 'active' *Marji'iyya*. Rather, the Sadrists sought to reduce the effectiveness of the *Marji'iyya* in determining the political position of the Shi'a. SCIRI and other Shi'a Islamists were very wary about the evolving crisis in Najaf and were unsure how they should publicly respond to it. The Sadrists had combined nationalist imagery with a Shi'a 'nativism' that was hard to overlook. The USA on the one hand wanted to eliminate the Sadrists once and for all, and on the other was anxious about the public relations disaster that might ensue if the city of Najaf, in particular the shrine area, was extensively damaged. At the same time, the superpower was concerned that the Interim Government would be fatally weakened if it made no move to contain the Sadrists, knowing full well that the brunt of any fighting would have to be borne by the MNF.

The Interim Government had other considerations in mind, not so much in terms of bolstering its authority but rather in demonstrating the efficacy of its new policy of the 'strong state' that would not brook any serious dissent. If the Sadrists could be eliminated, or at least reduced in size, then one more prop of a threatening future Islamist state would be removed. It was partly a divide and rule policy. By focusing on the Sadrists as a dangerous and undisciplined rabble, the Interim Government could peel them away from the mass of Islamists. It would then be able to 'domesticate' or marginalise the likes of SCIRI and the Da'awa Party far more easily. The Iranians watched all these events keenly.[14] A defeat of the Sadrists at this juncture would have been fatal to their ambitions in Iraq. They would lose a powerful proxy tool to put pressure on the USA, which would force them into either escalating their challenge to the USA through alternative routes or scaling down their ambitions and plans in Iraq. It is no surprise that they chose to throw their support behind the Sadrists in Najaf. Iraqis who were directly commanded by the Iranian *Pasderan* were secreted into the Mahdi Army, which stiffened their resistance.

Tensions between the Sadrists in Najaf and the governor had already begun to build in mid-July. The Mahdi Army was rumoured to be stockpiling weapons in the shrine of Imam Ali, in preparation for the possible eruption of fighting. Eighty Iranian agents were claimed by the governor to be in Najaf, training the Sadrists in advanced weapons, including Iranian-supplied anti-aircraft guns.[15] The Sadrists did not dominate the city in its entirety, but they did operate no-go zones. These included the vicinity of the Imam Ali shrine and the huge cemetery of Najaf, the *Maqbarat as-Salam* whose catacombs and crypts provided excellent hiding places for fighters and weapons stockpiles. But Najaf was not Sadr's domain. The residents of Najaf were dependent on pilgrim traffic for their livelihood, and this had dwindled to next to nothing. The old-established religious families of Najaf were also formidable competitors to Moqtada, and the immense influence of the *Marji'iyya* on the city's affairs did not work to his advantage.

The Najaf Crisis of August 2004

The second Najaf crisis started on 3 August, 2004, when one of Moqtada al-Sadr's aides, Sheikh Mahmoud Sudani, claimed that a joint Iraq–multinational force had surrounded Moqtada's house in Najaf the previous night and had started firing at it. The report was categorically denied by the MNF, but its command did say that they had been attacked by small arms fire while patrolling the city. Independent observers, however, confirmed that a loose MNF cordon around the city was already in place. A battle ensued in which a number of Mahdi Army followers were killed. Earlier, the MNF had arrested Sadr's associate in Karbala, Sheikh Mithal al-Hassnawi, and Najaf became engulfed in a demonstration demanding his release.[16] Arrests of Sadrists were quickly followed by the Sadrists' kidnapping eighteen policemen in a tit-for-tat retaliation. The governor of Najaf then called for the intervention of US Marines who were stationed thirty miles outside the town. Fighting spread, and within days a full-blown crisis had erupted, with battles in Najaf, Diwaniya, Nasiriya and Sadr City, where US F-15 fighter-bombers dropped their load.[17] The brunt of the fighting took place in Najaf itself, where fierce battles erupted for control over the vast cemetery area. Official statements were flying thick and fast about the demise of the 'thugs and terrorists' of the Mahdi Army. 'We will not negotiate,' said the Interior Minister, Falah Naqib. 'We have power to stop these people, and we'll kick them out of the country.'[18] The assumption was that the Mahdi Army was totally a foreign, or otherwise an Iranian, creature. In retaliation, Moqtada was calling for a nationwide insurrection against the American 'devils'. In his weekly sermon at the Kufa Mosque, which was read out by an aide, Moqtada said, 'I say America is our enemy and the enemy of the people, and we will not accept its partnership. . . . I blame the occupier for all the attacks going on in Iraq, such as the attacks on the churches and the kidnappings.'[19]

The fighting in Najaf coincided with the departure of Grand Ayatollah Sistani to London, to undergo heart treatment. Sistani arrived in London on 6 August but did not enter hospital immediately, raising questions as to the nature of his heart ailment and whether it required emergency action. Sistani's absence from Najaf at the onset of the battles sent a number of important messages. The first was that he was unwilling to provide a layer of protection to the Sadrists by his presence in the city. This led to widespread conjecture that Sistani was indifferent to the fate of Moqtada al-Sadr, and might well have wished to see the back of him.[20] But whether this implied prior knowledge of the crackdown on Moqtada, or even connivance at the attack on him, is highly questionable. Sistani's concerns about Moqtada had nothing to do with the street power of the Sadrists or their political programme. It did, however, have everything to do with the disruptions that the Sadrists were able to inflict on the carefully laid plans for the Shi'a to march into power through elections and a new constitution. Many did link Sistani's absence from Najaf as a 'green light' to the Interim Government from the *Marji'iyya* to strike at the Sadrists.

The choice of London for Sistani's treatment was read as a snub to Iran and, by implication, a rejection of the purported role of Iran in egging on Moqtada al-Sadr. This allowed the government to ratchet up its media attacks on the Sadrists, calling them 'outlaws who continued in their criminal and terrorist acts against the citizenry', and promising to bring 'a return of order, security and tranquillity to all parts of Iraq'.[21] The USA meanwhile advised all the residents of Najaf to leave the city, signalling that it was planning to launch an assault aimed at the centre of the city. By the second week of August, hundreds of people had been killed throughout southern Iraq and Baghdad as the Mahdi Army and the MNF, allied Iraqi police and National Guard forces fought in various towns and cities, but mostly in Najaf. There, the Sadrists were reduced to defending their entrenched positions around the shrine of Imam Ali, and inside the shrine itself.[22]

An assault on the shrine by the MNF, or even by Iraqi forces, would have had untold consequences. The signals from the Interim Government became blurred – bellicosity mixed with invitations to Moqtada to 'participate in elections next year'. The hour of reckoning was fast approaching. The Minister of Defence was playing the role of the 'heavy', announcing that they had captured hundreds of Mahdi Army and unidentified 'foreign' fighters, and that he had in his possession clear evidence of intervention by unnamed foreign countries in the unfolding crisis.[23] The Najaf police chief, General Ghalib al-Jazairi, chimed in with his bit of bravado. His forces were ready to deliver the final blow to the Sadrists. 'We will finish with them, control the city and no longer tolerate militias in Najaf'.[24] The Interim Government took to calling Sadr City by its old, pre-Saddam, name of 'Thawra' City. This was a highly provocative gesture, a clear sign that it did not recognise the renaming of the city in honour of the late Grand Ayatollah Muhammad al-Sadr. The Najaf crisis also had many of the features of a battle of wills between the Prime Minister and the Sadrists. In Hilla and Diwaniya, followers of Moqtada al-Sadr attacked the local offices of the INA, the Prime Minister's party, and burnt them down.

Defamation Campaigns and the Rubai'e Mission

At the same time as the Najaf crisis, and in a related effort to discredit politicians and groups potentially hostile to the Interim Government, a prosecutor in the judicial services, Ziad al-Maliki, laid a series of patently false charges against Ahmad Chalabi, including counterfeiting of currency – about three dollars' worth. An arrest warrant was issued against him and another entirely spurious warrant for conspiracy to murder was issued against Salem Chalabi, the Chief Executive of the Special Court to try Saddam and his associates. Both these charges were so contrived that the Interim Government's Minister of Justice threatened to resign if the prosecutor did not withdraw the indictments. Ahmed Chalabi's INC offices were closed down by the Interim Government. Chalabi, however, was not cowed by these measures and returned to Iraq where he tried to play a part in resolving the Najaf crisis. The arrest warrant was never implemented.

As the crisis evolved and the destruction of the shrine in a large-scale assault became a distinct possibility, mediators proliferated. Dr Mowaffaq Rubai'e, National Security Adviser and a former member of the Governing Council, was brought in. His mediation efforts were conducted with the full knowledge of the Prime Minister, the US Embassy and the MNF command. He prepared a list of conditions to present to Moqtada to end the fighting and, after amendments, obtained the approval of Ayad Allawi to present them to Moqtada.

After successfully arranging to meet with Moqtada (through Da'awa and Badr intermediaries), Rubai'e prepared a final draft agreement for the approval of the prime minister. Rubai'e then returned to Najaf, in the company of the intermediaries, to seal the agreement with Moqtada. A firm rendezvous point and time were agreed at the Najaf house of Moqtada's assassinated father. Just before the mediation party set off for the meeting, the rendezvous area came under intense bombardment by US Marines, and US Special Forces were seen heading in the direction of the rendezvous location. Moqtada, sensing a trap had been laid for him, scurried to find cover. He only just escaped with his life. Rubai'e himself believed that he was being set up to capture or kill Moqtada. It was only after what he thought was an attempt to kill him had failed that Moqtada al-Sadr, who had hitherto been in hiding in various safe houses, decided to move to the shrine and occupy it.[25]

Following this incident, Moqtada became intensely suspicious of the Interim Government, and his suspicions of the Americans were intensified. It took another set of negotiations, again conducted through the mediation of Dr Rubai'e, to produce a settlement document, which Moqtada then signed. This document, however, was abruptly renounced by the Interim Government, just as Rubai'e was about to hold a press conference to make its terms known. It became clear at that point that the Interim Government was determined to pursue a strategy of humiliating Moqtada al-Sadr and forcing him to accede to its demands. Rubai'e saw his position being undermined. He was seen to be out of tune with the prevailing security ethos of the Interim Government, which was increasingly seeking a decisive confrontation with the

Sadrists. Rubai'e was accused of exceeding his remit in negotiations with Moqtada al-Sadr and being in secret league with the Iranians. None of these charges could be substantiated, but the damage was done. Rubai'e was isolated and ignored in his office, while administrative measures were taken to curtail his financial and operational independence, effectively leaving him with no resources to carry out his duties.

Shi'a Islamists, the National Assembly and the Najaf crisis

As the battles were raging, so was concern about the direction into which the fighting was leading. Islamist Shi'a politicians, and even lay Shi'a, became increasingly worried about an Interim Government secret agenda, aimed at decimating the Sadrists as a preparation for redrawing the post-sovereignty political map in favour of a centralised, strongman government. Salama al-Khafaji, a former member of the Governing Council and a founder of the 'Shi'a Political Council',[26] held the American forces responsible for the fighting, and contravening the truce that had been reached earlier with the Mahdi Army. A more senior Shi'a leader, Ibrahim al-Jaafari of the Da'awa Party, one of Iraq's two vice-presidents, called on the US Marines to pull out of the city of Najaf. He had earlier termed the Marines' attack as 'not a civilised way' to rebuild the country.[27] Jaafari had refused to resign from the vice-presidency when Moqtada had called on him to do so. Former IGC member and leading Shi'a cleric Muhammad Bahr ul-Uloom, not known for his partiality to Moqtada al-Sadr, attacked the Interim Government and the Americans directly.[28]

As the assault on the city began to take shape, half the Najaf provincial council resigned in protest. The deputy governor of Najaf, Jawdat al-Quraishi, stated in his resignation statement, 'I resign from my post denouncing all the US terrorist operations that they are doing against this holy city'. As the denouement loomed, the opinions of the Shi'a political class became crystallised. The growing recognition that the destruction of the Sadrists would only strengthen the strong 'security' state advocated by Ayad Allawi galvanised the fence-sitters such as the Da'awa Party, who might have reaped some political gain from the elimination of a strong and popular rival. Similarly, independent Shi'a politicians, who had either been marginalised or had felt cheated by the formation of the Interim Government, saw that supporting Moqtada might result in improving their political fortunes. SCIRI held out the longest, torn between the desire to remove a rival from the scene and fear that the Interim Government might be empowered immeasurably by the destruction of the Sadrists. The organisation was also very concerned about the effects of the fighting on the shrine, and on the political prospects of the Shi'a in general.

The Interim Government was in a predicament. It had announced publicly that an all-Iraqi force was being prepared to seize the shrine from the Sadrists. But the belligerent rhetoric could not mask the deep anxieties that lurked underneath this statement. The public response to the assault on the Sadrists was not as sympathetic as had been anticipated. Moqtada was sitting defiantly inside the shrine, hurling epithets at the prime minister, while his followers continued to demonstrate around the country. Important Shi'a voices in the regions pitched in against the plans for an assault on the shrine. In Qom, Ayatollah al-Haeri, Moqtada's main *mujtahid* backer, issued a statement condemning to perdition any Muslim who participated in an attack on the shrine.

The critical situation in Najaf and in the South of the country coincided with the convening of a conference to elect a hundred-person National Assembly. The Association of Muslim Scholars and other major Sunni groups boycotted the process. The assembly was supposed to provide broad oversight power over the Interim Government, with veto powers over Cabinet decisions. It had specific responsibility for budgetary and financial matters. The halls of the conference centre reverberated with angry calls by Shi'a delegates to put an end to the fighting in Najaf, and denunciations of the Interim Government's threatened use of force against the Sadrists in the Imam Ali shrine. A four-person delegation from the conference met with Ayad Allawi, who issued a statement announcing that the Interim Government was holding any action against the Sadrists in abeyance. The preparations for the attack on Najaf might have been an elaborate ruse to cow the Sadrists into leaving the shrine complex. The Interim Government went so far as to demand that all foreign journalists and their Iraqi stringers leave Najaf, indicating an imminent assault on the shrine.[29]

In an orchestrated move with the government, the new National Assembly nominated eight of its members to head a delegation to meet Moqtada al-Sadr and present him with a three-point plan to resolve the crisis. The delegation was headed by Sayyid Hussein al-Sadr, a relative of Moqtada, and adviser to Allawi. The plan called for the Mahdi Army to evacuate the shrine of Imam Ali, with assurances that it would not be attacked during its withdrawal; turning the Mahdi Army and the Sadrist movement into a political party; and Moqtada al-Sadr's participation in the political process.[30] The delegation arrived in a military airfield near Najaf on 17 August, and drove through the deserted city to the shrine of Imam Ali. Moqtada al-Sadr refused to meet with them, leaving the negotiations to his top aides.

The Sadrist negotiators did not allow Sayyid Hussein al-Sadr to meet privately with Moqtada and deliver the proposal of the National Assembly by hand. Because they were so suspicious of the real intentions of the delegation, they claimed that such a visit might help others (presumably, the MNF) find out Moqtada's secret location. Fuelling their insecurity was their belief that

Moqtada had been targeted before the arrival of the earlier Rubai'e mediation mission. The Sadrists' suspicions about falling into a trap may have been further inflamed by an American artillery barrage against their positions, just as the delegation from the National Assembly was preparing to go to the shrine area.[31] The delegation did not meet Moqtada and returned empty-handed to Baghdad. This prompted an angry letter from the prime minister's office to the National Assembly, denouncing Moqtada's snubbing of the delegation.[32]

The high-risk confrontation continued. In private, the hawks of the Interim Government, prompted to a large extent by their mentors in the Anglo-American intelligence agencies, were demanding a full-blown assault on the Sadrists in the shrine, using Iraqi forces as a symbolic cover, while in practice relying on the Marines. No government could actually count on the loyalty of Iraqi forces under these circumstances. The Minister of Defence, Hazem Sha'alan, who had encamped in the vicinity of Najaf during the crisis, later confirmed that preparations were advanced for an assault on the shrine. 'We were about to implement a plan for an assault the shrine from four different gates after completing our siege of al-Sadr's militias,' he said.[33] The US ambassador, John Negroponte, was also calling for a decisive blow against Moqtada al-Sadr. He was backed by his superiors in Washington, even though certain reports claimed that the US Marines were responding to local challenges rather than implementing part of a detailed political plan. The calculations that governed the prime minister's actions were more nuanced. Attempting to diminish Moqtada's stature by drawing him into a process in which he had to abide by rules might not have necessarily worked to the prime minister's advantage. At the same time, although the Mahdi Army's defeat by the MNF would have been an almost foregone conclusion, it might easily have turned into a pyrrhic victory. The latter course of action ran the risk of the destruction of the shrine and turning Moqtada al-Sadr and his followers into martyrs. With a looming election where the Najaf outcome would feature largely in people's perceptions of Allawi's government, the choices were extremely difficult.

Sistani and the Najaf Crisis

It was Grand Ayatollah Sistani who came to the rescue of both Moqtada and the government. Sistani had undergone a minor operation in London but had kept abreast of developments in Najaf from his hospital bed. His representative in London, Sayyid Murtadha al-Kashmiri, issued regular bulletins about his condition and statements of his concern about the dangerous stand-off in Najaf. The confrontation between Moqtada and the Interim Government now revolved around control of the sanctuary, with

Moqtada insisting that he would not hand over the keys of the shrine complex to anyone other than the *Marji'iyya*. The head of the Sadrist office in Nasiriya, Sheikh Aws al-Khafagi, issued a televised challenge to the Americans and the Interim Government. 'We will not hand over the keys of the sanctuary to the American forces. This would be a historic mark of shame on us, and we will not hand them over either to the police or the National Guard who have violated all the bounds of sanctity and shed the blood of Muslims.'[34] He did, however, leave a way out of the confrontation. Khafagi continued: 'If they [the government] want the [keys] then they should contact Sayyid Sistani's office so that an authorised person from that noble office can collect the keys to the sanctuary.' Moqtada al-Sadr also categorically refused to accede to the Interim Government's demands that the Mahdi Army should be disbanded. Scenes of hundreds of Mahdi Army fighters milling around the sanctuary were televised, with a defiant subtext that they would fight to the death if need be.

Meanwhile the Interim Government was not to be outdone by the Sadrists' rhetoric. In a press conference held on 19 August in the governor's offices in Najaf, Qassim Dawood, the new Minister of State for Military Affairs and Ayad Allawi's point man on the crisis, issued a harsh set of conditions for Moqtada to abide by. Moqtada was to announce personally, at a specially convened press conference, the disbanding of the Mahdi Army; all the weaponry of the Mahdi Army in all the provinces was to be handed over to the police and the National Guard; his forces would have to evacuate the Imam Ali shrine and the cemetery of Najaf completely; Moqtada al-Sadr would have to confirm in writing that he would not undertake any armed action; all prisoners and those who had been kidnapped who were in the custody of the Sadrists would have to be released; and there had to be a complete disclosure of the 'trials' of policemen and ordinary citizens that had been held by the special Sharia courts of the Sadrists, including the death sentences that had been passed; and the affected families had to be compensated.

On 19 August, Sistani left his London hospital for an unknown destination in the city. His London representative, Sayyid Murtadha al-Kashmiri, issued a statement signalling a positive response from the Grand Ayatollah on the opening provided by Aws al-Khafagi's earlier offer to hand over the keys of the shrine to the *Marji'iyya*.[35] Kashmiri's statement significantly alluded to the Mahdi Army's occupants of the shrine as *al-Mutassimum* – a religious term implying they were in the shrine as a form of retreat. 'If the retreatants, of their own volition, leave the noble sanctuary and the shrine in the city of Najaf, lock the gates, and hand over the keys in a sealed envelope to representatives of Grand Ayatollah Sistani' then the ayatollah would accept taking control of the shrine complex.

It was a deft move that badly undercut the Interim Government. First, it did not refer to the Mahdi Army in a derogatory fashion, nor hold it responsible for the situation in Najaf. Second, it did not deem the armed presence of the Sadrists in the shrine as an occupation; rather as sanctuary-seeking. Third, it made no conditions on the Mahdi Army except for the evacuation of the shrine complex. The Grand Ayatollah's demand that such a move be made of the Sadrists' own free will, rather than be couched as an instruction, allowed the Sadrists to save face when withdrawing. Sistani refused to take sides in the struggle between the Interim Government and the Sadrists, but his declaration allowed the ground for a settlement to be narrowed down to the question of if and when the Sadrists would be prepared to accede to his conditions. Nevertheless Moqtada could not but be reminded that in the Ayatollah's absence his forces had been badly mauled, and the costs of holding out might now be too high. Any assault on the shrine would be out of the question as long as negotiations on the withdrawal of the Mahdi Army were taking place within the context of Sistani's statement.

The Interim Government, fearful of a serious political reversal, announced through its Ministry of Interior spokesman that it had seized the shrine complex without a fight. Its forces had arrested hundreds of Mahdi Army militiamen, 'but were unable to find Moqtada al-Sadr himself'. Moqtada was deemed to 'have escaped under the cover of darkness'.[36] It was a patently false claim. Reporters who reached the shrine complex on 21 August confirmed that it was still in the possession of the Mahdi Army, and that there was no evidence of any police or National Guard presence.[37] On 25 August, Sistani arrived back in Iraq in the city of Basra. The Interim Government clearly did not want him around while it planned the final phases of the Najaf stand-off. But Sistani's office announced that the Ayatollah was intent on moving on to Najaf from Basra as soon as possible, and his deputies were organising a huge welcoming reception along his route. Statements of support from religious, tribal and political dignitaries poured in. An irresistible momentum was clearly being established for the resolution of the Najaf crisis according to the terms and conditions of the Sistani statement.

With Sistani's arrival in Najaf, with thousands of pilgrims and attendees in tow, the Interim Government recognised that the initiative now belonged to Sistani. The Americans halted their combat operations on 26 August.[38] Sistani was closeted with Moqtada al-Sadr and on the same day a five-point agreement was hammered out between them.[39] The agreement called for the demilitarisation of Najaf and Kufa and the withdrawal of all armed groups from them; gave the Iraqi police the responsibility for the maintenance of law and order in the two cities; called for the withdrawal of all foreign forces from the two cities; demanded compensation from the Interim Government for all victims of the hostilities; and called for the mobilisation of all currents of opinion to complete a census upon which general elections to restore complete sovereignty could be based. The agreement was sealed by the two, and Moqtada added on the margins the following words: 'These are not the requests but the instructions of the *Marji'iyya* and I am prepared to implement whatever is in them in response to the *Marji'iyya*'s instructions, with my gratitude [to it].'[40] Moqtada couched his climbdown in terms of submission to the demands of the highest religious authority. The Interim Government had no choice but to accept the terms of the agreement, and within a few hours the shrine's loudspeakers were blaring out Moqtada's instructions to his followers to lay down their arms and join the throngs of pilgrims outside the shrine. Weapons were collected by pushcarts and then taken to the Sadrists' headquarters. The heavy and medium weapons were then moved to hidden stockpiles of the Mahdi Army. The keys to the shrine were delivered to Sistani's representatives, who took responsibility for the shrine in conjunction with the Shi'a *waqf* (endowments) foundation.[41] A few days later, several of Moqtada al-Sadr's deputies issued statements in his name calling on his followers around the country to cease fighting and to prepare to join in the political process.[42]

The Significance of the Najaf Crisis

The Najaf crisis was a decisive turning point. All the main protagonists – the Sadrists, the Interim Government and the USA – claimed success in one way or another. The only clear winner, however, was Grand Ayatollah Sistani. It was through the judicious and timely use of his authority that he unequivocally demonstrated his control over the Shi'a masses, and his ability to fashion a settlement that no one could refuse. The Interim Government had to swallow a bitter pill, for it had banked on its ability to contain, and then eliminate, the threat from the Sadrists. The Interim Government model for Iraq was like a version of the Arab authoritarian state with its semi-democratic embellishments. The Sadrists had no place in such a state. Such a version of a stable Middle Eastern order was subscribed to by the intelligence agencies and chanceries in western capitals, and found a resonating echo in the variety of authoritarian regimes of the area. In private, the leading luminaries in the Interim Government expressed their deep misgivings about democracy and whether it could ever take root in the rocky terrain of Iraq. But in public they were bound to pay more than lip service to the notion of electoral democracy, if for no other reason than that it was what the president of the United States had publicly demanded. The gross miscalculation of the Interim Government was that the destruction of the Sadrists would be viewed as an elimination of a dangerous rival by other Islamists, and even the *Marji'iyya*. The fear and contempt expressed by the leading Shi'a political groups towards the Sadrists was mistakenly assumed by the Interim Government to result in them turning a blind eye to the destruction of the Sadrists. In the early phases of the crisis, senior SCIRI officials broadly hinted that the removal of Moqtada would not be a very terrible outcome. As events moved towards a climax, however, the Shi'a Islamists, even SCIRI, began to realise that the Interim Government's plans for the Sadrists would ultimately include *them*. It was this realisation, more than any other, which led to a serious rethink of their earlier indifference to the fate of Moqtada. The Interim Government began to lose its Islamist cover at the very moment when it needed it most. Any attempt by the Interim Government to press its advantage militarily would have resulted in a closing of ranks on the part of all the Shi'a Islamist parties in a general rejection of the Interim Government's solution. Inadvertently, this would prepare the ground for a grand alliance of the Shi'a, prompted in no small degree by their common fear and anxiety about the intentions of the Interim Government and its backers. The cardinal mistake of the Interim Government was to enter the final stages of the confrontation with Moqtada with little or no support remaining from the Islamists.

The Shi'a Islamist parties were driven by the Najaf crisis to realise that they should either hang together or be hanged separately. It became clear that the upcoming elections were not so much a matter of which party was to come out on top as much as how to ensure that the Shi'a political agenda was not ignored by a resurgent authoritarian and secular state. After Najaf, efforts were redoubled to bring all the Shi'a groups into a single electoral bloc, even though there were still voices that argued for a different set of electoral alliances that might accommodate Ayad Allawi's INA and related secular groups. It took the Najaf crisis to bury the hatchet, at least for the short term, and for expediency's sake, between the mainline Shi'a Islamists and the Sadrists. Iran could also sense the harsh winds that would emanate from Iraq if it did not manage the electoral agenda so that the Shi'a groups, Islamists or otherwise, stood united. The Interim Government played an ambiguous game with Iran, with cordial visits by the Deputy Prime Minister and PUK stalwart, Barham Saleh, and belligerent outbursts from Sha'alan, the Minister of Defence. Ayad Allawi played the statesman's role with Iran, but his tone was notably cool and distant. It was clear that if another version of the Interim Government emerged from Iraq's forthcoming elections, it might spell disaster for Iran's interests in Iraq.

The USA also claimed victory, and could point to the exit of the Mahdi Army from Najaf as proof. This was the second time that the USA had called for the disbanding of the Mahdi Army and the elimination of Moqtada al-Sadr, however, with neither objective actually achieved. By letting Moqtada once again slip from the noose which it had tied around him, the USA showed that, when the chips were down, it would not, or could not, weather the potential storm of protest and indignation that might follow in the wake of the destruction of the Sadrists. Once again, there was a clear misreading of the implications of the apparent public exasperation with the crisis-ridden rise of the Sadrist movement. It did not translate into an authorisation for a frontal assault against the shrine of Imam Ali. The USA did, of course, finally understand the risks of such a move, and pulled away at the brink of catastrophe. Nevertheless, it showed itself an irresolute force that lacked subtlety in its approach to charged issues. It would be a long time before the superpower would seriously entertain the idea of a direct military confrontation with either the political wing of the Sadrist movement or the Mahdi Army.

Moqtada al-Sadr emerged at a clear advantage at the end of the crisis. He and his movement had survived, in spite of being under siege for weeks and hopelessly outgunned. The Mahdi Army was seen as recklessly brave and committed, though lacking in prudence and common sense, and was grudgingly respected by its enemies. It had held out against the most powerful force on earth – or, at least, that was how it was portrayed in the media. The body count of those killed in the Mahdi Army was trumpeted by the Interim Government and the MNF as a mark of the huge losses being inflicted on them. Instead, this turned into a badge of honour the longer the Sadrists held out. The mismanagement of the media by the Interim Government and the MNF during the Najaf crisis was another sign of misunderstanding public opinion. The bombastic and triumphalist rhetoric of the hawks of the Interim Government was heard by a suspicious and angry public.

Moqtada was strengthened in intra-Shi'a counsels, but he also understood the limits of his confrontational tactics. He had abused the sanctity of the shrine to advance his cause, and he knew that he could not deploy this avenue again. At the same time, by publicly deferring to Sistani, for the time being he had buried any distinction between the 'silent' and 'active' *Marji'iyya* of the Sadrist lexicon; there was now only one *Marji'iyya* and that was led by Sistani. The abrupt reversal of the Sadrists on this matter was ascribed to Iranian influence. It was considered that Iran did not want to have side battles between the main props of Shi'a power in Iraq, and used its power of patronage to force all of its allies and proxy groups to accept the ultimate authority of Sistani. But it was not necessary to impute this role to Iran. It was self-evident that the Shi'a groups had to accept a final arbiter if they were not to self-destruct before the upcoming elections. The Sadrists became part – albeit a difficult and prickly part – of the grand alliance of the Shi'a, something which would have been difficult to achieve in time for the elections had not the Najaf crisis accelerated the process.

The prestige and influence of Grand Ayatollah Sistani rose to unprecedented levels after his successful resolution of the Najaf showdown. He confirmed his position as the undisputed religious leader of Iraq's Shi'a, not only as an indispensable interlocutor with the government and the MNF, but also as an astute master of the political moment. He used his authority to affect a number of issues. By stymieing the Interim Government's thrust towards the destruction of a main component of the Iraqi Shi'a firmament, he drew a 'red line' around the permissible limits of the elimination of the government's opponents. The Interim Government, especially its Shi'a components, was placed in the awkward position of reluctantly acknowledging Sistani's authority, while privately seething at the unwarranted and meddlesome interference of an 'outsider' in Iraq's affairs. Acolytes of the Interim Government began to mutter about Iranian fifth-columnists, and the 'unacceptable' domination of the Iraqi political scene by a 'foreigner'. A senior official muttered, 'How can an Iranian be allowed this power in Iraq?' in a clear reference to Sistani. This line was also being heard increasingly in the Interim Government's backers in the Arab media, although couched with the usual faint praise for the Grand Ayatollah. Sistani was also seen as the person who 'tamed' Moqtada, and brought him into line with his increasingly public plans to instigate a grand Shi'a electoral alliance.

19

To Hold or Abort an Election

'It is unacceptable to use the pretext of elections to invade towns. . . . We will call on Iraqis to boycott the polls and to consider the results null and void in case of operations in Fallujah.' –

Statement by Association of Muslim Scholars, 21 October, 2004

'There will be a real catastrophe if the elections are delayed. . . . The safe areas [of Iraq] will be engulfed in flames if the elections are postponed.' –

Statement by the Office of Grand Ayatollah Muhammad Taqi al-Mudarressi, 5 November, 2004

The end of the Najaf crisis and the reaffirmation of Grand Ayatollah Sistani's dominant role in the Shi'a politics of Iraq focused attention on the crucial milestone of the upcoming constitutional elections. The Interim Government was seen as an unnecessary interlude in the process of restoring Iraq's sovereignty and establishing constitutional rule. Its behaviour, before and during the Najaf crisis, strayed far from the ideal of a caretaker government concerned mainly with presiding over a successful transition period. It became a party to the elections of January 2005, by positing a specific perspective for Iraq and promoting Ayad Allawi as the right leader to steer Iraq out of its crisis. The Najaf confrontation ended poorly for the government. It robbed it of an essential victory, and left the political agenda in the hands of the *Marji'iyya*. The Interim Government now had to scramble to regain the initiative. If it failed to do so, it would face a difficult electoral campaign which might well end in its defeat. Its problems were further compounded by the revival of the tensions in Fallujah, which increasingly began to be seen as the insurgents' capital. The Interim Government was now in a race against time to score a political victory that would strengthen its claim to the leadership of Iraq.

The Electoral Framework

The UN Security Council Resolution 1511 stipulated that Iraq's first-ever free and universal elections should be held by the end of 2004, and no later than 31 January, 2005. During the CPA's last few weeks, Bremer had signed Order 92 that authorised the creation of an election commission, the Independent Electoral Commission of Iraq (IEC). The IEC had a nine-member Board of Commissioners that included seven voting members who were Iraqi citizens, and two non-voting members.

The electoral law was embodied in another CPA order, Order 96, issued on 15 June, 2004. The key stipulation of the law was that Iraq would be treated as one electoral district rather than a series of constituencies or regionally based or provincially based electoral districts, to elect 275 members of a Transitional National Assembly. Sistani's office was unhappy about the CPA's choice of a single electoral district, which the CPA justified using a variety of considerations. Practically it would have been difficult to organise Iraq into electoral districts within the short time-frame allowed, given the absence of any census data or political agreements on the division of constituency boundaries. Another reason was the concern by senior CPA democracy and election advisers that a constituency-based election would produce a lopsided majority for the Islamists from both sects, and would seriously harm the prospects of liberal-minded groups and minorities.[1] The treatment of Iraq as a single electoral constituency obliged the political parties and groups to form alliances for the purpose of producing electoral lists. The CPA Order also called for every third candidate to be a woman. Whether this was done to promote gender equality, or whether in the hope that women would not favour the religious parties in the same ratio as men, was an open question. The latter smacked of the usual wishful thinking of CPA staffers and advisers, who tackled the 'women' issue in Iraq within the framework of western gender politics and the views of the few English-speaking, middle-class women professionals whom they came across.

Escalation in Insurgency Activity and the Elections

The autumn of 2004 saw a dramatic rise in the level of violence. In September and October 2004, there were more than thirty car bombs. More American soldiers had been killed in the three months since the transfer of sovereignty – 162 – than in the entire war.[2] The scope and scale of the attacks raised the question of whether elections could be held in such an atmosphere of relentless violence. In its early days, the Interim Government did not question the appropriateness of holding elections, even though insecurity was widespread. Rozh Shawys, the Kurdish vice-president, said that 'the next four months would provide sufficient time for positive developments to occur that would ensure free and fair and transparent elections.'[3] Ayad Allawi had also announced, in an earlier interview with the UK press, that violence would not lead to postponement of the elections. 'If 300,000 people are not able to vote because terrorists decided that, then frankly 300,000 people will not change the vote of 24 million people.'[4] But events during the next two months would sorely test the election dateline. Violence in Baghdad was continuing apace with a particularly horrific incident in Haifa Street, an insurgent stronghold near the Green Zone.[5] There, a Bradley-armoured vehicle was disabled by rocket-propelled grenade fire which led, inexplicably, to hovering US helicopters firing at civilians who were milling around the burning vehicle.

It was in Samarra, though, that the first crisis erupted after the Najaf confrontation had been defused by the Sistani initiative. The city had been rapidly falling out of control, and by September was considered an insurgent stronghold. Preparations to retake the city from the insurgents has been laid by the MNF for weeks previously. The plan was for the Interim Government to take the initiative, and show its commitment and willingness to participate in the security drive, with the MNF providing support and manning a cordon sanitaire around the city.[6] A further impetus for giving the Interim Government the lead in the Samarra action was the fact that the Minister of Interior, Falah al-Naqib, originated from Samarra and it was thought that his city and tribal affiliations would help the security forces in providing a coun-terweight to the insurgents. Great hope for a successful outcome on the part of the Interim Government was attached to the Samarra operation, with a clear message that it was in control and that the insurgents and foreign fighters were on the run. Several options were considered that would entail the deployment of Iraqi security forces in the lead in the retaking of the city. But the uncertain training and equally uncertain loyalty of the Iraqi troops continued to militate against the idea, which eventually was dropped. If the Iraqi forces failed to secure the city or, worse, disintegrated, the results would be calamitous.

The Interim Government promised control by November over all areas affected by insecurity and violence. Nearly 3,000 troops from the USA's First Infantry Division, backed by Iraqi National Guards forces and an Iraqi army battalion, seized the main buildings and installations of Samarra from insurgents after heavy fighting in which over 100 insurgents were killed. In reality, the victory was short-lived. Samarra had been 'liberated' many times during the past year, always to revert back to being heavily infiltrated by insurgents.

The evolution and spread of the insurgency was being met by a funda-mental reassessment of the MNF's military strategy. All talk of dead-enders and former regime elements gave way to a more sober assessment of the long-term threats that the insurgency posed to the political process. The belated recognition in Washington that the insurgency was only a part of a more generalised rejection by the Sunni Arabs of the post-invasion order in Iraq drove the reappraisal of the strategy. This was further reinforced by the political thinking of Ayad Allawi, who had all the time been calling for peeling off the foreign fighters and terrorists from the mainline insurgents, and enticing the latter into the political process.

An important element of his plan was the dismantling of de-Ba'athification – or at least limiting it to the absolute minimum of Saddam and his closest supporters, and to draw back into the new armed forces significant elements from the former regime's officer class. The new order that he envisaged was not necessarily a clone of the Ba'athist regime. It was more an alliance of groups that crossed ideological and sectarian boundaries, and formed the elements of a new political and ruling class. In foreign policy, the new Iraq would be strongly tied to the USA and to the USA's Middle Eastern security allies, including Jordan, Egypt and Pakistan. Iraq would have correct but limited relations with Iran. Islamists would be strictly restricted in terms of their access to power, and only allowed as a junior part of a ruling coalition. The *Marji'iyya* would be given its due status, but firmly kept from influencing the direction of political affairs. The ruling political elite would comprise 'reformed' Ba'athists, a professional and high-status officer class, and a group of apolitical technocrats in charge of the economy and the service ministries. Security would be provided through a revitalised intelligence apparatus, perhaps not as heavy-handed as before, but equally intrusive and pervasive. Tribes, or at least tribal leaders, would be co-opted into the process by the liberal use of large cash handouts. Economic policy would follow the pattern in countries such as Egypt, Tunisia or Morocco, which favour a few business tycoons, allied to the political class, who would be given access to state resources and preferential treatment in privatisations and licences. The leadership of the insurgents, and their Sunni Arab sympathisers, were offered a prominent, though not necessarily dominant, place in this framework. It was expected that they would accept these inducements to join the political process. Economic growth would be less than stellar; personal incomes would inch forward; liberties would be curtailed, but domestic stability would be ensured. In Washington, the resurgence of the familiar themes of stability and order in the Middle East ensured that this argument would find favour there.

The problem was that Iraq was about to launch an experiment in electoral democracy unique to its neighbourhood. The other countries where Allawi's model was pursued vigorously were either family-ruled autocracies or military-dominated dictatorships. The neo-conservative thesis was being quietly shed, if not yet fully discredited, and many in official Washington were coming around to seeing the 'virtues' of this model for Iraq. There were, however, two imponderables. The first was that progress in the political process was entirely dependent on the results of free and fair elections. This introduced the element of unpredictability into the outcome where radically different visions for Iraq would be contending for power. The second was that the main message underpinning the justification of the USA's presence in Iraq, now that WMD were no longer an issue, was the promotion of democracy – wherever this might lead. This created tensions between the desire for control and stability, and the willingness to accept the outcome of elections. Ayad Allawi's plan ran a serious risk of being derailed if the elections could not be 'managed' or delayed.

The Second Fallujah Crisis

The Interim Government was preoccupied with trying to reconcile conflicting objectives in a crowded agenda within a short space of time. It had promised to regain control of insurgent-held areas, and portrayed the retaking of Samarra in this vein. It now had to deal with the even more entrenched insurgency in Fallujah, which had grown far beyond the levels of the previous April, when the Coalition handed control over the city to the ill-starred Fallujah Brigade. The capture of Fallujah, however, perfectly illustrated the Interim Government's dilemma. The rooting out of insurgents was obviously a matter of great national interest. In any case, the MNF command was determined to retake the city and was pressing Ayad Allawi to acquiesce to a large-scale assault on the city.[7] The fighting was expected to result in high civilian casualties and large-scale destruction, which would most certainly incense wavering Sunni Arab opinion, an important constituency in the electoral strategy of Ayad Allawi. The Najaf crisis had ended in a debacle for the Interim Government, and permanently alienated large sections of Shi'a opinion. The image of the strong state that the Interim Government wanted to project was now flying in the face of the difficult trade-offs that had to be made.

The assault on Fallujah by the MNF was a long time in preparation. In September, the Interim Government had invited the Fallujah Shura Council, a coordinating body of the city's main civic and political groups, to talks in Baghdad aimed at ensuring the insurgents left the city.[8] The talks led nowhere. The media machine of the MNF had been announcing that Zarqawi and his group were holed up in the city and that retaking it would have a lethal impact on his capabilities and operations. A harsh rule was imposed on the city, leading many observers to talk of the 'Talibanisation' of Fallujah. Foreign fighters – Saudis, Tunisians, Lebanese and Syrians – had played a vital role in defending the city during the April siege by the US Marines. They stayed on in the city, dominating entire neighbourhoods by their armed presence.

As the MNF attack became inevitable, the foreign fighters mainly slipped away, as did the leading Iraqi insurgent leaders such as Sheikh Abdullah al-Janabi.[9] General Thomas Metz, commander of the MNF ground forces in Iraq, confirmed this by saying, 'I personally believe some of the senior leaders probably have fled'.[10] The population of Fallujah also fled. The Emergency Working Group for Fallujah (EWG), which grouped a variety of international humanitarian agencies and Interim Government ministries, estimated that out of Fallujah's normal population of 300,000, about 250,000 had fled, creating a crisis of internally displaced people. Most congregated in nearby towns and villages, as well as the western parts of Baghdad such as the heavily Sunni 'Amariya district, awaiting the outcome of the battle. Even so, 50,000 inhabitants stayed resolutely on in the city.[11]

The battle for Fallujah started on 7 November, 2004, when the MNF and Iraqi government support forces sealed off the town as well as nearby Ramadi city, the capital of Anbar province.[12] All water and electricity services to Fallujah were cut off. All men under the age of 45 were restricted from leaving the city. That night, the Iraqi National Guards' 36th Commando battalion attacked from the west and south of the city, capturing the general hospital. Shortly thereafter, on the morning of 8 November, four Marine battalions and two US Army mechanised cavalry battalions launched their attack on a broad front. By the following day the city had fallen into American hands, although fighting continued until the middle of the month. The insurgents apparently divided their forces in the city. About half stayed on to fight to the death.[13] The other half slipped away to fight another day. Insurgents fought in small teams, and relied on snipers to slow down the American advance. But there was no doubt about the outcome. The USA brought massive firepower to bear and pulverised insurgents holding out in buildings and mosques.[14] The damage to Fallujah was extensive. Nearly 60 of the city's 200 mosques had been destroyed. The MNF claimed that sixty-six mosques were discovered to hold insurgents' weapons caches. Half the city's homes were totally destroyed or suffered serious damage. Casualties on the US side were relatively heavy. Ninety-two Americans were killed, as were eight Iraqi security forces. Insurgent fighters killed, however, numbered over 1,200, and a further 1,000 were taken prisoner. The MNF was accused of using banned chemical weapons such as white phosphorus and incendiary bombs, a charge denied by the State Department but subsequently indirectly confirmed by the Department of Defense.

Sunni Arab Boycott of the Elections

The political fallout of the Fallujah battle was grave. Even though the Americans had planned and led the operation, Ayad Allawi, as prime minister of a nominally sovereign country, tried to maintain the impression that it was he who had given the final order to start the battle. The Islamic Party of Iraq withdrew from the government.[15] The Association of Muslim Scholars (AMS) went one step further by demanding that the forthcoming elections be boycotted. In fact the AMS had met in late October and had promised to boycott the elections if Fallujah were to be attacked. A momentum was developing amongst Iraq's Sunni Arabs to boycott the elections, thereby implicitly threatening the legitimacy of the vote.

The military objectives of the Fallujah battle were clear. The city was recaptured for the central government, the insurgents routed, and the preponderance of the MNF in any set battle was determined. There was also an element of Marine retribution for the incomplete operation in April that had badly backfired and had allowed the insurgents to regroup. But the political benefits that were supposed to accrue from the retaking of Fallujah began to seem distant. In fact, the entire episode was yet another manifestation of improper political planning and predictions that were widely off the mark. The retaking of the city neither crippled the insurgency nor led to the capture of its leading figures. The thought that 'taming' an insurgency stronghold would make holding the elections a safer proposition was preposterous. The idea that somehow hitting at Sunni extremists would separate the cooperative Sunni from the belligerent Sunni was a fundamental misunderstanding of the insurgency. The withdrawal of the Islamic Party of Iraq from the government was met with great dismay. It was the cornerstone of the USA's strategy of co-opting Sunni groups into the new political order. The attack on Fallujah, however, crystallised growing concerns amongst the Sunni Arabs that the dice were loaded against them in the upcoming elections, especially as the Shi'a were rallying to the *Marji'iyya*'s call for a united Shi'a front. The argument within the Sunni Arab community as to whether to boycott or participate in the elections was in fact settled by the Fallujah operation. By the time it was over, calls were being raised from nearly all Sunni quarters, even those sympathetic to the new order, to postpone the elections, if only for a few months. The Islamic Party of Iraq demanded that the elections be postponed for six months, so that they could be held under more auspicious conditions. Only a few Sunni figures or groups, those who consciously refused to identify themselves in sectarian terms, or those who were entrenched in the Interim Government's power structure, still called for holding the elections on their due date.

Sistani and a United Shi'a Electoral list

The elections for the constitutional assembly were the first occasion on which Iraq's Shi'a could demonstrate their numerical superiority and political preponderance and represented their best chance to determine the constitutional make-up of the country. Their anticipation of and expectations for the elections were diametrically opposed to the Sunni's fears and anxieties about these very same elections. Grand Ayatollah Sistani had insisted on elections as the only legitimate way forward. By the end of the summer of 2004, elections were no longer a distant possibility, and the mechanics of building winning coalitions loomed as the key challenge ahead. The *Marji'iyya* was aware that it had to tread a very fine line between political impartiality, non-intervention and making clear its concern about the broad outlines of a future Iraqi state. A silent war was launched for the *Marji'iyya*'s ear. Shi'a secularists and advocates of a strong, centralised state such as Ayad Allawi called for the *Marji'iyya*'s non-involvement, or at least its neutrality, in the upcoming elections. They held Sistani to account for his apparent advocacy of the principle of keeping the *Marji'iyya* away from politics. On the other hand, Shi'a activists and political figures wanted the direct involvement of the *Marji'iyya* in the elections, either by supporting particular groups or parties or by mobilising its resources to ensure a massive voter turnout. There was little doubt that the *Marji'iyya* would see the constitutional assembly elections as a watershed in the history of Iraq, and a critical step in the political emancipation of the Shi'a. They would not countenance a complete detachment from the political arena at this stage of the process. However the *Marji'iyya*'s reputation would be indelibly tarnished if it were to make the wrong policy choice. But the political quietism that so many expected or wanted from the *Marji'iyya* was not apparent.

Sistani built his roadmap for the elections in a deliberate and measured manner. There could be no viable electoral strategy for any avowedly Shi'a group without reference to Sistani and the *Marji'iyya*. All the main political groups trekked to Najaf to coordinate their actions with his office and find out the direction he was leaning towards. In mid-September, Sistani called for a meeting at his home with the other three grand ayatollahs, Muhammad Said al-Hakim, Ishaq Fayyadh and Bashir al-Najafi.[16] The meeting was also attended by SCIRI's leader Sayyid Abd el-Aziz al-Hakim. Sistani's office issued a general statement calling for 'holding the general elections in the country on their due date [in January 2005], broadening public participation and remedying the problems in the laws governing elections and political parties'.[17] A few days later Sistani met the representative of the Karbala-based Islamic Action Party, who claimed that the *Marji'iyya* would back a single electoral list if the Shi'a parties and groups produced such a list.[18] In an interview in *al-Hayat* in the same period, another leading cleric denied the existence of such a list, or even that the *Marji'iyya* had called for such a thing. He did say, however, that the main political and religious figures of the Shi'a would welcome such an initiative on the part of the *Marji'iyya*.[19]

All the same, an alternative proposal to a unified Shi'a list was being hatched. It was based on a grand alliance between the main political groups inside the old Governing Council, in fact reverting to the pre-invasion pact between SCIRI, the INA and the Kurdish parties. The main proponent of such an electoral alliance was SCIRI's Adel Abd el-Mahdi, the Interim Government's minister of finance. Mahdi was quoted as saying, 'The goal is to have a united front. We think that would be better for the unity of the country.'[20] Several political parties, including the Da'awa Party, were approached to join this project.[21] Sistani was deeply concerned by this alternative electoral plan for the Shi'a. He reckoned that the proposal would allow a cabal of politicians to hijack the elections, and gravely affect the Shi'a's constitutional rights as a prospective majority. A single party list, the core of which was Mahdi's tripod, would accommodate most of the political parties, but within a formula that would seriously under-represent the Shi'a. Sistani also believed that under the guise of insecure conditions and a possible Sunni boycott, the elections would be likely to be postponed to improve the chances of the 'grand alliance' if this were to come about. He expressed his fears to the UN's Lakhdar Brahimi and sought Brahimi's return to Iraq to address his concerns at these twin developments. He even went so far as to threaten that he would withdraw his support for the elections and declare them to be illegitimate.[22]

The *Marji'iyya*, faced with the possibility that the elections, upon which they had pinned so much hope, would be stifled by a single, all-party list, redoubled their efforts to push the quarrelling Shi'a political leaders into a *Marji'iyya*-backed list of their own. They also intensified their statements regarding the inviolability of the elections and the impermissibility of their postponement. Grand Ayatollah Ishaq Fayyadh issued a statement in early October linking improvement in security conditions 'with the holding of elections as elections will lead to a free and democratic government.'[23] Similarly, Grand Ayatollah Muhammad Said al-Hakim's son and spokesman, Muhammad Hussein, held a press conference where he stated that 'The elections will hold the destiny of the Iraqi people, because they will be held for the first time in their modern history.'[24] The next step in the *Marji'iyya*'s campaign to guide the election process was to mobilise the Shi'a rank-and-file to cast their votes as a religious obligation. Sayyid Ahmad al-Safi, one of Sistani's closest aides, in a Friday sermon in Karbala on 22 October, called for a heavy turnout, and labelled abstention from voting a form of high treason.[25] Participation in the elections, he said, 'has religious sanctity and abstention [from voting] will throw the transgressor into hellfire'.

The United Iraqi Alliance

The genesis of the United Iraqi Alliance (UIA) as an umbrella group for the Shia came from inside the *Marji'iyya* itself. According to Muhammed Redha Sistani, the Grand Ayatollah's son, the idea had been germinating in the *Marji'iyya*'s minds for several months.[26] Sistani adopted the principle that the UIA should act as the electoral vehicle for the Shi'a and should continue in any post-election government as a unified grouping that would govern the country and steer the writing of a new constitution through the assembly. Sistani's decision to back the UIA essentially put paid to any alternative political proposal, and the main Shi'a parties scurried to join in the deliberations for the new alliance.

A six-man committee was appointed, headed by Sistani himself, to hammer out the principles that would form the basis of the new alliance, and to bring the main Islamist parties closer. The main issue was how to fit the ambitions and claims of the various parties and individuals into an acceptable list for the 275 seats of the new assembly. This was far more problematic than the electoral programme which, by and large, followed the moderate Islamist tinge that marked the orientation of most of the established political groups. Sistani did not want to see the UIA dominated by the established parties, and early on decided that half of the UIA candidates should be independents unaffiliated to any of the political parties and groups. (Ayad Allawi had been approached to join the alliance, but showed no interest in being part of a Sistani-led political grouping.)

The six-man committee agreed on a formula that would allocate roughly equal shares to the main Islamist groups. The 'Shi'a Political Council' that Ahmad Chalabi had helped to organise and that grouped small Shi'a factions was also assigned a stake. Every third candidate was a woman. The selection of the 'independents' also had to be approved by the main political parties. Most were subsequently organised around the person of Hussein Shahristani, and formed a distinct faction inside the UIA. Moqtada al-Sadr's position on the elections was extremely ambiguous. While accepting a major stake in the UIA slate, he hedged his bets by having a number of other candidates running on separate tickets, including the one most closely associated with his movement, the Elites and Cadres list. But his signals to the Sunni community were that elections should be postponed while the fighting continued and Iraq remained under occupation. Eventually he announced that while he saw no purpose in participating in elections, he would not stop his supporters from forming their own tickets or joining the UIA. Sadr was planning to maximise his gains and was keeping all his options open.[27] On 8 December, 2004, the UIA formally announced its electoral list. It consisted of two hundred and twenty-eight candidates, headed by Abd el-Aziz al-Hakim of SCIRI. All the main Shi'a Islamist politicians and leaders were included. There was also a smattering of Sunni, mainly from the Mosul area, to give the ticket the semblance of inclusiveness. They were brought in mainly by Ahmad Chalabi. Shi'a leaders were jubilant about the UIA, sensing that it was the chosen vehicle to deliver them from decades, if not centuries, of disempowerment. 'We consider that this alliance has really made a historic impact on Iraqi society,' said Hussein Shahristani. 'This is a historic moment for the birth of a new, democratic and just Iraq.' [28]

Ayad Allawi, the Kurds and Calls to Postpone the Elections

But as the UIA list was being put together, rumblings became louder about the necessity to postpone the elections. The decision of the Iraqi Electoral Commission (IEC) to include non-resident Iraqis in the electoral register was interpreted as a measure to load the rolls in favour of the Kurds and the Shi'a, who constituted the largest part of the exiled community. The figures of exiled Iraqis were unreliable, but the International Organisation for Migration, which was helping the IEC to organise the elections abroad, estimated that there were about one-and-a-half million Iraqi voters abroad. The largest such concentrations were in Iran. This was interpreted as another measure to create a lopsided Shi'a majority that would alienate the Sunni Arabs from participating in the elections. In addition, the Fallujah battle and its aftermath further embittered Sunni opinion, and the prospects of a wide-scale Sunni boycott of the elections became real. The pressure to postpone the elections began to build up.

The Interim Government – or at least Ayad Allawi – was still calling for elections to be held on their due date, however. Barham Saleh, the Kurdish Deputy Prime Minister, regularly reaffirmed the Interim Government's commitment to elections, clearly reflecting the Kurds' insistence on holding them according to the TAL timeline. But other prominent figures in the Interim Government such as the Minister of Defence, Hazem Sha'alan, doubted they could be held on time, and cited the security situation in support of his contention. The forces that were now ranged in favour of postponing the elections could point to a number of justifications for their case: ensuring Sunni participation; producing a more 'balanced' electoral register; improving security considerations. There was also the deep anxiety that was felt about the true strength of the UIA, and whether the Shi'a would vote en bloc for it. This was greatly felt by Ayad Allawi who was putting together his own electoral list, the 'Iraqi List', and though aspiring to be non-sectarian and secular, competed for votes from the same broad Shi'a pool. Though Sistani would not publicly come out in support of any particular list, it was clear that his supporters and deputies would be pulling in the votes for the UIA.

With the increasing likelihood of a widespread boycott of the elections by Sunni-based parties, Ayad Allawi was offering a home for the secular Shi'a voter and the Sunni voter who did not believe in boycotting the elections. His electoral strategy was based on projecting his profile as a strong leader, with the potential of uniting the country behind a modernising and secular agenda. He knew that he could not seriously compete for the vote of the religious Shi'a but his calculations were that a large number of the Shi'a would be sufficiently concerned about clerical control, Iranian influence and the sectarian drift of Iraqi political life to vote for him en masse. It was a carefully crafted strategy, whose underlying premises would be soon tested. He would have much preferred a grand alliance of political parties with a single, dominating, slate, but this was torpedoed by Sistani. Joining the UIA list would have put him in an unwelcome or uncomfortable subordinate position to the preponderant Islamists and ultimately the *Marji'iyya*. Sistani himself had been consulted on the invitation to Allawi to join the UIA ticket and had raised no objection. There were rumours that Allawi would have been offered the premiership in the event of such a broad UIA ticket coming into office, but he knew that the UIA slate would not have been his natural political home. This was also understood by the main leaders of the UIA.[29] On 16 December, Ayad Allawi unveiled his programme in which he promised to work for national unity and away from 'religious and ethnic fanaticism'.[30]

The Kurds had decided early on to form a united list of all the main political parties in Kurdistan – the Kurdistan Alliance – anchored on the KDP and PUK, each with a third of the candidates on the list, to fight the elections. The Kurds anticipated that the constitutional assembly would need to tackle issues that were of momentous consequences for the Kurdish region. The need to maintain a united front, at least as it related to the constitutional status of Kurdistan in a future Iraq, overrode any special party interest. The Kurds relied on the scrupulous application of the TAL and the milestones that were embedded in it, foremost of which was the presentation of a draft constitution to a referendum by 15 October, 2005. The Kurds had also aspired to cement their status in the central government by lobbying for the post of president in the post-election transitional government.

The grand alliance that had been proposed by Abd el-Mahdi would have well suited the aspirations of the Kurds. They were more comfortable in dealing with known political quantities, and it was clear that in any power-sharing deal with the other main parties of the grand alliance they would have maintained their privileged status, as all sought to gain their support and goodwill. The formation of the UIA encouraged them, on the one hand, to pursue their own united list, but it also raised the spectre of a united Shi'a bloc, under the general supervision of the *Marji'iyya*, which had frequently

looked unfavourably at the idea of federalism in general and Kurdish 'exceptionalism' in particular. The struggle over article 61(c) of the TAL, where the
Marji'iyya was incensed about the extent of minority rights that were
conceded, was too recent an experience. The possibility that they might have
to deal with a UIA that was beholden to the Najaf religious hierarchy was an
irritant and a source of anxiety for the Kurds, and drove them further into
consolidating their electoral effort. A number of backdoor proposals were
floated about the possibility of a pre-electoral pact between the UIA and the
Kurdistan Front, but these fell foul of the *Marji'iyya*'s wish to see the members
of the new national assembly unfettered by secret deals and prior commitments. The Kurds' own intelligence was far more sanguine about the electoral
prospects of the UIA, and their plans were based on a UIA sweep of the Shi'a
vote. Others, including intelligence reports and professional western pollsters,
were predicting a very strong showing by Ayad Allawi's Iraqi List. One poll
gave the secularist parties 60 per cent of the vote, with the UIA at 40 per cent.

The campaign to postpone the elections was bolstered by musings of
American and British officials about the incompleteness of the elections if
the Sunni Arabs were to stay away in droves. The Americans began to
explore means by which the number of Sunni Arabs in the new assembly
could be increased through a formula that guaranteed them a fixed
percentage of seats.[31] In addition, removing some of the obstacles in the
face of potential candidates who had been Ba'ath Party members was also
mooted, including renunciation of previous affiliations. The *Marji'iyya* did
its best to stop a momentum for postponing elections from gathering pace.
'We have to deal with the security situation in Iraq, but not through the
postponement of elections. It has to be dealt with by other means,' said
Hussein Shahristani.[32]

The call to postpone the elections was embraced by Arab leaders who were
fearful of a lopsided UIA victory. However, the milestone-driven strategy of
the USA placed a huge premium on meeting the set dates in the political
process, and this was the first popular and democratic test for the efficacy of
the new order. The Islamic Party of Iraq, which had walked out of the government as a result of the Fallujah crisis, quietly formed its own list of candidates,
and indicated that it might participate in the elections. But seeing itself out of
sync with the trend in Sunni opinion, it withdrew its list from the elections.
There would be no Sunni Arab party contesting the election, apart from the
minor groups around the president, Ghazi al-Yawar's '*Iraqiyun*' list and Adnan
al-Pachachi's liberal and democratic list, which appealed to the small secular
and urbanised middle classes of Iraq.

The electoral prospects of the potentially fractious UIA did not rest on the
cumulative popularity of its constituent groups. Rather, its success would

hinge on two major assumptions. The first was that the mass of the Shi'a would respond to the call of the *Marji'iyya* in ways that would transcend their particular political, regional or ideological perspectives. The second was that the Shi'a would intuitively recognise the historic importance of these elections as the best chance they would have of reversing their community's legacy of disempowerment. None of the public opinion polls addressed these two critical points. Time and again the polls would show that the majority of Iraqis – frequently over 70 per cent – favoured a 'religious' state, but the correct inference was never drawn from these results.[33] Ayad Allawi was described as being 'effective' or 'somewhat effective' as prime minister by over 60 per cent of the sample. It was therefore assumed that his list would at least receive a major share of the vote. The opinion polls did not capture the burning issues of the times. For the Kurds there was no doubt that they would vote strictly in favour of the Kurdistan Alliance. For the Shi'a, the complex questions of identity, religious loyalty, Iraqi patriotism, fear of the return of the Ba'athists, were all mixed together in different measures. Ayad Allawi was banking on the desire for order, security, Arab identity and material progress to push the Shi'a (and Sunni) voters in his direction. It was not a bad strategy, but it missed the *zeitgeist*.

20

Corruption and the Potemkin State

'There is a sense, frankly, that there was some degree of corruption.' –

Lt General David Petraeus, Head of the MNF Training Support
Command, October, 2005

'It seems hard to understand to an outsider that this stuff could go on under our noses and Americans wouldn't know anything about it. But clearly, we didn't know everything.' –

US military official discussing the corruption charges at the
Ministry of Defence

In a probably apocryphal story, Catherine the Great's minister, Grigori Potemkin, was said to have erected a series of hollow facades showing prosperous villages along the Empress's route in the Crimea. The Crimea had been recently added to her empire. These facades were meant to fool the Empress into believing that the country was well-administered and the peasantry happy and thriving.[1] The Iraqi state that the CPA bequeathed to the sovereign Iraqi government was just such a hollow construct. The administrative machinery had been imploding over the past decade-and-a-half, a process further distorted by the CPA hiatus. Nevertheless, the state was deemed to be a functioning, purposeful and decisive entity. Bombastic statements were made by ministers about imminent improvements in services, about the launching of massive reconstruction work, about the build-up of the armed forces, but none of these claims had any substantive basis. Neither the ministers nor the bureaucracies over which they presided could deliver a fraction of what they had publicly promised. Iraqis were used to seeing the state provide them not only with jobs but also with the basic necessities of life. Ministers had an exalted status and their pronouncements were always given serious play. There was no alternative for the average citizen but to believe in the promises of the government. When their hopes were dashed, they would pin new hopes on the next set of ministers. With no civil society to speak of and little opportunity for work in the private sector, it was no wonder that Iraqis continued, against hope, to rely on their state and its promises. But the Iraqi state combined the worst features of a centralised bureaucracy with vestiges of the occupation, and a near collapse of the information, reporting and control mechanisms that underpin any functioning government authority. The legacy of corrupt practices, outdated management systems, incompetence and nepotism was neither seriously challenged nor bypassed. The CPA's appalling mismanagement of the country was handed over to the incoming administration. The foreign staff had mostly left, but a new administrative and political nexus was being assembled around the US Embassy and its agencies. Policy and administration in Iraq became even more fragmented under the Interim Government, beset as it was by never-ending security challenges. Under these conditions of jumbled reporting lines, policy confusion, legal limbo, uncertain mandates and corrupt agendas, the Iraqi state was degraded even further.

Administrative Failures and Inadequacies of the Iraqi Government

The 'capacity' issue was the catch-all word that implied that the Iraqi government was not necessarily what it was cut out to be. The word was used extensively by the battery of consultants who were employed to effect everything, from a national development strategy to the regeneration of the date-palm industry. The situation of a sovereign government that by and large was incapable of administering the state was camouflaged by behind-the-scenes efforts by foreign advisers to hammer out policy and programme positions covering a bewildering array of sectors. These would be passed off as Iraqi government initiatives, often translated verbatim into a strange 'techno-Arabic', without any serious internal discussions.[2] These reviews were probably pointless, in any case, as few in the bureaucracy understood, accepted, or appreciated their importance. A rearguard action was often fought by senior bureaucrats, frequently leftovers from the former Ba'ath regime, to block action on these expensively generated proposals. Incoming ministers, frequently former exiles, would also populate the ministries with their own cronies, placed in senior positions of power for which they were patently unsuited. This further exacerbated confusion and bureaucratic resentment, as those people pushed their own priorities, whether corrupt, political or simply technically or philosophically different. Failed former petty traders became senior advisers; adventurers and bankrupts ended up in charge of huge departmental budgets.[3] All this in the face of senior officials who prided themselves on 'knowing' how the Iraqi government operated and believed that only they had the skills to operate the machinery of government.

In as much as the USA and its allies had to accept the notional sovereignty of the government, they had to deal with the 'free' choice of the Iraqi government in selecting its own set of ministers, senior officials and advisers. Civil service recruitment standards were non-existent. Serious reform or restructuring proposals produced by foreign advisers languished until a forceful or accommodating minister would adopt them. If they were sufficiently important, however, they would become part of the agenda that the US ambassador or senior Washington officials would discuss with their Iraqi counterparts or with the prime minister. They would then be presented as a matter of great urgency, and government decision-makers would be manoeuvred into adopting them as Iraqi proposals. The end result was a curious mixture of initiatives that had little or no resonance with either the population's pressing needs or the real issue of structural reform.

The USA and its allies, mainly Britain, after June 2004, had to navigate through the murky institutions of the Iraqi government, pushing, cajoling and warning, if necessary, while paying something more than lip service to the sovereign government. The Interim Government, on the other hand, quickly understood the need to accept and adopt those policies that the Coalition deemed imperative. Otherwise, the Interim Government had a free hand in pursuing what they thought were important issues. In security matters, there was little or no debate. The Iraqi government simply did not have the data or resource base to be able to counteract any MNF proposals, initiatives or suggestions. Intelligence was entirely with the MNF, as the Iraqi Intelligence Services under Shahwani continued to report to the CIA. The basis for an alternative government policy would have had to be inadequate intelligence gathering and assessment of the political parties or security ministries. The latter were in no position to provide detached and objective information. In other fields, such as the economy, a few key issues were considered vital by the Coalition, mainly those related to Iraq's international economic relations and indebtedness. The lead in these matters was invariably taken by the US Treasury, which hovered around the Iraqi authorities, gingerly shepherding their every step. Other important US-initiated proposals, for example the reform of the Iraqi government's management procedures and the introduction of IT-based reporting and information systems, were not adopted or implemented speedily because of bureaucratic inertia, resistance or unwillingness to accept change. The USAID, in this instance, would plough ahead with its consultants, hoping that the government would sooner or later recognise the significance of these measures.

The transfer of control over Iraq's funds at the Development Fund for Iraq (DFI) was seen as an important milestone in the transfer of sovereignty to the Iraqi government. At the time, this was hailed as removing a major constraint on the Iraqi government's abilities to fashion, and implement, major reform and reconstruction programmes. A great deal of hope was riding on the Interim Government, as it was home-grown and supposedly more aware than the CPA of the nuances of the country's affairs. This perception was nurtured not only by Iraqi politicians but also by foreign advocates, who believed in the indigenous running of the country. An Iraqi-led government would be savvier than the CPA, more attuned to the needs of the people, more able to manage the complex politics of the country, more able to navigate the bureaucracy and deliver the goods. For all its faults and shortcomings, sooner or later the CPA had to account in detail for the disposition of Iraq's funds. The CPA's handling of the Development Fund was ultimately controlled by the US Congress together with a host of other related agencies and authorities. Once a sovereign Iraq government took over, however, the accountability nexus changed. The UN did establish a monitoring board over the Development Fund, the International Advisory and Monitoring Board (International Advisory Board), but this had limited powers to apply sanctions on either the CPA or subsequent Iraqi governments. The task of accounting for the proper management and use of Iraq's resources fell on nascent or weak Iraqi government overseeing bodies. Not infrequently, these were intimidated by the power of senior politicians and by the costs and complexity of the hundreds, if not thousands, of cases of incorrect financial dealings brought to their attention – some real, but a great many more completely spurious.

The enabling environment for the proper exercise of the powers of the state's oversight institutions was simply not there. The Office of the Inspector Generals, the Integrity Commission, the Bureau of Supreme Audit, and the judiciary were all, in one way or another, groping to find their role in the post-invasion order.[4] Their effectiveness in combating corruption was untested. However, the weaknesses of the state institutions of accountability and enforcement do not, in and of themselves, explain the explosion in corrupt practices, bordering on the open plunder of the state's resources, which accompanied the transfer of sovereignty. A more complete explanation has to include the legacy systems inherited from the Saddamist years. More importantly, it was the appalling ethical standards of those who were catapulted to positions of power and authority that must carry most of the obloquy. Most of these came from exile, most had had western training, and most held advanced degrees of one form or another. The naïve belief that an advanced education or exposure to western societies would somehow improve ethical standards in government was hopelessly misplaced.[5] The Brahimi government of technocrats changed into something entirely different. The Interim

Government did not invent corruption, neither could its successor govern-ments claim to have clean hands, but it did preside over a veritable avalanche of corrupt practices, some breathtaking in their range and size.

The Reconstitution of Corrupt Networks

The key to the enabling of large-scale corruption during the Interim Government was the re-weaving of the Saddam-era OFF complex of suppliers, banks and middlemen. The new mechanisms for siphoning off state resources did not necessarily mimic the old set of protagonists. But certain central institutions, such as the banking systems of Jordan and Lebanon, which had served the *ancien régime* well in hiding the rake-offs in the OFF programme, were drafted into the new dispensation.[6] At the same time, important middlemen based in Jordan, the UAE and Lebanon surfaced under the Interim Government to run the state supply contracts, now with new partners. These were the same people who had actually run the contracts for the old order. The OFF programme in the Saddam era was run, on the Iraqi side, by a few senior bureaucrats in the Ministry of Trade, the Ministry of Finance, the Central Bank, the Planning Ministry, and the State Oil Marketing Organisation (SOMO). Between them, they formed an insider cabal reporting to Taha Yassin Ramadhan, Saddam's deputy and henchman. The entire oper-ation had been supervised by the former *Mukhabarat*, Saddam's intelligence services, which kept tabs on where the money was flowing. The system relied on favoured suppliers who were prepared to over-invoice the Iraqis and then kickback the extra revenues into bank accounts held by individuals as proxies for the Iraqi government.[7] The extra cash would then be shipped back to Baghdad in sealed metal boxes, some of which would be seized at the border by Saddam's wayward son, Uday, for his own purposes.

Although the system generated huge cash flows, up to half a billion dollars per annum from essential imports alone, leakages were few as the *Mukhabarat* supervised closely. From time to time greedy middlemen, who may have dipped into the cash pot, would find themselves coming under the *Mukhabarat*'s lethal attention. The CPA did not seriously undermine the cohesion of this cabal, although individual ministers at Trade, Finance and Oil did try to dismantle their respective parts of the Saddamist insider network. A number of officials were removed from their positions, including a senior Ministry of Trade linchpin. In their eagerness to complete their ministerial line-up, which drew on 'technocrats' from the Saddamist years, Brahimi and Blackwill, wittingly or otherwise, brought in cabinet ministers who had been involved in the administration of the OFF programme. It was at the Ministry of Trade that the process of partially re-establishing the old networks would begin. A number of officials who had been dismissed or had retired on

cism from the media and the public for its consistent failure to meet its self-proclaimed targets. The auditors' report on its disbursement procedures was scathing. The Ministry of Electricity was unable to provide the auditors with bidding and award documentation for contracts valued at more than $245 million. No justification whatsoever could be provided for a further $229 million in contract awards.

High-level corruption was also suspected in the Ministries of Transport, Housing and Labour, and Social Affairs. The Ministry of Transport chartered, at huge mark-ups, aged aircrafts for the national carrier, Iraqi Airways, from Jordan-based leasing companies belonging to Saddam-era businessmen. This was visibly scandalous, as travellers had to ride on Boeing-727s dating from the early 1970s, which were barely airworthy. Iraqis became accustomed to the rickety planes that formed the Iraqi Airways 'fleet', while being fed with justifications about the difficulties in finding suitable aircraft for the dangerous flight to Baghdad. The Iraqi Airways crew who had to fly these planes were openly contemptuous of their nominal employer, the Ministry of Transport, for agreeing to lease and fly these planes. The Minister of Transport himself, a French-educated engineer, Louay al-'Iriss, fled the country before the end of the Interim Government's tenure. An international arrest warrant was later issued for him.[10]

It was clear that these massive transfers outside the control of Iraqi government institutions were part of a deliberate plan to undertake purchases of vital supplies without running the risk of being held accountable by Iraqi oversight institutions. The incidence of such transfers dramatically fell in the second half of the Interim Government's tenure, between the January and May 2005 period. The Interim Government ceased to be a fully empowered government after the January 2005 elections, and continued to act only in a caretaker capacity while the Transitional National Government was being organised. The auditors' report to the International Advisory Board for the period of January to June 2005 did not record any large or serious infringements of Iraqi government procurement rules. The implication was that the ministers concerned no longer felt that they had sufficient legal cover to continue brazenly to violate the procurement rules of the Iraqi state on the often unwarranted grounds of a national emergency. The auditors' reports were released towards the end of the Interim Government's tenure as a caretaker government, in April 2005. By that time, the damage had been done and the public and the media were too immersed in other issues and crises to pay much attention to the arcane disclosures of international auditors. Just after the formation of the Transitional National Government, a number of former Interim Government ministers fled the country, one step ahead of arrest warrants that were being prepared against them. A number of senior politicians such as Adnan al-Pachachi attributed this flight to the fear of score-settling by the new government.[11] Others claimed that these ministers feared for their lives from insurgents, given that their level of protection would be drastically reduced now that they had become ex-ministers. The scale of the wrongdoing that was exposed by the KPMG auditors, and later by Iraqi investigative bodies, was such, however, that there was a prima facie case of corrupt practices against a majority of the absconding ministers.

Another case of massive fraud was unearthed in the contracts awarded for the protection of the oil pipelines running from the Northern oil fields in Kirkuk to the refinery complex in the Baiji area, and to Turkey.[12] Mishaan al-Jubouri, a former regime operative and rumoured cigarette-smuggling kingpin working with Uday, Saddam Hussein's son, was approached by the Ministry of Defence to help in organising battalions to guard the oil pipelines. Initially, his role had been restricted to helping in nominating and recruiting officers and soldiers from the tribal areas through which the pipeline passed. The revised military doctrine that was being pursued by the MNF was that it would be more effective if pipeline security were given to tribal levies. They, it was claimed, would have a greater commitment to protecting these facilities, since they ran through their own tribal territory. But the theory was often belied by the practice. Local recruits, either independently or in partnership with insurgents, would scheme to disrupt the pipelines, both to justify the need for their 'protective' services and out of sympathy with the insurgents' cause. Jubouri extended his remit to the point where he had become the effective commanding officer of these battalions. According to the investigative committee's report on this affair, between January and October 2005, Jubouri siphoned off the first month's salaries of all the battalions, padded the battalion payrolls by up to 30 per cent, and took over the catering contracts – over-charging by up to 90 per cent for the food supplies. There was also a connection between the pipeline protection force and the insurgents. One of Jubouri's recruits, a battalion commander, was arrested and accused of organising attacks on the very pipelines he was supposed to protect. The Jubouri incident, however, which led to arrest warrants being issued for himself and his son, paled into insignificance compared to the rackets that were tearing up Iraq's oil industry and its misguided fuel imports programme.

Graft and Theft in the Oil Industry

The endemic corruption in the oil industry predated the Interim Government and continued unchecked into the Transitional National Government. A culture of secrecy and bureaucratic condoning of smuggling was carried over from the Saddam era into the post-invasion Iraqi administrations. The Oil Ministry was notorious for its opaque practices, and for being a historically elitist organisation that saw itself as both separate and above the ordinary ministries of the Iraqi government. To some extent this may have been warranted, given the signal importance of the oil industry. The best and brightest of students were selected for scholarships and advanced study abroad, destined for stellar careers as oil industry technocrats and administrators. In fact Iraq's main cadres of chartered accountants and financial analysts were not, as one might expect, to be found in the Central Bank or the Ministry of Finance but in the Oil Ministry, and similarly for a whole range of engineering and management talent. The *esprit de corps* in the ministry was always high, as the staff formed a charmed and privileged circle on the firmament of Iraqi bureaucracy. In contrast to the prevailing practices in other government departments, especially as the former regime became more dictatorial, participation in international conferences, liberal travel allowances, access to foreign technical and specialist publications, were all made freely available to oil ministry functionaries. No regime, no matter how brutal or incompetent, would mess with the oil industry, not even the Ba'athists, who tolerated the presence of 'apolitical' technocrats in high offices inside the oil ministry. The professionalism and competence of the Iraqi Oil Ministry, in its heyday, were well known and acknowledged in industrial circles worldwide.

All of this would unravel in the 1990s, as the international sanctions began to bite and the regime's need for discretionary funds that were not subject to international supervision became ever greater. The sanctions encouraged the development of illicit supply channels and organised oil smuggling outside the purview of the UN sanctions committee. In addition, the Ba'ath regime's craving for revenues pushed them into maximising oil production, even at the expense of prudent reservoir management and good oil field practices.[13] The emigration of senior oil industry talent added to the degradation of the capabilities of the Oil Ministry itself, as hitherto unacceptable practices became the norm. Complex oil pricing formulae, designed to ensure that Iraq received the best prices for its oil, were jettisoned. The former regime began to issue oil vouchers that entitled the holders to discounted oil, in order to entice people into its smuggling and skimming rackets. Good engineering practice went out of the window as the oil field operators were instructed to push for increased production, regardless of costs. What had been state-of-the-art equipment for the oil industry became increasingly dated, as the former regime deliberately under-invested in oil field renewal and upgrading. The corruption that became endemic to the sector came about because the senior management and technical cadres of the Oil Ministry had become tired, dispirited and often hopelessly compromised by their toleration of unethical and inappropriate practices. The frequent personnel changes that took place during the successive post-invasion governments added yet another dimension to the disorganisation in the oil industry.

Corruption in the oil industry took several forms. The most glaring was the unmetering of Iraq's oil exports. Crude oil exports were not precisely gauged by a series of tamper-proof control systems. A few operated at the wellhead or at the loading terminals, but none of the systems employed was complete or up to date. In some cases, the amount of oil that was loaded on to tankers was measured by a crude plumb line. This made it impossible to determine the amount of Iraq's oil exports accurately. No agency could give a satisfactory answer as to why this situation continued without remedy and why the CPA, during its tenure, tolerated this glaring oversight. Subsequent Iraqi oil ministers continued to stall on the metering issue, even as the IMF extracted promises from the Iraqi government to tackle this grave problem. The opportunities afforded to criminals and corrupt officials in the umetered export of crude oil were legion. Some of the more alarming reports about tens of thousand of tons of tanker loads of crude oil being smuggled out in 'rogue' ships may not have rung true, but the gist was true. Criminal gangs fitted out small tankers with false bottoms to carry unreported Iraqi crude oil. Most managed to slip away to tank farms in the lower Gulf and elsewhere, where Iraqi oil was blended with other crude oil and its provenance was lost. In other cases, rudimentary craft were rigged out in yards along the Shatt-al-Arab waterway, which made a few journeys with stolen oil cargoes and then sunk. Crude oil was also spirited out of the country from the northern oil fields. There, the pipelines would be regularly and accurately struck, disrupting supplies to the refineries. This forced the Oil Ministry to use trucks to carry the crude oil to the refineries, where they became prey to sophisticated networks of truck drivers, corrupt officials, smuggling gangs and insurgents. It was not in the crude oil sector that the vast smuggling rackets thrived, however, but in the oil products sectors.

The oil products sector in Iraq operated in an Alice-in-Wonderland world. A congruence of factors turned this sector into a near-perfect playground for large, organised and entrenched groups that garnered immense profits from the oil products racket. First was the incredible persistence of the subsidies for petroleum products that were inherited from the Saddamist years and continued unchanged until their reform towards the end of 2005. The result was a huge dent in the government's budget, where subsidising of domestic oil products ate up 15 per cent of the budget (rising to nearly 20 per cent by 2005). But the extent of the subsidies was such that the differential between Iraqi oil products prices and those of nearby countries ranged from a low of ten times to an unbelievable eighty times. Before the price reforms of late 2005, regular gasoline sold in Iraq at the equivalent of 1c per litre, compared to 10c in Iran, 40c in Jordan and 80c in Turkey. Both the CPA and the Interim Government shied away from any reform of the price structure, fearing wide-spread disturbances and unpopularity. The Interim Government had promised the IMF to revise the prices in its September 2004 negotiations for emergency support for its economic programme. It failed to act on its promise, however, and passed this politically controversial issue to the incoming Transitional National Government.[14]

Profits for the smugglers were incredible. A ton of diesel bought at the official price would cost the smuggler about $10; this same product would sell at a smugglers' port in southern Iraq at $250. Of course, with the rise in global oil prices starting in 2005, the margins would be even greater. A calculation made by the Ministry of Oil's Inspector General Department estimated that the net profit per truck of smuggled diesel delivered to the smugglers' port, after payments for officials and the truck driver, was $8400 *per trip per truck*.[15] Not all the oil products that fed into the smugglers' rings came from imports, refineries or state oil depots. Some business sectors, such as bakeries and fishing, would receive subsidised fuel from the government, often far in excess of their stated needs. They would either sell their surplus requirements into the black market, or simply not produce bread or catch fish. It would be more rewarding for them to simply sell their fuel quotas.

A second factor enabling the rampant criminality in the oil sector was the abysmal state of control systems throughout the chain of storing, moving, distributing, recording and accounting for oil products. Spot inspections would reveal huge discrepancies between reported amounts received and shipped. In one six-month period, the discrepancy amounted to 25 per cent of the reported products shipped. In one province, Babel, the amount of oil products received and shipped was out by an astounding 50 per cent.[16] Thirdly, the smuggling racket across Iraq's borders relied on corrupt border officials, connivance from the frontier authorities of Iraq's neighbours, and poor or non-existent management control and reporting systems of the concerned ministries of oil, interior and finance. The complete indifference of the MNF to the smuggling rackets, even though a large number of them were insurgency-linked or paid protection money to the insurgents, was a factor that emboldened the smugglers. The MNF would only rarely move against smugglers, and only after some particularly dire incident had occurred. Any smugglers caught would enter Iraq's labyrinthine, overloaded and inefficient judicial system. This was easily corrupted or threatened into acquiescence, and barely served to deter would-be miscreants. In one case, a truck convoy carrying $28 million of smuggled fuel was impounded, but released after the culprits agreed to pay a $4 million fine! Needless to say, the fine was never paid.[17]

The demand for oil products had nearly doubled after the invasion, primarily because of the large expansion in the number of cars and trucks, increased electricity demand and the use of private generators, because of the persistent and increasingly lengthy power cuts. This coincided with an insurgent-led campaign to damage Iraq's refineries, and with serious management and investment shortcomings in the refineries sector. The demand for imported products soared as Iraq's refineries were unable to meet the expansion in demand. Increasing domestic refinery output would not have, of itself, stopped the smugglers, but it would have removed one of the props of the smugglers' racket and would have reduced the budgetary burden. But the entire system was becoming rigged to favour the continuation of this absurd policy. In fact economists from the universities would be trotted out to back the arguments for free fuel as part of the welfare compact between the government and the people, while politicians would nod understandingly to the need for price reform, only to denounce its deleterious effects on people's living standards. The people, in fact, were getting the worst of all worlds. Fuel shortages persisted and reached monstrous levels, as motorists would often queue for twenty-four hours in front of petrol stations which sold subsidised fuel. Those who had the money to pay for black-market fuel would often be stuck with an adulterated product sold by kerbside operators from jerry cans or bottles. Periodic crises would affect the import programme as the Ministry of Oil, itself under pressure to guarantee oil products supplies, would import at levels way above its budgetary allocations. These would result in large IOUs accumulating to Turkish and Kuwaiti suppliers, who would then pressure their governments to pressure in turn the Iraqi Ministry of Finance to increase the allocations to the Oil Ministry to pay its bills. As the fuel shortages became more serious in Baghdad and other cities, and the fear that the public's anger would feed into more support for the insurgency, emergency committees met to 'resolve' the issue. Finally, the MNF would chip in with its estimates of the security consequences of an abiding fuel shortage, and the US Embassy would relay the threats from Turkey and Kuwait to shut out Iraqi fuel purchases in the future if their bills were not paid. Often, the arrears of the Ministry of Oil to these suppliers would exceed a billion dollars each. The bills would be paid by the Ministry of Finance from emergency budgetary reserves – only for this vicious circle to start up again. Everyone down the chain fed on the Iraqi government's resources as a result of atrocious policies, which would only be tackled by the Transitional National Government in its last days, at great political risk.

The oil sector rackets amounted to billions of dollars that were stolen from the Iraqi treasury. These ranged from the gamut of kickbacks on fuel purchase and transport contracts that went to senior officials at the Ministry of Oil to the theft of imported and domestic fuel products by smuggling gangs and to the illegal export of crude and fuel oil. The cost to the budget of Iraq's fuel imports ran at the annual level of $6 billion by the end of 2005.[18] About $200 million of that was probably skimmed off as commissions and kickbacks. The amount smuggled out of these fuel imports was nearly 30 per cent, while domestic fuel products and crude oil were siphoned off abroad at a rate of probably another $2 billion.[19] The size of the oil racket might have reached $4 billion – in an economy the GDP of which was about $30 billion by 2005. The theft and smuggling of fuel products involved thousands of people, and was a sophisticated and complex operation conducted by many groups inside and outside Iraq and by government departments. This was not the case, however, in one of the biggest cases of misappropriation of funds that took place in modern times, and which hung as a dark cloud over the Interim Government's probity. Nearly $1.2 billion of funds were allegedly embezzled from the Iraqi Ministry of Defence's arms procurement budget over a short six-month span in late 2004 and early 2005.

The Plunder of the Ministry of Defence

The Iraqi Ministry of Defence was reconstituted in April 2004 under the CPA. It operated under a budget set up by the CPA, which was premised on a small force of three light infantry divisions. With the advent of the Interim Government, pressure was afoot to increase the budget of the Ministry of Defence dramatically, in line with a revised security strategy that called for the establishment of 'rapid deployment forces' and mechanised divisions. These were assumed to form the elements of an expanded Iraqi army and an enhanced Iraqi involvement in counter-insurgency operations. The CPA's defence doctrine was jettisoned by the Interim Government, with little protest from the MNF advisers who had been assigned to the Ministry of Defence. General David Petraeus, who had been responsible for security in the Mosul area, between invasion and February 2004 as head of the 101st Airborne Division, was brought back to Iraq with new responsibilities. He commanded the group responsible for the training and expansion of Iraq's army, the Multinational Security Transition Command in Iraq, commonly known as 'Minsticky'. The Security Transition Command subscribed to the new military doctrine for the Iraqi army and signed off on the expansion proposals of the Interim Government. The Ministry of Defence assumed responsibility for procurement of the armaments and transport for the new Iraqi mechanised divisions, even though the Security Transition Command was supposed to have an oversight role. Petraeus was a firm believer in giving the new Iraqi government as wide a latitude as possible to make its own decisions, without intrusive involvement by the Security Transition Command. Writing in the *Washington Post* in September 2004, Petraeus waxed lyrical about the progress in setting up the new Iraqi army and the rapid equipping of these forces: 'Training is on track and increasing in capacity. Infrastructure is being repaired. Command and control structures and institutions are being re-established.'[20] But under the very noses of the Security Transition

Command, officials both inside and outside the Ministry of Defence were plotting to embezzle most, if not all, of the procurement budget of the army.

The new Minister of Defence, Hazem Sha'alan, had no experience either in the security arena or in the professional management of large organisations.[21] He was probably selected because of his loyal service to the intelligence agencies when he was the CPA-appointed governor of Qadissiya province. Sha'alan had been involved in a losing power struggle in the province with the ascendant Islamists, whom he deeply loathed. He brought Mishal al-Sarraf into the ministry as his special adviser. Al-Sarraf, born into a Najafi family, was a business adventurer with a murky background. He had previously been a real-estate speculator in war-torn Lebanon, a dealer in cardamom from Guatemala, a grower of spring onions on the Arizona–Mexico border, and a promoter of *halal* canned meats in Europe and Lebanon. As the war clouds gathered in early 2003, he popped up in Kuwait, hovering around the growing ORHA operation of Jay Garner, and became one of its numerous camp followers. Mishal al-Sarraf would boast, while in Kuwait, that he had become one of the CIA's recruits for Iraq. It is unclear what role he had played during the CPA period, but his appointment as senior adviser to the Minister of Defence was received with incredulity.

Fred Smith, the CPA-appointed senior adviser to the Ministry of Defence, was an effective and capable administrator, with impressive career credentials in national security and defence. He stayed on throughout the month of June 2004 during the handover of the Ministry of Defence to the incoming Minister, Hazem Sha'alan and al-Sarraf, his adviser. Smith was dismayed by the unfocused and grandiose security schemes that the new team at the Ministry of Defence was concocting.[22] The new staff was of uneven quality. They were seeded throughout the Ministry of Defence's headquarters to form the backbone of the new civilian-dominated administration. Five of these senior civilian appointments would feature, knowingly or unknowingly, in the unfolding embezzlement scandal. Two of them would be later murdered under mysterious circumstances, probably because of their knowledge of the details of the unfolding massive fraud. A third one would confess after her arrest and would provide most of the incriminating evidence against the key players.

As a harbinger of things to come, Dale Stoffel, one of the innumerable freelance military contractors who gravitated towards Iraq in search of El Dorado, received a contract from the Ministry of Defence for the refurbishment of mothballed Soviet-made tanks and other armoured vehicles of the former Iraqi army.[23] Stoffel was extremely proficient in this area, and had managed to land a number of contracts for the procurement of Russian and East European military equipment for testing by the Pentagon. He was introduced to al-Sarraf, who then brought him to the Minister of Defence. Sha'alan awarded a multimillion dollar contract to Stoffel's company, Wye Oak Technology, for the refurbishment of equipment for three battalions. It was the first substantial contract awarded by the newly sovereign Iraqi Ministry of Defence. Curiously, however, the Ministry of Defence insisted that Stoffel route his billing through a Lebanese middleman, Raymond Rahma Zayna, an associate of al-Sarraf and one of the band of fixers and commission agents that hung around the US military abroad. Stoffel performed part of the contract and was seeking payment for nearly $25 million of work already accomplished. The Ministry of Defence cut three separate cheques, routed through the Lebanese middleman for 'processing'. It was clear to Stoffel that this abnormal payment mechanism was for hiding commissions that would be kicked back to senior Ministry of Defence officials by Raymond Zayna. In any case, Stoffel did not receive his promised payment, and he complained to the office of Senator Santorum in Washington and to senior Pentagon officials. Following a meeting held in the Taji army base north of Baghdad to sort out the problem between Stoffel and Zayna, the British deputy commander of the Security Transition Command, Brigadier Clements, ordered Zayna to release the money to Stoffel. Stoffel never saw the money. Returning to Baghdad after their meetings, Stoffel and an assistant were ambushed and killed. Stoffel's computer was stolen. Investigators noted a number of unusual occurrences and concluded that the attacks were made in such a way as to disguise an assassination. The murders may have been ordered because of fear that Stoffel's 'whistle-blowing' might alert the MNF to the corruption inside the Ministry of Defence. Suspicion hung around the entire Wye Oak deal, but investigators probed it insufficiently, possibly because of the fallout that might have occurred on senior Ministry of Defence officials who benefited from the corruption. The Security Transition Command did not want to see its efforts tarnished by allegations against its Iraqi counterparts. Meanwhile, the Ministry of Defence was being systematically looted.

The Ministry of Defence's budget for 2004 was set at about $100 million by the CPA, a patently inadequate figure given the ambitious expansion plans for Iraq's military. This was subsequently adjusted as the Interim Government took over sovereignty, and a new budget for the ministry was set at about $450 million. Nevertheless, the main burden of financing Iraq's military fell on the USA. The Pentagon's budget included appropriations for the supply, equipping and training of Iraq's security forces, as well as for the building and refurbishment of bases. The US budgetary support for the Iraqi armed forces was possibly in the region of $8 to $10 billion.[24] The establishment of the mechanised divisions and the rapid deployment forces did not feature in the original plans for the Iraqi army, and the costs of setting them up had to be borne directly by the Iraqi treasury. The normal procedure, according to the TAL, was to submit requests for budgetary changes to the National Assembly, after they had been approved by the Cabinet. The National Assembly had been formed to act as a legislative and oversight body during the interim period, until elections in January 2005. The decision to form these divisions was taken unilaterally, without any reference to either the Cabinet or the National Assembly.

In a series of circulars issued by the Cabinet secretariat office, the Ministry of Finance was instructed to appropriate $1.7 billion in one lump sum and to put it at the disposal of the Ministry of Defence. The Ministry of Defence, in turn, was informed by the Cabinet secretariat that it had prime ministerial approval for the formation of two rapid deployment divisions, and that the Ministry of Finance would make available the necessary appropriations for these divisions. At no point did the Ministry of Defence present any detailed proposals for these forces, or justify the amounts involved. The MNF was not consulted about the details of these divisions and was purposely kept out of the loop. The entire procedure was at best irregular and contravened both the Financial Management Law and the terms of the TAL. Prior to receiving the approval for funding these divisions, the Ministry of Defence had sought and received exemptions from the standing instructions of the Ministry of Finance that limited ministerial discretionary spending to the equivalent of $350,000. The exemptions were predicated on the understanding that all Ministry of Defence expenditures beyond the applicable limits would need the approval of the prime minister and deputy prime minister. The stage was set for a mad shopping spree for armaments with an unlimited chequebook, all to be effected in the period of the last three months in the life of a supposedly 'interim' government.[25] With just enough procedural niceties out of the way, the Ministry of Finance, under Adel Abd el-Mahdi, imprudently allowed the Ministry of Defence access to $1.7 billion in funds to spend in an uncontrolled and unauthorised manner, contravening a number of laws and regulations.

The locus of activity now moved to the Ministry of Defence's own senior staff, to make these purchases actually happen. In a series of astounding and brazen decisions that broke every contracting and procurement rule, the Ministry of Defence started to award huge contracts without any bidding and with minimal documentation.[26] The CPA had appointed Bruska Shawys, the Secretary General of the Ministry of Defence, to his job, a unique position in the Iraqi civil service. In fact the post of secretary general of the Ministry of Defence was deliberately invested with extra powers that made the holder the chief operating officer of the ministry. Shawys was a KDP stalwart and a brother of the then vice-president of Iraq in the Interim Government. Shawys authorised his deputy, Ziad Qattan, to be the head of the Ministry of Defence's procurement department, in addition to his duties as the deputy secretary general of the Ministry of Defence. By his own admission, Qattan knew nothing about weapons procurement. 'Before, I sold water, flowers, shoes, cars – but not weapons. We didn't know anything about weapons', he said in an interview later with the *Los Angeles Times* newspaper.[27] Qattan ingratiated himself with the US military in his neighbourhood, and became one of those elected as a local councillor in the Coalition's attempts to foster grassroots democracy.[28] He was then recruited into the nascent Ministry of Defence by the chief Coalition talent scout, Colonel Dermer. Qattan distinguished himself in the early Ministry of Defence by arranging the purchase of office furniture. Following the transfer of sovereignty, Qattan's star in the Ministry of Defence rose rapidly.

As chief procurement officer and with a billion-dollar budget, Qattan turned to a recently established company, with no background in military procurement and with only $2,000 in paid-up capital, to provide the Iraqi army with equipment for its rapid deployment forces. The company, called the *'Ayn al-Jariah* (the 'Flowing Spring'), was established on 1 September 2004, with three shareholders: Abd el-Hamid Mirza, the secretary of the office of the then vice-president; Zina Fattah, a Jordanian-based Iraqi and associate of Mishal al-Sarraf, the senior adviser to the Minister of Defence; and Naer Muhammed Ahmed al-Jumaili.[29] This last shareholder was the operator of the sham company, which was to be the conduit for the equipping of two Iraqi divisions. In all, Ziad Qattan signed $1.12 billion in contracts with the *'Ayn al-Jariah* company and other front companies of Naer al-Jumaili. The contracts were awarded without any competitive bidding. Astoundingly, full payments of the contracts were often made *in advance*, with none of the usual requirements for performance bonds or guarantees. The legal department of the Ministry of Defence did not vet the contracts, and no original contract copies were lodged with it.[30] The contracts themselves were drawn entirely to the advantage of the intermediary company. For example, the supplier could change the origin of the military equipment at will, with no reference to the Ministry of Defence.

The payment terms for the contracts also followed an extraordinary route. Rather than lodging the contract value with the Iraqi government's bank, the Trade Bank of Iraq, which was organised for the very purpose of financing the letters of credit of the Iraqi government, the Ministry of Defence contracts were paid for in highly suspicious ways. The Ministry of Defence transferred the bulk of its financial appropriations to a branch of a local state-owned bank, Rafidain Bank. From this account, checks were drawn in hundreds of millions of dollars to the order of Mirza – one of the shareholders of the *'Ayn al-Jariah* company. He would then endorse the cheques to Naer al-Jumaili. The latter would deposit the proceeds, now amounting to nearly a billion dollars, into his personal account at a small Baghdad private bank, the Warka Bank. From his account at the Warka

Bank, Jumaili transferred about $480 million to his private account at the Housing Bank of Jordan, a publicly listed bank with significant Jordanian government shareholding. He also transferred $545 million from his account at the Warka Bank to the account of a confederate, a certain Mohannad Taha, in the same bank. Mohannad Taha then transferred all the money to Jumaili's account at the Housing Bank of Jordan. Jumaili also drew $100 million in cash from the Warka Bank. More than a billion dollars were transferred into the account of a private individual in the Housing Bank of Jordan, ostensibly to finance the purchase of equipment for the Iraqi rapid deployment forces. The Iraqi Ministry of Defence had parted with more than a billion dollars, moved into the accounts of unknown people in a foreign country.

The equipment that was purchased under these 'contracts' was of poor quality, and its real cost was a fraction of the money that was paid out by the Ministry of Defence.[31] The biggest supplier was a former Polish state-owned armaments company, Bumar. This company refused to acknowledge that the contracting counter-party was the Iraqi Ministry of Defence, and dealt only with the middlemen with whom they in turn contracted. The terms of the contract between Jumaili and the ultimate suppliers afforded Jumaili the widest possible scope for over-charging and gouging. Bumar's main contracts with Jumaili concerned the supply of helicopters for the rapid deployment force. In one notorious case, Iraq was sold twenty-four Soviet-era helicopters, over thirty years old, for $100 million. The Iraqi inspection team refused to take delivery of these helicopters, given their near-unusable state – even when their purchase price had already been paid in advance. In another case involving the purchase of twenty Polish-made Sokol helicopters, the supplier did not provide any bid bonds, and the helicopters were supposed to be delivered in one-and-a-half years' time. The premise that the rapid intervention divisions had to be quickly equipped was clearly thrown out of the window. Referring to Qattan's spending spree, John Noble, a British adviser to the Ministry of Defence, said, 'There is no doubt he took advantage of opportunities. Certainly millions, possibly even hundreds of millions of dollars were lost through Qattan's ventures.'[32] The litany of disastrous and outrageously overpriced equipment covered the entire spectrum of armaments, from machine guns that were copies of the ones actually contracted for, to armoured vehicles that were so poorly armoured that machine-gun bullets would easily pierce them. A related series of purchases, this time signed for unilaterally by the Minister of Defence, involved the purchase of nearly $80 million of equipment from the Pakistani government stockpile. There were no details regarding the number and condition of the equipment and vehicles being bought. The Iraqi army was saddled with vehicles equipped with right-hand drive steering, a British legacy to Pakistan from the days of the Raj, while Iraqis drove with left-hand steering!

Rumours about hundreds of millions of dollars of the Ministry of Defence's funds sloshing around and then vanishing began to surface in the days after the January 2005 elections. There were hints that something was afoot when Baghdad airport personnel intercepted a huge shipment of cash to Lebanese banks. The entire scandal would have probably been hushed up were it not for the investigations conducted by the Bureau of Supreme Audit (BSA). At great risk to its investigative staff, the BSA delved into the dark recesses of the Ministry of Defence's procurement and produced a damning report that it released only to the incoming administration of Ibrahim al-Jaffari.[33] The report, dated 16 May 2005, landed on the new prime minister's desk, where it was kept under close wraps. News of its findings, however, began to leak. On 15 July 2005, the intrepid Baghdad reporter for Knight Ridder (both an agency and a chain of newspapers), a young Egyptian–American woman journalist, broke the news. The incoming Defence Minister, Saadun al-Dulaimi, acknowledged the main points of the BSA investigative report.[34] Within a few months, the Integrity Commission reckoned that it had sufficient evidence to ask for arrest warrants to be issued against a host of people involved in the scandal, including the former Minister of Defence, Hazem Sha'alan, his adviser, Mishal al-Sarraf, the Secretary General of the Ministry of Defence, Bruska Shawys, his deputy, Ziad Qattan, and a number of other senior Ministry of Defence officials. The head of the Integrity Commission, Judge Radhi al-Radhi, said, regarding the alleged theft at the Ministry of Defence, 'What Sha'alan [the former Minister of Defence] and his ministry were responsible for is possibly the largest robbery in the world . . . . Our estimates begin at $1.3 billion and go up to $2.3 billion.'[35]

Most of the culprits fled the country, with Sha'alan heading for London and then Jordan, Sarraf for Lebanon and Qattan for Poland. There, Sha'alan and Qattan fulminated in the press about witch hunts by an Iraqi government now infiltrated by Iranian agents, and protested their innocence.[36] Sha'alan gave a theatrical press conference with Bumar executives in Poland, after reaching Warsaw on board a private plane provided, according to him, by 'well-wishers'. Their protestations began to sound hollow as more damning evidence emerged in the form of a secret tape recording of the main protagonists, talking openly about the theft from the Ministry of Defence. The tape implicated a number of very senior government officials, either as bagmen or as recipients of the looted cash. An accomplice who felt cheated by his partners probably provided the tape. Its authenticity was vouchsafed by a number of independent analysts. The Director General of Finance at the Ministry of Defence, Sawsan Jassim, was arrested and helped in exposing the involvement of senior Ministry of Defence officials. Two of her colleagues at the Ministry of Defence, the Director General of Planning, Issam al-Dujaili and the Inspector General of the ministry, Leila al-Mukhtar, were murdered. Mukhtar was killed in the Green Zone in an obvious inside job. Dujaili was murdered while driving to work.

The saga of the grand theft of the Ministry of Defence perfectly illustrated the huge gap between the harsh realities on the ground, and the Panglossian spin that permeated official pronouncements of the government, the US Embassy and the MNF. The optimistic assessments by General Petraeus concerning the equipping and training of Iraqi forces clashed with the huge squandering of the Ministry of Defence's resources and the abysmal and inappropriate equipment purchases for its rapid deployment forces. The latter, supposed to be the vanguard of the Iraqi commitment to the counter-insurgency effort, found that their much-vaunted helicopters were either inoperable or unavailable for eighteen months. They were driving right-hand steering vehicles, firing knock-offs of American machine guns, with bullet-proof vests that fell apart, and wearing toy helmets. Ministers who were chosen for their supposed technocratic prowess and competence ended up on the run from the law under serious indictment of fraud, embezzlement and theft. The military procurement budget was handed over to unscrupulous adventurers and former pizza parlour operators. Every single agency involved in the money chain that siphoned a billion dollars of Iraq's resources into offshore accounts was culpable, if not complicit, in this crime. The Ministry of Finance allowed nearly $2 billion to slip out of its control in flagrant disregard of its own rules and the financial and budgetary laws of the country. The MNF simply watched, while the Ministry of Defence was being plundered in front of their very noses, hiding behind the excuse that the Iraqis were now responsible for their decisions. As long as US money was not involved in the scams at the Ministry of Defence, there was no reason to protest. The message was all, and to be off-message was a cardinal sin in the war for the public's ear. Iraqi institutions, weak and continuously undermined by dishonest officials, became further degraded as corrupt practices appeared to go unpunished. Arab countries who shed crocodile tears about the plight of the Iraqi people did not bat an eyelid when a billion dollars plonked into secret accounts in their countries' banks. Officials in Lebanon and Jordan would later stymie repeated attempts to access the accounts of the main protagonists, claiming bank secrecy laws and immunities.[37] Meanwhile, the US Treasury set up a special unit to track insurgency financing – while overlooking the prima facie evidence that part of the corruptly derived funds of Iraqis in the banks of Jordan, Lebanon and the UAE were being diverted to insurgents and terrorists. The courage of the Bureau of Supreme Audit, a number of whose officials were assassinated, and of the judges of the Integrity Commission, was tremendous. These people would prove indomitable in the face of a chorus of accusations that their work of uncovering corruption was politically motivated – a common defence of criminals. They were, however, zones of hope in an increasingly corrupt, demoralised and fractious governmental apparatus.

21

Iraqi Society on the Eve of Free Elections

' *It's like Plato's republic in here, all of these well-meaning, smart people who want to do the right thing . . . . But they never leave here and they have no idea what's happening in the country they're supposed to be building. It's totally absurd.'* –

An anonymous contractor on life in the Green Zone,
quoted in Newsweek, 20 September, 2004

Eighteen months after the fall of the Ba'athist regime, and as Iraqis were preparing for the elections, the verities that underpinned Iraq's society and the relationships between its peoples had been violently upended. Every basic tenet of society had been disrupted in ways that would have a profound effect on the electoral outcome. For the first time, the most fundamental questions about who and what an Iraqi was were being seriously asked, behind a backdrop of escalating violence and resistance. The undoubted new liberties and freedoms that the overthrow of the Ba'ath brought had to be set against the accelerating disintegration in the most elemental relationships that are the mainstay of any stable society. Identities that had been smothered, suppressed, or simply overlooked bubbled to the surface. To be secular or religious, a Kurd, Arab, Turcoman, Shi'a or Sunni could literally determine whether you were to live or die, or whether you felt safe or had to flee your neighbourhood or town. Restrictions on personal freedoms were swept away, but this was not much use if a simple travel request to one of the Coalition partner countries were to be routinely rejected. Iraqis were now free, but apparently not good enough to be allowed into these countries. 'Iraqis could travel anywhere as long as it was to Jordan!' as the refrain went. Newspapers could write what they wanted, and they did, including outright lies, slander and calumnies, and rumour-mongering. The millions of Iraqi exiles from the Saddam era were now joined by hundreds of thousands fleeing the violence, or who simply could not abide life in the new order. It now seemed that the Ba'ath Party was not simply a small coterie that sat upon a repressive system of control. It had hundreds of thousands of adherents, sympathisers, fellow-travellers and beneficiaries of its largesse. A repressive and corrupt government was replaced by an equally chaotic, if not more corrupt, administration.

The lot of the average citizen when dealing with officialdom was still subject to the whims and bigotries of the bureaucrat. But access was far more daunting. Ministries had huge throngs milling outside, often in ferocious heat or engulfed in dust clouds, while people awaited their turn to be individually screened. What used to take hours to achieve now took days, if not weeks. And this in a climate of anxiety and stress, as a suicide bomber might mingle in the crowds, or a car packed with explosives might detonate while waiting in line in front of one governmental department or another.[1] Everywhere, there was cynicism mixed with disgust at the litany of broken promises made by the government. The abysmal level of services during the Saddam era began to look positively rosy in light of the appalling shortfalls in electricity, water, sanitation and policing services. The overthrow of the dictatorship was decidedly a mixed blessing. Ultimately, it depended on who you were.

The Green Zone

The rise and rise of the 'Green Zone' was the best indicator of the true state of affairs inside the country, at least as senior officials, foreign diplomats and the USA saw it. The 'Green Zone' was the euphamism given to a ten-square kilometre fortified area in the middle of Baghdad that served as the headquarters for successive Iraqi administrations and the numerous organisations and entities that served or liaised with them. The area was, in fact, the administrative centre for the Ba'ath regime and included a number of palaces, monuments, government buildings and officials' homes and villas. Following its collapse, the ORHA ensconced itself in the former Republican Palace, which later became the nerve centre for the CPA, and then for the US Embassy. The Iraqi government had more modest offices, including a pint-size prime ministerial office and cabinet meeting room, and a converted office building, formerly the Ministry for Military Industries that served the Governing Council and later the cabinet secretariat. Over time, the Green Zone harboured the head offices of the Ministry of Defence, and as the security condition deteriorated in the rest of the country – the 'Red Zone' – ministers and other high officials abandoned their residences and even their ministries and moved into homes and offices inside the Green Zone. The entire perimeter of the Green Zone was ringed with concrete blast walls, and access to and egress from the Green Zone was tightly controlled by US forces and their security contractors at a few entry points. There were badges for various categories of entrants to the Green Zone, and, within the Green Zone itself, sensitive buildings and sites required another set of identity badges. Inside the Zone, security was provided either by minor members of the Coalition, such as Georgians from Georgia in the Caucasus, or by security company personnel from Nepal or a variety of South American countries.

The Green Zone evolved into a world of its own, ever more distant and alien from the rest of the country. Incrementally, and even imperceptibly, it turned into an enclave where the culture of small-town America combined with the trappings of vice-regal administration. This created a curious 'bubble' environment divorced from the travails and life-threatening risks in the rest of the country, with ever more dense concentrations of Iraqi central government offices and officials, parliamentarians and politicians.[2]

While Baghdad was suffering endless power outages, filthy streets, untreated sewerage, random shootings and killings and bombings, residents of the Green Zone lived with uninterrupted power and services provided to international standards by professional, frequently foreign, contractors. The mortars that were periodically lobbed in by insurgents were wildly inaccurate and only a handful of people were either killed or injured by these attacks. The houses and villas of the Ba'ath regime's senior officials were seized by the government, and their disposition was given to the office of the cabinet secretary. In time, it ceased to be only ministers living in the Green Zone and commuting to their ministries. Entire ministerial head offices were moved into the Green Zone, and few ministers ever left the cocooned environment of their proxy offices.[3]

To some extent this was encouraged by the US Embassy as it sought to minimise the travel of its senior officials and contract workers to areas outside the Green Zone. Iraqi government leaders would live in a commandeered house or villa; work in a surrogate head office in one of the Green Zone's refurbished buildings; conduct meetings and other official business there; and, if lucky, be transported by helicopter to Baghdad International Airport to catch a flight outside the country, avoiding the unpleasant and often dangerous airport road. The Green Zone began to encroach on nearby areas, and these were incorporated into its security zone as ever more officials sought the relative safety and comfort of a secure area.[4] The murder of a few parliamentarians accelerated this process, as it became clear that the insurgents would likely target parliamentarians outside the Green Zone whenever the opportunity presented itself. The Green Zone became a symbol of a besieged administration cut off from its wellsprings, unable to comprehend the depth of the country's hardships and dangers. At no point did any senior leader contemplate restricting, or even dismantling, the Green Zone.[5] If the new political class had been prepared to share the burdens of the rest of the country and had not been afraid or intimidated by insurgent threats, this would have been a powerful signal for the Iraqi population. As it was, an embittered

Iraqi said, 'All the people in the Green Zone have their bodyguards . . . . We Iraqis remain here; it is just explosions and no security in the streets . . . . They protect themselves, but no one protects us, the Iraqis.'[6]

Violence and Mayhem

It was the unrelenting violence that most affected the daily lives of urban dwellers. The killings were not all insurgency-related. In the early days after the war, the violence was directed mainly against former regime operatives and those suspected of being informants or accomplices.[7] But the tempo and scale of the violence changed with the rise of the insurgency. As it gained traction, assassinations and kidnappings began to affect the normal lives of citizens, and added to the increasingly unsettled and anxious world in which most people existed. The security forces, especially the police, were relentlessly and deliberately targeted – to drive home the point that anyone working with or for the Coalition was treasonous.[8] Government employees became routine assassination targets, and, as the terror became more indiscriminate, all classes of workers for the government or the Coalition became fodder for the terrorists' bullets and bombs. Simple labourers, kitchen workers, factory hands, garbage collectors, teachers, were mowed down in a horrible campaign to frighten and intimidate often desperate people to abandon thought of government work. Later, workers in Iraq's small business sector would also feature in the terrorists' campaigns. Bakery workers and even barbers were routinely killed en masse. The latter were targeted supposedly because the Wahhabist wing of the insurgency took exception to trimmed beards and fashionable haircuts, considering them to be an affront to their religious scruples.[9] Kidnappings of civilians, for ransom as well as for terror-inducing purposes, surged in 2004. Bankers, businessmen and even would-be parliamentarians were kidnapped and released only after the payment of large ransoms.

Most Iraqis had neither the means nor the desire to change their daily routines, but they did worry about their children. The school run became fraught as parents fretted over whether their children would be caught up in the latest bombing or some similar outrage. The lives of the mass of people began to diverge greatly from those of senior officials. The latter could at least protect themselves with bodyguards, armoured vehicles, special phones and alarm devices, when they were moving about. The armoured vehicle business boomed, as Iraq became the leading market for specially protected cars and vans. The first set of armoured vehicles was provided by the CPA for a few political leaders, but later most ministers, deputy ministers and officials in sensitive or dangerous jobs would be issued with their own armoured cars, courtesy of the cabinet office.

The daily routine of travel to and from the place of work had to be changed constantly, to avoid a pattern that would be detected by terrorists and insurgents. The suicide bomber who killed the Governing Council president, Izzeddine Salim, had tracked his movement to and from the Green Zone.[10] His journey had become predictable and thus an easy target for the killers. But all the protection in the world still could not stop repeated attempts at the lives of senior officials. In one notorious area, the Tahrir Square roundabout and tunnel complex, convoys carrying ministers and senior officials would periodically become the targets of suicide bombers or rooftop ambushes. The stress of being on constant watch against terrorist attacks ate at the composure of bodyguards and drivers in convoys. They would routinely fire salvoes into the air to open a pathway for their convoys during Baghdad's notorious traffic jams, or drive at breakneck speed down the wrong lane of a highway. (Doing a 'wrong' was bodyguard slang for driving down the wrong or opposite lane in a divided highway.) The antics of ministerial convoys, which frequently ended in pile-ups and fatalities, became a deeply resented facet of Baghdad life, and drew the anger of commuters, ordinary drivers and passersby. Short journeys became a complex logistical nightmare, especially if road blocks had been thrown up by trigger-happy American troops or Iraqi government security forces. Many people would meet an untimely end because they failed to see the signal to stop from a Coalition soldier who, fearing suicide bombers, would open up against the oncoming vehicle.

Shortages of Basic Necessities and Services

The effect of the violence was compounded by the irregular supply of the basic elements for the functioning of an urbanised society: fuel, water and power. The supplies of these three essential services were interrelated. The absence of regular fuel supplies affected the workings of power plants and the flow of electricity, which in turn affected the operation of the water and sewerage treatment plants. By the end of 2004, the electricity supply in Baghdad was being cut to a four hours per twenty-four hour cycle. Generators proliferated, but these had to be fed with regular diesel supplies, which were scarce. Neighbourhoods often banded together to buy a large generator for a number of households. More common, however, was the rise of the generator entrepreneur, who would ensure the flow of expensive power at regular intervals to a number of households. These entrepreneurs would often own and operate the generators, which had sometimes been 'liberated' stock from government installations and depots during the chaos of the post-war days. Nobody would seriously challenge the generator entrepreneur's claim to these assets. This was not quite what the Green Zone economic planners had in mind when talking about 'encouraging private entrepreneurship'. Their performance, ruthlessness and purported greed became the stuff of urban legends. Petrol ran short to the point where filling a car with the government-supplied and subsidised product might easily take fourteen to sixteen hours of waiting in line in front of the state-owned petrol stations.[11] Senior officials, of course, had their own sources of gasoline and diesel, which were provided, regularly and abundantly, at special pumps inside the Green Zone. Water flows into peoples' homes was sporadic, and when the water did come, it was often at such low pressure that it would take hours to fill the water cisterns.[12] The hardships of daily life, especially for the middle classes, became ever more acute and a constant source of griping. It was the plight of the middle classes that captured the headlines and the attention of the world's media. The poor, of course, especially the denizens of Sadr City and other neglected neighbourhoods, had never had many of services in the days of the Ba'ath regime. They were therefore used to communal taps and electricity supplied through theft from the public grid in 'chattals' – cables illegally connected to the main power lines and drawing unmetered electricity into people's homes. The Ministry of Electricity estimated that up to half the power distributed by the transmission system in urban areas was stolen.[13] Not many people bothered to pay their electricity bills, which in any case were next to nothing and part of the absurd subsidies system inherited from the former regime.

One of the main concerns of the poor was the availability of cooking gas. Iraqis were used to using LPG cylinders for their cooking needs, as no national grid for natural gas distribution had ever been developed. The LPG came mainly from Iraq's refineries, and as these sputtered to meet the increasing demand for petroleum products, an acute shortage of cooking gas developed. There was a proliferation of adulterated gas, with frequent gas explosions reported on a regular basis. The gas distributor going around Baghdad's neighbourhoods in his donkey cart, loaded with rusting and battered gas cylinders, was a common sight. The government tried to regulate the supply of subsidised gas by a ration system that called on the users to take their coupons to depots where the gas would be dispensed. The depots were located with the authorised food distributors of the Public Distribution System (PDS), Iraq's omniscient system of providing subsidised food and other essential items.

It was the operations of the PDS that most impacted on the lives of the poor, with its inefficiencies and waste. Arcane Green Zone discussions about replacing the PDS with more economically efficient mechanisms were abandoned for fear that this would lead to public disturbances.[14] The PDS was not only politically popular but a lifeline for the poor, who were not prepared to gamble on losing the certainty of supplies from the PDS today for the promise of a better deal tomorrow. Trade ministers would spend their time publicly decrying any intention of changing the terms of the PDS, while privately insisting that the system had to be reformed. Nothing much happened, therefore, and the corruption, graft and theft that were embedded in the system continued with no serious let-up. From time to time, shortages of basic commodities would occur as the purchasing, transport or distribution mechanism broke down.

In some cases, shortages were artificially created as senior trade officials blocked purchases of basic commodities, mainly because sufficient commissions had not been paid. For example, no wheat was purchased for months on end in early 2005, which created a serious risk that the PDS would not be able to meet the flour quota for the ration card. As the crisis loomed, teams of buyers were hurriedly assembled by the government to make huge flour purchases from nearby countries, at prices that reflected the 'emergency'. Millions of dollars of commissions were raked off by unscrupulous officials and politicians, because of a previous decision to halt normal wheat purchases.[15] The PDS became a regular target of media ridicule.

Killings of Academics and Doctors

Iraqi governments were frequently castigated and held responsible for the poor living conditions inside the country. Some of this criticism was deserved, but the fact remained that social disruption, crises and anxiety-inducing acts of violence and criminality were an integral part of the insurgents' tactics. This was particularly evident in the assassination of scores of academics and professionals, especially doctors. The killings started just after the collapse of the Ba'ath regime, when a number of university rectors and professors were murdered. The assumption at that time was that they had been assassinated for being pillars of the former regime, but many hardly fitted the stereotypical bill of a Ba'ath Party *apparatchik*. Dr Muhammad al-Rawi, a noted cardiologist and former Rector of Baghdad University, Iraq's oldest and most prestigious institution, was one of the first to be killed.[16] He was gunned down in his clinic in July 2003. He had been removed from his post as a result of the de-Ba'athification orders, but, even before these came into force, students had demonstrated against his continuing presence at the head of the university. The relationship between the Ba'ath regime and universities was subtle and deep. It would have been improbable that senior academics, particularly those in administratively sensitive posts, would have been allowed their position had they not been supporters and proponents of the regime's policies.

Academics with Ba'ath party affiliations felt aggrieved by their subsequent treatment as stalwarts of the former regime and by their removal from their posts as part of the de-Ba'athification measures. Nearly 300 members of Baghdad University's academic staff alone were sacked. The new Rector of Baghdad University, Sami al-Mudhafar, said, 'We can cope with de-

Ba'athification, we can cope with the staff shortage but we hate it. [They] were professors first and Ba'athists a very distant second.'[17] This view was not necessarily shared by vengeance-seeking individuals or groups who started to assassinate academics. It was highly probable that the early victims of the killings were murdered for their presumed associations with the former regime, but, as time went on and the intensity and scope of the killings increased, other factors prevailed. The killings of elites is a tried and tested strategy of insurgents and terrorists, bent on disrupting ordinary life and creating a climate of fear and anxiety to show that normal life is impossible unless their demands are met. Referring to the assassinations Dr al-Sinawi, a university professor, said, '[The assassinations and dismissals] will lead to a disruption of higher education for years to come. This will dramatically affect the standards of teaching and research for generations.'[18]

A number of exiles and opponents of the Ba'athist regime, who had returned to senior academic posts, were also targets for the assassins. A case in point was the murder of Professor Abd el-Latif Mayah, a democracy and human rights activist and political science professor at Baghdad's Mustansiriyah University. He had opposed the regime and was imprisoned for his activities. The night before his murder he had been a guest at a talk show on an Arab satellite television station, where he had extolled Sistani's position on free elections.[19] Three other Mustansiriyyah University professors were killed, ostensibly because of their Ba'ath party affiliations, while the dean of Mosul University's Political Science Department was murdered for his association with the occupation authorities.[20]

Iraq's university system was the pride of its educational structure and had been considered amongst the best in the Arab world. Nearly a quarter of a million students were registered at Iraq's twenty universities and technical institutes. Students were of indifferent quality as Iraq offered a guaranteed university place to any secondary school graduate. By the time of the Ba'ath regime's overthrow, the university system, reeling from years of war and sanctions, had been chronically degraded. Teaching standards had fallen, with only a third of the academic staff holding doctoral degrees. Nearly 40 per cent of Iraq's professors had emigrated, while its institutes and research organisations were isolated from the international community. A 2005 report by the UN University in Tokyo on the state of higher education in Iraq laid out the scale of the problems faced by the sector.[21] Nearly 2,000 scientific laboratories had to be re-equipped, while the universities needed at least 30,000 computers. Nevertheless, students continued to go to the universities. Academic qualifications were critical for ensuring acceptable employment in the state sector, and were the basis of the state's salary scales. Under these circumstances 'degree inflation' proliferated in Iraq during the 1990s. Idle civil servants and others with time on their hand pursued doctoral programmes at Iraq's universities, which resulted in nearly every official of any consequence being addressed as 'Daktour'. It was expected that one could not possibly hold a senior position if one did not hold a postgraduate qualification of one form or another.

The absence of advanced qualifications did not deter returning exiles from seeking, and obtaining, senior civil service positions. Returning exiles, some with the barest of academic credentials, were propelled to the doctoral class by the simple act of being repeatedly addressed as such. Some even went to the trouble of producing false diplomas, acquired from Baghdad's thieves market. The habit of equating competence and knowledge with paper qualifications was endemic; the public had been drilled into this over decades. The habit would persist into the post-occupation era, with a vengeance. It was assumed that the more advanced the degrees held by the ministers the more competent the Cabinet would be. The CPA easily picked up on this cultural feature of Iraqi society when it proudly announced the number of PhDs in the Governing Council and Interim Government cabinets as an indicator of their quality and careful selectivity.

Within a few months after the end of the war, doctors began to be targeted by hit squads. As with university professors and lecturers, the assassination of doctors followed no discernible pattern. Doctors were believed to be high-income earners, and a number of kidnappings were for ransom. Conditions in hospitals and private clinics became fraught with danger, prompting thousands of doctors to emigrate or to leave their profession. 'We can either quit our jobs and stay at home, work under these circumstances and endanger our lives or leave the country altogether', an Iraqi surgeon, Dr Muhammad al-Baghdadi, said.[22] Doctors began to receive handwritten messages to leave the country or else. By early 2005, nearly 10 per cent of Baghdad's 32,000 registered doctors had left their work.[23] Doctors were also accosted by relatives of patients angry at the doctors' perceived inability to cure or effectively treat the patient. 'We try to avoid complicated operations. What if the patient dies? You're face to face with relatives with guns', as one doctor said.[24] The standards of medical care plummeted. A deteriorating physical infrastructure, inadequate supplies and medicines, continuous power outages, all added to the sense of a health system under siege. This was further compounded by the rampant corruption in the medicines' importing company, *Kimadiya*, a state-owned monopoly from the Saddam era. Pharmaceuticals were routinely hoarded by company officials and then diverted to the black market or illegally exported.

The Health Ministry itself became a bastion of Islamist political parties. In spite of heroic efforts by individual doctors, administrators and ministerial officials, the deterioration in the health system continued unchecked. The Health Ministry budget had exploded from a paltry $16 million in the last year of Saddam's rule to nearly a billion dollars in 2004, but this had to accommodate the massive losses to the health system's infrastructure and the theft or destruction of medicines and medical equipment. It also had to fund the huge increases in the salaries and wages of workers in the health care system. The difficulties in access to medical services became more acute outside the relatively well-endowed Baghdad area. Iraqis discovered self-healing, traditional remedies and self-prescription of potent drugs. The latter was a particularly dangerous phenomenon, as all manner of potent drugs were freely dispensed by unregulated pharmacists. Drug addiction, a hitherto minor problem in Iraq, became more prevalent. Loose border controls between Iran and Iraq encouraged smugglers to use Iraq as a conduit for the heroin trade going into Saudi Arabia and the Gulf countries. Pilgrims to the holy sites of Iraq also carried hashish and opium, to feed their habit, or for sale in the virgin Iraqi market.[25] Even so, drug addiction was not that widespread, in spite of the social turmoil and stressful living conditions, perhaps a testament to the still powerful taboos against drug use and the pull of clan and family ties, which proscribed such practices.

Growth in Civil Society and Private Sector Organisations

There were a number of salutary developments in post-war Iraq, especially the growth of non-governmental and civil society organisations. These would have been impossible under the Ba'ath and the regime's obsessive controls over the individual and society. Ever more Iraqis gravitated towards these non-state institutions to redress grievances, tackle special interest issues, and help to build the foundations of a hoped-for democratic society. To their credit, the CPA and, later, the USAID programme placed a great deal of emphasis on these institutions, and considerable resources were expended on establishing, supporting and strengthening them. Democracy promotion, women's issues, provision of microcredit, support for artists, media and journalism training – the list was wide-ranging and encompassed a variety of people in all walks of life. The experience was novel and welcomed by most Iraqis who were associated with these programmes and played a part in rooting the idea of a civil society in an historically authoritarian political culture. The first serious test of the efficacy of these programmes was in the run-up to the elections of January 2005. Tens of thousands of volunteers and workers were drafted into the tasks of election monitoring and supervision. The development of civil institutions attracted a large number of enthusiastic and dedicated workers and was, perhaps, the most effective of the tasks undertaken by the foreign aid community in Iraq. Iraqis were attracted into this work, not only by the higher salaries on offer but also by a genuine sense of commitment and service to the idea. There were cases, however, that ended in tragedy, as when a trainee reporter working for the Institute for War and Peace Reporting was killed by the MNF while covering a story.[26]

The growth of private businesses was also seen as a critical element in the economic and social revitalisation of Iraq. The CPA had spent considerable resources in private sector development, and the policy rhetoric favouring private enterprise was continued in the successor governments in Iraq. With the notable exception of the Kurdish north, which followed its own rules within the framework of the Kurdistan Regional Government, the private sector continued nevertheless to be stymied by red tape, conflicting policies, inadequate credit and a hostile security environment. Businessmen had a very low reputation in Iraq, the public being accustomed to seeing merchants described by the government and the media as greedy, grasping and steeped in unethical practices. The overwhelming preponderance of the state in the economic sphere was not materially dented in the post-war world. Attempts were made to kick-start privatisation programmes on a small scale, but they had been more or less abandoned after a number of false starts. A privatisation commission was established during the interim government but it did very little, and was subsequently disbanded by the Transitional National Government.

The USAID programmes for encouraging the private sector were wide-ranging and included support for privatisation, capital markets development, credit for small and medium-sized enterprises and business services development. The effect of these efforts was not readily measurable, in spite of the ream of impressive 'metrics' produced by the foreign aid community. Perhaps the most intractable issue facing the private sector was the total absence of credit through the banking system. The state-owned banks dominated the banking sector, accounting for well over 90 per cent of total deposits. They were in a deplorable condition and effectively bankrupt.[27] They barely functioned as payment conduits for the government and had next to no resources for on-lending to businesses. The private banking sector, in spite of a spate of new banking licenses issued by the Central Bank of Iraq to foreign banks, was still puny in terms of capital, resources and skills. These issues were not lost on USAID, but it was proving far more difficult than anticipated to revitalise the private sector in Iraq. Nevertheless, businesses were operating on a larger scale than before, although few existed outside the area of providing supplies and contracting services to the government or the MNF; or in the areas of trading, retailing and wholesaling.

Public Markets and Entrepreneurship

Baghdad markets were well-stocked at reasonable prices. Gone were the days of acute shortages, shoddy goods and exorbitant duties. The shortages were mostly government-induced and reflected the appalling mismanagement of the food import and distribution systems. Whenever these reached critical levels, for example when sugar was unavailable for months on end on the ration book, private importers would spring into action and sugar would be plentiful in the markets – but at international level prices. Consumers, accustomed to receiving free sugar, would then complain about price gouging by greedy merchants. The press would then pick up on queue and add to the cacophony of noises demanding price controls and the chastisement of traders. (The latter was a tried and tested method of the Ba'ath regime which frequently swooped on 'profiteers', and in a number of cases actually imprisoned or executed them.)

The memory of the glorious days of the merchant classes, when the views of the *Shorja*, Baghdad's main wholesale market, would be avidly sought by Trade and Finance ministers, had not been completely erased. The main pillars of Baghdad's old merchant classes had disappeared, but a new merchant community was in the making. This was not seen as an undisguised blessing by all sectors of society. A number of merchants who had been dispossessed and deported to Iran in the expulsions and purges of the 1970s and 1980s were feeling their way back into Iraq. This gave rise to alarmist reports – part of the insurgents' disinformation campaign – that the *bazaaris* of Iran were returning to dominate the Iraqi trading scene. The vast majority of wholesale traders had been Shi'a before the socialist experiments of nationalisation sapped the vitality out of the Iraqi economy, and there was a subtle sectarian undertone to these reports. The fanciful nature of these claims did not stop a massive case of arson from taking place in the *Shorja* market in early 2005, where hundreds of merchants' offices, warehouses and stores were destroyed. Losses ran into tens of millions of dollars. It was clearly a case of insurgent-inspired sabotage, aimed at undermining the consolidation of a new, privately operated, wholesale market.

One of the curiosities of the CPA was the emphasis given to the reopening and revitalisation of the Baghdad Stock Exchange, a Saddam-era market that traded in the shares of private and partly state-owned companies. Stock markets, in the lore of proponents of radical economic overhaul were seen as showcases for Iraq's new economy and as a visible sign of the vitality of capitalist institutions. The total market capitalisation was pitiful, a grand total of $140 million by 2003.[28] The market was kept closed after the war as the CPA initiated a programme for its computerisation and the upgrading of its systems and procedures. Responsibility for overseeing the revamp of the exchange was first given to a US army reservist whose previous job had been with an armoured security company.[29] Later the job went to a twenty-four-year old political science major with no knowledge or experience in finance.[30] The appointment was received with incredulity by Baghdad's fraternity of stockbrokers. One of them said, 'I had thought the Americans would send someone who was at least 50 years old, someone with grey hair!'[31] The market finally opened in February 2004, temporarily housed in a converted restaurant inside a hotel before moving to its permanent quarters a year later.

By 2005 the exchange grew in size and activity, and although trading was restricted to four-and-a-half hours per week, volumes increased impressively and market capitalisation reached $1.5 billion.[32] Nearly ninety companies were listed in a number of sectors, including hotels, banks and construction materials. Given the poor security and policy environment that affected the real economy, the Baghdad exchange, now renamed the Iraq Stock Exchange, became a favourite haunt of speculators and traders with time and money on their hands. Nearly half the brokers were women, and active investors numbered over 10,000. The market had its ups and downs, sometimes moving, astonishingly, in a contra-cyclical pattern to the increased violence. Investors, especially those who visited the exchange, were ever conscious of the security dangers outside. 'When I go to the exchange I read the Quran, verses that can protect me', as one investor said.[33] The trading was still done by hand and prices posted on blackboards. By 2005, the CPA's promised electronic trading system had still not been installed.

But new businesses did spring up at the edge of the 'new' economy, such as the installation and maintenance of TV satellite systems, internet service providers and internet cafes. Enterprising young people became net savvy very quickly, and some relayed this into successful small businesses. As yet, there were no broadband services because of the indecision of the Ministry of Telecommunications which offered and then withdrew licences to private contractors, and its inability to provide a state-operated alternative. Installing a satellite dish might cost a significant amount of money – a minimum of $3,000 – so companies would install a dish and have the costs shared by a number of houses hooked up to a central dish.

Educational Policy and the Teaching Profession

An area which was mostly a success for the Iraqi government, USAID and the international aid community, and which had a significant impact on the lives of families, was the rehabilitation and expansion of Iraq's primary and secondary schools. The strategy for the rehabilitation of this sector had been set out by a detailed survey by UNESCO, which identified the main bottle-necks, problems and opportunities. In a one-year period, USAID rehabilitated about 2,400 schools, nearly one-fifth of Iraq's schools, and distributed nearly nine million science and maths textbooks. Millions of teacher and student 'kits' were handed out.[34] The World Bank also chipped in with a $40 million loan, funded by grant aid, for the provision of textbooks, and a further $60 million for schools rehabilitation. The programme was nevertheless dogged with criticism, especially as a large portion of the textbook contracts were awarded to printers outside Iraq. Similarly, the costs of rehabilitating the schools were grossly in excess of the norms in Iraq, mainly due to the 'layering' and high personnel costs implicit in aid-financed projects. The impact on Iraqis, however, was immediate and positive. School enrolment and participation increased; the acute shortage of textbooks and teaching materials was relieved; and a stab at improving the standards and quality of teachers was taken.

On the other hand, de-Ba'athification had a major impact on the educational sector, as large numbers of teachers were affected by the Party's orders. Teachers were a favourite target for Ba'ath Party recruiters, and featured prominently in the indoctrination, mobilisation and propaganda policies of the former regime. At the same time, a fair proportion of the Ba'ath regime's victims were teachers, as the Ba'ath Party tried to weed out proponents of a different ideology or teachers who would not toe the party line. The plight of newly dismissed teachers and the return to service of formerly purged teachers became a running sore in the successive post-war governments.[35] There were well over a quarter of a million teachers in Iraq's school system, and they occupied an important position in Iraqi society. The teaching profession had been held in high esteem in the past, but, as in nearly every area in Iraq's society, had suffered grievously over the previous twenty years. Teachers' salaries fell to next to nothing in the era of sanctions. Moonlighting, offering private tuition, and even sale of exam questions became accepted methods of augmenting a teacher's income. Many would leave the profession as conditions in the educational sector plummeted in the 1990s. In Kurdistan, following the end of internecine warfare in 1996, the sector began to revive but it was not significantly better than the rest of the country by the time the war had ended.

Educational policy, in particular curriculum and textbook reform, were high on both the CPA and subsequent governments' lists of priorities.[36] The textbooks of the Saddam era were full of references to Saddam and the Ba'ath Party, and the indoctrination, hero worship and militarisation reached into the furthest nook and cranny of the system.[37] The textbooks themselves reflected the extreme Arab nationalism of the Ba'ath Party, anti-Americanism and especially anti-Zionism, and a version of history that effectively ignored Shi'a and Kurdish sensibilities. There was no doubt that the system needed a complete overhaul. But, as in most initiatives launched by the CPA and subsequently continued by its successor governments, curriculum and textbook reform became mired in controversy and partisanship.

Essentially, the CPA had wanted a 'modern' curriculum, shorn of any sectarian, national or religious bias and stripped of all politically resonant phrases. Such a curriculum would form the basis for creating a new Iraqi citizen, filled with democratic ideals, politically moderate and partial to the west. The CPA's zeal for ecumenical education hit a rough patch, however, when the Education Minister of the Governing Council, the indomitable Dr Alaa Al-Alwan, later the Health Minister, criticised the CPA for removing references to Islam and proscribing verses from the Quran in the new textbooks that it provided.[38] The idealist zeal of some CPA officers mixed with a naïve effort to import the best of 'international practice'. The neo-conservative educational staffers and advisers of the CPA might have also, rather clumsily, attempted to slip in their ideological proclivities into Iraq's textbooks.

The battle over textbook content would continue into the Interim Government as the 'modernisers' and secularists tried to stake a claim to the effort, avoiding the minefields of the alternative historical and religious narratives of Iraq's Shi'a and Sunnis, Arabs and Kurds. Religious groups and Islamists meanwhile were insisting on a wholesale revision of the history taught to Iraq's children, to emphasise the under-reported and ignored aspects of the Shi'a narrative. Meanwhile, Kurds were ploughing ahead with their own educational curriculum, which naturally gave pride of place to their own language, culture and history. The content of textbooks became a leitmotif of the Iraqi condition. Issues of secularism and religion, the privileged position of Islam in society, liberal values versus traditional cultures, coexistence of Arab and Kurdish nationalisms, the varying Shi'a and Sunni interpretations of historical and religious issues – the list went to the heart of the Iraqi dilemma.

Religiosity and Increased Community Solidarity

The march towards increased religiosity helped to crystallise religious and sectarian affiliations in the multiple identities of Arab Iraqis. These, more than anything else, would determine the outcome of the elections. Religious observance became a matter of affirming one's particular identity, transcending other considerations and scruples. Young men would crowd into mosques on Fridays in huge numbers to hear preachers extol the virtues of their particular version of Islam. Mosques associated with charismatic clerics would be full of worshippers listening to sermons that demanded justice and redress of grievances for their sect. The Buratha Mosque in Baghdad became a centre for expressing the outrage of the Shi'a at their historic victimisation, and a determination to use the electoral mechanism to remedy the powerlessness that they felt. Sheikh Jalal al-Saghir, the Imam of the mosque, was particularly eloquent, delivering powerful sermons which thousands of people would hear in person or on tapes. His fearless espousal of the 'rights of the majority' was nothing less than a demand for Shi'a rule. He was not deterred by at least a dozen attempts on his life, and the Buratha Mosque itself would be the target of two devastating suicide bombings and mortar attacks which left scores killed.

The tactics of the extreme wing of the insurgents, which targeted the Shi'a in particular, played a large part in increasing their community solidarity. The truth was that the majority of the Shi'a no longer saw the bombings carried out by the insurgents as part of a broad destabilisation strategy. It was increasingly perceived that their group alone was being targeted, and that the devastation and killings were an expression of a generalised Sunni refusal to allow the electoral process to determine the distribution of power. The luke-warm condemnation of these attacks by the Sunni religious establishment greatly added to the suspicion that, although they may have disagreed with the indiscriminate nature of the killings, they did not necessarily object to their political purpose. In many ways the *takfiri* ideology of the extremist Salafis and Wahabbis which the Shi'a found so abhorrent was having an important counter-effect in solidifying the Shi'a politically.

The fulcrum of Shi'a opinion moved decisively towards a religious and communal understanding of their identity, leaving other considerations – tribal, political, or regional – to play a distant and secondary role, at least for the time being. It took some time before the changing reality of the Shi'a sank in. Most Shi'a secular politicians, together with the US and UK governments, were in deep denial about this fundamental shift in the persona of the Shi'a of Iraq. The UK ambassador, for instance, was adamant about the prevalence of an 'Iraqi' identity over other considerations, insisting that people were not as sectarian as they seemed.[39] At the same time, the usual arguments affirming the existence of a broad centre that grouped the two communities (the Kurds were always left out of the equation) were paraded as if they would somehow mitigate the effects of political polarisation. The common Arab and tribal identities of the Shi'a and Sunni were also produced to confirm the ephemeral nature of a sectarian political line-up. The removal of the dictatorship was supposed to lead to a common democratic and liberal future for the Arabs of Iraq, as if the legacy of decades, if not centuries, of misrule and tyranny could be wished away.

A similar reaction was at work within the Sunni community. While publicly adhering to the common roots of the Arabs of Iraq, their visible leaders, in particular the clerical classes and the Islamists in their midst, were profoundly shaken by the possibility of loss of power. The build-up to their boycott of the elections was cast in terms of rejecting elections held under the auspices of an illegitimate government working under a law that was drawn up during the occupation. But it was the increasingly evident demographic realities in Iraq that exercised their leadership. The methods of the terrorists and insurgents may not have been the ones that would have been chosen by the rank and file of the Sunni Arab community, but blocking the rise of the Shi'a was seen as a patriotic duty if majority rule was to mean Iranian interference, Shi'a clerical authority over the political process, and a distancing of Iraq from its Arab roots. It was now the turn of the Sunni community to feel under siege. Stripped of the props of central authority, an indifferent if not antipathetic America, and with enfeebled Arab allies, the Sunni leaders of Iraq were determined to stop the march towards what they perceived to be a majority dictatorship. Middle-class Sunnis stayed true to their heritage of denying the prevalence, or even the existence, of sectarianism in Iraq. They continued to blame the occupation forces, Iranian machinations, or formerly exiled politicians for this state of affairs, all the while pointing to the Shi'a members of their own extended families or their visits to the holy shrines as positive proof of the absence of sectarian feelings on their part. The litmus test was not whether they had Shi'a relatives, probably of a secular bent and equally middle-class in disposition, but how they perceived the denizens of the slums of Baghdad and the underclass of poor and dispossessed Shi'as. The idea that these people might come into power filled them with dread – as it did with quite a few of the Shi'a middle classes. A post-Ba'athist mindset was evolving, which welcomed the secularisation, even westernisation, of Iraq, but which was not prepared to accept the consequences of free elections. As long as the western presence in Iraq was associated with free elections, which might bring the dreaded Islamists to power, the cultured middle classes of Baghdad would be ranged against the democratic process.

The increasingly poisonous environment between the two communities began to affect the lives of mixed families and neighbourhoods. Tensions bubbled to the surface within families that had both Shi'a and Sunni members, and the beginnings of population shifts in mixed neighbourhoods could be discerned. The string of small towns and villages around the southwest periphery of Baghdad, the control of which was vital for the evolving insurgency, was the first to see people driven out of their residences.[40] At first it was a trickle, but within a year the trickle would turn into a flood. Clusters of refugees from these towns could be seen outside the shrine cities and in the poorer parts of Baghdad. The pattern involved placing threatening notes ordering these hapless people to leave within a few hours, followed by selective killings to drive the point home. The process crept northwards into Baghdad itself, especially within the district of Dora, an industrial suburb lying to the south of the city.

Iraqi society was severely jolted by the invasion and occupation of Iraq, probably more so than at any other time in the past millennium. More people were affected more intensively than in the wars of the Saddam years, in the coups and countercoups of the 1950s and 1960s, or in the two world wars. It would be necessary to return to the Mongol invasion to discern a similar cataclysmic upheaval that spread to every corner of the country. The striking feature now was the inability of the occupying authorities to impose central control and, in the process, allow free rein to the repressed passions of the country to boil over. Neither the occupying authorities nor the successor government could articulate a vision of the country that took into account the changes that had indelibly occurred. The Americans repeated the mantras used to justify the occupation of the country, even as the Iraqi peoples' hopes, fears and anxieties signalled other preoccupations and concerns. The democratic and liberal-minded political class that thought the people would give it a hearing was impervious to the changes that had occurred. They did not, and could not, acknowledge that longer-term trends were consolidating, which would spring to the fore in the elections. The elections were neither a referendum on the occupation and its garbled message nor a vote of confidence in the new democratic structures so laboriously hammered out. They were about the empowerment and disempowerment of entire peoples; rectifying historical wrongs and affirming age-old verities; suppressed national rights and the identity of an entire country. The battle lines over Iraq's identity were being drawn everywhere, and it was on the fundamental issue of Iraq's identity, more than on any other, that the outcome of Iraq's first post-war elections would be determined.

22

The Vote

'Taking part in elections like these means nothing but to grant legitimacy to a completely illegal situation.'

Muthanna al-Dhari, spokesman for the (Sunni) Association of Muslim Scholars, speaking on December 10, 2004 referring to the January 2005 elections

'We won't have a secular constitution. We'll have an Islamic constitution; the majority in this country is Shi'a. Anybody who wants to liberate Iraq should vote for this list [the 'Sistani' list]' –

SCIRI leader, speaking in a Kirkuk mosque, January 2005

The election boycott call by the main Sunni parties would obviously have a major influence on the level of participation by the Sunni Arabs. An election for a constituent assembly without significant Sunni Arab involvement might be seen as seriously impaired. At the same time, as the election date approached, the strength of the UIA – the party list ostensibly backed by Sistani – appeared to be gathering momentum and threatened a clean sweep of the Shi'a vote. Alarm bells arose, not only amongst the secular parties but also in Washington.[1] There the administration was caught in a predicament of its own making. On the one hand, the obsessive determination to meet each and every milestone of the TAL on time made Bush impervious to arguments for delays to the political process; on the other hand, the gathering strength of the Shi'a religious parties, and their shadowy connections to Iran, made a mockery of the claim that elections would lead to a secular, pro-western government. The efforts to stiffen up Ayad Allawi's campaign thus became more urgent, and led to a decision by the USA and Britain, backed by friendly Arab regimes and groups, to support his campaign covertly.[2] The insurgents were bent on destroying the credibility of the elections. A marked escalation of bombings, assassinations and sabotage marked the weeks that preceded the elections, and included the murder of the governor of Baghdad province. Would-be voters were threatened with certain death if they dared to cast their ballot, and people were warned off polling stations, which became insurgent targets. As late as the middle of January, barely a fortnight before the elections, the Interim Government was still hinting that the 'security situation' might lead to the postponement of the elections. But George Bush was determined that there would be no delays, and Ayad Allawi backed off from suggesting a postponement to the elections.[3] A postponement would have certainly been interpreted as a ploy to stop the Shi'a groups ranged around the UIA list from achieving their goals through the democratic process. In the event, the elections went ahead anyway – in spite of the widespread Sunni Arab boycott; the near certainty of the UIA achieving a dominant position in the new assembly; and the insurgent campaign of intimidation. Now there were the questions of who was going to form Iraq's first popularly elected government and what kind of government it was to be.

The Boycott of the Sunni Arabs

The decision by the main Sunni Arab groups and political parties to boycott the elections was disastrous. It effectively shut out the Sunni Arabs – from the inner counsels that determined the pace and direction of the political process, at a critical juncture when a new constitution was being drafted. The factors that underlay the boycott decision were many and varied. The extreme wing of the insurgency denounced the entire democratic process and was totally unwilling to participate in any shape or form in electoral politics – at least not until the terms of the political process were altered to its advantage. The forty-seven mainly Sunni groups that convened at Baghdad's Um al-Qura mosque, in mid November 2004, under the auspices of the AMS, had denounced the elections whose results were 'settled in advance in favour of the collaborators' and which were 'imposed' by the occupation forces.[4] They repeated that there could be no free and fair elections within a political process that was determined by the occupying powers. Groups that had gingerly sidestepped the issue of cooperating with the Americans, such as the Iraqi Islamic Party, only decided to boycott the elections when they could not engineer their postponement. The demand for postponing the elections was linked to the unsupportable claim that the insurgency would subside over the next few months.

The hypothesis was that the mainline Sunni parties should be given enough time and leeway to convince the more amenable insurgents to participate in the election process. But underneath these apparently valid concerns lurked the unspoken truth – namely that the umbrella Shi'a alliance, the UIA, together with the Kurdish parties, were likely to sweep more than two-thirds of the seats in the new assembly, and would therefore determine the course of Iraqi politics. The boycott of the elections was a rearguard action, designed to achieve a number of objectives: first, to deny the legitimacy of the elections, given that the Sunni community would stay away in droves and any parliament would be unrepresentative. Second, the boycotters were not prepared to participate in a process that would publicly confirm the demographic reality of the Shi'a's numerical advantage. This would undermine their constantly repeated refrain that the Shi'a claim to a majority status was illusory. Once the elections became a foregone conclusion, however, the boycott severely hampered the Sunni Arabs in participating in the constitution-drafting process. They had to await the arrival of a new American ambassador who would be prepared to pick up on their objections and insist on their involvement in the drafting of the constitution. Tactical voting considerations would have dictated that they should have voted for Ayad Allawi's list, but this was not to be. Most Sunni Arabs chose to sit out the elections.

The United Iraqi Alliance, the Kurdistan Alliance, and the *Iraqiyya* List

The United Iraqi Alliance (UIA) list grouped all the main Shi'a leaders in Iraq, except for the Prime Minister, Ayad Allawi. The UIA was hard pressed to come out with a coherent campaign theme. Its symbol was that of a shining candle, designed for easy identification by simple or illiterate voters. Its platform was a hodgepodge of platitudes that promised rebuilding Iraq's economy and social services, strengthening the security forces and a demand for a clear timetable for the withdrawal of the MNF.[5] The latter point was quickly forgotten, as were nearly all the promises made, as soon as the prospects for governing the country became closer to fulfilment. The UIA's political programme was unrealistic and unachievable for an eleven-month transitional government, the principal mandate of which was to preside over the country as a constitution was being drafted. But the UIA had an extremely potent ally: Grand Ayatollah Sistani. Three of his closest *wakils* (agents) were on the list. Statements by other parties, especially Ayad Allawi's list, that the UIA was unfairly using religious symbols in its campaign were summarily dismissed. Sistani's deputies and his entire organisation inside Iraq were mobilised to get people to vote. When asked by Sistani's followers whom to vote for, the deputies would invariably praise the UIA and 'recommend' people to vote for them. On 4 January 2005 the *hawza* of Najaf also mobilised voters for the UIA list.[6]

The election was becoming a straight contest between the UIA and Ayad Allawi's *Iraqiyya* list. The Kurdistan Alliance ticket was not a direct competitor, as both parties had basically conceded the Kurdish vote to them. There was some question about the Fayli (Shi'a) Kurdish voters and whether they would choose their ethnic over their sectarian affiliations. Eventually, the majority of Fayli Kurds went for the UIA. Ayad Allawi's campaign was the most professional and polished. This was because it was receiving considerable support from the USA and Britain, in a variety of ways. Private polls of the US Embassy were showing a dramatic sweep by the UIA, and anxiety gripped the main coalition partners. The scruples about directly interfering in the electoral process melted away, as it became increasingly obvious that the democratic process would likely lead to the 'wrong' outcome. The objective became one of denying the UIA a clear electoral victory that would allow them to govern unchallenged. The presence of a strong countervailing force in the form of secular and pro-western parties became essential.[7] However, US financial support for certain candidates was highly controversial and smacked of fixing the elections.

The Prime Minister's campaign had a slick sheen that was a contrast to the rank amateurism of the UIA's election campaign. Trading on the image of Ayad Allawi as a 'strongman', his election posters focused on his piercing gaze, with various slogans that called into mind an image of a decisive and virile leader. The elections were of an epoch-making nature, more a referendum on identity than a straightforward issues-related election. In the privacy of the polling booths, the most unexpected of people would find themselves voting for the UIA as a mark of community solidarity. A young man of mixed Iraqi and European parentage, who had left Iraq as a child for the west and had only recently returned to Baghdad as part of the CPA contingent, was a case in point. He was totally irreligious, an avid partygoer, and could barely speak Arabic. Nevertheless, he cast his vote for the UIA. 'I had planned to vote for one of the liberal parties but when the time came, I could not betray my Shi'a origins', he sheepishly admitted in defence of his vote.[8]

The January 2005 Elections and their Aftermath

The actual elections went off quite successfully, in spite of a near-universal boycott in the majority Sunni areas of Iraq and the terrorist incidents that marred the process in parts of the country. About 8.5 million Iraqis cast their vote, nearly 60 per cent of the eligible voters.[9] Iraqis overseas, however, of whom nearly 1.2 million were eligible to vote, did not participate in the anticipated numbers. Only a quarter of a million cast their votes. By and large, accusations of ballot-rigging were few, given the importance of the elections. In Mosul, however, irregularities were widely reported, including the non-delivery of ballot papers that affected Christian voters, leading to widespread protest demonstrations. The final results of the elections were being tallied throughout the month of February, but early on it became clear that the major winners were the UIA and the Kurdistan Alliance. A 111 slates competed for the parliamentary seats, but only handfuls were able to gain any representation. Out of the 275 seats in parliament, the UIA had initially garnered 133, which would later increase by the addition of a few more seats according to a complex vote distribution formula. A small, independent Sadrist list with three seats also joined the UIA, as well as others, pushing the UIA to 148 seats, well above 50 per cent of the new parliament. The Kurdistan Alliance obtained seventy-five seats while Ayad Allawi's *Iraqiyyah* list managed forty seats, a respectable showing of nearly 15 per cent of the parliamentary seats.

Nevertheless, the Allawi list was embittered by the intervention of Sistani in favour of the UIA. Imad Shabib, a former officer and associate of Ayad Allawi, said, 'We lost the elections because of the influence of Sistani on the voters . . . The Shi'a list [the UIA] won three million votes because of his personal influence and the election results do not reflect reality.'[10] Ayad Allawi later rued the baneful influence of Sistani's deputies on the electorate. 'Frankly, I know in the south we have a lot of good Iraqi people who wanted to vote for us, but they [Sistani's representatives] told them that their wives would divorce them, they would be sent to hell.'[11] The UIA was now poised to ensure that its nominee for the prime ministerial post would be the country's first freely elected prime minister for over fifty years.

The focus now switched to the internal dynamics of the UIA where a number of contenders were preparing themselves for being the list's nominees for the post of prime minister. The UIA had early on decided to constitute itself as a parliamentary bloc with its own internal rules and procedures. Immediately after the elections, as it became clear in preliminary results that the UIA would be the largest bloc, meetings of those assured of a seat in the national assembly were called at the behest of Sayyid Abd el-Aziz al-Hakim. The fact that Hakim took the lead in this matter and that the parliamentary bloc met at SCIRI's headquarters in Baghdad gave him de facto leadership of the UIA. The consensus inside the UIA and in Najaf was that the transition phase required that the UIA held the premiership, which ensured control over the executive branch. The principles for selecting a prime ministerial candidate were also set, which included a commitment to work for rectifying the historical disadvantage of the Shi'a.[12] The early expectation was that Abd el-Mahdi would secure the nomination.

The SCIRI was determined to control the main security portfolios, in particular the Interior Ministry. Its Badr organisation, with its thousands of trained militiamen, was poised to increase its role in internal security matters. The organisation was prepared to withdraw Abd el-Mahdi's nomination in favour of Jaafari, knowing that it would have a number of Cabinet portfolios, especially the Interior Ministry, allocated to it. Jaafari was convinced that he would be the best prime ministerial candidate, and even thought of this as a 'calling' and as a culmination of decades of political activity and opposition to the Ba'ath regime. On 22 February 2005, Ibrahim al-Jaafari became the UIA candidate for prime minister, and was virtually assured of forming the next government. Ahmad Chalabi was the UIA's candidate for deputy prime minister.

The selection of Jaafari as the UIA's candidate for prime minister was replete with significance and symbolism. The head of the Da'awa Party, Saddam's most implacable historical enemy, who was indelibly associated in the public mind with the decades-long Islamist struggle to achieve legitimacy and power, was now poised to lead the first truly democratic government in Iraq's history. It was not what the Americans had expected or wanted. The containment of Iran, one of the cornerstones of US, and indeed western, policy since the 1979 Revolution, and for which Iraq was an essential prop, went on the backburner. Iran had played a significant behind-the-scenes role in assuring the electoral success of the UIA, and had a great deal riding on the UIA's choice of prime minister. In fact, Iran played a contributing role in the selection of Jaafari. Both the USA and Britain were resigned to accepting the UIA's selection and prepared for thwarting a possible Islamist agenda by relying on the spoiling role of the Kurds in any new Cabinet.

The neo-conservatives in Washington were at a loss to explain the outcome of the elections, which by all reckoning had handed power to a group that was completely out of their reckoning. One of the principal myths that underlay the justification for the invasion and occupation of Iraq now lay in ruins. When given the choice, the Shi'a did *not* vote for the secular, liberal or pro-western parties. Instead, they voted in ways diametrically opposed to the original hypothesis of the war's ideological promoters. The spin doctors of Washington sprang into action, praising the Iraqi people for going to the polls in the teeth of terrorist threats. They belittled the UIA victory by churlishly claiming the UIA's 48 per cent of the vote count did not actually constitute a majority. Washington was not prepared to acknowledge publicly that the election results opened up an entirely new set of issues that had to be considered. A very prescient observer of the Shi'a scene, Professor Juan Cole of the University of Michigan, who had come out strongly against the war and the occupation, accurately summed up the post-election situation. 'This is a government that will have very good relations with Iran . . . In terms of regional geopolitics this is not the outcome that the United States was hoping for.'[13]

The Formation of Ibrahim al-Jaafari's Transitional National Government

The UIA quickly formed a series of internal committees that would map out the policy framework for Jaafari's government. The most important of these was called the Coordination and Follow Up Committee, and it comprised representatives of all the main UIA factions. Lip service was paid to the limited duration of the Transitional National Government and its main responsibilities of managing the country during a period when the new constitution was being drafted. The Islamists' experience in the Interim Government period had been embittered, and the UIA was intent on rectifying what they saw as its errors and excesses. For example, the nascent security institutions of the country were still packed with Ba'athists and Ba'ath regime operatives.[14] The head of the Iraqi Intelligence Services was accused of forming a brigade-sized force that reported only to him and, presumably, his American overseers. The Ministry of Interior was full of people who were loyal to the former minister, Falah al-Naqib, and had twelve battalions that were considered inimical to the Shi'a.

The UIA developed a seven-point plan as the basis of its governing platform.[15] The first and most vital was the 'security' file. The UIA called for a thorough springcleaning of the security forces and asked that elements from outside, obviously meaning the Badr Organisation, join the security forces en masse. It was a cardinal principle that the UIA, rather than other coalition partners in the government, should dominate the security policy of the Transitional Government. The second point called for a reform of the institutions of the state, which meant the intensification and implementation of the de-Ba'athification measures. (These had been either reversed or allowed to lapse during the Interim Government months.) In addition, there were the usual demands of improving the level of services and accelerating reconstruction, and the UIA government was obliged to support the families of those who lost their lives in the struggles against Saddam and terrorism, and to improve the lot of the deprived southern provinces and Baghdad.

The prime minister-designate was also bound by a set of promises that governed his and his Cabinet's policies. An acceptable candidate from the UIA's perspective was one who was able to 'express the patriotic and Islamic identity of the country'.[16] He was also bound to have 'a positive view on the *Marji'iyya*, and act in accordance with its views and decisions'.[17] Essentially, the UIA would only join a government that was run by an Islamist – who was close to the *Marji'iyya*. The prime minister also had to agree to accept that two or three representatives from the UIA would be embedded in every ministry presided over by a UIA minister. The UIA wanted to ensure that the prime minister would not operate outside of the control of the UIA's main bodies. In practice, this would prove impossible to achieve as the prime minister sought to establish, and then enhance, his own authority. Jaafari acceded to these conditions and set about trying to form his cabinet. The first port of call was the Kurdistan Alliance. No government was possible without their involvement. The Kurds did not have a blocking veto on the formation of the government as, according to the TAL's terms, a two-thirds majority would be needed for electing the presidential council. But it would be extremely difficult to conceive of a government not anchored on the Kurds. The discussions with the Kurdistan Alliance were long and laborious with a number of false starts.

The Kurdistan Alliance presented a detailed working paper that regulated the relationship between them and the UIA.[18] It was divided into two parts. The first dealt with the principles for a governing partnership between the two blocs, and the second with a joint effort at managing the drafting of the new constitution. The working paper listed eleven principles for the operations of the Transitional Government. These included abiding by the terms of the TAL; forming a unity government that would include other parties; accelerating the process for launching the trial of Saddam and his henchmen; and defining the circumstances that would call for the resignation of the government. The Kurd's main concern was in the drafting of the constitution. Here the Kurds called on the UIA to accept a number of guiding principles for the constitution-writing process, and pushed for the inclusion of Sunni groups that had boycotted the elections. The Kurds insisted on respect for the existing federal arrangements for Kurdistan; that the status of Kirkuk should be quickly settled, and that their *pesh merga* forces should be inducted, as an organised force, into the new army. The Kurds sought eight cabinet posts and wanted the UIA's support for their candidate, Jalal Talabani, for the presidency. The Kurds' demands for a 'national unity' government were actually a call to include the *Iraqiyya* list in the government. This may have been prompted by the Americans, who wanted to ensure the presence of a countervailing force in a UIA-led government.

The discussions with Ayad Allawi on his participation in the government led nowhere. The *Iraqiyya* list presented its own ten-point working paper, most of which carried positions that were diametrically opposed to that of the UIA.[19] The talks foundered on a number of issues, including de-Ba'athification, the role of the *Marji'iyya* in politics, federalism for the south, the status of militias, and the role of Iran. The list was too long and the gaps too wide. Eventually, Ayad Allawi chose to stay in opposition, while the UIA redoubled its efforts to reach a final deal with the Kurds. The Sadrists were also an issue, playing a spoiler role by threatening to bolt from the UIA and join the *Iraqiyya* bloc in forming a government. They had to be appeased with a number of cabinet posts, including Transport and Health. The National Assembly had convened on 16 March to elect its speaker and his deputies. A number of candidates had been presented for what was to be a 'Sunni Arab post'. Hachem al-Hassani, a prominent member of the *Iraqiyya* list, was elected as the Speaker. Ghazi al-Yawar, the former President of Iraq in the Interim Government, accepted the post of vice-president in the

Transitional Government, as did SCIRI's Adel abd el-Mahdi (there are two vice-presidents). On 6 April 2005, the National Assembly chose Jalal Talabani as President. On the following day, Talabani designated Ibrahim al-Jaafari to form his cabinet.

The actual formation of the cabinet was a drawn-out affair. Although National Assembly members should have been concentrating on the writing of the constitution, there was a scramble for high-level positions. A five-person UIA committee was appointed to look into the resumes of candidates for ministerial positions. The committee included nominees from SCIRI, the Da'awa Party and the independents caucus inside the UIA. The idea was to shortlist three candidates for each ministerial post, while giving the prime minister the final choice of candidate. Most posts were quickly filled but a major issue still loomed. The absence of the *Iraqiyya* list from the cabinet removed a number of Sunni Arabs from possible consideration for cabinet posts. The SCIRI had insisted on the Interior Ministry for its candidate Bayan Jabr, leaving the Ministry of Defence as the preserve of the Sunni Arabs. The post became a tussle between the UIA, which sought a Sunni Arab who was at least supportive of the political process, and outside groups which wanted to have either a professional officer or a person who could lay claim to access to the insurgents.

The Jaafari cabinet was cobbled together as a result of a series of compromises. Factions inside the UIA had to be appeased; the Sadrists had to be included; the Kurds had to be given their due; the Sunni representation had to be reasonable both in number and quality. A number of Sunni groups, seeing the manifest error that had been made by their community in staying away from the voting, scrambled to be given a place in the new cabinet. It was proving difficult, however, to achieve a consensual list that most Sunni Arab groups would accept as being representative. The US Embassy took a particular interest in the key ministries, the so-called 'sovereign ministries', of foreign affairs, defence, interior, oil and finance, and it exercised a subtle veto if the candidate was seen to be too partisan or divisive. The rhetoric of the UIA political leaders promised the public a cabinet of competent, effective and honest ministers, as an antidote to the excesses of the Brahimi/Blackwill selections of the Interim Government. The reality was compromises and deals, and frequently the demands of balance and representation took precedence over the qualities of the ministers. Ali Allawi was the new finance minister. Bayan Jabr's tenure at the Interior Ministry would prove contentious, especially as the Ministry of Interior came under increasing fire from the Sunni Arab parties – and the US Embassy – for allowing large-scale infiltration of Shi'a militias and alleged 'death squads' into its ranks.

Jaafari and his cabinet were sworn in on 3 May, 2005 in front of the National Assembly. The fragility of the coalition government was apparent, even as it was being sworn in. A key phrase in the oath calling for a 'democratic and federal' Iraq was surreptitiously dropped by Jaafari's aides, much to the anger and consternation of the Kurds. It seemed to confirm their suspicions about Jaafari and his less-than-sterling commitment to a federal future for Iraq. Jaafari followed the swearing in with a speech that laid out, vaguely and grandiloquently, the government's plans over the transition period. The commitments made were completely unrealistic and unnecessarily bound the Transitional Government to reforms and improvements in services, jobs and incomes in ways that would prove difficult to achieve. The government, after all, only had an eleven-month life, and three months had already been spent in bickering and manoeuvring. The unfortunate pattern of over-promising and under-delivering had begun with the CPA and the Governing Council, and continued with the Interim Government and, now, with the Jaafari government. It was a case of politicians making expedient or wild promises that took no notice of the prevailing conditions of insecurity, administrative chaos and dysfunctional government. A tired and weary citizenry stood back and hoped against hope for some reprieve from lawlessness, violence, power blackouts, gasoline lines and water shortages.

The Jaafari government was beset with serious crises from the day it came into office. Many groups had wanted it to fail. It was the first Islamist-led government, and the expectation by secularists and Arab nationalists was that it would be mired in squabbling and ineffectiveness. It was an article of faith on the part of the secularists and liberals that Islamists had no governing programme or abilities, and that the task of 'real' government should be given to others who knew how to handle power and run a state. Patently false and mocking rumours began to spread about the Islamists' unsuitability for the task in hand and their obsession with the trivia of dress codes and Islamic forms of conduct and address. It was claimed that the prime minister had insisted that women who worked in the prime minister's office wore the *hijab*, an obviously false accusation. Crucial meetings were supposedly broken up for prayers, and it was said that rough clerics and uncouth provincials from the southern governorates were having the run of the place.

Zalmay Khalilzad and the Shift in US Policy

The US and British embassies maintained a formal correctness, but were still unsure as to how they should engage with a government run by Islamists. In time, however, they learnt that the ways of power can accommodate strange bedfellows. This became most evident after US Ambassador John Negroponte was replaced by Zalmay Khalilzad.[20] The latter's arrival in May 2005 coincided not only with the formation of the Transitional Government but also with the return of the main Sunni groups to the political process. Khalilzad, with his wealth of experience in Iraqi politics and personalities, was the right diplomat for the task at hand. His fluency in Farsi gave him access to Islamist leaders with no English, and his mannerisms and mindset were seen, naïvely, as enabling him to be empathetic to the ways of the Iraqi political class. As Adel Abd el-Mahdi, the vice-president, said, 'Zalmay presents himself as from the region . . . He understands the culture here and knows he can invite himself to come and see us.'[21] Iraqis often forgot that Khalilzad was an American envoy under instructions from an American president with a specific mandate to bolster the American project in Iraq – or at least to stop its deteriorating position.

Khalilzad decided to be a hands-on ambassador, not quite vice-regal, but certainly not a detached diplomat. In essence, his stance tracked the changing perceptions in Washington, which was now moving into a district third phase in America's encounter with post-war Iraq. The first phase had involved acting out the neo-conservatives' extraordinary conceit that the Shi'a of Iraq would provide the strategic Arab ally in the Middle East that America was seeking after 9/11. The ill-will manifested by the neo-conservatives towards the Saudi Arabian monarchy, which was seen as the guilty party in the radicalisation of Sunni Islam worldwide and as an 'un-indicted co-conspirator' in the 9/11 outrages, could partly account for the decided tilt towards the Shi'a and the Kurds in the immediate post-war environment in Iraq. This was reinforced by talk about the 'Greater Middle East' and the new American emphasis on promotion of democracy and human rights in the region. Bush's stated determination to end America's mollycoddling of dictators and tyrants in the Middle East added further suspicion to the belief that America was preparing to jettison its long-term allies, or at least reduce its reliance on them. Iraq, with a majority population supposedly grateful for its liberation from the Sunni-dominated world of Saddam, and with plenty of oil, would prove the perfect foil to the sclerotic regimes of the area. This naïve picture collapsed against the realities of the Shi'a situation in Iraq and the increasing tensions between the USA and Iran. By April 2004, America had abandoned most of the underpinnings that had informed its early Iraq strategy. The *Marji'iyya*'s insistence on elections; the rise of the Sadrists; the strength of Iranian influence on a broad swathe of Shi'a Iraqi groups; the weakness of the liberals, secularists and democrats – all pointed to the need for revising the assumptions that lay at the base of the American position in Iraq.

The second phase in America's diplomatic profile in Iraq coincided with the formation of the Interim Government, which, at its heart, involved the abandonment of the former policy tilt and its replacement with support for creating a 'national security' state in Iraq. By the time this shift occurred, however, the USA had already committed itself publicly to a political process based on a series of electoral milestones. This second phase was to provide the maximum support for the premiership of Ayad Allawi and for work on the measured rebuilding of the security forces – which included the return of Ba'athists into public service – in a radical departure from the original blueprint. But this fell foul of the limited time available for the Interim Government to consolidate itself; the milestone of the upcoming elections; and the existence of empowered Shi'a groups lurking in the wings. The failure of the secularists and nationalists to perform in the elections of January 2005 put paid to this second strategy, which was effectively abandoned after Ayad Allawi failed to secure the premiership and to have an important say in the Transitional Government. A new policy and a new person were needed to check the apparently unstoppable march of the Shi'a Islamists. This was coupled with the need to produce an effective political counter to the insurgency, which was not being contained by military means and which translated into a new opening towards the 'moderate' wing of the insurgency and its political allies.[22]

The USA now adopted a new policy direction, premised on coaxing credible representatives of the Sunni Arabs into the political process. The presence of only seventeen Sunni Arab representatives in the National Assembly provided the rationale for an opening towards the Sunni political and religious parties that had boycotted the elections. A new policy orientation could be discerned. It was the prime mandate of Khalilzad to increase the participation of Sunni Arabs in the political process, and in particular in the constitutional talks, as a prelude to a more 'even-handed' approach that would be more inclusive and accepting of the demands of the Sunni Arabs. A number of Sunni groups, prompted by the USA, rose to the occasion, and laid the groundwork for their re-engagement in the political process. In late May 2005, nearly 1000 Sunni Arabs – clerics, political and tribal leaders, even former military officers – met in Baghdad and demanded that they be included in the drafting of the new constitution. They were led by the Iraqi Islamic Party and Adnan Dulaimi. 'The country needs Sunnis to join politics . . . The Sunnis are now ready to participate', he said.[23] Ironically, the Sunnis would use the same arguments as the Shi'a for engaging in politics, referring to their marginalisation and loss of influence if they did not. The Sunnis who had already participated in the Jaafari government were pointedly not invited. They were cast as collaborators and 'court Sunnis'. The new Sunni grouping now had one major advantage. They would have a powerful advocate for their position in the person of the US ambassador.

Weaknesses of the Jaafari Government

The Jaafari government came into being after a difficult process that saw challenges at each step of the way. To some extent, this was due to the inexperience of Iraqi political leaders in negotiating and forming governments; more importantly, it was due to the sheer complexity of the rules governing the transition process and the myriad forces that had to be balanced. Any government emerging out of such cumbersome initial conditions could not also be expected to have an ambitious governing programme, unless led by someone with extraordinary leadership qualities. The leadership style of Jaafari was the opposite of Ayad Allawi's. He cultivated the air of a thoughtful scholar and moved in deliberate, cautious steps. His public pronouncements were vague. He hardly ever responded directly to a question and kept his options open on every conceivable issue. He seemed more comfortable in his Islamist certainties, and his speeches and interviews were liberally laced with religious terms and symbols. At first, his diffidence and obvious sincerity were endearing to a public that had seen too many strong men and 'men-of-action'; but later on these traits were reckoned to indicate indecisiveness and uncertainty. Jaafari had entered office as Iraq's most popular politician according to a number of opinion polls, but his lot, together with that of all of Iraq's political class, would precipitously fall.

It was unclear where the Transitional Government was heading. As a government, it did not articulate a single political and economic programme. The early Cabinet meetings were short on substance and long on procedure and the minutiae of administration. Ministers had considerable leeway in the running of their departments, without being subject to a set of commonly agreed policy precepts and objectives. Given this situation, the performance of the Transitional Government was a function of the relative success of each of its components rather than of the government as a whole. Success, therefore, was directly dependent on the qualities of the individual ministers and their ability to articulate and implement a coherent plan for their departments. Jaafari's management style also involved considerable delegation of his powers to trusted aides and ministers. There was also the abysmal security situation. Terrorism and violence surged at the time of the formation of the Transitional Government, not so much because of a sudden deterioration in the capabilities of the security forces, but more so because of a concerted effort by the insurgents to discredit and undermine Iraq's first democratically elected government. The fact that the Transitional Government was led by Shi'a Islamists added further layers of viciousness and cruelty to the insurgents' campaign. There was also a leap in the scale, gruesomeness and wantonness of the terror attacks on civilians.

In broad outline, therefore, the Transitional Government suffered from the same set of problems that afflicted the Interim Government, and it ended up committing the same mistakes – but for different reasons and purposes. In one important respect, though, it had an advantage over the Interim Government. It was not an appointed but an *elected* government which, despite the widespread Sunni Arab boycott, could still claim a democratic legitimacy that the Interim Government had lacked. Nevertheless, it was dogged by the problem of a limited mandate – in this case for overseeing the drafting of a constitution – which had to be achieved within a short period of time. Unlike the Interim Government, however, three months of its life-term were taken up with simply getting organised. In the remaining period it could do no more than set a realistic number of achievable targets and be content with them. What it did do, however, was to follow the Interim Government's route of promising everything to everyone. Political leaders were not prepared to accept the limiting nature of the words 'interim' and 'transitional', and they governed as if there were no time and objective constraints to their power. The Shi'a Islamists had suspected that Ayad Allawi would extend the duration of his government by postponing elections. It was now his turn to suspect that the Transitional Government would play for time and extend its mandated life. One of the conditions for the participation of Ayad Allawi's group in the Transitional Government had been that 'a consensus is reached [between the parties]' not to extend the duration of the transition period'. By ignoring the constraints on its ability to deliver on public promises of improvement in the citizens' lot, the Transitional Government set itself up to being judged on the basis of meeting impossible targets. At the same time, both the Interim Government and the Transitional Government were determined to impose their stamp on the government's security forces. The Transitional Government was determined to reverse the Interim Government's 're-Ba'athification' and attempts to pack the Defence and Interior Ministries with its cronies and supporters. The UIA reckoned the Interim Government's security measures were aimed particularly at the Islamists, and were designed to tie Iraq into the US security alliances in the Middle East. UIA's intent was not to rectify or reverse these appointments, or to improve the functions and efficiency of these institutions, but rather to turn the security ministries into UIA bastions. The short duration of the Transitional Government's life made these measures even more urgent.

In the end, therefore, both post-war Iraqi sovereign governments wanted to put their particular slant on the state machinery, to the detriment of the professional and non-partisan conduct of the government. Ideological affinity, partisanship, personal loyalties and cronyism were more important than competence and professionalism. Given Iraq's uncertain and tumultuous conditions, the desire to 'manage' the political process and use the machinery of government to advance the narrow political interest of those already ensconced in power, however, was not an altogether incomprehensible sentiment. Leadership that could match the country's difficult circumstances was simply not there to impart a unifying vision on the process. The USA kept a worried presence in the background. Its enormous investment of prestige and resources in the Iraqi 'project' were now challenged by a new imponderable – that of an Islamist-led government and the direction in which it would take the country during the following few months. Damage limitation became the order of the day, and there was a redoubled insistence on meeting the milestones of the TAL. The next hurdle in this marathon was the writing of the constitution. According to the TAL, the draft of the constitution had to be ready by 15 August 2005, scarcely three-and-a-half months away.

23

Negotiating a Constitution

'*We're watching an amazing event unfold: That is the writing of a constitution which guarantees minority rights, women's rights, freedom to worship in a part of the world . . . in a country that only knew dictatorship. And so, you're seeing people express their opinions and talking about a political process.'*–

George W. Bush on the writing of the Iraqi constitution, August 2005

'*We declare that we don't agree and we reject the articles that were mentioned in the draft and we did not reach consensus on them in what makes the draft illegitimate. We call upon the Arab League, the United Nations, and the international organisations to intervene so that this document is not passed. . .'* –

Joint statement issued by the fifteen-member Sunni constitution negotiating team, August 2005

The writing of a permanent constitution by an elected assembly was the main reason for the creation of a transitional period in the Iraqi political process. It had been Sistani's key demand, and was infused with extraordinary significance and symbolism. Through a permanent constitution, it was reasoned, the Iraqi state would be refashioned in ways that would reflect the values and aspirations of its myriad communities. The constitution was also the vehicle through which historical wrongs would be redressed and a new democratic dispensation established. Many people subscribed to Sistani's view, even including parts of the political establishment. But what was supposed to be a grand compact between Iraqis, which would usher in a new period in the history of their troubled country, was overwhelmed by the virulent political struggles of the times and the constraints of an impossibly short deadline. The TAL had set a theoretical period of nearly seven months between the end of the elections for the transitional assembly and the presentation of the final draft of the constitution by its drafting committee. After ratification by the assembly, the constitution was supposed to be approved by a national referendum on 15 October 2005, giving the public a two-month period in which they could formulate their opinions on it. The TAL drafters had allowed no margin for surprises in the political timetable; neither had they provided for the deterioration in inter-communal relations that accompanied the run-up to the constitutional elections. It took three months after the constitutional elections before a government could be announced. This, in turn, postponed the establishment of an all-party parliamentary constitutional drafting committee until the composition of the Transitional National Government could be determined. The process was further complicated by the efforts to find the mechanism through which Sunni Arabs could participate in the drafting process, given that their representation in the assembly was patently inadequate. The intervention of the US ambassador in the process was both necessary and problematic, for, although he played a smoothing interlocutor's role between the various factions, he was also accused of partisanship and glossing over fundamental differences in the interest of moving the process forward. These issues detracted a great deal from the promise of the new constitution, impaired its credibility, and turned what should have been a unifying agreement into a controversial and divisive document.

Sunni Arabs and the Constitution-Drafting Process

On 10 May 2005, the National Assembly nominated fifty-five of its own members to form the drafting committee.[1] The UIA had an absolute majority on the committee. Only two of the original fifty-five members were Sunni Arabs. On 24 May, Sheikh Humam Hammoudi, a cleric on SCIRI's central council, was selected as the committee's chairman. Hammoudi had joined Islamist politics after coming under the influence of Ayatollah Baqir al-Sadr, and had been jailed in the 1970s. After his release he fled Iraq to Iran. Foregoing his earlier preoccupations, he chose to pursue religious studies during his several years in exile in Iran. He was a thoughtful and deliberate politician, world-weary, and gave the impression that he was in conflict with his dual role as a man of politics and a man of religion. But he had seen his present position as a vindication of decades of struggle against dictatorship and as an historic opportunity to reclaim his community's rights in Iraq. Behind a ready smile lay a steely determination to push through with the constitution as the only and best chance to establish a framework for a new Iraqi state.

The issue of Sunni representation bedevilled the workings of the constitutional committee from the beginning. Grand Ayatollah Sistani had called on the leaders of the UIA to include more Sunni Arabs into the drafting process, and the USA was fearful that the lopsided Shi'a and Kurdish majority in the committee would destroy the chances of the constitution's legitimacy in the Sunni community.

The question remained as to how the Arab Sunnis were to be represented. Two major groupings that had boycotted the elections were now revising their stance.[2] The AMS had made condemnatory remarks about the constitutional process, but behind the scenes it was signalling that it would not be averse to having a role in the drafting committee. The Iraqi Islamic Party, which was the major Sunni group closest to the political process, favoured its involvement in the drafting committee, but it did not want to be seen as breaking Sunni ranks. It did not help matters when its former leader and Governing Council member, Mohsin Abd el-Hamid, was briefly arrested by US forces on suspicion of supporting the insurgents.

A new Sunni group, the National Dialogue Council, had also sprung up, led by an outspoken and fearless lawyer (and former Ba'athist), Saleh al-Mutlaq. Mutlaq was unashamed about the Ba'ath Party, going so far as to claim that it was the best party in Iraq's history. 'I still see the Ba'ath Party as the best party we have seen. If you compare them, they are much better than the parties that are governing the country now', he said.[3] Another person preparing to join the constitution-writing process was Adnan al-Dulaimi, a religious scholar. He emerged in the post-war tumult to head the Sunni Endowments Trust. He fell foul of the Jaafari government which saw him as being increasingly partisan after he had participated in conferences that were critical of the government. 'I have been chased out of my job because I defend the Sunnis', Dulaimi told a news agency.[4] He struck an incongruous figure as he harangued the media with his shaky voice, wearing a *siddara*, a strange and out-of-fashion hat that the *effendi* or official classes wore in the early monarchical period.

Initially, the majority Shi'a bloc, the UIA, was less than enthusiastic about accepting anything other than a symbolic participation on the part of unelected Sunnis in the drafting process. After fitful negotiations, however, it was agreed that an additional thirteen Sunnis could be added to the drafting committee, to put them roughly on a par with the Kurds. The thirteen additional members would, however, be non-voting.[5] This was rejected out of hand, in spite of promises that all the major decisions affecting the constitution would be consensual. After further rounds of negotiations, with the ever-present US Embassy advisers in the background, an agreement was reached whereby a total of twenty-five Sunnis would be added to the drafting committee. Ten of them, though, would be non-voting counsellors. This put the voting number of Sunni Arabs in the constitutional drafting committee at seventeen. The Sunnis were being assiduously wooed by the US Embassy to accept these terms and join the constitutional talks. The alternative was that the UIA, with the tacit approval of the Kurds, would plough ahead without the Sunnis.[6]

The three major groups that led the Sunni contingent agreed on a list of candidates and formally joined the constitutional drafting committee.[7] They had been kept abreast of developments.[8] The drafting committee inducted its new members only by early July, which left less than six weeks to write a constitution. Some of the new members were accused of being former Ba'athists, while the selection of candidates did not even pay lip service to a consultative process within the Sunni community. They were simply nominated by the kingpins of the Sunni side: the Islamic Party, Adnan al-Dulaimi's contingent, and the National Dialogue Council of Saleh al-Mutlaq. The situation appeared dire as each of the major blocs, including the Americans, had already provided their own drafts of a constitution, each differing greatly in the problematic areas.

Calls for Extending the Deadline for Writing the Constitution

The Kurds always saw the TAL as the basis of a permanent constitution. The UIA, on the other hand, wanted to do away with the less attractive features of the TAL but was stymied by its built-in veto. In essence, the constitution could not be passed in a referendum if three provinces voted against it. This stipulation was originally used by the Kurds to allow themselves the right to block a constitution with which they did not agree, as they could easily muster the majority needed in three provinces to override a new constitution. The USA also expected the TAL to be the base of a new constitution. During Deputy Secretary Zoellick's May visit to Baghdad, he stated that the Iraqis he had met had subscribed to this view. 'There's a general sense with everyone I talked to about using the Transition Administrative Law as a cornerstone.'[9] Sheikh Humam Hammoudi, the head of the drafting committee, showed the UIA's ambivalence about the TAL in an interview with the International Crisis Group. 'We will rely on general principles of the Transition Administrative Law but in the drafting of the constitution it will be only one of several sources.'[10] The TAL became in fact the basis for a large part of the new constitution, especially in those articles dealing with fundamental rights of Iraqis and the various freedoms associated with a liberal constitution. These were never seriously debated as they were taken as self-evident or innocuous. The attention of the drafters was elsewhere – on matters of federalism, ownership of natural resources, the role of religion in the state, nationality and citizenship, and the status of Kirkuk. The extraordinarily ambitious programme would have taxed a much larger, better organised and prepared drafting committee. Other countries took months, if not years, to fashion such a constitution. The *New York Times* summed up the case for extending the deadline for writing the constitution in an article by J. Alexander Thier of Stanford University's Project on Failed States, formerly a legal adviser to the Afghanistan constitutional commission. 'If the nascent government is able to devise a constitution by mid-next month, then they're probably missing the point. A constitution cannot be written in a few weeks by a handful of politicians at a conference table; creating a founding document requires the long ordeal of reaching political compromise and building trust . . . If Iraq's leaders end up with a constitution that looks good on paper but doesn't reflect a real political agreement, they will have failed.'[11]

The campaign to extend the deadline for writing the constitution coincided with the expansion of the drafting committee. The International Crisis Group, a respected conflict resolution NGO, was the first international organisation to call for a six-month extension of the deadline. This was followed by hints from the UN in Baghdad that a deadline extension might be appropriate. Nevertheless, senior Iraqi politicians, especially the Shi'a, were insistent on keeping to the incredibly short time-frame. There was concern that, if the momentum imposed by the tight timetable were not maintained, a Pandora's Box would be opened that might derail the entire transition process. A prolonged transitional process was also seen as working against the interests of the established parties who were positioning themselves for the December 2005 elections.

People who thought that a thorough-going legal, philosophical and intellectual airing of the issues would precede the promulgation of a new constitution were sorely disappointed. The discussions in the media were perfunctory, and the conferences that were called by western NGOs and foundations to explore the constitutional options remained limited in their impact on the participants. The TV campaign that was financed by the 'Future of Iraq Committee', an obvious front for American aid money for democracy-promotion, was not only insipid but inexplicably voiced over by people with a recognisably non-Iraqi accent. Meaningless slogans such as 'Vote Iraq', and shots showing bricklayers building walls, with reference to the reconstruction effort, did nothing to raise people's awareness of the burning issues that had seized the country and intruded on people's lives. The TAL had allowed for a possible extension of the deadline for writing the constitution. The drafting committee was supposed to notify the National Assembly by 1 August whether it felt that it would be able to produce a draft by the middle of August. Otherwise it could request a six-month extension of the deadline. The Sunni Arabs were clearly in favour of the extension. They had been effectively involved for only a few weeks in the drafting committee.

In public, the UIA bloc was ambiguous about the possibility of the drafting committee asking for an extension, but it held to the deadline in private. In a move that would pre-empt the call for an extension, however, Sheikh Humam

Hammoudi announced on 27 July that a number of important chapters of the constitution had already been agreed upon, and he circulated a draft relating to the personal law chapter of the constitution.[12] This seemed to indicate that the constitution-writing process was advancing at a faster rate than antici-pated. As the date of 1 August loomed, the drafting committee informed the National Assembly that it did not need an extension to the deadline, and that it would be able to produce a final draft by 15 August. The USA had played an important behind the scenes role in ensuring that the timelines of the political process would not be significantly changed. There was deep concern about any slippage in the TAL milestones lest it be seen as a loss of traction and therefore an encouragement to the insurgents and other ill-wishers. Rumsfeld, in his imitable way, bluntly said, 'We don't want any delays . . .. They're going to have to make the compromises necessary and get on with it.'[13] Once again, the milestones of the TAL appeared to be set in concrete. Jalal Talabani had met with US Ambassador Khalilzad. 'We discussed the issue of drafting the constitution on time and without delay', Talabani said. 'We agreed that on 15 August, the constitution's draft will be ready.'[14] The irony that the American ambassador had confirmed that the constitution was to be produced on time was not lost on people.

The Issue of Federalism for the South

The constitutional drafting committee was still wrestling with the most contentious issues that had been inherited from the TAL, when another bombshell erupted. On 11 August, four days before the deadline for presenting the draft constitution to the National Assembly, Sayyid Abd el-Aziz al-Hakim, leader of SCIRI and the head of the UIA, stood up in front of a large crowd in Najaf and made a startling announcement: 'To keep the political balance of the country, Iraq should be ruled under a federal system next to the central government . . . We think it is necessary to form one entire region in the South.'[15] Until that day, no senior political figure had publicly demanded that the Shi'a of Iraq should have a region of their own with commensurate powers and status like Kurdistan. Hakim's comments went against the prevailing current within Islamist circles that emphasised central rule. The Shi'a region he was demanding would embrace the entire South, and would hold the major oil fields and reserves, and the ports of the country. It built on the residue of frustration and anger that southerners felt at their neglect and impoverishment by successive central governments, which had continued in a more pronounced form since the fall of the Ba'ath regime. The scheme also dovetailed into SCIRI's own political supremacy in the south where it controlled, alone or in alliance, a number of provincial councils.

The TAL, which had basically limited federal regions to amalgams of not more than three provinces, was now being superseded in this most crucial of areas. Hakim was insisting that the constitution be drafted in ways that would allow the formation of 'super regions'. Grand Ayatollah Sistani had, apparently, been consulted on this matter, and while no formal statement was issued by his office, it was presumed that Sistani did not raise any objections. But Hakim's demand for a federal solution to the Shi'a's notion of being disadvantaged did not automatically translate into separatism and the establishment of a Shi'a state. In any case, there was scant support for such an entity; the belief that the Shi'a were specially targeted by the radical Sunni insurgents, however, grew in intensity, and this certainly played a part in the increasing alienation of the Shi'a from the idea of a centralised state.

The idea of a federal and multi-region solution for the structures of the Iraqi state was first mooted in an essay entitled 'Federalism' by Ali Allawi in 1992.[16] Decentralisation and strengthening of local government were important elements of the 2002 *Declaration of the Shi'a of Iraq*.[17] Ahmad Chalabi was also a proponent of a regional solution to the Iraqi state, and had made a number of speeches in favour of a three-province region in the deep south of the country. But none of the early proponents of federalism for the south had the mass base to promote these notions. The agenda was still dominated by Sistani's broad principles for political involvement. It fell to SCIRI, a party with a large base of followers in the Shi'a community, to take the lead in moving away from the generalised demands for elections and a constitution to a specific plan of action. By pursuing a regional agenda, SCIRI, of course, had to abandon the idea of a non-sectarian and unitary state, which was always an important element in its political platform.

The possibility that Iraq would be divided into two regions, Kurdish and Shi'a, with the resource-poor, mainly Sunni, rump provinces left to fend for themselves, raised serious alarm bells with the Sunni Arab negotiators. It seemed to confirm their worse fears about the new constitution.[18]

The Sunni Arab position on federalism was uniformly negative. It rankled those who believed in the binding unity of the country and the ever-present dangers of break-up if the centrifugal forces that threatened the country were given free sway. Of course the idea of a central state was indissolubly linked to the historical control that their community had exercised over the state, but it was also connected to the sense that it was they, uniquely, who had held the stewardship over a united Iraq identity. Now this was being threatened in a new compact, the consequences of which might reverberate for a very long time. But the Sunni Arab leadership had come around to accepting, grudgingly, that the Kurds did have an exceptional case, and by the time negotiations for the new constitution were afoot, the issue of Kurdistan's semi-independent status was no longer seriously questioned. The details were vigorously discussed, especially the territorial boundaries of Kurdistan and the case of Kirkuk's status, but the main issue of a confederal status for the Kurdistan region had been conceded. The Shi'a 'super region', however, was another matter altogether. It challenged the very heart of the Iraqi identity and the proposition that the Arabs of Iraq were at least united by their common ethnicity.

The response by the Sunni Arabs to Hakim's call for a nine-province region, the first time that the idea of federalism had been expressly linked to a sectarian rather than a geographical, administrative or ethnic base, was imme-diate and loud. Sunni clerics fulminated in their Friday sermons about plots to break up Iraq, and promised to foil the plan by fair means or foul. The resource argument, also a vital consideration for the Sunni Arabs, was played down in the public debate, mainly to concentrate the public's attention on the issue of unity and not on the division of resources, for which an accommo-dating formula had been found. The gauntlet was thrown down: SCIRI could now define the terms of the debate on regionalism, and for the first time the idea of an autonomous Shi'a region, albeit one in the context of a federal Iraq, was seriously broached.

The Hakim demands for a Shia region did not materially affect the progress towards completing the constitution, as it came well after the outlines of the new constitution were in their final draft form. A multiple province region had already been agreed in the draft, with the Kurds being its main propo-nents at first. They were looking to adding Kirkuk, and even parts of other provinces such as Mosul and Diyala, to their region. This would have necessitated that the TAL's three-province limit to regions be dropped.

The Status of Kirkuk

The Kirkuk issue was one that might have threatened the Kurdish and Shi'a constitutional pact.[19] The TAL made specific references to the issue of Kirkuk, and committed the Iraqi transitional government to 'act expeditiously to take measures to remedy the injustice caused by the previous regime's practices in altering the demographic character of certain regions, including Kirkuk'. In addition, Article 58(c) of the TAL stipulated: 'The permanent resolution of disputed territories, including Kirkuk, shall be deferred until after these measures are completed, a fair and transparent census has been conducted and the permanent constitution has been ratified.'[20] The Kurds had expected action on this matter by the Jaafari government as part of their joint governing agreements with the UIA. The prime minister, however, was very hesitant about accepting Kurdish claims to Kirkuk, or prepared to acknowl-edge the need for large-scale population movements to rectify the demo-graphic changes wrought by Saddam and, to a lesser extent, by other post-monarchy governments. These involved resettling Arabs from the southern regions and redefining the nationality of residents of Kirkuk, in order to increase the 'Arab' component of the city and the province of Kirkuk. The city was estimated to have a population of nearly a million, while the province had a population of about one-and-a-half million. Kirkuk sat on one of Iraq's biggest oil fields, accounting for nearly 15 per cent of its oil production. The Kurds were vociferous in demanding that Kirkuk be drawn into Kurdistan.

The Kurds were prepared to accept the Turkomen, Arabs and Christian populations of pre-monarchical Kirkuk as legitimate residents, but insisted that the resettled Arabs of the Saddam era and earlier should be removed. On the other hand, Kurds who had been displaced from Kirkuk had an absolute right of return, while Arabised neighbourhoods of Kirkuk that had been taken away from the province had to be reattached. To underscore their commitment to the return of Kirkuk to the Kurdistan region, they anticipated that Kirkuk would become the capital of Iraqi Kurdistan. The territorial limits of Iraqi Kurdistan, as presented by the Kurdish negotiators during the constitutional talks, were to extend beyond the limits of Kirkuk province. They were also to include areas of Mosul and Diyala provinces such as the Tel Afar area, Khanaqin and Mandali.

Both the Turkoman and the Arab stories of Kirkuk's identity were at loggerheads with the Kurdish version. The Turkomen claimed Kirkuk on historical grounds, and considered the Kurds migrants, in the city and province solely because of the oil boom. They deeply resented the Kurds' pell-mell rush into the city after the fall of the Ba'ath regime, and seriously disputed the right of all the resettled Kurds to be considered residents. Arab tribes of the Kirkuk area disputed the extent of the expulsions of the Kurds from Kirkuk, claiming that the figures had been grossly exaggerated by the Kurds for self-serving purposes.[21] They sought to keep Kirkuk as part of a central Iraq state and outside the limits of the Kurdistan region. The prospects for the resettled Arabs were dismal.

The Kurdish negotiators entered the constitutional talks determined to resolve the uncertain status of Kirkuk and to implement the provisions of the TAL. Their position had been immeasurably strengthened by the provincial council elections that gave the Kurds nearly 60 per cent of the votes and control over the main levers of power in the provincial assembly. The KDP and PUK buried their rivalries and presented a united set of demands to the constitutional talks, partly expecting that their unwavering support for the USA and its allies would lead to a reciprocal support for their positions. The Turkomen and Arabs were more disorganised, and were unable produce a coherent alternative to the Kurdish position. The Turkomen in particular had suffered from the excesses of the Ba'ath regime and were also subject to discrimination and smaller-scale expulsions. The Kurdish strategy was to try to win them over to accepting that Kurdish rule over Kirkuk would be better than central, or Arab, rule over the city. The Kurds also benefited from the apparent split in the UIA on the Kirkuk issue – between the more accommodating SCIRI position, strongly advocated by the pro-Kurdish Adel Abd el-Mahdi, and the position of the Sadrists and the Da'awa Party. The Sadrists were hostile to the Kurdish demands and in fact to all regionalist claims. Eventually it was felt that the Kirkuk problem could not be settled within the time-frame for the constitutional process, and the issue was left unresolved. The constitution extended the life of the TAL articles dealing with the status of Kirkuk, but stipulated that a census and referendum on the status of Kirkuk by its residents be completed before 31 December 2007.

Finalising the Draft Constitution

Another issue which received a late airing was the place of Islam in the new state. The TAL had lukewarmly endorsed Islam as one of the sources of legislation in Iraq, but this time the *Marji'iyya* was insistent on a more strongly pronounced wording.[22] The fear that the Iraqi constitution would enshrine Sharia law and its purported negative effects on women's rights was greatly overblown. In reality, not even the supposedly 'secular' Kurds wanted to jettison the role of Islam in providing a moral framework for legislation, and they readily acquiesced to a role for Islam in the relevant chapters of the constitution. The Kurds were an overwhelmingly Muslim people and socially conservative. Their daily lives and mores were based on the precepts of Islam. In spite of their secular political leadership, the pull of Islam on the mass of the people was very potent. Making Islam a moral basis for legislation was a popular position to take. For most Iraqis, a generalised statement that gave Islam a privileged status was welcome, and numerous opinion polls showed large majorities in favour of such a position. The draft constitution's wording on this matter reflected the need to strike a balance between Islam and democracy, without alienating the powers which were pushing for a secularised constitution, namely the USA and Britain. The constitution affirmed Islam as the religion of the state, and stipulated that no law could be passed that violated its commonly agreed precepts, a formulation that obliged the two sects of Islam to agree on a definition of what these common principles were. There were two other matters that the *Marji'iyya* had sought to cover in the constitution, and on both of these its position was respected and reflected in the final draft. The first had to do with providing a special status for the holy shrines of the Shi'a; and the second was to grant the *Marji'iyya* itself, as an institution, a constitutionally recognised position.

Other constitutional principles were not debated at length. Wherever the TAL provided a suitable wording to a thorny issue or a resolution of a difficult problem, its formulations were accepted by the drafting committee.[23] In essence, the drafting committee confined itself to technical and non-controversial issues. There were a series of deals and compromises that were thrashed out by politicians. The divisive issues were pushed to the conclave of the political leaders of the main blocs: Talabani and Barzani for the Kurds; Hakim and other UIA leaders for the Shi'a; and Saleh al-Mutlaq, Adnan al-Dulaimi and the Islamic Party leadership for the Sunni Arabs. The Kurds brought along their key adviser, former US Ambassador Peter Galbraith, a noted advocate for maximum autonomy for Kurdistan, as a prelude to formal independence later, as and when conditions would be propitious. Deals were struck which were then announced or given to the drafting committee, to be included in the final document. Federalism, the issue of Kirkuk, religion and state, oil and natural resources, water rights were all handled by the political leaders, with the views of the Sunni Arabs noted, but not necessarily acted upon.[24] The Sunni Arabs were unable to block the passing of the constitution, at least at the parliamentary level.

The Iraqi constitution of 2005 was not the national compact that many had thought necessary and desirable, but a document arising from a series of political deals. It was seen as a necessary step in the political process and was not vested with the quasi-sacred status that such documents had in other countries. Nevertheless, it enshrined basic rights and opened up the possibility of a different type of Iraqi state from the one that had gone so disastrously awry. A version of the draft constitution was released to the press before the National Assembly had seen it. This was partly to assure the Iraqi public that there would not be inordinate delays. As the 15 August deadline loomed, however, the committee's chairman, Sheikh Humam Hammoudi, requested an extension of a further week, which was granted by the National Assembly.[25] The extension was primarily for the purposes of convincing the Sunni Arabs to go along with the draft, especially the articles dealing with federalism and the possibility of forming large regions. As it was, Saleh al-Mutlaq, one of the main Arab Sunni leaders, said: 'I think that if this constitution passes as it is, it will worsen everything in the country.'[26] Dulaimi went further and demanded international intervention to block the passing of this document.[27] But the Shi'a-Kurdish bloc was determined to pass the document and confronted the Sunni negotiators in no uncertain terms. It was felt that the Sunni Arabs wanted to derail the constitutional talks as part of a plan to stop the political process. The Sunni call for more time to examine in detail the various constitutional issues was seen as an attempt to thwart the process, rather than a legitimate concern for more substantive discussions. This reinforced the Shi'a-Kurdish feeling that the deadlines must be respected. In turn, the Sunnis felt that they had entered belatedly into the talks and that the Shi'a and the Kurds had settled on a set of principles for Iraq's constitution after their years of joint political action. The Sunnis had wanted to empower the drafting committee, where they had a significant presence, with the final disposition of the constitution, rather than give the National Assembly that power.[28] This was, of course, resisted by the Shi'a and the Kurds, but, even so, the Shi'a-Kurdish bloc did not push it to the limit where they could railroad the constitution through the assembly.

Eventually, the National Assembly and the government granted the drafting committee more time to reach an accord between the Shi'a-Kurdish bloc and the Arab Sunnis. Bush himself intervened by calling Hakim and urging him to compromise with the Sunni Arabs. America's strategy of drawing the Sunni Arabs into the constitutional negotiations partly to sap the insurgency's support would be seriously threatened if the Sunni Arabs pulled out of the talks or boycotted the referendum. On 28 August, 2005, the draft constitution was finally read to the National Assembly with only three of the fifteen Arab Sunni members present. The draft which was accepted was not the final draft, but only the last of many working drafts that had been circulating since the end of July. Yet another draft was given to the National Assembly on 13 September, but by that time the changes were hitting the law of diminishing returns. With barely a month to go before the referendum, Iraqis had still not seen the document that was supposed to be their new national compact.

The Constitutional Principles of the New Iraq

The constitution that was presented to the Iraqi public, even in its not-quite-final forms, was a document with embedded ideas and principles that would have been unthinkable in the recent past. But it was not, by any stretch of the imagination, a national compact. The thrust of the new constitution, apart from enshrining individual and human rights, was the adoption of federalism and decentralisation as the guiding paradigms for the new Iraq. Powers were devolved to the regions and provinces, which would enjoy considerable autonomy from the centre. The limits on the size of regions were removed, opening the way for the Shi'a super region which so worried the Sunni Arabs. In case of disputes between the federal and regional authorities, it was the region's laws that would hold sway. A region would be responsible for its internal security, paving the way for the institutionalising of the *pesh merga* and Shi'a militias such as the Badr Brigade.

In the area of natural resources, and especially oil, the constitution was silent about who had control over all undiscovered and unexploited oil fields. Existing oil fields would continue to be operated by the central government, but new fields, or expansion of existing fields, were presumed, at least by the Kurds and the Shi'a advocates of a super southern region, to be within the jurisdiction of the regions. Natural resources were stated to belong to 'all the people of Iraq in all the regions and governorates', presumably allowing the citizens of the regions to claim these rights. The ambiguity in the constitution on this most vital of areas, however, was because it was presumed that the underlying issues would be sorted out later, after the political map of the country had been settled. It would have to await the formation of other regions, the passage of regional oil and natural resources laws, and the institutionalisation of federal-regional arrangements, before the ownership and control over oil fields could finally be established.

The boycott of the January elections by the Sunni Arab community was now seen to be a disaster. Even in a reduced form, the presence of forty or fifty Sunni Arab parliamentarians, together with the secularised, or moderate, groups of the Shi'a, might have placed a formidable brake on the sweep of the new constitution. But this was not to be. The Sunni Arabs were angry and sullen. They were confronted with yet another dilemma – whether to boycott the referendum on the constitution, or to organise for its defeat in their majority provinces. The extreme wing of the insurgency would always denounce the political process, regardless. The Sunni Arab parties, on the other hand, were this time determined to stick to the political process.

The Sunni Arabs deeply objected to the treatment of the Ba'ath Party in the constitution. The original draft included a blanket ban on all parties that called for terrorism and anathemisation, especially the 'Saddamist Ba'ath and its symbols'. Subsequent versions of the constitution were more accommodating to the concerns of the Sunni Arabs. The de-Ba'athification Commission was placed under the control of parliament, and could be dissolved by a majority vote and former party members would have judicial protection. Changes were also incorporated that addressed some of the fears of the Sunni Arabs that the new state would not be institutionally biased against their community. Most of these changes were effected as a result of intense pressure from the US, which was fearful that the constitution might be rejected in the Sunni Arab provinces, with disastrous consequences. For most Sunni Arabs these changes were too little or too late to have any effect on their decision to vote against the constitution in the referendum.

The Referendum on the New Constitution

A massive voter registration drive began in the Sunni Arab areas. In the Anbar province, where participation in the earlier elections had been negligible, nearly 90 per cent of all the eligible 715,000 voters had registered to vote in the referendum.[29] The same story was replicated in other provinces with large

Sunni Arab populations, including Salahuddine, Nineveh and Diyala. The majority of the Sunni Arab parties were calling for a No vote. The Iraqi Islamic Party, however, left the door open, so that, if enough changes were to be secured before the referendum date, they might change their position on the No vote. The Sunni Arabs' enthusiasm to vote was very nearly derailed by a National Assembly decision on 2 October on the voting rules for the referendum.[30] A No vote tally would be related to the base of registered voters rather than actual voters. The Sunni leadership was outraged. 'There is no point in participating in a referendum when the result has already been determined', said Saleh al-Mutlaq.[31] The USA was publicly sceptical about the ruling, but, in private, Khalilzad was working diligently to have it reversed. Three days later the National Assembly changed its definition of the voter base: it would now show actual rather than registered voters. Last-minute changes to the constitution, such as the agreement to allow the incoming parliamentarians after the December elections a four-month period to propose amendments, were pursued, to increase both Sunni Arab participation and their Yes vote. The Islamic Party was mollified by these changes, and recommended to its supporters to vote in the affirmative on the constitution. But most of the other Sunni Arab groups were very hostile to the constitution, in spite of concessions that had been made to address their fears and anxieties.

Voting for the constitution took place, as planned, on 15 October, 2005. Turnout was at 63 per cent of the registered voters, a better result than in the January elections, but still short of expectations.[32] It was clear, even in the early days after the referendum, that the Yes vote had won the day by a significant margin. The question was whether three provinces could muster the two-thirds votes needed to block the constitution from being adopted. In the majority Shi'a provinces, the Yes vote was invariably above 90 per cent, even in those provinces with a supposedly large secular Shi'a population, such as Babil and Basra. The constitution in toto was seen as a positive document by the vast majority of Shi'as, even if some had some misgivings about the nature and extent of federalism. A similar thumping majority for the draft constitution was recorded in the Kurdish areas. In the three Kurdish provinces of the Kurdistan Regional Government, the majorities were at 99 per cent. Even in Kirkuk, nearly 63 per cent of the electorate voted Yes. A surprising result was achieved in Baghdad, a city supposedly evenly divided between the Shi'as and the Sunnis. The Yes vote was nearly 78 per cent of the total, an eye-opener as to the true sectarian demographics of Baghdad. The Sunni Arab provinces of Anbar and Salahuddine predictably voted against the constitution, the former by over 96 per cent and the latter by 82 per cent. All attention was now focused on the province of Nineveh and its capital, Mosul. After accusations of fraud and irregularities that delayed the announcement of the final tally, the Independent Electoral Commission gave the finishing results. The province of

Nineveh had voted against the constitution, but not in sufficient numbers to scupper it: 55 per cent voted against and 45 per cent for.[33] The constitution was therefore ratified by referendum. The next milestone in Iraq's interminable political process would be elections for a four-year parliament and a permanent government.

The saga over the constitution and the tumultuous crowding of events over a short period of time were symptomatic of the whole post-war period. Matters of an epoch-making nature were crammed into an impossibly short timetable, which could nevertheless be justified by the imperative of moving the country forward. A constitutional document of enormous import was put together by a group of people who were in many ways accustomed only to forging deals behind closed doors. They would often stumble into formulations that were inspiring and also self-serving. An unelected foreign party with its own interests, whose presence was necessary and yet intolerable, was always hovering in the background, and often the foreground. Yet the constitution, in its own peculiar way, was representative of the wishes of the majority of the population and reflected, by and large, the desire of the people to turn a page in Iraq's history. It is possible that more time and effort would have produced a more inclusive document, given the deep anxieties of the Sunni Arab community about the post war political order. In the final analysis, the constitution was a document that had all the hallmarks of a series of deals by political operatives. On the other hand, the constitution did stumble on the elements of a new Iraqi compact: civil and human rights; decentralisation; wealth-sharing, and a fairer share for the country's historically disadvantaged peoples. But these were not sufficient to dispel the gloom and despondency of the Sunni Arab community.

24

Crises and the Jaafari Government

'An observer of the country's affairs would be deeply saddened and shocked at the state of the security situation and the failure of plans to tackle this problem . . . .What makes the situation more deplorable is the isolation of senior officials from the people . . . with a significant number living in the Green Zone and avoiding their place of work . . . .The situation of the public services is no different from the security situation, with crises affecting the people from electricity to water to fuel supplies . . . .The Iraqi people feel that they have gained nothing from the fall of the dictatorship except freedom of expression and a free press.' –

Memo by Abd el-Latif Rashid, Minister of Water Resources, sent to the Prime Minister and the Cabinet, August 2005

A range of crises and new, or inherited, problems immediately buffeted the Transitional National Government. Although it had a popular mandate, the terms of the TAL obliged the UIA to seek partners in the process of forming the government. Its main ally, the Kurdistan Alliance, was intensely wary of Jaafari's true intentions, while Ayad Allawi's *Iraqiyya* list had moved into ineffective, but hostile, opposition. The other main power broker, the US Embassy, while concerned about an Islamist-led government, was also sceptical about the prospects for Jaafari's government. They were, however, pinning their hopes on the permanent government to be installed after the December elections, rather than taking much notice of the present government. Their position, therefore, was to express their support for the government publicly, and hope to influence its policies and decisions through close monitoring of the government's activities.

At the top of the Transitional Government's agenda was security, especially in view of the intensification of insurgency and terrorist attacks which were clearly aimed at undermining the public's confidence in the government. The economy was sputtering along, with no real investments or job-creation opportunities, while the reconstruction effort was beset with implementation issues. There was no resource-gap as such, thanks to continuing oil exports, but public finances suffered from lack of budgetary discipline. The legacy of poor spending controls and the accompanying corruption and waste had reached astounding levels. The insurgency attacks combined with administrative incompetence and chaos to create unprecedented crises in the public services sector. Shortages in petroleum products and a running power outage problem became exacerbated to the point where they seriously undermined the credibility of the government.

At another level, the Transitional Government came under increasing pressure from the IMF and the US Treasury to implement the agreements that the Interim Government had reached with the IMF. The entire Iraqi external debt reduction programme was at risk if Iraq did not reach an agreement with the IMF for a 'Standby Arrangement' (SBA) by the end of 2005. The successful conclusion of an SBA with the IMF was dependent on Iraq raising petroleum prices and reducing the subsidies by the end of 2005. There were also other areas where the Transitional Government's performance came under intense scrutiny. The growth of the Shi'a militias and their infiltration into the state security apparatus was an issue that intensely discomfited the USA and the main Sunni Arab groups. This was a new dimension to the counter-insurgency war, and clearly jeopardised inter-communal reconciliation. How the Transitional Government would tackle the problems it faced would play a large part in determining the outcome of the December elections.

Election Promises

The installation of the Transitional Government accompanied high expectations. Improvements in administrative performance were not the main reason that drove people to vote for the UIA. Nevertheless voters were led to expect that the new government would be more effective at tackling the problems facing the country than previous administrations since the Ba'ath regime had been. The public expected that the Transitional Government would immediately start to remedy the services and security situation, and the message was that conditions would rapidly improve.[1] A realistic and cold-blooded assessment of the actual situation inside the country would have led to a different conclusion, one that might have been painful for politicians to admit to, but which was nevertheless necessary to make if the expectations of the public were not to be raised too high. The counter-insurgency campaign could not be made more credible by the announcement of yet another 'Security Plan for Baghdad', as if the Transitional Government were introducing an entirely new security doctrine that was different in substance both from that of the MNF and the previous government's own plans. Neither could the electricity supply be assured by introducing 'new' measures to stop corruption and sabotage, when these were nothing more than a rehash of previously failed policies. There was a deep reluctance to accept that the administrative rot had set so deep inside the government that only a full-scale revamp of the machinery of government would be adequate. At the same time, the Transitional Government's ministers were asked to emphasise the achievements of their ministries when the public could see precious little in terms of improvements.[2]

Some of the promises were difficult for the government to fulfil, such as a rapid improvement in public services, or a wholesale clear-out of government departments that were seen to have been flooded with ex-Ba'athists during the Interim Government. The UIA firmly believed that government institutions had been subverted by returning Ba'athists and opponents of the Islamists during the Interim Government, and that it was now time to drive out those who might be fifth-columnists inside the new Transitional Government. The solution proferred was to crowd government departments with thousands of job-seekers attached to UIA parliamentarians and their fellow-travellers or relatives. Ministers were provided with lists of hundreds of supplicants and job-seekers carrying the imprimatur of parliamentarians, political parties and various notables and worthies. Some were indeed competent, and had been cruelly mistreated by the former regime or by insidious officials; most, however, were either unqualified or unsuitable for the jobs they sought. This did not stop ministries from being packed with these people, resulting in over-crowding and under-performance that compounded the problems of government departments. This state of affairs contrasted abysmally with good news stories about the revival of the economy and the private sector. In fact, there were precious few jobs either in the private sector or in the much-vaunted reconstruction programme. The best indicator was that less than 100,000 people were employed in all the US-funded reconstruction projects: granted, not a small figure, but woefully inadequate given the unemployment conditions throughout the country.[3] The stated policy of the government on employment was that the state 'was in great need of expertise, competence and effectiveness, and that priority should be given to those with the right qualifications and skills', a most worthy sentiment that was honoured only in the breach.[4]

Early Security Measures

The government's new security measures, code-named 'Operation Lightning', were unveiled by the Minister of Interior, Bayan Jabr, in early June 2005.[5] They were based on a change in emphasis, from what had been claimed to be a formerly 'defensive' strategy to what was now an 'offensive' strategy. Baghdad was divided into twelve zones, patrolled by a mixed force from the Ministry of

Defence and the Ministry of Interior. The new security plan was based on a show of force and the coordinated actions of all the security forces, commanded and controlled in the 'Adnani' Palace complex inside the Green Zone by elements from the MNF and the security ministries. The twenty-four entry points into Baghdad were to be controlled by both fixed and mobile forces, and insurgent strongholds inside the city would be regularly raided. This was meant to scupper the insurgents' and terrorists' intentions by a relentless war of attrition and wide-scale arrests and incarcerations. Success was prematurely announced when Baghdad was claimed to be 'under the total control' of the security forces and it was reported that hundreds of suspect terrorists and insurgents had been captured. Ahmad Chalabi, the Deputy Prime Minister, asked rhetorically in cabinet 'why the level of insurgent action had been hardly dented compared to the previous year, even when the number of battalions had gone up from 3 to a 107'.[6] No one had an answer. A weak response to the continuing insurgent mayhem was to reactivate the death penalty for capital and terrorist offences, which had been suspended by Bremer. This, however, hardly affected the counter-insurgency campaign. Few people were sentenced to death by fearful judges, and even fewer, perhaps a dozen, were actually executed for terrorist-related crimes or mass murder. In any case, the death penalty would hardly be a deterrent to suicide bombers and hardened insurgents.

'Operation Lightning' had patchy results. In the Doura suburb of Baghdad, an insurgent hotbed, nearly a thousand people were arrested, but 500 had to be released almost immediately because of insufficient evidence or interventions by influential Sunni Arab parties. A number of Saudi *jihadis* were arrested in the operation. One was carrying $50,000 in cash from 'well-wishers', organised by a mosque in Mecca, one of the innumerable conduits for financing the insurgency. The virulence of the insurgency and its increasing violence drove the Ministry of Interior to adopt a more radical policy for containing and defeating the insurgents, as well as cementing control over the internal security forces. The demarcation between the militias and the formal police and special security units became increasingly blurred, as one merged into the other. This alarming development accelerated the process of politicising the internal security apparatus. The former Interior Minister of the Interim Government, Falah al-Naqib, who acquiesced in, or promoted, the formation of special police battalions loyal to himself or his group, had initiated this.[7] This process was thorough and widespread involving not just the police and security units but the established militias of the Islamist political parties.

The process had started with the chaotic reformation of Iraq's police forces after the end of the war. In spite of hundreds of millions of dollars expended on training, the revamped police was nowhere near to being an impartial law-enforcement and crime-prevention force. The poorly led and poorly motivated police, especially in the provinces, became an easy prey to infiltration by the Islamist political parties. In Basra, Nasiriya, 'Amara, and elsewhere in the South, the police forces came under the sway of local alliances and political groups, which used the police as a means of extending and exercising their authority. Men wearing police uniforms, riding in police cars, and carrying police-issued weapons might easily be militiamen performing either a party or a public-order function.[8] Both the Badr Organisation and the Mahdi Army were implicated in the infiltration of the police forces, while leadership of the local police fell under the power of provincial councils dominated by political parties.[9] In many respects, the increased role of the militias was in response to the collapse of security and the inability of the MNF and the formal Iraqi security forces to combat lawlessness and terror. The militias' intelligence was frequently better than that of the MNF or of the local authorities, and they could track and apprehend culprits more effectively and quickly. But this did not stop the protests that the militias, either directly or through the police force, were targeting hundreds of people for killings and arrest without due process.

In Basra, the gradual slippage of the province's entire security force into the control of political parties affiliated with SCIRI, the Sadrists or the Fadhila Party was seen as a direct threat to the British forces responsible for overall security in the South. Basra became a scene of large-scale killings and assassinations attributed to the police and shadowy groups that were clothed in policemen's uniforms. The activity of the police, militias and other armed gangs was also linked to the rampant criminality and oil-smuggling rackets, which were so damaging to the society and economy of the South. The relative calm in the South in the immediate post-war period had been touted as an example of the peace that prevailed in most of the country, and a refutation of supposedly biased media reporting about the scale of violence in Iraq. But the South was now slipping into a dangerous combination of lawlessness and raw power struggle, as well as turf wars between the leading Islamist protagonists.

The covert war being waged by the militias and their proxies in the Ministry of Interior became publicly manifest. In November, American forces in the posh Jadriya neighbourhood of Baghdad discovered a 'secret' prison.[10] The prison, in the basement of a government building, held over 200 detainees in various states of distress. They were mostly Sunni Arabs, malnourished. A number had signs of torture. They were being held as terrorist suspects. There was a worldwide media outcry, but the response of most Iraqis was muted. The use of non-conventional, even brutal, tactics was held to be justified in the fight against terrorists. The Interior Minister, the dapper Bayan Jabr, who was becoming increasingly vilified in the Arab press and privately by the USA, was regarded as a hero by many Iraqis for his unapologetic and resolute stance against terrorists.[11] But the Sunni Arab community, the US and the British, and even parts of the political establishment, saw matters differently. The Interior Ministry had fallen under the control of the militias, and the state was now being used to settle scores and run a campaign of intimidation, abductions and assassinations against innocent Sunni Arabs. The sight of Interior Ministry commandos and special forces was most unwelcome in the Sunni areas of Baghdad.[12] A high US official estimated that 90 per cent of the 35,000 police officers working in north-east Baghdad were affiliated with the Mahdi Army.[13] It was common knowledge that Baghdad's 60,000 strong police force was divided between the Mahdi Army and the Badr Organisation. The former was grouped around a unit called the 'Punishment Committee', while Badr controlled the Ministry of Interior's *Maghawir* (commandos unit), with about 12,000 members. This much was admitted by Haider al-'Abadi, a former telecommunications minister and now spokesman for the prime minister's office. 'We are investigating that. We know there is infiltration in our security forces – we know that for sure', he said in an interview with the *Los Angeles Times*.[14]

Sunni Arab organisations, notably the AMS, began to collect grisly evidence of the hundreds, later known to be thousands, of people who were summarily killed or abducted and had disappeared. The Sunni community began to feel extremely targeted, and did not hesitate to use the term 'death squads' to refer to the militia-dominated units in the Interior Ministry. On the other hand, most Shi'as saw the Interior Ministry as a bulwark against terrorists and killers, and justified the brutalities and excesses of their special forces as a necessary concomitant to the fight against *takfiris* and insurgents. The polarisation of opinion between the two communities increased significantly as the hitherto muted Shi'a response to the suicide bombings and killings of innocent people was now matched by a campaign to eliminate individuals who were considered to be insurgents or terrorists. These 'selective' assassinations and disappearances quickly moved on to a larger canvass, where entire groups became targeted simply for their communal affiliations.

Managing the Crises in Petroleum Products and Electricity Sectors

The sense of a country under siege was exacerbated by the continuing problems in securing adequate power and petroleum products supplies. The Transitional Government formed a number of committees headed by the Deputy Prime Minister, Ahmad Chalabi, which tackled the crises in the energy and infrastructure sectors and tried to introduce spending disciplines in the government's contracting procedures. The problems were correctly seen to be systemic and interlinked. Energy shortages fed into refinery shutdowns. Pipeline disruptions and attacks on power lines and sub-stations were directly connected to corruption and infrastructure protection forces being compromised or infiltrated. Smuggling of fuel products was linked to price distortions and subsidies, which, in turn, were defended by vested interests – some inside the Transitional Government. Even so, the work of these committees, by any objective standard, was a noticeable improvement on the past, and a determined start was made to remedy the situation in a variety of sectors, not always successfully. The Iraqi military and the MNF were drawn into the deliberations of the energy and infrastructure committees. In June 2005, the MNF came up with its 'Infrastructure Protection Plan'.[15] It called for the allocation of $70 million for oil pipeline protection and the enhancement of the capabilities of the Strategic Infrastructure Battalions (SIB). Control over the entire plan would be assigned to Iraq's Ministry of Defence. The plan was accepted in its entirety and the appropriate funding provided by the Ministry of Finance, but there was actually little impact on the level of attacks and disruptions. The truth was that the US army did not have sufficient troops to provide the necessary level of protection, and infrastructure protection and securing electricity supplies was not at the top of their lists. Plans would be made to protect various stretches of pipelines, only to see the pipelines blown up time and time again.

In the Latiffiyya area, a hotbed for insurgents and an important terminus for pipelines bringing in petroleum from the South, insurgents murdered the commander of the protection battalions. In the northern stretch of the pipeline complex, the commander of the battalion charged with protecting the facilities was arrested for complicity with the insurgents.[16] There were daily attacks on pylons, high-tension towers, pipelines, storage tanks and fuel depots, and they were met by a resolute and often uphill struggle by the infrastructure and energy committees to come up with counter-measures. Without the work of these committees and their determination to continue to craft solutions to the never-ending crises, the shortages and outages would have been far worse. In a number of instances, the crises reached potentially catastrophic levels, when, for instance, the fuel supplies in Baghdad in November 2005 were estimated to last for only a few days. The insurgents had managed to disrupt the supply complex in a series of coordinated attacks, which dovetailed with a refusal from Turkey to provide further fuel on credit. Eventually, the energy committee muddled through with a mixture of improvised solutions, partial payments of outstanding claims – and by introducing a drastic measure that banned non-essential driving in Baghdad except on alternate days.

Following the January elections, there was a dramatic increase in attacks on the power sector. By the summer of 2005, such attacks were leading to intolerable power outages in Baghdad. In August 2005, the hottest month of the year, Baghdad was receiving only six hours' power per day. Total electricity demand was estimated at about 6,150 MW, but production was only 3,725 MW.[17] Power output had remained static between 2004 and 2006, in spite of the completion of a number of grant-financed projects. To add to the problems, Iraq's hydroelectric generating capacity, principally from the dams at Mosul (on the Tigris) with a 613 MW capacity and Haditha (on the Euphrates) with 300 MW capacity, were affected by the reduced water flows from Syria and Turkey. The Haditha dam, located in the heart of the insurgency, often had to be shut down for days on end. The power sector was on the verge of collapse, and it was impossible to maintain power supplies in an environment which was fraught with instability, violence and corruption. Power generation issues and the slow commissioning of new plants were now compounded by distribution issues and, at the consumer end, by rampant power theft and non-payment of bills.

The power sector's problems could not have possibly been resolved in the time-frame of the Transitional Government, and it was actually a sign of success that the entire sector did not collapse. The committee's emphasis on the deployment of rapid repair teams to re-erect pylons and towers that had been knocked down was a notable achievement. The delays in repairing destroyed towers did not exceed a week, in spite of the numerous, and often fatal, attacks on the repair teams. The administrative chaos in the electricity ministry was partly mitigated by the dedication of its technical teams and the ministry's professional engineers. Muhsin Shlash, the new Transitional Government electricity minister, was, however, unable to halt the slide in power output. He was effectively sidelined after three months in the job, and was banned from Cabinet meetings. But he could not be replaced, as the 'Independents' bloc of the UIA insisted that he stay on the job, and Jaafari was not prepared to confront an important component of his governing coalition. In effect, the energy committee acted as the de facto ministry, while the struggle for control over the Electricity Ministry continued to simmer. It was finally resolved by the Shlash returning to his job towards the end of 2005, but by then the elections were drawing near and the damage done to the government's public relations by the continuing power crisis could not be contained.[18]

The oil and petroleum products sector also preoccupied the energy committee. The major oil pipelines from Kirkuk to al-Fathah were constantly attacked and were inoperative for long periods of time. Pipelines carrying crude oil and products from the Baiji refinery to Baghdad were also sabotaged regularly, passing as they did through insurgent-controlled areas, as was the pipeline carrying crude oil from Naft Khaneh to the Doura refinery in Baghdad. The petroleum products situation in Baghdad often became critical, as a simultaneous attack on the oil infrastructure on these multiple fronts had a cascading effect on the Baghdad fuel situation.

426 THE OCCUPATION OF IRAQ

Controlling Public Sector Tenders and Contracts

The energy committee's work merged with that of the contracts committee. Part of the resolution of both the power and petroleum products crises was related to the pace of contract awards and implementation for equipment and supplies for these sectors. The establishment of the cabinet's contracts committee was determined by the need to reduce corruption drastically, increase the rate of contract awards and implementation as part of the reconstruction effort, and ensure the increased level of participation by the Iraqi private sector in the government's procurement and supplies. The committee was headed by Ahmad Chalabi and included the Ministers of Finance and Trade, the Governor of the Central Bank of Iraq, and the Managing Director of the Trade Bank of Iraq. The contracts committee's first order of priority was to ensure that the proposals brought to its attention met the Iraqi government's own standards for tendering and contracts awards. Iraq's well-established procedures had been undermined during the sanctions years and fatally ignored by the CPA and the Interim Government. The CPA introduced completely alien contracting procedures, and the chaotic award of huge contracts with no Iraqi involvement or oversight bred a culture of ignoring the rules in the interest of speed in contract implementation, resulting in poor contracts and coruption. The committee insisted that all ministries follow the procedural rules, while assuring them that their urgent requests would be vetted within a week of submission. The discipline imposed on ministries became an important part in re-establishing a modicum of concern and probity when presenting the contract proposals. Independent observers from the US mission vouchsafed the decline in the incidence of corruption, in spite of the constant grumblings by ministers about delays in approving contract awards. After a number of clearly padded contracts were firmly turned down, the ministers concerned towed the line, at least when it came to large-scale contract awards. The contracts committee now turned to the Trade Ministry, the most corruption-prone of Iraq's ministries, and its multibillion dollar budget for the import of staples for the ration programme.

Rooting out the endemic corruption in the Trade Ministry was a difficult task, given the public's sensitivity to disruptions in supplies of the food and provisions basket. The incoming Minister of Trade, Abd el-Basit Karim, was energetic and effective. He soon uncovered the harsh realities inside the ministry, and declared that 'the warehouses of the Ministry of Trade were empty of products'.[19] Basic rations such as sugar and rice had not been delivered for months on end, while the twilight weeks of the Interim Government were marked by paralysis in decision-making and the artificial build-up of shortages. The urgency of purchasing products had to be balanced against reinforcing dependence on the newly re-entrenched nexus of corrupt suppliers.

This was tackled in two ways. First there was the introduction of guidelines for suppliers which emphasised size, reliability, competence and, above all, financial scale and stability. This latter measure required suppliers to produce audited accounts. In one fell stroke, a large army of middlemen and agents who crammed the Ministry of Trade's supplier lists were eliminated. Then, the committee insisted that all tenders be divided into goods and carriage. The scams of the OFF programme had revealed that a great deal of fraud was caused by goods being delivered to Iraq using transport monopolies, so competition was introduced into the shipping of products into Iraq. The overcharging on Iraq's transport bill for its food basket imports was estimated at a staggering $600 million. The transport cartels, which had infiltrated and subverted senior personnel in the Transport Ministry, were incensed by this move and fought it tooth and nail. It was also discovered that the Australian Wheat Board had been using these shipping cartels as part of its supply arrangements with Iraq during the OFF period and overcharging Iraq by hundreds of millions of dollars.

The rotten undergrowth of the Ministry of Trade's supply chain had been exposed, but nevertheless attempts to defraud the state would continue unabated. The contracts committee also sought to help the Iraqi private sector by allowing Iraqi traders and businessmen to contract directly with the Ministry of Trade on its supplies. The principle established was that eligible Iraqi companies would be allowed to sell commodities for the food basket if the goods were inside Iraq and met the quality and price constraints of the ministry. If the private sector, it was reasoned, were to become accustomed to managing a complex logistics chain and supply the necessary volume and range of goods, then the privatisation of the food basket would be that much more realistic and achievable. The trial was met with great enthusiasm, and Iraqi businessmen began to supply nearly a quarter of the requirements of the food basket through direct purchases.

Iraq's Debt

Throughout the Transitional Government period, the Ministry of Finance sought to reinforce its authority as the main determiner of macroeconomic and fiscal policy. The relationships with the Central Bank of Iraq (CBI), under the able Sinan al-Shabibi, were very cordial and close. (The CBI had been given an independent status in the early CPA months, and was therefore exclusively responsible for monetary policy.) Nowhere was this more evident than in the negotiations involving Iraq's indebtedness and the relationships with the multilateral agencies, especially the IMF. Shabibi was committed to the cancellation of 'odious debt', that is, debt incurred by dictatorial regimes for strengthening their domestic control or engaging in war. Nearly all Iraq's debts were incurred during the 1980s, as Iraq was engaged in fighting the Iran–Iraq War and Saddam was extending his tyrannical authority. The odious debt argument was not acceptable inside the US Treasury, however. An early decision was therefore made by the CPA that Iraq should try to recognise, reconcile, quantify and then settle the debt on terms that allowed for a large, though not complete, write-off.

The debt was classified into four categories, each of which had particular features and characteristics. The first category amounted to a total of about $40 billion, and was owed to a number of western countries and Japan which had combined under the 'Paris Club'. This was a grouping of industrial countries that negotiated common positions with indebted countries that had defaulted on their loan obligations, or sought debt restructurings. The second category related to Iraq's debt to sovereign countries that were not prepared to join the lead of the Paris Club countries and sought bilateral deals with Iraq. Large creditors such as China, Turkey and a number of former Soviet Bloc countries, who were mainly arms suppliers to Saddam, formed the core of this group. This category of creditors held about $20 billion in debt. The third category involved the hundreds of private sector creditors to Iraq, ranging from banks to trade suppliers from over fifty countries. They were owed about $20 billion by Iraq. The fourth category consisted of the claims on Iraq by Saudi Arabia, Kuwait, the UAE and Qatar. These governments claimed over $50 billion in debt, with Saudi Arabia at $39 billion and Kuwait at $8 billion accounting for the bulk of it. This debt was to be treated differently from the other categories, as it was considered more amenable to a 'political' solution.

The resolution of Iraq's debt was one of the unalloyed successes of the entire post-war period. The Interim Government had worked closely with the US Treasury in finalising the terms of the Paris Club deal, whereby the creditor countries had agreed to write off 80 per cent of Iraq's indebtedness to them. The deal with the Paris Club countries was signed in November 2004. The terms and conditions of the deal were extremely significant, as they would act as a benchmark for Iraq's negotiations with all other creditor countries. In summary, Iraq was to be given an immediate write-off of 30 per cent of its reconciled indebtedness to the Paris Club creditors. The balance of 50 per cent of the debt write-off was contingent on Iraq reaching a deal with the IMF on a series of structural reforms that were encompassed within a Standby Arrangement (SBA), and on the successful implementation of the SBA. The Interim Government, which had committed Iraq to the SBA, had sought a cash settlement for commercial creditors.

When the Transitional Government's Minister of Finance assumed his responsibilities, however, he immediately put a stop to the cash settlement proposals, as their funding requirements, probably up to $3 billion in cash and including a forced loan from the state-owned Rafidain Bank, would have put an enormous strain on public finances. A new policy of issuing bonds in settlement of the debts of the commercial creditors was then pursued. A size-able bond issue would not only allow Iraq to develop a creditor profile in international capital markets and establish a price for Iraq's debt but would also encourage the formation of debt management capabilities within the Ministry of Finance. In January 2006, Iraq issued its first ever international bond, with a value of $2.8 billion, a twenty-two-year term and a coupon of 5.8 per cent in settlement of nearly $19 billion claims by commercial credi-tors. The London *Financial Times* described the debt deal for Iraq as an 'effort to remove an obstacle to Iraq's economic recovery [that] has been one of the few successful projects undertaken in post Saddam Iraq'.[20]

The Budget

The debt negotiations ran the risk of absorbing all the time and motivation of the Ministry of Finance senior staff at the expense of other areas of vital domestic concern. Senior staff preferred to deal with Iraq's international economic relations, which involved extensive international travel and absences from Baghdad, rather than the difficult task of managing the budgetary process, assigning spending priorities and controls, reforming the subsidies system, removing regional disparities, and launching banking sector restructurings. An early decision was made by the Transitional Government's Finance Minister, Ali Allawi, to use the budget as a tool to manage the macroeconomic and fiscal priorities of the government. The first attempt to address the issues of the government's economic programme, in the form of a supplemental budget presented to the cabinet in July 2005, was stymied by a fear that the reform of the petroleum subsidies would be polit-ically hazardous. A supplemental budget was also necessary to contain public spending within specific limits and to accommodate the new government's priorities. In late August 2005, the Minister of Finance presented a strategic perspective for the 2006 budget, in a paper approved by the Cabinet. This formed the basis for the 2006 budget. For the first time in modern Iraq's history, a budget was developed on the basis of an underlying economic vision.[21]

The central problems facing the Iraqi budget after the fall of the former regime were the twin issues of revenue generation and the burden on the budget of large, untargeted entitlement and subsidy programs. No govern-ment since April 2003 had been able to present a meaningful program to tackle these problems, and the budgets that had governed the state's expendi-tures and revenues since that date had been stuck together without any coherent framework that bound the parts. A crude amateurism prevailed, which had contributed a lot to the prevailing confusion over the previous two years as to the existence (or absence) of any coherent economic program for the country. For example, at the outset it was claimed that Iraq only needed to increase oil production to generate all the revenues it needed for reconstruction. This idea was quickly dropped as it was realised that Iraq's economy had been devastated, and that no amount of oil exports would be able to resolve the capital and investment gap. The Madrid Conference that followed produced impressive headline figures as to the amount of donor assistance that would be forthcoming. That was the beginning of the myth of the flood of donor cash that was going to solve Iraq's reconstruction problems. A whole raft of reforms were then announced by the CPA, designed to increase the flow of foreign investment, restructure public finances, and reorganise the banking system, but none of them was pursued with any vigour, and their impact on revenue generation and expenditures were minimal.

It took some time to convince the cabinet that the budget was the only mechanism through which the government's fiscal and investment programme, and its priorities and policies, could be manifested in a direct way. The allocation of planned revenue realisations and the patterns of expenditures were the only real, substantive expression of the government's actual intent, constrained as it was by the financial and monetary (and legal) realities it faced. From the outset, the argument that a Transitional Government should stick to a limited mandate and not undertake any serious initiatives beyond what was necessary was dismissed. A budget ought to be a catalyst for introducing necessary changes and reforms. Four key assumptions underlay the 2006 budget. First, it was assumed that grant assistance and aid would seriously taper off over the following two years. Second, non-oil revenues were not expected to be a significant source of budget revenues for the following four years. Thirdly, security expenditures were to continue at a high level. Fourthly, the universal entitlement programs (the PDS and the petroleum products subsidies) would become unsupportable at their current levels. On the revenue side, the budget proposed a radical expansion of petroleum production and exports; a major effort to improve revenue yields from non-oil sources; and an increase and acceleration of grant and loan flows.

It was on the expenditure side that the budget proposed to reflect the economic and social priorities of the country. Seven key variables governed the spending side of the budget. They included: the introduction of a phased plan for the gradual reduction or elimination of the PDS and the petroleum products subsidies programme; the establishment of cash limits for the combined costs of the PDS and the petroleum products subsidies; limiting capital spending in the non-oil sectors and increasing oil sector investment allocations; providing for a firmer basis for regional and provincial financing; restructuring of the state-owned banking sector; and increasing security related expenditures. The budget would also introduce, for the first time, a comprehensive social security programme for the very poor in the form of cash grants. Nearly a million families would be covered.

The most contentious issue overall was the increase in petroleum products prices, a *sine qua non* for the SBA with the IMF. The US Treasury was concerned that the entire Paris Club debt deal would be in jeopardy if the IMF did not approve an SBA by the year's end, while the IMF was rightly concerned about perpetuating the massive subsidies that encouraged waste, corruption and inefficiencies. The IMF was also wary about the civil disturbances that might occur if the price reforms were poorly managed. Many in the Cabinet were concerned about the electoral impact of price increases in an environment of shortages, outages, joblessness and rampant insecurity. Eventually, the economic arguments were overwhelming and were buttressed by a $500 million social safety net to insulate the poor from the price increases. The budget was passed by the Cabinet, but the price increases were to take effect only after the elections.

The next hurdle was the National Assembly. The UIA leadership was concerned about the apparent paucity of allocations to the provinces in the budget. The reality was somewhat different, as the budget had made an emphatic commitment to regional development. Apart from block grants of a billion dollars for the provinces, a further $500 million were allocated to capitalising regional development banks, and $300 million to a fund to support the families of victims of the former regime. The UIA wanted more. Eventually the National Assembly passed the budget together with increased regional allocations. The petroleum products price increases were put into effect on 18 December. After several days of riots and disturbances, the price increases stuck. Iraq had begun the long and painful process of reforming its unsupportable subsidies programme, something which both the CPA and the Interim Government had shirked from. The Transitional Government had bitten the bullet.

Tragedy on the Bridge of the Imams

On 31 August 2005, crowds of Shi'a pilgrims converged on the Bridge of the Imams connecting the 'Adhamiyya district of Baghdad with Kadhimain, the site of the shrines of the two Imams. They had been marshalled from all corners of Iraq by the Shi'a political parties, partly to commemorate a religious occasion and partly to demonstrate the crowd-mustering and street power of the Shi'a masses. The crowd had had a few mortars lobbed at it, but nevertheless the processions took place, in spite of the seven people killed by the shelling. The bridge in question had been closed for vehicular traffic for a while; pedestrians had to navigate a number of concrete barriers before they could get on to the bridge. It was certainly not possible to accommodate the throngs that were expected, and orders had remained for the bridge to be closed to all traffic. For some unexplained reason, however, the concrete barriers had been removed, and the crowds began to stream towards the bridge as it was the shortest route to the marchers' destination. The bridge became crammed with people, but the flow was continuous into Kadhimain. Just before midday, rumours swept the masses on the bridge that a suicide bomber was in the midst of the crowd. Panic and pandemonium ensued, and in the resulting crush more than a thousand people were killed. They were crushed to death or suffocated and many of those who had hurled themselves into the Tigris were drowned. It was the worst such tragedy in Iraq's history. The Cabinet met in an emergency session. Two of the Sadrist ministers made exceptionally strong statements, condemning the Interior and Defence Ministers, who were held responsible for the marchers' security. Jaafari promised an investigation. The families of the victims were promised compensation, but the results of the enquiry were never released.[22] The enquiry put the blame squarely on the Ministry of Defence, in particular the commander of the Second Brigade, General Jawad al-Roumi, who was responsible for the area on the eastern side of the bridge. The Minister of Defence, Saadoun al-Dulaimi, was also implicated. It was a unilateral decision on their part to open the bridge to the marchers, probably to facilitate the pilgrimage and to avoid any confrontation with elements of the Mahdi Army. It was known that they were planning to participate in the procession and to raise anti-government and anti-occupation slogans. Dulaimi was seen as a vital element of the Transitional Government and Jaafari (and others) were not prepared to see him publicly chastised for his decision. In any case, Dulaimi had accepted the responsibility for this tragedy and had tendered his resignation even before the committee of enquiry had formally convened. But it was not accepted. Ordinary Iraqis were shocked at the scale of the tragedy, even though they had been inured to years of violence. An attempt was made to use the tragedy to bring the two communities together. Unsubstantiated news reports began to circulate that some brave individuals from the predominantly Sunni 'Adhamiyya area had jumped into the river to save the drowning Shi'a pilgrims. This was played up by the government-controlled media, but to little effect. The sectarian violence was now incessant.

The Trial of Saddam Hussein

On 19 October, 2005 the long-delayed trial of Saddam Hussein opened, to intense worldwide interest and media coverage. Formal charges against Saddam and a number of co-defendants, including his half-brother Barazan Ibrahim and Taha Yassin Ramadhan, were filed on 17 July by the Iraq Special Tribunal, in relation to the 1982 massacres in the town of Dujail. The road to the trial had been for a long time in the making. It was way back in 1993 when Warren Christopher, the then US Secretary of State, had sought to prepare a war crimes charge sheet against Saddam and other Ba'athist leaders.[23] Throughout the 1990s, various organisations sprang up with the mission of prosecuting the Iraqi leadership. As the lead-up to the war accelerated, the Department of Defense began to develop a master list of about 300 persons who would be arrested after the overthrow of the regime. Salem Chalabi, a notable US-trained Iraqi lawyer, worked closely with this group, and continued to be involved in the process of developing a framework for a war crimes tribunal after the fall of Baghdad. The UN itself held a number of sessions in Baghdad in July 2003, where the subject of the regime's war crimes and justice for victims were discussed. The major international human rights organisations, such as Amnesty International and Human Rights Watch, were involved.[24]

Soon after the establishment of the Governing Council, a committee to look into the former regime's crimes was formed under the Governing Council member and judge, Dara Nureddine, advised by Salem Chalabi. The Iraq Special Tribunal law was passed by the Governing Council on 9 December, 2003, in one of the few cases where the CPA actually ceded its powers to legislate to the Governing Council. Salem Chalabi was appointed as the first chief executive of the Special Tribunal. For the next few months, Chalabi was deeply engrossed in setting up the machinery of the court in the face of some opposition from the Iraqi judiciary. Most members of the judiciary had little belief in the idea of war crimes, seeing in it a form of victor's justice, and lobbied to have the prosecution of the former regime officials, including Saddam, handled under ordinary Iraqi criminal law. Others thought that the Iraqi judiciary did not have the capacity to take on such complex cases, or were concerned about their personal safety if they joined the tribunal's panel of judges. On 30 June, 2004, the Coalition formally transferred its authority over the former regime's leaders, whom it held in custody, to the new Interim Government. The defendants themselves continued to be held by the Coalition in various prisons, mainly at Camp Victory near the Baghdad airport. The Special Tribunal had its first crisis when Salem Chalabi was ousted from his position during the Interim Government and was accused in a patently false charge of conspiracy to murder a Finance Ministry official. It later transpired that Salem Chalabi's ousting had been engineered by two of his deputies, who worked closely with the American intelligence agencies. The Special Tribunal's management fell into chaos, until direct intervention by the Americans in its affairs rectified the situation. By the summer of 2005, the Special Tribunal felt it was ready to take on the trial of Saddam.

The trial was initially led by a Kurdish judge, Rizgar Amin, who presided over a court that frequently descended into chaos, histrionics, interminable speechifying and grandstanding. The defendants took every opportunity offered them to denounce the Special Tribunal, the Occupation, the laws under which they were tried, and the 'collaborators' who were judging them. At one point, Barzan Ibrahim showed up in his long johns, and turned his back to the judge's podium throughout the day. Amin, ever concerned about the appearance of impartiality and fairness of the trial in front of the world's media, was seen to be too lenient in his management of the court. Roauf Abd el-Rahman, who replaced Amin in January 2006, was far more forceful. The antics in the court deflected attention from another set of issues: whether the Special Tribunal was in fact necessary with its eclectic and cumbersome mixture of Iraqi and international law, and whether Saddam and his henchmen should have been tried in Iraq in the first place. The Special Tribunal's defenders tried to portray the court as a window on the new Iraq, where the most heinous crimes would not prevent the perpetrators from getting a fair trial and where their rights would be respected.

The first case brought up to the Special Tribunal dealt with the events that accompanied the failed assassination attempt on Saddam in the town of Dujail in 1982. The defence team's strategy was to relate the crimes that the defendants were accused of to the emergency conditions of a country at war. The assassins were portrayed as Iran's accomplices, and their attempted act a form of high treason during war. The harsh response of the state was that of a country fighting for its survival. The strategy was to some extent successful, but it couldn't address the overwhelming evidence of killings of minors, deportations of innocent townsmen to distant areas and the wholesale destruction of the town.

In many ways, the Special Tribunal was yet another example of the failed projects of a well-meaning crowd, which sought to transform the political culture of Iraq at lightning speed. The Tribunal was clearly not totally impartial, as when a complex legal manoeuvre involving arcane excuses was employed to the effect that Iran's charges against the former regime could be ignored.[25] The charge of 'Crimes of Aggression' under which Saddam could have been tried for his start of the Iran–Iraq War was dismissed, as there was no underlying UN Security Council resolution. These crimes did not feature in the charge sheets against the former regime. At the same time, the trial had the effect of polarising opinion in Iraq and the Arab world, and gave a platform for the former regime's leaders to raise the increasingly irksome question of whether this was indeed victor's justice. The Special Tribunal was held inside the Green Zone, protected by US troops. Traces of western – American – legal theories, procedures and norms were everywhere. A far more suitable outcome, though probably more difficult logistically, would have been to hold the trials outside Iraq, even if a capital sentence could not be passed, using mainly international judges. This would have de-politicised the process and improved the technical management of the court. In private, the vast majority of the new political establishment dismissed the notion of a trial for Saddam out of hand. Most would have preferred him to be quietly disposed of.

The Jaafari government was beset with problems and crises that marred an assessment of its true performance. It had an atrocious press, unfortunately accentuated by the ramblings and vague pronouncements of the prime minister. The prime minister's staff was of indifferent quality and was unable to cope with the massive load and complexity of the issues that tumbled into his office. Jaafari's instinctive predilection for compromise made decision-making difficult. This was further exacerbated by the backlog of work that piled up in the cabinet secretariat. Some ministers were patently unsuitable for the job, and cabinet sessions were frequently confused affairs that dealt inordinately with inconsequential matters. Jaafari had a tense relationship with the Kurdistan Alliance. The days of the government were thought to be numbered, but the government did in fact survive, no doubt helped by the imminence of national elections and the political risks of overturning the Shi'a–Kurdish governing pact. Jaafari was a complex and enigmatic person who was unable, in public, to address an issue directly. A stickler for upholding the law, he would refer any cabinet decision or issue to his legal adviser to ensure that the proper procedures were followed. But Jaafari's common decency showed through. He entered office as Iraq's most popular politician. He may have left office with his stature diminished, but on leaving he was still Iraq's most popular politician. The government itself had a number of notable achievements; in the budgetary and finance area; in its international economic relations; in fighting corruption; and even in the provision of services, which would have totally collapsed without the Herculean efforts of the energy and infrastructure committees. But the government also presided over a period of increased lawlessness and insurgency attacks, and it was not able to stop the unbridled growth of the power of militias.

25

Into Uncharted Waters

'I call on you to participate broadly in the forthcoming elections so that we can safeguard Iraq, its mosques and its clerics, and so that we can end the rule of one sect without the others; and so that we can make a common stand and say to the Occupier, 'Leave our country!' –

Sheikh Mahmoud Mahdi al-Sumaidei'i,
of the AMS, speaking in November, 2005

'. . . And for this purpose [participating in the elections], *do not split your votes and cause them to be wasted. . .'* –

Statement from the Office of Grand Ayatollah Sistani,
encouraging his followers to vote in the 15 December elections

'I'll choose 555 [United Iraqi Alliance – the 'Shi'a' list] *because it gathers together qualified and religious people. . . . We want security for all Iraqis, but especially for the Shi'ites because they are targeted.'* –

Mahmoud Hadi, an accountant, when asked about
his voting intentions for 15 December, 2005 elections

The elections on 15 December, 2005 were a watershed in Iraq's history and the final milestone in the political process that had begun with the transfer of sovereignty in June 2004. Unlike the earlier elections of January, which were Iraq's first free elections after the war, the December 2005 elections were considered more representative. The January elections had suffered from a near-universal boycott by the Sunni Arabs, but in the December elections, the Sunni community participated enthusiastically and in great numbers. No one could doubt the inclusiveness of these elections. The December elections would not only demonstrate the relative size and power of the various communities, but would also provide the basis for the formation of Iraq's permanent government. At the same time, the spotlight was on the performance of the Jaafari government, which, whether fair or not, had been widely vilified. The credibility gap between its promises and what it actually might deliver came back to haunt the government, especially in the area of public services, and it was uncertain whether the Najaf religious hierarchy would once more affirm its commitment to the UIA. Nevertheless, the UIA survived as the main Shi'a electoral grouping, and its cohesion, though only on the surface, was a model for the main Sunni Arabs groups. They emulated the UIA and formed their own exclusively sectarian grouping, the *Tawaffuq* ('Accordance') bloc to fight the elections. Although there was a huge turnout for the elections, they were marred by clamorous calls of fraud and irregularities, and it was several weeks before the final results were announced. This opened up another problem, as the UIA was torn by a bitter internal power struggle for the post of prime minister. The choice of the prime minister of Iraq preoccupied the US Ambassador in Baghdad – as well as George Bush, as did the composition of the government, and the nature and scope of the participation of the Sunni Arab groups. The battles over the new government were played out against the rising tide of violence. On 22 February 2006, extremists blew up one of Shi'a Islam's holiest sites, the shrine of the Two Imams in Samarra. The savagery of the response to this unprecedented outrage shocked everyone. Civil war seemed inevitable.

A Governing Plan for Iraq

In September 2005, a remarkable document began circulating within the UIA, which mapped out a governing programme for a new Iraq.[1] It was supposedly written by Adel Abd el-Mahdi, the vice-president, who also doubled up as SCIRI's chief theoretician. The document was entitled 'Perspectives on the Principles of Governance in Iraq', and it set out a vision of Iraq with power and authority structures determined by the emancipation and empowerment of the Shi'a. Mahdi identified the coming phase in Iraq's development as a transitional period, a movement from tyranny to democracy and from centralism to federalism and local government. It was a period that would call for a grand compromise between the three main components of Iraqi society: the Shi'a, the Sunnis and the Kurds. The mindset of opposition that had dominated the political establishment had to give way to a recognition that the Shi'a were now the new governing class, and should think and act accordingly. The marginalisation of the Shi'a and their institutions, rites and symbols would give way to their recognition and elevation. The security state of the Ba'ath would be dismantled and replaced by the secure state based on the rule of law. False myths and gods – of

Arabism, racism and sectarianism – would be dethroned. Iraq would be at peace with itself and with its region.

Mahdi postulated that no 'national project' could succeed without a group that could embody its principles and carry them forward. He then asked a rhetorical question: 'Should those [the Shi'a] who carry the 'national project' be driven by their Islam . . . their Shi'ism . . . or their patriotic identity? In other words what are the right assumptions upon which a new governance paradigm should be based?' Ultimately he concluded, 'Iraq is the Shi'a . . . . And the Shi'a are Iraq.' The political emancipation of the Shi'a necessarily leads to the emancipation of the entire country. Once the majority was clear about its governing principles and intentions, particularly if they provided sufficient latitude for the aspirations of others and democracy was ensured, the remaining groups would be able to outline their own vision within this broader framework. In time, the idea of a common citizenship would arise. This would supersede the division of society into majority and minority sects. Communities would organise themselves around a Shi'a axis. In turn, the Shi'a would seek political partners from other groups that were capable of articulating a vision of their communities which respected Shi'a interests. The document basically posited a fundamental re-ordering of the Iraqi state, towards lesser dependence on it by the citizenry, a more equitable distribution of power and jobs, and a radical devolution of power to local government and provinces.

The Mahdi document was the first major attempt to go beyond the numbing platitudes of politicians and try to articulate a vision for the country, no matter how controversial. The ideas and theories in the document were radically different in form and intent from those that underpinned the entire political process. The logic of Mahdi's argument was that the minority ultimately had to acquiesce in the vision of the majority. This was a radical departure from the principle of compromise, in seeking the lowest common denominator in order to draw all groups into the political process. It also marked the abandonment of the western ideal of citizenship, in favour of a constellation of lesser sects and ethnicities revolving around a Shi'a sun. The document came perilously close to equating Iraq with the natural abode of the Arab Shi'a, only a small step removed from the call for a 'Shi'a Nation of Iraq'. The harsher edges of the Mahdi vision were smoothed over by his insistence on democracy, legality and civil rights.

It was unclear whether the road-map laid out in the Mahdi document had been accepted as policy by the SCIRI central council, but tell-tale signs could be discerned about the effects – and acceptance – of the paper in subsequent developments. This was especially true in relation to the devolution of powers from the centre to the region, and to the encouragement given to the forma-tion of regions, as part of the federalisation of Iraq. Mahdi was viewed with suspicion by many, but he was deeply persuasive. The position people took as regards Mahdi and his thoughts would prove critical in the struggle for mastery over the UIA, and ultimately for the premiership of Iraq.

The Remaking of the United Iraqi Alliance

The Jaafari government was not popular with the UIA parliamentarians. There were frequent complaints that Jaafari had ignored or bypassed the formal coordinating mechanisms between the UIA's parliamentary contingent and the government.[2] If the UIA was called upon to provide a new prime minister, SCIRI was determined that the candidate would be vice-president Adel Abd el-Mahdi. The lines to Washington were also cleared, with Mahdi making a low-key visit to the USA, where he met senior officials of the Bush administration. Jaafari's visit to Washington in May had left Bush with a negative impression of him.

The UIA underwent a drastic make-over in preparation for the elections. When it came to configure the make-up of the 'second' UIA, it was clear that there would have to be a redistribution of influence within the party. Islamists had felt that it was they who had provided the 'muscle' for the UIA's electoral triumph.[3] The Sistani factor appeared to be no longer at play. The *Marji'iyya* had kept its distance throughout the months that had preceded the December elections. In fact it was rumoured that the *Marji'iyya* was not intervening at all in the December elections, and that the UIA was to be left to its own devices. This encouraged the looser elements inside the UIA to stake out positions for themselves as independent electoral lists, or at least to threaten their departure from the UIA list if their demands were not met. But this had been an incorrect reading of the *Marji'iyya*'s position. The *Marji'iyya*'s apparent lack of inclination to endorse any particular list masked a determination not to let the UIA fail.

The UIA fell under the sway of its main groups, and was now an electoral alliance of the six major political units that comprised the Islamist Shi'a movement. These were SCIRI, the Badr Organisation, the Da'awa Party and the Da'awa Party–Iraq Organisation, the Sadrists, the Fadhila Party, and the Independents, who had mainly gathered around Hussein Shahristani. The latter continued to enjoy the support of Sistani's son, to the detriment of other putative leaders of the 'Independents' bloc.[4] The SCIRI, however, was the main force behind the regrouped UIA.[5] Candidates for the regrouped UIA were then apportioned on the basis of the relative power of the six constituent groups, providing SCIRI/Badr and the Sadrists with the largest numbers, followed by the Da'awa Party in its two components, and the Fadhila Party. A loose coalition of thirty would-be UIA parliamentarians was grouped around Shahristani. A large number of Shi'a political groups that had sought an independent existence outside the UIA, relying on the neutrality of the *Marji'iyya* in the upcoming elections, were now confronted with the *Marji'iyya*'s late change of position in favour of the UIA.

The fear of a break-up of the Shi'a vote was further compounded by the poor performance of the Jaafari government in providing essential services and security. A backlash of the voters might lead to the dispersal of the Shi'a vote in favour of other groups, and therefore reduce the chances of a working majority in the new parliament. The *Marji'iyya* began to call for its followers to vote for the UIA list. Sistani's office began to campaign in both oblique and obvious ways for the UIA, and to great effect – the other groups were caught flat-footed, and stood by helplessly as their base of support eroded away. For the third time within a year, the *Marji'iyya* cast its weight behind the UIA and its works.[6]

Sunni Arabs Electoral Preparations

The elections were now to be based on provincial lists rather than a single national list, thus providing some leeway for local figures and parties to compete for the parliamentary seats. Three main Sunni Arab parties joined together to form one electoral list, under the leadership of the Iraqi Islamic Party, which was now led by the strong-willed and taciturn Tarek al-Hashemi. A former army officer and supporter of the Muslim Brotherhood movement, he was bitter about the treatment of the army during the Saddamist period, and even more embittered when the CPA disbanded it.[7] Hashemi also had a successful business career before he emerged as one of the leaders of the Islamic Party in the post-war period. The Islamic Party had maintained links with the US Embassy and was one of the key elements of Khalilzad's strategy to engage the Sunni Arabs in the political process. Hashemi's presence at key functions confirmed the 'even-handed' approach of the US to Iraq's varied political factions.

Hashemi knew that the Sunni Arabs had to redouble their efforts to gain a foothold in the political process after the disastrous decision to boycott the January elections. The *Tawaffuq* front was built on three pillars of Sunni support: the Islamic Party, Adnan al-Dulaimi's 'Conference of the People of Iraq', and a third group led by Khalaf Olayan, which represented senior officers from the former Iraqi army and tribal elements. The *Tawaffuq* front clearly had connections with the 'nationalist' insurgency, which appeared to welcome the presence of a friendly voice in the counsels of government. Hashemi himself often talked about the 'honourable resistance' when referring to the acceptable face of the insurgency, but would not countenance a blanket approval of their extremist tactics. He called for a new religious dispensation for acts of resistance, away from the ideology of the extreme Salafists and *takfiris*.[8] Hashemi paid dearly for his break with the terrorist wing of the insurgency. Two of his brothers, and a sister, were murdered.[9]

The Sunni religious establishment pulled out all the stops to ensure broad Sunni participation in the elections.[10] In Fallujah, a centre for insurgent sentiments, Sheikh Abd el-Sattar Athaab demanded that his townsmen turn out in full force to vote. 'Consider my words as a *fatwa*', he said. 'Those who disobey it will be held to account under Islam.'[11] Even the insurgents got into the act. A statement from the 'Islamic Army' issued an order to its followers 'to avoid targeting polling stations and the spillage of the blood of believers'. They were careful to qualify their statement, however, by saying 'this does not mean that we support the so-called political process, and we stress that the *jihad* operations against the Americans and their collaborators will continue'.[12] The extreme wing of the insurgency, especially Zarqawi's al-Qaeda group, was bent on disrupting the process, this time targeting Sunni figures who had declared their support for the elections. A number of figures from the Islamic Party and its associates were murdered.[13] A similar campaign of terror and intimidation targeted other political parties, including Ayad Allawi's *Iraqiyya* list. Saleh al-Mutlaq, whose National Dialogue Council contested the elections on a separate ticket, said, with regard to the assassinations, 'This is a message to all the Sunni currents and personalities to pull out of the elections.'

The 15 December Elections

The December elections were critical in determining a number of factors: whether sectarian sentiments would prevail; whether the *Marji'iyya*'s writ would continue to hold sway; and what the relative strength of the Shi'a lists would be. Observers were also watching the elections as an indicator of the balance of Sunni Arabs in Iraq's population, especially in Baghdad. Above all, there was the question of whether some stability could be created in the face of increasingly ominous signs of impending civil war. The elections were expected to result in the loss of seats by the three main winners in the January elections, primarily to accommodate what was regarded as a good showing by the Sunni parties. The Kurdistan Alliance held to its January format, but included a number of Kurdish Islamists, such as Ali Babir, a founder of the 'Ansar al'Islam' group, a proscribed terrorist organisation.[14] The elections took place in a relatively safe environment, with minimal terrorist disruptions. A turnout of nearly 80 per cent of voters was recorded, an astonishing figure by any reckoning. But no sooner had the polls closed than a cacophony of complaints arose about voter irregularities and fraud.[15] Sheikh Mahmoud al-Sumaidaei of the AMS said, during Friday prayers, '[We] are living a conspiracy based on lies and forgeries. You have to be ready during these hard times and combat forgeries and lies for the sake of Islam.'[16] The preliminary results in Baghdad showed a huge UIA lead, once again deflating the repeated claim about the even sectarian split in Baghdad. But there was no doubt about the hardening of sectarian and ethnic opinion. Shi'as voted for the UIA; Sunnis voted for the *Tawaffuq* bloc or Saleh al-Mutlaq's group; and the Kurds voted for the Kurdistan Alliance.

The final uncertified election results were not announced until 20 January 2006, well over a month after the elections. It took a further two weeks before the certified results were announced. There were inevitable cries of fraud and cheating from many quarters. In the end, out of 275 seats in the new Council of Representatives, the UIA had 128 and a further 2 from the proto-Sadrists, the *Rissaliyyun* group. The biggest relative losers were the *Iraqiyya* list, the cross-sectarian and secular list of Ayad Allawi, which lost 40 per cent of its seats. The other great losers in the elections were the small Shi'a lists, who had counted on the *Marji'iyya*'s strict neutrality in the elections. Ahmad Chalabi did not gain a seat; neither did Ali al-Dabbagh. For these groups, the elections were a veritable debacle.

The De-Selection and Nomination of a Prime Minister

Once the elections were over, the spotlight again focused on the UIA and its candidate for prime minister. Both SCIRI and the Sadrists were determined to have their candidate win. Furious lobbying went on behind the scenes to secure the nomination of their candidate. The SCIRI candidate, Adel Abd el-Mahdi, appeared to be the favourite, and he was already behaving as the prime minister-in-waiting. But the numbers were not necessarily in his favour.[17] Jaafari was able to count on the solid support of the Sadrists and the two wings of the Da'awa Party. This gave him fifty-five out of a total of sixty-five votes needed to secure the nomination. Mahdi, on the other hand, could only count on the SCIRI/Badr bloc, with thirty votes, together with the Fadhila Party at fifteen votes in tow. But even these were not totally secure. Eventually, the unpredictable Independents bloc held the decisive vote. When informed that there was a good chance that Jaafari might win, senior officials in the US Embassy were shocked. They were planning on a Mahdi premiership.[18] But it was not to be. On 12 February, 2006, a secret ballot was held. Jaafari won the UIA's nomination by a single vote, with 64 votes against 63, with two blank votes.

Jaafari won by a secret ballot in a clearly democratic and legitimate way. But he had powerful enemies: within the UIA, the US administration, and the Kurdish groups. They now conspired to reverse the decision of the UIA, on the spurious grounds that he was a divisive figure. The fact that the Sadrists gave their support for Jaafari was a damning indictment for his candidature, at least in American eyes. 'It will be harder to take on the Mahdi Army with

Jaafari as prime minister', a western official in Baghdad was quoted as saying.[19] The Kurds were certain that, if Jaafari were to remain the prime minister, the issue of Kirkuk would continue to remain unresolved and that he would chip away at their region's powers. The opponents of Jaafari had a powerful weapon against him. He could only form a government if the president-elect were to nominate him, and the president-elect had to be voted in with two-thirds of the parliamentary vote. There was thus a built-in blocking veto for the Kurds that could only be circumvented by some improbable parliamentary arithmetic, for example, by giving the presidency to a non-Kurd. The USA was also working diligently to block the formation of a Jaafari government, but this was proving more difficult than anticipated. Moqtada al-Sadr, in turn, was determined that Mahdi would not become the UIA's prime ministerial candidate. The SCIRI kept up the pretence that it continued to respect the choice of the UIA parliamentarians, but in practice it was clearly ranged against Jaafari's having a new term in office. Jaafari stuck to his position, determined to ride out the storm. There was now a serious possibility of an irreversible split in the ranks of the UIA.

The US now began to pile on the pressure. Khalilzad was instructed to inform Hakim that Bush 'doesn't want, doesn't support, and doesn't accept' that Jaafari should form the next government.[20] Splits in the UIA began to appear soon after, as one after another of the UIA's top leadership began to call for Jaafari's withdrawal. Mahdi himself, still sitting as vice-president, demanded that Jaafari should go, in the interest of the UIA's unity. The *New York Times*, in a vitriolic editorial, demanded that Jaafari be driven out of office.[21] On 20 April, Jaafari finally agreed to step down – but not in favour of Mahdi. In a series of meetings it was agreed within the UIA that the Da'awa Party would continue to provide the candidate for prime minister. On 21 April 2006, Nuri (Jawad) al-Maliki became the UIA candidate for prime minister. It was a totally unexpected turn of events for a person who had laboured in the shadows for a number of years, and probably neither expected nor aspired to be prime minister. Maliki had stood firmly behind Jaafari, going so far as to act as his most vocal and staunch supporter outside and inside the counsels of the Da'awa Party. Once Jaafari knew that he was fighting a losing battle, he threw his considerable weight inside the party to Maliki's advantage.[22]

The Destruction of the Samarra Shrine

The saga of who was to head Iraq's first permanent government, or what the spin doctors called its 'national unity' government, coincided with a disastrous collapse in the security situation. This was aggravated by the destruction of the shrines of the Two Imams in Samarra on 22 February, 2006 at the hands of extremists linked to al-Qaeda.[23] The Askariyya shrine was the tomb of the tenth and eleventh Imams of the Shi'a, and the place where the twelfth Imam was believed to have gone into occultation. It was one of the four 'atabats (thresholds) in Iraq, and the destination of millions of pious Shi'a pilgrims. Sunnis also venerated the shrine and visited it in large numbers. The news of the bombings of the shrine which made its magnificent golden dome collapse, spread very quickly. Within a few hours, Shi'a militias were on the streets, and in a paroxysm of violence and rage nearly 1,300 people, the majority of whom were Sunni Arabs, were killed in immediate retaliation.[24] The extent of the slaughter was unprecedented, and seemed to signal an end to the reticence of the Shi'a in taking revenge. As a perceptive analyst of the world of the Shi'a commented, 'This could be the tipping point . . . . At some point, the Shiite street is going to be so fed up that they're not going to listen any more to calls for restraint.'[25] It wasn't the proverbial 'street' that was doing the killing, however, but organised units of the Shi'a militia of the Mahdi Army.[26] The dance between the Sunni Arab parties and the Sadrists, where the former saw Moqtada al-Sadr as a nationalist leader, and the latter saw the Sunnis as natural partners and allies against the American presence, came to an abrupt end. The AMS rapidly changed its tune and directly accused the Mahdi Army of complicity in the killings and of the destruction or takeover of dozens of Sunni mosques. The Sunnis began to feel increasingly vulnerable in a state where the two other communities had their own militias and armies. A senior leader of the *Tawaffuq* bloc, Mahmoud al-Mashhadani, said, 'The Kurds have their militia, and they're part of the army. The Shi'ites run the government. We [the Sunnis] have been left alone with our mosques in the field.'[27] Most Shi'as, however, felt that the Sunnis needed no militias, given that the insurgency was overwhelmingly a Sunni Arab affair.

The Americans became greatly alarmed by the turn of events and the brazen display of street power by the militias. Khalilzad had already made it clear that he expected the Interior and Defence Ministries to be run by professionals. He was particularly incensed with the infiltration of the Ministry of Interior and held the minister, Bayan Jabr, personally responsible for this state of affairs. 'The ministers, particularly security ministers, have to be people who are non sectarian, who are broadly acceptable, who do not represent or have ties to militias', said Khalilzad in a news conference in February.[28] The Sunni Arabs, feeling bereft of official support and with no significant power base inside the government, moved to seek protection from the Americans. One of the *Tawaffuq* leaders, Salman Jumaili, said, 'We would refuse the withdrawal of American forces during this period. They have to fix what they destroyed . . . and guarantee that no sect will dominate the other sects and no party will dominate another party.'[29] In some respects, the apparent helplessness of the 'official' Sunni Arabs played to their advantage, as the Americans sought to offer them more than token representation in the new government.

The participation of Sunni Arabs in the government involved two tactics. The first was the establishment of a political council for national security to group the leaders of all the major parliamentary blocs alongside the government. The presence of the major political leaders on the council would give the council policy-making roles that could supersede the prime minister's prerogatives: it could play the role of overseeing the government's security measures. The second method was to create the positions of deputy prime ministers responsible for sectoral policies. There were two deputy prime ministerial positions established, one for security affairs and the other for economic and public service maters. These would be filled by a Kurd and a Sunni Arab, with the latter being assigned the security portfolio. A double oversight role on security matters would considerably dampen the Sunni Arabs concerns with being left high and dry in a government dominated by the Shi'a and the Kurds. The USA was now trying to mollify the Sunni Arabs, hoping they would be able to influence the insurgency and draw more of the insurgents into the political process. But the killings by the militias and death squads continued unabated, as did the mindless terror of the insurgents. The killing of Abu Musab al-Zarqawi in an air strike on 8 June 2006 only temporarily quelled the virulence of the insurgency. Increasingly, the signs of a civil war were there for all to see, even affecting remarks made by the normally very cautious US military.[30] It was under these inauspicious conditions that Nuri al-Maliki was called upon to form his 'national unity' government.

The Maliki 'National Unity' Government

Nuri al-Maliki was largely an unknown quantity before his return to Baghdad from Damascus after the fall of the regime. In Syria he was known for taking radical anti-American positions, and his mistrust of American intentions in Iraq continued even after he had joined the de-Ba'athification Commission as its deputy. He emerged into the limelight as a senior parliamentarian both in the unelected National Assembly, which tracked the Interim Government, and later on in the Transitional National Assembly, where he headed the security committee. He was known for his maximalist positions on the treatment of former senior Ba'athists, and was uncompromising about the need to confront the insurgency with all necessary force. Maliki's past political positions hardly featured in his assessment for the post, and all those who sought, and obtained, the downfall of Jaafari welcomed his nomination with great relief. Maliki recognised that the country had been without an effective government for nearly five months since the elections, and committed himself to forming a 'national unity' government within a three-week period. His government was a brave attempt to square a circle, drawing on all the parliamentary factions, with the exception of Saleh al-Mutlaq's group, to form his administration. Even Ayad Allawi's *Iraqiyya* list saw fit to participate this time. The cabinet he put together was sworn in on 20 May. Talabani stayed on as President, as did Adel Abd el-Mahdi as vice-president. The *Tawaffuq*'s Tarek al-Hashemi was also sworn in as vice-president, replacing the outgoing Ghazi al-Yawar. One of the *bête noires* of Khalilzad and Washington was the former Interior Minister Bayan Jabr, who was seen as the guiding spirit behind the infiltration of the militias, especially the Badr Organisation, into the Ministry of Interior.[31] The US would not countenance him keeping his job. He was removed but then given the Finance Ministry in compensation. The Ministry of Defence went to a serving general, Abd el-Qadir Jassim, an American nominee. The new Minister of Interior was Jawad Bolani, whose appointment caught everyone by surprise as he had been an aircraft engineer with little experience in security related matters. The Sunni Arabs appeared satisfied with their portion of power and felt that they could block any tendency of the state to veer away from their interests. The final milestone in the political process was now reached. A permanent government that would shepherd Iraq over the next four years was in place. But neither the violence nor the drift towards communal strife and low-grade civil war could be stopped.

The anxiety about the future was all too palpable, and was evident during Maliki's visit to Washington in late July 2006. A gruff but decent man with none of the circumlocutions of his predecessor, he was carrying the burden of holding Iraq together, from a position he had neither sought, nor expected nor trained for. It was almost too much for a single person, shorn of any meaningful support, with an inexperienced staff, and surrounded by enemies and ill-wishers on all fronts. But Maliki had an inner resilient core. He recognised his short-comings and sought to remedy them as best as he could. He accepted advice from his American minders, but not uncritically. He was direct in his demeanour and decisive in his actions. At first, he could devote all his time to the matters and crises at hand rather than expend his energies protecting his flanks and watching out for conspirators – as rivals were wrongfooted by his appointment. The Americans recognised that they had to support Maliki whatever the cost, and pulled out all the stops to back his government.

Maliki announced a number of confidence-building measures to draw the communities of Iraq together and bridge sectarian divides. Shortly after he had formed his government, he announced the prime minister's initiative for national reconciliation, and sought to establish the parameters whereby elements of the insurgency and the former Ba'athists might enter the polit-ical process. At the same time, he had been prevailed upon to make strong statements about the need to tackle the problem of the militia. It was not quite clear how he was supposed to achieve that, given that the two biggest Shi'a militias, those of Badr and the Mahdi Army, were controlled by parties who formed the backbone of the UIA.

'Civil War' and the Militias

The spiral of violence was spinning out of control. Debates raged about whether Iraq had entered the phase of 'civil war'.[32] For most people, it was immaterial whether the dictionary definition of civil war applied. In many respects, Iraq's violence was worse than a civil war, where at least some civil peace usually prevailed behind the front lines. But applying this epithet mattered for the self-image of Iraqi politicians, and to official Washington. The latter studiously avoided using this loaded term, for it undermined whatever remained of the tattered credibility of the official line. Acknowledging that civil war conditions in Iraq did indeed prevail would inevitably raise the question as to what US troops were doing in an internal conflict. Even so, leading senators and congressmen no longer shied from using this term.[33] Senator Reid, a Democrat, announced emphatically on 20 July, 2006, that 'There is a civil war going on in Iraq.'[34]

The first flashes of an incipient civil war could be traced to a little-reported series of incidents that took place in late 2004, in the aftermath of the second battle for Fallujah.[35] Refugees leaving Fallujah had converged on the western Sunni suburbs of Baghdad, 'Amriya and Ghazaliya, which had come under the control of the insurgency. Insurgents, often backed by relatives of the Fallujah refugees, turned on the Shi'a residents of these neighbourhoods. Hundreds of Shi'a families were driven from their homes, which were then seized by the refugees. Sunni Arab resentment against the Shi'a's 'collaboration' with the occupation forces had been building up, exacerbated by the apparent indifference of the Shi'a to the assault on Fallujah. In turn, the Shi'a were becoming incensed by the daily attacks on policemen and soldiers, who were mostly poor Shi'a men. The targeting of Sunnis in majority Shi'a neighbourhoods began in early 2005. In the Shaab district of Baghdad, for instance, the assassination of a popular Sadrist cleric, Sheikh Haitham al-Ansari, led to the formation of one of the first Shi'a death squads. These comprised individuals associated with the Mahdi Army, who were organised for their grisly task by a local religious leader, the imam of a Shi'a *husseiniya* (meeting hall).[36] At first the killings were limited to recalcitrant Ba'athists, insurgent suspects and Salafists. But a momentum had developed whereby the cycle of killings, assassinations, bombings and expulsions fed into each other, quickly turning to a full-scale ethnic cleansing of city neighbourhoods and towns. In Baghdad, the Shaab district became nearly Sunni-free, and similarly for the Maalif and Shu'ula areas and most of the Hurriya district. Shi'as were driven out of 'Amriya, and most of Dora and Ghazaliya. A rough map of Baghdad would show an overwhelming Shi'a presence on the east bank of the river, and a majority Sunni presence on the west bank of the Tigris. The situation had not yet deteriorated into a clear division of the city, but a mental redrawing of the map of the city according to sectarian criteria began to impose itself on the minds of most Baghdadis. Sentiments were hardening and calls for inter-sectarian concord began to sound extremely hollow. Sermons of both sects were increasingly inflammatory, and code words for the enemy were flying fast and furious. Shi'a imams would routinely denounce 'Wahhabis, Takfiris and Nawasib'; Sunni preachers would rant about 'Safawis, Buwayhis and Persians' in their midst. One Sadrist cleric, who had been jailed by the Americans, said, 'After I was in jail I knew who was my enemy and who was not. The Americans are not my enemy . . . . Our enemies are the Wahhabis.'[37]

A decisive turning point in community relations took place after the January 2005 elections. The UIA sweep handed over key ministries of the government to political parties with armed wings. The expansion of the police forces by the Transitional National Government opened the door to a huge flow of new recruits, drawn mainly from the Shi'a poor. Frequently, these were members of the Mahdi Army or had been sympathetic to it. A similar, though less noticeable, pattern was followed in the recruitment for the army. Although the senior officer grades were vetted to some extent by the MNF recruiters, the rank and file of the soldiery were also drawn from poor Shi'as, with their built-in loyalties to tribes and to the Islamist parties. The attacks on Sunni targets by the Mahdi Army entered a determined phase in 2005. By then, the distinction between the 'national resistance', which had earlier called for inter-sectarian cooperation in resisting the occupation, and the extreme wing of the insurgency, with its anti-Shi'a polemics, had blurred. Moqtada as-Sadr's demands that the Sunni ulema brand Zarqawi and his followers as infidels were ignored. This further fuelled the suspicion that Zarqawi's thesis about the Shi'a's 'perfidy and treachery' to Islam was implicitly accepted by the ranking Sunni ulema.

In March 2005, in Madain, a town south of Baghdad with a Sunni majority, clashes between insurgents and Shi'a migrants led to wide-scale expulsions and killings of Shi'a residents. The newly elected Transitional National Assembly broke up in uproar as news filtered through of dozens of corpses floating downstream on the Tigris as a result of the killings. Sunni Arab organisations, including the AMS, denied that expulsions were taking place, putting the stories coming out of Madain down to malicious fabrications. Units of the Ministry of Interior that had been sent to restore order behaved in an obviously partisan way, arresting Sunni men at random. The Ministry of Interior's special units had now become indelibly connected with the Shi'a Islamist parties. The police force as a whole was also falling under the militias' sway. As one American adviser said, 'To be perfectly honest, I'm not sure we're ever going to have police here that are free of militia influence.'[38] But a range of other factors would also contribute to the exacerbation of sectarian feelings. The wrangles over the constitution; SCIRI's demands for a federal region in the

South of Iraq; the perceived tilt of the US Ambassador to Sunni groups when enticing them into the political process; the mooted rehabilitation of Ba'athists; all these and other factors heightened sectarian feelings and misgivings.

The Mahdi Army had evolved considerably since its start as a rag-tag militia attempting to confront the US military in Najaf. A core of the Mahdi Army became professionally organised and structured. Rumours abounded that some of its key leadership were being trained in Iran and in Hizbollah camps in Lebanon. 'We do know that Shi'a extremist groups have received training through some sort of third element associated with Iran', said the MNF's Baghdad spokesman, Major General William B. Caldwell. 'We do know that weapons have been provided.'[39] Moqtada al-Sadr maintained titular control over the Mahdi Army, but his key subordinates were probably more influential in the command structure.[40] At the same time, the Mahdi Army became a 'franchise', with local groups springing up that were only loosely connected to the main body of the Mahdi Army. They would be organised by local clerics, petty businessmen, street toughs and sometimes criminal gangs who acted frequently outside the framework of the Mahdi Army proper. The Badr Organisation of SCIRI, on the other hand, was less involved in the sectarian killings and cleansings of later times. SCIRI was ever conscious of the need to tread carefully and had scrupulously avoided any military confrontation with the Americans. Badr insinuated itself into command structures of the Ministry of Interior and local and provincial forces. It left the 'muscle' to the Mahdi Army.

The 'militia issue' loomed large in the security and stabilisation plans of the MNF and USA. The sectarian revenge killings, especially after the Samarra bombings, began to dwarf the deaths perpetrated by the insurgents. According to reports, the number of those killed in execution-style murders in the aftermath of the Samarra bombings was eight times the level of deaths caused by insurgent attacks.[41] To the Shi'a political class, this seemed to be a reversal of America's priorities in the battle against the overwhelmingly Sunni Arab insurgents. American casualties were caused by the insurgents and not the militias, went their oft-repeated complaint. But the USA was turning a deaf ear. Militias not only meant a dangerous armed threat to the US military presence in Iraq; a principal factor in sectarian killings; a threat to the authority of a central government – but, ominously, a tool in the hands of the US foe, Iran.[42] The US could not produce definite evidence of its accusation that Iran was behind Iraq's Shi'a militias. General Caldwell's earlier comments about the possibility of Iranian collusion in the training and arming of the militias were now superseded by direct accusations. In August 2006, Brigadier General Michael Barbero claimed that there was 'irrefutable' evidence of Iranian collusion with Iraqi militias, but he could not provide any specific examples.[43] Zalmay Khalilzad, the US Ambassador, added that militias were the greatest threat to

Iraq's stability and demanded that the government move to disband them.[44] Maliki made the requisite noises against the presence of militias, but the government could not convince itself, let alone its parliamentary base, about the necessity or urgency of confronting the militias. They were seen to be part of the Shi'a arsenal against a possibility that the balance of forces – inside the state or in terms of their relations with the USA – would tilt against them.

Control of the Shi'a Islamist parties over the state structures was still hesitant, especially as the Iraqi army appeared to be entwined with the MNF command and would not normally accede to the orders of the Iraqi government. In one particular case, an order given to an army unit by the prime minister, in his capacity as commander-in-chief of the Iraqi armed forces, was countermanded by the MNF. Another order, given to an Iraqi commander by the prime minister and acted upon, resulted in the summary dismissal and imprisonment of the officer concerned by the MNF.[45] With the army effectively out of the government's control, the militias appeared to be ever more important for the Shi'a groups. Maliki hesitated and procrastinated, in essence refusing to act out the demands of the MNF and the US Ambassador to allow them to tackle the militias – especially the Mahdi Army – head on. 'We have told the Americans that we don't mind targeting a Mahdi Army cell inside Sadr City', Maliki said. 'But the way the multinational forces are thinking of confronting this issue will destroy an entire neighbourhood. Of course it [a planned attack on Sadr City] was rejected.'[46] A battle between MNF-led Iraqi army units and the Mahdi Army in Diwaniya in August 2006 resulted in casualties on both sides; still, the Maliki government would not sanction an assault on the Mahdi Army. Provocative or pre-emptive attacks by the MNF against the Mahdi Army would continue throughout 2006, frequently angering the government.

Killings, Internal Population, Displacements and Emigration

In October 2006, the noted British medical journal *Lancet* published a very disturbing report on the killings in Iraq.[47] This followed on an earlier report that the journal had made in 2004, when it surmised that deaths attributable to the war in Iraq in the period March 2003 to September 2004 had exceeded 100,000 people. In the October 2006 report, the *Lancet* reached an even more frightening approximation. The journal estimated that the total deaths in Iraq in the period between March 2003 and July 2006 *may have exceeded 650,000 people*. The figure was astounding, as it easily surpassed all the previously published figures of casualties, which ranged from 50,000 (from the unofficial Iraq Body Count) to 100,000. The *Lancet* used statistically acceptable methods, which had been employed with good effect in other conflict zones. The report was immediately condemned by officials in Washington and London as being grossly exaggerated. Even so, the *Lancet* study seemed credible to many experts, and the numbers of Iraqi deaths began to creep upwards towards a much higher consensus figure. For the first time, the level of Iraqi deaths as a result of the war began to loom large in the minds of both the war's critics and its dwindling band of supporters. The war and the post-war mayhem were killing off Iraqis at a far higher level than had been predicted or reported. The Iraqi public was strangely mute about this. Few Baghdad papers or TV stations dwelled on the matter. Iraqis had become inured to the terrible carnage in the country, and indifferent to the on-going controversy over the scale of casualties.

The bloodshed in the country was not the only grief that Iraqis had to suffer. They were being displaced in an unparalleled campaign of sectarian and ethnic cleansing that affected all sections of society. In another report, dated October 2006, the Brookings Institution–University of Berne Project on Internal Displacement submitted another startling finding on the scope of the internal refugees' problem in Iraq after the Samarra bombings of February 2006.[48] The UN's High Commissioner for Refugees had estimated that nearly 1.6 million people had been displaced internally since March 2003.[49] The Brookings–Berne report dealt only with those displaced as a direct result of sectarian-induced violence. The report stated that, by September 2006, nearly 250,000 people had fled their homes because of fear, intimidation or threats. (By November 2006, the head of the Iraqi Red Crescent Society informed the author that the figure had gone up to nearly 500,000 people.) Most of the displaced people had come from mixed neighbourhoods of major cities, especially Baghdad and Mosul, and the provinces of Babil, Diyala and Salahudin. The report emphasised that most of those displaced since the Samarra bombings were Sunnis fleeing from Shi'a areas, reversing an earlier pattern whereby Shi'a had come under pressure in predominantly Sunni areas and accounted for the largest number of displaced people. The bonds that had previously kept Iraqi society resilient were fraying alarmingly. Intolerance was spreading throughout the two communities, and, even when friends or neighbours tried to protect those marked for eviction, they would come under the scrutiny of militias later on. In Mosul, it was the Kurds and Christians who came under attack from radical Sunni groups. West Mosul had been effectively 'cleansed' of its Kurdish and Christian populations, just as the city began to receive large numbers of Sunni Arab refugees from Baghdad and other provinces. Hundreds of thousands of Iraqis were fleeing their country. According to the UN High Commissioner of Refugees, somewhere in the order of 1.8 million Iraqis were now outside the country since the end of the war.[50] By November 2006, nearly 1,000 Iraqis were being displaced by sectarian violence, while 2,000 Iraqis were leaving for Syria and 1,000 for Jordan on a daily basis.[51]

452   THE OCCUPATION OF IRAQ

In an ominous development, the Najaf hierarchy appeared to have had its fill of politics, denouncing the succession of governments that they, in no small part, had encouraged. 'The government formed after the fall of the regime hasn't been able to do anything, just make promises. And people are fed up with the promises . . . One day we will not be able to stop a popular revolution', said Grand Ayatollah Bashir al-Najafi in early August 2006.[52] Sistani put out a statement which came as close as he could make it to pushing the alarm buttons, without creating a crisis of confidence in the political process entirely. It was a long and anguished cry from the heart and a plea to end the mayhem. 'I address myself to all the proud people of Iraq in all their sects and ethnicities to face the dangers that confront the future of their country, and to show solidarity in combating hatred and violence and to replace them with peaceful dialogue and amity.'[53] The Grand Ayatollah's office, ever sensitive to changes in the public mood, sensed that something new was afoot. Grumblings against the government, though not necessarily against the person of Maliki, increased throughout the summer and autumn of 2006, with many regretting giving their vote to the UIA – or even voting at all. The cynicism and anger of the populace were palpable, as public services deteriorated even further. Gasoline queues, power shortages, insecurity, lawlessness, car bombs, internal exile – Iraq appeared to be nearing total bedlam. It was a far cry from the euphoria that had accompanied the January 2005 elections, or even the determination with which 80 per cent of voters went to the polls a scant seven months previously. The flimsy and often jerry-built structures that were put together to house the 'political process' were showing dangerous signs of instability. The process that began with the Transition Administrative Law, or even earlier when the Governing Council had been formed, had come to an end with the formation of the permanent government. There were no more milestones left.

Epilogue

'*Those who cannot remember the past are condemned to repeat it.*' –
George Santayana, philosopher and poet, 1905

As 2006 drew to a close, the backdrop to the crisis in Iraq began to change. Death squads and the infiltrated police force began to match – and exceed – the insurgents in the scale and viciousness of their attacks on civilians. In terms of the government's credibility, the Maliki government was called upon to address the lawlessness and violence emanating from the militias as a matter of even greater priority than the counter-insurgency campaign. The USA, the Sunni Arab parties and their regional supporters in the Arab world would all join in demanding that the Maliki government tackle the Mahdi Army directly, or at least give the MNF the green light to mount an assault on their strongholds. Maliki, however, was acutely aware both of his dependency on the Sadr bloc in parliament and of the deep unpopularity of such a move with the Shi'a masses. The state's institutions continued to atrophy, and the much-expected 'standing up' of the Iraqi army's combat units, which were being so laboriously and expensively trained, was still a long way off. Three years into the training of the Iraqi security forces, the same problems remained: absenteeism, poor communication between the American trainers and the Iraqis, and doubtful institutional loyalties.

Meetings between senior Washington officials and the Baghdad government multiplied throughout the autumn of 2006, culminating in a visit to Baghdad by Stephen Hadley, Bush's National Security Adviser, in late October 2006. This trip followed after the apparent failure of combined American and Iraqi units to pacify Baghdad, in the latest plan to reassert government control over the capital. Maliki loudly complained that he had no effective control over the Iraqi armed forces, that he was unable to move a company of troops without prior approval from the MNF command. It was a moot point whether increasing Iraqi government control over the armed forces would have the desired effect of countering the insurgency or the militias.

There was a marked shift in the American public's attitude towards the Iraq war. The shift certainly influenced the outcome of the November congressional elections, which handed control over Congress to the Democrats – who had campaigned with the promise of fashioning a new Iraq policy. But they still had to contend with Bush's determination not to change strategic directions. There was a real fear that a retreat from Iraq, in whatever guise, would be interpreted as an American defeat, and would consign Bush's presidency to the ranks of the failed presidencies of the past. The Iraq Study Group, a panel of eminent individuals co-chaired by the former Secretary of State James Baker and by Lee Hamilton, a former Congressman, had been authorised by Congress in March 2006 to examine the options available to America in Iraq. The report's findings were seen to provide the essential bi-partisan cover to undertake a major shift in American policy, particularly with regard to its proposals for a gradual withdrawal of America's combat functions, and an increased emphasis on training and strengthening the Iraqi armed forces. Bush met Maliki once again in Amman, Jordan, in late November. The meeting was partly overshadowed by a leaked memo, written by Hadley on his return from his October visit to Baghdad. Hadley questioned Maliki's sincerity in pursuing a non-sectarian agenda, but he still held out the possibility that Maliki could be enticed into forming a new alliance of mildly religious Shi'a, SCIRI, the Kurds and the government-allied Sunni Arab parties. It was a sign of the times that a former Da'awa Party stalwart could be seen as the catalyst and leader of a movement whose main aim would be to isolate, and perhaps eliminate, the Sadrists. In Amman, Bush reiterated his support for Maliki as the 'right guy for Iraq', and seemed ready to act upon the recommendations of the Hadley memo. Both Sayyid Abd el-Aziz el-Hakim and Vice-President Tareq al-Hashemi were invited to Washington for further consultations. Bush was deeply reluctant to acknowledge the role that either Iran or Syria might play in stabilising Iraq. He came close to vetoing any regional conference that would allow these two countries a formal role in the resolution of the Iraqi crisis. As the fourth anniversary of the start of the war approached, a new phase of the war had begun: George Bush was now pitted against the growing army of sceptics and opponents in Washington.

The tumultuous events of 2006 were capped by another extraordinary episode in the tortured passage of the country through the labyrinths of its past. Saddam Hussein, who had been sentenced to death by the Iraq Special Tribunal in early November for ordering the Dujail massacres, lost his appeal. On December 30, 2006, he was hanged in a dank and rancid execution room in the former headquarters of the *Istikhbarat,* the military intelligence services in the Kadhimain area, a site chosen for its symbolic significance. Hundreds of people had met their end in its dungeons. Rather than providing 'closure' for the years of his tyranny and terror, the circumstances surrounding his execution, and the actual moments before he was hanged, were to provide further grist to the mill of Iraq's conflicts and civil turmoil. The Maliki government was insistent that the hanging proceed forthwith, in spite of American concerns about the political fallout from a hasty execution. The timing of the execution was unfortunate as it coincided with the beginning of the holidays commemorating the end of the Hajj, marked by most of the Islamic world even though the Shia of Iraq would celebrate on the following day. The official version of the execution showed a subdued Saddam quietly mounting the gallows. However, a video shot from one of the witnesses' mobile phones showed an entirely different picture of Saddam's last minutes. He was seen to be taunted by the guards and some of the witnesses as he mounted the scaffold, all the while maintaining his composure and a remarkable degree of equanimity and courage in the face of certain death. The assembled witnesses were nearly all Islamists mainly from the Da'awa Party and the Sadrist movement. Some of the chants hurled at Saddam included paeans to Moqtada, leading some to question whether the execution party was state-sponsored or one dominated by the Mahdi Army. The Shi'a of Iraq were, in the main, uncritically supportive of the execution. The Kurds though, while welcoming the demise of their tormentor, were concerned that with his death the *Anfal* campaign and other atrocities against the Kurds would not receive the fulsome court exposure they deserved. The Sunni Arabs as well as most of the Arab and Muslim World reacted very negatively to the manner of Saddam's execution. The crimes of the Saddamist regime were overlooked as they focussed on the questionable juridical basis of the execution warrant. What they saw was victor's justice, vengeance-seeking, sectarian gloating and the attempts of a weak government to impose its writ. It was the mismanagement of the execution process that allowed for the deflection of attention from the crimes of his years in power to the manner of his death.

This book began with scholars. The late Edward Said famously attacked the arcane world of Orientalist studies and single-handedly launched the debate on the role of scholars in fashioning the justification for the imperial drive to dominate the Middle East. Ever since, it has become almost a commonplace to look for academics and their theories lurking behind the decisions and actions of politicians and national leaders. George Bush had a legion of academic and think-tank cheerleaders for his Iraq venture. They drew their inspiration from radical conservatism and an unapologetic defence of western – mainly American – values. Their description of the Arab Middle East bordered on caricature. It was of a reactionary, anti-modern, even nihilistic, culture. If left to its own devices it would create profound instability in the world. It was the duty of the United States, the world's superpower, not to shirk from the challenge that this region posed. Washington was where the battles for the modern Middle East have usually started, and the Iraq war was no exception.

When America's foray into the heartland of the Middle East began to go awry, these very same apologists for the war scuttled for cover, perhaps mindful of history's indictment of their prescriptions and prognoses. Some neo-conservative luminaries heaped blame on the Bush administration for faulty execution of their impeccable conceptions. Others actually blamed the Iraqis, in a variation on the theme that Iraqis were an ungrateful lot and did not deserve the gift of freedom. 'Scholars are, of all people, those least familiar with the ways of politics', said Ibn Khaldun, the fourteenth-century Muslim philosopher of history. But he meant real scholars and not this curious new breed of mandarin that flits between universities, think-tanks, law offices, corporations and the upper echelons of government. These people were supremely political and knew when the game was up.

Nearly four years after the war was launched, a new set of experts has emerged to dominate the discussions on Iraq. These are experts on the last days of an earlier American expedition that ended in anguish. The disputes over how the Vietnam War ended are returning with a nearly forgotten vehemence. The lessons of that earlier war are drawn as a parallel to the circumstances in Iraq. The elements of a stab-in-the-back thesis are being prepared, in warning to a Congress now controlled by Democrats, in case it might decide to cut off American support for the Iraq venture unilaterally. The battle lines on who 'lost' Iraq are already being demarcated – if this eventuality actually materialises.

The law of unintended consequences broke out in Iraq with a vengeance. The US invasion and occupation of Iraq broke the thick crust that had accreted over the country and region as a whole, and released powerful subterranean forces. The emergence of the Shi'a after decades, if not centuries, of marginalisation was perhaps the most profound outcome, closely followed by the massive spur given to the drive for a Kurdish nation. On another level, the divisions within the world of Islam became far more pronounced. They are about to move on to an altogether different plane of mutual antipathy and internecine warfare. Aligned to this was Iran's insistence on its claims to a privileged role in regional counsels. The already fearful Arab countries of the Middle East had to ponder over this new demand by a potentially nuclear-armed Iran, and whether to accommodate or challenge it. It was the Bush Administration that acted as the unwitting hand-maiden to history and denied, ignored, belittled and misunderstood the effects of what it had created.

The Bush Administration shared with others a gross misconception related to the response of the Sunni Arabs to their loss of power and prestige. This was probably most disturbing to observers, not least to those Iraqis who thought that after a sullen period of resentment the Sunni Arabs would adjust to the changed circumstances and seek to find a place in the new constellation of forces in the country. The insurgency was almost an exclusively Sunni Arab affair, notwithstanding the two half-rebellions of Moqtada al-Sadr in 2004. The sense of loss and defeat was made even more poignant by the fact that it was a totally unexpected force that achieved the impossible – the dethronement of the community from centuries of power in favour of, as they saw it, a rabble led by Persianate clerics. It was almost too much for them, and certainly too much for the neighbouring Arab countries. Resistance might have been expected, but the extreme violence of the insurgents' tactics was truly shocking. It was to do with some form of existential struggle, where the Sunni Arabs' entire history and identity were at stake.

The elevation of mass bombings and indiscriminate killings to foment sectarian warfare stumped the military. It was an altogether different form of 'asymmetrical' war, which could not be seriously contained without disregard for the basic civil rights of people. Such warfare was also relatively cheap to deploy, relying on individual fanatics and improvised explosive devices: the IED's of military jargon. Fear of US retribution did not stop the terrorists and insurgents from receiving ample logistical and financial support from a range of neighbouring countries. The insurgency continues – with no let-up. It is now matched or even superseded by the explosion of sectarian killings by death squads and out-of-control militias. For those who design and execute its strategy and tactics, the insurgency seems to be a winning ticket. After all, it has forced the Americans to push for greater inclusiveness and representation of the Sunni Arabs in government. Whether this will satisfy the insurgents, who are still the real power in the Sunni Arab community, remains to be seen.

The Arab countries of the Middle East have been unable to adjust to the events in Iraq, but not so much because of the contagious effect of the changes that have taken place. Iraq cannot, by any stretch of the imagination, be seen as a model for anything worth emulating. The Arabs' inability to adjust has less to do with the instability that might spill over from the raging violence in Iraq, and more to do with accommodating an unknown quantity into a regional system that can barely acknowledge pluralism and democracy, let alone a Shi'a ascendancy, in Iraq. Egypt, Saudi Arabia and Jordan, linchpins of the American security order in the Arab world, cannot accept the principle of a Shi'a-dominated Iraq, each for its own reasons. These countries will do their utmost to thwart such a possibility, and, failing that, will probably try to isolate such an entity from any effective role in the region. They still entertain hopes of fashioning an alliance between secular, Iran-bashing politicians and the more acceptable face of the old Ba'athist and militarist order, to create a

458 THE OCCUPATION OF IRAQ

majority that might pull the country – or at least the Arab part of it – away from an overt Shi'a identification.

This is a path that the USA may also pursue, except that it is stymied by the very processes that it has set loose. Democracy and elections can produce unexpected and unwelcome results, and so far they have delivered the Shi'a vote to the Islamist parties. But the coalition within the UIA is unstable and there is an elemental hunger for power by rival Shi'a Islamist groups. Already the spoils of office are being jealously guarded by the rival groups. According to the constitution, it is uncertain whether Iraq should be a majoritarian democracy or a democracy-by-consensus. The central authority may crumble, as frustrated Shi'a political leaders, blocked from gaining undivided power in Baghdad, seek to find different formulae to run the country. One such possibility is a new alliance between the SCIRI Islamists, the *Tawaffuq* bloc and the Kurdistan Alliance, to push for a federal resolution of the crisis. Alternatively, and encouraged by the USA, they may choose to monopolise power and smash the political base of their rivals. Two highly contentious questions are posed: can the Shi'as in power actually confront the Sadrists, and can the Sunni Arabs in government face off the insurgents?

A federal solution as envisaged is, in reality, a confederal solution. It postulates the three-way division of the country into large administrative units, taking the Kurdistan Regional Government as the model. This has all the attributes of an independent state, bound to the centre by ties of convenience and interest rather than by a commitment to a unitary Iraq. Baghdad may have to be given a special status as the federal region, but, even here, an administrative division between mainly Shi'a east Baghdad (the Rusafa area) and mainly Sunni west Baghdad (the Karkh area) may be necessary to accommodate the ambitions and interest of various groups. The Sadrists have, up to now, stood against the idea of federalism, partly because of their distrust of SCIRI, which may come to dominate the southern region. They may accept the inevitable and stake a claim to power in Baghdad through their control over Sadr City and other Shi'a neighbourhoods.

Whatever outcome might evolve, the least stable one would be the continuation of the current desperate attempts to maintain a degree of integrity for the central state. The Iraqi state that has evolved as a result of the tumultuous changes over the past few years is not one to which many people are prepared to give their allegiance. It is unloved by the Sunni Arabs, who have lost control over it, and barely tolerated by the Kurds. 'We can already smell the scent of the free state of Kurdistan', as a Kurdish minister said to the author. Even the Shi'a, who have been the greatest gainers in the central state, see it mainly as a jobs and spoils dispensing institution. The increasing instability, and the state's own feebleness, alienate more and more people – who leave Iraq for other horizons.

The rules of a just war could have been applied to Iraq if the issues that had propelled America to invade Iraq were clearly ethical. But this was not the case. The explicit reason that was used related to Iraq's phantom arsenal of nuclear and biological weapons, and to the risks they posed to the national security of the United States. All other arguments were ex post facto, and were not part of the overt reasons given to validate the decision to invade Iraq. Removing tyranny, building a democracy, introducing human and civil rights, writing a progressive constitution – these were all subsequent justifications for maintaining the presence of America in Iraq. But they were not part of the original brief. Neither did they feature prominently in backroom discussions on the war. It is for this reason that, when Bush sought a public validation from Iraqis for America's mission in the country, there were few takers – except the Kurds, who had always been different.

It is not that the Shi'a are ungrateful that they have finally been freed from generations of oppressive control, but they will always see their 'freedom' as incidental to something else that America was seeking. Being an afterthought does not give rise to gratitude and celebration; and similarly for democrats, liberals, modernisers, champions of free markets and all the others who might have believed in the American mission if its substance had matched its rhetoric. But none now gives any credence to the claims that the purpose of America's occupation of Iraq was somehow related to America's espousal and promotion of democratic values. On the ground, these claims ring hollow. The rhetoric of change and reform came easily to the spokesmen for the occupation and to those in official Washington, but it was equally quickly dropped when it clashed with whatever were the exigencies of the moment. No wonder that cynicism runs deep regarding America's true motives. Seizure of the oil fields, building Iraq as a base to subvert Iran, breaking up the country as part of a redesigned, fragmented Middle East, removing Iraq as a threat to Israel, these were all arguments held out as the 'real' motives behind America's push into Iraq. There was no 'American party' in Iraq, no people who were open advocates of an alliance with America because it was in the manifest interest of the country to have such an arrangement. America's only allies in Iraq were those who sought to manipulate the great power to their narrow advantage. It might have been otherwise.

America's 'civilising mission' in Iraq stumbled, and then quickly vanished, leaving a trail of slogans and an incomplete reconstruction plan. The billions that America had spent went unrecognised, and therefore not appreciated. Iraqis heard about the billions, like some memorable banquet to which only a few are invited. But what they experienced was the daily chaos, confusion, shortages, and the stark terrors of life. Death squads now compounded vicious attacks by terrorists. Opinions and divisions were hardening. No-go areas, ethnic cleansing, emigration, internal displacement were now happening under the watch of 150,000 MNF troops. No power on earth, except the USA, could have withstood the stresses of the Iraqi war and its aftermath. The Americans could do so only because they had a surfeit of resources and military power, which they could bring to bear on problems that would have sunk many other countries trying their hand at 'nation-building'. But the Iraqis had already turned their backs on their would-be liberators.

In all of these struggles for Iraq's future, the new Iraqi political establishment was notably silent about how to extricate the country from its current predicament. The dependency on a foreign power to tackle Iraq's existential questions was embarrassingly evident, even after three sovereign governments had been in power. The Iraqi political class that inherited the mantle of the state from the Ba'athist regime was manifestly culpable in presiding over the deterioration of the conditions of the country. The absence of leadership on a national scale was glaring. The search for that will-o'-the-wisp, the Iraqi national leader, predictably got nowhere. There were only Shi'a, Sunni and Kurdish politicians, a smattering of self-styled liberals and secularists, each determined to push their particular agenda forward. There was no national vision for anything, just a series of deals to push forward a political process, the end state of which was indeterminate. There was also no governing plan. The corroded and corrupt state of Saddam was replaced by the corroded, inefficient, incompetent and corrupt state of the new order. The *Marji'iyya* managed to maintain its stature and dignity, but only just. It was the only institution that most of the Shi'a respected and acknowledged most of the time. It pushed people to vote, to participate in the political life under the new dispensation.

Time is running out. The monumental patience of the Iraqi people has nearly ended. They have endured so many hardships and broken promises, but they have still kept the light of hope flickering. They are very near a terminal breaking point.

Bush may well go down in history as presiding over one of America's great strategic blunders. Thousands of servicemen have been the casualties of a failed policy. A new Iraqi political establishment is emerging. It is a mixture of former oppositionists, carpetbaggers and profiteers, cunning bureaucrats who avoided or thrived on de-Ba'athification, and previously angry young men and women who are now deputies and councilmen, keen to taste the fruits of power. They may shrug off the lost opportunities for their country and fellow citizens, and sink further into their mendacious and supremely egotistical ways. But it is Iraq and the Iraqis who have paid most for the failed policies of their erstwhile liberators and their newly minted governors.

Notes

Chapter 1: The Great Divides

1. Abd el-Karim al-Uzri, *Mushkillat al-Hukm Fi il-'Iraq* (The Problem of Governance in Iraq), self published, London, 1991, pp. 2–9. The Faisal memorandum was first reproduced by the Iraqi historian Abd el-Razzaq al-Hassani, in his work on the cabinets of Iraq. This version by al-Uzri is the first complete treatment of the subject by a former minister. Al-Uzri was deputy to the Royal Chamberlain in the last years of Faisal I.
2. There are a number of excellent surveys on the ancient history of Iraq. For the general reader, the most accessible is George Roux's *Ancient Iraq*, Penguin, Harmondsworth, 1993.
3. Saddam fancied himself as a reincarnation of several historic heroes. Murals of him in the guise of Salahuddin, the legendary Muslim warrior of the Crusades, and as Nebuchadnezzar, the Babylonian king, were ubiquitous. On many of the bricks in the walls of Babylon, Saddam had the following inscription made: 'This was built by Saddam Hussein, son of Nebuchadnezzar, to glorify Iraq'.
4. For the military history of Iraq during World War I, see A. J. Barker, *The Neglected War*, Faber & Faber, London, 1967. There are a number of recent studies on Iraq in the aftermath of World War I and the establishment of the mandate system. See Toby Dodge, *Inventing Iraq: The Failure of Nation-building and a History Denied*, Hurst and Co., London, 2003; Ghassan al-'Attiyya, *Al-Iraq: Nasha'at ad-Dawla 1908–1921*, Laam Books, London, 1993.
5. For the referendum on Faisal, see Nur Masalha, 'King Faisal I of Iraq: A Study of His Political Leadership 1921–1933', unpublished Ph.D. dissertation, pp. 61–3, School of Oriental and African Studies, University of London, 1988.
6. There are a large number of works on the Arab Revolt in World War I. A general survey of the fall of the Ottoman Empire in the Middle East is David Fromkin's *A Peace to End All Peace: The Fall of the Ottoman Empire and the Creation of the Modern Middle East*, Henry Holt & Co., New York, 1989. For the Arab view on the Revolt, see Suleiman Musa, *'Al-Haraka al-'Arabiyya 1908–1924* (The Arab Movement 1908–1924), Dar-al-Nahar, Beirut, 1970. For a general survey on the modern Middle East, see William Cleveland, *A History of the Modern Middle East*, Westview Press, New York, 1994.
7. For Faisal and the short-lived Arab State in Syria, see Khairiyya Qasimiyya, *'Al-Hukkuma al-Arabiyya fi Dimashq 1918–1920* (The Arab Government in Damascus 1918–1920), Beirut, 1983; also, Sati'al-Husri's *Yawm Maysalun* (The Day of Maysalun), Beirut, 1964.
8. See Masalha, op. cit.
9. See al-Uzri, op. cit.
10. The best non-polemical survey on the succession to the Prophet Muhammad is Wilfred Madelung's *The Succession to Muhammad – A Study of the Early Caliphate*, Cambridge University Press, Cambridge, 1997.
11. The tragedy of Karbala is a central theme in all works on Shi'a Islam. It has also entered into the religious symbolism of moderate Sunnism. A good survey in English of the development of early Shi'sm is S. H. M. Jaffri, *The Origins and Early Development of Shi'a Islam*, Oxford University Press, Oxford, 2002.

12. The Imami line of the Shi'a, accounting for perhaps 95 per cent of all the Shi'a, affirms that there are twelve Imams who were infallible guides for the interpretation of Islam. Imams must be lineal descendants of Ali (the first Imam) and Fatima (the Prophet's daughter). Each Imam must designate his successor directly. The Imams were all either killed, imprisoned, or closely watched by both the Ummayad and Abbasid Khalifs. The Shi'a believe that the twelfth Imam went into 'occultation' – that is, he vanished from the physical to appear in another, spiritual realm. They also believe that his return will herald the establishment of a just society, the defeat of the Dajjal –the embodiment of evil or the Anti-Christ – and the end of time before Judgement Day. Most Sunnis accept that some of the Shi'a Imams were noted religious scholars, but do not subscribe to their infallibility or to their special role in guiding Muslims.

13. For the establishment of Shi'ism in Iran, see Said Amir Arjomand, *The Shadow of God and the Hidden Imam: Religion, Political Order, and Societal Change in Shi'ite Iran from the Beginning to 1890*, University of Chicago Press, Chicago, 1987.

14. A number of specialist works on Iraq during the Ottoman period cover the relationships between the Shi'a and the Ottoman authorities. See Yitzhak Nakash, *The Shi'is of Iraq*, Princeton University Press, Princeton, NJ, 1994; Stephen Longrigg, *Four Centuries of Modern Iraq*, Gregg International Publishers, Farnborough, England, 1968; Meir Litvak, *Shi'i Scholars of Nineteenth-Century Iraq: The 'Ulama of Najaf and Karbala*, Cambridge University Press, Cambridge, 2002. The best work in Arabic (and in any language) on this period is the magisterial study of Ali al-Wardi, *Lamhat Ijtimai'yya min Tarikh al-Iraq al-Hadith* [Sociological Glimpses from the Modern History of Iraq], Baghdad, 2004.

15. The struggle between the various schools of Shi'ism, especially the Akhbari and Usuli, is covered in Arjomand, op. cit. Also, the topic is covered in extensive detail in Hamid Algar, *Religion and State in Iran 1785–1906*, University of California Press, Berkeley, CA, 1969. For the messianic and eschatological tendencies in Shi'ism, see Abbas Amanat, *Resurrection and Renewal: The Making of the Babi Movement in Iran, 1844–1850*, Cornell University Press, Ithaca, NY, 1989.

16. For the mass conversion of the tribes to Shi'ism, see Nakash, op. cit., pp. 25–48.

17. For the role of the Shi'a *ulema* in calling for *jihad* against the British in World War I, see ibid., pp. 55–61. Earlier, in 1910, the Shi'a *mujtahids* had called for a joint position with the Sunni *ulemas* to stop European encroachments on Ottoman and Persian territory.

18. The failure of the 1920 rebellion and its effects on the Shi'a clerical classes is covered in a number of studies, including ibid., Masalha, op. cit., al-'Attiyya, op. cit. A view from a participant in the 1920 rebellion is Muhammad Mahdi al-Basir, *Tarikh al-Qadhiyya al-Iraqiyya* (History of the Iraq Question), Laam Books, London, 1990. A powerful and more wide-ranging work is Hassan 'Alawi, *Al-Shi'a wa ad-Dawla al-Qawmiyya fi il-Iraq* (The Shi'a and the National State in Iraq), CEDI France, Paris, 1989.

19. On the early development of the Islamist movement in Iraq, see Abd el-Halim al-Ruhaimi, *Tarikh al-Haraka al-Islamiyya fi-il Iraq 1900–1924* (The History of the Islamic Movement in Iraq 1900–1924), Beirut, 1985. For a survey on the evolution of Islamic political thought, see Hamid Enayat, *Modern Islamic Political Thought*, I. B. Tauris, London and New York, 2005. For the development of Shi'a political thought, see Fouad Ibrahim, *Al-Faqih wa ad-Dawla- Al Fikr al-Siyassi al-Shii* (The Jurisprudent and the State-Shi'a Political Thought), Beirut, 1998.

20. The origins and growth of the Muslim Brotherhood in Iraq is covered in Basim al-'Azami, 'The Muslim Brotherhood', in Faleh Abd el-Jabbar, ed., *Ayatollahs, Sufis and Ideologues: State, Religion and Social Movements*, Saqi Books, London, 2002.

21. The most authoritative source book on the Islamic Da'awa Party is Salah al-Kharsan, *Hizb ad-Da'awa al-Islamiyya: Haqaiq wa Wathaiq* (The Islamic Da'awa Party – Facts and Documents), Damascus, 1999. See also Joyce N. Wiley, *The Islamic Movement of Iraqi Shi'as*, Lynne Rienner Publishers, Boulder, Colo., 1992.

22. See al-Kharsan, op. cit. See also Chibli Mallat, *The Renewal of Islamic Law: Muhammad Baqer al-Sadr, Najaf and the Shi'i International*, Cambridge University Press, Cambridge, 1993. Al-Sadr himself was a prolific author. In 1996 a group of researchers under the auspices of the Dar al-Islam Foundation in London produced a collection of essays for Ayatollah al-Sadr, *Muhammad Baqir al-Sadr: Dirassa fi Hayatihi wa Fikrihi* (Studies on his Life and Thought), Dar al-Islam Foundation, London, 1996.

23. See J. F. Devlin, *The Ba'ath Party: A History from its Origins to 1966*, Hoover Institution Press, Stanford University, Calif., 1976.

24. See Abdulaziz A. Sachedina (translator), *The Prolegomena to the Quran*, Oxford University Press, Oxford, 1998, pp. 3–22, on al-Khoei's life and thought.

25. Khomeini's lectures on Islamic government are in *Islam and Revolution: Writings and Declarations of Imam Khomeini*, translated by Hamid Algar, Mizan Press, Berkeley, CA, 1981.

26. See al-Kharsan, op. cit., for a full discussion of the Ba'ath attack on the Shi'a Islamists, especially pp. 273–91.

27. The best single volume on the modern history of the Kurds is David McDowall, *A Modern History of the Kurds*, I. B. Tauris, London and New York, 2000. The text of the Treaty of Sèvres relating to Kurdistan called for producing a 'scheme for local autonomy of the predominantly Kurdish areas'. Within a year, the Kurds of this area would have the right to demand independence from Turkey if the majority of the people so wished.

28. See McDowall, op. cit., for the rise and fall of the Mahabad Republic, pp. 231–48. For a detailed analysis of the Republic, see William Eagleton, Jr, *The Kurdish Republic of 1946*, Oxford University Press, Oxford, 1963. For the great power rivalries in Iran after World War II, see Bruce R. Kuniholm, *The Origins of the Cold War in the Near East*, Princeton University Press, Princeton, NJ, 1980.

29. See McDowall, op. cit., pp. 302–13.

30. Ibid., pp. 323–37.

31. See Edmund Ghareeb, *The Kurdish Question in Iraq*, Syracuse University Press, New York, 1981 for a detailed discussion of the events leading to the 1974–75 war between the Ba'ath and the Kurds, the Algiers agreement between the Shah of Iran and Saddam, and the aftermath to the Kurdish debacle.

32. Iraqi exiles spawned a number of short-lived journals and news-sheets that chronicled the activities, struggles and internecine fights of the opposition. The most consistent in its policies of opposition and the best produced and edited was *Tayar aj-Jadid*, published by Saad Saleh Jabr in London. Jabr was a fierce critic of the Ba'ath and Saddam. He spent his considerable fortune on the financing of the opposition abroad. During particularly bleak periods, it was Jabr with his optimism and moderation who kept the liberal and democratic opposition alive. The other main journal was the weekly newspaper *Jihad* put out by the Da'awa Party in London, edited by Sami al-Askari. A number of Iranian-financed journals that covered the Iraqi opposition were also published in London. The most important of these was the news magazine *Al-'Alam*.

33. See Jon Lee Anderson, 'Letter from Iran: Dreaming of Baghdad – What Regime Change Means to the Iraqi Opposition', *New Yorker*, 10 February, 2003, on the Hakim family and their sufferings in Iraq.

34. The assassination of Sayyid Mahdi al-Hakim took place in broad daylight in the lobby of the Khartoum Hilton Hotel. The assassin walked calmly towards Sayyid Mahdi and shot him at near point-blank range. A relative of Hakim, Sayyid Abd el-Wahhab al-Hakim, was also wounded in the attack. It was quickly established that the murderer was a professional assassin attached to the Iraqi Embassy in Khartoum. He was spirited out of the country immediately after the assassination.

35. The killings in Dujail were the subject of the first war crimes charges levelled against Saddam and his accomplices. The Dujail trial, presided over by the Iraq Special Tribunal, concluded in July 2006. In November 2006, the trial judges found Saddam guilty of the charges and sentenced him to death by hanging.

36. Hanna Batatu was a lifelong Marxist, and tended to see Iraq through the prism of class analysis and conflict. His book, *The Old Social Classes and the Revolutionary Movements of Iraq*, Princeton University Press, Princeton, NJ, 1978, is not for the faint-hearted. Its encyclopaedic scope covers nearly 1,300 pages in the paperback edition.

37. Halabja became a byword for the atrocities of the Ba'athist regime. Human rights organisations, journalists and foreign chanceries amply documented the chemical warfare against the Kurds. See, for example, Human Rights Watch (HRW), 'Whatever Happened to the Iraqi Kurds?', 11 March, 1991, at http://www.hrw.org/reports/ 1991/IRAQ913.htm.

38. The *Anfal* campaign was also widely covered. Human Rights Watch published a particularly shocking indictment of the regime's crimes as regards the *Anfal* in its July 1993 report, 'Genocide in Iraq – The *Anfal* Campaign Against the Kurds', http:// www.hrw.org/reports/1993/iraqanfal/. The *Anfal* campaign was the subject of the second war crimes trial against Saddam and his accomplices. It began in August 2006.

Chapter 2: The Rise of the Opposition

1. See Patrick E. Tyler, 'Officers Say US Aided Iraq in War Despite Use of Gas', *New York Times*, 18 August, 2002. The extent of US support for Iraq during the Iraq–Iran War was also confirmed by the former head of Iraqi military intelligence, General Wafiq al-Samaraei, who had defected to the opposition in 1995 and was later appointed security adviser to President Talabani in 2005.
2. On 3 July, 1988, the *USS Vincennes* shot down an Iranian civil airliner flying from Dubai to Bandar Abbas. For the Iranians it was a prima facie case that the USA had entered the war on the side of Iraq. The Iranian allegations were partly corroborated by a *Newsweek* article on 13 July, 1992, which accused US authorities of a cover-up. Iran filed suit at the International Court of Justice, which in November 2003 found that the actions of the superpower were unlawful. The USA agreed to compensate the victims of the disaster in 1996, before the decision of the Court had been handed down.
3. The costs to Iran alone of the war were estimated at $350 billion. See Farhang Rajaee, *The Iran–Iraq War: The Politics of Aggression*, University Press of Florida, Gainesville, FL, 1993. Dilip Hiro, in his book *The Longest War*, Grafton Books, 1989, estimates the cost of the war at $1.1 trillion for both parties.
4. See Bruce Maddy-Weitzmann, *The Inter Arab System and the Gulf War: Continuity and Change*, The Carter Center, Atlanta, Ga, November 1991.
5. See HRW, 1991, op. cit.
6. See Tyler, op. cit.
7. The most detailed analysis of the west's involvement with the regime of Saddam Hussein during the Iran–Iraq War can be found in Kenneth Timmerman, *The Death Lobby: How the West Armed Iraq*, Houghton Mifflin, New York, 1991.
8. The coup plot of 1969 involved a number of officers led by General Abd el-Ghani al-Rawi, a former Cabinet minister in the Aref era, in alliance with civilians led by Saad Saleh Jabr. The plotters were closely coordinating with Mulla Mustafa Barzani and Iranian intelligence, SAVAK. The plotters were betrayed by a double agent. Dozens of people were subsequently executed by the Ba'ath regime in response to the attempted coup.
9. The cost of the bailout of the bank was nearly $400 million. The collapse of Petra Bank generated an official enquiry in Jordan. A military court subsequently tried and sentenced most of the defendants, including Chalabi and his managers, *in absentia*. Chalabi always insisted on his innocence and laid the blame squarely on the blunderings of the Central Bank. He published a detailed tract refuting the charges against him. The stand-off between Jordan and Chalabi in this matter continued with no resolution in sight.
10. The State Department continued formally to refuse to meet any Iraqi opposition figures. Leaders of the Iraqi opposition would meet furtively with low-grade functionaries, where only notes of the Iraqis' views would be made. The CIA, though, working mainly through Britain's intelligence agencies, did not have the same compunction. Congressional leaders were far more open to these contacts.
11. For a listing of Iraq's major opposition groups in the 1990s, including the formation of the Joint Action Committee, see http://middleeastreference.org.uk/iraqiopposition.html.
12. The best survey on the origins and evolution of the Supreme Council for the Islamic Revolution in Iraq (SCIRI) can be found in Adel Raouf's *Al-'Amal al-Islami fi il-Iraq bayn al-Marji'iyya wa al-Hizbiyya* (Islamist Action in Iraq between the *Marji'iyya* and Party Organisation), Damascus, 2000, pp. 305–61. This is a formidable study of the Iraqi Islamist movement and the interplay between the Najaf hierarchy and political parties.
13. There are no authoritative surveys of the March 1991 uprisings. The best single document on the uprisings and their aftermath is HRW, 'Endless Torment: The 1991 Uprising in Iraq and its Aftermath', June 1992, at http://www.hrw.org/reports/1992/Iraq926.htm. Journalists were few on the ground but a number were able accurately to report the drama from positions in Kuwait, Khoramshahr and Amman. See Alan Cowell, 'Unrest in Iraq Reported to Spread from Basra to Three Other Cities', *New York Times*, 4 March, 1991; Rodney Pinder and Karl Waldron, 'Crisis in the Gulf: Shi'a Muslims Rise Up Against Saddam in Basra', *Independent* (London), 4 March, 1991; William Claiborne, 'Anti-Saddam Uprising Spreads in South Iraq: Refugees Say Opposition Has Seized Some Towns', *Washington Post*, 5 March, 1991.
14. See HRW, 1992, op. cit.; Claiborne, op. cit.

15. See HRW, 1992, op. cit.; R. W. Apple Jr., 'Iraqi Clashes Said to Grow as Troops Join in Protests', *New York Times*, 5 March, 1991; Bob Drogan and Mark Fineman, 'Uprisings Spread Anarchy in South Iraq, Refugees Report', *Los Angeles Times*, 5 March, 1991.
16. See HRW, 1992, op. cit.
17. See ibid.
18. See ibid.
19. See ibid.
20. See Marion Farouk-Sluglett and Peter Sluglett, *Iraq since 1958 – from Revolution to Dictatorship*, I. B. Tauris, London and New York, 2001, pp. 289–90.
21. See Raouf, op. cit., pp. 447–66 on Grand Ayatollah al-Khoei's dealing with the uprising.
22. The speech can be retrieved in full from the Bush Library website at http://bushlibrary.tamu.edu/research/papers/1991/91021504.html.
23. See Steve Coll and Guy Gugliotta, 'Iraq Accepts All Ceasefire Terms', *Washington Post*, 4 March, 1991. The full text of the meeting at Safwan can be sourced from: http://www.gulflink.osd.mil/declassdocs/centcom/19960424/DOC_80_CEASE_FIRE_DISCUSSIONS_WITH_IRAQIS_AT_SAFWAN_AIRFIELD_001.html.
24. See HRW, 1992, op. cit.
25. A videotape of Saddam's conversation with Grand Ayatollah al-Khoei, based on the televised meeting, was widely circulated.
26. HRW, 1992, op. cit. For an eyewitness account of the battle for Karbala, see Zainab al-Suwaij, 'Memories of a Free Iraq – The Fire Last Time', *New Republic*, 10 February, 2003.
27. This was widely reported and quoted in Farouk-Sluglett and Sluglett, op. cit., p. 289. Abd el-Aziz Kadhem, a Karbala restaurateur, was an eyewitness who confirmed this to journalists from the Institute for War and Peace Reporting's *Iraq Crisis Report*, 13 April, 2004.
28. HRW, 1992, op. cit.
29. Ibid.
30. The frequent refrain was: *Al-Amrikan mu jiddiyyin* (The Americans are not serious (about overthrowing Saddam)). It took nearly a decade before the Islamist parties accepted that the United States was indeed serious.
31. A profile of Ayad Allawi is carried in Jon Lee Anderson, 'A Man of the Shadows', *New Yorker*, 24 January, 2005.
32. Ibid.
33. Interview: author with Francis Brooke, political adviser to the INC, April–June 2004.
34. The articles were unsigned, but the suspicion was that they had been written by Saddam himself, or probably Tariq Aziz, the Deputy Prime Minister. See Jon Lee Anderson, 'Letter From Baghdad – Saddam's Fears', *New Yorker*, 5 May, 2003. Anderson interviewed Saddam's personal physician, Dr 'Ala Bashir, who stated that it was Saddam who penned them. 'The next morning, and for two consecutive days, articles appeared in the Ba'athist newspaper *Thawra*. They were unsigned, but they were written by him [Saddam].'
35. The Sadr family was one of the most illustrious of the religious families in Iraq, as well as Lebanon, and, in earlier periods, Iran.
36. See Raouf, op. cit.
37. The theological development of Ayatollah Muhammad Muhammad Sadiq al-Sadr is also covered in a compendium of essays in his honour called *Ayatollah Muhammad Muhammad Sadiq al-Sadr Rajl ul-Fikr wal Maydan* (Man of Thought and Action), Amin Press, Tehran (?), 2001, especially the essay on the political thought of Ayatollahs Baqir and Muhammad Sadiq al-Sadr, pp. 191–259, by 'Aref al-Sadiqi.
38. Raouf, op. cit.
39. Cited in al-Sadiqi, op. cit., p. 227. Also, Mukhtar al-Asadi, '*Al-Sadr al-Thani, al-Shahid wal Shaheed* (The Second Sadr, the Witness and the Martyr), Amin Press, Tehran (?), 1999. The book deals with the later sermons of Ayatollah al-Sadr, his assassination and its aftermath.
40. See al-Sadiqi, op. cit., pp 236–9. Also al-Asadi, op. cit., p. 69.
41. Al-Asadi, op. cit., devotes considerable attention to the attacks on Ayatollah al-Sadr by other religious figures, and his response to them.
42. The assassination of the two ayatollahs was well reported in the western press and was taken up by human rights organisations. The UN Special Rapporteur on Human Rights in Iraq also highlighted these murders. See the report distributed to the UN General Assembly on 24 September, 1998 A/53/433.

43. See al-Asadi, op. cit., pp. 99–105.
44. See ibid., pp. 157–8. See also Nabil Yasseen's detailed article on the assassination of Ayatollah Muhammad Sadiq al-Sadr that appeared in the London *al-Hayat* newspaper on 2 February, 1999.

Chapter 3: The Build-up to War

1. Author interviews with Francis Brooke, political adviser to the INC, April–June 2004. See also David Wurmser, *Tyranny's Ally: America's Failure to Defeat Saddam Hussein*, AEI Press, Washington, 1999.
2. Interviews: author with Warren Marik, April 2004.
3. The details of the failed coup attempt of the INA are in Scott Ritter, *Endgame*, Simon and Schuster, New York, 1999; and in James Bone, 'MI6 "proposed Iraqi coup" to topple Saddam', *The Times* (London), 18 March, 1999. The INC's version was given in Warren Marrik's interviews with the author, April 2004.
4. See Martin Indyk *et al.*, 'Symposium on Dual Containment: US Policy Toward Iran and Iraq', *Middle East Policy*, Vol. 3, No. 1, 1994; and Anthony Lake, 'Confronting Backlash States', *Foreign Affairs*, Vol. 73, No. 2, March/April 1994. For a critique of the dual containment policy, see Barbara Conry, 'America's Misguided Policy of Dual Containment in the Persian Gulf', Cato Institute, Cato Foreign Policy Briefing no. 33, November 1994. (Also at http://www.cato.org/pubs/fpbriefs/fpb033.html.)
5. The 'Clean Break' report is widely available on the WorldWideWeb. Other signatories of the report included David Wurmser, a fellow at the American Enterprise Institute, and Douglas Feith, later to become Under Secretary of the Department of Defense in the Bush administration.
6. This argument was extended to include the whole arena of Middle East Studies at American universities. These were also held complicit in developing an 'Arabist' orientation in foreign policy. See Martin Kramer, *Ivory Towers on Sand: The Failure of Middle Eastern Studies in America*, Washington Institute for Near East Policy, Policy Papers No. 58, 2001.
7. Interviews: author with Francis Brooke, April–June 2004. Also interviews: author with Zaab Sethna, INC media adviser, April–July 2005.
8. Interviews: author with Francis Brooke, April–June 2004.
9. See the interview with Francis J. Ricciardone, *Al Ahram Weekly* (Cairo), Issue 439, July 1999, pp. 22–8.
10. See the Ricciardone interviews in *Milliyet* and *Cumhuriyet*, 1 March, 1999. With reference to the possibility of a coup against Saddam he said, 'Most probably, there will be a military coup. . . . It will be very sudden and without warning. . . . The United States does not have a candidate [to replace Saddam] . . . A military regime will be in power for some time after the coup.' The full transcript of the interview was made available to the author by the US Embassy in London.
11. The pan-Arabist newspaper *Al Quds al Arabi* led the charge, but nearly all the London-based Arab press, as well as the Gulf newspapers, were vehemently against the implications of the Iraq Liberation Act and the Act itself.
12. Personal notes taken by the author, and conference papers, on the New York meeting.
13. See the Ricciardone interview in *al-Ahram Weekly* (Cairo).
14. The abuses of the OFF programme became the subject of a huge internal enquiry by the UN, headed by the former head of the US Federal Reserve Board, Paul Volcker. The enquiry, the findings of which were published in September 2005, implicated a large number of companies and individuals in sanctions-busting and accepting bribes and kickbacks from the Ba'ath regime. The reports can be accessed at www.iic-offp.org.
15. The most complete archived source on sanctions on Iraq can be found at www.casi.org.uk.
16. The literature on the UN's weapons inspection programme for Iraq is vast. The best survey from the point of view of an insider is Hans Blix, *Disarming Iraq*, Pantheon, New York, 2004. Blix's conclusions are an indictment of the intelligence apparatuses of the USA and the UK. He comes out strongly against the war and affirms the work of the UN weapons inspectors in discovering, dismantling and destroying Saddam's WMD.
17. For example, the conference held in London, July 1997, on the theme 'The Broad Outlines of an Islamic Political Project for a Future Iraq'; the conference on the theme of 'An Alternative Vision for Iraq', London, October 1998; the seminar on 'The Future of Iraq', held under the auspices of the Foreign Office, London, February 2000.

18. The Da'awa Party produced an entirely revised manifesto in 1995.
19. The Declaration was widely circulated and had its own website. Thousands of copies were printed and distributed in Iraq after the fall of the regime. It can be accessed at http://www.al-bab.com/arab/docs/iraq/shia02a.htm.

Chapter 4: The Invasion

1. The memo was entitled: 'Regarding the Suspension of the Iraq National Accord's Membership in the National Conference'. Copy in the author's possession.
2. Elliott Abrams, a signatory to the PNAC statement, joined the National Security Council and in 2002 became Senior Director for Near East and North African Affairs. John Bolton, a board member of PNAC, became Under Secretary of State for Arms Control and International Security Affairs. Paula Dobriansky, another PNAC supporter, became Under Secretary of State for Global Affairs, responsible for the spreading of democracy. Zalmay Khalilzad, a former RAND Corporation senior analyst, who went on to become ambassador in Iraq, joined the National Safety Council (NSC) as its Director for the Gulf and Southwest Asia and Other Regional Issues. Richard Perle became the head of the Pentagon's Defense Policy Board. Peter Rodman, another PNAC signatory, became the Assistant Secretary of Defense for International Security Affairs. Donald Rumsfeld became the Secretary of Defense.
3. See 'Iraq Sanctions Saga Continues amid Policy Confusion', *Middle East Economic Survey*, Vol. 45, No. 23, 10 June, 2002; also Colin Rowat, 'How the Sanctions Hurt Iraq', MERIP Note 65, 2 August, 2001, accessed on http://www.merip.org/mero/mero 080201.html; and 'Making Targeted Sanctions Effective: Guidelines for the Implementation of UN Policy Options', The Special Program on the Implementation of Targeted Sanctions (SPITS), Stockholm, February 2003.
4. The most complete description of Bush's determined insistence on linking Saddam to the 9/11 plotters comes from Richard Clarke, *Against All Enemies: Inside America's War on Terror*, Free Press, New York, 2004.
5. See Bob Woodward, *Plan of Attack*, Simon & Schuster, New York, 2004, and Clarke, op. cit.
6. See Blix, op. cit.
7. The INC's role in providing faulty intelligence was consistently used against the organisation by opponents of Chalabi in the Bush administration. See Kenneth Pollack, 'Spies, Lies, and Weapons: What Went Wrong', *Atlantic Monthly*, January/February 2004. Pollack's article was a form of *mea culpa*. He had earlier written a book calling for the invasion of Iraq as a precautionary move against Saddam's acquiring nuclear weapons (*The Threatening Storm: The Case for Invading Iraq*, Random House, New York, 2002).
8. One of the most apparently credible sources was Khidir Hamza. He was a noted nuclear scientist who worked with the Iraqi Atomic Energy Commission. He defected to the USA in 1994 and co-authored a book, *Saddam's Bombmaker: The Terrifying Inside Story of the Iraqi Nuclear and Biological Weapons Agenda*, Scribner, New York, 2000. Hamza became a media celebrity and a witness in congressional committees in the run-up to the war, finding out that Saddam was on the verge of acquiring a nuclear capability. He later joined the Coalition Provisional Authority (CPA) as a senior adviser to the Ministry of Science, but his tenure was unhappy and short-lived. Others who had worked on the Iraq nuclear weapons programme seriously questioned his claims.
9. The Northern Alliance in Afghanistan was based on the minority Tajik community who overthrew the Taliban. The USA gave them logistical and other support, without at first actually committing any ground troops to the war.
10. Based on the author's personal dealings with the Foreign Office's Arab/Iraq experts.
11. See the profile on Paul Wolfowitz by Bill Keller, 'The Sunshine Warrior', *New York Times Magazine*, 22 September, 2002.
12. Formally known as 'The Report on the Transition to Democracy in Iraq', adopted by the Coordinating Committee of the Democratic Principles Workshop, 4 October, 2002.
13. The de-Ba'athification paper was written by Ali A. Allawi.
14. The section on the London conference of December 2002 is based on the personal notes and conference papers of the author.
15. It should be noted here that although the UK is part of the EU, with regard to Iraq the UK maintained a completely different and uncoordinated policy from the rest of the EU. The UK and the rest of the EU each sent its own set of representatives.

16. An excellent profile of Zalmay Khalilzad can be found in Jon Lee Anderson, 'American Viceroy: Zalmay Khalilzad's Mission', *New Yorker*, 19 December, 2005.
17. See Roula Khalaf, 'Iraqi Opposition to Haggle over Go-Between Committee for US', *Financial Times* (London), 14 December, 2002.
18. See Peter Slevin and Daniel Williams, 'Key Exiles Agree U.S. Should Not Run Postwar Iraq; Leaders Jockey to Succeed Hussein', *Washington Post*, 15 December, 2002. See also Salah Nasrawi, 'Iraqi Struggle Over Plan for Interim Baghdad Government in Post-Saddam Iraq', *Associated Press*, 15 December, 2002.
19. See Lydia Georgi, 'Iraqi Opposition to Meet in Kurdistan After Sealing US-Brokered Deal', *Agence France-Presse*, 17 December, 2002; Anthony Shadid, 'Exiles Set Up Unwieldy Council; Internal Opposition Gets Look From US', *Boston Globe*, 18 December, 2002; also Hussain Hindawi, 'Iraqi Opposition Still Divided', *United Press International*, 20 December, 2002.
20. See Daniel Williams, 'U.S. Army to Train 1,000 Iraqi Exiles', *Washington Post*, 18 December, 2002.
21. Christopher Dickey and Colin Soloway, 'Friends or Foes', *Newsweek*, 23 December, 2002. The article gives an in-depth survey of US relations with the Da'awa Party in the preparations for war.
22. Judith Miller, 'Hussein's Foes Put off Talks in North Iraq; Safety Is Issue', *The New York Times*, 16 January, 2003. Also Guy Dinmore and Gareth Smyth, 'Opposition to Meet Inside Iraq', *Financial Times* (London), 20 January, 2003.
23. Robin Wright and Warren Vieth, 'Iraqi Opposition Falling Short of U.S. Expectations', *Los Angeles Times*, 23 January, 2003.
24. 'Allawi: The Opposition Meeting is Useless', *Turkish Daily News*, 28 February, 2003.
25. Stefan Smith, 'US Role in Post-Saddam Iraq Dominates Opposition Talks', Agence France-Presse, 26 February, 2003.
26. Interview: author with Salem Chalabi, November 2004.
27. The most detailed account of the military aspects of the invasion and occupation of Iraq is in Michael Gordon and General Bernard Trainor, *Cobra II: The Inside Story of the Invasion and Occupation of Iraq*, Atlantic Books, London, 2006.
28. See ibid., pp. 338–43.
29. Interview: author with Bayan Jabr, SCIRI Consultative Council member, Baghdad, January 2006.
30. Ayad Allawi, the head of the INA, did state though in an interview that the INA was responsible for the surrender of a few units and mentioned in particular the 14th Brigade in the 'Amara area.
31. Interview: author with Zaab Sethna, INC media adviser, May 2004.
32. See Joshua Hammer, 'Murder at the Mosque', *Newsweek*, 19 May, 2003.
33. See Glenn Frankel and Nora Boustany, 'Mob Kills 2 Clerics at Shiite Shrine', *Washington Post*, 11 April, 2003. See also Joshua Hammer, 'Murder at the Mosque', *Newsweek*, 19 May, 2003. The article can also be accessed on http://msnbc.msn.com/id/3068555.
34. Interview: author with Ayatollah Baqir al-Nasiri, London, August 2006.
35. Notes from discussions with Abd el-Karim Mahoud al-Muhhamadawi, Baghdad, November 2003–June 2004.

Chapter 5: Occupation Authorities

1. See the testimonies of Grossman and Feith, 11 February, 2003, available from Federal Document Clearing House Congressional Testimony, *The Future of Iraq*, Hearing of the Senate Foreign Relations Committee. The full text can be accessed at: http://www.iraqwatch.org/government/US/HearingsPreparedstatements/sfrc-021103.htm.
2. Ibid.
3. Thomas E. Ricks, 'Army Historian Cites Lack of Postwar Plan', *Washington Post*, 25 December, 2004.
4. Michael R. Gordon and John Kifner, 'U.S. Warns Iraqis against Claiming Authority in Void', *New York Times*, 24 April, 2003.
5. Henry Hamman, 'US Will Place Advisers in Iraqi Ministries', *Financial Times* (London), 20 March, 2003. Also Trudy Rubin, 'U.S. as Postwar Occupiers Would Quickly Alienate Many', *Philadelphia Inquirer*, 23 March, 2003.
6. David Rennie, 'Retired US General Moves In As "Governor"', *Daily Telegraph* (London), 9 April, 2003.
7. Interviews: author with Salem Chalabi, November 2004. Chalabi was bivouacked with the Garner field team in Kuwait in early 2003.

8. See Public Broadcasting Service (PBS) Interview with Jay Garner, 17 July, 2003. The transcript of the interview can be accessed on http://www.pbs.org/wgbh/pages/frontline/shows/truth/interviews/ garner.html. Bob Woodward, in his book, *State of Denial*, Simon and Schuster, New York, 2006, p. 128, claimed that it was Cheney's office which actually blocked Warrick's appointment.
9. Dhia gave a detailed description of the activities of the IRDC during a visit to Washington in July 2003. See Federal News Service, Defense Department Special Briefing, 7 July, 2003. The IRDC was a favourite of the right-wing media in Washington. See Michael Rubin, 'Self-Fulfilling Prophecy: State vs. Iraq Planning', *National Review Online*, 3 May, 2004.
10. Interview: author with Salem Chalabi, op.cit.
11. Ibid.
12. Guy Dinmore, 'US to Meet Opposition Leaders Over Interim Authority', *Financial Times* (London), 10 April, 2003; also CNN.com, 'Iraqi Opposition Leaders to Discuss New Government', 13 April, 2003.
13. Sacha Bagilli, 'Conference of Iraqi Exiles Ends with 13-Point Statement But Continued Uncertainty', *World Markets Analysis*, 16 April, 2003; also Marc Santora with Patrick Tyler, 'Pledge Made to Democracy by Exiles, Sheiks and Clerics', *New York Times*, 16 April, 2003.
14. Santora with Tyler, op. cit; also Robin Wright, 'Powell Says the U.S. Will Select Leaders to Shape a New Government, Leaving U.N. Lesser Role', *Los Angeles Times*, 10 April, 2003.
15. Ibid; also, Paul Watson and Tony Perry, 'Iraqi Troops Surrender Major City', *Los Angeles Times*, 12 April, 2003; Patrick Cockburn, 'American Soldiers Fire on Political Rally, Killing at Least 10 Civilians', *Independent* (London), 16 April, 2003.
16. The transcript of the press conference can be sourced at cnn.com; http://transcripts.cnn.com/ TRANSCRIPTS/0304/24/se.02.html.
17. Phil Reeves, 'Americans Arrest "Mayor" as Garner Struggles for Control', *Independent* (London), 28 April, 2003.
18. Interview: author with Hoshyar Zebari, Iraqi Foreign Minister, May 2005. Zebari, a senior aide to Massoud Barazani, was present in all the key discussions between the Kurds and Garner.
19. Patrick Tyler, 'Opposition Groups to Help to Create Assembly in Iraq', *New York Times*, 6 May, 2003.
20. Matthew Lee, 'US to Convene First Meeting to Set Up Interim Iraq Government Next Week', Agence France-Presse, 11 April, 2003.
21. Rajiv Chandrasekaran and Monte Reel, 'Iraqis Set Timetable to Take Power: Meeting to Come Within a Month', *Washington Post*, 29 April, 2003.
22. Jane Perlez, 'Iraqis Set to Meet to Pick Transitional Government', *New York Times*, 29 April, 2003; also Alissa J. Rubin and Michael Slackman, 'After the War: Iraqis Agree to Agree on a New Government', *Los Angeles Times*, 29 April, 2003.
23. Douglas Jehl with Eric Schmitt, 'U.S. Reported to Push for Iraqi Government, With Pentagon Prevailing', *New York Times*, 30 April, 2003; also Douglas Jehl with Eric Schmitt, 'U.S. Pushing Creation of Iraqi Government: Shift Reflects Viewpoint of Pentagon', *New York Times*, 1 May, 2003.
24. Interview: author with Zebari, op. cit; also Niko Price, 'Five Key Iraqi Political Leaders Meet in Baghdad', *Associated Press*, 1 May, 2003.
25. Quoted in the *Guardian*, 14 March, 2006.
26. Barry Schweid, 'Former State Department Counterterrorism Official to Head Transition in Iraq', *Associated Press*, 30 April, 2003; also Robin Wright, 'U.S. Will Add Iraq Overseer', *Los Angeles Times*, 2 May, 2003.
27. Patrick Tyler, 'In Reversal, Plan for Iraq Self-Rule Has Been Put Off', *New York Times*, 6 May, 2003.
28. The arrival of Bremer in Baghdad and the announcement of his appointment as CPA administrator were more than a little confused. On 6 May, 2003, Bush announced that Bremer was going to be 'presidential envoy' to Iraq, and that he would be the senior leader there. Bremer, when he arrived in Baghdad on 12 May, was thus the presidential envoy. On the following day, however, 13 May, Bush announced that Bremer was to be the CPA administrator.
29. Stephen F. Hayes, 'New Sheriff in Town: Paul Bremer is Quick on the Draw', *Weekly Standard*, 26 May, 2003; also Karen DeYoung, 'U.S. Sped Bremer to Iraq Post; Move Reflected Worries Over Rebuilding Efforts', *Washington Post*, 24 May, 2003.
30. See L. Paul Bremer III, with Malcolm McConnell, *My Year in Iraq: The Struggle to Build a Future of Hope*, Simon and Schuster, New York, 2006, Chapter 2.
31. See Rajiv Chandrasekaran and Peter Slevin, 'A Month After Baghdad's Fall, U.S. Efforts Founder', *Washington Post*, 9 May, 2003.

32. Bremer, op. cit., Chapter 2.
33. Patricia Sullivan, 'Ambassador Hume Alexander Horan Dies', July 25, 2004. Also Donald R. Norland 'Appreciation: Hume Alexander Horan', *Foreign Service Journal*, September 2004.
34. See Hume Horan, 'Restoring a Shattered Mosaic', *Foreign Service Journal*, March 2004; also 'Interview: Hume Horan', *Religion and Ethics Newsweekly*, Public Broadcasting Service, Episode 716, 19 December, 2003.
35. Interviews: author with Sheikh Humam Hammoudi, January 2006. Hammoudi was a member of SCIRI's central council and a close associate of Ayatollah Baqir al-Hakim.
36. Babak Dehghanpisheh and Christopher Dickey, 'The Shi'ite Shockwave', *Newsweek*, 5 May, 2003; also Douglas Jehl with Nazila Fathi, 'Ayatollah Presents Quandary for U.S.', *New York Times*, 8 May, 2003.
37. Soraya Sarhaddi Nelson, 'An Exiled Leader Comes Back, Calls for Unity Among Shi'ites', *Philadelphia Inquirer*, 11 May, 2003; also Susan Sachs, 'Back in Iraq, a Cleric Urges Islamic Rules', *New York Times*, 11 May, 2003.
38. Interviews: author with Hammoudi, op. cit.
39. Ibid.

Chapter 6: A Collapsed State – a Ruined Economy – a Damaged Society

1. See Douglas Feith's testimony to the Foreign Relations Committee, 11 February, 2003. He said: 'The governmental structures that exist right now may be, as I mentioned in my testimony, may be usable to some extent within a reconfigured Iraq.' See also the United States Institute of Peace (USIP) interview with Sherri Kraham, former Iraq desk officer at the State Department and Deputy Director, CPA, 5 November, 2004, available on the USIP website, www.usip.org. Kraham was detailed to work on post-war planning at the Pentagon.
2. Some *Mukhabarat* people were well known – and well integrated – in the ministries. Senior Ba'athists, who sometimes doubled up as *Mukhabarat* operatives, would wear green fatigues and openly carry pistols.
3. See USIP interview with Ambassador Robin Raphel, 13 July, 2004, available on the USIP website. Raphel was responsible for the Ministry of Trade in the immediate post-war period.
4. Personal notes of the author whilst Minister of Trade; see also ibid.
5. Personal notes of the author whilst Minister of Trade.
6. The CIA was especially egregious in this matter, placing a number of its Iraqi agents as provincial officials and, in one case, a governor.
7. See USIP interview with Kraham, op. cit.
8. See USIP interview with Raphel, op. cit. The senior directors general that the CPA kept on at the Ministry of Trade were all subsequently implicated in serious accusations of corruption after the war.
9. See USIP interview with Joe Rice, 31 July, 2004, available on the USIP website. Rice, a colonel in the army reserve, was responsible for setting up local councils.
10. Ibid.
11. See CPA, 'Administrator's Weekly Report on Governance', various dates. Available on the CPA website http://govinfo.library.unt.edu/cpa-iraq/government/weekly_updates/conso/index.html.
12. Marian Wilkinson and Matthew Moore, 'AWB Knew Iraq Deal Suspects', *The Age* (Melbourne), 20 January, 2006.
13. USIP's interviews with former CPA staffers and advisers give a good cross-section of the type of people who were attracted to Iraq. They are part of USIP's oral history project on the war. They can be accessed at http://www.usip.org/library/oh/iraq.html.
14. By ideological, I here mean those who were driven by a preconceived ideology, for example an extreme right-wing libertarianism or religious fundamentalism. I use the word 'idealists' to mean people who were naïve, with vague romantic and humane motives.
15. See Elizabeth Rubin, 'Fern Holland's War', *New York Times*, 19 September, 2004.
16. The most exhaustive treatment of the OFF programme can be found in the Volcker reports of 7 September, 2005. They can be accessed at www.iic-offp.org. The Volcker report on the programme, which came after sustained pressure on the UN to account for its management of the OFF programme, implicated a huge swathe of individuals and companies in corrupt practices. They included Benon Savon, the UN official in charge of the programme.
17. See Keith Crane and Danilo Roseano on Iraq's food distribution system, 'Replacing Iraq's Public Distribution System', National Defense Research Institute (NDRI) paper, RAND Corporation, December 2003.

18. See US House of Representatives Committee on Government Reform Special Investigations Division, 'Rebuilding Iraq: US Mismanagement of Iraqi Funds', prepared for Henry A. Waxman, 21 June, 2005.
19. Ibid., also 'Disorder, Negligence and Mismanagement: How the CPA Handled Iraq Reconstruction Funds', *Iraq Revenue Watch*, Report No. 7, September 2004.
20. Waxman Report, op cit.
21. See The Campaign Against Sanctions website for the variety of NGOs working on Iraqi humanitarian aspects prior to the war: http://www.casi.org.uk/reader/, especially the Red Cross and the 'Garfield' reports.
22. The reports of the UN and the World Bank on the Iraqi economy were vital resources for the CPA. They later became part of the UN/World Bank 'Joint Iraq Needs Assessment', report, October 2003.
23. The East European model of 'shock therapy' was where radical reforms were announced and implemented in a very short period of time, to shock the economy and society into accepting irreversible changes from the Soviet-era to a market-led system. The idea behind this was that the bitter medicine should be given quickly and in large doses, rather than slowly and in more measured amounts.
24. See USIP interview with Hugh Tant, October 22, 2004. Tant was assigned to the Central Bank of Iraq to handle the logistics of the currency exchange programme.
25. See the United Nations Development Programme (UNDP), 'Iraq Living Conditions Survey 2004'; also, UN/World Bank, op. cit.
26. UNDP, op. cit.
27. Ibid., Section 3, and UN/World Bank, op. cit.
28. Amal Hamdan, 'The Hidden Victims of Iraq's War', reported on AljazeeraNet, 22 February, 2004.
29. John Howley, 'The Iraq Jobs Crisis: Workers Seek Their Own Voice', reported in Foreign Policy in Focus, 8 September, 2004. The report can be accessed on: http://www.fpif.org/commentary/2004/0409iraqlabor_body.html.
30. Roberta Cohen and John Fawcett, 'The Internally Displaced People of Iraq', The Brookings Institution, Iraq Memo 6, 20 November, 2002.

Chapter 7: Deepening Rifts in a Brittle Society

1. The most complete exposition on the sectarian issues affecting the Iraqi state and identity are the writings of Hassan al-'Alawi. See especially, *Al-Shi'a wal ad-Dawla al-Qawmiyya fil-Iraq 1914–1990* ('The Shi'a and the Nationalist State'), CEDI (France), Paris 1989; also Abd el-Karim al-Uzri, *Tarikh fi Dhikriyat al-Iraq* (Reminiscing Iraqi History), self-published, London, 1982.
2. Al-'Alawi, op. cit.
3. Ibid., pp. 233–303.
4. See, for example, Karim Baqradouni, *Ma'arakat Baghdad-wa Yawm al-Hisab* (The Battle for Baghdad and the Day of Reckoning) *Asharq al-Awsat*, London, 29 March, 2003.
5. Robert Fisk, 'Baghdad: The Day After', *Independent*, 11 April, 2003.
6. Michael R. Gordon and Bernard E. Trainor, *Cobra II: The Inside Story of the Invasion and Occupation of Iraq*, Atlantic Books, London, 2006, pp. 448–54.
7. Mark Baker, '"Liberator" Garner a Hit with the Kurds', *Sydney Morning Herald*, 23 April, 2003.
8. See Michael Rubin, 'The Islamist Threat in Iraqi Kurdistan', *Middle East Intelligence Bulletin* (*MEIB*), Vol. 3, No. 12, December 2001. The article can be accessed at http://www.meib.org/articles/0112_ir1.htm.
9. See Council on Foreign Relations, New York, 'Ansar al-Islam', accessed on http://www.cfr.org/publication/9237/ansar_alislam_iraq_islamistskurdish_separatists_.html; also Andrew Apostolou, 'Who Lost Zarqawi?', *National Review Online*, 2 November, 2004.
10. A frequent refrain of the Sunni Arab community was 'If Saddam was equitable in anything, it was in his equitably oppressive treatment of all Iraqis'.
11. Sati' al-Husri occupies a unique position in Iraqi history. He is loathed and loved in equal measure, loathed mainly by the Shi'a and loved mainly by the Sunni. For his pernicious influence on Iraqi life, read al-'Alawi, op. cit., pp. 286–90. His admirers organised a conference in his honour: *Sati' al-Husri: Thalathoon 'aam 'ala al-raheel* (Sati' al-Husri: Thirty Years After His Death), Arab Centre for Unity Studies, Beirut, 1999. For a western perspective see William Cleveland, *The Making of an Arab Nationalist: Ottomanism and Arabism in the Life and Thought of Sati' al-Husri*, Princeton University Press, Princeton, NJ, 1972.

12. David Blair, 'Thousands Join Baghdad Protests', *Daily Telegraph* (London), 19 April, 2003. The slogan most chanted was *La Sinniyya wa La Shi'iya – Wihda Wihda Islamiyya* (No Sunnism, No Shi'ism – Only Islamic Unity).
13. Babak Dehganpisheh and Christopher Dickey, 'The Shi'ite Shockwave', *Newsweek*, 5 May, 2003.
14. Ewen MacAskill, 'Shi'a Clergy Push for an Islamist State', *Guardian* (London), 3 May, 2003.
15. Juan Cole, 'Shi'ite Religious Parties Fill Vacuum in Southern Iraq', *Middle East Report Online*, 22 April, 2003.
16. Nir Rosen, *In the Belly of the Green Bird: The Triumph of the Martyrs in Iraq*, Free Press, London, 2006, pp. 7–36. Rosen, a young freelancer who wrote mainly for the *Asia Times*, moved widely across Baghdad and the South in the war's aftermath; also Juan Cole, 'The United States and Shi'ite Religious Factions in Post-War Iraq', *Middle East Journal*, Vol. 57, No. 4, Autumn 2003.
17. Todd Richissin, 'Shi'ite Pilgrims See Promise of New Iraq on Islam's Path', *Baltimore Sun*, 1 May, 2003.
18. See Rosen, op. cit. and Cole, 'The United States and Shi'ite Religious Factions in Post-War Iraq'.
19. Anthony Shadid, 'Clerics Vie with U.S. For Power', *Washington Post*, 7 June, 2003.
20. Interviews: author with with Bayan Jabr, a SCIRI leader, Baghdad, January 2006.
21. Ibid.
22. 'Iraq's Weapon Caches Abound', *Associated Press*, 1 November, 2004.
23. See 'Iraq's Legacy of Terror: Mass Graves', USAID. The report can be accessed at www.usaid.gov/iraq/pdf/iraq_mass_graves.pdf.
24. Human Rights Watch, 'The Mass Graves of al-Mahawil', May 2003. This report can be accessed at http://hrw.org/reports/2003/iraq0503/. It is the most complete exposition on the Mahawil mass graves.
25. Scott Wilson, 'Iraqis Killing Former Baath Party Members', *Washington Post*, 20 May, 2003.

Chapter 8: Dismantling the Ba'athist State

1. Jon Lee Anderson, 'Letter From Iraq: Out on the Street', *New Yorker*, 15 November, 2004. Alusi, a Sunni Arab and former Ba'athist, turned against the party in the 1970s. Before the fall of the regime, he had participated in the seizure of the Iraqi mission in Berlin in 2002, for which he was jailed. After his release, he returned to Baghdad and served as an INC nominee on the de-Ba'athification Commision. Alusi broke with the INC after he made an ill-advised visit to Israel in September 2004. He survived an assassination attempt in February 2005, in which two of his sons were killed. In the elections of December 2005, Alusi was elected to the National Assembly as an Independent.
2. Ahmad Chalabi was appointed head of the Commission. Jawad (Nuri) al-Maliki of the Da'awa Party was the deputy. Sheikh Jalal al-Saghir of SCIRI was also on the board of the Commission.
3. Bremer, op. cit., pp. 39–42, 44–5.
4. Kenan Makiya had explored the workings of the Ba'ath Party in his influential book *The Republic of Fear: The Politics of Modern Iraq*, University of California Press, Berkeley, 1988, and in his follow-up work, *Cruelty and Silence: War, Tyranny, Uprising and the Arab World*, Penguin, Harmondsworth, 1994.
5. The author had an extensive exchange on this matter with Professor Rebecca Boehling of the University of Maryland, an expert on de-Nazification. Boehling warned of the consequences of sweeping de-Ba'athification. She is the author of *A Question of Priorities: Democratic Reform and Economic Recovery in Postwar Germany*, Berghahn Books, Oxford and New York, 1998.
6. Bremer, op. cit., p. 39.
7. The full text of Feith's testimony can be accessed at: http://www.internationalrelations.house.gov/archives/108/feith0515.htm.
8. Quoted in Jon Lee Anderson, 'A Man of the Shadows', *New Yorker*, 24 January, 2005.
9. David Sanger and James Dao, 'US Is Completing Plan to Promote a Democratic Iraq', *New York Times*, 6 January, 2003.
10. Rory McCarthy, 'US Puppet Health Minister Forced Out as Doctors Rebel', *Guardian* (London), 12 May, 2003.
11. See 'The Iraqi Media Three Months After the War: A New But Fragile Freedom', *Reporters without Borders for Press Freedom*, www.rsf.org.
12. Ibid.

13. Ibid.
14. Anthony Borden, 'Iraq Media Free-For-All', *Global Journalist Magazine*, Fourth Quarter, 2003. Borden was the executive director of the Institute for War and Peace Reporting, which had a pioneering programme for young Iraqi journalists.
15. SalamPax would later be given a column in the *Guardian* (London) newspaper.
16. Other notable Iraqi bloggers were the girl blogger Riverbend, with her Baghdad Burning portal, and 'Omar', with his Iraq-the-Model blog. Civilian bloggers of some note included that associated with Dahr Jamail, a journalist. The most authoritative blogger on Iraq was Juan Cole, an expert on Shi'a Islam and a Professor of Islamic History at the University of Michigan. His news blog on the country was comprehensive and authoritative.
17. Neil King Jr, 'US-Backed Media Take Root With the Launch of Radio Station', *Wall Street Journal*, 16 April, 2003. The IMN was operated by a defence contractor, the San Diego-based Science Applications International Corporation, under a $108 million contract from the Defense Department.
18. A comprehensive expose of the troubles at the IMN can be found in Kathleen McCaul, 'Iraq; Troubles at Iraq Media Network', *Baghdad Bulletin*, 21 July, 2003. The article can be accessed at http://www.corpwatch.org/article.php?id=7880.
19. The same Order that dissolved the Ministry of Information also dissolved the armed forces.
20. Bremer, op. cit., pp. 54–9.
21. Ibid.
22. The formation and role of the army in the development of modern Iraq is treated in a number of studies, including Toby Dodge, *Inventing Iraq: The Failure of Nation-Building and a History Denied*, Columbia University Press, New York, 2003; Reeva Simon, *Iraq between the Two World Wars: The Creation and Implementation of a Nationalist Ideology*, Columbia University Press, New York, 1986; and Mohammad A. Tarbush's *The Role of the Military in Politics: A Case Study of Iraq to 1941*, Kegan Paul International, London, 1982. Several studies in Arabic covered the sectarian foundations of the Iraqi armed forces, notably Hasssan al-'Alawi's *The Iraqi Shi'ite and the National State, 1914–1990*, CEDI (France), Paris 1989.
23. The so-called Rashid 'Ali Movement and the Golden Circle of officers who carried out the coup featured prominently in Iraqi nationalist and anti-colonialist lore.
24. In 1948, Iraqis had held the Janin front in Palestine. In 1973, the Iraqi army's belated deployment on the Syrian front was held to have 'saved' Damascus from falling to the Israelis.
25. Internal document from the Iraqi Ministry of Defence, based on information from CPA advisers.
26. Ibid.
27. None of the opposition conferences called for the dissolution of the armed forces; rather their reorganisation and changes in their military doctrine.
28. Gregg Easterbrook, 'Sweet Surrender', *New Republic Online*, 5 July, 2004.
29. Charles Clover, 'Violence Prompts Policy Shift on Iraqi Army', *Daily Telegraph* (London), 24 June, 2003.
30. Patrick Tyler, 'After the War: The New Army', *New York Times*, 24 June, 2003.
31. Cherif Bassiouni, 'Iraq Post-conflict Justice', January 2004. The report can be accessed at: http://www.law.depaul.edu/institutes_centers/ihrli/_downloads/Iraq_Proposal_04.pdf
32. Sharia law is the corpus of Islamic rules and decrees that govern personal status laws, and often other areas of law such as commercial contracts, torts and criminal law. Only a few countries, such as Iran and Saudi Arabia, claim to operate only on the basis of Sharia law. In most Muslim countries, the Sharia is the basis of personal status laws, such as marriage, divorce and inheritance. The imposition of Sharia law versus the adoption of western law has been an ongoing struggle for the last two centuries, with no resolution in sight. Those who want to Islamicise society frequently demand the reintroduction of the Sharia to govern all aspects of law, while modernisers insist that only secular codes are appropriate for contemporary times.
33. Bassiouni, op. cit.
34. See Interview with Cherif Bassiouni, 13 February, 2004 on PBS 'Religion and Ethics' programme, episode 724. The transcript is available on PBS's website, www.pbs.org. Bassiouni was a law professor at Chicago's De Paul University and an expert on international criminal tribunals, war crimes trials, and the justice systems of Arab countries.
35. This was particularly evident in ministries with large discretionary budgets, such as Electricity, Trade and Oil.

Chapter 9: The Formation of the Governing Council and the Rise of the Insurgency

1. 'Iraq Politics: Rebuilding with the UN', *Economist Intelligence Unit*, 23 May, 2003.
2. UN transcript of press conference by Secretary General Kofi Annan and Special Representative for Iraq Sergio Vieira de Mello, 27 May, 2003. It can be accessed at: http://www.un.org/News/Press/docs/2003/sgsm8720.doc.htm.
3. Ibid.
4. Patrick E. Tyler, 'Attackers Wound an Iraqi Official in a Baghdad Raid', *New York Times*, 21 September, 2003.
5. Ibid.
6. Personal communication to the author from Governing Council members.
7. Interview: author with Salem Chalabi, who had been present in most of the meetings that preceded the formation of the Governing Council. Chalabi stated that there was an unsigned protocol between Bremer and the Governing Council. This set out the powers that the Governing Council would actually have in the running of Iraq.
8. Bremer, op. cit., p. 101.
9. Minutes of the Governing Council, 21 July, 2003.
10. Robert McMahon, 'UN: Iraqi Governing Council Takes First Steps Toward International Recognition', Radio Free Europe, 24 July, 2003.
11. Nir Rosen, *In the Belly of the Green Bird: The Triumph of the Martyrs in Iraq*, Free Press, New York, 2006, pp. 31–3.
12. Bremer, op. cit., p. 122.
13. Charles Recknagel, 'Iraq: Al-Najaf Demonstration Highlights U.S. Difficulties in Winning over Iraqi Shi'a', Radio Free Europe, 21 July, 2003.
14. Sistani website http://sistani.org/html/eng/.
15. Ibid.
16. Ibid.
17. See Bremer, op. cit., p. 242.
18. The most comprehensive report on the events of Fallujah is Human Rights Watch's 'Violent Response: The US Army in al-Falluja', Vol. 15, No. 7(E), June 2003. The report can be accessed at www.hrw.org.
19. Ahmed Hashim, *Insurgency and Counter-Insurgency in Iraq*, Cornell University Press, Ithaca, NY, 2006, p. 107.
20. Rosen, op. cit., p. 44 and pp. 60–62.
21. Ahmed S. Hashim, 'The Sunni Insurgency in Iraq', Center for Naval War Studies, 15 August, 2003.
22. Dexter Filkins and Robert F. Worth, '11 Die in Baghdad as Car Bomb Hits Jordan's embassy', *New York Times*, 8 August, 2003.
23. The UN conducted a full internal investigation of the attack. The report, entitled 'Report of the Independent Panel on the Safety and Security of UN Personnel in Iraq', 20 October, 2003, is available on http://www.un.org/News/dh/iraq/safety-security-un-personnel-iraq.pdf.
24. Anita Sharma, 'The UN Baghdad Bombing: One Month On', *Open Democracy*, 17 September, 2003, available on http://www.opendemocracy.net/democracy-un_iraq/article_1488.jsp.
25. Neil MacFarquhar, 'Bomb Meant for Top Cleric Kills 3 Guards', *New York Times*, 25 August, 2003.
26. Quoted in *Asharq al-Awsat* (London), 16 October, 2003.
27. Harry de Quetteville, 'Maverick Cleric Gathers Shiite Army to Oppose the US', *Daily Telegraph* (London), 7 August, 2003.
28. Neil MacFarquhar and Richard Oppel Jr, 'Car Bomb in Iraq Kills 95 at Shiite Mosque', *New York Times*, 30 August, 2003.
29. Minutes of the Governing Council, 31 August, 2003.
30. Michael R. Gordon and Bernard E. Trainor, 'Even as U.S. Invaded, Hussein Saw Iraqi Unrest as Top Threat', *New York Times*, 12 March, 2006.
31. Ibid.
32. Brian Bennett and Michael Ware, 'Life Behind Enemy Lines: An Inside Look at the Ba'athists, Terrorists, and Disaffected Iraqis Fighting U.S. Troops', *Time Magazine*, Vol. 162, No. 24, 15 December, 2003.
33. See the chronology of attacks on oil installations at Iraq Pipeline Watch, http://www.iags.org/iraqpipelinewatch.htm.

34. Jeffrey B. White and Michael Schidmayr, 'Resistance in Iraq', *Middle East Quarterly*, Fall 2003, and Anthony H. Cordesman, 'Iraq's Evolving Insurgency: The Nature of Attacks and Patterns and Cycles in the Conflict', Center for Strategic and International Studies, Washington (work-in-progress). The work can be accessed on http://www.comw.org/warreport/fulltext/0602 cordesman.pdf.
35. Cordesman, op. cit., and White and Schidmayer, op. cit.
36. See Hashim, 2006, op. cit., especially pp. 59–125, for an excellent treatment of the base of support for the insurgents. Also the articles on the insurgents from *Time Magazine's* Michael Ware, available at www.time.com.
37. See, for example, Christian Parenti, 'Two Sides: Scenes from a Nasty, Brutish and Long War', *The Nation*, 23 February, 2004.
38. There is a strong connection between Douri and the *Jaysh Muhammad* insurgency organisation. See the report of Charles Duelfer of the Iraq Survey group to the Director of Central Intelligence, available at: https://www.cia.gov/cia/reports/iraq_wmd_2004/chap5_annxE.html.
39. Saddam's family and cronies, sympathetic businessmen and the former intelligence services themselves had large stashes of cash abroad, just for this eventuality. In addition, sympathetic businessmen, charities and influential religious leaders in nearby Arab countries volunteered funds for the incipient insurgency.
40. See Dana Priest, 'Violence, Turnover Blunt CIA Effort in Iraq', *Washington Post*, 4 March, 2004.
41. Ibid.
42. Jonathan S. Landay, 'More Iraqis Supporting Resistance, CIA Report Says', *Knight Ridder Newspapers*, 12 November, 2003.
43. Greg Miller and Bob Drogin, 'CIA Struggles in Iraq, Afghanistan', *Los Angeles Times*, 20 February, 2004.
44. There are a number of internal Iraqi government documents on the composition and make-up of the insurgency. The discussion draws on all these reports.
45. Jody K. Biehl, 'Abducted in Iraq: Four Months on Planet Bin Laden', *Spiegel Online*, 21 January, 2005. The article can be accessed at: http://www.spiegel.de/international/ 0,1518,337867,00.html.
46. See Rod Norland, Tom Masland and Christopher Dickey, 'Iraq: Unmasking the Insurgents', *Newsweek*, 7 February, 2005.
47. Ibid.
48. Ibid. As one of the leaders of the insurgents in the Baghdad neighbourhood of al-'Adhamiya said to Parenti, 'The Shi'a know nothing! The Sunni must govern Iraq.'
49. See Rosen, op. cit., pp. 60–69.
50. Roel Meijer, 'The Association of Muslim Scholars', *Middle East Report*, 237, 15 October, 2005. The report can be accessed at www.merip.org.
51. The *fiqh al-muqawamma* articles are available on the AMS website: http://iraq-amsi.org/.
52. Department of Defense News Transcript, 23 July, 2003.
53. Warren P. Strobel and Jonathan S. Landay, 'Intelligence Agencies Warned About Growing Local Insurgency in Late 2003', *Knight Ridder Newspapers*, February 28, 2006.
54. Sean Loughlin, 'Bush Warns Militants Who Attack U.S. Troops in Iraq', *CNN.com*, 3 July, 2003.
55. Strobel and Landay, op. cit.
56. See RAND Corporation, *Establishing Law and Order After Conflict*, Santa Monica, CA, 2005. Chapter 5 deals with Iraq.
57. Hashim, 2006, op. cit., pp. 271–76.

Chapter 10: The Shadow of Real Power

1. See Bremer, op. cit., for his views on the Governing Council. Nearly all Governing Council members blamed Bremer for his poor policies and decisions.
2. The Arab media were, with a few exceptions, universally hostile to the Governing Council. The most negative of the mainstream media were the *Al-Quds al-'Arabi* newspaper, the al-Jazeera TV channel, and the independent press of Jordan.
3. For a transcript of Pachachi's speech at the UN, see US Department of State, International Information Programs, 25 September, 2003.
4. Quoted by Washington File, Bureau of International Information Programs, US State Department, 25 September, 2003.

5. Available on the UN Security Council website: http://www.un.org/Docs/sc/unsc_resolutions 03.html.
6. Bremer and other members of the CPA thought the exiles, with the exception of the Islamists – whom they were not prepared to acknowledge – could never represent the country at large, and had no support base in the country.
7. Minutes of the Governing Council, 3 August, 2003.
8. Minutes of the Governing Council, 4 August, 2003.
9. Available on the official CPA website, http://govinfo.library.unt.edu/cpa-iraq/budget/.
10. See Bremer, op. cit., pp. 109–11.
11. See Linda Bilmes and Joseph E. Stiglitz, 'The Economic Costs of the Iraq War', p. 1, available on http://www2.gsb.columbia.edu/faculty/jstiglitz/cost_of_war_in_iraq.pdf.
12. This became obvious in the tone and content of questions that the author and others in the Iraqi delegation had to field from the media.
13. Rory McCarthy, 'Foreign Firms to Bid in Huge Iraqi Sale', Guardian (London), 22 September, 2003.
14. Paul Krugman, 'Who's Sordid Now?', New York Times, 30 September, 2003.
15. The Iraqi business community in Dubai met with the Iraqi delegation during the IMF meetings, and expressed their profound dislike, and rejection of, the Bremer orders authorising unrestricted foreign investment.
16. See the interview with the author, who was then Iraq's Minister of Trade, in Thomas Crampton, 'Iraq Official Warns on Fast Economic Shift', International Herald Tribune, 14 October, 2003.
17. The text of Bremer's statement can be accessed at the CPA website. The Minister of Trade, for example, warned that 'This push to sell everything is the political stance of economic fundamentalism. A plan based on ideology, not economics, is, of course, naturally wrong.'
18. See Crampton, op. cit.
19. Meeting with the Minister of Trade, November 2003.
20. Quoted in Herbert Docena, 'Spoilers Gatecrash the Iraq Spoils Party', Asia Times, 28 October, 2003.
21. Minutes of the Governing Council, 4 September, 2003.
22. Office of Grand Ayatollah Sistani. The text can be accessed at http://www.sistani.org/messages/hakim.htm.
23. Minutes of the Governing Council, 4 September, 2003.
24. Bremer, op. cit., p. 161.
25. The size of the FPS force in 2003, according to the CPA, was 40,000 people. See http://www.cpa-iraq.org/security/MOI_Info_Packet.html.
26. See Scott Johnson, 'Phantom Force', Newsweek, 25 April, 2006.

Chapter 11: The Enigma of Ayatollah Sistani

1. Interview with Salem Chalabi, November 2004. Chalabi was an early attendee at meetings at the Shi'a House.
2. Muhammad Redha, the Grand Ayatollah's son, acted as the point of contact for the Baghdad politicians. The Ayatollah maintained a wide network of advisers and well-wishers, who kept his worldwide offices informed of all major developments.
3. Al-Shi'a akhadhu al-wattaniyya wa dhaya'u al-Watan.
4. The press tried to assess Sistani's political views. See Philip Kennicot, 'The Religious Face of Iraq', Washington Post, 18 February, 2005.
5. Biographical details can be accessed at Sistani's official website http://www.sistani.org/ html/eng/.
6. See Reider Visser, 'Sistani, the United States and Politics in Iraq', Norwegian Institute of International Affairs, 2006. Visser debunks the notion of a 'quietist' orientation for Sistani, pp. 2–6.
7. The Iranian exile commentator and neo-conservative sympathiser Amir Taheri was a noted proponent of these views. He wrote a widely read column in the London Arabic daily Sharq al-Awsat.
8. The report is available on the Internet, http://www.uga.edu/islam/sachedina_silencing.html.
9. Available on the Sistani website.
10. See Visser, op. cit.
11. Ibid.

12. Ibid.
13. Quoted in Juan Cole's blog 'Informed Comment', 10 October, 2003, available on http://www. juancole.com/2003/10/senior-member-of-college-of-ayatollahs.html.
14. Bremer exclaimed this to the author during the April 2004 crisis with Moqtada.
15. Cole, 'Informed Comment', October 2003.
16. See David Ignatius, 'Cracking Down on a Cleric', *Washington Post*, 31 October, 2003.
17. Howard LaFranchi, 'One of the Harshest Critics of the United States Is Now Willing to Work With the Americans', *Christian Science Monitor*, 19 November, 2003.
18. Cole, 'Informed Comment', November 2003.
19. Available on the CPA website, http://www.iraqcoalition.org/.
20. Cole, 'Informed Comment', op. cit.
21. Discussions at the Shi'a House. Also, minutes of the extraordinary session of the Governing Council, 22 November, 2003.
22. Available on the official Sistani website.
23. Ibid.
24. Quoted in *Sharq al-Awsat* (London), 28 November, 2003.
25. Minutes of the extraordinary session of the Governing Council, 22 November, 2003.
26. Quoted in Cole, 'Informed Comment', November 2003.
27. Ibid.
28. *Al-Sabah* (Baghdad), 12 December, 2003.
29. Alissa Rubin and Sonni Efron, 'U.S. Asks U.N. to Go to Iraq, Assess Feasibility of Vote', *Los Angeles Times*, 20 January, 2004.
30. Cole, 'Informed Comment', February 2004.
31. Marc Carnegie, 'Annan Considers UN Mission to Iraq', Agence France-Presse, 20 January, 2004.
32. Interview on National Public Radio, 9 March, 2004.
33. See his press conference at the UN on 19 January, 2004, available on http://www.un.int/usa/04_008.htm.
34. Elaine Sciolino and Warren Hoge, 'UN to Send Expert Team to Help in Iraq, Annan Says', *New York Times*, 28 January, 2004.

Chapter 12: A Constitution in Waiting

1. Interviews: author with Salem Chalabi, November 2004.The Agreement itself was mainly drafted by Roman Martinez, one of Bremer's aides.
2. Ibid.
3. Interview: author with Adnan al-Pachachi, February 2005.
4. Interviews: author with Salem Chalabi, November 2004.
5. Galbraith was not new to Iraqi Kurdish issues. He had played an important part in highlighting the 1988 Halabja and Anfal attacks, and the mass movement of Kurds into Iran and Turkey after the collapse of the March 1991 uprisings. From 1979 to 1993 he had been a senior adviser to the Senate Foreign Relations Committee. In 1992, Galbraith brought fourteen tons of captured Iraqi secret police documents out of northern Iraq that detailed atrocities against the Kurds.
6. Interviews: author with Salem Chalabi, November 2004.
7. Peter Galbraith, *The End of Iraq: How American Incompetence Created a War Without End*, Simon and Schuster, New York, 2006, p. 140.
8. Interview: author with Pachachi, February 2005. He couched his involvement in the TAL in purely secular and democratic terms.
9. Ibid.
10. Interviews: author with Salem Chalabi, November 2004.
11. Statement by Grand Ayatollah Sistani's office, 8 March, 2004, available on www.sistani.org.
12. The situation arose because the Kurds were negotiating on a parallel line with the CPA, with few Shi'a aware of what they were up to. When the issue arose, Adel Abd el-Mahdi played a large part in convincing the other Shi'a on the Governing Council to go along with it. He thought this was a 'deal-breaker' for the Kurds – and the Shi'a could not afford to alienate the Kurds (or the CPA, for that matter) at this late stage. Abd el-Mahdi effectively played the part of the Kurds' advocate, and believed that the *Marji'iyya* would go along with the plan. The *Marji'iyya* was not privy to these discussions.

13. Bremer, op. cit., pp. 304–8.
14. Ministers and visiting dignitaries were kept waiting for hours before being told that the signing ceremonies had been postponed.
15. Bremer devotes an entire index entry to 'Governing Council, ineffectiveness of'. See Bremer, op. cit., p. 407.
16. Ibid., p. 171.
17. The Minister for Electricity, Ayham al-Samarrai'i, an Iraqi-American, was especially close to Bremer. He would later be arrested for corruption.
18. Quoted in an interview by Professor Noah Feldman, a one-time adviser to the CPA, with *Mother Jones Magazine*, 16 January, 2005. The interview, entitled 'What We Owe Iraq', can be accessed at: http://www.motherjones.com/news/qa/2005/01/feldman. html.
19. Interview: author with Salem Chalabi, November 2004.
20. Bremer himself was a late convert to Catholicism, but he did not wear his faith on his sleeve.
21. 'Evangelical Missionaries Rush to Win Iraq as Middle East Mission Base', quoted in *Christian Today*, 22 March, 2004, accessed on www.christiantoday.com.
22. The CPA in public did not discuss the proselytisation of missionaries, and kept a careful distance from them. In private, however, it was another matter.
23. Interview: author with Adnan al-Pachachi, February 2005.
24. Rajiv Chandrasekaran, 'U.N. Envoy Stresses Need For "Credible" Iraq Elections', *Washington Post*, 13 February, 2004.
25. The statement can be accessed at the AMS website: http://iraq-amsi.org/. See also the interview with its leader, Hareth al-Dhari, in *Sharq Awsat* (London), 3 May, 2004.
26. UN Security Council, 23 February, 2004, S/2004/140.
27. The full text of the letter is available on the official Sistani website, www.sistani.org.
28. The statement is posted on the official website of the Grand Ayatollah Sistani at: www.sistani.org/messages.
29. Noah Feldman, 'The Democratic Fatwa: Islam and Democracy in the Realm of Constitutional Politics', *Oklahoma Law Review*, Vol. 58, No. 1, Spring 2005. Feldman, a professor of Law at New York University, worked as an adviser to the CPA in its early days, but quit abruptly, evidently at loggerheads with the powers-that-be. He went on to write a book *What We Owe Iraq: War and the Ethics of Nation-Building*, Princeton University Press, Princeton, NJ, 2004.

Chapter 13: The Fires of Sectarian Hatreds

1. The text of the Zarqawi letter is widely available on the Internet, for example at www.global security.org.
2. Nicholas Blanford, 'Huge Blasts Attack Iraq Unity', *Christian Science Monitor*, 3 March, 2004.
3. Zarqawi letter, op. cit.
4. Ibid.
5. The funds that the Saudi state made available for the propagation of Wahhabism have not been made public, but they certainly run into hundreds of millions of dollars per annum. In testimony to the US Senate Sub-Committee on Terrorism on 26 June, 2003, Alex Alexiev, a senior fellow at the Centre for Security Policy, estimated that the Pakistani Islamic school system, the *madrassah*, alone received $350 million per annum from Wahhabi sources.
6. The press conference transcript is available at the official CPA website: http://www.cpa-iraq.org/ transcripts/20040302_Mar2_KimmittSenor.html.
7. 'Who Are The Insurgents?', USIP Special Report, April 2005, pp. 9–10.
8. The classic texts on *takfir* are very explicit about the narrow conditions that have to apply. See Sherman Jackson, *On the Boundaries of Theological Tolerance in Islam: Abu Hamid al Ghazali's Faysal al Tafriqa*, Oxford University Press, New York, 2002. This is an exposition of the work of the great scholar Abu Hamid al-Ghazali on this subject.
9. Quoted in Shmuel Bar, 'Sunnis and Shiites – Between Rapprochement and Conflict', *Current Trends in Islamist Ideology*, Vol. 2, 2005, p. 87, Hudson Institute, New York.
10. Martin Kramer, *Islam Assembled: The Advent of the Muslim Congresses*, Columbia University Press, New York, 1985, Chapter 11, 'In Defence of Jerusalem'.
11. Kate Zebiri, *Mahmud Shaltut and Islamic Modernism*, Oxford University Press, New York, 1993. The Shaltut *fatwa* was widely circulated in Iraq.

12. Nir Rosen, 'The Battle for Sunni Hearts and Minds', *Asia Times*, 16 April, 2004.
13. See Rosen, op. cit., Chapter 2. See also 2006, Hashim, 2006, op. cit., pp. 108–20.
14. Edward Wong, 'Sufis Under Attack as Sunni Rifts Widen', *New York Times*, 21 August, 2005.
15. The full transcript of Powell's speech at the UN is available at: http://www.white house.gov/news/releases/2003/02/20030205–1.html.
16. Nir Rosen, 'Iraq's Jordanian Jihadis', *New York Times Magazine*, 19 February, 2006.
17. A number of studies have appeared that explore the Zarqawi and Maqdisi connection. Most emanate from the Hudson Institute's Center on Islam, Democracy and the Future of the Muslim World. See Nibras Kazimi, 'A Virulent Ideology in Mutation: Zarqawi Upstages Maqdisi', in *Current Trends in Islamist Ideology*, Vol. 2, 2005, Hudson Institute, New York; Stephen Brooke, 'The Preacher and the Jihadi', *Current Trends in Islamist Ideology*, Vol. 3, 2006, Hudson Institute, New York. An important interview with Mishari al-Dhayedi, a Saudi who knew Maqdisi, was carried in the London *Sharq al-Awsat* newspaper, 7 July, 2005.
18. Kazimi, op. cit.
19. Ibid.
20. Ibid.
21. A great deal of information about the insurgency is classified and highly secret. The best-published sources are Ahmed Hashim's 'Insurgency and Counter-Insurgency in Iraq'; Anthony Cordesman's web-based project, 'Iraq's Evolving Insurgency'; and Michael Eisenstadt and Jeffrey White, 'Assessing Iraq's Sunni Arab Insurgency', available at http://www.washingtoninstitute.org/html/pdf/PolicyFocus50.pdf. An entire website devoted to the Iraqi insurgency with links is available at: http://www.comw.org /pda/0603insurgency.html. The Cordesman project can be accessed via this website.
22. Daniel Williams, 'In Sunni Triangle, Loss of Privilege Breeds Bitterness', *Washington Post*, 13 January, 2004.
23. Author's discussions with Ahmad Chalabi and Rubai'e.
24. Quoted in Scott Johnson, 'Inside an Enemy Cell', *Newsweek*, 18 August, 2003.
25. Christian Parenti, 'Two Sides: Scenes From a Nasty, Brutish and Long War', *The Nation*, 23 February, 2004.
26. Zaki Chehab, 'Inside the Resistance', *Guardian* (London), 13 October, 2003.
27. Hashim, 2006, op. cit., pp. 104–8.
28. 'Who Are the Insurgents?', USIP Special Report, April 2005, pp. 6–9.
29. Anthony Shadid, 'In Searching Homes, U.S. Troops Crossed the Threshold of Unrest', *Washington Post*, 30 May, 2003.
30. Saddam had encouraged the construction of large state-sponsored mosques in the Shi'a South. Some of them became haunts for radical Sunni Islamists and Wahhabis. In the shrine city of Karbala, these mosques were seen as an affront to the Shi'a creed. Most of them were seized by various Shi'a factions after the fall of the regime.
31. See Amatzia Baram, 'Who are the Insurgents? Sunni Arab Rebels in Iraq', United States Institute of Peace, Special Report 134, April 2005.
32. David Rhode, 'After Effects: Mosul: Free of Hussein Rule, Sunnis in North Flaunt a Long-Hidden Piety', *New York Times*, 23 April, 2003.
33. Hashim, 2006, op. cit., pp. 108–20.
34. The Association of Muslim Scholars condemned attacks on civilians, but held the occupation ultimately responsible. 'If there were no occupation, these crimes would not have happened' went the refrain.
35. A case in point is the pre-World War II career of Emir Shakib Arslan. See William Cleveland, *Islam Against the West: Shakib Arslan and the Campaign for Islamic Nationalism*, University of Texas Press, Austin, Texas, 1985.

Chapter 14: A Marshall Plan for Iraq?

1. Diane B. Kunz, 'The Marshall Plan Reconsidered: A Complex of Motives', *Foreign Affairs*, May/June 1997. Most of the works on the Marshall Plan are laudatory. For a contrary view see Alan Milward, *The Reconstruction of Western Europe, 1945–51*, Methuen, London, 1984.
2. Milward, op. cit.
3. The interview transcript is available from ABC News, New York. At niteline@abc.com. It can be accessed at: http://www.mtholyoke.edu/acad.intrel/iraq/koppel.htm.

4. Bremer, op. cit., p. 119.
5. See Martin Schain, ed., *The Marshall Plan: Fifty Years After*, Palgrave, New York 2001.
6. The gap between pledged amounts at international donor conferences and the actual disbursements has always been huge. Headline targets are always misleading. Actual disbursements fall in the range of 20 to 30 per cent of commitments. The gap is caused by a variety of factors, including conditionalities, budgetary procedures in aid-granting countries, and absorptive capacity.
7. Bremer's *My Year in Iraq* sets out the impossible timetable that was set for the development of an Iraqi reconstruction plan. But he misses the irony.
8. Iraq Revenue Watch, 'Disorder, Negligence, and Mismanagement: How the CPA Handled Iraq Reconstruction Funds', Report No. 7, September 2004, p. 3.
9. Personal discussion of the author with Iraqi subcontractors to the US military.
10. Patrick E. Tyler and Raymond Bonner, 'Questions Are Raised on Awarding of Contracts in Iraq', *New York Times*, 4 October, 2003.
11. As Minister of Trade, the author held a number of meetings with CPA advisers on the subject of equal treatment to Iraqi suppliers. The CPA could not breach the Pentagon's procurement habits and patterns.
12. A company based in Kuwait used to handle the laundry for Garner's staff in the Republican Palace.
13. See the Bechtel/Iraq website http://www.bechtel.com/iraq.htm, and the USAID website on Iraq http://www.usaid.gov/iraq/contracts/.
14. See 'Rebuilding of Iraq – Status of Funding and Reconstruction Efforts', US Government Accountability Office (GAO), Report to Congressional Committees, July 2005 – the GAO Report; and 'Rebuilding Iraq: US Mismanagement of Iraqi Funds', US House of Representatives, Committee on Government Reform, prepared for Rep. Henry A. Waxman, June 2005 – the Waxman Report.
15. GAO Report, pp. 13–20.
16. See Valerie Marcel, Royal Institute of International Affairs, Chatham House Briefing Paper No. 5, 'The Future of Oil in Iraq: Scenarios and Implications', December 2002.
17. Paul Wolfowitz, Testimony to the U.S. House Appropriations Committee, 27 March, 2003.
18. Walid Khadduri, 'The Iraqi Oil Industry: A Look Ahead', *Middle East Economic Survey*, Vol. XLVII, No. 48, 29 November, 2004.
19. GAO Report, op. cit.
20. See Isam al-Khalisi, 'Decentralizing And Restructuring of Iraq's Electricity Supply System' *Middle East Economic Survey* (MEES), Vol. XLVIII, No. 1, 3 January, 2005. The article can be accessed at: http://www.mees.com/postedarticles/oped/v48n015OD01.htm.
21. GAO Report, pp. 20–26.
22. Isam al-Khalisi, 'Decentralizing and Restructuring of Iraq's Electricity Supply System', op. cit.
23. T. Christian Miller, 'Iraq Power Grid Shows US Flaws', *Los Angeles Times*, 12 September, 2004.
24. GAO Report, p. 24.
25. GAO Report, p. 25.
26. Aram Roston, 'Baghdad Sewage Plant Offers Example of Problems in Iraqi Reconstruction', NBC News, 3 September, 2004.
27. United States Government Accountability Office (GAO), 'Rebuilding Iraq – Water and Sanitation Efforts Need Improved Measures for Assessing Impact and Sustained Resources for Maintaining Facilities', Washington DC, September 2005. The report can be accessed at: http://www.gao.gov/new.items/d05872.pdf.
28. Roston, op. cit.
29. GAO, 'Rebuilding Iraq–Water . . .'.
30. T. Christian Miller, 'Million Said Going to Waste in Iraq Utilities', *Los Angeles Times*, 10 April, 2005.
31. Ibid.
32. Iraq Revenue Watch, Report No. 7, September 2004, p. 7.
33. The SIGIR reports started in June 2004, but the major exposés were in spring 2005.
34. USIP Special Report, 'The Coalition Provisional Authority's Experience with Economic Reconstruction in Iraq', April 2005, available on USIP's website, www.usip.org.

35. See Peter Galbraith, 'The Bungled Transition', *New York Review of Books*, 23 September, 2004 in reference to the poor quality of the CPA's staff. Galbraith was a frequent visitor to Iraq after the fall of the former regime.
36. This was communicated directly to the author by Olin Wetherinton, the US Treasury's then senior adviser on the Iraqi economy.

Chapter 15: April 2004 – the Turning Point

1. *Al-Zaman* newspaper (London and Baghdad), 4 November, 2003. Moqtada made a number of gushing statements addressed to the American people on the occasion of Ramadhan, the fasting month, which fell in October/November 2003. The Americans in Iraq were 'guests in our big home', he said.
2. An internal Iraqi government document entitled '"Sadr City" – An Iraqi Strategy', undated, probably July 2004.
3. Theoretically, Baghdad includes Sadr City within its boundaries. If Sadr City were separated from Baghdad, however, it would probably be the second biggest city in Iraq.
4. '"Sadr City" – An Iraqi Strategy', op. cit.
5. Ibid.
6. Internal Iraqi government document on the tribes of Sadr City, undated, probably May 2004.
7. See George Packer, 'Letter from Baghdad', *New Yorker*, 17 May, 2004, for the support of professionals – doctors in this case – for the Sadrists.
8. '"Sadr City" – An Iraqi Strategy', op. cit.
9. Nir Rosen, 'Iraq's Cleric Who Would Be Heard', *Asia Times*, 16 August, 2003. The report can be accessed at www.atimes.com.
10. Internal Iraqi government document on the names of the leaders of all the mosques and meeting halls of Sadr City, undated, probably May 2004.
11. Juhi had developed an impressive pictorial and forensic file on the case. In private, he thought the accusations against Moqtada to be an open-and-shut case. But the CPA was clearly encouraging him in this.
12. Ayatollah Hussein al-Sadr was an exceptionally tolerant and moderating influence in the politics of Iraq. He had a mystical bent that allowed him to work easily with other faith groups both inside and outside Iraq. During the Saddam era, he was obliged to appear on television during religious occasions. This was used against him by more radical and opportunistic Shi'a leaders in the post-war environment. In November 2003, he met with the Secretary of State, Colin Powell, at the Ayatollah's house in Kadhimain. His influence, however, was restricted to the Kadhimain area.
13. Nir Rosen, ' Muqtada's Powerful Push for Prominence', *Asia Times*, 18 March, 2004.
14. Alissa J. Rubin, 'US Shutters Iraqi Newspaper', *Los Angeles Times*, 29 March, 2004. Rubin speaks of the *Hawza* circulation as well below 50,000. The 15,000 figure is from private sources.
15. Nir Rosen, 'US Newspaper Ban Plays Into Cleric's Hands', *Asia Times*, 31 March, 2004.
16. Ibid.
17. Rosen, 'Muqtada's Powerful Push for Prominence'.
18. Jeffrey Gettleman, 'Violent Disturbances in Iraq from Baghdad to Southern Cities', *New York Times*, 4 April, 2004.
19. Press conference of Paul Bremer, 4 April, 2004. The transcript can be accessed at the CNN website at: http://transcripts.cnn.com/TRANSCRIPTS/0404/04/se.00.html.
20. Charles Recknagel, 'Symbol of Insurgency', *Asia Times*, 9 April, 2004.
21. See Kimmitt–Senor press briefing on 5 April, 2004, accessible at: http://www.cpa-iraq.org/transcripts/20040405_Apr5_KimmittSenor.html.
22. Anthony Shadid, 'U.S. Forces Take Heavy Losses as Violence Spreads across Iraq', *Washington Post*, 7 April, 2004.
23. The CPA could not produce conclusive evidence about the involvement of Iranian operatives in the uprising. Moqtada received several delegations from Iran and Lebanon's Hizbollah, but according to intelligence sources, these were not able to persuade Moqtada to follow their directives by offering him logistical and financial support.
24. David Gombert was the main adviser to Bremer on these matters.
25. The account of the rest of the section is based on internal documents made available to the author.
26. The document was entitled 'A Political Plan for Moqtada and JAM'. JAM was the acronym for *Jaysh al-Mahdi*, the Mahdi Army.

27. Internal document of the Ministerial Committe for National Security.
28. Jeffrey Gettleman, ' Sunni–Shi'ite Cooperation Grows, Worrying US Officials', *New York Times*, April 8, 2004.
29. The rest of the section is mainly based on internal documents made available to the author, except where otherwise indicated.
30. Alissa J. Rubin and Doyle McManus, 'Why America Has Waged a Losing Battle on Fallujah', *Los Angeles Times*, 24 October, 2004.
31. Donna Miles, 'Abizaid Swannack Escape Injury in Fallujah Attack', *DefenseLINK News*, 12 February, 2004.
32. Rubin, op. cit.
33. Ibid.
34. Thanassis Cambanis, 'UN Envoy Offers Plan for Interim Government', *Boston Globe*, 15 April, 2004.
35. Rubin, op. cit.
36. This was true also on the Security Committee, where the tension between the two was palpable.
37. Quoted in Rubin, op. cit.

Chapter 16: The Interim Iraqi Government

1. Rajiv Chandrasekaran, 'Shi'ite Politicians' Objections Lead Candidate to Withdraw', *Washington Post*, 28 May, 2004.
2. A number of these documents were found in his sister's house. The house, in the Mansour area of Baghdad, had been used as a document storage and interrogation centre by the Ba'ath Party.
3. Claude Hankes-Drielsma, a noted investment banker, was recruited by the Governing Council to investigate abuses in the OFF programme. The initial findings of Hankes-Drielsma were corroborated in the Volcker report on the UN's OFF programme.
4. Quoted in Agence France-Presse, 'Brahimi a Controversial Figure, Says Chalabi', 26 April, 2004.
5. See Bremer, op. cit. In the index on Chalabi, p. 404, Bremer has an entry for 'Chalabi, intriguing of. . .'.
6. See Brian Bennett and Michael Weisskopf, 'Inside the Takedown', *Time Magazine*, 7 June, 2004. The article can be accessed at: http://jcgi.pathfinder.com/time/magazine/article/0,9171,994338,00.html.
7. Jane Mayer, 'The Manipulator', *New Yorker*, 7 June, 2006.
8. Ibid. Bremer denied any knowledge of the raid to the Minister of Defence, Ali Allawi. The latter had an apartment at the Chalabi residence that was also raided at the same time.
9. Bremer, op. cit., p. 341.
10. Interview: author with Adnan al-Pachachi, February 2005.
11. Rajiv Chandrasekaran, 'Former Exile is Selected as Interim Iraqi leader', *Washington Post*, 29 May, 2004.
12. Ibid.
13. Interview: author with Adnan al-Pachachi, February 2005.
14. The official translation is poor. It uses the term 'the sons of the soil of Iraq', a typical Arab expression.
15. The full statement is available on Sistani's official website, www.sistani.org.
16. The full text of UN Resolution 1546 can be accessed at: http://www.un.org/Docs/sc/ unsc_resolution04.html.
17. Ayad Allawi's letter to the UN is part of the addendum to the UN Security Council Resolution 1546, and can be accessed at: http://www.un.org/Docs/sc/unsc_04.html.
18. Colin Powell's letter to the UN is part of the addendum to the UN Security Council Resolution 1546, op. cit.
19. David Ignatius, 'Allawi's Bold Bid for Stability in Iraq', *Washington Post*, 14 July, 2004.
20. This strategy was discussed at length in the Security Committee under Bremer. The author, then the Minister of Defence, presented a detailed strategy paper on the insurgents' objective of encircling Baghdad. The paper was called 'The Belt Around Baghdad – The Evolving Security Threat', dated 5 May, 2004.
21. Based on internal government documents made available to the author.
22. Syrian support for the insurgency was regularly discussed at the CPA's Security Committee. A plan entitled 'Curtailing Syrian Assistance to the Insurgency' was prepared for the incoming Interim Government.

Chapter 17: Arabs and Persians

1. Ghaith Abdul-Ahad, 'Outside Iraq But Deep in the Fight', *Washington Post*, 8 June, 2005.
2. Promoting democracy in the Middle East became almost an industry. Every self-respecting think-tank had to have a conference, seminar, symposium or colloquium on one aspect or another of democracy in the Middle East. Elizabeth Cheney, Dick Cheney's daughter, was made a Deputy Assistant Secretary of State in 2005 specifically to promote modernisation and development in the Middle East.
3. See, for example, Joseph McMillan, 'Saudi Arabia and Iraq: Oil, Religion, and an Enduring Rivalry', United States Institute for Peace, January 2006, available on http://www.usip.org/pubs/special reports/sr157.html.
4. Private discussions in summer of 2004 of the author with a US ambassador to a GCC country.
5. Ayad Allawi had met with Sistani in the immediate aftermath of the war. Later, he preferred to delegate his relationships with the Najaf hierarchy through intermediaries, not all of them trustworthy.
6. The figures were compiled by internal Iraqi government sources. See also Christopher Boucek, 'The Presence of Saudi Nationals in the Iraqi Insurgency', *Terrorism Monitor*, 20 April, 2006, available on http://www.jamestown.org/terrorism/news/article.php. A report dated September 2005, by Anthony Cordesman and Nawaf Obaid of the Centre for Strategic and International Studies, puts the Saudi percentage of the overall foreign contingent in the insurgency at only 12 per cent. The discrepancy has not been satisfactorily explained. It may be that Cordesman and Obaid's figures are estimates, while the death figures are actual; or that the Saudis were more prominent in suicide and other deadly operations. The report can be accessed at http://www.globalpolicy.org/security/issues/iraq/resist/2005/0919saudimilitants.pdf.
7. Quoted in Cordesman and Obaid, op.cit.
8. Prince Saud al-Faisal, Saudi Arabia's Foreign Minister, delivered these remarks at the Council on Foreign Relations, New York, on 23 September, 2005.
9. See McMillan, op. cit.
10. The literature on the Wahhabi distaste for other Muslim groups, but especially the Shi'a, has been widely reported and studied. The Internet is crammed full of these extremist views. A good intro-duction to the doctrines of the Wahhabis can be found in Hamid Algar, *Wahhabism: A Critical Essay*, Islamic Publications International, 2002.
11. Quoted on the BBC, 28 September, 2004, accessed at http://news.bbc.co.uk/1/hi/world/middle_east/3695634.stm.
12. Quoted in Rasha Saad, 'Questioning the Conference', *Al-Ahram* (Cairo), 7–13 October, 2004.
13. See Gordan and Trainor, *Cobra II*, op. cit., on the extent of the cooperation of these countries with the invasion plans.
14. 'Arab League Head Does Not Rule Out Arab Troops in Iraq', Reuters, 31 May, 2004.
15. Associated Press, 14 September, 2004.
16. US Department of State, 'Country Reports on Terrorism 2004', issued in April 2005.
17. Reported on the BBC News, 18 December, 2003, accessed at http://news.bbc.co.uk/1/hi/world/middle_east/3329671.stm.
18. Quoted in *Sharq al-Awsat* (London), 27 July, 2004.
19. 'Iraq Accuses Iranian Embassy of Killing Agents', Agence France-Presse, 14 October, 2004.
20. This incident occurred at a meeting of the Ministerial Committee for National Security in April 2004, at which the author was present.
21. Robin Wright and Peter Baker, 'Iraq, Jordan See Threat to Election From Iran', *Washington Post*, 8 December, 2004.
22. An excellent analysis of Iran's influence in Iraq can be found in International Crisis Group (ICG), 'Iran in Iraq: How Much Influence?', 21 March, 2005. The report can be accessed at the ICG site, www.crisisgroup.org.
23. Quoted in ibid., p. 5.
24. See 'Iraq Accuses Iranian Embassy of Killing Agents', Agence France-Presse, 14 October, 2004.
25. ICG report, op. cit., pp. 22–3.
26. Ibid., p. 22.
27. This was a legacy from Iraq's earliest days as an independent state. The early nationality laws clas-sified all Iraqis into two categories – those holding Ottoman citizenship and those who were Persian subjects at the end of the World War I. The latter category were Iraqis, who, mainly to

avoid conscription into the Ottoman army, selected to be treated as Persian rather than Ottoman subjects. Nearly all these people were Iraqi Shi'a. This became the origin of the subsequent stigma of being a *taba'iyah*, a dependent subject of another country, Iran. This status was passed from one generation to the next. The database of such Iraqi citizens was used to expel the *taba'iyah* from Iraq in the 1970s and 1980s. The new nationality laws passed in the Transitional National Assembly in 2005 removed all these distinctions.

28. Ma'ad Fayad, 'Iraqi Political Activist: Religious Interference is Harming Iraq', *Asharq al-Awsat* (London), 4 August, 2005.
29. Ibid.
30. Personal notes of the author, who at that time was the Minister of Trade.

Chapter 18: Showdown at the Shrine

1. Numan al-Haimus, '*Allawi: Lannaqif maktufi al-aydi amam al-tamarrud*' ('Allawi: We Will Not Stand Idly By In The Face of This Mutiny', *Asharq al-Awsat*, 19 August, 2004.
2. Ann Scott Tyson, 'Sadr's Militia Regrouping, Rearming', *Christian Science Monitor*, 15 July, 2004.
3. USIP interview with Larry Crandall, 20 September, 2004. Available at the USIP website, www.usip.org.
4. Press briefing by General Ricardo Sanchez, Baghdad, 25 September, 2003, accessed at the CPA website, http://www.cpa-iraq.org/transcripts/20030928_Sep25Sanchez.html.
5. Spencer Ackerman, 'The US Failure to Disarm Iraq's Militias', *New Republic*, 11–18 July, 2005.
6. Ibid. See also the USIP interview with David Gombert, 25 August, 2004, available at www.usip.org.
7. A special inter-ministerial committee was formed, the Transition and Reintegration Implementation Committee, which met regularly to coordinate the DDR proposals. It died a slow death.
8. Spencer Ackerman, op. cit.
9. Peter Maass, 'The Salvadorization of Iraq?', *New York Times Magazine*, 1 May, 2005.
10. Ibid. Maass accompanied raids with the elite units of the Ministry of Interior, where he saw considerable human rights abuses and very questionable interrogation techniques of suspect insurgents.
11. Edward Cody, '5 U.S. Troops Killed in Baghdad Attack', *Washington Post*, 5 June, 2004.
12. Ibid.
13. Somini Sengupta, 'In the Ancient Streets of Najaf, Pledges of Martyrdom for Cleric', *New York Times*, 10 July, 2004.
14. See Edward Wong, 'Iran Is in Strong Position to Steer Iraq's Political Future', *New York Times*, 3 July, 2004.
15. Scott Tyson, op. cit.
16. *Al Mada* (Baghdad), 4 August, 2004.
17. *Al Mada* (Baghdad), 8 August, 2004.
18. Rory McCarthy, 'Sadr Comes Out of the Graveyard', *Guardian* (London), 7 August, 2004.
19. Quoted in Juan Cole's blog, 'Informed Comment', August 2004.
20. Author: discussion with the Iraqi National Security Adviser, 7 July, 2006.
21. *Al Mada* (Baghdad), 12 August, 2004.
22. John F. Burns, 'Iraqi Conference on Election Plan Sinks into Chaos', *New York Times*, 16 August, 2004.
23. *Al Mada* (Baghdad), 19 August, 2004.
24. Cole, 'Informed Comment'.
25. Interviews: author with the Iraqi National Security Adviser.
26. Cole, 'Informed Comment'.
27. The Shi'a Political Council was organised mainly by Ahmad Chalabi in the summer of 2004, to group a number of independent Shi'a politicians and smaller Shi'a parties into a political bloc and pressure lobby. As an organised group, the Council could lay claim to a place with the major Shi'a Islamist parties in devising the strategy for the upcoming elections of January 2005.
28. Ibid.
29. Burns, op cit.
30. Statement by Qassim Dawood, Minister of State, carried in the Arabic news website, elaph.com, 19 August, 2004.
31. Author: discussion with the Iraqi National Security Adviser, 7 July, 2006.

32. *Asharq al-Awsat* (London), 19 August, 2004.
33. *Asharq al-Awsat* (London), 31 August, 2004.
34. Elaph.com, 19 August, 2004.
35. Kuwait News Agency, 20 August, 2004.
36. *Al Mada* (Baghdad), 22 August, 2004.
37. Ibid.
38. Dexter Filkins and John F. Burns, 'Tentative Accord Reached in Najaf to Halt Fighting', *New York Times*, 27 August, 2004.
39. *Asharq al-Awsat* (London), 28 August, 2004.
40. Ibid.
41. Ibid.
42. *Asharq al-Awsat* (London), 31 August, 2004.

Chapter 19: To Hold or Abort an Election

1. This was one of the principal concerns of Larry Diamond, the democracy and elections adviser to the CPA. In meetings with the author and the National Security Adviser, Diamond showed an inordinate anxiety about an Islamist sweep of the elections.
2. Anthony H. Cordesman, 'Iraq's Evolving Insurgency and the Risk of Civil War', Centre for Strategic and International Studies, 23 March, 2006.
3. Interview in the *Al Mada* (Baghdad), 16 September, 2004.
4. Rory McCarthy and Luke Harding, 'Thirteen Die in US Attack on Baghdad Crowd', *Guardian* (London), 13 September, 2004.
5. *Al Mada* (Baghdad), 13 September, 2004.
6. Embodied in an internal Iraqi government report entitled 'Samarra – Course of Action', 29 July, 2004.
7. Dexter Filkins, 'U.S. Plans Year-End Drive to Take Iraqi Rebel Areas', *New York Times*, 19 September, 2004.
8. *Al Mada* (Baghdad), 18 September, 2004.
9. For the views of Abdullah al-Janabi, see his interview by Scott Johnson, *Newsweek*, 7 August, 2004.
10. Edward Wong and Eric Schmitt, 'Rebel Fighters Who Fled Attack May Now Be Active Elsewhere', *New York Times*, 10 November, 2004.
11. The report can be accessed at http://www.uniraq.org/documents/Falluja.
12. The sequence of events of the battle for Fallujah can be traced at, for example, http://www.globalsecurity.org/military/ops/oif-phantom-fury-fallujah.htm.
13. Wong and Schmitt, op. cit.
14. Robert F. Worth and Edward Wong, 'Assault Slows, but G.I.'s Take Half of Falluja', *New York Times*, 11 November, 2004.
15. Edward Wong, 'Sunni Party Leaves Iraqi Government Over Falluja Attack', *New York Times*, 10 November, 2004.
16. Karbala News Agency, September 16, 2004 accessed at www.karbalanews.net.
17. The statement can be accessed at Sistani's official website at: www.sistani.org/messages.
18. Karbala News Agency, 20 September, 2004, accessed at www.karbalanews.net.
19. Quoted in Karbala News Agency, 23 September, 2004, accessed at www.karbalanews.net.
20. Dexter Filkins, 'Top Shiite Cleric Is Said to Fear Voting in Iraq May Be Delayed', *New York Times*, 23 September, 2004.
21. Interview: author with Sami al-Askari, MP, an independent Islamist, August 2006.
22. Filkins, op. cit.
23. Karbala News Agency, 9 October, 2004, accessed at www.karbalanews.net.
24. Ibid.
25. Karbala News Agency, 22 October, 2004, accessed at www.karbalanews.net.
26. This section is based on several interviews: author with, amongst others, Mowaffaq al-Rubai'e, National Security Adviser, Sami al-Askari, an independent MP for the UIA, Sheikh Humam Hammoudi, MP for the UIA, and Hussein Shahristani. The latter was interviewed for this purpose on January 25, 2006.
27. Edmund Sanders, 'Cleric Hedges Bets on Iraq Vote', *Los Angeles Times*, 26 December, 2004.

28. Anthony Shadid and Karl Vick, 'Candidate Slate Shows Shiites Closing Ranks', *Washington Post*, 7 December, 2004.
29. Interview: author with Sami al-Askari, MP, August 2006.
30. Quoted in Juan Cole's blog, 'Informed Comment', December 2004.
31. Steven R. Weisman, 'U.S. Is Suggesting Guaranteed Role for Iraq's Sunnis', *New York Times*, 26 December, 2004.
32. Karbala News Agency, 17 November, 2004, accessed at www.karbalanews.net.
33. The IRI polls on Iraq are all available on the website: http://www.iri.org/countries.asp?id =7539148391.

Chapter 20: Corruption and the Potemkin State

1. See Simon Sebag Montefiore, 'An Affair to Remember', *New York Review of Books*, Vol. 52 , No. 3, 24 February, 2005.
2. A case in point is the Iraqi National Development Strategy, 30 June, 2005, a worthy document, but entirely the work of consultants.
3. The Ministry of Defence in the Interim Government was a particularly egregious case in point. In another instance, a former grocer was appointed a deputy minister to the Minister of State for National Security Affairs.
4. These were all established or reconstituted during the CPA period, and were important and worthwhile institutional reform initiatives.
5. The term *muthaqaf* (educated in the modern way) was used historically to define the new elites, and these were juxtaposed against the traditional, supposedly ignorant, rest of society. The term carried with it intimations of modernity, westernisation, probity and competence. It is ironic that the biggest culprits in the sad story of corruption in post-war Iraq were of the *muthaqaf* class.
6. The main banks in Jordan were the Housing Bank, partly government-owned, and the Jordan National Bank. In Lebanon, the preferred banks were Fransa Bank, Bank al-Mawarid, and First National Bank of Lebanon.
7. The system is described in detail in the Volcker Report on the OFF scams. The reports are available at www.iic-offp.org.
8. The auditors' reports can be accessed at: http://www.iamb.info/.
9. Ayham al-Samarrai was subsequently arrested for corruption in August 2006. He was taken in custody awaiting trial. In October 2006, he was sentenced to two years' imprisonment. In December 2006, he escaped from jail.
10. BBC News, 27 June, 2005.
11. Quoted on the Iraqi Economy website, www.iraqieconomy.org, 9 May, 2005.
12. See Ellen Knickmeyer, 'Graft Alleged in Iraq Oil Protection Effort', *Washington Post*, 5 February, 2006. See also Robert F. Worth and James Glanz, 'Oil Graft Fuels the Insurgency, Iraq and U.S. Say', *New York Times*, 5 February, 2006.
13. See Walid Khadduri 'The Iraqi Oil Industry: A Look Ahead', *Middle East Economic Survey*, Vol. XLVII, No. 48, 29 November, 2004.
14. The agreement between the Iraqi interim government and the IMF for an Emergency Post-Conflict Assistance programme (EPCA), in which the interim government made its commitments, is on the IMF website at http://www.imf.org/external/pubs/ft/scr/ 2004/cr04325.pdf, p. 15.
15. Ministry of Oil, Iraq, Inspector General's Office, April 2006.
16. Ibid.
17. Ibid.
18. Iraq Ministry of Finance estimates.
19. These Ministry of Finance estimates were broadly confirmed by the US Government Accountability Office. See the testimony of its head, the Comptroller General David Walker, to the US House of Representatives, Committee on Government Reform, 25 April, 2006, available on the GAO website as GAO report number GAO-06-697T, entitled 'Rebuilding Iraq: Governance, Security, Reconstruction, and Financing Challenges'.
20. David H. Petraeus, 'Battling for Iraq', *Washington Post*, 26 September, 2004.
21. Sha'alan had left Iraq under murky circumstances. He was on the periphery of the Iraqi opposition in the 1990s, working as a part-time journalist in London. He also dabbled as a real estate broker without much success.
22. Personal exchanges and discussions with Fred Smith, July and August 2006.

23. Ken Silverstein, T. Christian Miller and Patrick J. McDonnell, 'U.S. Contractor Slain in Iraq Had Alleged Graft', *Los Angeles Times*, 20 January, 2005.
24. These figures are based on estimates by the Iraqi Ministry of Finance, extrapolated from the 2006 budgetary support for the Iraqi armed forces. Total expenditures by the Iraqi armed forces were estimated at about $12 billion, of which $4 billion was provided by the Iraqi treasury. The rest came from the Pentagon's budget.
25. The full details of the chain of transactions had to be reconstructed later. The key document was a report written by the Bureau of Supreme Audit (BSA), addressed to the prime minister and dated 16 May, 2005. The BSA Report carried the number 1/1/3/2282 and was entitled (in Arabic) 'The results of the audit and supervision on the operations and accounts of the Ministry of Defence for the period June 28 2004 until February 28, 2005'. Other sources of information included the Rafidain Bank, the Central Bank and the Ministry of Finance.
26. BSA Report.
27. Solomon Moore and T. Christian Miller, ' Before Rearming Iraq, He Sold Shoes and Flowers', *Los Angeles Times*, 6 November, 2005.
28. Breme in his memoirs, *My Year in Iraq*, devotes considerable space to his relationship with Qattan, whom he praises for returning to Iraq to 'rebuild the nation' (p. 178). Bremer later denied that he knew Qattan. The entire disgraceful episode is exposed by the researcher Nibras Kazimi in his blog 'Talisman Gate', accessed at http://talismangate.blogspot.com/2006/01/in-new-book-bremer-mistakenly-exposes.html.
29. BSA Report and information from the Companies Registrar, Ministry of Trade.
30. BSA Report.
31. Ibid. Also, discussions with the author and senior Ministry of Defence officials.
32. Hannah Allam, 'Iraq Seen Wasting $300 Million on Substandard Military Equipment', Knight-Ridder newspapers, 15 July, 2005.
33. See n. 25 above.
34. Allam, op. cit.
35. Quoted on the website on the Iraqi economy, www.iraqieconomy.org, 19 September, 2005.
36. Muhammad al-Shafi'i, *Ghadhab polandi min tashkik fi aslihatihm* ('Polish Anger at Suspicions about Their Weapons'), *Sharq al-Awsat*, London, 30 September, 2005.
37. The author, as the Minister of Finance of the Transitional National Government, addressed a detailed request to the Jordanian authorities in September 2005 for information regarding the details of the Jordanian bank accounts of Jumaili, the main culprit in the theft. The request was co-signed by Sinan al-Shabibi, the Governor of the Central Bank of Iraq. The Jordanians stonewalled, however, and refused to divulge any information. This was in violation of the inter-Arab treaties enforcing the disclosure of information in criminal cases.

Chapter 21: Iraqi Society on the Eve of Free Elections

1. Zarqawi specialised in suicide bombings in crowded places. Explosions aimed at police or army recruits were soon augmented by attacks on public markets, mosques, and busy streets. See, for example, Jim Krane, 'Car Bombings Suggest Change in Tactics', *Associated Press*, 18 June, 2004.
2. William Langewiesche, 'Welcome to the Green Zone: The American Bubble in Baghdad', *Atlantic Monthly*, November 2004.
3. The Ministry of Defence was entirely inside the Green Zone. It occupied the premises of the former Saddam-era National Assembly. The building had been attacked by missiles during the war, and was renovated at great expense. The Minister of Interior chose to occupy the 'Adnan Palace' inside the Green Zone.
4. The Foreign Ministry maintained its offices adjacent to the Green Zone, but it was within its boundary security arrangements. Several ministers lived in the houses and villas attached to the Foreign Ministry compound.
5. A few senior officials insisted on living outside the Green Zone. They included the Deputy Prime Minister in the Transitional National Government, Ahmad Chalabi, and the Minister of Finance, Ali Allawi.
6. Layla Ahmad, 'Iraq: Green Zone Offers Uncertain Refuge from Baghdad Violence', Radio Free Europe, 10 July, 2006.
7. Scott Wilson, 'Iraqis Killing Former Ba'ath Party Members', *Washington Post*, 20 May, 2003.

8. See International Crisis Group, 'In Their Own Words: Reading the Iraqi Insurgency', February 2006, available at their website, http://www.crisisgroup.org/.
9. Patrick Cockburn, 'Iraq: The Aftermath: Iraqi Barbers in the Firing Line as Fanatics Target Western Symbols', *Independent*, 13 May, 2005.
10. The assassination of Salim was a classic case of a lookout spotter and a parked car that swerved in front of the target vehicle.
11. The Riverbend blog, 'Baghdad Burning', had a running commentary on the shortages and difficulties of daily life in Baghdad. See http://riverbendblog.blogspot.com.
12. Ibid.
13. Ministry of Electricity: 'Master Plan for the Electricity Sector, 2006-2015, June 2006 (limited circulation).
14. For example, the RAND Corporation December 2003 Report, 'Replacing Iraq's Public Distribution System for Food with a Monetary Payment'. See Chapters 11 and 15 for a more thorough treatment of this subject.
15. In one particularly blatant case, the team that was sent to Dubai in April 2005 during the last days of the Interim Government was determined to buy flour from a large miller in the UAE at prices that were 20 per cent above the prevailing levels. They managed to achieve most of their purchases before the new Trade Minister, Abd el-Basit Karim, put a stop to it.
16. Brussels Tribunal, Madrid International Seminar on the 'Assassination of Iraqi Academics', 22 to 23 April, 2006.
17. Quoted in Turi Munthe, 'Will Harsh Weed-Out Allow Iraqi Academia to Flower?', *The Times Higher Educational Supplement*, 25 July, 2003.
18. Quoted in Tabitha Morgan, 'Murder of Lecturers Threatens Iraqi Academia', *The Times Higher Education Supplement*, 10 September, 2004.
19. Nicholas Riccardi, 'Another Voice of Academia Is Silenced in Iraq', *Los Angeles Times*, 21 January, 2004.
20. Ibid.
21. UN University, Tokyo, February 2005. The report is entitled 'The Current Status and Future Prospects for the Transformation and Reconstruction of the Higher Education System in Iraq'. It can be accessed at http://www.unu.edu/news/ili/Iraq.doc.
22. Quoted in Ahmed Mukhtar, 'Where Is This Going?', *Al-Ahram Weekly*, 10–16 June, 2004.
23. Sabrina Tavernise, 'Facing Chaos Iraq's Doctors Are Quitting', *New York Times*, 31 May, 2005.
24. Ibid.
25. Mona Mahmoud and Melanie Eversley, 'Hospitals Wage a Different War: Against Addiction', *USA Today*, 23 June, 2005.
26. The NGO Reporters without Borders maintained a running list of the journalists killed in Iraq both during the war and in the post-war period. Their site can be accessed at http://www.rsf.org.
27. A detailed analysis of the state-owned banks was made by the US Treasury, USAID and Bearing Point, the consultants. The report, entitled 'Assessment of Iraqi State-Owned Banks', was issued on 15 November, 2005.
28. Jeremy Kahn, 'Stocks & Bombs Behind the Struggle to Open the Baghdad Stock Exchange', *Fortune Magazine*, 29 September, 2003.
29. Ibid.
30. Yochi Dreazen, 'Grad Has Bigger Job Than He Bargained For', *Wall Street Journal*, 28 January, 2004.
31. Ibid.
32. Borzou Daragahi, 'Tiny Baghdad Stock Market Is a Hot Spot', *Nation & World*, 4 May, 2005.
33. Patrick Frost, 'Violence Sends Baghdad Stocks into the Basement', Agence France-Presse, 31 July, 2006.
34. Details on USAID's work in Iraq's education sector can be accessed at http://www.usaid.gov/iraq/accomplishments/education.html.
35. Bremer makes this the main reason why he began to question the scope of de-Ba'athification. See Bremer, *My Year in Iraq*, op. cit., p. 341.
36. See the Ministry of Education, 'Second National Seminar on Strategies and Curriculum Reform of the New Education System', 30 March, 2004. This can be accessed at www.cpa-iraq.org.
37. See Tina Wang, 'Rewriting the Textbooks - Education Policy in Post-Hussein Iraq', *Harvard International Review*, Vol. 26, No. 4, 2005.
38. Ibid.

39. In discussions with the author, October 2005. The ambassador later seemed to change his mind. In his farewell memorandum to Downing Street before his departure as the UK's ambassador in Iraq in August 2006, he predicted greater polarisation of the sects and the possibility of civil war.
40. Sectarian strife first began in the string of towns to the south and southwest of Baghdad. Initially, they did not constitute large-scale 'ethnic cleansing'. The Karbala News Agency ran a graphic story on the early expulsions in the town of Yussufiya (www.karbalanews.net), dated 10 October, 2004. Within a year the expulsions turned into a flood, affecting both Shi'a and Sunni communities. See Sabrina Tavernise, 'Sectarian Hatred Pulls Apart Iraq's Mixed Towns', New York Times, 20 November, 2005.

Chapter 22: The Vote

1. Richard A. Oppel Jr. and David E. Sanger, 'Iraqi Premier Calls Bush to Discuss Obstacles to Election', New York Times, 4 January, 2005.
2. Seymour M. Hersh, 'Get out the Vote', New Yorker, 25 July, 2005.
3. Dexter Filkins and David E. Sanger, 'Amid Tensions Iraqi Leader Affirms Jan. 30 Vote Plan', New York Times, 6 January, 2005.
4. Mazen Ghazi, 'Forty-Seven Bodies Boycott Iraq Elections', Islam Online, 18 November, 2004.
5. In its preamble about its vision for Iraq, the UIA platform called for 'the establishment of a clear timetable for the withdrawal of the Multinational Forces'.
6. Anthony Shadid, 'Iraq's Shi'ite Clergy Push to Get out The Vote', Washington Post, 7 December, 2004.
7. Seymour Hersh, op. cit.
8. In personal conversation with the author, July, 2005.
9. The election results are drawn from the official website of the Iraqi Independent Electoral Commission, www.ieciraq.org.
10. Agence France-Presse, 'Jaafari Edges Closer to Iraq Premiership', 23 February, 2005.
11. Anthony Shadid, 'Iraq Must Unify Or Face "Disaster", Premier Warns', Washington Post, 18 February, 2005.
12. Internal UIA documents.
13. Robin Wright, 'Iraq Winners Allied with Iran Are the Opposite of U.S. Vision', Washington Post, 14 February, 2005.
14. Ellen Knickmeyer, 'Iraqi Alliance Seeks to Oust Top Officials of Hussein Era', Washington Post, 18 April, 2005.
15. Internal UIA document.
16. Internal UIA document.
17. Internal UIA document.
18. The document is dated 15 March, 2005.
19. The document is dated 21 March, 2005.
20. See the detailed profile of Khalilzad in Jon Lee Anderson's 'American Viceroy: Zalmay Khalilzad's Mission', New Yorker, 12 December, 2005, by accessing www. newyorker.com.
21. Ibid.
22. The insurgency was being increasingly assessed as an alliance of convenience between varieties of groups, the goals of which were divergent and even incompatible in the long run. On the one hand, the extremist terrorist groups represented by the al-Qaeda network had to be fought and vanquished. But the door could be left ajar to those insurgent groups that were tribally based, or were led by former military or intelligence officers. It was felt that some of these groups had been driven into resistance and violence because of the erroneous policies of the early occupation period. With the right incentives, many of them could be co-opted into the political process.
23. Ellen Knickmeyer and Naseer Nouri, 'Sunnis Step off Political Sidelines', Washington Post, 22 May, 2005.

Chapter 23: Negotiating a Constitution

1. International Crisis Group, 'Iraq: Don't Rush the Constitution', Middle East Report, No. 42, 8 June, 2005.
2. Ellen Knickmeyer and Naseer Nouri, 'Sunnis Step off Political Sidelines', Washington Post, 22 May, 2005.

3. James Glanz, 'Baathists May Be Joining Iraq's Constitution Drafters', *New York Times*, 30 June, 2005.
4. Agence France-Presse, 'Iraq Fires Top Sunni Official', 30 July, 2005.
5. Interviews: author with Sami al-Askari, member of the National Assembly and of the constitution drafting committee. The interviews took place in July and August 2006.
6. Ibid.
7. Ibid.
8. Ibid.
9. Neil MacDonald, 'Iraq Constitution Will Draw Heavily from Transitional Law, Says Zoellick', *Financial Times*, 20 May, 2005.
10. International Crisis Group, 'Iraq: Don't Rush the Constitution'.
11. *New York Times*, 14 July, 2005.
12. Ellen Knickmeyer and Omar Fekeiki, 'Iraqi Charter to Give Religion a Big Role', *Washington Post*, 28 July, 2005.
13. Quoted in the Department of Defense News link, http://www.defenselink.mil/transcripts/2005/tr20050727–secdef3541.html, on 27 July, 2005.
14. Radio Free Europe/Radio Liberty, 'Iraq: Commission Chief Says Constitution to Be Ready on Time', 1 August, 2005.
15. Edward Wong, 'Top Shiite Politician Joins Call for Autonomous South Iraq', *New York Times*, 12 August, 2005.
16. Ali Allawi, 'Federalism', in Fran Hazelton, ed., *Iraq Since the Gulf War: Prospects for Democracy*, Zed Books, London, 1994.
17. The Declaration can be accessed at http://www.al-bab.com/arab/docs/iraq/shia02a.htm.
18. Dexter Filkins and James Glanz, 'Charter Talks in Iraq Reach Breaking Point', *New York Times*, 26 August, 2005.
19. See International Crisis Group, 'Iraq and the Kurds: The Brewing Battle over Kirkuk', *Middle East Report*, No.56, 18 July, 2006.
20. The full text of the TAL can be accessed at: http://www.cpa-iraq.org/government/TAL.html.
21. International Crisis Group, 'Iraq and the Kurds', pp. 4–5 and 19–21.
22. Interviews: author with Sami al-Askari in July and August 2006. Askari, an independent Islamist and fomer Da'awa Party leader, was close to the religious groups in Najaf and the south of Iraq.
23. Ibid.
24. Ibid.
25. CNN, 'Iraq Constitution Deadline Extended', 15 August, 2005.
26. Robert Reid, 'Iraq Finishes Constitution but without Sunni Approval', *Associated Press*, 29 August, 2005.
27. Oliver Poole, 'Sunnis Pledge to Fight Iraq's Constitution', *Daily Telegraph* (London), 30 August, 2005.
28. Interviews: author with Sami al-Askari, July and August 2006.
29. Ellen Knickmeyer and Bassam Sebti, 'Iraq's Sunnis Register to Vote in Droves', *Washington Post*, 8 September, 2005.
30. BBC News, 'Sunni Anger at Iraq Vote Change', 3 October, 2005.
31. Adrian Blomfield, 'Boycott Threat to Iraq Poll as Voting Rules Are Changed', *Daily Telegraph*, 5 October, 2005.
32. The referendum results are drawn from the official Iraqi Independent Electoral Commission tallies. They can be accessed at www.ieciraq.org.
33. Some doubt continued to be raised about the results of Nineveh province. See Gareth Porter, 'Vote Figures for Crucial Province Don't Add up', *Inter Press Service News Agency*, 19 October, 2005.

Chapter 24: Crises and the Jaafari Government

1. Jaafari's speech to the new National Assembly tried to give the impression of a fresh start. He revelled in indirect and obscure allusions, as when he concluded, 'I love Iraq and all that is sacred in it. Its people, its waters, its palm trees. And the most wonderful aspects of a palm tree are its

fruits and its bounty. And the palm tree dies while standing upright. And I hope that I will be martyred standing upright.'
2. Instructions to this effect came from the Cabinet office regularly.
3. USAID, Iraq weekly status reports. This can be accessed at the USAID website, www.usaid.gov/iraq.
4. Cabinet minutes for 11 May, 2005.
5. The details of the plan were kept mainly secret from the Cabinet, although its broad outlines were discussed with ministers.
6. Cabinet minutes for 9 June, 2005.
7. Naqib later complained to Rumsfeld about the dangers of militia infiltration of the Ministry of Interior, ignoring, of course, his own role in launching this process. See Michael Moss, 'How Iraq Police Reform Became Casualty of War', *New York Times*, 22 May, 2006.
8. Ibid.
9. See Solomon Moore, 'Killings Linked to Shiite Squads in Iraqi Police Force', *Los Angeles Times*, 29 November, 2005. Also Moss, op. cit.
10. Moore, op cit.
11. Jabr dismissed the charges of torture and maltreatment in the Jadriya prison episode. Referring to the case of a supposedly invalid detainee, Jabr said that the man in question was responsible for the murder of sixty-six people. For good measure, he flatly denied the charge that the Badr militia had infiltrated his ministry.
12. Dexter Filkins, 'Armed Groups Propel Iraq towards Chaos', *New York Times*, 24 May, 2006.
13. Moore, op. cit.
14. Ibid.
15. The 'Infrastructure Protection Plan' was dated 16 June, 2005, as a Ministry of Defence document. It was clearly the work of the MNF.
16. James Glanz and Robert F. Worth, 'Attacks on Iraq Oil Industry Aid Vast Smuggling Scheme', *New York Times*, 4 June, 2006.
17. Data are from the Ministry of Electricity, 'Master Plan for the Electricity Sector', June 2006.
18. Shlash was later indicted for corruption by the Integrity Commission. He fled the country before the warrant for his arrest was issued. The previous electricity minister, Ayham al-Samarrai, was not so lucky. He was arrested in Baghdad in August 2006 for corruption.
19. The Minister of Trade went public with his bleak assessments in a number of interviews on Iraqi television in May 2005.
20. Joanna Chung and Stephen Fidler, 'Restructuring Under Fire: Why Iraqi Debt Is No Longer a Write-Off', *Financial Times*, 16 July, 2005.
21. The document was entitled 'Strategy and Policy for the 2006 Budget' and dated 20 August, 2005.
22. Neither did the Cabinet see the report. The information in this section was pieced together through discussions with the main security ministers and the National Security Adviser.
23. Interview: author with Salem Chalabi, June 2006.
24. Ibid.
25. Ibid.

Chapter 25: Into Uncharted Waters

1. The document was unsigned, but widely attributed to Adel Abd el-Mahdi. It was dated 11 September, 2005.
2. The elaborate mechanism for ensuring the UIA's involvement and oversight of the Transitional Government came to nothing. Jaafari did not act out the commitments he had made to the UIA parliamentarians to secure the premiership.
3. Interview: author with Sami al-Askari, August 2006.
4. There was a tussle for control of the 'Independents' between Hussein Shahristani and Ali al-Dabbagh. Shahristani won out, forcing Dabbagh either to accept a secondary role inside the UIA or to form his own party list. He chose the latter course.
5. Interview: author with Sami al-Askari, August 2006.

6. Ashraf Khalil, 'Iraqi Mosques Flex Election Muscle', *Los Angeles Times*, 3 December, 2005.
7. Hashemi gave an extended interview on his background and career on *al-Iraqiyya* TV channel, July 2006.
8. See Hashem's interview (above).
9. The last of his siblings to be murdered was General Amr Bakr al-Hashemi. He had been appointed chief of staff of the Iraqi army in May 2004 by Ali Allawi, then Defence Minister. He was subsequently removed by the Interim Government. At the time of his murder in October 2006, he was acting as senior adviser to the defence minister.
10. *Asharq al-Awsat* newspaper (London), 5 November, 2005.
11. Fadil al-Badrani, 'Clerics Use Friday Prayers to Urge Big Iraqi Vote', Reuters, 10 December, 2006.
12. *Asharq al-Awsat* (London), 29 November, 2005.
13. *Asharq al-Awsat* (London), 22 November, 2005.
14. Jonathan Steele, 'Rise in Poll Complaints Troubles Iraq Vote Monitors', *Guardian*, 19 December, 2005.
15. Quoted in *Associated Press*, 'Iraq to Remove 90 Former Ba'athists From Ballots', 24 December, 2005.
16. Interviews: author with Sami al-Askari, July and August 2006. A number of interviews were also held with senior Jaafari advisers. The full details of the back room manoeuvrings inside the UIA for the selection of the prime minister involved bewildering shifts of allegiance and last-minute switches of the vote.
17. Interviews: author with Sami al-Askari, July and August 2006.
18. Robert F. Worth and Sabrina Tavernise, 'Radical Cleric's Influence Grows in Iraq', *New York Times*, 16 February, 2006.
19. Juan Cole, 'Informed Comment', 6 March, 2006.
20. Edward Wong, 'Shiites Say U.S. Is Pressuring Iraqi Leader to Step aside', *New York Times*, 28 March, 2006.
21. Editorial, *New York Times*, 2 April, 2006.
22. Interview: author with Adnan al-Kadhimi, political adviser to Jaafari and senior Da'awa Party member, March-April 2006.
23. Dan Murphy, 'Attack Deepens Iraq's Divide', *Christian Science Monitor*, 23 February, 2006.
24. Ellen Knickmeyer and Bassam Sebti, 'Toll in Iraq's Deadly Surge: 1,300', *Washington Post*, 28 February, 2006.
25. The quote is from Juan Cole, *Christian Science Monitor*, 23 February, 2006.
26. Edward Wong and Sabrina Tavernise, 'Religious Strife Shows Strength of Iraq Militias', *New York Times*, 25 February, 2006.
27. Ibid.
28. The transcript of the press briefing, 19 February, 2006, can be found on the MNF website at http://www.mnf-iraq.com.
29. Megan Stack, 'Iraq's Besieged Sunnis Now Looking to U.S.', *Los Angeles Times*, 5 March, 2006.
30. Borzou Daragahi, 'In Iraq, Civil War All But Declared', *Los Angeles Times*, 19 July, 2006.
31. Edward Wong and Sabrina Tavernise, 'Religious Strife Shows Strength of Iraq Militias', *New York Times*, 25 February, 2007. Jabr was the subject of a lengthy piece in *Harper's Magazine* by Ken Silverstein, 'The Minister of Civil War', August 2006.
32. See, for example, Edward Wong, 'A Matter of Definition: What Makes a Civil War and Who Declares It So?', *New York Times*, 26 November, 2006.
33. Senator Joseph Biden, a Democrat, and Senator Richard Lugar, a Republican, had indeed warned of civil war threatening in Iraq as early as April 2004. See Justin Webb, 'US Senators Warn of Iraq Civil War', *BBC News*, 5 April, 2004.
34. Senator Reid's comment can be accessed at: http://www.cnn.com/2006/POLITICS/07/20/iraq.democrats/index.html. See also the transcript of Senator Hagel's interview with George Stephanopolous of *ABC News*. 'This Week' programme can be accessed at: http://www.rawstory.com/news/2006/GOP_Sen_Low_grade_civil_war_0319.html.
35. See Nir Rosen, 'Anatomy of a Civil War: Iraq's Descent into Chaos', *Boston Review*, November/December 2006. This is one of the most accomplished reports on the incipient civil war.
36. This *husseiniya*, the Mustafa *husseiniya*, was controversially raided in March 2006 by a mixed US–Iraqi force, when several people were killed. The Mustafa *husseiniya* housed the local offices of the Da'awa Party, the party of the then prime minster, Ibarhim al-Jaafari.

37. Rosen, op. cit.
38. Amit R. Paley, 'In Baghdad, a Force under the Militias' Sway', *Washington Post*, 31 October, 2006.
39. Sudarsan Raghavan, 'Iran Said to Support Shiite Militias in Iraq', *Washington Post*, 15 August, 2006.
40. See Sabrina Tavernise, 'Influence Rises but Base Frays for Iraqi Cleric', *New York Times*, 13 November, 2006.
41. Farah Stockman and Bryan Bender, 'Iraqi Militias' Wave of Death', *Boston Globe*, 2 April, 2006.
42. Raghavan, 'Iran Said to Support Shiite Militias in Iraq.
43. See Aparisim Ghosh, 'Is Iran Controlling Iraqi Militias?', *Time Magazine*, 25 August, 2006. The article can be accessed at: http://www.time.com/time/world/article/ 0,8599,1333861,00.html.
44. Damien Cave and Edward Wong, 'Shiite Militia Clashes with Iraqi Troops', *New York Times*, 28 August, 2006.
45. Private communication to the author from a highly placed Iraqi source.
46. Rick Jervis, 'Iraq Will Wait to Disarm Militias', *USA Today*, 20 October, 2006.
47. The report was compiled by researchers from the Johns Hopkins University School of Public Health and the Mustansiriya University School of Medicine in Baghdad. The full report can be accessed at: www.thelancet.com.
48. Ashraf al-Khalidi and Victor Tanner, 'Sectarian Violence: Radical Groups Drive Internal Displacement in Iraq', The Brookings Institution–University of Berne Project on Internal Displacement, October 2006. The report can be accessed at: http://www.brookings.edu/fp/projects/idp/200610_DisplacementinIraq.htm.
49. Walter Pincus, '1,000 Iraqis a Day Flee Violence, U.N. Group Finds', *Washington Post*, 24 November, 2006.
50. Ibid.
51. Ibid.
52. Nancy A.Youssef, 'Shiite Leaders Distance Themselves from Iraqi Government', McClatchy Newspapers, 1 August, 2006.
53. The statement can be accessed at www.sistani.org/messages.

Index

Note: The prefixes 'Al-' and 'El- are ignored in the alphabetical ordering or names. For abbreviations, the reader is referred to the list on pp. xvii–xix. Page references in *italics* indicate the List of Characters; those in **bold** type indicate maps.

hatreds 233–48, 432; and Shi'a 177,
183, 188, 268, 269, 271–75; and
Sunnis 169–70, 177, 178, 183, 188,
189, 234, 242, 266, 456, Islamist 180,
181–82, and political process 337, 389,
399, 414, 444, 457, and Sadrists 271,
444, Salafi 180, 181, 187, 385, and
Tawaffaq front 440–41, 444, *ulema*
245–48; support for 176–78, 189,
296–97, 456; and Transitional
National Government 400, 418, 419,
421, 435, 448; and tribes 243–45; and
weapons 140, 174–75; and Zarqawi
233–35, 239–40, 338, 441
  see also Fallujah; Najaf; resistance to
  occupation
intelligence: CPA 117, 179, 187; Iraqi *xxiii*,
46, 58, 60, 115, 123, 154, 157, 172,
305; US 80–81, 187, 189
Interim Iraqi Administration (IIA) xi,
98–99, 100–1, 103; and Governing
Council 169
Interim Iraqi Government xi, 263, 280–93;
and administrative failures 349–52,
396; Arab states 290, 292, 295–301;
Cabinet 286, 289, 297; and corruption
349–56, 361–68; CPA legacy 290, 320,
349; and defamation campaigns
323–25; and economy 419; and
education 384; and elections 286, 288,
301, 309, 315, 334, 340–42; and
Fallujah crises 277, 279, 338–39; and
Governing Council 280, 286;
inauguration 286: and insurgency
286, 289, 290–92, 335; and Iran
304–8, 313; and Moqtada al-Sadr 290,
320, 324–25, 327–28; and Najaf crisis
316, 320–21, 324, 325–33, 334;
policies 289–90, 292; powers and
functions 287–89; president 280, 285;
prime minister 280, 283–85; and
security 288–89, 291–92, 319–20, 336,
349–50, 394, 401; and al-Sistani 284,
286–87, 309, 323; and sovereignty
283, 286–88, 295, 320, 334, 351; and
tenders and contracts 426; and
Transitional National Government
401; and war crimes tribunal 433
  see also elections
Interior Ministry: and Bridge of the
Imams tragedy 432; and Interim
Government 394; and militias 421–23,
444, 446, 449; and national unity
government 446; and security 202–3,

289, 319, 420–23, 448; and
Transitional Government 392, 396
International Advisory Board 261–62, 351,
353–55
International Atomic Energy Agency
(IAEA) 71
International Crisis Group 307, 406–7
International Monetary Fund (IMF)
124–25, 196, 200, 358–59, 427; and
Standby Arrangements 419, 428, 431
International Organisation for Migration
344
internationalism, US 4
Internet, access to 154
invasion of Iraq x–xiii, 2, 89–95; build-up
to 62–76, 77–89; and collapse of
central authority 93–95; costs 194–95,
255; errors in 8, 114; factors in 4–6;
and ideological imperative 9–10; and
immediacy of interest 9; insufficient
troop numbers 91, 97; and Iraqi
opposition forces 87, 89–90; and
Islamists 90–3; motive and purpose 1,
4, 10; opposition to 2, 94–95, 166,
229, 301, 303; planning for 87–88,
114–15; and self-fulfilling prophecies
10; and Shi'a 137–38, 174; and Sunni
Arabs 135–37; support for 2, 134,
176–77, 295, 455, 458; and
unintended consequences 7, 8, 10, 94,
114–31, 445, 460
investment, post-war 125, 196, 199,
256–57, 263, 430
iqlim (region) *xxiii*
Iran: and Arab states 296, 298–99, 301,
303, 456; and Chalabi 282–83;
containment 64–65, 393; and CPA
303–4, 312–13; and Governing
Council 304, 305; and Imami Shi'ism
25, 32; influence in Iraq 10, 207, 272,
332, 393; and Interim Iraqi
Government 304–8, 337; and Kurds
33, 34, 41, 50; and militias 449; and
Moqtada al-Sadr 306; nuclear
programme 305, 306, 307; and
post-war Iraq 86, 292, 303–13;
Revolutionary Guard 44, 47; and
Sadrists 321; Safavid rule 25; Saudi
fears 298–99; and SCIRI 44, 69, 306,
318; and Uprising of March 1991 47;
and US 3, 9, 39, 86, 306–7, 398, 454, 459
Iran–Iraq War x, 3, 31–32, 34–38, 39–40,
434; economic impact 40, 121, 127,
428; and human rights violations 144;

opposition, Iraqi *cont.*
  and Iran–Iraq War 34–37, 38, 39–40;
  and Iraq Liberation Act 67; Islamist
  35–37, 43–44, 46, 50–51; Kurdish 35,
  36, 37–38, 39, 41, 51; and Kurdish
  autonomy 73; leadership 35–36, 41,
  44–45, 47, 51–52, 53, 61, 69, 85–86,
  100; mobilisation of Shi'a masses 56,
  57–59; rise 39–61; and Sadiq al-Sadr
  54–57, 58, 59–61; and sanctions 70;
  and Sunnis 135; Uprisings of March
  1991 45–50; and USA 42, 43, 45,
  50–53, 63, 64–68, 69–70, 76, 78–82,
  87
  see also Chalabi, Ahmad; leadership
    council; Supreme Council for the
    Islamic Revolution in Iraq
Organisation for Islamic Action 44
Ottoman Empire 21, 22, 25, 26, 33
Oviatt, Mark 260

Al-Pachachi, Adnan xvii, 72–73, 78, 88; and
  de-Ba'athification 147; and elections
  346; and Fallujah crisis 277; flight
  from Iraq 355–56; and Governing
  Council 165, 191–92, 222, 225, 285;
  and Interim Government 285; and
  Saddam Hussein 242; and transfer of
  sovereignty 213, 217, 221, 227
Al-Pachachi, Muzzahim 72–73
Pakistan, and USA 337
Palacios, Ana 192
Parenti, Christian 243
parties, political: Islamist 111–12, 191; and
  media 153; and security forces
  421–22, 448
  see also Ba'ath Party; Da'awa Party;
    Fadhila Party; Iraqi Islamic Party;
    Kurdish Democratic Party; Patriotic
    Union of Kurdistan
partition, and sectarianism 132, 224
Patriotic Union of Kurdistan (PUK) 34, 35,
  36; and constitution 411; and
  elections 345; and Halabja 37; and
  Iran 304; and Iraq Governing Council
  191; and KDP 53; and Syria 43; and
  Uprising of 1991 50; and USA 67
patriotism, Iraqi 176–77, 243, 347, 438
Pentagon 84, 97, 98–100, 152, 161; and
  Chalabi 281; and de-Ba'athification
  147, 151; Defense Intelligence Agency
  81; and INC 85, 87, 90, 99; and
  insurgency 240; and Interim
  Government 101, 104; and Iraqi

economy 124; and Iraqi troops 87;
  military contractors 252–53, 362; and
  reconstruction 252, 263; and UN
  agencies 124; and weapons of mass
  destruction 83
  see also Office for Special Plans
Perle, Richard 66, 67, 455, 467 n.2
Persian language 309
pesh merga (Kurdish partisan army) 46–47,
  89, 134, 316–18, 395, 414; weapons
  140, 158
Petraeus, Lt Gen. David H. 348, 361–62,
  368
Pickering, Thomas 69
pipeline war 175–76, 255, 356, 358, 423–25
Plan 459 175
Planning Ministry 194
pluralism, in Iraq 53, 72, 101, 209, 222
police, Iraqi 94; attacks on 180, 181, 373;
  and insurgency 188–89, 202, 272–73,
  291; and militias 421–23, 448, 453
politics: Islamist 26, 27, 35–37, 45, 93–94,
  111–13, 139, 191; and Sistani 205–6,
  208–10, 215–18, 311–12
population 18–20, *19*, 25, 267, 390
poverty: and public services 375; and
  social security 431
Powell, Colin xviii; and CPA 105, 107, 200;
  and Iraq Governing Council 192; and
  Madrid Conference 200; and MNF
  288; and Nasiriya Conference 101;
  and possibility of Iraqi coup 79–80;
  and Zarqawi 238
power supply: and CPA 126, 268; insurgent
  attacks on 175–76, 257–59, 423–25;
  and Interim Government 354–55,
  371, 374–75; and oil industry 255,
  359–60, 423–25; and ORHA 102, 104;
  and reconstruction 252, 257–59; and
  Transitional National Government
  419, 423–25
president: and Interim Government 280,
  285; and Kurds 345; and Transitional
  National Government 396
Presidential Council 224
prime minister: candidates 280, 283;
  Interim Government 280, 283–85;
  and Iraq Governing Council 284–85;
  Shi'ite 283; and United Iraqi Alliance
  392–93, 394–95, 396, 437, 439, 442–43
  see also Allawi, Ayad; Al-Jaafari, Ibrahim;
    Jabr, Saad Saleh; Al-Maliki, Nuri
prisoners, degrading treatment 186
privatisation 264, 337, 380, 427

Shi'a *cont.*
and Saudi Arabia 298–99; street
power 138–39, 267, 269, 309, 431; and
Sunni 237–38
see also Islamism; Sadrist movement;
United Iraqi Alliance; Al-Zarqawi
Shi'a House: and Iraq Governing Council
205–6, 221; and Najaf stand-off
274–75, 320; and Sistani 205, 221
Shi'a Political Council 325, 343
Shineski, Gen. Eric 91
Shlash, Muhsin 425
shortages 374–76, 380, 419, 426
shoura (consultation) *xxiv*
shrines, Shi'a *xxi*, 13, 49, 92, 172, 272,
274–75, 309–10, 412
Shulsky, Abram 81, 100
shu'ubbi (Shi'a) *xxiv*
Shu'ubiyya movement *xxiv*
shuyukh (elders) *xxiv*
siddara (hat) *xxiv*, 405
Siffin, battle (657) 23
Al-Sinawi, Sahil 377
Al-Sistani, Grand Ayatollah Ali xii, xvii, 55,
59, 92–93, 206–7; and Baqir al-Hakim
111, 113; and Brahimi 227, 229,
230–31, 342; and constitution 210–11,
221, 223, 403, 404–5; and CPA
168–69, 202, 206, 210–11, 267; and
democracy 209–10; and elections 216,
284, 312, 335, 390, and Brahimi
217–18, 227, December 2005 436,
439–40, and November 15 Agreement
219, and single Shi'a list 340–42,
344–45, 392, time scale 226, 230; and
federalism 409; and Interim
Government 284, 286–87, 309, 323;
and Iran 311–12; and al-Khoei 207,
208, 209; as *Marji' al-Taqlid* 61, 112;
and Moqtada al-Sadr 171, 212, 267,
270, 322–23, 327–30, 332–33; and
politics 205–6, 208–10, 215–18,
311–12, 332–452; and religion and
state 208–10; as scholar 207; and Shi'a
House 205, 221; and UN 217, 229, 230
Sistani, Muhammad Redha xvii, 168, 206,
274, 343, 439, 476 n.2
Slocombe, Walter 158, 317
Smith, Fred 362
smuggling: of drugs 379; of oil 123,
357–61; of petroleum products 424
society: and assassinations 376–79;
collapse of middle class 127–28;
deepening divisions 132–46, 151–52,

182; dislocation 114, 129–31, 370–87;
and education 382–84; and
entrepreneurship 374, 380–82;
increasing violence 373–74;
militarisation 156; and religiosity
384–86; and shortages 374–76, 380
souq el-mraydi (thieves' market) *xxiv*
sovereignty, Iraqi 103, 168–69, 171,
191–93, 204–5, 266; and constitution
169, 193, 204, 213, 214, 219–32; and
Governing Council 191–93, 213, 226,
287, 294–95; and Interim
Government 283, 286–88, 295, 302,
320, 334, 351; time scale for 214–15,
220–22, 224–26, 231; and TNA
215–16, 224
see also elections
Soviet Union 3, 31, 35
Special Coordinator for Transition in Iraq
68
Special Inspector General for Iraq
Reconstruction (SIGIR) 262
Special Police Commando Unit 319
Special Republican Guard 142, 156, 290–91
Standby Arrangements (SBA; IMF) 419,
428, 431
state: and religion 208–10, 308, 347,
412–14; and Sadiq al-Sadr 56, 57,
59–61; and Shi'a 137–38, 177; and
society 114, 133, 145, 147; and tribe
14
State Department (US): and Da'awa Party
74; and de-Ba'athification 151–52;
and Defense Department 83, 99; and
insurgency 187, 281; and interim
government 101, 105, 109, 293; and
Iraqi economy 124; and Iraqi
opposition 66, 67, 69, 77–78, 79–80;
and legality of occupation 106, 164;
and MEK 304; and post-war Iraq
83–84, 120; and realist policy 77, 79,
83, 85, 108, 111; and reconstruction of
Iraq 253, 260; and regime change
67–68; and war on Iraq 80
Stock Exchange 381–82
Stoffel, Dale 362–63
Strategic Infrastructure Battalions (SIB)
424
Strauss, Leo xviii, 5–6, 81
Sudani, Sheikh Mahmoud 322
Sufi orders 56–57, 134, 236–37
suicide bombings 371, 374, 385, 423; and
CPA 202; and murder of de Mello
170–71; and al-Qaeda groups 180; in